GREAT LIVES
FROM
HISTORY

GREAT LIVES FROM HISTORY

Ancient and Medieval Series

Volume 3
Hes-Nie

Edited by
FRANK N. MAGILL

SALEM PRESS

Pasadena, California   Englewood Cliffs, New Jersey

Library of Congress Cataloging-in-Publication Data
Great lives from history. Ancient and medieval
series / edited by Frank N. Magill.
   p. cm.
Includes bibliographies and index.
   Summary: A five-volume set of biographical
sketches, arranged alphabetically, of 459 individ-
uals whose contributions influenced world culture
and the social development of societies flourishing
in earlier centuries.
   Biography—To 500. 2. Biography—Middle
Ages, 500-1500. [1. Biography—To 500. 2. Biog-
raphy—Middle Ages, 500-1500. 3. World history.]
I. Magill, Frank Northen, 1907-   .
CT113.G74 1988   920'.009'01—dc19   88-18514
[B]
[920]
ISBN 0-89356-545-8 (set)
ISBN 0-89356-548-2 (volume 3)

LIST OF BIOGRAPHIES IN VOLUME THREE

LIST OF BIOGRAPHIES IN VOLUME THREE

GREAT LIVES
FROM
HISTORY

HESIOD

Born: Fl. c. 700 B.C.; Ascra, Greece
Died: Date unknown; Ozolian Locris, Greece
Area of Achievement: Literature
Contribution: Hesiod organized and interpreted the Greek myths which form
the basis for European civilization and examined with moral conscience
the working life of Greek society at the dawn of modern history.

Early Life

In the centuries after his death, Hellenic historians and writers added to
the legend of Hesiod's life so that a moderately detailed portrait of him developed through commentary and speculation. The work of more recent
classical scholars has demonstrated that most of this material cannot be sub-
stantiated through historical records. While it is not inconceivable that
subsequent archaeological discoveries will provide additional information, it
seems reasonable to assume that the autobiographical information provided
by Hesiod himself in *Erga kai Ēmerai* (c. 700 B.C.; *Works and Days*) is the
only basis for drawing an outline of his life. Like some of the work traditionally attributed to him, it is fragmentary and sketchy, but as one of Hesiod's
best translators, Apostolos Athanassakis, contends, it is "better than all fan-
ciful conjecture." Although some scholars maintain that even this work cannot be positively authenticated, without it, "there is no poet named Hesiod,"
as P. Walcot argues.

In *Works and Days*, four assertions about Hesiod's father are presented—
that he made a living as a merchant sailor, that he came from the province of
Cyme in Aeolis, that "grim poverty" drove him from Asia Minor, and that he
settled in Ascra in the region known as Boeotia, an initially inhospitable but
visually striking district near Mount Helicon. Considering the fact that others
who followed this migration pattern moved on to establish Greek colonies in
Italy when they were unable to make a living, it is reasonable to assume that
Hesiod's father was comparatively prosperous, an assumption corroborated
by the story of the division of his estate between Hesiod and his brother
Perses in *Works and Days*. Although Boeotia was thought to be something of
a backwater by scholars possibly influenced by the prejudices of its neighbors, there is convincing evidence from artistic and poetic sources that it was
actually more like a cultural center. Boeotian verse shared many of the traits
of epic poetry associated with the Ionian region, and the region's geographic
location on the trade route to the Near East provided many opportunities for
cultural advancement, including an earlier adoption of the alphabet than
many other parts of the Hellenic world.

In both *Works and Days* and *Theogonia* (c. 700 B.C.; *Theogony*), the
crucial moment of transformation in Hesiod's life is presented as a justifica-

tion for his work. While tending sheep, probably in early manhood, Hesiod was visited by the Muses, who gave him the gift of song (that is, wisdom in poetic language) and charged him with the responsibility to instruct his countrymen. Hesiod combines the perspective of the common man—the "country bumpkin," the "swag-bellied yahoo," who the Muses address—with the poet's power to create pleasure which counters the pains of human existence and the orator's eloquence, which reconciles citizens to the necessity for compromise in a social community. Thus, when Hesiod found himself in a dispute with Perses over the division of their father's estate, he took the occasion to criticize the nobles (or "kings") who presided as judges for accepting bribes and not rendering true justice. He develops *Works and Days* as a poem in which he counsels his brother and his fellow citizens about the kind of society in which, through the gods' justice, they may all have an opportunity to live relatively comfortably.

There are hints in *Works and Days* and *Theogony* that Hesiod lived much of his life as a bachelor, although he briefly speaks as if he had a son, and there is an account of a visit to Chalcis in Euboea for funeral games, in which he won a handsome prize. M. L. West argues that the poem he performed was the *Theogony*. Beyond that, a number of inferences may be made from the sensibility that emerges through his work. As West observes in explaining the style of his translation, "If I have sometimes made Hesiod sound a little quaint and stilted, that is not unintentional: He is." The obscurity that wreathes Hesiod's life is an intriguing invitation to conjecture. As long as it is based on a careful reading of the work in its known historical context, it is a kind of modern equivalent of the mentally active participation of the audience in that earlier era of oral communication.

Life's Work

Most of the poems which were originally attributed to Hesiod in the centuries after he lived have been designated the work of other writers by modern scholarship. From an original oeuvre consisting of eleven fragments and two titles, only the *Catalogue of Women*, which was appended to *Theogony*, and *Ornithomanteia* (*Divination by Birds*), which was appended to *Works and Days*, may have been based on something Hesiod wrote. Athanassakis mentions that both works, which were thematically connected and impressive imitations by anonymous writers, were often amalgamated into the work of a commanding literary figure, as is the case with Homer and Hippocrates. Athanassakis observes that the *Shield of Herakles* is included in most standard editions of Hesiod, "thus paying homage to ancient tradition," but he makes a plausible case that it is a visionary poem of apocalyptic power which stands comparison with Hesiod's finest writing.

In any event, *Theogony* stands as the beginning of Hesiod's work. It carries out the Muses' injunction to "sing of the race of the blessed gods" and "tell of things to come and things past," in return for their fabulous gift. This gift, however, like most divine bounty, carries the burden of its own mystery, and *Theogony* is not only a form of thanks and worship but also an attempt to understand the import and consequence of the action of the gods in the affairs of humans. To do this, Hesiod reaches back to the creation of Time and Space from an immeasurable, primordial flux to chart the origins of cosmic history. As he describes the beginning of the known universe, the elemental aspects of the cosmos, Earth (Gaia), Sky (Ouranos), and Sea (Pontos), are not only physical components of firmament and terrain, but gods, with all the attributes of divinity (and humanity) common to the Hellenic vision of deity. This merging compels him, in composing a poem on the birth and genealogy of the gods, to create also cosmogony, or an account of the development of the shape and form of the universe through time. As a correlative, without actually identifying the precise moment of the emergence of the human race, *Theogony* also presents an early history of humanity set amid and sometimes parallel to the genealogy of the Olympian deities.

Because the eighth century B.C. was a time of rapid economic expansion and increasing mobility for Greece, with contacts with the Orient already in process for more than a hundred years, it is not surprising that elements of creation myths from the Hittite *Song of Ullikummi* (the castration motif), the Babylonian *Enuma Elish* (activity versus entropy), the Indian *Rgveda*, and even the Norse *Elder Edda* appear in *Theogony*. Hesiod was working at the apex of a tradition, but his singular contribution was to place—above the diversity of the separate families of gods, shaping the chaos of turmoil and struggle—the controlling power of Zeus's sovereignty. The argument of the poem is the rightness and justice of Zeus's reign, the intelligent ordering of what had been a saga of endless, almost random violence. The structure of the poem itself contributes to this sense of order, beginning with the world in Hesiod's time, then moving back to show the evolution from Chaos, and then concluding with a reaffirmation of Zeus's wise aegis.

The direction of cosmic evolution is from a focus on the form of the natural world to a concentration on the structure of an anthropocentric one. This is a reflection of the imposition of the will of Zeus, since, as Hesiod presents it, the first "beings"—Chaos (Void), Gaia (Earth), and Eros (immanent creative energy)—are essentially elemental impulses, unbound and undirected. Hesiod does not postulate what preceded this condition, but sees Eros as a crucial catalyst to the proceeding procreation. First, Hesiod lists the progeny of Chaos and the progeny of Earth. The birth of the Mountains and the Sea by parthenogenesis, and then the birth of the Titans through Earth's incestuous union with her son Sky, are actions apparently without purpose, more impulse than vision. The lineage of Zeus is established with the castration of Kronos (Time)—an act challenging order—who is the last of the Titans, son of Sky and father of Zeus. Parallel to this, the children of Chaos arrive, dark and gloomy, negative in impact, a plague to humankind.

The story of the ascendancy of Zeus involves a shift from the maternal line with an obscure partner to a patriarchal lineage much more in accordance with Hesiod's own society. Zeus, a male sky god, is ultimately evolved from Mother Earth, an evolutionary process directed toward male dominance, which Hesiod justifies as necessary for law and order. Zeus, "the father of gods and men," generates the seasons (emblems of regularity and predictability) by his second wife, Thetis, herself an embodiment of wisdom which he assimilates. Their children symbolize the constants of civilization: Eunomia (Law), Dike (Justice), and Eirene (Peace). Thus, the history of Zeus is also a progression from chaos to law, as Zeus stands in antithesis to his defeated but still dangerous rivals, who are expressions of wild energy. As *Theogony* concludes, Zeus divides his spoils—titles and spheres of influence—with some principles of fairness that lead gradually to a civilized order of governmental succession. The union of Zeus with noble women produced the race of heroes which drew humankind closer to the immortals, but as the children of Night remain on the scene, strife and sorrow will always be the lot of humans. For this reason, the Muses have given the poet the gift of song to provide some relief.

Works and Days is a shift of emphasis from the cosmological and eternal to the local and specific. Hesiod examines the ways in which a man might lead a reasonably satisfying life. Working within the larger pattern of the universe as presented in *Theogony* and assuming a familiarity with it, Hesiod confronted the limitations imposed by often unfathomable forces and offered a program of sorts for survival. Because the only style of literary expression available was the dactylic hexameter of the Homeric epic, the poem follows that form, but it is essentially didactic in tone and style, a series of instructions regarding the proper conduct of a man's working life in an agricultural economy controlled by not always scrupulous nobles or "kings." The form is not ideal for Hesiod's purposes, and the poem tends to ramble, but it contains fascinating lessons designed as guidance for men who were prepared to commit their lives to productive industry proscribed by moral behavior.

Works and Days is developed out of the sense of divine justice elaborated in *Theogony*. It accepts the concept of order in human existence and sees work as "the action to fulfill that order." The rationale behind the poem is that conditions have steadily deteriorated since the Golden Age. As Hesiod tells it, men have progressively weakened through the "Five Ages," their working conditions becoming harder, their physical strength diminished, and such afflictions as hunger and disease, unknown in earlier times, now plaguing humankind in the Iron Age. These banes occur as a consequence of human deviousness as expressed in the myths of Prometheus and Pandora. Hesiod sees violence and injustice emerging from Prometheus' challenge and, without being specific, names Pandora (meaning woman) as a source of increasing complexity in human affairs for the introduction of sexual and artistic matters. Bound by the thinking of his era, he describes the feminine role as one of distraction, undermining a man's clarity of purpose and, by implication, his control. A woman's "glamor" and guile encourages dissipation and waste which restricts independence. For Hesiod, woman is "the other," an outsider, who must be taught "right" ways. That is, she must eradicate the singularity in her nature that makes her different from a man. Once a similarity is achieved, she will become valuable property, because she contributes to the permanence of the home. The perspective is very male-oriented and very narrow. A larger view of the two myths suggests that Prometheus introduces the technical to the natural and Pandora introduces the beautiful or ecstatic to the rational, each complicating but also deepening human experience. In a sense, Zeus has used Pandora as a tactic in his contest with Prometheus, and both myths are part of Hesiod's explanation for the current condition of the world.

In order to overcome these unpleasant conditions, Hesiod stresses justice as the crucial virtue, the essential value in all endeavor. Focusing on his own life, he decries the local politicians, subject to bribes, who have unjustly favored his brother Perses in dividing their father's legacy. The entire poem is supposedly addressed to Perses, who is exhorted to follow a life of honest work because without it, men would scheme to gain riches and justice could not exist. The central text of the poem is a series of maxims, suggestions, folk sayings, and specific advice about how to function in a grain-growing or wine-making world. Rather than a manual, however, it is more an outline of operations framed by a reliance on the right time of the year for a particular action. The purpose is really to inculcate a sense of appropriateness and propriety in everything. Similarly, the long, expressive descriptions of the harshness of winter and the pleasures of summer are designed to reconcile human nature to the larger patterns of the natural cosmos. The "works" section is a kind of astronomical guide for plowing, planting, and harvesting, that places man in harmony with his environment, thus putting him in synchronization with the will of Zeus. The part of the poem known as the "Days" is less impressive because it is rooted in the "science" or superstition of Hesiod's world. It is a forerunner of astrological prediction—an attempt to make sense of mysterious, perplexing aspects of existence. It represents a variety of superstitions, particularly numerology, extant in Mesopotamia and Egypt. Hesiod is recording the folk wisdom of the tribe, another valid task of the didactic poet.

Summary

The fifth century judgment of Herodotus, that "Hesiod and Homer are the ones who provided the Greeks with a theogony, gave the gods their names, distinguished their attributes and functions, and defined their various types," is still valid. The mythic truth that Hesiod established is the basis for the origin of the European mind and worldview, the beginning of a definition of Western civilization. In his work, the strong thread of value and principle that distinguishes the most admirable attributes of culture can be traced back to its inception. The ultimate lessons of his philosophy, organized through reflection upon astronomical phenomena, are to live in harmony with the visible, the regular, the knowable, and to acknowledge and forbear the illusive, the abrupt, the terrible. Speaking across the gulf of time, Hesiod remains the "great teacher and civilizer," the poet as embodiment of the divine voice that offers access to universal truth which humankind ignores at its own peril.

Bibliography
Athanassakis, Apostolos N. *Hesiod: Theogony, Works and Days, Shield*. Baltimore: Johns Hopkins University Press, 1983. An imaginative modern translation, combined with lucid, thorough notes and an incisive introduction. The author's familiarity with historic and contemporary Greece enables him to offer many relevant details from folk culture.

Brown, Norman O. *Theogony*. New York: Liberal Arts Press, 1953. A reliable translation with a detailed, interpretive introduction that contains perceptive commentary on the poem's meaning.

Burn, Andrew Robert. *The World of Hesiod: A Study of the Greek Middle Ages*. London: K. Paul, Trench, Trübner and Co., 1936. An early study that examines the poet in his historical context. Much basic background information.

Evelyn-White, Hugh G., ed. and trans. *Hesiod, the Homeric Hymns, and Homerica*. Cambridge, Mass.: Harvard University Press, 1914. The translation considered standard through most of the twentieth century.

Frazer, R. M. *The Poems of Hesiod*. Norman: University of Oklahoma Press, 1983. A somewhat ornate but reliable recent translation with informative commentary.

Havelock, Eric. *Preface to Plato*. Cambridge, Mass.: Harvard University Press, 1963. An excellent discussion of "oral acoustic intelligence," the tradition in which Hesiod composed.

Janko, R. *Homer, Hesiod, and the Hymns: Diachronic Development in Epic Diction*. Cambridge: Cambridge University Press, 1982. Solid scholarship and interesting speculation about the development of the hexameter tradition, with many theoretical assertions about dates and origins.

Lamberton, Robert. *Hesiod*. Fort Lauderdale, Fla.: Hermes Books, 1988. An accessible introduction to Hesiod's works. Historical background of the poems and problems of dating them are discussed. Major subsidiary works are analyzed.

Pucci, Pietro. *Hesiod and the Language of Poetry*. Baltimore: Johns Hopkins University Press, 1977. An extremely detailed examination of the meaning of words in Hesiod. Primarily for the specialist but clear in presentation.

Thalmann, William G. *Conventions of Form and Thought in Early Greek Epic Poetry*. Baltimore: Johns Hopkins University Press, 1984. A comprehensive, carefully annotated examination of the form and structure of the poetry of Homer and Hesiod, illuminating parallel approaches in the work of both poets and providing many incisive comments on the meanings of their poems. An impressive assimilation and extension of much previous scholarship on the subject.

Walcot, P. *Hesiod and the Near East*. Cardiff: Wales University Press, 1966. The important influences of Oriental literature and thought on Hesiod are traced and explained. Good background information on life in Boeotia in Hesiod's time as well.

West, M. L. *Hesiod: "Theogony" and "Works and Days."* New York: Oxford University Press, 1988. An excellent translation of Hesiod's major work by one of the leading experts on Hesiod's writing. Includes a short but very enlightening introduction and notes.

──────────. *The Hesiod Catalogue of Women: Its Nature, Structure, and Origins*. New York: Oxford University Press, 1985. A definitive study of a work previously attributed to Hesiod.

──────────. *Theogony*. Oxford: Clarendon Press, 1966. A critical edition with an extensive, informative introduction.

──────────. *Works and Days: With Prolegomena and Commentary*. Oxford: Clarendon Press, 1978. A companion to the author's *Theogony*.

Leon Lewis

HILDEGARD VON BINGEN

Born: 1098; Bermersheim bei Alzey
Died: September 17, 1179; Rupertsberg bei Bingen
Areas of Achievement: Religion, literature, and music
Contribution: The first major German mystic, Hildegard, in her prolific writings and extensive preaching, exerted a widespread influence on religious and political figures in twelfth century Europe.

Early Life

Born in 1098 in Bermersheim bei Alzey, Rheinhessen (now in West Germany), Hildegard von Bingen was the tenth and last child of Hildebert von Bermersheim, a knight in the service of Meginhard, Count of Spanheim, and his wife, Mechtild. At her birth, her parents consecrated Hildegard to God as a tithe. As early as the age of three, Hildegard had her first vision of a dazzling white light, which she was later to call the *umbra viventis lucis* (shadow of the living Light), which appeared to her as reflected in a *fons vitae* (shining pool). Other visions followed, along with accurate premonitions of the future. When she was eight years old, her parents entrusted her to the care of the learned Jutta of Spanheim, a holy anchoress attached to the Benedictine Abbey of Mount Saint Disibode.

Hildegard's visions continued during her adolescence, but, embarrassed when she began to realize that she was alone in seeing them, she began to keep them to herself, confiding only in Jutta. In spite of her ill health, Hildegard began her studies under Jutta, learning to read and sing Latin. Her further education was entrusted to the monk Volmar of Saint Disibode, who, over time, became her lifelong friend, confidant, and secretary. At age fourteen, she took vows and received the veil from Bishop Otto von Bamberg, the hermitage of Jutta having by this time attracted enough followers to become a community under the Rule of Saint Benedict.

The next two decades were formative years for Hildegard: She acquired an extensive knowledge of the Scriptures, the church fathers and later church writers, the monastic liturgy, science, medicine, and philosophy. From her later writings it is possible to trace specific writers she studied during this period: Saint Augustine, Boethius, Saint Isidore of Seville, Bernard Silvestris, Aristotle, Galen, Messahalah, Constantine the African, Hugh of Saint Victor, Alberic the Younger. Meanwhile, she continued to experience the charisma of her mystical visions. When Jutta died in 1136, Hildegard, at thirty-eight, was unanimously elected abbess by the nuns of her community.

Life's Work

The turning point in Hildegard's life came in 1141, when she received a commandment from God: "Write, what you see and hear! Tell people how to enter the kingdom of salvation!" She initially went through a period of self-doubt—how could she, *ego paupercula feminea forma* (a poor little figure of a woman), be chosen as a mouthpiece for God?—and was concerned as to whether others would give credence to her visions. She finally confided fully in her confessor, the monk Godfrey, who referred the matter to his abbot, Kuno. Kuno ordered Hildegard to write down some of her visions, which he then submitted to the Archbishop of Mainz. The archbishop determined that Hildegard's visions were indeed divinely inspired, and Hildegard ultimately came to accept a view of herself as a woman chosen to fulfill God's work.

A ten-year collaboration between Hildegard and her secretary Volmar began, as she dictated to him her principal work, *Scivias*, an abbreviation for *nosce vias* [*Domini*], or "know the ways of the Lord," (1141-1151; English translation, 1986), consisting of twenty-six visions dealing with the relationships and interdependence between the triune God and humans through the Creation, Redemption, and Church. The visions also contained apocalyptic prophecies and warnings, which would motivate Hildegard to begin an extensive correspondence of more than one hundred letters to popes, emperors, kings, archbishops, abbots, and abbesses; she also began to journey throughout Germany and France preaching against the abuses and corruption of the Church. As her visions led her to an active role in church and social reform, she came to accept her link with the tradition of the female prophets (Deborah, Olda, Hannah, Elizabeth).

In 1147, when Pope Eugenius III held a synod in Trier, he appointed a commission to examine Hildegard's writing. Bernard of Clairvaux, with whom Hildegard had corresponded, spoke affirmatively of her. Subsequently, in a letter to Hildegard, the Pope approved her visions as authentic manifestations of the Holy Spirit and, warning her against pride, gave her apostolic license to continue writing and publishing. Hildegard, in return, wrote the Pope a long letter urging him to work for reform in the Church and the monasteries. The woman who initially had felt timid serving as a mouthpiece for the Word of God was beginning to speak with the uncompromising sense of justice that was to characterize her prophetic and apostolic mission for the rest of her life.

With the Pope's endorsement of her visions, Hildegard's renown and the number of postulants at her convent grew, and she determined to separate from the monastery of Saint Disibode and to found a new community at Rupertsberg, near Bingen, a site which had been revealed to her in a vision. Despite the objections of the monks of Saint Disibode and their abbot, Kuno, who would lose prestige and revenue with her departure, Hildegard used family connections with the Archbishop of Mainz to secure the property and personally oversaw the construction of a convent large enough to house fifty nuns. In 1150, she moved to Rupertsberg with eighteen other nuns. As abbess, Hildegard managed to obtain exclusive rights to the Rupertsberg property from Abbot Kuno in 1155, and several years later it was arranged that she would respond directly to the Archbishop of Mainz as her superior rather than to the abbot of Saint Disibode.

Under Hildegard's leadership, the new community flourished, as did her own work and creative production. In 1151, she completed *Scivias*, concluding the work with a liturgical drama set to music. *Ordo virtutum* (1151) is the earliest known morality play and a dramatic work of considerable originality and merit. Between 1151 and 1158, seventy-seven individual hymns and canticles which she had written for her nuns were collected in a lyrical cycle entitled *Symphonia harmonia caelestium revelationum* (the harmonious symphony of heavenly revelations), which, according to Peter Dronke, contains "some of the most unusual, subtle, and exciting poetry of the twelfth century." Her music, ranging in mood from tranquil lyricism to declamatory intensity, includes some of the finest songs written in the Middle Ages.

Hildegard, who in addition to her responsibilities as abbess served in the convent infirmary, commenced work on two books on natural history and medicine. Characterized by careful scientific observation, Hildegard's medical and scientific studies contain the prototypes of some modern methods of diagnosis and anticipate certain later discoveries such as circulation of the blood and psychosomatic illness.

She also wrote a commentary on the Gospels, an explication of the Rule of Saint Benedict and one of the Athanasian Creed, and the lives of Saint Rupert and Saint Disibode.

It was primarily for her mystical trilogy that Hildegard was known in her day: that is, *Scivias*, a treatise on ethics entitled *Liber vitae meritorum* (1158-1163; book of life's merits), and *De operatione Dei* (1163-1173; *Book of Divine Works*, 1987), a vast cosmology and theodicy. It is these works, together with her letters, that primarily account for the late twentieth century renaissance in Hildegard scholarship. The illuminated manuscript of *Scivias* that was prepared at her scriptorium in 1165 is of interest not only to modern theologians and art historians but also to the lay person desiring access to her prolific and sometimes abstruse work.

Known by her twelfth century contemporaries as the *prophetissa Teutonica*, the Sibyl of the Rhine, Hildegard continued, into her seventies and eighties, to travel widely in Germany and France, providing spiritual direction and preaching. Pilgrims flocked to her convent; her advice was sought by popes and archbishops, emperors and kings, religious and lay persons of all classes. Her influence in twelfth century Europe was considerable. Through the years, she corresponded with four popes—Eugene III, Anastasius IV, Adrian IV, and Alexander III—and with two German emperors, Conrad III and his son and successor Frederick I Barbarossa, whom she rebuked for supporting an antipope. She also sent letters to Henry II of England and his queen Eleanor, the divorced wife of Louis VII. She corresponded with Bernard of Clairvaux and preached his crusade in her travels. She corresponded continuously with the Archbishop of Mainz and with bishops and clergy throughout Germany, the Low Countries, and central Europe. Moreover, she maintained a personal correspondence with twenty-five abbesses of various convents. Constant and uncompromising themes in her letters were condemnation of the abuses and corruption within both church and secular government and the need for social justice, compassion, and wisdom.

The year before her death, when she was in her eighties, Hildegard faced a difficult ethical trial. Her community was placed under interdict for having buried in the convent cemetery a revolutionary youth who had been excommunicated. Hildegard refused to have the body exhumed and removed as ordered; instead, she blessed the grave with her abbatial staff and removed all traces of it. In her view, although the young man had been excommunicated, because he had been absolved and reconciled with the Church before dying, he merited a sacred burial. The interdict forbade the community to hear Mass, receive the Eucharist, or sing the Divine Office. As painful as the interdict was to Hildegard, her sense of justice and her fidelity to her "living Light," no matter what the cost to her, led her to withstand the pressure to give in; she would not let the letter of the law stand before the spirit of the law. Hildegard wrote numerous letters of protest to the appropriate authorities, until finally her argument prevailed and the interdict was removed. Six months later, in 1179, she died.

Summary

The first major German mystic, Hildegard von Bingen has never been formally canonized (three proceedings were initiated in the thirteenth and fourteenth centuries, but none was ever completed), yet she is included in the martyrologies and in the Acta Sanctorum under the title "saint," and in 1979 Pope John Paul II, on the eight hundredth anniversary of Hildegard's death, referred to her as "an outstanding saint." Through her preaching, writings, and correspondence, she actively influenced the decisions and policies of religious and political leaders of her day. The founder of the Rhineland mystic movement, she influenced later medieval mystics, including Mechtild of Magdeburg and Meister Eckehart. Further, the themes of ecology, social responsibility, the cocreativity of human beings, feminine aspects of the divine, and the interconnectivity of the cosmos in her visionary writings have been noted by Creation-centered theologians in the twentieth century.

Although philosophically Abbess Hildegard accepted the Catholic medieval view of woman's subordination to man, based on the doctrine of the Fall, her visions encouraged her to become highly independent in her thinking, actions, and creations. She made significant contributions in her medical writings. Her poetry, music, and liturgical drama *Ordo virtutum* are original

in form and ideas. Her visionary works, while they also provide a compendium of contemporary thought, are a unique phenomenon in twelfth century
letters, as are the manuscript illuminations which accompany them. Considering the originality of her visionary cosmology, it is not surprising that Hildegard of Bingen has been compared to both Dante and William Blake.

Bibliography

Chicago, Judy. *The Dinner Party: A Symbol of Our Heritage*. Garden City,
N.Y.: Doubleday and Co., 1979. Describes the creation of "The Dinner
Party," a monumental work of art celebrating the contributions of thirty-
nine significant female figures in Western civilization, including Hildegard
of Bingen as "one of the greatest and most original thinkers of medieval
Europe."

Dronke, Peter. *Poetic Individuality in the Middle Ages: New Departures in
Poetry, 1000-1150*. Oxford: Oxford University Press, 1970. An excellent
study of the poetic imagery of Hildegard's lyrics, with numerous textual
examples in the Latin original and in translation. Analyzes the *Ordo
virtutum* as a fusion between a morality play and the expression of mystical
experience. Contains the complete Latin text of the *Ordo virtutum* and the
musical transcriptions of two of Hildegard's melismatic sequences from the
Symphonia harmoniae caelestium revelationum.

_____. *Women Writers of the Middle Ages*. Cambridge: Cambridge
University Press, 1984. A substantial study of the nature of Hildegard's
visionary experiences and their influence on the development of her
cosmological thought. Focuses on Hildegard's autobiographical writings,
her letters, and her medical treatises, including excerpts from selected
texts and letters in the Latin original and in translation.

Gies, Frances, and Joseph Gies. *Women in the Middle Ages*. New York:
Thomas Y. Crowell, 1978. A sociological view of women's lives in the
Middle Ages, with selected significant figures as examples of various social
roles; Hildegard represents female monasticism.

Hildegard of Bingen. *Book of Divine Works, with Letters and Songs*. Translated and edited by Matthew Fox. Santa Fe, N.M.: Bear and Co., 1987.
Contains translations of important primary source material: Hildegard's
third major visionary opus, forty-two selected letters; and twelve songs.
Also contains a good summary introduction to Hildegard's life and works.

_____. *Illuminations of Hildegard of Bingen*. Edited by Matthew
Fox. Santa Fe, N.M.: Bear and Co., 1985. Color reproductions of the illuminations of Hildegard's visionary manuscripts, accompanied by extensive
commentary on the themes of her cosmology.

_____. *Scivias*. Translated by Bruce Hozeski. Santa Fe, N.M.: Bear
and Co., 1986. The translated text of Hildegard's major visionary cycle,
accompanied by black-and-white illustrations of the text's illuminations.

Introductory essays include a biographical sketch, a review of her work, and an analysis of the structure and contents of *Scivias*.

Kraft, Kent. "The German Visionary: Hildegard of Bingen." In *Medieval Women Writers*, edited by Katharina Wilson. Athens: University of Georgia Press, 1984. An interpretive study of significant events in Hildegard's life and their influence on her works. Provides a summary review and analysis of her important creative work, followed by selected excerpts from her works.

Lagorio, Valerie M. "The Medieval Continental Women Mystics: An Introduction." In *An Introduction to the Medieval Mystics of Europe*, edited by Paul E. Szarmach. Albany: State University of New York Press, 1984. An insightful survey of important European women mystics from Hildegard of Bingen in the twelfth century to Saint Catherine of Siena in the fourteenth century.

Newman, Barbara. *Sister of Wisdom: St. Hildegard's Theology of the Feminine*. Berkeley: University of California Press, 1987. A comprehensive scholarly study which examines Hildegard's contributions within the context of twelfth century thought and also as part of the sapiential tradition.

Schmitt, Miriam. "Hildegard of Bingen: A Prophetic Sign for Her Times." *Benedictines* 41, no. 1 (1986): 31-40. Examines Hildegard's developing recognition of the significance of her visions, her spiritual awakening to her call as a prophet, and her increasing consciousness of the importance of her ministry of justice to the Church and to the world.

Jean T. Strandness

HIPPARCHUS

Born: 190 B.C.; Nicaea, Bithynia, Asia Minor
Died: 126 B.C.; possibly Rhodes
Areas of Achievement: Astronomy, mathematics, and geography
Contribution: Hipparchus was the greatest astronomer of ancient times. He
was the founder of trigonometry, which he used in a method for determin-
ing the distances from Earth to the moon and sun, and the first to use
consistently the idea of latitude and longitude to describe locations on
Earth and in the sky.

Early Life

Very little is known about Hipparchus' life. He was born in Nicaea, a
Greek-speaking city in Bithynia (modern Iznik, Turkey), in the northwestern
part of Asia Minor. Calculations in his works are based on the latitude of the
city of Rhodes, on the island of the same name, so many historians believe
that he spent a major portion of his life there. Rhodes was a merchant center, a convenient port from which to make voyages. At least one of Hipparchus' observations was made in Alexandria, so it seems that he visited and
perhaps spent time as a student or research scholar at that great nucleus of
scientific inquiry. Since he was intensely interested in geography, it is likely
that he traveled to other places in the Mediterranean basin and the Near
East. He seems to have been familiar with Babylonian astronomy, including
eclipse records, but it is impossible to say how he came to know these.

Life's Work

Most of what is known of Hipparchus comes from the *Mathēmatikē
suntaxis* (c. A.D. 150; *Almagest*) of Ptolemy, whose work depends to a considerable extent on that of the earlier scientist, and from the *Geōgraphica*
(c. 7 B.C.; *Geography*) of Strabo. Of Hipparchus' own writings, only the
Tōn Araton kai Eudoxou phainomenōn exēgēsis (*Commentary on the Phaeno-
mena of Eudoxus and Aratus*) survives, in three books. It criticizes the less
accurate placement of stars and constellations by two famous predecessors. It
is certainly not one of his most important works, but it contains some information on his observations of star positions, which were the basis of his lost
star catalog. Other lost works of Hipparchus include *Peri eviausiou
megethous* (on the length of the year) and *Peri tēs metabaseōs tōn tropikōn
kai isēmerinōn semeiōn* (on the displacement of the solstitial and equinoctial
points). He is also credited with a trigonometrical table of chords in a circle,
a work on gravitational phenomena called *On Bodies Carried down by Their
Weight*, an attack on the geographical work of Eratosthenes, a compilation
of weather signs, and some aids to computational astrology.

A number of achievements are attributed to Hipparchus by Ptolemy and other ancient writers. A new star appeared in the constellation Scorpio in July, 133 B.C. Hipparchus realized that without an accurate star catalog, it was impossible to demonstrate that the star was indeed new, so he set about producing a complete sky map with a table of the positions of the stars, including the angle north or south of the celestial equator (latitude) and the angle east or west of the vernal equinox point (one of the two intersections between the celestial equator and the sun's path, or ecliptic). In order to do this, he needed a means of measuring celestial angles, which led him to invent many of the sighting instruments, including the diopter and possibly the armillary astrolabe, used by astronomers before the invention of the telescope in the seventeenth century. He also knew how to calibrate water clocks. Hipparchus' star catalog included about 850 stars, along with estimates of their brightness. He divided the stars into six categories, from the brightest to the dimmest, thus originating a system of stellar magnitude. He also made a celestial globe, showing the locations of the fixed stars on its surface.

In comparing his own measurements of positions of stars with those of earlier astronomers, Hipparchus discovered that there had been a systematic shift in the same direction in all of them. He noticed the phenomenon first in the case of the bright star Spica. In 283 B.C. Timocharis had observed the star to be eight degrees west of the autumnal equinoctial point, but Hipparchus found the figure to be six degrees. He found a displacement for every other star which he was able to check. These discrepancies, he established, were the result of a shift in the position of the equinoxes—and therefore of the celestial equator and poles. In modern astronomy, this shift is called the precession of the equinoxes and is known to be caused by a slow "wobble" in the orientation of Earth's axis. The spot to which the north pole points in the sky (the north celestial pole) describes a circle in a period of more than twenty-six thousand years. Hipparchus was first to describe and to attempt to measure this phenomenon. He was, however, unable to explain its cause, since he held the geocentric theory which postulates a motionless Earth at the center of a moving universe.

From the beginning of theoretical astronomy, the geocentric theory had been the accepted one. It assumed that the sun, moon, planets, and stars were carried on vast transparent spheres that revolved at different but constant speeds around Earth. Unfortunately, in order to explain the observed motions of the planets, which vary in speed and sometimes are retrograde relative to the stars, astronomers had to postulate the existence of additional spheres, invisible and bearing no celestial bodies but interconnected with the other spheres and affecting their motions. An Alexandrian astronomer, Aristarchus, had proposed the heliocentric theory, which holds that Earth, with its satellite the moon, and all the other planets revolve around the central sun. The main appeal of this theory was its simplicity; it required fewer imaginary spheres to make it work.

Hipparchus rejected the heliocentric theory and instead adopted modifications of the geocentric theory to make it accord better with observations,
perhaps following Apollonius of Perga. The main feature of the Hipparchan
system is the epicycle, a smaller sphere bearing a planet, with its center on
the surface of the larger, Earth-centered sphere and revolving at an independent speed. He also postulated eccentrics, that is, that the centers of the
celestial spheres do not coincide with the center of Earth. The geocentric
system with epicycles is often called "Ptolemaic," since Ptolemy made observations to support the theory developed by Hipparchus. Aristarchus' heliocentric theory is closer to the picture of the solar system provided by modern astronomy.

In developing his astronomical system, Hipparchus observed the period of
revolution of the celestial objects that move against the background of the
stars. That of the sun, which is the year, he found to be 365 ¼ days, less ⅟₃₀₀
of a day, a figure which was closer to the true one than that of any previous
astronomer. He noticed the inequality in the lengths of the seasons, which he
correctly attributed to the varying distance between Earth and the sun but in-
correctly explained by assuming that the center of the sun's sphere of revolution was eccentric to the center of Earth. These conclusions were, perhaps, a
step in the direction of recognizing that the relative motion of the two bodies
describes an ellipse. He also achieved a measurement of the length of the
lunar month, with an error of less than one second in comparison with the
figure now accepted. The Roman scholar Pliny the Elder wrote that Hipparchus countered the popular fear of eclipses by publishing a list which demonstrated their regularity over the preceding six hundred years.

Hipparchus attempted to measure the distances of the moon and sun from
Earth by observing eclipses and the phenomenon of parallax (the shift in the
apparent position of the moon against the background of the stars under
changing conditions). His figure for the distance of the moon (60.5 times the
radius of Earth) was reasonably accurate, but his estimate of the sun's distance (2,550 times Earth's radius) was far too small. (The true ratio is about
23,452 to 1.) In fairness to Hipparchus, it should be noted that he regarded
his solution to the problem of the sun's distance as open to question.

In order to make the mathematical computations required by these problems, it was necessary for Hipparchus to know the ratios of the sides of a
right triangle for the various angles the sides make with the hypotenuse—in
other words, the values of trigonometrical functions. He worked out tables of
the sine function, thus becoming, in effect, the founder of trigonometry.

Geography also occupied Hipparchus' attention. He began the systematic
use of longitude and latitude, which he had also employed in his star catalog,
as a means of establishing locations on Earth's surface. Previous geographers
show evidence of knowing such a method, but they did not employ it consis-

tently. Hipparchus was able to calculate latitudes of various places on Earth's surface by learning the lengths of the days and nights recorded for different seasons of the year, although the figures given by him were often in error. As the base of longitude, he used the meridian passing through Alexandria. He was especially critical, probably too much so, of the descriptive and mathematical errors in the work of Eratosthenes. He even had some quibbles with the famous measurement of the spherical Earth, which is the latter's most brilliant achievement. It may be Hipparchus rather than Eratosthenes who first described climatic zones, bounded by parallels of latitude north and south of the equator.

Summary

Hipparchus was a careful and original astronomer whose discoveries, particularly that of precession, were of the greatest importance in the early history of the science. He was a meticulous observer who produced the first dependable star catalog and who determined the apparent periods of revolution of the moon and the sun with an exactitude never before achieved. As a mathematician, he originated the study of trigonometry, compiling a sine table and using it in an attempt to measure distances in space beyond Earth which was, at least in the case of the moon, successful. Both as astronomer and as geographer, he pioneered the systematic use of the coordinates of latitude and longitude. He devised instruments for use in these observations and measurements.

Unfortunately, almost all Hipparchus' writings have disappeared, so modern assessments of his work must depend on ancient writers who happened to mention him. His influence was important enough to cause several later scientists whose works survive to refer to and summarize him. Most notable among these were Ptolemy and Strabo. It is sometimes hard to tell when these authors, particularly Ptolemy, are following Hipparchus and when they are going beyond him to present their own conclusions. Ptolemy's work became the standard textbook on astronomy down to the time of Nicolaus Copernicus in the sixteenth century; thus Hipparchus' name was deservedly remembered. One of Hipparchus' most important mathematical successors was Menelaus of Alexandria (fl. c. A.D. 100), who developed the study of spherical trigonometry.

Bibliography

Dicks, D. R. *Early Greek Astronomy to Aristotle*. Ithaca, N.Y.: Cornell University Press, 1970. Hipparchus is not given major treatment, although he does appear as an important figure in the history of astronomy. The discussion of his criticisms of Eudoxus and Aratus is particularly good.

Dreyer, John L. E. *A History of Astronomy from Thales to Kepler*. Rev. ed. New York: Dover Publications, 1953. This fine, accessible study places

Hipparchus clearly in the context of the development of astronomy. Dreyer differs from common interpretation in crediting Ptolemy, not Hipparchus, with the theory of epicycles.

Heath, Thomas. *A History of Greek Mathematics.* 2 vols. Oxford: Clarendon Press, 1921. Includes a section on Hipparchus in the second volume, emphasizing his probable contributions to the origin of trigonometry and establishing his place in the history of mathematics.

Lloyd, G. E. R. *Greek Science After Aristotle.* New York: W. W. Norton and Co., 1973. Rather than giving a separate treatment to the subject, this work discusses the contributions of Hipparchus as they arise in a general study of ancient science from the fourth century B.C. to the end of the second century A.D. The attention given to Hipparchus is appropriate and appreciative.

Neugebauer, Otto. *A History of Ancient Mathematical Astronomy.* 3 vols. New York: Springer-Verlag, 1975. This work contains a section on Hipparchus in volume 1, briefly discussing what little is known about his life and chronology and devoting the rest of its space to a careful consideration of his astronomical work. There are some mathematical and astronomical symbols and formulas which the layperson may find difficult.

_____. "Notes on Hipparchus." In *The Aegean and the Near East: Studies Presented to Hetty Goldman*, edited by Saul S. Weinberg. Locust Valley, N.Y.: J. J. Augustin, 1956. An important discussion of the extent to which Hipparchus knew Babylonian astronomy.

Ptolemy. *Ptolemy's "Almagest."* Translated by G. J. Toomer. New York: Springer-Verlag, 1984. Much of what is known about Hipparchus is based on Ptolemy's words. This fine translation has complete notes and a useful bibliography.

Thompson, J. Oliver. *History of Ancient Geography.* Cambridge: Cambridge University Press, 1948. Gives adequate notice to the geographical theories and contributions of Hipparchus in various parts of a more general study.

J. Donald Hughes

HIPPOCRATES

Born: Probably 460 B.C.; Cos
Died: Probably 377 B.C.; Larissa, Thessaly
Area of Achievement: Medicine
Contribution: Hippocrates is credited with separating the practice of medicine from magic and superstition, inaugurating the modern practice of scientific observation, and setting the guidelines for high standards of ethical
medical practice.

Early Life

Hippocrates was born in Cos; he lived during the period spanning the end
of the fifth century and the first half of the fourth century B.C., according to
two references to him in Plato's dialogues. Though little else can be thoroughly documented, many legends, possibly true in parts, have been offered
by commentators regarding Hippocrates' early life. According to tradition,
Hippocrates was one of several sons of Praxithea and Heracleides. He probably had the education suitable to one of his background, which would
include nine years of physical education, reading, writing, spelling, music,
singing, and poetry. After another two years at a gymnasium, where he
would have had intensive training in athletics, it is conjectured that Hippocrates studied medicine under his father, a member of the priest-physician
group known as Asclepiads. This training was a form of apprenticeship in a
medical guild.

In addition to his training, which consisted of following a physician and
observing his treatment of patients, Hippocrates is believed to have traveled
to the nearby islands of the Aegean Sea, to the Greek mainland, and possibly to Egypt and Libya, to study the local medical traditions. He is thought
to have met the philosopher Democritus and the rhetorician Gorgias.

His sons Thessalus and Draco carried on the family tradition of medical
practice. As testimony to his fame, legend also has it that King Perdiccas of
Macedonia asked Hippocrates and another physician, Euryphon, to examine
him and that Hippocrates helped him to recover from his illness.

Hippocrates was equally renowned as a teacher, giving rise to the image of
the "Tree of Hippocrates" beneath which students sat and listened to him.
Plato, a younger contemporary, referred to Hippocrates the Asclepiad as the
very type of the teacher of medicine. Some historical accounts suggest that
Hippocrates habitually covered his head with a felt cap, though the reason
for this habit is only a matter of speculation. This description did, however,
help twentieth century archaeologists to identify a likeness of him.

Life's Work

That Hippocrates was a well-known Greek physician who lived in the
period of golden achievements in Greek history is undisputed. The rest of his

achievements remain a matter of scholarly debate, centered on the problem of *Corpus Hippocraticum* (fifth to third century B.C.; Hippocratic collection), a substantial body of writings whose authorship seems to be spread out over different historical periods.

Thus the medical views expressed in this collection are carefully referred to as the ideas of Hippocratic medicine, acknowledging the complete lack of confirmation about the identity of his actual writings. Of the approximately seventy unsigned treatises which constitute the collection, only two are definitively known to have been written by Hippocrates' son-in-law, Polybus, because another famous ancient writer, Aristotle, quoted from them.

The normal historical tendency has been to attribute those which are written with authority and good sense and which seem to be of the approximately right time period to Hippocrates and the rest to other authors. The debate over the authorship of the *Corpus Hippocraticum* itself has produced an enormous body of scholarship; one tentative point of agreement is that the earliest essays are from the fifth century B.C. and the latest about two centuries later. To cloud the matter even further, the Hippocratic writings themselves are inconsistent, suggesting that the collection incorporates the thinking of different schools of medical practice.

The collection is historically important precisely because it had more than one purpose: to establish medicine as a practice distinct from philosophy and religion and, in furtherance of this goal, to collect information about this separate discipline in writing for the future edification of patients and physicians. Part of this effort involved debate with other schools of thought, such as the Cnidian school.

The centers of medical teaching were often in the temples of healing known as Asclepieions. The two most famous ones of the time were on Cos and Cnidus, between which there was a traditional rivalry and a fundamental difference in approach to medical practice. The Cnidus practitioners, under the guidance of the chief physician, Euryphon, seemed to have been much concerned about the classification of diseases and continued the tradition of deductive knowledge of disease derived from the practice of ancient Greece, Babylonia, and Egypt. Hippocrates was of the Coan school, which worked more inductively, concentrating on observation and treatment of the entire patient and taking into account the mental as well as the physical state.

The first important contribution of the Hippocratic writers—to separate medicine from the shackles of religion, superstition, and philosophy—is apparent in the first text of the collection, *Peri archaies ietrikes* (fifth or fourth century B.C.; *Ancient Medicine*), which is a reminder that medicine had previously been very much a matter for philosophical speculation. This essay establishes medicine as a branch of knowledge with its own rational methods and describes a practice that calls for skill and craft and art, one based on observation.

Hippocratic medicine recognized disease as a natural process and further suggested that most acute diseases are self-limited. The symptoms of fever, malaise, and other apparent sicknesses were not considered to be mysterious spiritual symptoms but merely the body's way of fighting off the poison of infection. Epilepsy, for example, much feared as a mysterious, sacred affliction, is discussed as a medical problem. The focus of Hippocratic medicine was on regulation of diet, meaning not merely nutrition but exercise as well. The adjustment of diet to the physical state of the patient was thus viewed as the original function of medicine and the importance of the kind of food and its preparation to treat sickness was recognized early.

The Hippocratic writers mention other ideas equally surprising in their modern relevance and influence, such as the notion that great changes, whether in temperature, periods of life, or diet, are most likely to lead to illness. Thus the collection of four books entitled *Peri diaites* (fifth or fourth century B.C.; *Regimen*) starts with the argument that health is affected by the totality of diet and exercise; the age, strength, and constitution of the individual; the seasonal changes; variations in wind and weather; and the location in which the patient lives. The Hippocratic idea that a local condition must be treated in conjunction with the general condition, the whole constitution (*physis*) and the complex relations to the environment, is also remarkably similar to the modern notion of holistic healing.

Though many of the other practices and theories have been discarded medically, some were influential for so long that they have been incorporated into the history of Western culture. For example, among the most influential theories set forth in the Hippocratic collection is the idea that the human body is composed of four fluid substances: blood, phlegm, yellow bile, and black bile. Perfect health results from the balance of these fluids in the body. Concomitantly, an excess or deficiency or imperfect mixture results in pain, sickness, and disease. The influence of this theory is apparent in many classics of Western literature, such as the plays of William Shakespeare and Ben Jonson.

Hippocratic medicine was also conservative, seeking primarily to help the sick when it would be beneficial. Medicine was defined by three purposes: It should relieve suffering, reduce the severity of the illness, and finally, abstain from treating that which was beyond the practice of medicine. The physician's job was to help the natural recovery process with diet and regimen, to be administered only after careful observation of the individual symptoms and the patient's constitution. The remedies recommended were mild and adapted to the various stages of the disease; drugs were relatively rare. Most important, sudden and violent measures to interrupt the natural course of the disease were forbidden. The Coan school believed in prognosis, in predicting, from the experience of long and careful observation, the course of the disease and furthermore in telling the patients and their friends, so that they could be mentally prepared for what might follow, even if it were death. This dictum prevented the physician from prescribing ineffective or expensive treatments simply to remain busy; it is thought that the Hippocratic physician would not even undertake the treatment of a hopeless case, though he probably did his best to make the patient as comfortable as possible.

The most important view in the Hippocratic collection—the most important because it is still unchanged over the course of two thousand years—is the clearly expressed concept of the medical profession as it is summed up in the Hippocratic oath. The doctor is defined as a good man, skilled at healing. Perhaps for this definition alone, the man who is thought to have written or inspired the Hippocratic writings has been called the father of medicine, a title that suggests the ideal of the philosopher-physician—similar to the ideal of the philosopher-king—a person with moral character as well as practical skills.

Summary

Hippocrates was a much-admired physician whose contemporaries were also giants in their fields: Aeschylus, Sophocles, and Euripides in tragedy; Aristophanes in comedy; Thucydides in history; Pericles in government. Leaving aside the question of authorship of the Hippocratic writings, it is clear why the figure of Hippocrates, for whom the collection is named, is so revered: The keen observations of human behavior and health recorded in these pieces remain fruitful reading.

The Hippocratic writings include a book of more than four hundred aphorisms, pithy observations which have been absorbed, though sometimes in a mutilated form, into the English language, influencing those outside the medical field. The most famous of these, popularly remembered as "Life is short, Art long," started as

> Life is short, whereas the demands of the (medical) profession are unending, the crisis is urgent, experiment dangerous, and decision difficult. But the physician must not only do what is necessary, he must also get the patient, the attendants, and the external factors to work together to the same end.

Others reveal a common sense which has been proven over and over again: "Restricted or strict diets are dangerous; extremes must be avoided"; "People who are excessively overweight (by nature) are far more apt to die suddenly than those of average weight"; "Inebriation removes hunger (for solid foods)."

If much of the rest of the body of medical knowledge represented by Hippocrates has long since been surpassed, its spirit has not. Hippocrates and his colleagues changed the attitude toward disease, freeing medicine from magic and superstition and insisting on the importance of observation over philosophical speculation. The Hippocratic writings established medicine as a separate discipline with a scientific basis, setting down in writing the medical knowledge of the time regarding surgery, prognosis, therapeutics, principles of medical ethics, and relations between physicians and patient, thus laying the foundations and formulating the ideals of modern medicine.

Bibliography

Coulter, Harris L. *Divided Legacy: A History of the Schism in Medical Thought*. Vol. 1, *The Patterns Emerge: Hippocrates to Paracelsus*. Washington, D.C.: Wehawken Book Co., 1975. The subtitle of the first volume refers to two patterns of thought, rational and empirical, dominating medical history. The author places Hippocrates in the empirical tradition. Provides an extensive bibliography and index. Lists quotations from original writings.

Edelstein, Ludwig. *The Hippocratic Oath: Text, Translation, and Interpretation*. Baltimore: Johns Hopkins University Press, 1943. This monograph argues that the Hippocratic oath represented the opinion of a small segment of Greek medical society, was based on Pythagorean principles, and served as a voluntary oath of conscience between teacher and student.

Goldberg, Herbert S. *Hippocrates, Father of Medicine*. New York: Franklin Watts, 1963. A short, simplified overview of the life and work of Hippocrates, his times, and his relevance to modern health practice. Index.

Heidel, William Arthur. *Hippocratic Medicine: Its Spirit and Method*. New York: Columbia University Press, 1941. Heidel discusses the close connections among science, philosophy, history, and medicine in the period of Hippocratic medicine. Provides notes and sources.

Jones, W. H. S., trans. *Hippocrates*. 4 vols. London: Heinemann, 1923-1931. Among the best English translations and critical editions of Hippocratic writings, this work is part of the Loeb Classical Library edition. Greek texts face their English counterparts.

Levine, Edwin Burton. *Hippocrates*. New York: Twayne Publishers, 1971. Levine introduces the problems of scholarship in identifying authorship of the Hippocratic writings. The discussion focuses on ideas presented in various selected essays. Includes notes, an index, and an extensive annotated bibliography.

Moon, Robert Oswald. *Hippocrates and His Successors in Relation to the Philosophy of Their Time*. London: Longmans, Green and Co., 1923, reprint 1979. A series of lectures delivered by a physician to physicians, this work briefly categorizes the philosophies underlying the practice of ancient medicine before and after Hippocrates. Index.

Petersen, William F. *Hippocratic Wisdom for Him Who Wishes to Pursue Properly the Science of Medicine: A Modern Appreciation of Ancient Sci-*

entific Achievement. Springfield, Ill.: Charles C Thomas, Publisher, 1946. A physician's discussion of Hippocratic tenets and their relevance to modern physicians. Includes a glossary, illustrations, and an index.

Phillips, E. D. *Greek Medicine*. London: Thames and Hudson, 1973. Phillips traces practical and theoretical achievements of Greek medicine up to Galen. Includes selected references to the Hippocratic collection, an appendix on the cult of Asclepius, illustrations, an extensive bibliography, and indexes.

Sargent, Frederick, II. *Hippocratic Heritage: A History of Ideas About Weather and Human Health*. New York: Pergamon Press, 1982. A history of human biometeorology, this study traces from the ancient Hindus to the twentieth century the Hippocratic idea that the atmospheric environment influences people. Includes figures, portraits, tables, appendices.

Shakuntala Jayaswal

HIPPOLYTUS OF ROME

Born: c. 170; place unknown
Died: c. 235; Sardinia
Areas of Achievement: Religion and philosophy
Contribution: Initiating Christian commentary on the books of the Old Testament, Hippolytus also provided the first systematic handbook regulating the ordination of the ministry and the conduct of worship. In addition, he elaborated the connections among the Greco-Roman philosophical schools and popular practices and the diversity of opinions which divided the Christian communities.

Early Life

While it remains impossible to construct an early life for Hippolytus, it is possible to identify what he studied and when. It is instructive to compare his education with those of the great Alexandrians who were his contemporaries, Clement (c. 150-c. 215) and Origen (c. 185-c. 254). Hippolytus' more spirited and argumentative character does not suggest an eastern Mediterranean origin. Yet Hippolytus did write in Greek—the last Christian author in Rome to do so. He is often thought to have been a student of Saint Irenaeus in Gaul; both tackled the subject of heresy, which at that time meant simply a variety of opinions or practices. Nevertheless, Hippolytus' work *Kata pasōn haireseōn elenkhos* (*The Refutation of All Heresies*, 1885, also known as *Against All Heresies*), written before 199, took on its own character.

Two special dimensions gave focus to his thought. In order to elaborate the catalog of heresies and extend it into his own time, Hippolytus had sought the intellectual bases for that "diversity of opinions" from Greco-Roman philosophers, from what he could learn of the inner working of the "mystery religions," from the highly popular behavior of magicians, and from astrological inquires. His quotations, extensive though disjointed, remain a principal source for studies of pre-Socratic and later ancient intellectual tendencies.

Hippolytus' study of astronomy and astrology preserved what had taken shape in the centuries near the turn of the common era. He cataloged details of horoscopes and their attempted applications as well as the calculations of the sizes of Earth and planets and their respective distances from one another. These calculations led to arithmetic considerations, including the interrelationship between numbers when expressed by letters of the alphabet and words or names. The role of magicians, with their amulets and contrivances for illusion, indicated other activities competitive with Christianity.

The summary of these alternative inquiries was not Hippolytus' major concern, but he provided large enough selections that he might use their words as a basis for his theory that Christian intellectual formulations at odds with his own teaching originated in this environment. His conclusion is that the truth is found by a method of intellectual contrast: Let the other side speak and demonstrate its own inherent falsity. His books belong to his mature years; his method illustrates how and what he learned in his early life.

The other dimension of his formative years was the practice of the "Apostolic Tradition." In it were patterns for administering both the internal core of Christian worship and the external requirements necessary for church structure. Hippolytus' later account of the tradition indicated the status of developments within the expanding Christianity of the second century, in which his religious practice was grounded, and the reason that in later years he critically opposed every alternative form with such vigor.

Life's Work

Hippolytus was already a mature thinker and author when he became well-known. The Roman emperor Septimus Severus (reigned 193-211) initiated a Christian persecution in 202, the tenth year after his power was secured against rivals. Hippolytus' response was a treatise on the Antichrist and a commentary on the Book of Daniel. These works illustrate how Hippolytus perceived that the imperial demand for acts of obedience (emperor worship) violated the inhabitants of the Roman world. He reflected Greek concerns that went back to the power of the *demos* (urban people in *ekklesia*, or "assembly"); he recognized that the Roman state, with "feet of clay," had usurped the divine prerogatives, in a manner analogous to the example first propounded in the Book of Daniel. His interpretation was cautioned by his own chronological considerations: Like others of his day, he affirmed the world to be not more than fifty-seven hundred years old, so that the millennium remained at least three hundred years in the future. His discussion of the Antichrist is the most comprehensive written in antiquity.

Severus' persecution was severe in Alexandria, where it touched the life of an adolescent whose father was executed and who, but for his mother's intervention, would have followed in his father's path. That youngster was the budding biblical scholar Origen, who became in spite of his youth the director of the greatest Christian school. Origen spent considerable time in hiding. Accompanied by his principal benefactor, Ambrose, Origen came to Rome to hear Hippolytus speak. When Origen returned to Alexandria, Ambrose provided funding for secretarial staffing and encouraged Origen to emulate Hippolytus in the production of biblical commentaries and other works against critics of Christianity, especially those of greatest intellectual impact, such as Celsus.

Hippolytus is known for commentaries on many biblical books. A close examination of these studies reveals an emerging New Testament. He recognized twenty-two books as authoritative: four Gospels, thirteen of Paul's Epistles, one Acts of the Apostles, three catholic Epistles, and Revelation. Yet he also knew and used the Gospel of the Hebrews, the Epistle to the Hebrews, Second Peter, James, Jude, Shepherd of Hermas, Revelation of Peter, and Acts of Paul. The distinction seems to be based on what was allowed to be read in "our churches" and what, while proper for private reading, could not be publicly used since such had come into being "in our own times."

In the period of Severus' persecution and the following relative prosperity for the Church, Zephyrinus was Bishop of Rome (199-217). By the early third century, urban Rome counted some million people, with thirty to forty thousand estimated to be Christian. Administratively, this number was spread throughout the metropolis and not located in any single area. The tradition of "house churches," which goes back before the Constantinian revolution in 325, provides evidence for this diversity of location, as does the development of catacomb burial grounds.

Hippolytus described Zephyrinus as "an ignorant and illiterate individual," one "unskilled in ecclesiastical definitions," "accessible to bribes and covetous," and "incapable of forming his own judgment or of discerning the designs of others." The bishop also apparently represented a theological stance, relative to the interrelationship of Father and Son within the Christian Godhead, which was at odds with Hippolytus' understanding, so that there were continual disturbances among the diverse Christians of the capital. The theoretical formulation developing during the third century that there was but one bishop for each conurbation prevented the ancient acknowledgment that Hippolytus was a rival bishop in Rome itself; in modern times, he receives the designation "first antipope."

His principal rival was Callistus, also known as Calixtus, who became Bishop of Rome on the death of Zephyrinus. The controversy began during the reign of the emperor Commodus (180-192) and his urban prefect Sejus Fuscianus. Callistus was a slave to Carcophorus, a minor official in the imperial household; both were Christian. Carcophorus handled money deposited by widows and others toward burial expenses, and Callistus was directed to make a profitable return on these deposits through banking transactions. A failure led to his flight and capture, a further confrontation with the law, scourging, and sentencing to the mines on Sardinia. While Victor was Bishop of Rome (189-199), an imperial concubine, Marcia, also a Christian, obtained release for the captives from Commodus. As a "martyr," Callistus came to the attention of Victor, who pensioned him to Antium. When Zephyrinus became bishop, he brought Callistus into his service to take charge of the clergy and of the one principal asset held by the churches—the cemetery catacombs.

At Zephyrinus' death, none of these men was any longer young. Callistus officially succeeded, but Hippolytus held a rival claim, leading directly to theological disputes; Callistus claimed that Hippolytus' view of the relation of Father and Son was "ditheistic," while Hippolytus accused Callistus of so unifying the Persons of the Godhead that the Father could be said to have suffered equally when the Son was crucified. Some of the confusion may have been the difference between the Greek of Hippolytus and his followers and the Latin of Callistus and his followers. (There was a sizable Greek-speaking population in officially Latin Rome.)

Conflict of theology moved into conflict of administration. The actual role of Hippolytus became more evident, especially in his linguistic use of the episcopal "we" for pronouncements against the decisions of Callistus. These decisions included permission for those married more than once to enter the clergy, for clergy to marry and remain in orders, for women to live in concubinage with slaves (since Roman law did not permit full marriage to occur between slaves or between them and free persons), and for second baptism of those reconciling with the Church after lapse. In Hippolytus' opinion, such decisions were bad enough, but Callistus on his own authority determined that as Bishop of Rome he could forgive any sin, including that of abortion.

Like his North African contemporary Tertullian, Hippolytus was a champion of old causes in a rapidly changing world; tradition was encountering a variety of internal opinions and external pressures. This conservatism is nowhere better illustrated than in _Apostolikē paradosis_ (second or third century; _The Apostolic Tradition of Hippolytus_, 1934). This handbook contains the most ancient forms and prayers for the ordination of bishops, presbyters, and deacons; for the consecration of confessors; and for the appointment of widows and readers. It also contains instructions for catechumens for baptism and first participation in the Lord's Supper and for fasting and praying.

Callistus died naturally and was buried not in the catacomb which bears his name but in a crypt on the Via Aureliana; his feast day is October 14. Hippolytus outlived Callistus and his successors Urban and Pontian. When Maximinus became emperor in 235, severe persecution was resumed, going after the ranking leadership. Both Pontian and Hippolytus were sent to the mines of Sardinia, where they were worked to death. Anterus was bishop for three months during this upheaval, before Fabian, a layman, was elected directly into the episcopal office in 236.

Fabian was able to recover the bodies of both Pontian and Hippolytus and bring them back to Rome. Pontian was interred in the papal crypt of Saint Callistus. In 236 or 237, Hippolytus was interred in the cemetery on the Via Tiburtina that subsequently carried his name. The date of his burial, August 13, remains his feast day.

Summary

The historical testimony to Hippolytus' role within the Church, even to location, became vague. The church historian Eusebius, Bishop of Caesarea, writing less than a century later, identified Hippolytus as a bishop of "some" church; that vagueness might be excused were it not that Eusebius knew directly of Hippolytus' writings from the library at Aelia Capitolina (Roman

Jerusalem) and of his contemporaneity with Zephyrinus and the Roman persecutions of that era. A century after Eusebius, the Latin biblical scholar, Jerome, in *De viris illustribus* (392-393; lives of illustrious men), repeats this vague affirmation of Hippolytus' bishopric—"the name of the city I have not been able to learn"—in spite of extending the list of publications and confirming the correlation with Origen, whom Jerome knew had called Hippolytus his "taskmaster."

In 1551 a statue of a person seated on a throne was discovered in Rome. Since the throne base had engraved upon it Hippolytus' table for computing the date of Easter and a list of his writings, the statue was reconstructed with a bearded head—as though it were Hippolytus—even though the statue in body and dress is that of a woman, probably a follower of the philosopher Epicurus.

It was not until the mid-nineteenth century—an era refueled with conflict centering on the Bishop of Rome and pronouncements of "infallibility"—that the personality and concerns of Hippolytus were rediscovered. Those of his works that had survived had in the interim been confused with the writings of others, and only a chance manuscript-discovery permitted his own works to be disentangled from the hodgepodge of other writings. Work on the recovery of Hippolytus continues, and complete editions of his principal writings are gradually appearing.

Bibliography

Easton, Burton Scott. *The Apostolic Tradition of Hippolytus*. Cambridge: Cambridge University Press, 1934. Along with a readable edition of the text concerning the earliest Christian liturgical practice, this work provides a discussion of it with an account of its rediscovery and its centrality to Hippolytus' thought.

Eusebius. *The Ecclesiastical History and the Martyrs of Palestine*. Translated by Hugh Jackson Lawlor and John Ernest Leonard Oulton. 2 vols. London: Society for Promoting Christian Knowledge, 1927-1928. The text of Eusebius' history in English translation appears in the first volume. Eusebius sets in time, space, and circumstance the earliest Christian figures, including the "succession from the apostles" and the variety of alternative opinions ("haeresies") as well as the Roman imperial context with its intermittent persecutions. The second volume provides extensive notes.

Grant, Robert. *Augustus to Constantine: The Thrust of the Christian Movement into the Roman World*. New York: Harper and Row, Publishers, 1970. By placing the history of early Christianity within its widest socioeconomic context, Grant provides the reader with an interpretation of Christianity within rather than apart from its world. Chapters 10 through 13 most concern Hippolytus, though he informs many other sections.

Quasten, Johannes. *Patrology*. Vol. 2, *The Ante-Nicene Literature After*

Irenaeus. Utrecht, Netherlands: Spectrum Publishers, 1953. This handbook presents in chronological and geographical order those Christian authors who provide the literature and thought of the ancient Church. Hippolytus is a major figure in this volume.

Salmond, S. D. F. *The Ante-Nicene Fathers: Translations of the Writings of the Fathers down to A.D. 325*. Vol. 5, *Hippolytus, Cyprian, Caius, Novatian*. Buffalo, N.Y.: Christian Literature Publishing Co., 1885-1897. Reprint. Edited by Alexander Roberts and James Donaldson. Grand Rapids, Mich.: Wm. B. Eerdmans Publishing Co., 1971. This volume includes a nineteenth century translation of *The Refutation of All Heresies*. Regrettably, it remains almost the exclusive access to this work for anyone not reading either the original languages or a foreign translation.

Wordsworth, Christopher. *St. Hippolytus and the Church of Rome in the Early Part of the Third Century*. London: Francis and John Rivington, 1853. This first reconstruction of the life of Hippolytus is significant for the history of the Church in the mid-nineteenth century. A major feature is the Greek text and English translation of the ninth book of *The Refutation of All Heresies*, which includes autobiographical information.

Clyde Curry Smith

HOMER

Born: early ninth century B.C.; possibly Ionia, Greece
Died: late ninth century B.C.; Greece
Area of Achievement: Literature
Contribution: Homer wrote the *Iliad* and the *Odyssey*, Greek epic poems
  which played a crucial role in the birth of classical Greek civilization.
  These works greatly influenced history, theology, and literature in Greece
  and the entire Western world.

Early Life

The Greeks were not sure where Homer was born, when he lived, or even
if such a person actually existed. The name "Homer" may simply be a ge-
neric term denoting "one who fits a song together." Still, various sources pro-
vide some information about the provenance of the *Iliad* and the *Odyssey*.
The language of the poems is Ionic and Aeolic Greek, which points to an
East Greek origin. (In antiquity, East Greece included the west coast of Asia
Minor and neighboring islands.) Greek tradition named either the island of
Chios or the town of Smyrna, both in eastern Greece, as Homer's birthplace.
Chios boasted a guild of rhapsodists who recited the Homeric epics and who
claimed, without any proof, to be directly descended from Homer himself.
The geographical references in the poems, particularly the *Iliad*, are most
specific and correspond to the Ionian area and thus also support an East
Greek origin.

Homer's precise dates are no easier to ascertain than his birthplace. At
first sight, twelfth century features in the poems, the Mycenaean geography
of the *Iliad*'s Catalogue of Ships and ancient weapons such as Ajax's great
body shield and Odysseus' curious boar's tusk helmet, seem to suggest that
the poems were composed around the time of the Trojan War. Yet archaeological discoveries have shown that certain features of weaponry and
warfare described in the poems were not in use before 900 to 700 B.C. For
example, the Shield of Achilles in book 18 of the *Iliad* clearly depicts the law
courts and agricultural life of an eighth century city-state, not the twelfth
century monarchy of Agamemnon. The internal evidence from the poems
points to a poet working in the eighth century but trying to paint a picture of
the Mycenaean era more than four hundred years before his own time. The
fact that there are virtually no references to events after 700 B.C. indicates
that the poems must have been completed by that date.

Life's Work

The obscurity surrounding the author of the *Iliad* and the *Odyssey* is partly
a product of the conventions of the epic poetic genre itself. An epic poet was
expected simultaneously to create and sing a poem on a heroic subject before

an audience, without the help of writing. This astonishing feat was possible because generations of epic poets had developed traditional language, phraseology, and motifs with which to tell the stories of the great Greek heroes. Such poetry placed a premium on the ability to create poems orally, not on the development of a unique individual style. Hence, any trace of the personality of the author of the *Iliad* and the *Odyssey* has vanished.

Greek epic poets may have sung their songs at the dinner gatherings of the aristocracy, as do the bards in the *Odyssey*, as well as to members of their own artisan class. How the *Iliad* and the *Odyssey* moved from oral performance to their final written forms is not fully understood. The poems are clearly not an assemblage of stories stitched together by a collector. Since both poems develop organically around a central theme and exhibit a sophisticated handling of poetic techniques, they are most likely the creations of a single monumental composer at the end of a long poetic tradition.

In creating the *Iliad* and the *Odyssey*, Homer employed the various conventions of epic style in a skillful and flexible manner, which satisfied both aesthetic expectations and the need for fluent oral composition. The artificial dialect mixture of the poems was created for the epic and was never used by anyone in actual conversation. The mixture of dialect forms gives the language of the poems a unique "epic" quality and provides metrically convenient words for the poets to use in oral composition. Composition is also aided by ornamental epithets which are applied to divinities, people, and objects. Such adjectives not only satisfy metrical demands but also illuminate beautifully the unchanging nature of the heroic world. Thus, ships are "swift" even when standing still, and Odysseus is already "much-suffering" in the *Iliad*, before starting his ten-year trek home. Even the sequence of events in the poems is structured in a way which helps the poet compose aloud. Frequently repeated traditional scenes, such as arming for battle and sacrificing to the gods, possess a constant order of elements which is easily remembered. This regularity of events creates a strong sense that both nature and human life proceed along a carefully ordered path and makes anomalous behavior such as Achilles' seem especially jarring.

Even the major plot elements of both the *Iliad* and the *Odyssey* are very likely traditional. Both poems employ a "withdrawal-devastation-return" framework with a revenge motif at the end, a format typical of many epic poems. Scholars have found evidence for other earlier Greek epics which contained many of the thematic elements of both the *Iliad* and the *Odyssey*, but the Homeric poems are unique in their tight organization around one major theme: the *Iliad* around the wrath of Achilles, the *Odyssey* around the homecoming of Odysseus.

The action of the *Iliad* covers only fifty-three days in the last year of the ten-year siege of Troy, although the poet cleverly inserts references to the events of the previous decade which make the listeners believe they have experienced the entire war. The abduction of the Greek queen Helen by the Trojan prince Paris forms the backdrop for the events of the *Iliad*, which takes as its subject the wrath of one individual, Achilles, the greatest Greek warrior at Troy, and the devastation it wreaks on him and all heroic society.

The leader of the Greek army, Agamemnon, has taken away Achilles' concubine after he is forced to give up his own. Achilles responds to this slight by laying down his arms, a correct response according to the heroic code of honor. Yet he errs when refusing the fabulous ransom Agamemnon offers him to return to battle. The result is devastation: Patroclus, Achilles' closest companion, dies at the hands of the Trojan hero Hector while trying to take Achilles' place. This catastrophe finally goads Achilles to return to battle. He is, however, now fighting not for the Greeks but for personal revenge, a crucial difference. He abandons the civilized humanity of the heroic code and crosses over into inhuman frenzy, which the poet likens to the uncontrollable force of nature. Although he kills Hector, the embodiment of the civilized humanity which he has left behind, he continues to rage out of control, until the gods intervene to persuade him to give Hector's body back to the aged king Priam. Thus, the *Iliad* is more than a tale of heroic exploits: It is a profound meditation on life and death, culture and nature, and individualism and society.

The *Odyssey* tells the story of the return of Odysseus to his wife, Penelope, and son, Telemachus, on the island of Ithaca after ten years of fighting at Troy. It is the only surviving story of many which narrated the experiences of the Greek heroes returning home after the Trojan War. Odysseus' return itself took ten years, but, by using a technique seen in the *Iliad*, the poet compresses the time frame of the *Odyssey* into forty days in the tenth year of the journey, while casting many backward glances over the events of the preceding decade. While the poem centers on the return of Odysseus from Troy, the content of the *Odyssey* is thematically more diverse than that of the *Iliad*, and its structure is correspondingly more complex. It contains four major themes: the journey of Odysseus on his way home, replete with fantastic monsters, beguiling sorceresses, and a trip to the underworld; a parallel journey of Telemachus, who is now twenty years old and trying to grow to adulthood despite an absent father; Odysseus' actual return to Ithaca and his winning back of home and wife; and his revenge, aided by his son and faithful retainers, on the suitors who were vying for Penelope's hand. The amalgamation of all of these elements into a coherent whole is most skillfully accomplished. Frequent changes of scene and an exciting narrative of his adventures by Odysseus create suspense and keep the plot moving quickly.

The *Odyssey* paints a vivid picture of life in Greece. It focuses on the city-state Ithaca and, in particular, on the nuclear family represented by Odysseus, Penelope, and Telemachus—and includes moving portraits of slaves and other nonaristocratic characters. The center of attention, however, is always Odysseus, who is not a tragic hero such as Achilles or Hector. He is a survivor who lives by his wits and his tongue. He confronts death on a daily basis but is never in danger of dying before accomplishing his goals. In later Greek literature, Odysseus became a symbol of persuasion, trickery, and deceit.

The *Iliad* and the *Odyssey* thus focus intently on the role of the individual in society. This theme is rooted in the events of the eighth century, the very beginnings of classical Greek society. The great Mycenaean Greek kingdoms had collapsed by 1150 B.C. for reasons which are not understood but which probably included intense internecine warfare. The absence of the palace bureaucracies forced small separate groups of people to fend for themselves but ultimately allowed them to grow from 1150 to 800 B.C. into the city-states of classical Greece. The ninth and eighth centuries, during which the heroic epic tradition probably took shape, saw the formation of many city-states composed of individual households, much like that of Odysseus and in contrast to the extended Mycenaean family of the Trojan king Priam seen in the *Iliad*. Each member of such a household bore a great responsibility for its maintenance and, by extension, that of the city-state. Hence, the *Iliad* and the *Odyssey* devote much attention to the crucial question of the proper behavior of individuals in society.

An awareness of the common Greek heritage shared by all the city-states sprang up alongside the growth of the different separate political units. The Olympic Games, to which every city sent athletes, were founded in 776 B.C. The Panhellenic oracle at Delphi began dispensing political as well as personal advice around the same time. The Homeric epics, which record an expedition of many Greek heroes united against a common enemy, may be seen as both an affirmation of the connections between all the Greeks and support for the hero-founders of the new city-states.

Summary

Homer bequeathed to the West the beginnings of its literature. Countless works have been inspired and influenced by the epics, in which may be found the seeds of narrative, comedy, and tragedy. The sheer genius of the *Iliad* and the *Odyssey* becomes obvious in comparison with other epic poems which have survived from ancient Greece. Fragments of other epics, known collectively as the Epic Cycle, indicate that the Homeric epics were the originals around which the poems of the cycle were fashioned. These other poems were much shorter and, judging from the scanty remains, inferior in scope and style.

Homer also gave both history and religion to the ancient Greeks, and through them to Western civilization. Little has been said here about the gods mentioned in the poems, because humans are so clearly the focus of the poet's interest. The gods, who have the same emotions and social structure as the struggling mortals, appear frequently as mirrors for human activities and emotions, but there is one essential difference. The gods will never die, whereas death is the inevitable portion of every hero. Heroic life is merely a brief and shining prelude to a long and shadowy afterlife in Hades. Immortality for humans is obtainable only in heroic song. The gods' immortality underscores the mortality of the heroes, adding emphasis and pathos. The gods watch avidly the events unfolding on the Trojan plain, but they cannot rescue anyone—even their own offspring—from death when it is fated.

Bibliography
Clarke, Howard. *The Art of the Odyssey*. Englewood Cliffs, N.J.: Prentice-Hall, 1967. General introduction to the *Odyssey*, with a chapter comparing the *Iliad* and the *Odyssey*.

Homer. *The Iliad*. Translated by Richmond Lattimore. Chicago: University of Chicago Press, 1951. Literal translation of the *Iliad*, with a detailed introduction.

_____. *The Odyssey*. Translated by Richmond Lattimore. New York: Harper and Row, Publishers, 1965. Similar to his translation of the *Iliad*, with an introduction.

Kirk, G. S. *The Songs of Homer*. Cambridge: Cambridge University Press, 1962. The standard introduction to the Homeric poems, focusing on their language and composition. Illustrated.

Nagy, Gregory. *The Best of the Achaeans*. Baltimore: Johns Hopkins University Press, 1979. Sophisticated but stimulating analysis of the hero in Greek civilization and how the language of Greek epic defines his role.

Schein, Seth. *The Mortal Hero: An Introduction to Homer's Iliad*. Berkeley: University of California Press, 1984. An introduction to a literary interpretation of the *Iliad*. Explores questions of mortality, the gods, and heroism in detail. Excellent references.

Snodgrass, Anthony. *Archaic Greece: The Age of Experiment*. Berkeley: University of California Press, 1980. Economic and social history of the age in which the epics were composed, based on the archaeological evidence. Well illustrated.

Wace, Alan J. B., and Frank H. Stubbings, eds. *A Companion to Homer*. London: Macmillan, 1962. Essays on language, transmission of the text, and especially the archaeological evidence pertaining to the Homeric poems, by authorities in each field. Slightly dated but still authoritative. Illustrated, with many references.

Julie A. Williams

HORACE
Quintus Horatius Flaccus

Born: December 8, 65 B.C.; Venusia, Italy
Died: November 27, 8 B.C.; Rome, Italy
Area of Achievement: Poetry
Contribution: The most important Roman lyric poet, Horace took an appealing, deceptively casual approach to poetry. His odes, epistles, and satires became a beloved source of proverbial wisdom and a model for Renaissance and neoclassical poets throughout Europe.

Early Life

Horace was born in Venusia, a military colony in southern Italy. Nothing is known of his mother or siblings. His father was a freed slave whose profitable post as an auctioneer's assistant enabled him to buy land and to send his son to school in Rome. There, with the sons of senators and knights, Horace was educated in the Greek classics. Horace asserts in his *Satires* (35, 30 B.C.) that he received better education from his father, who accompanied him on walks through Rome's bustling marketplace while commenting on the character, appearance, and manners of passersby.

Sometime in his late teens or early twenties, probably in 45, Horace went to the Academy in Athens to study moral philosophy. Since this education was unusual for a freedman's son, it is likely that Horace's father recognized his son's brilliance and wished to give him every chance for success. In Athens, Horace began to write Greek poetry. In 44, Marcus Brutus came to Athens after the assassination of Julius Caesar. He recruited young Romans studying there to fight with him against Caesar's successors, Marc Antony and Octavian. The call to fight for freedom and the Republic stirred Horace to join Brutus' forces in 43. Though young and inexperienced, he became military tribune (that is, an officer capable of commanding a legion) and probably rose at the same time to the social rank of knight. At the pivotal Battle of Philippi, in 42, Brutus was killed and his army defeated. Rather than continue a hopeless cause, Horace returned to Rome.

His prospects were not bright. He had chosen the losing side. His father was dead. The farm in Venusia had been confiscated for distribution to a loyal legionnaire or officer. Yet Horace still had equestrian rank and must have had some money because he soon purchased the post of scribe in the quaestor's office, where public financial records were kept. In 39, a general amnesty for Brutus' followers removed whatever stigma attached to Horace's military service.

While a scribe, Horace began writing verse again, Latin imitations of the satirical, witty Greek poet Archilochus. Horace and the poet Vergil were physical as well as poetic contrasts. Horace was ruddy-faced, short, and stout; Vergil was dark-haired, tall, and lean. A long friendship showed that these differences made them complements, not opposites.

Life's Work

What drew Horace and Vergil together was a common interest in poetry. Vergil was at work on the *Eclogues* (43-37 B.C.), idealized poems about rural life, while Horace was writing realistic, trenchant observations of urban mores. Though their topics differed, these young writers shared an interest in the craft of poetry. Vergil was acquainted with Gaius Maecenas, one of Octavian's counselors, who acted as patron to promising poets. In 39 or 38, Vergil introduced Horace to Maecenas. At their second meeting Maecenas invited Horace to join his literary circle. Horace, still without a published poem, accepted the offer. The decision shaped the rest of his life.

In late 35 or early 34, Horace published the first book of *Satires*. It is a misleading title for most modern readers, who associate satire with ridicule and attack. To Horace, the word meant a mixture, or medley, indicating that the work lacked a narrative structure, consistent characters, and interrelated themes. Horace also referred to these poems as *sermones* (conversations), which suggests their casual tone and varied subject matter. One poem describes a trip with Vergil, another tells a ribald story about witches, a third is a fond remembrance of his father, a fourth a witty portrait of a boor. All the poems display a mastery of metrical form and reveal a good-humored and congenial persona. The poems are like conversations over dinner, and the poet is a most attractive host.

In 33, Maecenas rewarded Horace's skillful and popular poetry: He gave Horace land in the Sabine Valley. Prudently Horace leased most of it to tenant farmers and built himself a house. The so-called Sabine Farm became his beloved retreat from the world, where he lived simply but comfortably amid attentive servants and good friends, with leisure to concentrate on writing. Maecenas also gave Horace property in Rome and a house in Tibur. All the evidence indicates that Horace and Maecenas not only were mutually useful acquaintances but also possessed a deep friendship based upon a mutual love of literature.

Horace published two works in the year 30. One was a second book of *Satires*, less personal and more consciously literary in subject matter than the first book. This volume includes the famous story of the Country Mouse and the City Mouse as well as a parody of Homer's *Odyssey* (c. 800 B.C.). The second work was the *Epodes* (or "after-songs"), which was actually written ten or twelve years earlier. Shorter and more lyrical than *Satires*, these seventeen poems treat a miscellany of topics: the pains and pleasures of love, impatience with pretenders and sycophants, tribulations of the Civil War. The poems reflect a variety of moods as well as topics, but this variety does not result in incoherence. Rather, the contrasts create the sense of balance, the portrait of personality that cannot be moved from the golden mean either by life's follies or by its tragedies.

Horace himself testifies that these years were the happiest of his life. He spent most of the time at Sabine Farm, reading and composing. Maecenas' circle remained intact for more than a decade. Most educated Romans, including Octavian, who—after 27—called himself Augustus, admired Horace.

During this productive period Horace worked on the *Odes* (23, 13 B.C.) and the *Epistles* (c. 20, 13 B.C.). The *Odes* display Horace's poetic virtuosity: Eighty-eight poems in a variety of traditional and experimental meters demonstrate Horace's absolute control of language and his ability to suit expression to subject matter. Like previous works, the *Odes* treat a spectrum of political, personal, and social topics. Whatever the topic, the theme is that piety, moderation, and fellowship undergird the good life. The spirit of the *Odes* is autobiographical; the poems reflect Horace's contentment with life. Fortunately, contentment does not breed complacency or conceit in the poet. If life is good, it is not the poet's doing: Honest friends, a peaceful state, and kindly gods bestow this gift. It is somewhat surprising that Horace's contemporaries found the poems unsatisfactory, though perhaps that can be explained by the poems' unfamiliar style. Subsequent generations reversed the verdict and regarded the *Odes* as a personal and national masterpiece.

The *Epistles* return to the conversational tone of the early *Satires*. Addressed to friends, the poems engage Horace's companions one by one in reflection upon literary and philosophical topics. Perhaps the verses were a return to the atmosphere of the Academy, where the pleasurable speculation upon life's puzzles was interrupted by Brutus' politics. The *Epistles* are leisurely, intelligent poems—indeed, compliments, tributes, memorials to the discussions they record.

Ironically, the world these collections describe rapidly vanished. A plot against the life of Augustus was indirectly linked to Maecenas. He and his circle lost their privileged place near the ruler. Vergil died in 19, while Maecenas himself seems to have been distracted by a new favorite, the poet Sextus Propertius.

In 17, Augustus himself prompted Horace to begin writing again. Horace's relationship with Augustus was never easy. Though Horace admired Augustus' efforts to reunify the country after the Civil War, he maintained his distance. Horace never flattered the emperor openly and obsequiously as other poets did, though Augustus teased him about the omission. In this year, Augustus declared that Rome, the world's capital, would hold the Secular Games. Augustus requested Horace to write a hymn for the gods' blessing. Horace's *Carmen Saeculare* (17 B.C.), sung by a chorus of twenty-seven girls and twenty-seven boys, prays that fertility, morality, tranquillity, and glory may be the gods' gifts to Rome. The final book of *Odes*, published in 13, repeats this idea of festivity and ritual as bonding devices of community and celebrates poetry as itself a festive ritual.

Horace's last work was a second book of *Epistles*, also published in 13. These three long poems discuss the art to which Horace devoted his life. The first epistle calls upon Augustus to be the patron of developing poets rather than to enshrine a set of classics. The second epistle is Horace's moving envoi to poetry: He senses that his career is done. The third epistle is the famous *Ars poetica* (*The Art of Poetry*), in which Horace advises both readers and writers on the appreciation of poetry. It contains opinions (for example, that poetry should be pleasing as well as instructive and that a poet should set a work aside for nine years before trying to publish it) that subsequent generations would take, in very un-Horatian fashion, as a consistent philosophy of criticism. Maecenas died in the year 8 B.C., without having regained Augustus' full confidence. Horace died within months of his friend and was buried beside him.

Summary

Horace was spokesman for a generation of the Roman leadership class. He expressed its fears, its hopes, its discontents, and its pleasures. Because his poems interwove autobiography, social commentary, philosophy, and politics, they provided succeeding generations with insights, precepts, and bons mots on topics of enduring interest. Horace was remembered, therefore, in fragments. Readers quoted him and poets imitated him on particular topics (love, sex, the gods, wine, friendship) which overlapped with their own concerns. Horace appealed to different audiences for different reasons: to second century Romans for patriotism, to medieval monks for piety, to seventeenth century gentlemen for rakish self-indulgence.

Beyond the classical period Horace was most influential among aristocratic writers in European countries between 1500 and 1850. He appealed to them on several levels. His character showed how a congenial, generous temperament draws together like-minded and similarly talented men. His biography showed that one could become important and yet live independent of the world's demands. His career showed that art and politics were allies in fostering a sense of national identity and culture. His secular philosophy made clear that one could live morally without religious faith—an especially important idea to educated Europeans, who, for three centuries, watched Christian countries war with one another and split into hostile denominations. Thus, Horace was a poet whose life and art illustrated universal themes. When a society made urbanity and leisured culture its goals, its poets chose Horace as their guide.

In the twentieth century, Horace attracts attention for an additional reason. Modern scholars appreciate him as a verbal craftsman; his work is valued for the scope of the whole more than for the cleverness or beauty of the parts. Criticism today tends to value poets less as seers and legislators of mankind than as fabricators, the makers of meaning out of confusion. Contemporary critics study Horace's work in search of the unity in each volume of *Odes*, *Epistles*, and *Epodes*. The diversity of subjects and moods is no longer the sign of miscellaneous disquisition but the sign of subtle coherence. Critics aim to recover the poet's reason for grouping his poems and to gauge their aesthetic impact upon the reader. Like Shakespeare, like Cervantes, like every great author, Horace is always freshest to those who encounter him again and again.

Bibliography
Commager, Steele. *The Odes of Horace*. New Haven, Conn.: Yale University Press, 1962. Commager's book is widely regarded as the most substantial, incisive commentary on Horace's verse in English. Commager approaches Horace as a "professional poet," one committed to art as a vocation. Horace's distinctive characteristic is that he writes poetry about poetry, as if he wants to define the idea and demonstrate verbal craftmanship at the same time.
Fraenkel, Eduard. *Horace*. Oxford: Clarendon Press, 1957. This important book is for the serious student. Fraenkel approaches Horace as a poet who wrote for a few highly educated men rather than for general readers. He traces the development of his poetry from the experimental epodes and satires to the mature epistles and odes.
Hadas, Moses. *A History of Latin Literature*. New York: Columbia University Press, 1952. The chapter on Horace demonstrates why he is the most beloved of Roman poets. It articulates the virtues of common sense, good fellowship, and literary pleasure that generations of European writers have found in the poetry.
Highet, Gilbert. *The Classical Tradition: Greek and Roman Influences on Western Literature*. Oxford: Clarendon Press, 1949. Through judicious use of the index, the curious student can survey European attitudes toward Horace's poetry since the Renaissance. Highet is an opinionated and lively critic who inspires a return to primary texts.
Horace. *The Complete Works*. Translated by Charles E. Passage. New York: Frederick Ungar Publishing Co., 1983. This volume offers an unusual translation: without rhyme, in the original meter, with notes about the context of and allusions in each poem. Passage makes Horace accessible to the new reader and offers a fresh perspective to readers familiar with other translations.
Newman, J. K. *Augustus and the New Poetry*. Brussels: Latomus, revue d'études latines, 1967. This important book discusses the literary and social background to Horace's poetry. In the light of the rivalry between the Hellenistic, Alexandrian school of poetry and the old Roman traditions, Horace seems unsure of his own poetic purposes. Sometimes heavy going be-

cause Newman frequently argues with previous commentators, this study nevertheless richly repays close reading.

Noyes, Alfred. *Horace: A Portrait*. New York: Sheed and Ward, 1947. Himself a poet, Noyes tries to re-create Horace's real experiences from the topics, persons, and places recorded in the poetry. Noyes's reading is, therefore, fascinating, idiosyncratic, and largely unreliable. Noyes detects a proto-Christian sensibility in Horace that anticipates the end of the pagan worldview.

Perret, Jacques. *Horace*. Translated by Bertha Humez. New York: New York University Press, 1964. A good work for the general reader beginning the study or reading of Horace. Perret mixes biography and literary criticism without sentimentalism or pedantry. Perret delights in Horace's complex personality and multifarious poetry. The book contains a lengthy (though dated) annotated bibliography.

Putnam, Michael C. J. *Artifices of Eternity*. Ithaca, N.Y.: Cornell University Press, 1986. Putnam presents a detailed analysis of Horace's last work, the final book of *Odes*. Traditionally the fourth book is considered not unified and is said to show Horace bowing to Augustus' influence. Putnam argues that Horace remakes Augustus as the poet sees him. The approach has interesting biographical implications for interpreting Horace's last years.

Reckford, Kenneth J. *Horace*. New York: Twayne Publishers, 1969. Reckford's brief, appreciative study attempts to chart the growth of Horace's imagination and thought by a survey of his poetry. The emphasis is on theme rather than poetic technique. Some of Reckford's interpretations are more impressionistic than scholarly. The author provides useful notes and bibliography.

Rudd, Niall. "Horace." In *The Cambridge History of Classical Literature*, edited by E. J. Kennedy and W. V. Clausen, vol. 2. Cambridge: Cambridge University Press, 1982. Rudd attacks the tendency to see linear development in Horace's poetry and consistency in his opinions. Rudd argues that Horace was exploring new genres in Latin poetry and that the poems contain contradictory opinions and values.

Wilkinson, L. P. *Horace and His Lyric Poetry*. 2d ed. Cambridge: Cambridge University Press, 1968. Though this study is intended for the student who can read Latin, the first four chapters are accessible to the general reader. Wilkinson's Horace is neither the patriotic versifier of Augustus' policies nor the contented gentleman farmer addicted to ease and companionship. Wilkinson provides valuable summaries of Horace's thoughts on subjects ranging from religion to love to the state to poetry.

Robert M. Otten

HSIA KUEI

Born: c. 1180; Ch'ien tang, Chekiang, China
Died: c. 1250; Hangchow, Chekiang, China
Area of Achievement: Art
Contribution: Together with Ma Yüan, Hsia Kuei formed the Ma-Hsia school of painting, which was extremely influential in the subsequent development of landscape painting in China and Japan.

Early Life

Known as the younger contemporary of Ma Yüan (fl. 1200), Hsia Kuei served the Southern Sung emperors Ning Tsung (reigned 1195-1224) and Li Tsung (reigned 1225-1264). Little information exists about Hsia Kuei's life. It is known that, like Ma Yüan, Hsia received the Golden Girdle honor from the court and was artist-in-attendance at the imperial palace in Hangchow. Unlike Ma, however, who came from northwestern China, Hsia was apparently born very close to the capital, and Chinese art critics intimate that Hsia received imperial honors earlier in his life than did Ma.

Hangchow had become the capital in 1126, when an alliance between the Chinese of the Northern Sung and the Tungusic Juchen turned sour, and North China fell to the Juchen. The Northern Sung rulers fled to the Yangtze and settled into what was, at the time, an unimposing provincial capital situated at the mouth of the Che estuary. The imperial court apparently chose the town in part because it was easier to defend against "barbarians" but also because of the beauty of its location. Hangchow is surrounded by scenic hills and lies just east of what is perhaps China's most attractive lake, Hu.

In keeping with the generally favorable climate for commerce which characterized the Northern Sung period, trade continued to flourish during the Southern Sung era. As a consequence, Hangchow grew into a bustling trade center and by the middle of the thirteenth century had a population of more than half a million people. It also became what many consider to be China's most beautiful city, with scenic canals winding through the town. The wealthy led luxurious lives, living in multistoried villas replete with servants, gardens, and amenities brought to China from all over the globe. Scholars, poets, and painters lived near or within the court, and the favored professionals led fairly comfortable lives, with fancy titles and imperial stipends. Undoubtedly, Hsia was one of the favorite artists of the Southern Sung court, and like Ma Yüan, he chose subject matter which reflected his life-style and that of his patrons. Many of his paintings are found on fans, album leaves, and silk scrolls. Like Ma Yüan, Hsia Kuei used ink and slight traces of color on silk. He often depicted night scenes of China's elite enjoying the scenic splendors of Hangchow or diverting themselves with pleasant pastimes.

This idyllic situation was, however, somewhat deceiving, as the Chinese during the Southern Sung chafed at the fact that North China was in barbarian hands. After 1234, the situation grew progressively worse, as the Juchen Dynasty, known as the Chin, succumbed to the Mongol successors of Genghis Khan. From 1234 on, as the Mongol Empire continued to expand, the threat to the Southern Sung was never really far from the minds of China's literati, and Hangchow exhibited an almost *fin de siècle* atmosphere. Hsia's paintings, perhaps even more than those of Ma Yüan, reflected a sense of impending change. Whereas Ma was a northerner who had moved to the imperial court in the south, and was therefore strictly a courtier, Hsia was a native of Chekiang Province, presumably with a less sophisticated background.

Life's Work

Despite the fact that less is known about Hsia Kuei than about Ma Yüan (and fewer of Hsia's paintings are extant), in many ways, Hsia revealed more of himself through his art than did Ma. In fact, Hsia went beyond Ma in exploring new avenues of self-expression. Like Ma, Hsia used the "ax-stroke" technique of painting mountains, generally attributed to the great Northern Sung painter Li T'ang (fl. 1100). This technique has been likened to hacking out the angular features and crevices of the rocks with the side of a brush. Hsia also adopted Ma's tendency to emphasize one corner of his painting, though not nearly to the degree that Ma did.

Hsia's paintings tend to be much simpler and yet more emotional than those of Ma. Whereas Ma tended to be elegant and subdued, Hsia exhibited what one could almost call humility in his work. Perhaps Hsia was deferring to Ma's age; perhaps the difference in style merely reflects Hsia's humbler background. It is equally possible, however, that Hsia Kuei held different Taoist beliefs and avoided the occasional vanities which appear in Ma Yüan's paintings. As Max Loehr has pointed out, in Hsia Kuei's paintings,

> the dramatically bent and twisted pines of the Ma school are replaced by less conspicuous types of deciduous trees; . . . Ma's architecture gives way to rustic abodes. . . . Even Hsia's figures appear to be humbler folk than Ma's aristocratic types.

Chinese critics have suggested that Hsia was clearly more expressive than Ma and that the former's paintings had a greater sense of urgency and passion. Moreover, it appears that Hsia was less interested in humans than in nature, and, like nature, Hsia could exhibit changing moods, even within one work.

In some of Hsia's works, for example, one may find a soft setting of mountains bathed in an evening mist, while a lone fisherman's boat drifts gently in a quiet stream. As with Ma, the empty spaces become as important as the painted areas, for the viewer is expected to determine, using his own imagination, whether these are clouds, rain, or a mystical Taoist-Ch'an void. In such paintings, there is economy without affectation, subtlety without mannerism, and a sense of peace. In other works, Hsia seems anxious to show flux and movement by suggesting ominous possibilities. Here, there is distortion, asymmetry, and passionate uncertainty. Trees are larger than they should be, the rocks seem ready to fall, mountains vie with one another, and the water is turbulent and uninviting. These works are a reminder that fall and winter, in providing the eternal changes of life, do not always do so in a gentle fashion. In keeping with this genuinely Taoist understanding of nature's vagaries, there are some works by Hsia which suggest transitional stages, where serenity lies juxtaposed to passion. Always, however, as yin is to yang, one is in ascendancy while the other is subordinated and therefore lies in the background.

As with Ma, Chinese explanations of Hsia's motifs range from the poetical-philosophical to the dreary political. Again, Hsia may have been reacting to the circumstances north of the Southern Sung Empire. If this was so, however, it is far less pronounced than in Ma's works. It may be that Hsia felt less compelled to reflect the court's political sentiments in his paintings than did Ma. Hsia's family did, however, enjoy imperial patronage, and at least one of his sons, Hsia Sen, was also a court painter. Only a few of Hsia Sen's paintings have survived, and little is known about him.

In the United States, works attributed to Hsia Kuei can be found in the Boston Museum of Fine Art, the Freer Gallery, the Metropolitan Museum in New York, and galleries in Cleveland, Fort Worth, Indianapolis, Kansas City, and San Francisco. Unfortunately, some of these are probably forgeries, copied from the originals during the Ming (1368-1644) or early Ch'ing (1644-1912) dynasties. Because of the great Japanese admiration for Hsia, which began during the Ashikaga period (1338-1573), many more of his works are located throughout Japan. In particular, several private Japanese galleries have excellent examples of Hsia's work. Fortunately, the Beijing and Taipei palace museums also have fine collections by Hsia Kuei.

Summary

During several centuries subsequent to the fall of the Southern Sung Dynasty in 1279, Hsia Kuei, together with Ma Yüan, suffered the stigma of having labored for a weak and ultimately supine imperial court. Furthermore, Chinese critics labeled the two as being leaders of the so-called northern school of painters, which the critics considered substantially inferior to the southern, or proper, school. In measure, this was not as much a criticism of their style as it was a suggestion that gentlemen-scholars do not paint for a living, but rather pursue art only as a hobby to complement scholarship. Another reproach which later critics aimed at the two, although perhaps more at Ma than at Hsia, was that they were academic painters whose technique could be learned. This criticism, however, misses the mark, for there is no question that the totality of a Hsia painting is unique, and its spirit defies imitation.

Much like Ma Yüan, Hsia Kuei drew upon existing styles and techniques. In addition to the aforementioned ax-stroke and one-cornered methods, Hsia used the squeezed-brush technique to paint mountains, and his water was of the "fighting-water" style. The sum total of his work, however, marks him not merely as one of the two luminaries of the influential Ma-Hsia school but also as one of the dominant figures in Chinese landscape painting. Hsia's greatest influence, however, may not have been on subsequent Chinese painters, but rather on numerous schools of Japanese art. Initially, during the Ashikaga shogunate, the works of Ma Yüan were more in demand in Japan than were those of Hsia. By the time of Nōami (1397-1494), however, a definite shift had occurred, and Hsia Kuei had become a legendary figure among Japanese artists. Several of his techniques were of great importance in the development of Japanese painting from the late fifteenth century through the Tokugawa shogunate (1603-1867). To this day, Hsia's paintings are greatly admired by Japanese collectors.

By the middle of the Ming Dynasty, there was already substantial praise for Hsia Kuei among Chinese art critics. The considerable interest in Hsia shown by the Japanese and, more recently, by Western critics, has led to an even greater admiration of Hsia in China itself, and Chinese critics today are rightfully proud of this great artist.

Bibliography

Bush, Susan. *The Chinese Literati on Painting: Su Shih, 1037-1101, to Tung Chi Chi-ch'ang, 1555-1636.* Cambridge, Mass.: Harvard University Press, 1971. Quotes several Chinese scholars' views of Ma Yüan and Hsia Kuei.

Cahill, James. *An Index of Early Chinese Painters and Paintings: T'ang, Sung, and Yuan.* Berkeley: University of California Press, 1980. Contains a lengthy list of paintings attributed to Hsia Kuei which are located in museums and private collections.

Gernet, Jacques. *Daily Life in China on the Eve of the Mongol Invasion, 1250-1276.* New York: Macmillan, 1962. Simplistic but useful description of Southern Sung and Hangchow during and after Hsia's life.

Lee, Sherman. *Chinese Landscape Painting.* Cleveland, Ohio: Cleveland Museum of Art, 1954. Contains examples of Hsia's art, together with a brief critique of his technique.

Loehr, Max. *The Great Painters of China.* New York: Harper and Row, Publishers, 1980. Contains a very brief sketch of Hsia Kuei's life and an excellent discussion of his technique. Also has several photographs of Hsia's paintings.

Munsterberg, Hugo. *The Landscape Painting of China and Japan.* Rutland,

Vt.: Charles E. Tuttle Co., 1955. In Munsterberg's chapter on the Southern Sung period, there is a very brief discussion of Ma Yüan and Hsia Kuei, their paintings, and their impact on later Chinese art.

Paine, Robert. "Hsia Kuei and Motonobu." *Revue des arts asiatiques* 9 (1935). Contains a discussion of Hsia's influence on Japanese painting.

Sirén, Oswald. *Chinese Painting: Leading Masters and Principles*. Vol. 2. London: Lund, Humphries and Co., 1956. Contains a critique of Hsia Kuei and his art.

_____. *A History of Early Chinese Painting*. Vol. 2. London: E. Weyhe, 1932. Contains a brief discussion of the Ma-Hsia school with examples of their work.

Sullivan, Michael. *The Arts of China*. London: Thames and Hudson, 1973. Contains a brief passage about Ma Yüan and Hsia Kuei with examples of their work.

Swann, Peter C. *Art of China, Korea, and Japan*. New York: Praeger Publishers, 1963. Contains a brief discussion of the Ma-Hsia school, with examples of their paintings.

Waley, Arthur. *An Introduction to the Study of Chinese Painting*. New York: Grove Press, 1958. Authoritative discussion of the Ma-Hsia school.

Hilel B. Salomon

HSIEH LING-YÜN

Born: 385; Commandery of Ch'en, Yang-chia, Honan Province, China
Died: 433; Kuang-chou, Nan-hai, China
Areas of Achievement: Literature and philosophy
Contribution: Ling-yün was the first and greatest of China's nature poets, the
founder of the school of *shan-shui* verse. A philosophical syncretist, he
blended elements of Confucianism and Taoism with Buddhism to produce
a uniquely Chinese synthesis.

Early Life

A scion of one of China's most powerful and illustrious aristocratic families
of the Six Dynasties (420-589), Hsieh Ling-yün was born in Honan Province.
As secretary of the Imperial Library, his father was the least prepossessing
member of the Hsieh clan, which had included a host of distinguished poets,
calligraphers, and high-ranking imperial officials. The Liu, Hsieh Ling-yün's
mother's family, was distinguished by its calligraphers, notably Wang Hsi-
chih (321-379). In the light of his familial background, Ling-yün surprised no
one by his precocity. As a small child, he was placed under temporary adoption in Hang-chou with Tu Ming-shih, a devout Taoist. Calligraphy was an integral part of Tu Ming-shih's Taoism, and Ling-yün proved an apt pupil. The
boy remained with his foster family in the splendid aristocratic environs of
Hang-chou until he was fifteen.

In 399, a rebel faction led by Sun En invaded Chekiang and Kiangsu provinces, and in the ensuing struggle Ling-yün's father was killed. His family
decided to send Ling-yün to the safety of their house in the capital, Chien-
k'ang (now Nanking). There he came under the decisive influence of his uncle, Hsieh Hun, a handsome, aristocratic figure who was recognized as one
of China's foremost poets. Married to an imperial Chin princess and secure
in worldly ways, Hun had drawn together a lively, exclusive literary salon,
into which Ling-yün was inducted. He was soon recognized as a stellar member. The precocious Ling-yün cut a swath around Chien-k'ang even in an age
notorious for social ostentation and eccentricity. He had inherited the title of
Duke of K'ang-lo; as such, he drew revenues from more than three thousand
households. Hsieh Ling-yün affected foppish dress, extravagant behavior,
and a languor that challenged the efforts of scores of attendants. Dukedom
also brought government appointments: He was made administrator to the
grand marshal and, more important, administrator in the Redaction Office,
a post that ensnared him in the political fortunes of Liu Yi. It was thus that
he was forced to endure a chain of misfortunes that dramatically altered the
course of his life.

Life's Work

When Ling-yün entered service with Liu Yi, Yi had emerged as the most distinguished leader of a revolt against another rebel, Huan Hsüan, who founded the abortive Ch'u Dynasty in 404. Yï's victories against Huan brought him the dukedom of Nan-p'ing as well as a military governor generalship, these posts devolving upon him from Liu Yü, the titular restorer of the Chin Dynasty in 405. Ling-yün's fortunes might have been assured if Liu Yï had accepted Liu Yü's political supremacy. He did not. Thus, between 405 and 411, a series of complex plots and inevitable military clashes between partisans of the two men resulted in Yï's defeat and disgrace. Through the course of these events, Ling-yün served on his staff, ultimately suffering the consequences of his fall. Moved to the periphery of power, Yï, with Ling-yün in tow, was obliged in 412 to establish his headquarters at Chiang-ling in Hupei Province. There, Ling-yün's life changed decisively.

While posted to Chiang-ling, Ling-yün visited the famed Buddhist center at the nearby Mount Lu. The Eastern Grove Monastery, which eventually became the most influential southern center of Chinese Buddhism, had been founded by Hui-yüan (334-416), himself the principal disciple of Tao-an (312-385), who had been the first to emphasize the basic distinctions between Indian Buddhism—essentially an alien doctrine—and the casual versions of Buddhism that had been integrated with mainstream Chinese culture. Hui-yüan devoted himself to making the Chinese aware of the foreignness of Buddhist thought, hoping to make the purer form of its teachings and practices acceptable to well-educated Chinese aristocrats. Ling-yün found that this transcendental, poeticized Buddhism, with its many concrete images, appealed to him far more than the intellectualized Buddhism common to the capital and his native region.

Moreover, Ling-yün's poetic sensibilities were overwhelmed by the beauty of the Eastern Grove's setting—craggy, forested mountain peaks enshrouded in mists, lush gorges filled with tumbled boulders and riven by pure, roaring streams—and the austere way of life of its devotees. The contrast with the corruptions and hostilities of court life was compelling. In his poetic "Dirge for Hui-yüan," Ling-yün revealed his yearning to immerse himself in Buddhist study and to accept a place even as the least of Hui-yüan's disciples.

As Ling-yün was falling under the spell of Eastern Grove Buddhism, however, the fact that he and the Hsieh family had thrown in their lot with the wrong leader was becoming all too clear. Liu Yü, having consolidated his position, crushed Liu Yï, Ling-yün's mentor, on December 31, 412; Yï eventually was killed. Liu Yü spared Ling-yün, however, and coopted him into his service in 413, first as administrator to the commander-in-chief, then as assistant director of the Imperial Library. During the time that Ling-yün held these posts, the Chinese monk Fa-Hsien, after fourteen years in Afghanistan, returned to Chien-k'ang rich in Buddhist lore. He reported having seen a gigantic image of Buddha, in a cave, shining with brilliant light and casting mysterious shadows. Hoping to replicate this image, Hui-yüan arranged a similar shrine for the Eastern Grove. Painted shades of green on silk, the Buddha image was consecrated on May 27, 412. As a noted poet and calligrapher, Ling-yün was invited to produce a poem that he entitled "Inscription on the Buddha-Shadow," one of his earliest surviving metaphysical verses.

As always, Ling-yün's fortunes were linked to political events. In 415, he was dismissed from office, and the following year Hui-yüan died. Ling-yün's fortunes improved, however, with new administrative posts. More important was Yü's liberation of Ch'ang-an, the center of Northern Buddhism. Many of its monks thereupon traveled southward, bringing about the mingling of the two schools of Buddhist thought from which a distinctive Chinese version was to emerge. Amid this intellectual and religious excitement, however, Ling-yün was held responsible for eruption of a scandal and was again dismissed. Nothing is known of him for the next eighteen months. In 419, Liu Yü strangled the imbecilic Emperor An, ending the Chin Dynasty and allowing his assumption of power as Wu-ti, first of the Sung Dynasty.

In accordance with customary treatment of aristocrats after a coup, Ling-yün was demoted to the rank of marquess over only one hundred households. Subsequently, the rise of his cousin Hui as the chief of the emperor's henchmen and the courtly influence of a number of other relatives and friends drew him into succession politics. Unhappily, Ling-yün's romanticism, imprudence, and willful personality led him to back the wrong forces. Shortly after Yi-fu's ascension to the throne, the clique with which Ling-yün associated was disgraced. Ill and impoverished, he was banished to the lowly post of grand warden to Yung-chia, a backward town in Chekiang Province.

The mournful poems written during Ling-yün's exile from the capital reveal a distressed man confronting reality in full maturity. Middle-aged, bereft of significant income, beyond the pale of elusive political power, stricken by tuberculosis, and plagued by ulcerous legs, he had only his literary talents and religious beliefs to sustain him. Indeed, in accordance with esoteric Taoist and Buddhist teachings, he thereafter sought consolation in a search for truth in the wilderness into which he was exiled. The two months of hard travel that it took him to reach Yung-chia evoked a series of fine nature poems, elegantly descriptive and brooding. Upon arrival, he also commenced his "Pien-tsung Lun" (c. 423-430; "On Distinguishing What Is Essential"), a major philosophical work.

Many earlier Chinese philosophers had wrestled with problems examined in Ling-yün's "On Distinguishing What Is Essential," and in this sense it is a work of many authors. This fact, however, does not diminish the value of Ling-yün's contribution to Chinese philosophical discourse. Two versions of truth preoccupied him: truth that was acquired gradually and truth that was revealed instantaneously. Many Buddhists believed that an arrival at truth (Nirvana) required several lengthy stages of spiritual and bodily preparation, involving faith, study, and good works. That, Ling-yün acknowledged, was the gradualism that Siddhārtha Gautama, the Buddha, had taught. Yet Buddha, he argued, had used that explanation when teaching Indians, a people with a facility for learning but with scant predilection for intuitive understanding. Had Buddha preached to the Chinese, a people who had difficulty in acquiring learning but who were masters of intuitive comprehension, his message would have been different. Ultimate enlightenment—a state of nonbeing, or *wu*—although doubtless assisted by learning, would have been presented by Buddha to the Chinese as attainable in a flash, by a quantum leap in faith.

As his health improved and his literary reputation increased, Ling-yün also became more intriguing because of his new character. He was neglectful of his official duties, despite some efforts to plant mulberry trees, improve local agriculture, and undertake hydraulic works. His change in priorities had to do less with an implicit criticism of the state than with an honest desire to withdraw from worldly vexations in a mystic pursuit of truth. The climbing boots with removable studs that he designed for expeditions into the mountains became fashionable at court, and a broad-brimmed peasant hat, knapsack, and staff came to be his personal hallmarks. Soon, he resigned from office. His Taoism, which promised immortality for the body as well as the soul, required a spartan regimen of yoga, breathing exercises, and preparations of drugs, herbs, and elixirs. His "Fu of the Homeward Road" and "On Leaving My District" signaled his return in 424 to the decayed family estate at Shih-ning. There, moving toward a richer inner life, he labored assiduously in the mountainous wilderness. During the next several years, a number of monks joined him in his idyllic anchorite life. His continuous investigations into Buddhist meanings made him the most learned layman of his day.

The regard in which Ling-yün's poetry was held, added to the renown of his family name, made him useful to Emperor Wen upon his ascension to power. Ling-yün's presence not only would grace the court with a leading poet and calligrapher but also would solidify support for the emperor among many who had wavered. Accordingly, Ling-yün was offered the directorship of the Imperial Library. Since rejection would have constituted an affront to the emperor and meant peril for his friends, he accepted reluctantly. For several years, he collected and collated documents, including major Buddhist sutras; he wrote poems and painted for the emperor. Court life wearied him, however, and in spite of an impending promotion, he begged a sick leave, which in 428 allowed a return to Shih-ning. He conceived of himself during this time as free from official obligations and lived healthily and actively as a result, but the emperor viewed his conduct as defiant. Eventually, Ling-yün fell afoul of conflicts among the local gentry. In serious danger, he begged Wen-ti's forgiveness, and for a time the emperor protected him while he helped translate major sutras of Mahayana Buddhism into Chinese. Even his translations, however, were offensive to sectarians; the emperor found him a liability, and he was exiled to the wilds of Kiangsi Province. There Ling-yün once again courted disaster by engaging in defiant conduct. Falsely implicated in a rebellious plot, he was called to Nan-hai in 433. Philosophical, courageous, and aristocratic to the end, he was publicly executed the same year; he was buried in Kuei-chi, among the mountains he loved.

Summary

Of the thousands of Hsieh Ling-yün's writings and poems, relatively few survive. Those extant clearly confirm his repute as China's greatest nature poet. Nature poetry—descriptive, mystical, impressionistic, and simultaneously reflective and mood-stimulating—in Ling-yün's hands, was a disciplined, highly developed art form, particularly the five-word poem and the *yueh-fu*. Along with Pao Chao and T'ao Yüan-ming, he was in his own time—and has continued to be—recognized as one of the greatest poets in a uniquely Chinese genre.

As the most learned Buddhist layman of his day, Hsieh Ling-yün exerted a major influence—through his poetry, calligraphy, essays, translations, associations, and later anchorite life-style—in the Sinicization of Buddhism. His profound understanding of Buddhism, always melded subtly with his Confucianism and Taoism, allowed him to translate and reinterpret main tenets of the religion for a distinctive Chinese context. Only a quintessential Chinese could have accomplished this task.

Bibliography

Bingham, Woodbridge. *The Founding of the T'ang Dynasty*. New York: Octagon Press, 1970. Good background on the fall of the Sui Dynasty and early T'ang, with observations on contributions of the Sung. Lacks critical balance, but is accessible and gives the reader an accurate sense of the importance of the period. Limited bibliography; useful appendices.

Frodsham, J. D. *The Murmuring Stream: The Life and Works of the Chinese Nature Poet Hsieh Ling-yun (385-433), Duke of K'ang-Lo*. 2 vols. Kuala Lumpur: University of Malaya Press, 1967. Definitive scholarly study; eminently readable. Volume 1 is largely biographical; volume 2 translates and examines Ling-yün's poetry extensively. Helpful footnotes throughout. Adequate appendices and index.

Fung Yu-Lan. *A History of Chinese Philosophy*. Translated by Derk Bodde. 2 vols. Princeton, N.J.: Princeton University Press, 1973. Chapter 7 of the second volume of this excellent scholarly work carefully examines various aspects of Buddhism and Ling-yün's role and influence in its interpretations. Splendid comparative chronological tables of the period of classical learning; informative notes throughout; superb bibliography; fine index.

Clifton K. Yearley
Kerrie L. MacPherson

HSÜAN-TSANG

Born: c. 602; Lo-yang, Honan, China
Died: 664; Ch'ang-an, China
Areas of Achievement: Exploration, religion, and literature
Contribution: A pilgrim and scholar, Hsüan-tsang brought the wisdom of the Sanskrit Buddhist scriptures from India to China, producing a huge legacy of Chinese sutras and a record of his travels. His works stand as testaments to his faith and courage as one of China's greatest travelers in the physical and spiritual quest for religious truth.

Early Life

Hsüan-tsang was born with the secular name Ch'en Yi; he is also known by the honorific names Tripitaka and T'ang San-tsang. He was descended from a prominent Honan provincial family. Beginning with the Han Dynasty in the first century, several of his relatives had served in local and national governmental positions. His great-grandfather was a prefect in Shansi Province during the Northern Wei (386-534), and his grandfather served the Ch'i (479-502) court as an academician at the national academy, a position which gave the Ch'en family a hereditary sinecure in Lo-yang, Ch'en Yi's birthplace.

Ch'en Yi's father, Ch'en Hui, was a Confucian scholar during the short but politically tumultuous Sui Dynasty (581-618). Not wanting to get involved in the unsettled politics of the time, Ch'en Hui, on the pretext of illness, turned down the posts of magistrate, prefect, and garrison commander, preferring to stay at home and pass his learning on to his four sons. Ch'en Yi, the youngest, showed early signs of brilliance. At the age of eight he could recite the Confucian *Hsiao Ching* and conscientiously practiced the moral maxims he learned from his father. Instead of engaging in childhood pastimes, it is said that he spent his time studying the Confucian classics.

When Ch'en Yi was twelve, his second brother, Ch'en Ch'ang-chieh, took Buddhist vows at the Pure Land Monastery in Lo-yang, the eastern capital. Ch'en Yi went to his brother's temple and also studied to become a monk, but, at a time when the government was fearful of the economic and political power of Buddhist institutions, court decree permitted only twenty-seven out of hundreds of candidates to be accepted for ordination. Cheng Shan-kuo, the imperial envoy, found the younger Ch'en outside the monastery gates and, impressed by his erudition and piety, permitted him to take the lower Buddhist orders. From then on he was known by his religious name, Hsüan-tsang.

Hsüan-tsang continued his studies at Lo-yang, mastering scriptures and gaining fame for his scholarship and preaching. By this time the Sui Dynasty was under attack by the rebellious forces of Li Yüan, and Ch'ang-an, the western capital, fell in 617. A year later, Li Yüan mounted the throne as T'ang Kao Tsu (reigned 618-626) and proclaimed at Ch'ang-an the founding of the T'ang Dynasty (618-907). Because of the fighting that eventually led to the overthrow of the Sui and the consolidation of T'ang power, after a brief visit to Ch'ang-an, Hsüan-tsang and his brother retreated to the southwest province of Szechwan. There, at Ch'eng-tu, many refugee monks found haven from the famine and warfare affecting the rest of China. Hsüan-tsang took advantage of their presence to deepen his understanding of the sutras. In 622, at the age of twenty, Hsüan-tsang took his final vows, becoming a full-fledged monk.

The more he learned, the more Hsüan-tsang became preoccupied with certain knotty theological questions that his teachers could not answer to his satisfaction. Could all sentient beings attain Buddhahood, and if so, how? Were the ancient Hinayana teachings emphasizing personal religious zeal and commitment to life in the *sangha* (Buddhist monastic community) indeed inferior to the current Mahayana emphasis on salvation through faith in the saving grace of the bodhisattva Maitreya? Hsüan-tsang was especially interested in the emerging Fa-hsiang school of Buddhist thought derived from the Yogācāra school of Indian Mahayana teachings. Studying the extant Chinese textual versions of Yogācāra Buddhism convinced him that only by becoming familiar with the great *Yogācārabhūmi śāstra*, a fourth or fifth century text available only in India, could he understand the mysteries of his faith. Accordingly, seeking further enlightenment and disregarding his brother's reluctance to let him go, Hsüan-tsang left Ch'eng-tu, preaching and visiting famous religious teachers in the provinces of Hupeh, Honan, and Hopeh until he reached Ch'ang-an. At the Great Enlightenment Monastery he studied Mahayana and Hinayana tenets further under the capital's greatest theologians. Finally, Hsüan-tsang decided that he must go to the source of Buddhism—India—to learn at first hand the solutions to the metaphysical and religious questions perplexing him and to read in the original Sanskrit the words of the Buddha and the commentaries on these scriptures.

Life's Work

The so-called Western region, the area beyond China's borders leading to India, was off-limits, and imperial permission was required for any travel there. Hsüan-tsang did not have permission, but, taking advantage of a decree ordering some of the crowded capital's population to be dispersed to other areas, he set out for the West in 629. Before departing, he was encouraged by a dream about the holy Mount Sumeru foretelling that he would conquer all difficulties on this arduous pilgrimage.

Hsüan-tsang made his way to Kansu along the trade route linking Central Asia with China. Word had reached the T'ang officials there that a monk was attempting to circumvent the embargo on travel to the West. The Prefect of

Liang-chou, a pious Buddhist, overlooked the orders for Hsüan-tsang's detainment, permitting him to pass by the last T'ang military posts en route to India. His passage was at first assisted by a foreigner named Bandha and an old roan horse which had made the trip west numerous times, but they soon abandoned him.

Hagiographic accounts of Hsüan-tsang's travels through Central Asia are replete with tales of miraculous escapes from numerous life-threatening perils: sandstorms, landslides, glaciers, marauding tribesmen, demons, robbers, and the constant problem of insufficient food and water. Yet as he crossed through parts of modern-day southern Russia, Afghanistan, Pakistan, and other lands to the northwest of India, Hsüan-tsang's travels were assisted by sympathetic khans, princes, tribal chieftains, holy men, and others who gave the traveling cleric timely help and provisions as he in turn impressed them, through sermons and theological discourse, with his deep knowledge and holiness.

India in the seventh century was not a unified country but a land of competing kingdoms and dozens of smaller principalities. Hsüan-tsang was not the first Chinese to visit there, though he would be the first to travel through the five major political divisions of the Indian subcontinent. It is not recorded when exactly he reached India (631 is a possibility). He began his task of studying the earliest Hinayana texts, the Vedas, the scores of Mahayana Buddhist writings, and other religious literature as he passed through northern India, visiting monasteries and important cities on his way to the Buddha's birthplace. His travels were not easy, since attacks by pirates, wild animals, and Hindu zealots—among other obstacles—were common.

In the foothills of the Himalayas sacred places associated more than a millennium earlier with the life of the Buddha, Siddhārtha Gautama, were visited. Northern India had since become a bastion of Hinduism, giving the Chinese pilgrim many opportunities to meet Brahmans and observe Hindu customs. When he reached the sacred Ganges River, he was appalled by the ritual suicide Hindu devotees practiced there. After arriving at Magadha, the site where Siddhārtha attained enlightenment under a bodhi tree, Hsüan-tsang received an invitation to go to the great monastery of Nālandā, the largest Buddhist center in India.

Nālandā was a huge monastic community of more than ten thousand religious and laymen engaged in studying and propagating Mahayana teachings. The entire population turned out to welcome Hsüan-tsang to Nālandā, and Silabhadra, the respected master of Buddhist idealism, accepted him as a student-disciple. The venerable Silabhadra, a disciple of Dharmapala, a famous Mahayana theologian of the preceding generation, personally instructed him for fifteen months in the intricacies of the Yogācāra and Abhidhamma. That is exactly what Hsüan-tsang desired, and during the intermittent five years he spent at this citadel of learning he mastered prodigious amounts of texts and dogmas, even composing in Sanskrit three learned religious treatises of his own.

Using Nālandā as a base, he made side trips to other parts of India. After going to Bengal, he followed the eastern coast of the subcontinent southward. A planned trip to Ceylon was canceled because of the death of the king there, so he proceeded to the northwest before returning to Nālandā. By that point, Hsüan-tsang had been exposed to the full range of Indian scholarship, including grammar, logic, mathematics, medicine, and astronomy. His reputation grew with his scholarship. Eventually, realizing that it was time to consider returning to his homeland, he asked a fortune-telling Jain when he would return to China. The response was that it was propitious for him to leave at this time, if he wished; moreover, his return would be assisted by a king who would arrange for him and his possessions to return safely. He told his Nālandā hosts of his plan to leave; they protested his return to a "barbarous land" where the Buddha had not deigned to appear or be reborn. Hsüan-tsang countered their protestations with the argument that it was his duty to propagate the dharma among all creatures, including the Chinese, a people not as backward as the Indians presumed.

His departure was delayed by the demand of King Kumara that he come to Assam to convert him. King Harsha, a rival of Kumara, wanted Hsüan-tsang to preach in his lands south of the Ganges. Hsüan-tsang could refuse neither. After bringing Kumara into the Mahayana fold, Hsüan-tsang went to Harsha's capital at Kanauj in 642 to participate in a syllogistic debate to establish the validity of Mahayana beliefs over Hinayana, or "lesser vehicle," teachings. Offering his head if his arguments could be refuted, Hsüan-tsang dazzled a conclave of several thousand vassal kings, monks, Brahmans, and Jains with his command of logic. After eighteen days no one could counter his arguments. Hsüan-tsang was showered with gifts, but he accepted none of them. Harsha, after inducing Hsüan-tsang to participate in an almsgiving ceremony at Prayāga, finally, in 643, permitted him to start on his journey back to China. Accepting only a buffalo-skin coat to protect him from the rain and a sturdy elephant to transport his canonical library and possessions, Hsüan-tsang, after fifteen years away from China, finally set out for home.

A cavalry escort of northern Indian kings accompanied Hsüan-tsang as far as the Punjab. Though he lost many precious books while crossing the Indus River, his return trip across the Oxus River, along historic caravan routes and over the Pamir range, was less dangerous than his earlier one. He made his way to the oasis at Khotan, where he decided, probably with great apprehension, to send a letter via a Chinese messenger to the T'ang court reporting his imminent return and suggesting that his accomplishments should save him from chastisement. After about eight months, he received a reply inviting him to the capital for an imperial audience. Whereas he had left China furtively on a forbidden spiritual odyssey, he was to be officially escorted home, welcomed as a heroic pilgrim returning with invaluable sutras from the holy land of the Buddha. Hsüan-tsang, anxious to get back to Ch'ang-an to report to the emperor, unexpectedly arrived in the first month of 645, before plans for his official reception were completed. It was reported that so many turned out to greet him that initially he could not enter the city.

Kao Tsu, the founder of the T'ang Dynasty, had been ousted in 626 by a son who was now reigning as T'ang T'ai Tsung. This new emperor, unlike his father (who was a Taoist believer), was supportive of Buddhism. A month after the relics, Buddhist images, and 657 Indian books Hsüan-tsang brought with him had been ensconced at Hung-fu Monastery near Imperial Park, T'ai Tsung met Hsüan-tsang at Lo-yang. At a longer meeting soon after, fulsome praise again was heaped on him while the emperor debriefed his returned subject about the history, climate, geography, customs, and languages of lands visited. So impressed was the emperor with the returned pilgrim—he also recognized the strategic intelligence the monk could provide for his wars of expansion in the West—that he tried to induce him to become a layman and serve as an imperial official. In fact, he wanted the monk to accompany him as an adviser on his current military campaign, an offer the pacifist bonze declined. Hsüan-tsang, instead, asked permission to retire to a monastery southeast of Lo-yang to begin his task of translating his Sanskrit library into Chinese. First, though, on imperial command, he wrote a description (completed in 646) of his travels through 280 "countries." This work, titled *Ta T'ang Hsi-yü-chi* (the great T'ang records of travels to the western lands), constituted the most thorough account at that time of Central Asia and India.

The emperor offered him use of the Hung-fu temple complex in Ch'ang-an, and there a committee of some twenty specialists in lexicography, grammar, and Sanskrit was assembled to help Hsüan-tsang. When the encyclopedic *Yogācārabhūmi śāstra*—the quest for which Hsüan-tsang had launched his journey—was rendered into Chinese, T'ai Tsung had it disseminated throughout the empire with a laudatory preface of his own. The translation project was continued by Kao Tsung (reigned 649-683), Tai Tsung's successor, and after a period of about nineteen years a corpus of seventy-six books in 1,347 sections was produced. These books were stored in the Wild Goose Pagoda, a brick structure built on T'ai Tsung's orders, about 652. At the request of some Indian emissaries, Hsüan-tsang translated the Taoist classic *Tao-te Ching* from Chinese into Sanskrit.

Bothered by ailments incurred on his journeys and racing against time, Hsüan-tsang hoped to fulfill his goal of translating into his native language all the books he had brought from India. In 664, however, after a long illness, he died blissfully in the company of his fellow monks. More than one million people attended the interment of his remains in the Monastery of Great

Beneficience in Ch'ang-an at a ceremony presided over by Emperor Kao Tsung.

Summary

Hsüan-tsang was not the first Chinese to make the trip to India, nor was he the last. His uniqueness, therefore, lies not in the considerable accomplishment of his pilgrimage but in the effects of his subsequent writings and translations. The large number of Indian religious and philosophical texts and related commentaries rendered by him and his colleagues into Chinese made up approximately a quarter of all Chinese books on Buddhism extant at that time. Some remain the only versions of lost originals.

The record of Hsüan-tsang's travels became an invaluable compendium of facts and impressions about central and southern Asia, informing later travelers and diplomats and influencing T'ang foreign policy. He fostered ongoing cultural contacts between China and several of the lands he visited by receiving visitors and emissaries, thereby contributing to diplomatic goodwill. Chinese and Indians still honor him as the initiator of friendly contact between their countries.

Ironically, though he labored long and hard to translate the writings of the Indian "consciousness-only" school into Chinese and to propagate these teachings in China, within a generation after Hsüan-tsang's death, this sect, with its narrow interpretation that certain sentient beings were unable to attain salvation, had lost its foothold in China.

The life of Hsüan-tsang ultimately transcended the histories and clerical biographies in which it was recorded and took on the characteristics of literary hyperbole as it was retold for centuries in poetry, drama, and prose. By the Ming Dynasty (1368-1644), the exploits of Hsüan-tsang had been transformed into a hundred-chapter fictitious narrative called *Hsi-yu chi* (*The Journey to the West*, 1977-1983), written by Wu Ch'eng-en (c. 1500-c. 1582). In this literary reincarnation, Hsüan-tsang becomes a Chinese Don Quixote, Tripitaka, leading his cohorts Monkey and Pigsy on a comic journey replete with supernatural events, vengeful ogres, magical deliverances from life-threatening predicaments, and other trappings of high adventure set in exotic realms. This novelistic narrative, published in 1592 (and as popular now as then), has become the received interpretation of Hsüan-tsang's life in the popular imagination of many Chinese people, who today delight in his deeds as recounted in comic books, opera, animated films, and folk art, all based on *The Journey to the West*, one of the great works of Chinese literature.

Bibliography

Chan, Wing-tsit. *A Source Book in Chinese Philosophy*. Princeton, N.J.: Princeton University Press, 1963. An interpretative overview of the consciousness-only school of Buddhist idealism championed by Hsüan-tsang and a partial translation of his treatise on the establishment of this doctrine (*Ch'eng wei-shih lun*) are presented in section 23.

Grousset, René. *In the Footsteps of the Buddha*. Translated by J. A. Underwood. London: Routledge and Sons, 1932. Rev. ed. New York: Grossman Publishers, 1971. This work covers the life of Hsüan-tsang (called Hiuan Tsang, according to French romanization) from the perspective of Chinese and Indian history, with particular emphasis on relating his stay in India to milestones in the life of Buddha, supported by numerous photos of sacred Buddhist iconography. Includes a picture of Hsüan-tsang but no bibliography. The first edition has a foldout map tracing the route of his travels.

Hui-li. *The Life of Hiuen-Tsiang*. Translated by Samuel Beal. London: Kegan Paul, Trench, Trübner and Co., 1911. Prior to the appearance of scholarship by René Grousset and Arthur Waley, this work was the prevailing account of Hsüan-tsang's life in English. It is quite dated, and the stilted English is difficult to follow, a situation not helped by an inconsistent method of romanizing names. It is essentially an incomplete translation of Hsüan-tsang's biography by the monk Hui-li, compiled during the latter years of Hsüan-tsang's life.

_____ . *The Life of Hsüan-tsang*. Translated by Li Yung-hsi. Peking: Chinese Buddhist Association, 1959. Although perhaps difficult to locate, this is a readable, direct translation of the biography written by Hui-li. Paperback edition includes reproductions of a traditional painting of Hsüan-tsang and a fourteenth century woodcut showing him translating scriptures. Limited footnotes assist in identifying ancient place-names with modern counterparts.

Waley, Arthur. *"The Real Tripitaka" and Other Pieces*. London: Allen and Unwin, 1952. A synopsis of Hsüan-tsang's life, interspersed with many direct quotes, based on T'ang era Chinese biographies and modern Japanese secondary accounts. Waley prepared a lively partial translation of Wu Ch'eng-en's novel about Hsüan-tsang and wrote this historical account of Hsüan-tsang's life to complement the fictitious version. Presents sound background material to assist in relating Hsüan-tsang's career to the political and religious events of the time. Full notes and technical bibliography. Undoubtedly the best English account; written by a respected Sinologist.

Wright, Arthur F., and Denis Twitchett, eds. *Perspectives on the T'ang*. New Haven, Conn.: Yale University Press, 1973. Essays by Wright and Stanley Weinstein analyze Hsüan-tsang in the context of the domestic development of Chinese Buddhism and imperial politics. Latter essay probes impact on Chinese religious history of Hsüan-tsang's espousal of the Fa-hsiang sect's teachings.

Wu Ch'eng-en. *The Journey to the West*. Translated by Anthony C. Yu. 4 vols. Chicago: University of Chicago Press, 1977-1983. The most authoritative, complete translation of the *Hsi-yu chi*. The introduction to volume 1, "Historical and Literary Antecedents," traces the evolution of the novel's story and literary forms from the T'ang era historical facts to the Ming Dynasty work of fiction. With a reliable overview of Hsüan-tsang's life.

William M. Zanella

HSÜN-TZU

Born: c. 313 B.C.; Chao, China
Died: After 238 B.C.; Lan-ling, China
Area of Achievement: Philosophy
Contribution: Through his development and modification of Confucian teachings, Hsün-tzu built a synthesized and more realistic foundation for Confucian ideology that was influential throughout China during the Han Dynasty.

Early Life

Although Hsün-tzu is undoubtedly a great figure in Chinese philosophy, the basic facts of his life are still controversial among scholars. According to most Chinese scholars, he was born in the northern state of Chao around 313 B.C., and the period of his activities as a philosopher and politician covers sixty years, from 298 to 238. The most reliable sources about his life are his own writings, published posthumously, and Ssu-ma Ch'ien's *Shih chi* (c. 90 B.C.). Yet almost no information about his early life, his education, or even his family background can be found in these early sources, which provide an account of his life beginning at the age of fifty, when he first visited the state of Ch'i and joined a distinguished group of scholars from various philosophical schools at the Chi-hsia Academy. This lack of information about his early life prompts some modern scholars to doubt the accuracy of the *Shih chi* and suggest that Hsün-tzu first visited the Chi-hsia Academy at the age of fifteen, not fifty. These scholars contend that either Hsün-tzu's age was erroneously recorded in the first place or the *Shih chi* text was corrupted.

Life's Work

Whether Hsün-tzu first appeared on the stage of history at fifty or fifteen does not change much of his historical role, for he did not really affect his contemporaries or his immediate environment during his lifetime. Like his predecessors in the Confucian school, Confucius and Mencius specifically, Hsün-tzu traveled from state to state, trying to persuade the rulers of Ch'i, Ch'u, Chao, and even the Legalist Ch'in to adopt his brand of Confucian statecraft. The dating of his various visits to these states is again an area of endless academic debate.

There are, however, two reliable historical dates in Hsün-tzu's public career. In 255, he was invited by Lord Ch'un-shen of Ch'u to serve as the magistrate of Lan-ling. He was soon forced to resign the post when Lord Ch'un-shen gave credence to some slanderous rumors about the potential danger of the benevolent Confucian policy. Hsün-tzu then left for his native Chao. He stayed as an honored guest in the Chao court until Lord Ch'un-shen apologized for his suspicion and invited him to resume the magistrateship. Hsün-tzu remained in the position until 238, the year Lord Ch'un-shen was assassinated. Hsün-tzu was immediately dismissed from office, and he died in Lan-ling, probably soon after the coup.

The most immediate impact of Hsün-tzu on the political situation of the ancient Chinese world came, ironically, from his two best students, Han-fei-tzu and Li Ssu. Both men deviated from his teachings of Confucian benevolence and turned his emphasis on pragmatic sociopolitical programming into realpolitik. Han-fei-tzu became a synthesizer of Legalist thought, and Li Ssu became a prime minister who helped Emperor Cheng set up a totalitarian state after China was unified.

Hsün-tzu's greatest contribution to Chinese civilization lies in the field of philosophy, or, more generally, in the intellectual formation of Chinese sociopolitical behavior. His writings were perhaps compiled by himself in his later years but were definitely supplemented with a few chapters from his disciples. The standard edition of Hsün-tzu's works is the end product of a Han scholar, Liu Hsiang, who collated and edited the available sources into thirty-two chapters. Since Hsün-tzu lived through a period of fierce political strife, constant warfare, and tremendous social change on the eve of China's unification (also the golden age of Chinese philosophy known as the period of the Hundred Schools), his approach to the social and ethical issues of Confucian philosophy was markedly more realistic than those of Confucius and Mencius. In his defense of Confucian doctrine, he not only refuted the arguments and programs of other schools but also criticized the idealistic strain of thinking within his own camp, particularly in Mencius' philosophy. With an admirable command of scholarship and a powerful mind for critical analysis, Hsün-tzu demonstrated the Confucian way of thinking in a most systematic and pragmatic manner.

In opposition to Mencius' contention that human nature is innately good and man need only go back to his original psychological urges to achieve goodness and righteousness, Hsün-tzu states that human nature is evil and that only through education can man distinguish himself from animals. Despondent as it appears, Hsün-tzu's conception of human nature is quite complex and far removed from pessimism. For him, human nature—though evil—does not determine human destiny, for man has a capacity for reasoning and learning and for attaining a higher and more civilized order. That man has created civilization and sloughed off his barbarism is clear testimony to the possibility of a brighter future for mankind, as long as the civilizing order is maintained and continued. The whole process of education and socialization thus becomes the focus of Hsün-tzu's ethical concern.

It seems that when Hsün-tzu addresses the question of human nature, he has no preconceived illusions and deals squarely with human psychology as such. The evil of which he speaks is simply a composite body of animal drives and has no likeness to the Judeo-Christian concept of Original Sin. With such a no-nonsense and down-to-earth approach, he is interested in human nature less as an ontological issue than as an epistemological one. His particular emphasis on "artificial endeavor" for humanity also attests this interest, which some scholars describe as a "moral epistemology."

Hsün-tzu's interest in education and socialization centers on the Confucian concept of *li*, which has been translated in different contexts as propriety, decorum, rite, and etiquette. It is Hsün-tzu's belief that proper social behavior is foundational for moral gentlemen and that institutionalized rites regulate human relations for a better society. Thus, education is not only a way of acquiring external knowledge for its own sake but also a process of internalizing all the knowledge for the molding of a good and moral person. On the other hand, society is not merely a background against which one develops his intellectual faculty or moral character: Society is the main source of personality development. Through interaction between the individual self and the social norm, a functioning structure takes shape and reveals a pattern of *li* which serves as the very basis of social order.

How did *li* first come into existence? Confucius did not talk about its origin. Mencius was not interested in it. For Hsün-tzu, however, this question was of primary importance. In his treatise on *li*, Hsün-tzu offers the following explanation:

> Man is born with desires. If his desires are not satisfied for him, he cannot but seek some means to satisfy them himself. If there are no limits and measures of regulation in his seeking, then he will inevitably fall to wrangling with other men. From wrangling comes disorder and from disorder comes exhaustion. The ancient kings hated such disorder, and therefore they institutionalized *li* and righteousness in order to define the relationship between men, to train men's desires and to provide for their satisfaction.

This explanation supports his argument that human nature is evil and also shows his concern for law and order.

For Confucius and Mencius, *li* is the internalized moral code that impels people to exhibit proper social behavior; it has nothing to do with the penal code, or law, imposed by government from outside to regulate social order. Hsün-tzu's practical concern for institutionalized law and order greatly transformed this Confucian concept of *li*. Confucius and Mencius could not bear to see a society's peace and order being enforced by law, while Hsün-tzu would acquiesce on this practical matter. Hsün-tzu, however, was by no means a Legalist entrusting the programming of social order entirely to the institution of law; he always placed the benevolence of the ruling class, the moral behavior maintained by a gentlemanly social elite, and the education of the people ahead of the enforcement of law, a necessary evil.

Hsün-tzu's concept of nature also complements his realistic approach to social and ethical issues. He believed that nature exists independent of human will. Heavenly matters have nothing to do with social and ethical issues, and, therefore, human beings are solely responsible for their behavior. This attitude underlies logically his idea that human nature is evil and that the good is the product of man's artificial endeavor. It also implies the unlimited potential of "evil-natured" mankind to do good and better the human world, because there is no supernatural force to hinder such a human endeavor. In this sense, Hsün-tzu should be taken seriously as an ardent optimist with regard to human progress.

Summary

During his lifetime, Hsün-tzu did not have any major effect on historical events. War, suffering, and political intrigue continued in his country. It was during this time of chaos and disintegration that Hsün-tzu developed his systematic reinterpretation of the Confucian tradition. If the unification of China and the institutionalization of the Legalist program toward the end of the third century B.C. can only be partly credited to his students Han-fei-tzu and Li Ssu, at least Hsün-tzu can claim a lion's share in the formation of the Confucian system during the Han period, after the Legalist Ch'in Dynasty collapsed. This Han Confucian system, with its strong emphasis on the blending of practical sociopolitical institutions with moral concerns, has served as the foundation of Chinese social and political norms for two millennia.

Bibliography

Cua, A. S. *Ethical Argumentation: A Study in Hsün Tzu's Moral Epistemology*. Honolulu: University of Hawaii Press, 1985. Contains a detailed and stimulating analysis of Hsün-tzu's ethical theory and the rationale and argumentative discourse in his philosophy. An in-depth study of an important but rarely touched area of Hsün-tzu's thought. With a bibliography, notes, and an index.

Dubs, Homer H. *Hsüntze: The Moulder of Ancient Confucianism*. London: A. Probsthain, 1927. A systematic study of Hsün-tzu's life and all aspects of his philosophy, this work is based on traditional Chinese scholarship and contains lengthy quotations from Hsün-tzu's writings. It is scholarly but quite cumbersome in explicating major Confucian concepts; it is also very disorganized. With notes and an index.

Hsün-tzu. *Hsün Tzu: Basic Writings*. Translated by Burton Watson. New York: Columbia University Press, 1963. Contains a basically reliable translation of ten chapters from Hsün-tzu. With a useful outline of early Chinese history, annotative notes, and an index.

_____. *The Works of Hsüntze*. Translated by Homer H. Dubs. London: A. Probsthain, 1928. Still the most complete English translation of Hsün-tzu, it contains only nineteen chapters from the original book of thirty-two chapters. With an out-of-date introduction on ancient Chinese history, good textual notes, lexical explanations, and useful marginalia.

_____. *Xunzi: A Translation and Study of the Complete Works*. Vol. 1. Translated by John Knoblock. Stanford, Calif.: Stanford University Press, 1988. This volume inaugurates a set of annotated translations and full-scale studies of the complete works of Hsün-tzu. Contains the first six chapters of Hsün-tzu's original work.

Munro, Donald J. *The Concept of Man in Early China*. Stanford, Calif.: Stanford University Press, 1969. A narrowly focused but valuable study of an important topic in early Chinese philosophy. It contains useful sections on Hsün-tzu. With a glossary, notes, a bibliography, and an index.

Schwartz, Benjamin I. *The World of Thought in Ancient China*. Cambridge, Mass.: Harvard University Press, 1985. A remarkable study in the field of ancient Chinese thought, this book is scholarly but never dull. It presents all the major issues in clear language and compares them with Western philosophical concepts without losing their original meanings. The chapter on Mencius and Hsün-tzu is informative. With a bibliography, notes, and an index.

Pei-kai Cheng

JÁNOS HUNYADI

Born: c. 1407; place unknown
Died: August 11, 1456; Zimony (Zemun)
Areas of Achievement: Warfare and government
Contribution: By organizing, financing, and leading the Hungarian and Central European military forces, Hunyadi halted the Ottoman Empire's advance at the Balkan Mountains, postponing for some seventy years the Turkish conquest of central Hungary.

Early Life

Popularly believed to be the son of Sigismund, King of Hungary and Holy Roman Emperor, János Hunyadi was in fact the eldest child of Vojk, a lesser noble of Walachian origin who had moved to Hungary around 1395 and then had married into a Hungarian noble family. Besides János, the marriage produced two sons, as well as at least one daughter. János' father became a royal soldier and counselor, and in 1409 he received for his services an estate in Transylvania—called Vajdahunyad—from which the family took its name.

Little is known of Hunyadi's youth, since few extant records of the period mention him. Nevertheless, since he was for the most part a resident at the court of Sigismund, he presumably received early military training. This is all the more likely since soldierly prowess was generously rewarded with sizable grants of land, which in turn meant wealth and power.

Said to have been a born soldier, Hunyadi cut an impressive figure. He was of medium height and had a thick neck, long chestnut-brown hair, large, penetrating eyes, and a well-proportioned body. He began his military career in the 1420's under Pipo of Ozora. Around 1428 he married Erzsébet Szilágyi, herself a daughter of a noble family. Their marriage produced two sons, László and Mátyás, the latter destined to become perhaps Hungary's most illustrious king as Matthias Corvinus.

In 1430, Hunyadi entered the service of the king, accompanying Sigismund to Italy. There the young soldier served Fillippo Maria Visconti, Duke of Milan, for a time. In 1433, Hunyadi was reunited with Sigismund and accompanied him on many trips, including one to Bohemia in 1437. By then expertly trained in mercenary warfare, well acquainted with the most up-to-date Italian and Hussite military tactics and procedures and experienced in the methods of the Turkish armies, Hunyadi dedicated himself to the struggle against the Ottomans.

Life's Work

In the fifteenth century, the Ottoman Empire was still dedicated to expansion and military conquest. This awesome momentum, created by economic need and religious fervor, had by Sigismund's time already carried the Turks deep into the Balkan Peninsula. The Ottoman wave would soon sweep over Hungary, whose own southern frontier reached into the Balkans.

Unfortunately, the Hungarian distribution of land and wealth, favoring the aristocrats at the expense of the Crown, did not seem a likely source for the centralized, unified effort that would be required to hold the great Turkish empire in check. Nevertheless, the single most powerful aristocrat in the country was a man both eminently qualified and highly motivated to stem the Ottoman advance: János Hunyadi.

According to the chronicler Thuróczy, Hunyadi's military virtues were great; the account cites his strength and courage as a soldier as well as his strategical and tactical acumen. Though an accurate portrayal of him, Thuróczy's account fails nevertheless to consider certain other necessary aspects of Hunyadi's character. He was also a crafty politician who, though disliked by his fellow aristocrats, managed to create important if short-lived alliances with his peers. Moreover, able to count on neither the king, whose own landholdings had seriously dwindled, nor the barons, who were reluctant to dip into their vast resources, Hunyadi organized and financed his armies himself, drawing on the revenue of his approximately six million acres of property.

Under Albert II of Habsburg (reigned 1437-1439), Sigismund's son-in-law and successor, Hunyadi and his brother served as joint military governors of Szörény (Severin). Hunyadi continued as Bán of Severin until 1446, protecting that area from the Ottoman menace. It was, from all accounts, these experiences which hastened his assimilation. To Hunyadi, himself an immigrant without a Magyar pedigree, the *patria* encompassed not merely the nobility but the people as a whole.

In 1440, a few months after Albert's death, the Polish king Władisław III was elected King of Hungary by the Diet. Władisław, who saw Hunyadi as the real leader against the Turks, put him in charge of the key fortress in Belgrade and of the southern border region as a whole. In 1441, he appointed Hunyadi both Voivode of Transylvania and Ispán of Temesvár (Timişoara), offices he would hold until 1446. Hunyadi organized and equipped an army composed mainly of Bohemian Hussite mercenaries, but he rounded it out with his own adherents, relatives, noble vassals, and even peasants. He enjoyed his first victory over the Ottomans in 1442, driving the invading army out of Transylvania. This was the first such defeat ever suffered by the Ottomans in Europe, and news of it quickly spread, reviving hopes that the Balkans would indeed be liberated from the Turkish yoke.

Doubting that a passive defense would be adequate to deal with the Turkish menace, Hunyadi decided to take the offensive. Pressing toward the heart of the Ottoman Empire, he led his forces to one victory after another, occupying as he went the towns of Nish and Sofia. Though his long march was stalled not long after, his victories persuaded Sultan Murad II to negotiate for peace. Unfortunately, the treaty had no sooner been signed with the sultan's emissaries in Szeged than, at the behest of the papal legate, Władisław broke his word and launched a new attack. The foreign support which had been promised failed to materialize, and Hunyadi's forces were routed at Varna in 1444. The king fell in battle, while Hunyadi managed a narrow escape.

Although the Diet of 1445 recognized the succession of Albert's son László, Emperor Frederick III, who had custody of the young Habsburg, refused to surrender him. The problem of the succession was given a temporary but happy solution the following year: Hunyadi was acclaimed the Hungarian regent, a result largely of the vigorous campaign of János Vitéz, Bishop of Várad (Oradea).

It was not until 1448 that Hunyadi built up sufficient strength for a new offensive. Leading his army deep into the Balkans, he engaged the Turkish army at Kosovo. Betrayed, however, by the Serbian despot George Brankovich, Hunyadi was not only defeated but taken temporarily captive as well. In 1450, Hunyadi concluded an agreement with Frederick III that recognized the legitimacy of László. In 1453, the once-vacant throne now occupied, Hunyadi dutifully resigned as regent but was appointed by László his commander in chief and royal treasurer.

Unfortunately, the king fell under the influence of Ulrich von Cilli, a longtime rival of Hunyadi. Cilli now became allied with several aristocrats against Hunyadi. In addition, Hunyadi's old friend and ally János Vitéz, always a staunch foe of baronial power, put forward a plan for centralization which would have seriously weakened Hunyadi's position. When the Hungarians learned that Constantinople had fallen (in 1453) and that Sultan Mehmed II was gathering his forces to attack Hungary, Vitéz's plan was prudently withdrawn from consideration.

In 1456, the Ottomans besieged Belgrade, sending forth an army one hundred thousand strong. Neither the king, who fled the country, nor the barons came to the aid of Hunyadi's hopelessly outnumbered army. Eventually, however, help came. Franciscan friar John of Capistrano, sent by the pope to organize a Crusade, managed to recruit into Hunyadi's army some twenty thousand soldiers. On July 21, the city's walls already penetrated, the Turks launched an all-out attack but were defeated and withdrew en masse.

Not for another seventy years would a major battle be fought between Hungarian and Ottoman forces. Hunyadi, who had saved Hungary from Turkish conquest, died of the plague not long thereafter.

Summary

Hungary in the fifteenth century was poised between the Middle Ages and the Renaissance. It was also the meeting place of Western and Eastern Europe. Themselves the scourge of the West some five centuries earlier, the

Hungarians, now Christian and in possession of one of the most powerful states in Europe, hoped to bar the way of the new terror of Europe, the Ottoman Turks. It was mainly through Hunyadi's efforts that Hungary survived and Western Europe was spared the Turkish scourge. Yet—and this cast a dark shadow over Hungary—virtually all the border fortresses had fallen to the Turks.

When Hunyadi died, his first son, László, was killed by anti-Hunyadi conspirators, while his other son, Mátyás, was imprisoned. Upon King László's unexpected death in 1457, however, the Diet elected Mátyás king. Exploiting the peace created by his father, Mátyás, called Matthias Corvinus, inaugurated a glorious era for Hungary. Not only did it grow stronger both militarily and economically, but it became the center of Renaissance culture in East Central Europe as well. That this era would not last, indeed would pass into a century-and-a-half-long nightmare beginning with the Battle of Mohács in 1526, was the result at least in part of Mátyás' almost total neglect of the slumbering, but by no means extinct, Ottoman threat.

Bibliography

Held, Joseph. *Hunyadi: Legend and Reality*. New York: Columbia University Press, 1985. The most up-to-date and detailed work on Hunyadi that exists in English. Includes an index, a list of place names, maps, illustrations, and a brief note on primary sources.

Macartney, C. A. *Hungary: A Short History*. Chicago: Aldine Publishing Co., 1962. An excellent overview of Hungarian history by an eminent British historian. Though it gives only a brief account of Hunyadi, it is stylishly written and includes an index, maps, photographs, tables, a comparative chronology, biographies, and a bibliography.

Sinor, Denis. *History of Hungary*. New York: Frederick A. Praeger, 1959. A crossover effort, this entertaining treatment of Hungarian history was written by an Inner-Asian specialist and it includes an account of Hunyadi. Includes both an index and a chronology of events.

Vambéry, Arminius. *Hungary in Ancient, Medieval, and Modern Times*. 2d ed. London: T. Fisher Unwin, 1887. In this readable but dated survey, a full chapter is devoted to the career of Hunyadi. Includes an index and illustrations.

Zarek, Otto. *History of Hungary*. London: Selwyn and Blount, 1939. Translated by H.S.H. Prince Peter P. Wolkowsky. The sixth chapter of this work is mainly devoted to Hunyadi. Features an index, a map, and an aid to pronunciation.

Gregory Nehler

JAN HUS

Born: 1372 or 1373; Husinec, southern Bohemia
Died: July 6, 1415; Constance (in modern Germany)
Areas of Achievement: Religion and church reform
Contribution: Through preaching and writing against the abuses of the medieval church attendant upon the divided Papacy, the greedy and indolent clergy, and the rigid anti-layperson doctrines, Hus laid the foundation for the Protestant Reformation one hundred years later. His martyrdom at the Council of Constance made him a national hero to the Czech people.

Early Life

Jan Hus derived his name from the small hamlet in which he was born, Husinec, which literally means "Goosetown." No agreement exists about his exact date of birth or the nature of his early schooling, but it is known that his family was poor and his mother vowed her son to the priesthood. In 1390, Hus entered the University of Prague, and by 1398, he had garnered both the bachelor of arts and master's degree to join the arts faculty as a full member. During the winter semester of 1401/1402 he served for a term as dean of the arts faculty before enrolling in the faculty of theology to pursue the highest degree available in a medieval university, the doctor's degree in theology. After earning the bachelor of divinity degree in 1404, as a first step, he began to lecture on the Bible and then, in 1407, on Peter Lombard's *Sententiarum libri IV* (1148-1151; four books of sentences). He was within a year or two of his goal when his life was engulfed in controversy. From humble origins, Hus had climbed to the top rung of the academic ladder in his native land.

What was going on in his mind and heart during these years? Not much is known about these personal matters. All students and faculty were members of the clergy at that time, which did not mean that they were ordained as priests or monks but which did preclude marriage and secular occupations. Hus does not tell how he survived his prolonged apprenticeship in the lower ranks of the university, and unlike his celebrated successors in the Reformation (especially Martin Luther, 1483-1546), he does not divulge his religious thinking. He was ordained as a priest in June of 1400 and appointed preacher at the Bethlehem Chapel on March 14, 1402. This privately endowed religious institution in Prague had only been established in 1391, but it had already become a center for the Czech reform movement. Hus was to become its most famous advocate.

Amid the disarray caused by the papal problems in the fourteenth century—the "Babylonian Captivity" in Avignon, France, from 1305 to 1378, which was sharpened by the Great Schism from 1389 to 1415—there were calls for church reform throughout Europe. Add to this the chronic political unrest caused by the Hundred Years' War (1337-1453) and the ghastly Black Death outbreaks beginning in 1347-1348, all of which spawned the peasant revolts of 1356 in France and 1381 in England, and the calls for reform became cries for revolution. It was out of this context that John Wyclif emerged to become the leading religious reformer and the spiritual mentor of Hus.

Life's Work

Hus's philosophy was formed by the Czech reform movement and the theology of Wyclif. The Czech reform movement had been started in 1363, when the Holy Roman Emperor Charles IV and the Archbishop Ernest of Pardubice called to Prague an Augustinian preacher from Vienna named Conrad Waldhauser. This preacher castigated the German clerics and merchants with electrifying zeal, and in the process he converted John Milíč of Kroměříž, who took up the call to exhort his own people to repent and reform. Following Milíč came Matthew of Janov, who in his short life translated the Bible into Czech and compiled five volumes of theology called *Regulae veteris et novi testamenti* (1388-1392). This full-fledged religious movement prepared Hus to receive and respond to the powerful message from across the English Channel.

Wyclif cast his heavy shadow over the life and career of Hus. Although the Czechs in general and Hus in particular were strongly attracted to Wyclif's views on church reform and Christian doctrine, they did not agree completely with him. Hus differed from Wyclif on most of the views certified as heretical, but he was labeled as a follower of Wyclif and burned at the stake as a heretic because of his sympathy for Wyclif.

As a moralist, Wyclif questioned the legitimacy of the Pope, the sacramental authority of the clergy, and even secular lords and kings, when corrupt. Although many of his followers in England, called "Lollards," were persecuted and suppressed, Wyclif himself managed to stay out of trouble and died just as his doctrinal pronouncements were beginning to disturb the peace of Christendom. The Czech religious leaders were learning about Wyclif when Hus was becoming a preacher.

As a theologian, Wyclif denied the doctrine of transubstantiation in the sacrament of Holy Communion. The Lateran Council in 1215 had pronounced that the bread and wine were "transubstantiated" into the body and blood of Christ. Wyclif, rejecting this dogma, argued that it was impossible for the "real" elements, that is, the bread and the wine, to be annihilated by their transformation into the body and blood of Christ. This denial of transubstantiation led him to question the legitimacy of priests who administered the sacrament, to challenge the Pope, who was the chief priest of the church, and even to attack the tithes which were collected to support the Church. Moreover, Wyclif proposed that Communion be offered to the laity "in both kinds," which meant giving wine as well as bread to the laity. Finally, he based his criticism of transubstantiation and other doctrines on the Bible, as well as on philosophical arguments. Emphasizing the need for Scriptural grounding of doctrine, he became a stout supporter of the translation of the Bible into vernacular languages.

Hus began as an orthodox teacher and preacher. From 1402 to 1408 he exhorted his parishioners at the Bethlehem Chapel to stop sinning and to improve their lives. Yet he did not confine his criticism to the meek and lowly of his parish and community. He recognized that many of the problems which led his parishioners to suffer and sin were caused by clerical abuses and the corruption of the clergy. Being a proud Czech in a world dominated politically and ecclesiastically by Germans, Hus did not hesitate to lambaste the German leaders, clerical and lay, for the evils of the world and the confusion in doctrine. In so doing, Hus became a leader of discontented poor people who wanted to revolt against tyranny and a spokesman for discontented Czechs of all classes who wanted to overthrow the German Holy Roman Emperor. Even though Hus himself entertained no such exalted revolutionary ambition, he was accused of being subversive.

Hus was actually a theologian rather than a political ideologue. He assumed that human wretchedness was a consequence of the Fall in the Garden of Eden. He believed that the sacraments of the Church could restore the spiritual virtues which were not entirely destroyed by Original Sin. Baptism and Communion were essential for salvation. While Hus did not deny the importance of the other five sacraments, he and his peers focused attention on these two. Baptism was not yet the issue it would become in the next century. The controversy which was going to convulse the Christian world for the next two centuries revolved around Communion.

Hus did not subscribe to Wyclif's rejection of transubstantiation, but he welcomed his anticlericalism and his reliance on the Bible. Because of his sympathy for Wyclif's reform sentiments, Hus defended Wyclif against the charge of heresy. That made Hus vulnerable to the ever-increasing assault from the theologians and ecclesiastical politicians who would ignore his fine distinctions. The assault began in 1402 in Prague and ended only at Constance in 1415.

When the new archbishop of Prague, Zbyněk Zajíc of Hasenburk, attacked Wyclif's theology in 1402, he provoked Hus to argue that the transubstantiated bread remained in the sacrament after its consecration. While Hus did not accept Wyclif's position theologically, for Hus did accept the doctrine that Christ's real body and blood were present physically, he did agree with Wyclif's position philosophically. That is, Hus did believe that it was "real" bread which contained Christ's physical remains. The theologians who were dominant in Bohemia and who prevailed at the Council of Constance were scandalized by the notion that there was anything "real" like bread in the sacrament. They held further that Christ's body and blood could be perceived only by faith.

Hus's opponents also insisted that even a wicked priest could confer a valid Communion sacrament, which was orthodox doctrine from Saint Augustine's pronouncements a thousand years earlier. Beginning in 1407, however, they provoked Hus to reply that a layman who knowingly receives the sacrament from a wicked priest is guilty of a grave sin. While Wyclif's original argument had verged upon a heretical denial of ordination, Hus remained orthodox by affirming the validity of ordination while denying the corrupt priest any possibility of salvation. Since Hus persisted in defending the Wyclifite excoriation of bad priests and sinfully obedient lay people, he opened himself up to be condemned as a Wyclifite.

The ecclesiastical politicians launched their successful assault in 1411 when they provoked Hus to oppose the papal crusade against the King of Naples, who supported Gregory XII. Not only did Hus protest against the secular use of papal power, but he also railed against the sale of indulgences which supported the enterprise. On October 18, 1412, Pope John XXIII excommunicated Hus for nonobedience (not for heresy) and placed Prague under interdict until Hus left. Hus went into exile in southern Bohemia, where he lived with many nobles in several different castles. During his exile, he wrote his principal work, *De ecclesia* (*On the Church*), and several polemical articles against his critics. Again, he vainly struggled to disentangle his respect for Wyclif the reformer from his nonadherence to Wyclif's heretical ideas.

On October 31, 1413, Emperor Sigismund compelled Pope John XXIII to call a new council to convene in Constance exactly one year later. The emperor then invited Hus to leave his safe retreats and attend the council. He promised him safe conduct to the conference, and he gave the impression that he promised him safe conduct to return home. It made little difference though, because once Hus had been lured to the conference, he was doomed. On November 3, 1414, Hus arrived at Constance, six weeks ahead of the emperor's entourage. The council was formally opened on November 16, and Hus was arrested on November 28 and imprisoned in a monastery dungeon from December 6 to March 24 of the next year. After many postponements, Hus was granted a public hearing on June 5, and another on June 7-8. There was no debate allowed. On July 6, 1415, Hus was formally condemned for Wyclifite heresy, and when he refused to recant, he was burned at the stake.

Summary

Jan Hus was a Czech leader in a political system dominated by Germans. He was a Wyclifite reformer in an ecclesiastical setting run by opponents of Wyclif, whose books were burned on February 10, 1413, in front of the basilica of Saint Peter in Rome. As a conscientious human being, Hus was unlucky to live at a time when religious reform was necessary to fight for but not possible to achieve. Yet Hus was not a failure in the ultimate sense. By the standards of his own age and religion, he was vindicated by his martyrdom.

As a child of his age, Hus shared the theologically shaped view of the world and differed from his peers mostly by placing greater emphasis on Scriptural authority and patristic teachings of the first five centuries of the Christian era. In this respect, he stood on the threshold of the Reformation, which preferred the Bible to the Pope. As the subsequent intellectual revolutions in science and democracy have repudiated the medieval worldview and superseded the authority of the Christian clergy, Hus the embattled Wyclifite theologian (who tried not to follow Wyclif into heresy) has faded away. All that remains is Hus the martyr. In his moral stature, his unyielding devotion to truth as he knew it, the purity and integrity of his character, and his unswerving loyalty to Christianity as he believed it, Hus has become an inspirational figure to many generations. In the last analysis, Hus was not the victim of the Council of Constance; he stands as its judge.

Bibliography

Loomis, Louise R. *The Council of Constance: The Unification of the Church*. New York: Columbia University Press, 1961. A primary source on the proceedings of the Council of Constance and the condemnation of Hus.

Lützow, Franz. *The Life and Times of Master John Hus*. New York: E. P. Dutton and Co., 1921. An older, highly readable biography.

Odložilík, Otakar. *Wyclif and Bohemia*. Prague: Nákladem Královské ceské spolecnosti nauk, 1936. A Czech view of Wyclif's impact on Christian reform sentiment in Bohemia.

Schaff, David S. *John Hus: His Life, Teachings, and Death After Five Hundred Years*. New York: Charles Scribner's Sons, 1915. This is the best older biography. It is very sympathetic to Hus and his cause.

Spinka, Matthew. *John Hus and the Czech Reform*. Chicago: University of Chicago Press, 1941. Spinka is the outstanding Hus scholar writing in English. This biography places Hus in his Czech setting, which Spinka believes is essential to understand Hus. Spinka writes in the shadow of the Munich Conference in 1938, and this event colors his interpretation of Hus's betrayal by the German emperor at the Council of Constance.

_____. *John Hus at the Council of Constance*. New York: Columbia University Press, 1965. Contains the proceedings of the Council of Constance and Hus's correspondence.

_____. *John Hus' Concept of the Church*. Princeton, N.J.: Princeton University Press, 1966. Spinka's presentation of Hus's theology attempts to establish Hus as a major medieval theologian who admired Wyclif but did not follow him into heresy. He points out that many of Wyclif's other

Czech followers were more heretical, even though they opposed Hus and supported Hus's condemnation.

Stacey, John. *John Wyclif and Reform*. Philadelphia: Westminster Press, 1964. Wyclif is seen as a religious reformer in theology who remained prudent in politics.

Thomson, Samuel Harrison. "Philosophical Basis of Wyclif's Theology." *Journal of Religion*, 1931: 86-116. This is the clearest exposition which relates theology to philosophy. The medieval controversy over realism and nominalism is explained in terms that any patient reader can understand.

Ullman, W. *The Origins of the Great Schism*. London: Burns, Oates, and Washbourne, 1948. Gives the background for the religious corruption and moral confusion which set the stage for Hus's career. It deals with the rise of two popes, two Colleges of Cardinals, and two papal genealogies in the century preceding Hus.

Wylie, James Hamilton. *The Council of Constance to the Death of John Hus*. London: Longmans, Green and Co., 1900. A comprehensive source in English for this subject.

David R. Stevenson

IBN AL-'ARABI

Born: July 28, 1165; Murcia, Spain
Died: November 16, 1240; Damascus, Syria
Areas of Achievement: Philosophy, religion, and monasticism
Contribution: Ibn al-'Arabi formulated and made explicit the inner doctrines
   of Sufism and was the link between the Eastern and Western schools of
   that philosophy.

Early Life

Abu Bakr Muhammad ibn al-'Arabi al-Hatimi al-Ta'i was born in Murcia,
in Islamic Spain, in 1165, to a well-to-do and respected family. He spent his
early years in Murcia, moving first to Lisbon and later to the more cosmopolitan Seville, where his family settled. There he received his formal
education and was given the leisure to pursue a developing interest in mystical approaches to religion and the teachings of Sufism. In search of spiritual
enlightenment, he sought out individuals known for their wisdom and spiritual insights who would be willing to take him on as a pupil and guide him in
his quest. One such figure, Fatimah of Cordova, an elderly yet vigorous
woman at ninety-five, became Ibn al-'Arabi's spiritual adviser for several
years.

Students of Islamic philosophy customarily pursued a formal program of
study in such subjects as cosmology, the metaphysical doctrines of Islam,
analysis of the Koran for hidden meaning, and the science of letters and
numbers. In addition, the student gained skills in the practice of private
activities such as meditation, vigil, fasting, and prayer. Upon fulfilling these
requirements, the successful aspirant was prepared to experience, understand, and control supersensory communications of several types. He was
empowered with such gifts as visions, precognition, communing with the
spirits of the dead, and healing. Ibn al-'Arabi is reported to have been a
proficient student who enjoyed numerous mystical experiences; he frequently visited cemeteries, where he spoke with the dead. It was during this
intellectually fertile period of his life that he married the first of three wives,
a woman named Maryam—the daughter of a man of influence and wealth—
who was eager to partake of her husband's spiritual experiences and quest.

At age twenty, and already initiated into the Sufi way, Ibn al-'Arabi began
to travel throughout Andalusia in search of greater enlightenment. During
one of his stays in the city of Cordova, he was invited to the home of
Averroës, the most celebrated Islamic disciple of Aristotelian philosophy of
the age and a friend of his father. The well-established scholar and the young
visionary represented opposite approaches to the question of knowledge:
Averroës proposed that reason was the foundation of wisdom, while to Ibn
al-'Arabi, true knowledge resulted from spiritual vision. Nevertheless, Aver-

roës fully understood Ibn al-'Arabi's goals and recognized that his visitor had attained a level of understanding superior to most. Ibn al-'Arabi describes Averroës' reaction to the visit thus:

> He had thanked God, I have been told, to have lived at a time when he could have seen someone who had entered into spiritual retreat ignorant and had left it as I had done. He said: "It was a case whose possibility I had affirmed myself without however as yet encountering someone who had experienced it. Glory be to God that I have been able to live at a time when there exists a master of this experience, one of those who open the locks of His doors. Glory be to God to have made me the personal favor of seeing one of them with my own eyes."

Ibn al-'Arabi continued his peripatetic existence in Andalusia and North Africa, visiting sages, holding debates, and writing. He was also subject to frequent visions. In one such vision, received in 1198, he was ordered to depart for the Orient. Heeding the command, he arrived in Mecca in 1201 and remained there for four years, devoting himself to study, public discussion of his views, and writing. During his stay in the holy city of Islam, he married his second wife, wrote several works—including a famous collection of love poems—and began composition of his most famous book, *al-Futuhat al-Makkiyah* (the Meccan revelations), a lengthy compendium of esoteric knowledge.

Life's Work

Sufism represents an Islamic tradition, as old as the religion itself, of a small group of devout believers—exemplified by the earliest followers of Muhammad the Prophet—who renounce the rewards and temptations of this world in order to lead a life of contemplation and prayer. The emphasis of the group is on the direct experience of God; its fundamental tenet is that "there is no reality but the Reality (God), and that all other realities are purely relative and dependent upon His reality." The cumulative experiences and insights of those who followed the early Sufis constitute a complex doctrine; as a tradition, it was wrapped in heavy symbolism and obscure references, accessible only to those who could receive the dogma orally from an enlightened master. Ibn al-'Arabi succeeded in changing the pattern of transmission by recording much of this wisdom in books, making it possible for the tradition, full of veiled allusion, to be communicated to wider audiences in clearer and more accessible form. He is known among the Sufis as "the greatest Shaikh" for his role as the first to set in writing the vast amount of doctrine contained in the Sufi oral tradition.

Ibn al-'Arabi was a prolific writer, believed to have authored 250 separate titles. Aside from his writings on Sufism, he composed short treatises, letters, poetry, and abstract philosophical works. His most impressive work, however, is *al-Futuhat al-Makkiyah*. The motivation for writing the book, as the title implies, came from a compelling outside source—divine revelation—and the author is spoken of as simply the vehicle through which the message was recorded. The lengthy treatise, considered the main source book of the sacred sciences of Islam, is made up of 560 chapters; it records the sayings of the earlier Sufis, explains the principles of metaphysics and various sacred sciences, and describes Ibn al-'Arabi's own spiritual development. A second important work, *Fusus al-hikam* (1229; bezels of wisdom), is Ibn al-'Arabi's spiritual testament. This twenty-seven-chapter book, which contains the basic doctrines of Islamic esotericism, was inspired by a vision of the Prophet holding a book and ordering the writer to transmit the word to future generations.

Since Ibn al-'Arabi's metaphysical doctrines came from inspiration rather than meditation, his works generally lack coherence and frustrate those who read them hoping to gather from them a systematic and comprehensive view of the universe. Students of Ibn al-'Arabi suggest that his aim was not to give a rationally satisfying explanation of reality. In fact, some would argue that he was not a philosopher at all, since he was not interested in constructing a complete and consistent system of thought. What he attempted to do, rather, was to present a vision of reality, the attainment of which depended on the practice of certain methods of realization.

At the core of Ibn al-'Arabi's thought, as for all Sufism, is the concept of the transcendent unity of Being: Though God is separate from the universe, He encompasses all of it. While God manifests Himself in the creation, He transcends it. While God is above all qualities, He is not devoid of them. The qualities, or Names, are infinite, yet they are summarized in the Koran to make them understandable. Knowledge of these Names, then, leads to knowledge of Him, and to spiritual realization. One who has attained this level, the Universal Man, is one who has understood the Names, has mastered all the stages of enlightenment, and has been able to combine the fullness of being and of knowledge. The Prophet Muhammad was such a Universal Man, as were the great saints of Islam who, over the generations, transcended the material reality and understood all the spiritual possibilities of the universe.

The goal of all Sufis is union with the Divine, achieved in the gradual ascent through several levels of spiritual attainment culminating in a state of complete contemplation of God. The desired union with the Divine Being only comes after the arduous ascent, as if climbing a mountain, toward spiritual purification. Prayer is the essential element of this climb and also its ultimate goal; man begins by praying to God and ends his search by purifying his soul and allowing God to pray within him. Man thus becomes the mirror of God and finally understands all of His Names.

Each step in this spiritual quest requires passage from the outward reality to the inner one, to the true essence of things: from the external, or exoteric, to the hidden, or esoteric. The nonmaterial nature of the quest makes the use of ordinary words insufficient. For this reason, the Sufis often rely on a language full of symbols, the only adequate tool to describe the hidden meaning of nature, the true significance of the religious experience, and the inner workings of a man's soul.

Ibn al-'Arabi's articulation of the ideals of Sufism brought him fame, notoriety, and even some enemies. He spent the last part of his life living and lecturing in different areas of the Middle East and Asia Minor, coming into contact with numerous influential writers and thinkers. One of his disciples, Sadr al-Din al-Qunawi, is considered the essential bridge between Western Sufism and the equally vigorous school developing in Iran during the thirteenth century. Ibn al-'Arabi eventually settled in Damascus in 1223, where he remained for most of the rest of his life. There he devoted himself to teaching and writing and, as a respected sage, was able to influence future generations of Sufis, both Eastern and Western. He was survived by two sons and a daughter. One of the sons became an accomplished poet; of the daughter it is said that she was able to respond to difficult theological questions at an early age.

Summary

It is evident that Sufism, like similar schools of thought whose goal is spiritual communion with an Absolute, defies a simple and precise definition. Moreover, the experiences its adherents seek cannot be understood easily or even appreciated by the uninitiated; nor can they be described, with any clarity, using ordinary everyday language. Ibn al-'Arabi's most notable contribution was to record his own understanding of how this communion with a Supreme Being was attained, recounting, in the process, centuries-old insights hitherto transmitted only orally by enlightened individuals. He thus gave later generations a language with which to describe their experiences and a definitive doctrine from which to continue to develop the theoretical foundations of Sufism.

Through the centuries, Ibn al-'Arabi's influence has been enormous; he has been read and studied as seriously by his detractors as by his disciples. Clear links have been traced from Ibn al-'Arabi to all subsequent Sufi schools of thought and religious orders throughout the Islamic world. In modern times, his works continue to be read as far east as India and Pakistan; his odes are recited in Sufi monasteries in Egypt and North Africa. Some scholars have suggested that Ibn al-'Arabi strongly, if indirectly, influenced Dante, whose works reveal parallels with the spiritual quest of the Sufi.

Bibliography

Affifi, Abul E. *The Mystical Philosophy of Muhyid Din-Ibnul 'Arabi*. Cambridge: Cambridge University Press, 1939. Reprint. New York: AMS, 1974. The first serious and comprehensive examination of Ibn al-'Arabi's philosophy, this work attempts to make the Muslim sage understandable to Western readers. Affifi refers to Ibn al-'Arabi as a pantheist and a typical mystic philosopher, labels that other scholars find difficult to justify. The book contains a useful, though dated, bibliography and an informative appendix suggesting possible sources for Ibn al-'Arabi's system.

Asín Palacios, Miguel. *Islam and the Divine Comedy*. Translated by Harold Sunderland. London: J. Murray, 1926. The English version of the seminal work by the distinguished Spanish Arabist and translator of Ibn al-'Arabi. Asín Palacios was the first scholar to suggest the link between Dante and Islamic mysticism; he traced the influence of the Muslim thinker on the Italian poet through a variety of channels, among them the Order of the Templars. A fascinating study of the transmission of philosophical and literary motifs.

Corbin, Henry. *Creative Imagination in the Sufism of Ibn 'Arabī*. Princeton, N.J.: Princeton University Press, 1969. Translated by Ralph Manheim. An English version of the original French, this book explores in great philosophical detail Ibn al-'Arabi's notion of the creative imagination, which, according to the author, is the goal of the mystical experience. A serious and erudite work displaying great familiarity with Eastern and Western schools of mystical philosophy; the author attempts to understand Ibn al-'Arabi's thought in relation to these traditions.

Ibn al-'Arabi. *Sufis of Andalusia: The "Ruh al-quds" and "al-Durrat al-Fakhirah" of Ibn 'Arabi*. Translated with an introduction and notes by R. W. J. Austin. London: Allen and Unwin, 1971. An English translation of one of Ibn al-'Arabi's most accessible works, his account of Hispano-Muslim sages who influenced and guided him in his search for enlightenment. Of particular interest to the modern reader is Ibn al-'Arabi's mention of numerous female role models, described as having reached high levels of spirituality within a tradition which generally excludes women from such pursuits. The volume contains a fairly informative biographical portrait of Ibn al-'Arabi.

Nasr, Seyyed Hossein. *Three Muslim Sages*. Cambridge, Mass.: Harvard University Press, 1964. The text of three lectures delivered at Harvard University. A third of the book is devoted to Ibn al-'Arabi. The author emphasizes the importance of the medieval thinker in the development of Sufism in particular and Islam in general; he dismisses much of the criticism against Ibn al-'Arabi by asserting that his thought is highly original and resulted from divine inspiration. It thus defies categorization and comparison and should be treated as the unique phenomenon it is.

Shah, Idries. *The Sufis*. Garden City, N.Y.: Anchor Books, 1974. A serious and readable account of the theories, development, and principal figures of Sufism; aimed at the non-Muslim reader. The author uses numerous examples of ways in which Sufi motifs and practices found their way into European letters and institutions. He suggests that Sufism was disseminated mainly by its poets and quotes Ibn al-'Arabi's poetry as a possible model for the development of the cult of the Virgin Mary.

Clara Estow

IBN BATTUTAH

Born: 1304; Tangier, Morocco
Died: c. 1377; Morocco
Area of Achievement: Exploration
Contribution: Driven by an exceptional wanderlust, Ibn Battutah became the greatest Muslim traveler. His peregrinations through India, Russia, China, the East Indies, North Africa, and the Near and Middle East were recorded in the most famous of all Islamic travelogs, the *Rihlah*.

Early Life

Abu 'Abd Allah Muhammad ibn 'Abd Allah al-Lawati al-Tanji, who came to be known as Ibn Battutah, was born in Tangier, Morocco. His family had a long tradition of serving as religious judges, and his educational training prepared him for such a career. Well before he undertook the first of his many journeys at the age of twenty-one, Ibn Battutah had studied Islamic theology and law in Tangier. His first journey, which commenced in June of 1325, took the form of a pilgrimage to Mecca, but it had much broader ramifications. In a fashion reminiscent of the grand tours which Europeans would undertake in later centuries to finish their education, his trip to Mecca supplied Ibn Battutah with diverse opportunities.

Ever the astute observer and inquisitive intellectual, Ibn Battutah talked and studied with scholars he encountered as he made an unhurried progress eastward. Evidently his family was an affluent one, with extensive connections throughout the Islamic world. Their belief—a view seemingly shared by Ibn Battutah—was that his experiences would be ideally suited to the duties of a magistrate, which he was expected to assume upon his return. His purse, personality, and contacts with powerful officials readily opened many doors for the young man, and his winning ways, together with a considerable degree of curiosity he aroused as an individual from the outer geographic reaches of Islam, stood him in good stead. He was greeted with hospitality wherever he went.

Ibn Battutah's initial journey was a momentous one in a number of ways. He traveled to Cairo, probably the greatest city of the time, making stops, en route from Tangier, in most of the major ports of the southern Mediterranean. He reveled in the time he spent in that renowned intellectual center of ancient times, Alexandria. His experiences in Egypt aroused in him an insatiable wanderlust. He reached Damascus in August, 1326, and it was there that he took his first wife. After a brief courtship and honeymoon, he joined a caravan of pilgrims wending their way to Mecca.

The pilgrims' travels were arduous in the extreme. After passing through what is now Jordan and Syria, the faithful rested for several days at Al-Karak, for the ordeal of a desert crossing lay before them. They managed the crossing of the Wadi al-Ukhaydir—Ibn Battutah characterized it as the valley of hell—by moving at night until they reached the Al-'Ula oasis. Thence they moved onward to the holy city of Medina and then progressed to Mecca. As was the case with all of his peregrinations, Ibn Battutah produced vivid accounts of his experiences in and impressions of Mecca. He departed from Mecca sometime in November of 1326, now a *haji* (one who has made the pilgrimage to Mecca) as well as a man determined to see much more of the world.

Life's Work

The essence of Ibn Battutah's achievement lies in his wide-ranging travels. Yet there was much more to his repeated journeys than merely visiting strange and faraway places. The reader of *Tuhfat al-nuzzar fi ghara'ib al-amsar wa-'aja'ib al-asfar* (1357-1358; *The Travels of Ibn-Battuta*, 1958-1980, best known as *Rihlah*) becomes immediately aware of Ibn Battutah's keen eye for detail; clearly, he was a man of rare curiosity and intellect. Anything and everything interested him. From unusual religious beliefs to the economies of the regions through which he trekked, from methods of dress to the basics of diet, he noted the varied aspects of the life-styles which he encountered. Indeed, what Ibn Battutah saw and reported is at least as important as where he went.

Returning with his two wives to Tangier, Ibn Battutah tarried only a short time before succumbing again to his desire to travel. His next major undertaking was a second *hajj*, and this time he gave himself ample time to sense and savor all Mecca had to offer. His visit lasted for some three years. This must have been quite expensive, but evidently the family fortunes were ample to support such extended periods of travel.

Next, Ibn Battutah decided to sail down the Red Sea to the renowned trading center of Aden. He provides a singular description of the strategically located seaport and the way in which it depended on great cisterns for its water supply. After some time in Aden, he continued southward along the African coast and visited the important trade centers of Kilwa and Mombasa. On his return journey, he stopped in the major cities of Oman and Hormuz. In fact, in a fashion which was to become characteristic of all his endeavors, he attempted to visit every reachable site of major significance.

After touring the Gulf of Aden and its environs, he traversed the considerable breadth of Arabia while making the *hajj* for a third time. A trip across the Red Sea followed, with a risky, demanding journey to Syene (modern Aswān) and thence via the Nile to Cairo. By this juncture, Arabia, Africa's Mediterranean coast, and the lower reaches of Nile had become familiar territory, and, not surprisingly for a man of his inclinations, Ibn Battutah began to look farther afield.

He passed through the various Turkish states in Asia Minor, crossed the

Black Sea to reach Kaffa (modern Feodosiya, the first Christian city he had seen), and moved northeastward into Kipchak. This Russian region was then under the control of Khan Muhammad Özbeg, and Ibn Battutah joined his peripatetic camp. In this way he was able to visit the outer reaches of Mongolia, where he marveled at the brevity of summer nights.

Upon leaving the khan's camp, Ibn Battutah linked his travel fortunes to a Byzantine princess, whom he accompanied to Constantinople. There, in what he considered one of the most important moments of his career, he enjoyed an interview with Emperor Andronikos III. From the emperor's court he journeyed eastward, crossing the steppes of southern Asia en route to Kabul and thence over the Hindu Kush. In September of 1333, he reached the Indus River. He had, in eight years of traveling, made three pilgrimages to Mecca, seen most of the southern and eastern Mediterranean, floated on the Nile, braved the desert sands of Arabia, and penetrated deep into Russia. It is at this juncture that he ends his first narrative, and by any standard of measurement his achievements had been considerable. Still, though he was probably the most traveled man of his time, the clarion call to adventure drew him as strongly as ever.

He wandered throughout the Sind and eventually moved on to Delhi at the invitation of the ruler, Muhammad ibn Tughluq. This capricious, bloodthirsty monarch was a bit too much even for Ibn Battutah's eclectic tastes: "No day did his palace gate fail to witness the elevation of some abject to affluence and the torture and murder of some living soul." Yet somehow he managed to get along with this extraordinary ruler, and he became *Qadi* (judge) of Delhi at a very high salary. He served in this capacity for the next eight years. Yet, far from prospering, he fell into considerable debt. Scholars have ascribed this to his extravagance, and his living beyond his means may have figured prominently in his eventual decline into disfavor.

Resilient soul that he was, however, Ibn Battutah turned potential ruin into what to him must have been a glorious assignment. He was chosen to head a delegation which was paying a visit to the last Mongol emperor of China. Leaving in 1342, the group made its way to Calcutta en route to China. Here fate intervened, however, in the form of a shipwreck that completely destroyed the junk on which he and the other envoys were to travel. This was a disaster of the first magnitude, for Ibn Battutah lost not only his personal possessions but also the lavish gifts he had been delegated to carry to China.

Accordingly, Ibn Battutah remained in the region, visiting various cities on India's western coast and also the Maldive Islands, where he rose to prominence as a judge and added four wives to his harem. Yet he did not tarry overlong, for August, 1344, found him leaving the Maldives for Ceylon (modern Sri Lanka). Further adventures followed, and eventually he reached Java after having stopped briefly in Burma. From Java he finally made his way to China, where he visited Amoy, Canton, and Peking, among other major sites. Returning westward, he revisited Sumatra, Malabar, Oman, Persia, and a host of other locations. Upon reaching Damascus, he learned of his father's death some fifteen years earlier. It was the first news of home he had had in that many years.

It was also during this period that Ibn Battutah witnessed, at first hand, the ravages of the bubonic plague (sometimes called the Black Death). His graphic reports on what he saw in Damascus, where more than two thousand unfortunate souls died in a single day, is one of the finest surviving accounts of the plague. Perhaps thereby reminded of his mortality, he then revisited Jerusalem and Cairo in the process of making a fourth *hajj*. Finally, having been away from home almost constantly for more than twenty-four years, he returned to Morocco on November 8, 1349.

Even then, his travels were not over. After spending a relatively short time in Tangier, he made his way to Spain and toured Andalusia. His final major journey was into central Africa. Journeying from oasis to oasis across the Sahara, he reached the fabled desert entrepôt of Tombouctou, where the mighty Niger River (which he wrongly called the Nile) begins its great westward sweep to the ocean. At this point, his king called him home, thereby bringing an end to nearly thirty years of travel encompassing an estimated seventy-five thousand miles. His final years were more settled; he was in his early seventies when he died in his native Morocco.

Summary

With the possible exception of the voyages of Marco Polo, there is nothing prior to the European Renaissance to compare with the nature and extent of Ibn Battutah's travels. He single-handedly made the world a smaller place, and thanks to his remarkable accounts modern knowledge of much of Asia during the fourteenth century is considerably richer than otherwise would have been the case. As the chronicler Muhammad ibn Juzayy, who recounted Ibn Battutah's travels by royal decree, stated: "This Shaykh is the traveller of our age; and he who should call him the traveller of the whole body of Islam would not exceed the truth."

Bibliography

Cooley, William D. *The Negroland of the Arabs Examined and Explained*. London: J. Arrowsmith, 1841. Although there are some problems with Cooley's transcriptions from the Arabic, this is a useful early English account of that portion of Ibn Battutah's travels devoted to the Sahara and Niger regions.

Gibb, H. A. R., ed. *Travels in Asia and Africa, 1325-1354*. New York: A. M. Kelley, 1969. A reprint of the 1929 edition in the Argonaut series, this work is a convenient, accurate account of the highlights of Ibn Battutah's career. Gibb's introduction and notes offer useful historical background.

Hamilton, Paul. "Seas of Sand." In *Exploring Africa and Asia*, by Nathalie Ettinger, Elspeth J. Huxley, and Paul Hamilton. Garden City, N.Y.: Doubleday Publishing Co., 1973. The section entitled "The Traveler of Islam" constitutes a useful, accessible account of Ibn Battutah's first journey to Mecca. This volume is part of the Encyclopedia of Discovery and Exploration series. Illustrated.

Ibn Battutah. *The Travels of Ibn-Battuta*. Translated and edited by H. A. R. Gibb. 4 vols. Cambridge: Cambridge University Press, 1958-1980. This careful, amply annotated translation is by far the most important English-language source of information on the man and his milieu. Part of the Hakluyt Society's series on early explorers.

Tucker, William. "Ibn-Battuta, Abu Abd-Allah Muhammad." In *The Discoverers: An Encyclopedia of Exploration*, edited by Helen Delpar. New York: McGraw-Hill Book Co., 1980. A succinct, useful summation of the high points of Ibn Battutah's career. This volume includes short biographies of many other explorers as well. Includes bibliographies and an index.

James A. Casada

IBN GABIROL

Born: c. 1020; probably Málaga, Spain
Died: c. 1057; probably Valencia, Spain
Areas of Achievement: Literature and philosophy
Contribution: Ibn Gabirol created a form of poetry written in biblical Hebrew. His version of Neoplatonic philosophy came to be integrated within Christian Augustinian thought.

Early Life

Solomon ben Yehuda ibn Gabirol was probably born in Málaga in 1020 or 1021. The sources for his biographical data are allusions in his poems, references in the works of the Jewish commentator Moses ibn Ezra (c. 1060-c. 1139) and the Arabic historian Ibn Sa'id (c. 1029-1070), and Hebrew legends, many of which were published in the sixteenth century in Italy and the Ottoman Empire.

Western scholars index his name in a variety of ways: Most list him as Ibn Gabirol, others as Gabirol, and a few as Solomon ibn Gabirol. His name in Arabic was Abu Ayyub Sulayman ibn Yakhya ibn Gabirul; in Latin, he was known as Avicebron, Avicenebrol, Albenzubron, and variations thereof. There is no agreement as to the meaning of the name Gabirol. Some have suggested that it is a diminutive of the Arabic word *yabir* (power), while others see it as affixing the Hebrew word *El* (God), to *yabir*. The uncertainty in dates is caused, in part, by the sources' use of different calendars. Ibn Ezra wrote of poets and poetics in the eighth century of the fourth millennium (4800 of the Hebrew year), which approximates A.D. 1040, while Ibn Sa'id used the Muslim calendar.

In 4800, according to Ibn Ezra, "lived Abu Ayyub Selomo son of Yehuda ibn Gabirol, the Cordoban." From this, it has been concluded that Ibn Gabirol's parents had lived in Córdoba, capital of Muslim Iberia, whence they fled, probably in 1013 during the fundamentalist revolution that shattered the unity of the Umayyad caliphate. The family went to Málaga, where Solomon was born—an inference from his custom of appending "Malki," meaning "of Málaga," to his name in his writings. His poems suggest that his father had been prominent in Cordoban society before the turmoil and that his parents suffered from something akin to tuberculosis.

According to his self-description, Ibn Gabirol was small, homely, and weak; he suffered from a skin disease. He was educated in Hebrew, Arabic, and Greek literature as well as philosophy, science, and theology; indeed, Ibn Gabirol was wont to complain that he was treated as a Greek. Various sources describe him as vain, argumentative, and hot-tempered.

Life's Work

By his own report, Ibn Gabirol's first five poems were written when he was sixteen or younger. The most significant of these is *Azharot*, a nonmetrical versification of the 613 Commandments. Shortly after this time, the family moved to Saragossa, where Mundir I (reigned 1029-1038) had established an independent kingdom which attempted to maintain the sophisticated life-style of the Umayyads. Mundir and his immediate heirs welcomed all poets and philosophers. One of the leading figures at court was the Jewish Yekutiel ibn Hasan, who befriended the young poet. During this period, Ibn Gabirol wrote several works, including elegies on the death of Hai ben Sherira Gaon (939-1038), leader of the Hebrew Academy at Pumbedita, and *'Anaq* (neck-lace), a four-hundred-line didactic poem on the importance of Hebrew gram-mar, of which only eighty-eight lines have survived.

Around 1039, Ibn Gabirol lost his father and his patron: His father appar-ently succumbed to tuberculosis, and Yekutiel was assassinated by rivals at the palace. In 1040, Ibn Gabirol wrote two elegies in honor of his former pa-tron. Around the same time, he wrote a poem which he dedicated and sent to Samuel ha-Nagid (Ibn Nagrella; 993-1056), vizier to Badis, King of Gra-nada, whose forces had just defeated the rival king of Seville. Samuel, one of the most influential Jews of the period, sent financial assistance to the poet, who remained in Saragossa completing, in Arabic, his major study of ethics, *Kitab islah al-akhlaq* (1045; *The Improvement of Moral Qualities*, 1901). About that time, Ibn Gabirol's mother died. Alone in the world and depen-dent upon a patron for support, he went to Granada. Apparently, Samuel had known Ibn Gabirol's parents in Málaga. He took the orphan under his protection, and Ibn Gabirol came to call him "my father."

After arriving in Granada, Ibn Gabirol wrote a long, mournful poem ex-pressing his feeling of despair upon leaving Saragossa. In 1048, Nissim ben Jacob ben Nissim ibn Shahim, leader of the Kairwan (Tunisia) Jewish com-munity, arrived in Granada to arrange a marriage between his daughter and Samuel's son. Nissim (c. 990-1062) was a noted theologian, and Ibn Gabirol spent a year listening to his public disputations and commentaries. It has been surmised that Samuel had abandoned Ibn Gabirol because of some uncomplimentary comments the poet had made about Samuel's poetic style, and that Ibn Gabirol became dependent upon Nissim. This interpretation, however, seems doubtful, since Nissim himself was dependent upon Samuel's largesse and Ibn Gabirol was not the type to sit at anyone's feet.

Ibn Gabirol was the first of the significant Hispano-Hebrew poets and philosophers who wrote in both biblical Hebrew and Arabic. At this time, all Jews could read Ibn Gabirol's Hebrew poetry, but Jews and Christians who lived outside the Arabic world could not read works written in Arabic. Dur-ing the period 1167-1186, Judah ben Saul ibn Tibbon translated *The Improve-ment of Moral Qualities* into Hebrew. Meanwhile, Christians had become interested in Ibn Gabirol's philosophical work. In the mid-twelfth century, his major philosophical study, of which no Arabic copy has surfaced, was translated from Arabic into Latin as *Fons vitae* (English translation, 1963). A century later, Shem Tov ben Joseph Falaquera translated portions of the Arabic manuscript into Hebrew, but the Hebrew reading public found it of little interest. As time went by, most of the Arabic manuscripts were either lost or destroyed by Muslim fundamentalists. Jews preserved the Hebraic poetic and ethical works and Christians the Latin philosophical works. The result was that Jews knew nothing of Ibn Gabirol's philosophical opera; certain fifteenth and sixteenth century Portuguese Jewish philosophers, for example, considered "Albenzubron" a Muslim. Christians, on the other hand, knowing nothing of his Hebrew poetry, considered "Avicebron" a Muslim or an Arab convert to Christianity. In the mid-nineteenth century, Solomon Munk realized that Falaquera's Hebrew translation and the Latin *Fons vitae* were based on the same lost Arabic source. Munk published an extensive work demonstrating that Ibn Gabirol and Avicebron were one and the same.

Ibn Gabirol worked simultaneously on religious and philosophical poetry and prose. Except where internal evidence is available, there is little indication as to the order of composition of his works.

Hebrew was not the daily language of Iberian Jews; most spoke Arabic. Biblical Hebrew and the Hebrew of the commentaries, however, were known to all Jews. Secular poetry, if it had existed in biblical times, did not survive. There developed in Palestine under Byzantine influence, however, a form of poetry (*payytanim*) which was used in religious services and for special occasions. This form, based on stress rather than meter, and with various patterns of rhyme, was brought to Iberia and flourished there. During the height of the Umayyad caliphate, Jewish courtiers employed this poetic form for secular purposes. Around the same time, Jewish scholars embarked on an intensive study of biblical Hebrew; the result was an expansion of the biblical vocabulary. Ibn Gabirol was a proponent of biblical Hebrew, and his earliest poems followed the model of the *payntanim*. Gradually, his poems took on the characteristics of the most sophisticated Arabic stylists, but the language was the expanded biblical Hebrew. His secular poems became models, and copies quickly spread throughout the Mediterranean.

It was in Ibn Gabirol's religious poetry, however, that he reached the summit of his creativity. Using biblical Hebrew but infusing the poems with imagery and meters derived from Arabic poetry, he created works of such lasting beauty that they are still used in Hebrew prayer books. There is a pessimistic quality to these poems. While this dark mood is consistent with the stylistic temper of Arabic poets during the last decades of Umayyad Iberia, it also reflects Ibn Gabirol's own experience of being forced into exile after the death of Yekutiel and his family's memories of the flight from Córdoba. There is a yearning for redemption in his poetry; the poems are mystical and personal. Unlike his secular poems, which are marked by bravado and arrogance, Ibn Gabirol's religious works are filled with longing and humility.

The poem *Keter Malkhut* (*The Kingly Crown*, 1911) is, in part, a restatement of Ibn Gabirol's philosophy and a confession of sins. In his system, the incorporeal God, derived from a Platonic or Neoplatonic conceptualization, is all-powerful: "Thou art Lord, and all creatures are Thy servants and adorers." Following Plato, Ibn Gabirol visualized the soul as temporarily inhabiting the body, but he did not fall into the Platonic concept of reincarnation. The work demonstrates Ibn Gabirol's knowledge of Islamic science, particularly astronomy. The last portion of the poem, the confession of sins, is used in some Sephardic prayer books at Yom Kippur (the Day of Atonement).

Ibn Gabirol was a Neoplatonist at a time when Jewish intellectual life was focused on Aristotelian ideas. Scholars such as Judah ibn Tibbon or Moses Maimonides (1135-1204) either did not know or thought unimportant Ibn Gabirol's philosophical writings, while Falaquera thought him a follower of Empedocles. In reality, one can trace Ibn Gabirol's philosophy to ideas in Aristotle, Galen, Plotinus, Proclus, and various Hebrew and Muslim philosophers and theologians. The form of *The Source of Life* is the Platonic dialogue, and Plato is the only philosopher mentioned.

Rejected by Jewish and Christian Aristotelians, Ibn Gabirol was quickly accepted by Christian Augustinians. Because he had developed a philosophical and theological system without reference to Hebrew tradition, Christians considered his work a valid instrument for bolstering Augustinian teaching. Starting with the translator/commentator Dominicus Gundissalinus, Ibn Gabirol's cosmology and methodology influenced thirteenth century Christian theologians such as William of Auvergne, Robert Grosseteste, Saint Albertus Magnus, Roger Bacon, Saint Bonaventure, and Raymond Lull. The Christians took Ibn Gabirol's concepts of light and of the plurality of forms and incorporated them into Augustinian Scholasticism.

The Improvement of Moral Qualities, an ethical work which has survived in both the Arabic original and Ibn Tibbon's translation, became popular among Jews. Because of the numerous biblical citations, it was clearly marked as Jewish and seemed to hold little interest for Christians. The work is original in that the author lists twenty personal traits, each of which he links to one of the five senses. In the Arabic original, there is a diagram which was later used by Cabalists in developing their theories.

If Ibn Gabirol wrote any biblical commentaries or Cabalist tracts, none has survived. Abraham ibn Ezra of Tudela (1089-1164), a noted theologian, cited Ibn Gabirol seven times in his comments on the Bible. There is extant a comment by Ibn Gabirol on the Garden of Eden passage in Genesis in which that passage is treated allegorically: Eden is dealt with not as a specific place but as a generalized preexisting atmosphere, while the garden represents the real world. There is also extant a satirical poem in which, like the Cabalist writers, Ibn Gabirol makes use of the fact that each Hebrew letter has a numerical value. The values of the letters in the word for water, for example, total ninety, while those in the word for wine total seventy, proving that water is superior to wine.

Through the years, scholars have been discovering bits and pieces of Ibn Gabirol's canon; a *diwan* (collection of poems), for example, was found in Cairo. References to many undiscovered poems exist. Ibn Gabirol boasted that he had written twenty books, but only two have been found. Two others attributed to him, a Latin translation titled *De anima* and a Hebrew translation titled *Mivhar Penim* (1546), are questioned by most authorities.

Ibn Gabirol never married; he averred that his only loves were poetry and philosophy, avenues to truth. According to Ibn Ezra, Ibn Gabirol was thirty years old when he died in Valencia. That would be around 1050 or 1051. Hebrew tradition places his death in the year 4830, or 1069/1070, when he was fifty. Ibn Sa'id states that "Sulaiman ibn Yakhaya, known by the name of ibn Gabirūl of Sarakotha . . . died . . . in the year 450," that is, between February, 1057, and February, 1058. Scholars accept the latter date because it is the most exact; moreover, whatever is reported regarding Ibn Gabirol after 1057/1058 seems to involve magic and fantasy: that he created a female golem out of wood, or that he was murdered in Valencia by a rival Arabic poet who hid the body under a fig grove, and the deed was discovered when a tree began to produce miraculous fruit.

Summary

Ibn Gabirol was the product of a sophisticated Arabic civilization which permitted intellectual and religious freedom. During its zenith, that society accepted Greek science and philosophy. The Iberian Jews not only adapted aspects of Arabic culture and learning but also began a renaissance of biblical studies. Ibn Gabirol was an extraordinary stylist in both Arabic and Hebrew. He helped fashion the philosophical vocabulary of Arabic and the sensual vocabulary of Hebrew. As the author of at least 175 religious and 146 secular poems in biblical Hebrew, he was known as "the Nightingale"; his philosophical works crossed sectarian lines. That the Muslim fundamentalists burned his manuscripts while the Jews rejected his philosophy and the Christians paid no attention to his poetry reflects the limitations of Muslim, Jewish, and Christian civilizations and not the genius of Ibn Gabirol.

Bibliography

Gilson, Étienne. *History of Christian Philosophy in the Middle Ages*. New York: Random House, 1955. A significant work, written by a leading Thomist who pays special attention to the Aristotelian aspects of Hebrew and Arabic philosophy but also includes a brief summary of Ibn Gabirol's Platonism and its impact upon Christian thinkers. There are scattered references to Ibn Gabirol throughout.

Husik, Isaac. *A History of Mediaeval Jewish Philosophy*. New York: Macmillan, 1916. Reprint. Philadelphia: Jewish Publication Society of America, 1946. One of the earliest studies of the subject. Includes an excellent chapter on the development of Ibn Gabirol's philosophy and ethics. The section on ethics is perhaps one of the best available.

Myer, Isaac. *Qabbalah*. Philadelphia: Isaac Myer, 1888. Reprint. London: Stuart and Watkins, 1970. Links Ibn Gabirol with the Cabalists. The work is interesting, though quite speculative. Myer's explanation of the drawings in Ibn Gabirol is significant.

Sarna, Nahum M. "Hebrew and Bible Studies in Medieval Spain." In *The Sephardi Heritage*, edited by R. D. Barnett. New York: Ktav Publishing House, 1971. An excellent study of the Hebrew renaissance in Muslim Iberia, placing Ibn Gabirol's work in the context of both that Hebrew renaissance and the dominant Arabic civilization.

Sirat, Colette. *A History of Jewish Philosophy in the Middle Ages*. Cambridge: Cambridge University Press, 1985. The author examines the intellectual sources of Hebrew philosophy: the Bible, tradition, Aristotelianism, and Platonism, demonstrating how each of these helped shape emerging philosophical positions. The section detailing Ibn Gabirol's fusion of Hebrew religious thought with Neoplatonism is clear.

J. Lee Shneidman

IBN KHALDUN

Born: May 27, 1332; Tunis, Tunisia
Died: March 17, 1406; Cairo, Egypt
Area of Achievement: Historiography
Contribution: Ibn Khaldun formulated highly original and widely acclaimed theories on the rise and fall of empires and established himself as one of the most distinguished intellectual figures of Western Islam in the late Middle Ages.

Early Life
Abu Zayd 'Abd al-Rahman ibn Khaldun was born in North Africa to a respected family of Muslim public servants and intellectuals. The Khaldun clan, believed to have resided in Andalusia, Spain, since the eighth century, had left the Iberian peninsula and settled in Tunis shortly before the last stage of the Christian reconquest of much of Muslim Andalusia in the mid-thirteenth century.

The successful advance of the Spanish Christian armies that displaced the Khaldun family was one of many factors leading to political instability in the western Mediterranean, a situation that continued to characterize the area throughout Ibn Khaldun's life. Centralized political power, in the once-extensive and glorious Islamic empire, had disintegrated, leaving a collection of small, often-poor kingdoms of indeterminate frontiers, constantly threatened from without and suffering from endemic political strife. Palace plots, court intrigue, political assassinations, armed revolts, and usurpations were commonplace.

The tumultuous career of Ibn Khaldun must be understood in the political context of the period. Much of what is known about his career comes from his own autobiographical recollections, wherein the author candidly shares his failures as well as his triumphs. Expected to follow family tradition and pursue a career in learning and public service, Ibn Khaldun received a classical education that included instruction in both religious and secular subjects. This dual orientation, and the conflict inherent in it, would be a permanent feature of Ibn Khaldun's career and thought. He was schooled in the Koran, Islamic law, and Arabic grammar, as well as in philology, poetry, logic, and philosophy. He received his first official appointment in 1352 at age twenty, when he was named sealbearer by the Hafsid ruler of Tunis. His duty was to sign and seal the sultan's chancery documents. Ibn Khaldun, however, soon became embroiled in the political maelstrom of the region, falling prey to his own restlessness and political ambitions.

After the defeat of the ruler of Tunis by the emir of Constantine, Ibn Khaldun moved to Tilimsan, where he accepted the patronage of Sultan Abu Inan, who appointed him to a post similar to the one he had held in Tunis. In

1357, however, Ibn Khaldun was discovered conspiring against his master and was kept in prison for nearly two years, gaining release after the sultan's death. When the Marinid Abu Salim became ruler of Morocco—a development Ibn Khaldun had supported—the ruler appointed the young scholar secretary of state and judge. Ibn Khaldun occupied these positions until 1362, when palace intrigues led him to seek protection in the Nasrid kingdom of Granada, across the Strait of Gibraltar. His stay in Iberia was marred, however, by a growing rivalry with the Granadine prime minister Ibn al-Khatib, leading Ibn Khaldun to accept the opportunity to become prime minister in the court of the newly successful Hafsid conqueror of Bejaia. Back in North Africa in 1365, Ibn Khaldun combined his ministerial duties with writing and teaching jurisprudence. It was a prolific and relatively stable period of his life.

After his benefactor was defeated and killed—at the hands of a royal cousin—Ibn Khaldun, who had initially welcomed the usurper and remained in his government, fell out of favor and left Bejaia to pursue a policy hostile to the ruler. After changing political sides several times, Ibn Khaldun decided in 1375 to retire from public life, at least temporarily, in order to devote himself to writing. He settled among nomadic tribes, where he composed the first drafts of his most important historical works. Growing tired of isolation after four years, he sought to return to a more active life in his home city of Tunis.

Life's Work

When, at age forty-four, Ibn Khaldun abandoned his political career to live among the nomads to reflect and write, he was motivated by a desire to understand and reconcile the conflict he had experienced between spiritual demands and political realities. He also wished to understand the social milieu of various periods in the past, an interest that led him to the study of history. His approach to the past, his emphasis on the role of social causation in particular, sets him apart from traditional historians. Ibn Khaldun perceived the writing of history as requiring two separate—and innovative—steps. The first was to ascertain the truth of a particular event; this step would be accomplished through the verification of all facts related to the event. The second was to understand the event as the logical outcome of the interplay of forces within the society in which it occurred. Pursuing this dual approach, Ibn Khaldun attempted to discover the value system of a particular society, to extract its first principles, believing that these were responsible for historical change. He was interested first and foremost in the Islamic world, the world with which he was most familiar. He examined the growth and development of Islam through the centuries in order to formulate a theory that would explain the rise and decline not only of the powerful Islamic state but also that of all great empires through the ages. His observations were re-

corded in *Muqaddimmah* (1375-1379; *The Muqaddimah*), a work that outlines the principles of what Ibn Khaldun called the "science of human association," a discipline he believed to be totally new.

The low ebb of Islam during Ibn Khaldun's lifetime, the fourteenth century, attributed by traditionalists to society's abandonment of the original
Islamic ideals, was perceived rather differently by Ibn Khaldun. He viewed
all historical events as a natural—and entirely nonspiritual—process resulting from history's own dynamics. While Ibn Khaldun believed that Allah,
omniscient and omnipresent, was behind all change, he dismissed as hypo-
critical those traditionalists who embraced an idealistic thought-style, insisting on the primacy of the spiritual in the material world. Truly pious men,
Ibn Khaldun argued, would retire from this world to devote themselves to
worship; they would not meddle in the affairs of society, because the spiritual
and the secular have different spheres. Even the Prophet Muhammad himself, according to Ibn Khaldun, operated within a particular social system,
achieving his sacred mission within the limits set by the system's rules.

Rather than appealing to spiritual causation, Ibn Khaldun believed that
societies are controlled by forces generated from inside the sociopolitical
group. Man, he stated, is a social being who seeks naturally to associate with
others and form a community. What follows is the emergence of a leader
who gives cohesiveness to the group, nurturing the growth of an essential
quality known as *'asabiyah*, or group spirit. It is the degree of *'asabiyah*
present in a society at a particular point in its history that determines its success. Change comes about when local chieftains, backed by their group's high
level of *'asabiyah*, attack neighboring tribes, grow, and eventually establish a
dynasty. Larger populations in turn lead to the founding of cities, greater
prosperity, division of labor, capital accumulation, and the flourishing of arts
and crafts. Larger populations also make possible the creation of empires.
Furthermore, while civilization (here contrasted to the primitive existence of
nomadic tribes, described as illiterate and violent) can only exist under the
auspices of an empire, it also contains the seeds of its own destruction.
'Asabiyah weakens with the passage of time, and the vigor and energy that
made for successful conquest give way to vice and moral laxity. Dynasties
also founder; by their fourth generation, qualities of leadership among the
rulers have usually dissipated and have been replaced by a desire to dominate
others. Empires thus weakened become the target of fierce and ambitious
new groups and are eventually defeated by them, and a new historical cycle is
ready to begin.

History, then, argues Ibn Khaldun, is the rise and fall of empires resulting
from the inevitable clash between civilization and nomadism. This process,
although essentially cyclical in structure, is not repetitive in its outcome; it
builds upon itself. Each new empire does not reject the accomplishments of
the one it replaces; instead, it absorbs and integrates many of those qualities

and uses them to refine its own institutions and values. Something new and different is thus created. Furthermore, a new empire, at least during its formative years, promotes novel forms of cultural and artistic expression and represents an unequaled opportunity for religious and moral renewal.

Perhaps in search of his own moral renewal, Ibn Khaldun left Tunis in 1382 to make a pilgrimage to Mecca. En route, however, he stopped in Cairo and was prevailed upon to stay there. His family, traveling from Tunis to join him, died in a shipwreck in 1384. During his time in Cairo, Ibn Khaldun devoted himself to preaching, teaching, writing, and carrying out the duties of a Malikite judge. Although he believed that during this stage of his career he had comported himself with the utmost honesty, he was unable to escape censure. Ibn Khaldun died in 1406, shortly after being named judge for the sixth time; he was buried in a Cairo cemetery.

Summary

Ibn Khaldun's views of the historical process emphasize the temporal over the spiritual and employ a relativist, nonabsolutist interpretation of Islamic principles. A case in point is the interpretation of the traditional dictum, traced to the Prophet himself, that a caliph must be from the tribe of Quraysh. Since there were no survivors of this group by Ibn Khaldun's time, a fact ignored by traditionalists, Ibn Khaldun argued that the reason that the Prophet had chosen the Quraysh was that this tribe was the strongest in Arabia during his lifetime. As conditions had changed markedly in the intervening seven hundred years, argued Ibn Khaldun, the caliph should come from a tribe whose present qualities of strength most resembled the Prophet's original choice. In this instance, as in countless others, Ibn Khaldun proposed a temporal and revisionist interpretation of the tradition and sayings of the Prophet.

The ambitious and universal qualities of Ibn Khaldun's quest for the causes of historical change have contributed to making *The Muqaddimah* a document of importance for several disciplines; the text has been adopted by sociologists, economists, and historians as a meaningful statement and antecedent of their own methodology. Through the centuries, the work has been used to support a wide array of ideologies, ranging from orthodox Marxism to supply-side economics.

Bibliography

Azmeh, Aziz al-. *Ibn Khaldūn in Modern Scholarship: A Study in Orientalism*. London: Third World Centre for Research and Publishing, 1981. Initially a doctoral thesis, this book sets out to reconstruct Ibn Khaldun's thought with reference to the intellectual and cultural climate in which he lived. The author aims both to inform the reader concerning the most distinguished and innovative elements of Ibn Khaldun's work and to reclaim (and rescue) Ibn Khaldun from thinkers in numerous disciplines who over the centuries have misappropriated his thoughts and misapplied his ideas. Includes a very useful eighty-six-page bibliography of works on Ibn Khaldun in various languages.

Fischel, J. Walter. *Ibn Khaldūn in Egypt*. Berkeley: University of California Press, 1967. In this specialized study, Fischel, a well-known student of Islamic culture, appraises Ibn Khaldun's contribution to the field of historiography. Asserting that Ibn Khaldun's life and experiences are closely related to his ideas, Fischel explores in great detail the historian's years in Egypt. The second part of the book is devoted to identifying the Egyptian influence in Ibn Khaldun's works.

Lacoste, Yves. *Ibn Khaldun: The Birth of History and the Past of the Third World*. Translated by David Macey. London: Verso Editions, 1984. Written by an eminent geographer, this book explores ways in which to apply Ibn Khaldun's analysis of the complex forces operating in fourteenth century North Africa to twentieth century problems of underdevelopment in the Third World. Lacoste considers the *The Muqaddimah* a work of extraordinary genius, without precursors and successors; he views the work as the outcome of Ibn Khaldun's struggle to reconcile rationalism and mystical tendencies both in his own thought and in the society in which he lived.

Lawrence, Bruce B., ed. *Ibn Khaldūn and Islamic Ideology*. Leiden, Netherlands: E. J. Brill, 1984. This collection of articles resulted from a symposium at Duke University to commemorate the 650th anniversary of Ibn Khaldun's birth. In "Ibn Khaldūn and His Time," Franz Rosenthal argues against efforts to view Ibn Khaldun in the light of recent theories or as a forerunner of some subsequent ideology. What is of interest, Rosenthal asserts, is the man Ibn Khaldun in relation to his times. Other noteworthy articles in this volume explore such topics as the literary merits of *The Muqaddimah*, Ibn Khaldun's attitude toward Jewish history, and the impact of his ideas on Islamic society.

Mahdi, Muhsin. *Ibn Khaldūn's Philosophy of History*. Chicago: University of Chicago Press, 1964. This work examines the philosophical principles on which Ibn Khaldun's new science of culture is based to demonstrate that he ultimately relied on philosophical principles to explain history. The author rejects as unproductive the efforts of other commentators who attempt to show that Ibn Khaldun should be considered the father of the modern social sciences. Mahdi treats Ibn Khaldun's religious and philosophical principles as essential components of his thought, not merely vestiges of the historian's medieval upbringing.

Rosenthal, Franz. Introduction to *The Muqaddimah: An Introduction to History*, by Ibn Khaldun. 3 vols. Princeton, N.J.: Princeton University Press, 1958, rev. ed. 1967. Rosenthal has provided an excellent and complete English translation of Ibn Khaldun's most important work—though at times his use of many modern expressions is rather baffling. He introduces the first volume with a long and informative section on the life and work of Ibn Khaldun and the many factors that might have influenced his views.

Clara Estow

AL-IDRISI

Born: 1100; Sabtah, Morocco
Died: Between 1164 and 1166; near Sabtah, Morocco
Areas of Achievement: Geography and cartography
Contribution: A world traveler, al-Idrisi eventually collaborated with the Norman king of Sicily, Roger II, to produce a major geography and several significant maps of the medieval world. These works served as models for productions in the field for more than five hundred years.

Early Life

Al-Idrisi, whose full name was Abu 'Abd Allah Muhammad ibn Muhammad 'Abd Allah ibn Idris al-Hammudi al-Hasani al-Idrisi, was born in 1100 in Sabtah (now Ceuta), Morocco. As his full name indicates, he was a Shi'ite Muslim, descended from the Prophet Muhammad, of the noble house of Alavi Idrisis, claimants to the caliphate. His family had migrated from Málaga and Algeciras in Spain to Sabtah and Tangiers in the eleventh century, and al-Idrisi studied in Córdoba, the capital of Islamic Spain.

He was a student of medicine, a poet, a world traveler, and a merchant-adventurer. His wanderings, which began at age sixteen, eventually took al-Idrisi on the routes of many of the historic Muslim conquests. He traveled far and wide across much of the known world—west to Madeira and the Canary Islands, north to France and England, and east to Asia Minor and Central Asia—and meticulously gathered information along the way about what he saw and what lay beyond.

A natural curiosity about the world, along with the wealth and freedom to satisfy it, was probably the principal motivation behind these journeys. Al-Idrisi's identity as a great noble and a descendant of Muhammad periodically put his life in danger from assassins hired by rival Islamic noble houses or religious factions. This ever-present danger probably kept him on the move. Whatever the cause of his wanderings, they gradually gained for him the reputation of a worldly-wise and learned man. Under the pretext of offering him protection from his enemies, but probably because of his growing fame as a scholar and traveler, in 1140 the Norman Christian king of Sicily, Roger II, invited al-Idrisi to join his court. Al-Idrisi's acceptance of the offer led to a twenty-year stay at the Sicilian court and initiated a fifteen-year geographic and cartographic collaboration with Roger.

Life's Work

Sicily had been granted to Roger II and the Normans under the Treaty of Saint-Germain in 1139, and he promptly made Palermo his capital. Before the coming of the Normans, Palermo also had been the capital of Islamic Sicily. During the Middle Ages, under both the Muslims and the Normans, Palermo was a major crossroads of the Mediterranean world. It was a traditional meeting place for sailors, merchants, pilgrims, crusaders, scholars, adventurers, and other travelers.

During Roger's reign, Palermo also became an intellectual center of medieval Europe. He was interested in fostering learning of any kind, and he was generous with his patronage. Perhaps for pragmatic reasons of expansionism and trade Roger was devoted to geography. Undoubtedly, he believed that al-Idrisi's princely status might help him further his own political aims. In any case, he seems to have been dissatisfied with the existing Arabic and Greek works on geography and cartography: hence one of the major reasons for the summons to al-Idrisi.

At Roger's court, al-Idrisi was honored as a noble, scholar, and traveler, and it was there that his real fame as a geographer and cartographer came. During the fifteen years of their collaboration, al-Idrisi produced a celestial globe, a disk-shaped 1.5-by-3.5-meter tablet map of the known world, and many other maps. The globe and the world map were made of solid silver, weighing 450 Roman pounds. The globe and map in turn were based on al-Idrisi's encyclopedic geography, *Kitab nuzhat al-mushtaq fi ikhtiraq al-afaq* (1154; the pleasure excursion of one who is eager to traverse the regions of the world; also known as *Kitab ar-Rujari*, or book of Roger), which was completed under Roger's patronage. The world map and presumably also the globe fell into the hands of a mob in 1160 and were smashed, but many of the seventy manuscript maps made by al-Idrisi from the world map shortly before Roger's death in 1154 luckily survived. Sadly, no complete version of *Kitab nuzhat al-mushtaq fi ikhtiraq al-afaq* survives in any language. It first appeared in the West in Rome in an abridged version in 1592 and was translated into Latin in Paris in 1619, but no full translation into English ever has been made.

After the death of Roger, al-Idrisi continued to work for his son and successor, King William I (William the Bad), and wrote another geographic treatise. No complete version of this second book survives either, but a shortened version, a seventy-three-map atlas, remains. In about 1160, al-Idrisi left Sicily for his native Morocco to live out his life, where sometime between 1164 and 1166 he died, probably near Sabtah.

Al-Idrisi's great world map was a monument to medieval Islamic geography and cartography, but today it exists only in several reconstructions created by scholars from the surviving fragments of his works. It was divided into seven horizontal climatic zones (probably derived from the classical Greco-Roman worldview and the works of Ptolemy), each divided vertically into eleven sections to create a primitive grid, a system of longitude and latitude for more accurate place location. The map also contained a wealth of information, an abundance of detail, and a degree of clarity rarely achieved previously. It was most accurate for the Mediterranean region; perhaps understandably, Sicily is shown as an exceptionally large island. Its accuracy and detail also extended elsewhere. For example, al-Idrisi showed the source of the Nile River as an unnamed lake in Central Africa. Yet, while his maps were drawn very correctly for the time, they were not drawn mathematically.

On al-Idrisi's world map, the Islamic and Norman worlds were joined. In preparation for the creation of al-Idrisi's maps and geographies, Roger had sent out reliable agents and draftsmen to collect data from many lands. Al-Idrisi relied heavily on classic Muslim sources, such as the works of al-Khwarizmi and al-Masudi, and classic Greek, Roman, and Hellenistic sources, such as the works of Ptolemy, the father of modern geography and cartography. Al-Idrisi's grid system (but not his projections) probably was based on those of Ptolemy and a copy of Ptolemy's altered version of the world map of Marinus of Tyre. As his great world map demonstrates, however, al-Idrisi was often much more than a mere modifier of Ptolemy. Al-Idrisi also utilized Indian astronomical studies. Yet, perhaps most important, he relied heavily on his recollections of his own journeys and those of other travelers for reliable information.

Summary

Al-Idrisi's work was far more influential than Ptolemy's in the East, but less so in Europe. Still, his maps opened European eyes to some of what the Muslims knew about Africa and Asia in the Middle Ages. Perhaps because he spent much of his adult life in the service of the Christian kings of Sicily, for centuries—even into the twentieth century—al-Idrisi and his achievements were ignored by Muslim scholars. In so doing, they deprived their Western counterparts of a fuller understanding of him as well. Only recently has al-Idrisi's full impact begun to be realized, especially within the context of the study of the history of science and the history of cartography.

In short, al-Idrisi represents by far the best example of Islamic-Christian scientific collaboration in the Middle Ages in geography. *Kitab nuzhat al-mushtaq fi ikhtiraq al-afaq* was the most important geographic work of the period, and in its various forms it served as a major European and Muslim textbook for several centuries. Maps clearly based on those of al-Idrisi were produced well into the seventeenth century. He applied scientific methodology and precision to the heretofore largely imaginative arts of geography and cartography. Al-Idrisi truly deserved the epithet "Strabo of the Arabs," which was applied to him in his own lifetime.

Bibliography

Badeau, John S., et al., eds. *The Genius of Arab Civilization: Source of Renaissance*. New York: New York University Press, 1975. 2d ed. Cambridge, Mass.: MIT Press, 1983. Contains a relatively brief but significant factual account of al-Idrisi and his work by Florence Amzallag Tatistcheff, putting them into perspective with the broader medieval Arab achievement. Plate of one map.

Bagrow, Leo, and R. A. Skelton. *History of Cartography*. Cambridge, Mass.: Harvard University Press, 1964. 2d ed. Chicago: Precedent Publishing, 1985. Contains a brief section on al-Idrisi and his work which only begins to put him into perspective in the history of cartography. Plates of four maps.

Curtis. Edmund. *Roger of Sicily and the Normans in Lower Italy, 1016-1154*. New York: G. P. Putnam's Sons, 1912. A very good biography of the much-neglected King Roger II, containing a significant section on his collaboration with al-Idrisi. Includes extensive excerpts from al-Idrisi's works.

Gillispie, Charles Coulston, ed. *Dictionary of Scientific Biography*. Vol. 7, *Iamblichus-Karl Landsteiner*. New York: Charles Scribner's Sons, 1973. Contains a rather extensive entry on al-Idrisi, with a brief bibliography of non-English secondary sources, by S. Maqbul Ahmad. Excellent discussion of al-Idrisi's early life and travels and also of his influence through the centuries.

Lock, C. B. Muriel. *Geography and Cartography: A Reference Handbook* (combined and revised edition of *Geography: A Reference Handbook*, 1968, and *Modern Maps and Atlases*, 1969). Hamden, Conn.: Linnet Books, 1976. Contains an entry on al-Idrisi. Especially helpful with regard to some of the various abridgments and other editions of his now-classic works.

Dennis Reinhartz

IGNATIUS OF ANTIOCH

Born: c. A.D. 30; Antioch, Syria
Died: December 20, A.D. 107?; Rome
Area of Achievement: Religion
Contribution: Ignatius served as Bishop of Antioch from the early 60's to the early 100's and was an important theologian and the exemplary martyr of the early Christian Church. By his writings and example, Ignatius strengthened the office of bishop in the church hierarchy, clarified many central Christian doctrines, such as the Real Presence and the Virgin Birth, and formulated the strategy and tactics of voluntary martyrdom.

Early Life

Ignatius was born to pagan parents at Antioch, the capital of Syria, during the second quarter of the first century, about A.D. 30. One of the largest cities of the Roman Empire, the terminus of both Eastern caravan routes and Mediterranean sea-lanes, Antioch was the center of commerce and Greek culture in the eastern Mediterranean region. It contained a large Jewish refugee population but was also the site of the first gentile Christian community, which became the mother church of Christian churches throughout the Roman Empire.

According to the earliest traditions, Ignatius was converted to Christianity by the Apostle John, whose theology certainly profoundly influenced him, and in the early 60's was consecrated Bishop of Antioch by Peter and Paul on their way to Rome and martyrdom under the emperor Nero. A charming but improbable story identifies Ignatius with the small child whom Jesus Christ presented to His disciples at Capernaum as a lesson in humility. It would appear that this story is a wordplay on the surname Theophorus (or "God-bearer") which Ignatius took later in life; the tradition shows that Ignatius was believed to have been born before the death of Christ. Ignatius, the eager young Christian convert, was blessed with strong faith and great abilities; these qualities brought him quickly to prominence in the Christian community at Antioch and to the attention of Saint Evodius, Bishop of Antioch, and Peter and Paul.

Life's Work

As Bishop of Antioch in the first century, Ignatius presided in dignity over the early gentile church, leading the greatest Christian community in the Roman Empire. Here he furthered Paul's work in transforming Christianity from a Jewish sect into a world religion. Ignatius was an exemplary bishop who maintained Christian order in the community and orthodoxy in doctrine; like a good shepherd, he protected his flock from the wolves during the persecution under the emperor Domitian (A.D. 81-96).

Bishop Ignatius of Antioch suffered martyrdom not then but later under the humane, progressive, and just emperor Trajan. Though a pagan, the emperor was a good man and an enlightened ruler who regarded himself as the servant and protector of his people. So admirable was Trajan that there would arise a popular legend in the Middle Ages that Pope Gregory the Great had interceded with God and secured Trajan's salvation. In *La divina commedia* (c. 1320; *The Divine Comedy*, 1802), Dante, following this legend, placed Trajan, though a pagan, in Heaven alongside certain eminently just Christian rulers.

Trajan's policy toward Christianity was both moderate and legalistic. He strongly discouraged active persecution of Christians, though he allowed the legal prosecution of those who had been publicly denounced to the Roman authorities. Trajan laid down this policy explicitly in 112 in his correspondence with Pliny the Younger, the Governor of Bithynia. Roman officials were forbidden to search out Christians. Those denounced to the state were to be prosecuted by their denouncers before Roman magistrates, but these Christians were given procedural guarantees and the opportunity and encouragement to recant Christianity and conform to the state religion. Thus, under Trajan, Christians could be punished if legally proved guilty and then only if obdurate in their belief.

Allegations against Christians included treason, sedition, unspecified crimes, impiety, depravity, and membership in illegal secret societies, but ultimately their real offense was their primary allegiance to the Kingdom of God instead of to the Roman Empire. Ignatius could not in good conscience pay reverence to the imperial cult and the divinities in the Roman pantheon because he believed them to be idols and demons. To the emperor Trajan, however, respect for the state religion was an important aspect of civic duty and a mark of patriotism; thus, to him, a gesture of respect was a very reasonable demand.

Ironically, Trajan's policy was probably more destructive than Domitian's and Nero's persecutions had been. It was neither sporadic nor localized but was spread throughout the Empire. It seemed reasonable, legal, and just. Nevertheless, Trajan's policy threatened to divide and demoralize Christian communities by encouraging apostasy and discrediting Christian martyrs. The prosecution that Ignatius of Antioch faced was much more insidious than other persecutions because it appeared humane and just.

Later Christian hagiographers imagined a dramatic personal confrontation between Ignatius and Trajan. Ignatius was prosecuted at a time when Trajan's recent victory in Dacia had occasioned enthusiastic displays of loyalty to the Roman gods throughout the Empire. Ignatius' trial as described by his biographers probably never occurred, but the fictitious confrontation did capture the global conflict between the City of God and the earthly city. In fact, not Trajan himself but one of his governors condemned Ignatius; Ignatius was sent to Rome rather than executed in Antioch simply because the many celebrations of Trajan's Dacian victory had caused a scarcity of gladiators and victims for the Roman games. Moreover, the Roman mob found it especially entertaining to watch the death of an old man such as Ignatius. Although mistaken in imagining the personal confrontation between Ignatius and Trajan, the hagiographers were perceptive in personifying the conflict between two cities, two systems of belief, and two ways of life. It was not so much good versus evil as the best of the temporal—Emperor Trajan—versus the best of the spiritual—Bishop Ignatius.

The most significant historical source for the life's work of Ignatius is the collection of his seven epistles, which he wrote around 107, during his journey under guard to Rome and his martyrdom. Ignatius' journey was triumphant and even ecstatic: Along the way, his Roman guards permitted him to visit important Christian communities in Asia Minor and the Balkans, where he preached, blessed, ordained, and was received enthusiastically. Pausing at Smyrna, Ignatius wrote four epistles, to the Christians of Ephesus, Magnesia, Rome, and Tralles. Traveling on to Lystra, he paused there and wrote three more epistles, to the Christians at Philadelphia and Smyrna, and in farewell to Polycarp, the Bishop of Smyrna, who was Ignatius' protégé and later would himself suffer martyrdom. The contents of the seven epistles cover Christian beliefs and practices and stress Christian unity in doctrine and hierarchical organization. The most poignant of the letters is the epistle written to the Romans, in which Ignatius begged the Christian community at Rome not to try to have him reprieved.

Ignatius' eagerness and joy to be a martyr, that is, publicly to witness his Christian faith even unto death, appears to some modern psychoanalytical commentators "disturbed" and "self-destructive." Ignatius welcomed not self-destruction but union with his Lord Jesus Christ, humbly and faithfully identifying his own martyrdom with Christ's sacrifice.

Ignatius anticipated his martyrdom, which he perceived in almost Eucharistic imagery. He would become as "God's wheat, ground fine by the teeth of the wild beasts, that he may be found pure bread, a sacrifice to God." Across the millennia ring his triumphant words:

> Come fire and cross, and grapplings with wild beasts, cuttings and manglings, wrenchings of bones, breaking of limbs, crushing of my whole body, come cruel tortures of the Devil to assail me. Only be it mine to attain unto Jesus Christ.

On December 20, 107, according to Greek tradition, on the last day of the public games, Ignatius of Antioch was brought into the Flavian Amphitheater, the infamous Colosseum, and thrown to the lions. He welcomed the two ravenous lions, which immediately devoured him, leaving in the bloody sand only a few of the larger bones. Reverent Antiochenes gathered up the relics and brought them to Antioch, where they were enshrined.

Summary

Ignatius of Antioch was among the greatest of the early fathers of the Church. Admirable as the Bishop of Antioch and brilliantly imaginative as a Christian theologian, his greatest contribution was doubtless his exemplary martyrdom. His fortitude, commitment, authenticity, love, joy, and ecstasy illustrate the maxim that the blood of the martyrs is the seed of the Church. Ignatius was an Apostolic Father, having met and been associated with the Apostles Peter and John and with Paul, the Apostle of the Gentiles. Ignatius proved the continuity and catholicity of the early Christian Church by bridging the distance between Jew and Gentile and between the Age of the Apostles and the Age of the Martyrs.

Bibliography

De Ste. Croix, G. E. M. "Why Were the Early Christians Persecuted?" *Past and Present* no. 26 (November, 1963): 6-38. This important analysis discusses early Christian voluntary martyrdom, with Ignatius of Antioch considered as a precursor.

Eusebius. *The Ecclesiastical History of Eusebius Pamphilus*. Translated by Christian Frederick Cruse. Grand Rapids, Mich.: Baker Book House, 1955. The standard narrative primary source for the first three centuries of Christianity, Eusebius' account includes some information on Ignatius of Antioch.

Frend, W. H. *Martyrdom and Persecution in the Early Church: A Study of a Conflict from the Maccabees to Donatus*. New York: New York University Press, 1967. A penetrating examination of the social and psychological dynamics of martyrdom. Includes an insightful discussion of Ignatius of Antioch.

Ignatius of Antioch, Saint. "The Epistles of St. Ignatius." In *The Apostolic Fathers*, translated and edited by Kirsopp Lake. 2 vols. London: Wm. Heinemann, 1925-1930. Of the many usable modern editions of Ignatius' epistles, this Loeb Classical Library edition is one of the most readily available. These epistles are the principal primary source for the life of Ignatius and also are important for the history of early Christianity.

Ignatius of Antioch, Saint, and Saint Clement of Rome. *The Epistles of St. Clement of Rome and St. Ignatius of Antioch*. Translated and edited by James E. Kleist. Westminster, Md.: Newman Bookshop, 1946. Part of the Ancient Christian Writers and the Works of the Fathers in Translation series. Differences in translation and especially in commentary make this edition of the epistles an independently useful and complementary work.

Lane Fox, Robin. *Pagans and Christians*. New York: Alfred A. Knopf, 1987. An ambitious synthesis of scholarship about the cultural and social context of early Christianity, Lane Fox's work is important for background information.

Thurston, Herbert, and Donald Attwater, eds. *Butler's Lives of the Saints*. 4 vols. Westminster, Md.: Palm Publishers, 1956. The standard hagiography in English, Alban Butler's eighteenth century collection has been shortened, edited, supplemented, and revised by the editors. It is arranged according to feast days (Ignatius' day is February 1).

Terence R. Murphy

IMHOTEP

Born: Twenty-seventh century B.C.; Egypt
Died: Twenty-seventh century B.C.; Egypt
Areas of Achievement: Architecture and medicine
Contribution: Imhotep, the priest-physician who was deified as the Egyptian god of medicine, was also an architect and is credited with starting the age of pyramid building.

Early Life

Little is known about Imhotep's early life except that his father, Kanofer, is believed to have been a distinguished architect and that his mother was named Khreduonkh. He was probably born in a suburb of Memphis, and his early training was most likely influenced by his father's profession. To judge by his later reputation, he received a liberal education and was interested and skilled in many areas.

That Imhotep was a real historical figure in an influential position and that he was evidently respected for his wisdom and talent are deduced from his position as the chief vizier for one of the most famous Egyptian kings, Zoser, (fl. 2686 B.C.) of Egypt's Third Dynasty. From what is known of the duties of viziers at a later period, it is likely that Imhotep had to be both efficient and extremely knowledgeable, for the vizier was in charge of the judiciary and the departments of the treasury, the army and navy, internal affairs, and agriculture. As a judge, Imhotep is reputed to have penned many wise proverbs, although unfortunately none is known to have survived.

The increasing stature of Imhotep during his lifetime is apparent in the changes in statuettes discovered. In some he appears to be an ordinary man, dressed simply; he looks like a sage, seated on a throne or chair with a roll of papyrus on his knees or under his arm and is depicted as reading or deep in thought. When he achieved full god status, he was shown standing, carrying a scepter and the ankh, with the beard typically worn by gods. His mother was then regarded as the mother of a god and his wife, Ronpe-nofret, as the wife of a god; following what appears to have been a tradition of Egyptian deities, Imhotep was considered to be the son of the god Ptah as well as the son of the mortal Kanofer.

Life's Work

Imhotep's reputation is remarkable not only because he was accomplished in so many fields but also because he is credited for his distinction in two distinct fields and in two distinct periods: his achievement as an architect during his lifetime and his high position as priest-physician, for which he was accorded a divine status several hundred years after his lifetime.

In his capacity as architect, Imhotep is credited with designing and implementing the building of the earliest large stone structure—the Step Pyramid of Saqqara—which inaugurated the age of pyramid building in Egypt.

A story much debated among scholars nevertheless reveals the reverence with which Imhotep was regarded. According to the Legend of the Seven Years' Famine, it happened that the Nile River had not risen to its usual level sufficient to irrigate the land for seven years, resulting in a shortage of food. King Zoser, distressed by the suffering of his subjects, consulted Imhotep about the birthplace of the Nile and its god. After absenting himself for a brief period of research and study, Imhotep revealed some unspecified "hidden wonders" which the king investigated; he offered prayers and oblations at the temple of the god Khnum and, promised by the god in a dream that the Nile would not fail again, endowed the temple of the god with land and gifts in gratitude.

Imhotep's achievement in the field of medicine is equally legendary. His reputation as a healer seems to be based almost entirely on his apotheosis from a wise and talented man who was a contemporary of Zoser, to a medical demigod, and then finally to a full deity of medicine in the period of Persian rule (about 525 B.C.). In the period of the Greco-Egyptian rule, he was called Imouthes and identified with Asclepios, the Greek god of medicine, resulting in a gradual assimilation of the two figures.

Imhotep's reputation as a wise healer is thus one that seems to have developed several hundred years after his death. The godlike status accorded him as a healer not only shows how he was revered but also points to the inextricable connection between medicine, magic, and religion in Egyptian medical practice. In addition to his other duties, Imhotep held an important position as the Kheri-Heb, or chief lector priest. Thus entitled to read holy religious texts which were believed to have magical powers, he served as a mediator and teacher of religious mysteries. Among the priest-physicians, two main classes predominated: the physicians who had some systematic training in medicine and the larger class of those who emphasized the power to cure with amulets and magic incantations. Because the names or achievements of other practitioners of medicine in ancient times have been discovered while the specific qualifications of Imhotep as a healer are not as clearly documented, it is thought that his duties as a priest who was regarded as a magician may have initiated his reputation as a medical man.

In all likelihood, his cumulative achievements as architect, physician, priest, sage, and magician led to the great reverence in which Imhotep was held and to his subsequent deification. The magic he was reputed to practice may well have been grounded in the considerably well-developed art of healing in ancient Egypt. A number of medical documents have survived in rolls of papyrus: the Ebers Papyrus, the Hearst Papyrus, the Berlin Medical Papyrus, the Kahun Medical Papyrus, the London Medical Papyrus, the Edwin Smith Papyrus, and another papyrus in Berlin. The Ebers Papyrus, the most important of these, was written about 1550 B.C. but appears to be a compilation of other books written centuries before; parts of it were already in existence during Imhotep's lifetime and may therefore be construed to reflect the kind of medicine and magic Imhotep practiced.

The Ebers Papyrus lists many prescriptions for a variety of ailments; approximately 250 kinds of diseases are identified in the various papyruses. The doses and modes of administration are specified, suggesting that clinical examination, diagnosis, and therapeutics were quite progressive. Drugs from herbs, vegetable products, minerals, and parts of animals were studied and administered in many forms, such as gargles, salves, lozenges, pills, and plasters. Simple surgery was performed and fractures were successfully treated. The custom of mummification, involving the dissection of bodies to remove the viscera, undoubtedly provided the Egyptians with a better working knowledge of the internal organs and practical anatomy than existed elsewhere for many centuries afterward.

While the papyruses demonstrate that empiric knowledge existed and medical treatment was widely practiced, they also reveal that such practical measures were always accompanied by magical formulas. Disease was treated primarily as a visitation of a malign spirit or god, not as a dysfunction of the body. The healer therefore had to identify the nature and the name of the evil spirit, determine how far it had invaded the body, take into account the times and seasons of the year in gauging the virulence of the attack, and then try to drive it out with every possible means—including magic, ritual, and material remedies. Some physicians would seek to differentiate between symptoms which called for drugs, magic, or temple sleep, suggesting that already in ancient times an elementary form of psychiatry was practiced.

Several legends show the importance of the Egyptian temples as a gathering place for the sick and the practice of incubation sleep as a form of cure. The writer of one of the Oxyrhynchus papyruses, written in Greek around the second century A.D., recounts two incidents involving Imhotep's power. The writer, a priest named Nechautis in the temple of Imhotep, and his mother both fell sick at different times. On both occasions, they went to the temple, where Imhotep appeared to them in dreams, suggesting a simple remedy; upon waking, both were cured. Other legends discovered by Egyptologists recount stories of infertile couples who sought help at the temple of Imhotep and conceived children afterward.

One explanation given for the demigod status of Imhotep during the New Kingdom (about 1580 B.C.) was the religious revival which increased the magnificence and wealth of the Egyptian gods to such a degree that they became inaccessible to the common people; in search of a superhuman but sympathetic friend, it is conjectured, the common people selected new demigods from the national heroes of the past—including Imhotep, who had a reputation as a wise man.

In at least three temples built to honor him, the cult of Imhotep flourished. The first one, at Memphis, was famous as a hospital and school of magic and medicine and was referred to as the Asclepieion by the Greeks. Two other temples, one at Philae and one at Thebes, and a sanatorium are believed to have been devoted to the worship of Imhotep. Stories similar to the one related above illustrate the power of the practice of incubation at Egyptian medical temples. People with all sorts of illnesses and others seeking protection from accidents went to the temples for help. During this natural or drug-induced sleep, it was believed that either the deity or a priest acting on behalf of the deity would appear and indicate a remedy. Temple sleep served as a powerful form of faith healing, the most effective for very high-strung patients.

It is thought that a practical man of affairs such as Imhotep, with his interest in astronomy and other sciences, probably leaned toward the scientific treatment of illnesses. From the records about the cult of Imhotep that grew hundreds of years after his death, it is apparent, however, that his greatest public achievements were in the capacity of a faith healer.

Summary

The name Imhotep means "he who cometh in peace"; the symbolic significance of the name is perhaps the best way to explain the enduring reputation of a person whom some scholars doubt even existed. For three thousand years, well into the Roman period, Imhotep was worshipped as the god of medicine, for a long time in temples devoted to him. This deification of a person who was not of the royal pharaohs was in itself a rare achievement, pointing to the great respect that a priest-physician could command. It is entirely conceivable, too, that the powerful fraternity of priest-physicians deliberately helped to create his reputation, spreading the word about the healing power of a man otherwise familiar to people as a wise and accomplished vizier in order to increase the contributions of the pharaohs to the temple coffers. The champions of Imhotep's reputation argue, on the other hand, that the civilization of ancient Egypt was unknown for hundreds of years, compared to the relative familiarity of scholars with Greek and Roman life and culture. According to this argument, Imhotep simply suffered the fate of the ancients, as the inexorable process of history dimmed his achievements and assimilated his fame with succeeding generations of medical practitioners.

Under the Ptolemies, six festivals were regularly held to honor the events of Imhotep's life, including his birthday on May 31 and his death on July 1, though there is no documentation to prove that these dates have any relation to real historical events. The elaborateness of the cult of Imhotep points, if not to his actual existence or achievement, to the power of his reputation as a healer. That reputation alone was worth much in terms of what could be called ancient psychotherapy. William Osler's often-quoted tribute to Imhotep, "the first figure of a physician to stand out clearly from the mists of antiquity," is a recognition of the power that people in pain and suffering are willing to attribute to a distinguishable healing authority who by virtue of that confidence in his skill is able to bring them a measure of peace.

Bibliography

Cormack, Maribelle. *Imhotep: Builder in Stone*. New York: Franklin Watts, 1965. A simply and imaginatively written account of Imhotep's development and achievements as an architect. Part of a series called Immortals of Engineering. Contains an outline of the chronology of Egyptian history from 3200 B.C. to A.D. 640 and an index.

Dawson, Warren R. *Magician and Leech: A Study in the Beginnings of Medicine with Special Reference to Ancient Egypt*. London: Methuen and Co., 1929. A short account of Egyptian medicine, based on the study of the Egyptian papyruses relating to medicine and on the study of techniques of mummification. Contains illustrations and index.

Garry, Gerald T. *Egypt: The Home of the Occult Sciences, with Special Reference to Imhotep, the Mysterious Wise Man and Egyptian God of Medicine*. London: John Bale, Sons and Danielsson, 1931. This study by a physician contains a substantial chapter on Imhotep. Outlines the scholarly arguments about the existence of Imhotep. Serves as a brief but useful introduction to the problems of Egyptology.

Hurry, Jamieson B. *Imhotep: The Vizier and Physician of King Zoser and Afterwards the Egyptian God of Medicine*. London: Oxford University Press, 1926. Rev. ed. New York: AMS Press, 1978. The single most informative source about Imhotep, this monograph contains a short bibliography, an index, illustrations, and appendices referring to the construction and variants of the name Imhotep, his pedigree as architect, and the statuettes and murals depicting him.

Sigerist, Henry E. *A History of Medicine*. Vol. 1, *Primitive and Archaic Medicine*. New York: Oxford University Press, 1951-1961. Written by one of the most promising historians of medicine (although he did not live to complete the series), this book includes a substantial chapter on ancient Egypt. Contains illustrations, an index, and appendices on histories of medicine, sourcebooks of medical history, museums of medical history, and literature of paleopathology since 1930.

Shakuntala Jayaswal

INNOCENT III
Lothario of Segni

Born: 1160 or 1161; Anagni, the Roman Campagna
Died: July 16, 1216; Perugia
Areas of Achievement: Religion and government
Contribution: At a period of crisis in the Catholic church, Pope Innocent III succeeded in affirming the power of his office against challenges from powerful lay rulers and from the Albigensian heresy, and in so doing became the most powerful pope of the Middle Ages. In addition, through sweeping ecclesiastical reform, he attempted to mute the arguments of the critics of an increasingly venal, poorly educated, and self-indulgent clergy.

Early Life

The future Pope Innocent III was born Lothario of Segni at Anagni, in the Roman Campagna, the son of Trasmondo of Segni and Claricia, née Scotti, both members of prominent Roman aristocratic families. Occasionally one encounters the surname of Conti for Lothario. This name, Italian for "count," was assumed by the family after Innocent III's pontificate. It was one of the most powerful Roman families and furnished several popes to the Church in the thirteenth century. The surviving fragment of a mosaic and a painting of Innocent III confirm that he was short of stature, with a round face, high-arched eyebrows, a straight nose, and a small mouth. Contemporaries also noted his ability to express himself verbally in an incisive fashion and a well-modulated voice that commanded the attention of his audience.

The young Lothario, who was vowed to the clergy, was able to indulge an appetite for learning that he exhibited at an early age. He first studied at Rome under Peter Ismael, whom, in recognition, he later named Bishop of Sutri. His happiest years, according to his later testimony, were spent at the University of Paris, where he studied theology under Peter of Corbeil, whom he later rewarded with two high ecclesiastical appointments. Innocent always retained a great affection for France and its people. After his time in Paris, he studied civil and canon law, two subjects in which he excelled, at the University of Bologna, mainly under the great canonist Huguccio of Pisa. Lothario did not forget his teacher and companions at Bologna when he became pope. Huguccio became Bishop of Ferrara, and Lothario's fellow students and companions were awarded other important posts in the Church. Lothario's studies in theology and the civil and canon law were to prepare him well for his later pontificate.

Upon completion of his studies at Bologna, Lothario returned to Rome, where his education, family contacts, and relationship with several cardinals assured his rapid advance as a cleric. In 1187, Pope Gregory VIII ordained him subdeacon. In 1189 or 1190, Pope Clement III made him cardinal deacon of the Church of Saint Sergius and Saint Bacchus in the Roman forum, where he served during the pontificate of Celestine III. His years there were devoted to the reconstruction and embellishing of his church building and, most important, to writing. While wisely maintaining a distance from the machinations and intrigues of the papal Curia (the administrative office of the Church), Lothario composed several theological treatises, including *De contemptu mundi* (also as *De miseria conditionis humanae*; *On the Misery of the Human Condition*) and *De sacro alteris mysterio* (*The Sacred Mystery of the Altar*). These works contributed to his growing prestige as a theologian, moralist, and writer and undoubtedly had something to do with his election as pope at the very young age of thirty-seven.

Upon the death of the nonagenarian Celestine III on January 8, 1198, several candidates were nominated to succeed him. The new pope was elected on the same day on the second ballot. Although Lothario received the greatest number of votes on the first ballot, concern over his youth necessitated a second. His learning, unquestionable morality, and vigor, however, overcame initial concerns about his age. Lothario of Segni was elected by a unanimous vote and ascended the papal throne as Innocent III.

Life's Work

Innocent became pope at a crucial time in European history. The institutions of manorialism and feudalism were succumbing to the economic and political forces of the growth of towns and a new merchant class and of monarchs bent on creating centralized territorial states. The secular authority of the Pope was being challenged by ambitious rulers, and the Church itself, and especially the clergy, increasingly came under attack from critics attracted to various heresies. In addition, the Muslims retained control over Jerusalem and the Holy Places. From the first day of his reign, Innocent recognized the necessity for strong papal leadership and immediately laid claim to broad powers in the exercise of his authority over ecclesiastical government and, as Vicar of Christ, over temporal affairs having a bearing on the Church's well-being.

Innocent has been accused by some historians of selfish and excessive ambition because of his attempt to exercise power over European lay rulers. Indeed, the Pope did devote considerable time to diplomatic and political matters, and he did not hesitate to use the powers of his office to force obedience. His actions were motivated, however, by his sincere conviction that spiritual issues were at stake and that Christian unity and tranquillity necessitated recognition of the Pope's supremacy as ruler and judge throughout the Christian world. Although Innocent intervened in the affairs of numerous European kingdoms, including Portugal, Aragon, Castile, Hungary, and Poland, his interventions in the Holy Roman Empire, England, and France most clearly illustrate his motives.

Innocent intervened first in the Holy Roman Empire over the election of the emperor, and he was to remain involved there during almost all of his pontificate because of a series of complex events. The emperor, Henry VI, who had extended his control over a large part of the Papal States and over Sicily, died a few months before Innocent's election. The electors split over two claimants to the imperial title, while ignoring Henry's young son, Frederick II of Sicily. Frederick, who as King of Sicily was a vassal of the Pope, became Innocent's ward. Innocent intervened in the disputed election for two reasons. First, he wanted to separate Sicily from the imperial holdings and to reassert control over the Papal States. Second, he claimed special rights within the empire dating to the papal coronation of Charlemagne in 800. Innocent interpreted this event as a transfer of power from the Eastern Roman Empire (Byzantium) to the West by papal authority. He asserted, therefore, that, although the princes of the Holy Roman Empire had the right to elect, their choice was subject to papal confirmation and that he should be the sole arbiter in a disputed election. Following a lengthy civil war, Innocent finally secured the election of his choice, Otto IV, whom he crowned in 1209. Otto, however, failed to keep his promise to restore the papal lands to the Church and even laid plans to invade Sicily. Innocent promptly excommunicated him and declared him deprived of the imperial title. Innocent then threw his support to Frederick II in return for his promise to separate the administration of Sicily from his German holdings and to undertake a crusade to the Holy Land. Frederick was crowned in 1220. Innocent had effectively asserted papal power against disobedient lay rulers and had, at least temporarily, restored tranquillity to a war-torn Europe. In addition, papal lands that had been lost earlier were restored.

Although Innocent found himself at odds on several occasions with his most troublesome lay adversary, King John of England, the bitterest and longest dispute was over the election of the primate of the English church, the Archbishop of Canterbury, following the death, in 1205, of Archbishop Hubert Walter. Ultimately, two archbishops were elected: the choice of a group of monks of the cathedral chapter and the king's choice, a subservient courtier and civil servant, John de Grey, Archbishop of Norwich. Innocent rejected both claimants. He offered his own candidate, the English scholar and ecclesiastical statesman Stephen Langton. Despite John's opposition, Innocent consecrated Langton as Archbishop of Canterbury and gave him the *pallium*, the symbol of his office, in June, 1207. John's rejection of Langton led to a long and complicated struggle between king and pope. In March, 1208, Innocent placed England under an interdict—a territorial excommunication that denied some of the sacraments to John's subjects. John responded by seizing all church properties in England and collecting the revenues they provided. In November, 1209, the Pope excommunicated the king. The conflict was not resolved, however, until 1213, when, under the threat of an invasion of England by Philip Augustus (Philip II of France), John gave in. He agreed to accept Langton, to return church properties, and to repay the revenues he had collected from them since the imposition of the interdict (this last promise, however, he failed to keep). John further agreed to recognize the Pope as his feudal lord and to receive his kingdom back as a fief from the Papacy. Thus, Innocent had used the powers of his office to force lay obedience and to secure recognition of the best candidate for England's highest ecclesiastical office.

Innocent also intervened in France, in the domestic problems of Philip Augustus. In 1193, Philip had married a Danish princess, Ingeborg, for money and political expediency. Tiring of his queen, Philip forced a group of French prelates to annul the marriage on the totally insupportable grounds of consanguinity. Ingeborg and her Danish relatives appealed to the Pope, and Celestine III voided the annulment. Philip, however, ignored the Pope and, in 1196, married Agnes, the daughter of a Bavarian nobleman. Upon his accession, Innocent quickly intervened. He sent a legate to persuade the king, under threat of an interdict, to accept Celestine's prohibition and recognize Ingeborg. Philip refused to yield, and the interdict was imposed in January, 1200. Six months later, however, Agnes died, the king submitted, and the interdict was removed. Philip, however, expressed his intention of reopening the case and did not formally restore Ingeborg as queen until 1213. Nevertheless, Innocent had won on an issue directly related to the spiritual authority of the Pope and the Church: the sacrament of marriage.

Innocent was also committed to asserting the power of the Church against the twin threats of heresy and Islam. The Cathari (Albigensians), a heretical sect which had its origins in one of Christianity's early competitors in the Roman Empire, Manichaeanism, enjoyed great popularity in areas of southern France. Rejecting the organization of the Catholic church and its sacramental system, the Cathari posed a significant, though localized, threat to the Pope's authority. Accordingly, in 1208, Innocent called knights of northern France to embark on a crusade against the Cathari. The Pope, whose intention had been to convert the heretics, was soon grieved to find his religious crusade degenerating into a bloody war of territorial conquest; he did not foresee the brutality of the Inquisition, established by his successor, which resulted in the total extirpation of the heresy. Earlier, in 1202, Innocent had preached a crusade (the Fourth Crusade) to capture Jerusalem and the Holy Places from the Muslims. This undertaking, to the Pope's disappointment, was diverted from its goal by the selfish interests of the Crusaders, especially the Venetians, who instead took Constantinople. Innocent was preparing to launch a new crusade against the Muslims at the time of his death.

Innocent's greatest and most enduring achievement, and the one in which he took greatest interest and pride, was in the sphere of ecclesiastical reform. Aware of the inroads of heresy which had gained impetus from the Church's failure to define its doctrines and discipline its clergy, Innocent convoked the Fourth Lateran Council of the Church in 1215. In attendance were more than four hundred bishops, eight hundred abbots, and representatives of all major European rulers. The council enacted extensive reform legislation. The main tenets of Catholicism were restated, and the seven sacraments were defined. The doctrine of transubstantiation, which enhanced the role of the clergy as joint participants in the miracle of transforming the bread and wine into the body and blood of Christ, was affirmed. In addition, Catholics were required to confess their sins annually to a priest. Clerical participation in judicial ordeals was prohibited, thus requiring secular courts to devise more rational methods of determining guilt. Vacant bishoprics were to be filled within three months, and in every church province an episcopal council was to meet yearly to discipline its wayward members. Steps were taken to improve clerical morality. Celibacy and sobriety were encouraged, and gambling, hunting, engaging in trade, frequenting taverns, and the wearing of flashy, ornate clothing were forbidden. In addition, clergymen were not to hold more than one benefice in which they were required to exercise pastoral responsibilities.

The work of the council, which owed its inspiration directly to Innocent, went far, at least temporarily, in muting criticisms of the Church. An unfortunate decree of the council, however, was that Jews should be distinguished as outcasts by being required to wear a yellow label. This was an affirmation of Innocent's earlier advocacy of the ghettoization of the Jews. The Fourth Lateran Council marks the culmination of the papacy of Innocent III. He died suddenly in Perugia, on July 16, 1216, probably from malaria.

Summary

Innocent III is perhaps the most controversial figure in the history of the Papacy. His exercise of the authority of his office, which he, as Vicar of Christ, regarded as all-encompassing, often involved him in temporal matters. Some historians have argued, therefore, that he was more concerned with enhancing the temporal authority of the Papacy than in fulfilling the spiritual and pastoral duties of his office. Others, however, have argued that Innocent regarded his intervention in temporal affairs as an extension of his spiritual duties. His interventions were motivated by moral concerns—his desire to punish sin or to prevent its commission.

Indisputably, Innocent became pope at a period of crisis in the Church and succeeded in effectively asserting the powers of his office and transforming the Church into the most powerful and respected institution in Europe. His program of ecclesiastical reform, reflected in the work of the Fourth Lateran Council, had it been implemented more thoroughly, might have helped the Church to avoid the divisions and corruption of the succeeding centuries which led ultimately to the Protestant Reformation and the division of Western Christendom, the unity of which Innocent had labored to assure.

Bibliography

Barraclough, Geoffrey. *The Medieval Papacy*. New York: Harcourt, Brace and World, 1968. This volume, by one of the foremost historians of medieval Germany, contains a comparatively brief, but cogent, account of the pontificate of Innocent III. It is also richly illustrated and contains especially informative bibliographical notes.

Carlyle, A. J., and R. W. Carlyle. *Medieval Political Theory in the West*. 6 vols. Edinburgh: William Blackwood and Sons, 1903. This classic in the history of political thought contains important material on Innocent III in volume 5. The authors assert that Innocent's elevated conception of his papal office provided for him the obligation to exercise his authority actively in all areas of human life.

McIlwain, Charles H. *The Growth of Political Thought in the West from the Greeks to the End of the Middle Ages*. New York: Macmillan, 1932. This great medievalist emphasizes the spiritual motivation for Innocent's actions. He refuses to subscribe to the contention of others that Innocent was motivated by selfish political considerations. His work is a refreshing antidote to the more hostile accounts of the great medieval pope.

Powell, James M., ed. *Innocent III: Vicar of Christ or Lord of the World?* Boston: D. C. Heath and Co., 1963. Part of Heath's Problems in European Civilization series, this indispensable work takes a historiographical approach. An introductory essay by Powell, in which he traces the widely conflicting historians' opinions regarding Innocent, is followed by excerpts from the works of Innocent's biographers and historians of the Church and the period. Especially important is Powell's inclusion of a section from the definitive biography, *Innocent III* (Paris: Librairie Hachette, 1905), by the great French historian Achille Luchaire, translated from the French by the editor.

Tierney, Brian. *The Crisis of Church and State, 1050-1300*. Englewood Cliffs, N.J.: Prentice Hall, 1964. A useful collection of documents pertaining to the medieval Church, accompanied by interpretation and a narrative by one of America's foremost historians of the Middle Ages and of the medieval Church.

J. Stewart Alverson

INNOCENT IV
Sinibaldo Fieschi

Born: c. 1180; Genoa
Died: December 7, 1254; Naples
Areas of Achievement: Religion and politics
Contribution: Throughout his pontificate, Innocent IV defended the temporal and spiritual authority of the Papacy and upheld its supremacy over secular rulers.

Early Life

Sinibaldo Fieschi, who would later take the name Innocent IV, was the sixth son of ten children of Hugo, Count of Lavagna, in northern Italy. The family was well connected in political and ecclesiastical circles, especially in Genoa, where Sinibaldo was born, probably around 1180. During the bitter and recurring struggles between the Holy Roman emperors and the pope, the Fieschi were generally regarded as being proimperial—an ironic situation in the light of Sinibaldo's later actions as pope.

Fieschi was an exceptionally intelligent and gifted young man, who showed particular aptitude for the law, especially church or canon law. He studied at Parma under his uncle, a bishop, and then at Bologna, where he became a master of canon law. He served as the canon at the cathedral in Genoa, and then at Parma, before being named Bishop of Albenga in 1225.

During the papacy of Honorius III (reigned 1216-1227), Fieschi was summoned to Rome to serve the pope. The next pontiff, Gregory IX (reigned 1227-1241), appointed Fieschi as his vice-chancellor, and elevated him to the position of cardinal priest of St. Lawrence in Lucina.

Fieschi's activities as jurist and diplomat were recognized by Gregory, himself a strong and able administrator. From 1235 through 1240, Fieschi was Governor of the March of Ancona, part of the secular territory under the rule of the Papacy. There he demonstrated his tough, realistic approach to government and politics, a foreshadowing of his later actions as pope.

During this time, Gregory IX and the Holy Roman Emperor, Frederick II of Sicily (1194-1250), were engaged in a deadly contest for supreme power, Frederick pointing to the precedent of the ancient empire, the pope claiming supreme authority through apostolic succession. Upon the death of Gregory in 1241, Frederick seized a number of cardinals, hoping to force them into electing a pope favorable to him. Their choice, Celestine IV, ruled for only seventeen days in 1241, and there followed an interregnum of almost two years. Finally, enough cardinals escaped from Frederick's control to hold a new election; their choice was Sinibaldo Fieschi, who was elected on June 25, 1243.

The new pope took the name Innocent IV, which was a telling choice, since the last pope to use that name, Innocent III, had brought the power of the Papacy to its greatest height, both spiritually and temporally. His successor was determined to do the same; this meant inevitable conflict with Frederick II.

The surviving portraits of Innocent IV show a clean-shaven, rather full-faced man with dark, intelligent eyes and a determined set to his mouth. Among his contemporaries he was noted for his intelligence, learning, and tenacity. He was attuned to the practical and administrative, rather than the spiritual or mystical, but was still a friend and protector of Saint Francis of Assisi. His overriding concern was to maintain the supreme position of the Church.

Life's Work

Frederick and Gregory had long been engaged in open hostilities, and the emperor hoped that Innocent would be more favorably disposed to his cause. Very soon after Innocent came to the papal throne, however, he made it clear that he would continue Gregory's policies of maintaining the supremacy of the Church.

The relationship between Innocent and Frederick quickly deteriorated, and within months of the election they were virtually at war. Repeated attempts at negotiation broke down, and in 1244 Frederick advanced on Rome hoping to take the pope hostage. Innocent slipped out of the city on June 28, 1244, and fled to Genoa with a number of his cardinals. In December, they moved to Lyons, technically a part of the empire, but actually ruled by its archbishop and protected by the French, who were officially neutral but favored the cause of the pope. Innocent thus became the first pope to receive official asylum outside Italy. He would not return to Italy until after the death of Frederick; for ten years, he remained in Lyons, making it the center of the Church's administration and the headquarters for his battle against the emperor.

Innocent summoned a general council of the Church. The Council of Lyons met from June 26 through July 12, 1245, and had a number of items on its official agenda: conversion of the Mongols, reunification of the Latin and Greek churches, and a new crusade to the Holy Land. These paled beside the dominant issue: the Church's struggle with Frederick. The emperor was accused of perjury, breach of the peace, sacrilege, and heresy. Although ably defended by the noted jurist Thaddeus of Suessa, Frederick was found guilty on all charges, excommunicated from the Church, and deposed from his throne. Innocent proclaimed a crusade against Frederick, and began raising money and support throughout Europe.

The rest of Innocent's pontificate was one long war with Frederick. The reaction from the emperor to his excommunication was muted (he had faced this action on several occasions before), but his deposition caused an all-out assault on the position of the Church: Within his domains he plundered churches and monasteries, dispersed monks, and abolished the clergy's exemptions from taxes and their authority over the laity. He sent messages to other rulers, urging them to join him in making a complete break between church and state, and so securing supreme power for the secular monarchs.

Frederick II was a remarkable man. Known to his contemporaries as *stupor mundi* (the wonder of the world), his kingdom in Sicily was one of the most advanced of its time, with a court that delighted in arts and learning. In addition to wearing the imperial crown, he was King of Jerusalem, having secured peace through negotiations with the Sultan of Egypt. His burning ambition was to establish the empire and its ruler as the supreme power in Europe, unbeholden in any way to the pope.

Supporters of the imperial cause were known as Ghibellines, a name taken from the territory of Waiblingen in Franconia, which had long been territory of Frederick's family, the Hohenstaufens. Their opponents, who favored the pope, were known as Guelphs. It was at this time that these two names first became widely used, especially in Italy, where the two factions tore the countryside apart in internecine struggles.

Frederick's position of separation of church and state is often regarded as the more modern or advanced theory, one which looked forward to the Renaissance and modern times. Innocent's quest for papal authority, on the other hand, is considered by many to be a throwback to the ideas of the Middle Ages. Actually, these views are possible only in hindsight. At the time, both Frederick and Innocent made compelling cases for their views.

After the Council of Lyons had deposed Frederick, Innocent maneuvered for the election of a new emperor. First, Henry Raspe, Landgrave of Thuringia, was selected, and following his death in 1247, William of Holland was chosen. This election helped weaken Frederick's power in the north, especially in conjunction with the tacit support of Louis IX of France, later canonized as Saint Louis.

It was in the south, in Italy, that the main struggle was conducted, with Frederick campaigning on the peninsula and Innocent directing events from Lyons. In 1248, Frederick suffered a serious defeat when the city of Parma revolted from his rule and was seized by the Guelphs. That undermined Frederick's position in northern Italy and forced him to spend the next two years repairing his fortunes. Innocent continued to favor rival kings and pretenders, and even encouraged disloyal nobles in an attempt to poison the emperor. Just as Frederick had begun to regain his position, he suddenly died on December 11, 1250, near Lucera. Innocent returned to Italy.

His victory, however, was not yet complete. Conrad IV, Frederick's son, assumed the crown of Sicily and aspired to the imperial throne. Sicily had once been a fief of the Papacy, and Innocent wished to restore that situation. He offered the crown to a number of persons, including Charles of Anjou in

France, England's Richard of Cornwall, and the English king Henry III. Henry accepted for his young son, Edmund, but on the death of Conrad in 1254, Frederick's illegitimate son Manfred took the crown and promised to recognize the pope as his overlord.

The peace was short-lived, for Manfred soon renounced his allegiance. Innocent wearily but determinedly began to prepare for yet another phase in this incessant struggle. He became ill, however, and he died on December 7, 1254, in Naples. He was buried in the cathedral in that city; on his tomb was carved the words, "He destroyed the serpent Frederick, Christ's enemy."

Summary

Many of the contemporaries of Innocent IV, as well as later historians, have seen him only as a pope intent upon securing and enlarging the secular power of the Papacy. Engaged in a ten-year struggle with Frederick, Innocent may have lowered the prestige and moral authority of the Church through his political manipulations, his demands for funds, and his unyielding tactics. In this view, Innocent IV was less a spiritual leader than a political one, and his concerns were with secular power and its preservation.

On the other hand, it must be noted that Innocent's actions were based on motives that were primarily theological and canonical. In his view, and as articulated by the Council of Lyons, the pope wielded an authority transcending that of secular monarchs, precisely because the pope's authority was spiritual: The vicar of Christ took precedence over the vicar of Caesar. As a practical matter, Innocent preferred that the pope rule as a sovereign in his own right, but he always insisted that the pope held ultimate authority over all secular monarchs.

Thus, the pope had the authority to depose kings and emperors. When Frederick was found guilty of exceptionally serious offenses, Innocent "translated" or removed the empire from him. Frederick, a firm believer in the divine right of kings, naturally rejected this and the pope's claims. There could never be the possibility of peace between the two great contenders.

Because of the preoccupation with political and military struggles during his pontificate, Innocent's other achievements have sometimes been ignored. Actually, he proved to be quite notable in several areas, and is regarded by church historians as important for a number of reasons other than his lengthy confrontation with Frederick.

Innocent made several serious efforts to reunify the Church, and some writers believe that had he not died at a critical moment in the talks, a breakthrough could well have been accomplished. Regardless of whether this is true, at least he made the most determined attempt at reunion during this entire period. More audacious and less successful were his efforts to have missionaries convert Kublai Khan and his Mongols to Christianity. While this aim may seem a fantasy today, it should be remembered that much of the eastern part of Europe had only recently been opened to Christianity, and there was reason to believe that the process of conversion might well continue.

It was in education and within the administration of the Church that Innocent made his most lasting impact. He was a learned man himself, and encouraged learning in others. During his exile in Lyons, he established schools for theology, canon law, and civil law. He founded a university at Piacenza, approved the establishment of another in Valencia, and granted to it and to the university at Toulouse the same rights as those enjoyed by the long-established University of Paris.

Innocent appointed outstanding and able men to the Curia and provided strong and capable government for the Church. One of his first but longest-lasting actions as pope took place in 1245, when he gave the cardinals the distinctive red hats which they wear today.

Finally, Innocent IV is remembered as an outstanding canon lawyer and scholar. He published three collections of his own judicial works as pope, and his most famous production is a commentary on the decretals (letters which contain a papal ruling, usually on a matter of canonical law) of his predecessor, Gregory IX.

An intelligent, practical man, Innocent defended the rights and authority of the Papacy through ten years of desperate struggle, and left the Church strong and vigorous upon his death.

Bibliography

Cheetham, Nicolas. *Keepers of the Keys: The Pope in History*. London: Macdonald, 1982. A brief but generally good overview of Innocent's pontificate, concentrating on the struggle with the Empire. Must be read in conjunction with other studies of Innocent IV and his times.

Gontard, Friedrich. *The Chair of Peter: A History of the Papacy*. Translated by A. J. Peeler and E. F Peeler. New York: Holt, Rinehart and Winston, 1964. Provides first-rate background on the dispute between Frederick II and the popes. The biography of Innocent IV includes notice of his many other accomplishments as well.

Hollis, Christopher, ed. *The Papacy: An Illustrated History from St. Peter to Paul VI*. New York: Macmillan, 1964. A solid, well-researched, and well-presented theory of the institution and the men who have served it. Gives a good sense of the spirit of the times in which Innocent IV lived.

Kelly, J. N. *The Oxford Dictionary of the Popes*. New York: Oxford University Press, 1986. Concise, filled with information, with a brisk narrative, this work is arranged chronologically. Readers would best be served by reading the biographies of the popes immediately preceding Innocent IV.

Mann, Horace K. *The Lives of the Popes in the Middle Ages*. Vol. 14, *Innocent IV, the Magnificent*. 2d ed. London: Kegan Paul, Trench, Trübner and Co., 1928. A highly positive life of the pope, drawing upon much original material in the church archives. The organization of the work is a bit rambling, and the sympathies of the author are obvious, but this is a valuable study.

Masson, Georgina. *Frederick II of Hohenstaufen.* London: Secker and Warburg, 1957. Since this biography has Frederick II as its hero, the treatment of Innocent IV is somewhat unfavorable; Masson sees him as a traditionalist "medieval" pope. Still, the information is valuable for an understanding of the period and the actors.

Walsh, Michael. *An Illustrated History of the Popes: St. Peter to John Paul II.* New York: St. Martin's Press, 1980. This work provides the reader with a clear and essential understanding of the philosophical differences in the struggle between Papacy and Empire. Includes a clear and generally favorable biography of Innocent IV that concentrates on his intellectual and theological accomplishments.

Michael Witkoski

SAINT IRENAEUS

Born: Between 120 and 140; probably Smyrna, Asia Minor
Died: 202; Lugdunum, Gaul (modern Lyons, France)
Area of Achievement: Religion
Contribution: As the first systematic theologian of the Christian church, Irenaeus laid the foundation for the development of church doctrine and effectively ended the threat that Gnosticism might substitute mysticism for faith in the resurrection of Christ.

Early Life

All that is known of the life of Saint Irenaeus derives from the *Historia ec-clesiastica* (before 300, revised 324; *Ecclesiastical History*, 1927-1928) of Eusebius, and from occasional comments made by Irenaeus himself in his works. Since Eusebius was less interested in biography than in recording the development and growth of the Church, he offers only a few tantalizing details. Irenaeus was born sometime after 120, in or near the trading city of Smyrna on the southwestern coast of Asia Minor, which was at that time part of the Roman Empire. His parents, who were probably Greeks, were also Christians.

In the century that had passed between the crucifixion of Christ and the birth of Irenaeus, the apostles of Jesus had spread His message throughout the Mediterranean world, and Peter and Paul, in particular, had transformed a minor Jewish sect into an established institution with churches, priests, and bishops throughout the Roman Empire. In fact, the rapid growth of the Church had frightened and angered the Roman authorities. Though most Christians tried to be good citizens of the empire, they refused to worship the old Roman gods; as a result, they were often regarded as traitors and were frequently persecuted. The early history of the Church is filled with heroic and miraculous tales of these martyrs. One of them was Polycarp, a renowned Christian teacher and bishop of Smyrna, who was burned at the stake in 156. As a young man, Irenaeus was apparently brought to Polycarp for instruction in the faith and was deeply influenced by him. Because Polycarp had known several of the apostles, he was able to transmit their teaching with a personal vigor. Irenaeus' belief that the books of the apostles accurately present the true message of Christ probably derived from Polycarp. In his later years, Irenaeus' memories of his old teacher were still so sharp that he could vividly describe Polycarp and the lessons he had taught. It may have been Polycarp who sent Irenaeus as a missionary to the city of Lugdunum in the Roman province of Gaul.

Life's Work

After his arrival at Lugdunum, Irenaeus was ordained as a priest by

Pothinus, the bishop, and he soon began a lifelong career of converting the pagans of southwestern Gaul to Christianity. In 161, however, the expansion of the Church was endangered by the appointment of a new Roman emperor, Marcus Aurelius. Though in many ways a very admirable man, the emperor saw the Christians as a threat to the strength and unity of the empire, and he initiated an especially cruel series of persecutions against them. In 177, it was the turn of the churches of Gaul, and it is said that the streets of Lugdunum ran with the blood of thousands of Christians who had been tortured and killed.

Fortunately, though, Irenaeus had been sent by the leaders of the Church on a mission to Pope Eleutherius at Rome, so he escaped the time of persecution. The purpose of the mission is somewhat unclear: Eusebius says only that Irenaeus acted as a mediator in a dispute over an issue related to Montanism, which was one of many heresies in the early Church.

Montanists, who took their name from their leader, Montanus, believed that they were under the direct influence of the Holy Spirit, and their worship services, like those of the nineteenth century Shakers, were often characterized by emotional outbursts and "speaking in tongues." Some modern authorities have stated that the Pope had become a Montanist and that Irenaeus tried to persuade Eleutherius to return to a more orthodox view; others assert the opposite—that Irenaeus tried to convince the Pope not to excommunicate the Montanists. In any case, while in Rome, Irenaeus saw that heresies were threatening to tear the Church apart, and he determined that he would do everything he could to eliminate them.

The problem of heresies had arisen, Irenaeus believed, because the Church had as yet no established body of doctrine accepted by all Christian churches. In the modern world, many Christian denominations coexist peacefully and are drawing closer together through the ecumenical movement. This degree of unity has only been possible because Christians of nearly every denomination acknowledge and share certain fundamental beliefs. In the early days of Christianity, however, these common beliefs had not yet been clearly or systematically articulated. Without an authoritative body of doctrine, Christians could be led astray by religious leaders who claimed to have a new revelation or a superior interpretation of the Gospels. While Montanism was a relatively minor, and even tolerable, deviation from orthodoxy, Christianity itself was but one of several competitors in a great theological contest occurring throughout the Roman world. Among the others were the pagan religions, such as that of the old Roman state gods. Despite attacks from Roman imperial authorities, Christianity had been making steady advances against these religions, because they offered no vision of eternal life. A much more dangerous threat to the Church came from the various sects called Gnostics.

Gnosticism comprised a vague system of ideas about the nature of the universe; these ideas predated Christianity and had spread throughout the Mediterranean world by the second century after Christ. A central feature of this system was a belief in the salvation of the soul through the acquisition of a *gnosis*, or secret knowledge. This mystical revelation of the origins and fate of the cosmos would be communicated by a "divine redeemer" to an elite group of individuals ready to receive it. Gnosticism had become popular, particularly among intellectuals, through a gradual process of absorbing elements of other religions, as well as some aspects of Greek philosophy. When Gnostics encountered Christianity, they attempted to integrate it into their system by identifying Christ as the "divine redeemer" and by accepting only those portions of the Scriptures that agreed with their views. In addition, they claimed to possess secret books that augmented and improved upon the Christian message. Often, Gnostics even called themselves Christians. Yet Christianity and Gnosticism were fundamentally opposed: For the Christian, salvation was achieved through faith in Christ's resurrection and cooperation with the will of God, rather than by gaining some body of esoteric knowledge.

Irenaeus had become especially distressed about Gnosticism during his visit to Rome because one of his childhood friends and fellow students of Polycarp, Florinus, had fallen under the influence of a Gnostic leader. Florinus had become a Roman consul and was thus in a position to do great harm to the Christians of the city. Irenaeus wrote his old friend a long letter explaining some of his objections to Gnosticism and reminding Florinus that Polycarp had taught them to adhere only to the teachings of the Church established by the apostles. Unfortunately, Irenaeus was unsuccessful in dissuading Florinus from leaving the Church.

In 178, after returning to Lugdunum, Irenaeus was elected to replace Pothinus, who had been martyred, as bishop, and he also continued his missionary work. In 190, he again acted as a mediator for a new pope, Victor I, in a dispute between the churches of the eastern and western parts of the empire over the determination of the proper date for the celebration of Easter. Irenaeus suggested that such differences were not particularly important and, in any case, would probably disappear eventually. Eusebius notes that through his efforts, Irenaeus certainly lived up to his name, which means "peacemaker."

The constant appearance of such controversies reinforced Irenaeus' belief that the Church must have a consistent body of doctrine. Throughout his career, the problem of heresy, and especially Gnosticism, continued to weigh on his mind. As a result, he wrote a large number of letters, treatises, and books, all building toward a clear exposition of orthodox Christianity and a refutation of heresy. Though most of these works have been lost, several Latin translations of Irenaeus' most important treatise, which was originally written in Greek, have been preserved. *Elenchou kai anatropes* is most commonly known by its Latin title, *Adversus haereses* (*Against Heresies*, 1869). The exact date of its composition is unknown; Irenaeus began the work as a response to a request from a friend for information, but he continued to expand on his ideas during a period of several years. It was finally completed by about 190.

Against Heresies is the most important exposition of Christian theology prior to the Council of Nicaea in 325. As the Greek title implies, it is both a detailed discussion of the doctrines and history of Gnosticism and a rigorous refutation of Gnostic theory. In the first section, Irenaeus demonstrates the inconsistencies and lack of logical coherence of Gnostic belief. The more important portion of the book, however, contains, in essence, the first complete and systematic articulation of Christian theology. This system is relatively familiar to every educated Christian, for it is, in essence, still the basis of Christian belief: There is only one God, of which Christ as the Son is a part. God created humanity in His image, and He created the world for man's use. Yet, through the sin of disobedience, humanity fell away from God into the clutches of Satan, an angel who had been envious of humanity. God therefore sent His Son so that humanity might be saved from damnation and ultimately rejoin God. Through the Holy Spirit, people are drawn into Christ's victory over Satan and can ultimately attain salvation.

To Irenaeus, the biblical tradition is the only source of faith; no additional "gnosis" is either necessary or compatible with biblical truth. The Old and New Testaments form a continuous unity with a clear purpose: The Old Testament predicts the coming of Christ, whose oral teachings were written down by the apostles to form the books of the New Testament. They, in turn, established the Church, which preserves and disseminates the pure Christian message of redemption through faith. This apostolic tradition, passed on through the succession of bishops of the Church, ensures the correct interpretation of Scripture against the perversions and distortions of the Gnostics and other heretics. Thus, Irenaeus not only refuted heresy; in doing so, he also became the first theologian to defend the Church as an institution.

It is not clear how *Against Heresies* became well-known, yet the fairly large number of Latin manuscripts containing it, a translation in Armenian made in the third or fourth century, and numerous fragments in other languages all testify to its popularity. The fact that Eusebius reproduced sizable portions of it in the *Ecclesiastical History* demonstrates that by the early fourth century it had become part of the standard canon of Christian dogma. Irenaeus' other works seem also to have been well-known to the ancients, yet he himself drops out of sight after about 190. A tradition which originated in the fourth or fifth century states that Irenaeus was martyred in 202 in the general persecution orchestrated by the emperor Septimus Severus, but there is no solid evidence for this. On the other hand, no evidence contradicts the story, and it would be entirely consistent with Irenaeus' devotion to his faith.

Summary

Irenaeus is regarded by most authorities as the most important Christian theologian of the second century, as well as the founder of Catholic doctrine. Chronologically, he stands at a critical point in the history of the Church. The apostles and their immediate disciples had founded Christian communities all over the Mediterranean world, but without any central doctrine or authority, some of these had begun to accept competing and very different theologies. The mystical-philosophical system of Gnosticism, as well as pagan religions newly arrived from the East, such as Mithraism, had begun to make inroads in Christian congregations, while Roman imperial policy sought to wipe out Christianity. Irenaeus' coherent expression of Christian belief and his justification of the Church as an institution provided exactly the impetus toward consolidation needed by Christians if their faith was to survive.

What was required was a concept of what "the Church" meant to Christians. In *Against Heresies*, Irenaeus provided such a definition. He stated, first, that the Church is guided by the "rule of faith," a statement of belief to which all Christians subscribe, and he offered a creed which differs very little from the Apostles' Creed used to this day. Because the creed was given by the apostles to the Church, it expresses a tradition descended directly from Christ's own disciples. Second, the churches were established by the apostles themselves, who appointed their successors, the bishops. Thus, an unbroken line of succession was established which guarantees the rule of faith and guards against any notions of "gnosis." If Jesus had been the "divine redeemer" of the Gnostics, surely He would have given the "gnosis" to His disciples, who would have passed it to their successors. Third, what the Church has instead of some secret knowledge is the Gospels of the apostles, who were eyewitnesses to Christ's resurrection, which itself fulfills the predictions of the Old Testament. Because many books claimed apostolic authorship, Irenaeus made an important contribution to the determination of what exactly would constitute the New Testament by limiting the Gospels to those written by Matthew, Mark, Luke, and John and using as accepted apostolic writings most of the other books now included in the New Testament.

In developing this threefold definition of the Church, Irenaeus not only debunked heresy but, much more important, also provided the average Christian with dependable means through which to attain salvation: the Church, its rule of faith, and the Scriptures. According to Irenaeus, these means may be trusted because the rule of faith is the essence of apostolic teaching, because the Church has descended directly from the apostles, and because the Scriptures were written by the apostles. With this explanation of the sources of Christian theology, Irenaeus provided the fundamental structure of Church doctrine and ended the early period of uncontrolled Christian diversity.

Bibliography

Coxe, Arthur Cleveland, ed. *The Ante-Nicene Fathers*. Vol. 1, *The Apostolic Fathers with Justin Martyr and Irenaeus*. New York: Charles Scribner's Sons, 1884. Reprint. Grand Rapids, Mich.: Wm. B. Eerdmans Publishing Co., 1967. Contains the only complete English translation of *Against Heresies* and fragments of other works by Irenaeus. Also includes a useful, if overly enthusiastic, introduction which explains the plan and ideas of *Against Heresies* and places the work in its historical context. The translations of works of the other church fathers who preceded Irenaeus also provide helpful material for comparison.

Eusebius. *The Ecclesiastical History*. Translated by Kirsopp Lake. 2 vols. Cambridge, Mass.: Harvard University Press, 1959. Eusebius is the primary source for nearly all information on the life of Irenaeus, and the *Ecclesiastical History* also reveals how other early Christian writers built upon his work. Eusebius is an essential source for early church history. For those who might also wish to read him in the original Greek, this Loeb Classical Library edition provides it on facing pages.

Hägglund, Bengt. *History of Theology*. Translated by Gene J. Lund. St. Louis, Mo.: Concordia Publishing House, 1968. Treats the history of Christian doctrine topically, within a chronological context. While possibly difficult for a reader with no background in theological or philosophical study, Hägglund is worth the effort. Provides the clearest explanation of Irenaeus' reasoning in *Against Heresies* and helps to show how it relates to that of other early theologians.

Quasten, J. *Patrology*. Vol. 1, *The Beginnings of Patristic Literature*. Utrecht, Netherlands: Spectrum Publishers, 1966. The most complete discussion of early Christian literature, including poetry and stories, in addition to theological works. Details on texts, translations, and history of editions of each work covered. Extensive bibliographies for each section. Includes excellent discussion of *Against Heresies* and other works by Irenaeus.

Schaff, Philip. *History of the Christian Church*. Vol. 2, *Ante-Nicene Christianity* A.D. *100-325*. New York: Charles Scribner's Sons, 1884. Reprint. Grand Rapids, Mich.: Wm. B. Eerdmans, 1967. Though extremely dated in both its approach and its style, Schaff's is perhaps the most complete history of the Church in English. This volume discusses in great detail all aspects of the growth and spread of Christianity and the development of the Church in the period covered. Contains helpful sections on early Christian heresies, including Montanism and Gnosticism, and a chapter on Irenaeus.

Tyson, Joseph B. *A Study of Early Christianity*. New York: Macmillan, 1973. An excellent and very readable discussion of the historical and theological context in which Christianity developed, early Christian literature, the varieties of early Christianity, and the place of Jesus Christ in the development of the Christian tradition. Includes an evaluation of the contribution of Irenaeus.

Wolfson, Henry Austryn. *The Philosophy of the Church Fathers*. Vol. 1, *Faith, Trinity, Incarnation*. Cambridge, Mass.: Harvard University Press, 1956. Wolfson is considered by many authorities to be the greatest historian of Christian philosophy. This massive study of the relationship of Greek philosophy and Old Testament theology to the development of Christian philosophy is extremely thorough and may therefore be more detailed than some readers need. Organized topically; thus, references to Irenaeus and his thought are scattered through several sections.

Thomas C. Schunk

ISAIAH

Born: c. 760 B.C.; Jerusalem, Judah
Died: c. 701-680 B.C.; probably Jerusalem, Judah
Area of Achievement: Religion
Contribution: Because of his clear grasp of political reality and the power of his poetic utterances, Isaiah is generally considered to be the greatest of the Old Testament prophets.

Early Life

Although there are sixty-six chapters in the book which bears his name, Isaiah, the great prophet of the eighth century B.C., probably wrote only the first thirty-nine of them. Stylistic and historical evidence indicates that the later chapters were written in the sixth century B.C., after the people of Judah had passed into the Babylonian captivity predicted at the end of Isaiah's own works. The author of chapters 40-55 is probably a single anonymous prophet, called for want of a name "Deutero-Isaiah" or "Second Isaiah." The final chapters, called "Trito-Isaiah" or "Third Isaiah," are probably by various hands. At any rate, although these later chapters are clearly in the tradition of Hebrew prophecy, they have no other claim to the name of the great prophet Isaiah. In actuality, they may have been attached to the earlier chapters simply for the sake of convenience.

Isaiah was the son of Amoz; evidently he was a native of Jerusalem. Beyond that, very little is known about the life of Isaiah before he was called to prophesy around 742 B.C. Because he obviously had access to the inner area of the Temple, some scholars conjecture that Isaiah was a member of a priestly family and may even have studied for the priesthood himself. As a young man, he might have been a "wisdom teacher." Certainly he was familiar with the wisdom literature which was so much a part of Hebrew education.

The tone of Isaiah's poetry suggests that he was of aristocratic background. His pronouncements regarding specific rulers and councillors, his comments on statecraft, and his exposures of international intrigues all reveal the knowledge of an insider. Although the prophet Isaiah, like Amos and Hosea, forecast doom if the people of Judah did not reform, his warnings were often addressed to the ruling classes in words which evidence firsthand knowledge of their self-centered, luxurious, and corrupt way of life.

Even if Isaiah had not been an insider in court circles, he would have attracted attention because of his intellectual brilliance and his poetic genius. His social status, however, gave him an additional sense of security in his dealings with councillors and with kings. Even when God Himself spoke to him, Isaiah did not hide behind false modesty but volunteered with confidence for whatever mission God had in mind. It is undoubtedly this confidence which sustained him when God sent him out naked and barefoot, supposedly for three years, in order to attract the attention of his countrymen to the predictions which they had ignored.

Aside from this unusual episode, Isaiah seems to have lived a godly yet normal life. He was married—whether before or after his call is not clear. He had two sons, probably after he began to prophesy, since their names reveal his preoccupation with God's intentions toward his people. He maintained his court contacts, at times being called upon to advise the king.

It is clear that when Isaiah became the prophet of Judah, he did not emerge wild-eyed from the wilderness, nor did he change except in the intensity of his dedication. The rulers of Judah could not complain that God had not given them every chance to turn to Him; He had sent to them a prophet who spoke their language and understood their problems, a moderate, rational man who insisted only that private and public life should be subject to the will of God.

Life's Work

In the sixth chapter of Isaiah, the prophet describes the experience which directed his life. The moment is dated as falling within the year of King Uzziah's death (probably 742 B.C.). After seeing a vision of God enthroned, surrounded by angels, Isaiah's first reaction was the sense of his own uncleanness in the sight of God. After being forgiven, he heard God ask, "Whom shall I send? Who will go for Me?" Isaiah's immediate response was to utter the well-known words, "Here am I! Send me!"

During the next four decades, Isaiah took his advice, his satirical comments, his diatribes, and his predictions of doom to the people of Judah, later expanding his warnings to address the neighboring Jewish state of Israel, as well as pagan lands ranging from Egypt and Syria to powerful Assyria. Because so many manuscripts were lost after the fall of Jerusalem to Babylon, scholars cannot be certain of the chronology of Isaiah's thirty-nine chapters. Specific historical references date some segments, however, while others reflect themes which clearly preoccupied the prophet throughout his life.

Shortly after Isaiah began his life of prophecy, Judah was threatened by the allies Israel and Syria, who had joined forces in the hope of conquering Judah and placing a puppet on the throne and eventually defeating the powerful nation of Assyria. Isaiah was troubled by the fact that Israel's intended puppet was not of the house of David; furthermore, he was convinced that Assyria was in the ascendancy with the permission of God. Thus, on both counts Israel and Syria were defying God.

Given these convictions, it fell to Isaiah to convince King Ahaz that God would protect Judah. Taking his son Shear-jashub (whose name means "a remnant will return"), Isaiah went to meet Ahaz, carrying the reassurances that the king needed. Later, at the command of God, Isaiah fathered a second son, whom he named Maher-shalal-hash-baz (the spoil comes, the prey hurries). Isaiah then explained to the nervous king that the baby's name had been assigned by God, who thereby promised that before the child learned to speak, the defiant countries would be despoiled by Assyria.

Such messages from God, dictating specific directions which Judah's foreign policy should take in troubled times, evidently alternated with advice in domestic matters. God's protection could only be depended upon if Judah obeyed His moral laws. At court, in the streets of Jerusalem, and on the outlying estates of the wealthy, Isaiah saw the real danger to Judah. In Isaiah 5:8-24, he points out the inner rottenness of his people: the atheism and drunkenness of its men, the triviality and extravagance of its women, the smugness and greed of its elite. In the country, the great landholders extended their properties, squeezing out the poor; in Jerusalem, corrupt judges dispensed injustice; at the Temple, priests offered worthless sacrifices which could not substitute for righteousness; and at court, great officials served their own interests. Such a society, the prophet warned, would not be protected by the God to whom Judah gave lip service.

In chapters 10 and 11, Isaiah expresses his preoccupation with a later threat, that of Assyria, which was no longer threatened by alliances against it. Realizing its own vulnerable position, Judah was fearful. Again, Isaiah warned that military might and political stratagem would be useless; only God's intervention on behalf of a righteous people could save Judah.

The power of Isaiah's God, however, was not limited to dealings with Judah or even Israel. Isaiah's warnings were addressed to Moab and Samaria, to Egypt, and even to Assyria itself, a nation which he saw as the tool of God, currently powerful but destined eventually to be destroyed. In 711, Isaiah walked naked and barefoot through the streets of Jerusalem in order to point out the approaching fall of Egypt, which had betrayed a confederate to the Assyrians (Isa. 20:1-6). Not only their unrighteous cowardice but also their defiance of the governing plan of God had doomed the Egyptians.

For a country as defenseless as Judah, Isaiah's warnings about defying Assyria made sense. In 703, he advised King Hezekiah against sending an embassy to Egypt in order to plot against Assyria, which clearly would constitute a rejection of common sense as well as of God's plan (Isa. 30:1-7). In 701, the Assyrian king Sennacherib and his army were at the gates of Jerusalem. Isaiah urged Hezekiah to depend on patience and righteousness, not the Judaeans' inferior military forces, as the appropriate defense. When Sennacherib's men suddenly began to die, perhaps because of a plague, he withdrew, and Isaiah's God was appropriately credited with having saved the city.

Isaiah's role at Hezekiah's court is illustrated in chapter 38. Sick and believing that he was about to die, Hezekiah was visited by Isaiah, who brought a message from God: Put your spiritual house in order, and you shall be spared. The repentant king turned to God and was promised another fifteen years of life. Still, death would at last come to him, as it would to Jerusalem itself. Isaiah's portion of the book concludes with a prophecy of the Babylonian conquest and captivity, with the promise—reflected in the name of Isaiah's first son—that a remnant would return.

Isaiah's thirty-nine chapters contain no specific references to events in his life after about 700 B.C. Whether he continued his work into old age, whether he ceased to prophesy, or whether there is truth to the legend that he was cut in two during the reign of Manasseh is not known. It is ironic that this man who spent his life transmitting God's directions to the heads of nations should disappear so silently from the stage of history.

Summary

Isaiah is considered the greatest of the Old Testament prophets not only because of the fact that so much of his work remains but also because of his stature as a poet and as a representative of the God he served.

Unlike prophets of a humbler station, Isaiah could speak to the aristocracy as one of them. He could rebuke the daughters of Zion for their frivolity with references to their tinkling anklets; he could rebuke the great landowners by detailing their greedy appropriation of land. No pretense, no hypocrisy was proof against his penetrating eye; no foreign intrigue was too complicated for his mind to fathom.

The exactness of Isaiah's perception is one of the qualities which makes him a great writer. It is not known whether all of his work was in poetic form or whether segments were deliberately written in prose. It is undisputed, however, that all of his work is evidence of a remarkable talent. His style is so individual that scholars have been able to separate his own words from later additions with a surprising degree of agreement.

Although Isaiah's words continue to be significant to the faiths which depend upon the Judaic tradition, they would be far less significant if they had come from a lesser person. Even more important than the intellectual brilliance and the poetic genius of Isaiah is the quality of his obedience to God. When God asked who would go as His messenger, without argument his greatest prophet answered, "Here am I. Send me."

Bibliography

Church, Brooke Peters. *The Private Lives of the Prophets and the Times in Which They Lived*. New York: Rinehart, 1953. Though admittedly conjectural, a plausible reconstruction of the life of Isaiah based on a scholarly study of the chapters generally attributed to the prophet. Church differs from other commentators in rejecting the usual division of the book into three parts and insisting that only forty-two excerpts can be attributed to Isaiah with any degree of certainty. Despite this skepticism about the text, the work is imaginative, readable, and useful.

Cohon, Beryl D. *The Prophets: Their Personalities and Teachings*. New York: Charles Scribner's Sons, 1939. In three chapters, the author treats the three separate bodies of work into which the Book of Isaiah is usually divided. Using fairly lengthy excerpts from the text, Cohon reconstructs the historical setting of the prophecies in prose which sometimes has almost the force of fiction.

Herbert, A. S. *The Book of the Prophet Isaiah 1-39*. Cambridge: Cambridge University Press, 1973. Part of the Cambridge Bible Commentary on the New English Bible. A passage-by-passage explanation of the text. Clear and uncluttered. Contains a useful chronological table of events in the eighth century B.C., as well as a number of maps.

——————. *The Book of the Prophet Isaiah 40-66*. Cambridge: Cambridge University Press, 1975. This installment in the Cambridge Bible Commentary on the New English Bible deals with Deutero-Isaiah and Trito-Isaiah, the chapters attributed to writers of the sixth century B.C. Helpful maps, as well as a table of historical events from 626 B.C. to approximately 500 B.C.

Kraeling, Emil G. *The Prophets*. Chicago: Rand McNally and Co., 1969. A scholarly work dealing with the prophets in chronological order. Each Isaiah segment is handled in the historically appropriate section of the book. The emphasis is on the prophets' response to external and internal pressures. Begins with a convenient chronology.

Phillips, J. B. *Four Prophets, Amos, Hosea, First Isaiah, Micah: A Modern Translation from the Hebrew*. New York: Macmillan, 1963. The famous translator of the New Testament here has cast four prophetic books in modern poetic form. The translation of First Isaiah ceases after chapter 35 because of the close parallel between chapters 36-39 and 2 Kings.

Scott, R. B. Y. *The Relevance of the Prophets*. New York: Macmillan, 1944. An excellent background study, ranging in subject matter from the definition of prophecy and the significance of prophecy in Hebrew life to the relation of the prophets to society, to history, and to conventional religious structures. The final chapter, which bears the title of the book, is a lucid argument for the importance of the Old Testament prophets in the modern world.

Smith, J. M. Powis. *The Prophets and Their Times*. Chicago: University of Chicago Press, 1925, 2d ed. 1941. An important study by a great biblical scholar. Places the prophets within their historical periods. Although no single prophet is treated at length, the book is extremely valuable as a panoramic re-creation of prophetic times.

Rosemary M. Canfield-Reisman

SAINT ISIDORE OF SEVILLE

Born: c. 560; Seville, Spain
Died: April 4, 636; Seville, Spain
Areas of Achievement: Education, literature, and religion
Contribution: Through his defense of education, Isidore of Seville not only preserved the classical traditions of his people but also helped to forge a national identity.

Early Life

Isidore, the second son of prominent Hispano-Roman parents, was born in the city of Seville, where his parents had fled after the sacking of their native Cartagena by the Arian Visigoths. All the children in Isidore's strongly orthodox family committed themselves to service in the Church: The only daughter, Florentina, entered a convent, and the three sons, Leander, Isidore, and Fulgentius, became priests. After the early death of their parents, Severian and Theodora, Leander, already a priest, assumed complete responsibility for the education of his sister and brothers and enrolled them in convent and monastery schools. Fulgentius, the youngest, became Bishop of Écija, while both Leander and Isidore became archbishops of the See of Seville and, later, primates of all Spain. Both also were canonized.

Although Isidore's entire life was dedicated to the Church, the world around him was definitely not a Catholic one, nor even predominantly Christian. The Roman Empire in the West had been divided into many Germanic kingdoms. In the old Roman territory of Hispania, it was the Visigoths, perhaps the most Romanized of the Germanic peoples, who finally became the dominant power. By the time of Isidore's birth, they had managed to subdue most of the peninsula except for a small enclave of the Suevi in Galicia, the Byzantines in the south and east, and the Basques, who remained independent in their mountain strongholds. This military success was only a beginning. The Visigoths, in order to achieve their goal of a united Hispanic state, faced formidable religious and cultural differences. They were the ruling class, but their Hispano-Roman subjects, who greatly outnumbered them, considered them to be little more than heretics and barbarians.

After much internecine warfare, including a civil war among members of the royal family itself, the religious question was at least superficially settled by the conversion of Recared to orthodox Catholicism in 587. This act, which did much to mitigate Hispano-Roman tensions, was brought about largely through the efforts of Leander, Isidore's brother and Bishop of Seville. Although completely disparate in outlook and heritage, Leander and Recared did share one ideal: a unified Spain. It was a concept that Leander was to pass on to Isidore, who was not only his brother but also his fervent disciple. Therefore, after his brother's death, it was only natural for Isidore to succeed to the See of Seville and take his place as the spokesman of the orthodox Christian tradition. Although little is known of Isidore's early life, his ascension to the most influential religious post in Hispania brought Isidore to the forefront of his country's history. His desire was not only to record that history but also to alter its direction.

Life's Work

Isidore's main achievements were his defense of education and his preservation of knowledge that he gleaned from the writings of ancient pagan authors and of the church fathers. His concepts were seldom abstract or esoteric. He used his learning, influence, and great writing skill to further specific practical ends. He was perhaps the preeminent scholar of his time.

Isidore's first major achievement after his ordination as a bishop was the reorganization of the educational system, which the Church controlled. At the Fourth Council of Toledo in 633, he ordered that schools specializing in the liberal arts be set up in the cities of all dioceses of Hispania and that the course of study for priests be formalized and strengthened. Since the Catholic clergy represented or influenced almost all literate people, this decree brought about a rise in the standard of literacy for the entire peninsula. Isidore himself wrote many treatises outlining specifically the duties and obligations of the clergy as well as several commentaries on the Old and New Testaments. Isidore's also was the guiding hand in the much-needed revision and standardization of the old Spanish liturgy.

The bishop then turned from the education of the common man to the education of princes. After Leander's death, Isidore became the adviser, both spiritual and political, to the Visigothic monarchs. Notwithstanding his Hispano-Roman descent, Isidore considered himself to be a Spaniard. He admired the Visigoths for their courage and driving energy in unifying his beloved country. At the beginning of his historical chronicle of the Goths, there are the famous words of his "De laude Hispaniae" (in praise of Spain): "Of all the lands that extend from the west to India, thou are the fairest, oh sacred Hispania, ever-fecund mother of princes and peoples, rightful queen of all the provinces, from whom west and east draw their light."

A great nation needed a just and wise king, and to Isidore fell the task of shaping the Visigothic concept of kingship and of civilizing its barbaric nature. He wrote that a king must not only defend his people against outside attack but also serve as an example by his ethical Christian conduct. Isidore even went so far as to insist that a king who ruled unjustly had surrendered all rights of kingship, and therefore his people had the moral obligation to overthrow him. The bishop also advocated hereditary monarchy in order to ensure political stability. Many of his concepts were far ahead of his time. Any attempt by the Visigoths to abandon their old elective system of leadership generally ended in bloodshed. It is interesting to note, however, that it is not to the Visigothic reality but to Isidore's idealized rendering of that reality that later generations would turn in the quest for unity against the Moors.

In legal matters, Isidore was more immediately successful. One of the stumbling blocks to the true unification of the Hispano-Roman and Gothic peoples of the peninsula had been the lack of a uniform code of law. Finally, about 654, Recceswinth promulgated the first binding body of laws for the entire state, a code influenced significantly by Isidore's writings. The Liber Judiciorum, better known as the Fuero Juzgo, was to serve as the law of the land until modern times. So important had Isidore's contribution been that later generations adopted the custom of taking oaths in both criminal and civil cases on the saint's shrine in León. It was believed that any perjury would cause the death of the miscreant within the year.

Isidore also served as the Visigothic historian, producing an informative chronicle entitled *Historia de regibus Gothorum, Vandalorum, et Suevorum* (624; *History of the Kings of the Goths, Vandals, and Suevi*, 1966). He wrote many religious, scientific, and historical studies, but it was his last and most comprehensive work, *Etymologiae* (partial translation in *An Encyclopedist of the Dark Ages*, 1912), which earned for him lasting fame and the title of "Egregious Doctor." Edited and divided into twenty books after his death by his friend and former student, Braulio, Bishop of Saragossa, *Etymologiae* is a summarization of all the knowledge available to Isidore in the seventh century. The first of the medieval encyclopedias, it attempted to synthesize classical Greco-Roman traditions with Christian morals and doctrine. The subjects range from cosmology, language study, anthropology, the liberal arts, psychology, medicine, and shipbuilding to the planning of country gardens. *Etymologiae* was the standard reference work of its time; one thousand medieval manuscripts still survive, and the actual number was exceeded only by copies of the Vulgate Bible. Much of the information recorded in the encyclopedia is now only of intellectual curiosity. Nevertheless, it served as a beacon of classical learning throughout many centuries of scholarly twilight and, in its painstaking attention to detail and observation, provided a base upon which various disciplines could be built. For example, Isidore's discussion regarding medicines is remarkably free from magical or religious influences; thus, he continued the tradition of medicine as a scientific discipline and transmitted and expanded a universal medical terminology which could be understood by all of its practitioners.

Isidore died on April 4, 636. The Visigothic kingdom which he described and defended was to vanish soon after with the coming of the Moors in 711. His fame and influence, however, continued to grow. He was canonized by the Church, and because of his ardent support of Spanish nationalism, he became a symbol of the Reconquest. During the Middle Ages, the liberation of his remains from Muslim territory became a cause célèbre. Finally, in 1063, his tomb became a shrine on the pilgrim road to Santiago de Compostela. Word of his miracles spread all through Europe. Visions of Saint Isidore before a battle were said to ensure victory for the Christian forces. A Leonese legend tells how before the important Battle of Las Navas (1212), El Cid Campeador himself knocked on the door of the shrine to summon Saint Isidore to the fight.

Isidore's fame as a scholar also increased with Luke, Bishop of Tuy's biography, compiled centuries after the saint's death. Dante numbered him among the great theologians, and, in 1722, Isidore was declared a Doctor of the Church by Pope Innocent XIII. His feast day is April 4, but in Spain it has traditionally been celebrated on July 25 or December 30.

Summary

There are, in reality, two Isidores: the pragmatic scholar and educator and the legendary warrior-saint. Both personae converge in his influential role as a developer of Spanish culture and identity. His countrymen were to draw on his vision of a unified Spain as a rallying point in later battles for national identity. He was ahead of his time in understanding the value of education as a tool for forging cultural union; it was this awareness that motivated him to compile and make accessible the information necessary for a literate society.

A strong believer in tradition, Isidore wished to preserve the great classical heritage of learning which he had received from his Hispano-Roman forebears. Although not original in content, his encyclopedic writings achieved this purpose and became part of the foundation for the new intellectual awakening of the Renaissance.

Isidore's true originality lay in his concept of welding the contemporary to the classical. His history of the Visigoths offers valuable insight into his times, an era which he himself did so much to shape. He was the principal adviser to several kings and tried to use his prestige and scholarship to elevate Visigothic culture. Drawing on tales of the great leaders of Rome, he created the ideal of the perfect Christian prince. Though the Visigothic kings proved intractable, Isidore's ideas served as the basis for numerous future philosophical writings on the essence of kingship and power.

Isidore's influence on daily affairs was enormous. He revised the educational system of his jurisdiction, instituted clerical reform, and insisted on the standardization of religious texts. This influence was not limited to his own time and place. With the adoption of the Fuero Juzgo, the official law of all Christian Spain, Isidore's precepts on law and justice held sway until the twentieth century.

Little is known of Isidore's personality. By the testimony of his own words, it is evident that he could be ruthless and cynical. He exercised almost absolute control over the Spanish church and at times was unforgiving of religious nonconformity. In cultural and scientific fields, however, Isidore exhibited a rare tolerance and openness which merit praise.

Bibliography
Isidore of Seville. *History of the Kings of the Goths, Vandals, and Suevi.*
  Translated with an introduction by Guido Donini and Gordon B. Ford, Jr.
  Leiden, Netherlands: E. J. Brill, 1966, 2d rev. ed. 1970. A helpful English
  translation of Isidore's chronicle of the Visigothic monarchy.
_____. *The Medical Writings.* Translated and edited with an intro-
  duction and commentary by William D. Sharpe. *Transactions of the Ameri-
  can Philosophical Society* 54, no. 2 (1964): 3-75. Sharpe, a physician, has
  compiled and translated portions of the *Etymologiae* having to do with
  medicine. He presents useful background information on Isidore's sources.
Lear, F. S. "The Public Law of the Visigothic Code." *Speculum* 26 (1951): 1-
  23. Analysis of the law code which Isidore influenced so greatly.
O'Callaghan, Joseph F. *A History of Medieval Spain.* Ithaca, N.Y.: Cornell
  University Press, 1975. Contains a chapter on the Visigothic era with special emphasis on the drive for unity.
Starkie, Walter. *The Road to Santiago: Pilgrims of St. James.* New York:
  E. P. Dutton, 1957. Reprint. Berkeley: University of California Press,
  1965. Very readable, impressionistic description of Saint Isidore's shrine
  and legends associated with it.
Thompson, E. A. *The Goths in Spain.* Oxford: Clarendon Press, 1969. A
  good general history of the rise and collapse of the Visigoth empire.

Charlene E. Suscavage

ITZCÓATL

Born: c. 1382; place unknown
Died: 1440; probably Tenochtitlán (modern Mexico City)
Area of Achievement: Government
Contribution: As the founder of the Mexican state, Itzcóatl was largely responsible both for the strengths which enabled it to survive until the Spanish conquest and for the weaknesses which contributed to its destruction.

Early Life

Itzcóatl (obsidian serpent) was the illegitimate son of Acamapichtli, the first king of the Mexica, the Aztec tribe that founded Tenochtitlán and came in time to dominate central Mexico. His mother was a seller of herbs or vegetables and apparently a slave, but Itzcóatl distinguished himself as a military commander and statesman before he himself became king of the Mexica about 1427. Except for the remarkable fact of his parentage, nothing is known of his personal life, and his public life can only be understood in relation to the political development of Mexico in his lifetime.

The early struggle of the Mexica to establish themselves in the Valley of Mexico and to achieve hegemony over its various tribes must not be understood as a war among nations but as a conflict of city-states which fought each other in loose alliances. The arena of this struggle was a relatively small area in the vicinity of modern Mexico City, the heart of which is the site of Tenochtitlán.

The various chronicles of early Mexican history, all written from memory after the Spanish conquest, do not agree as to dates. The Mexica entered the Valley of Mexico from the north in the latter half of the thirteenth century, the last Náhuatl-speaking tribe to make this migration. They were in their beginnings a poor tribe of nomads, without the complex social and political structure or the elaborate system of religious ritual which they developed later. When they arrived, the valley was dominated by Azcapotzalco, the premier Tepenecan city on the west shore of Lake Texcoco; Tlacopán, on the mainland due west of Tenochtitlán; Coyoacán, on the southwest shore; Xochimilco and Chalco, in the south; and Texcoco, the intellectual center of the valley and the dominant power east of the lake. The Mexica, possessing no lands, indeed no resources but the prowess of their warriors, enlisted as mercenaries in the employ of other cities. In the early fourteenth century, one faction of the Mexica, defeated by the enemies of their employers, fled to a swampy area in the lake and began the slow process of building up the land upon which they established the town of Tlatilulco. Later—in 1369, according to one account—another faction, also forced to flee from their mainland enemies, established a second town nearby: Tenochtitlán.

In their wanderings and their early years in central Mexico, the basic organs of civil and military management of the Mexica were the clans, each of which was governed by its own council of elders, a headman, and a "speaker" who represented it in the council of the Mexica. After the founding of Tenochtitlán, however, a steady process of centralization began, and by 1375, when Acamapichtli was chosen the first king of Tenochtitlán, this process was virtually complete, so that a great gulf had opened between the council and the commoners, with real power concentrated in the hands of an oligarchy composed of a few great families who dominated the council and monopolized all administrative and religious power.

Acamapichtli's successor was his son, Huitzilhuitl, who became king in 1404, married the daughter of Tezozómoc, the king of Azcapotzalco, and was succeeded in 1416 by his ten-year-old son Chimalpopoca, during whose reign the inevitable conflict with Azcapotzalco came to a head.

Life's Work

Itzcóatl may have been speaker under Huitzilhuitl, and he certainly filled this post during the reign of Chimalpopoca. In that role, he astutely and cautiously extended the trade and influence of the Mexica to the shore towns while avoiding an open clash with Azcapotzalco. In 1426, Tezozómoc of Azcapotzalco died and was succeeded by his son Maxtla, who was determined to end the rivalry of the upstart Mexica and, according to one account, arranged the murder of Chimalpopoca in 1427.

Another account, however, suggests that Chimalpopoca was murdered by the war faction in the Mexican council. According to this story, the Mexica demanded materials from Tezozómoc for building a causeway to bring water from Chapultepec, on the west shore of the lake. The allies of Azcapotzalco, realizing that such a causeway would strengthen Tenochtitlán, resisted this demand and determined to destroy the Mexica. They cut off all trade and other contact with Tenochtitlán, and when Tezozómoc died, Chimalpopoca, no longer able to count upon his grandfather's protection, was murdered. In any case, the council of the Mexica elected Itzcóatl as his successor. Itzcóatl was recognized for both his bravery and his prudence; in fact, one source gives credit to him as a military leader and an important administrator as early as 1407. Another says that he had commanded armies for three decades. These achievements probably account for his election in spite of his illegitimacy. He was at that time about forty-five years old.

Itzcóatl's situation when he became king was precarious because of the forces arrayed against the Mexica, but he had strong allies in Tlacopán and in the king of Texcoco, his nephew Nezahualcóyotl, who was putting together an alliance of all the cities east of the lake. It was also at this time that Itzcóatl succeeded, perhaps by marriage to a princess of the other Mexican city in the lake, Tlatilulco, in achieving an alliance which led eventually to the merger of the two cities. Itzcóatl's further achievement of a triple alliance of Tenochtitlán-Tlatilulco with Texcoco and Tlacopán was perhaps his greatest political achievement, and it survived, with Tenochtitlán the dominant force in the alliance, until the Spanish conquest.

In 1428, Itzcóatl gathered the council in Tenochtitlán and demanded war against Azcapotzalco and its west-shore allies. Strong arguments were made in the council for peace, but the military party had everything to gain from a war. The power of the state, in the hands of the oligarchy, had been partially thwarted by certain elements in Tenochtitlán society which would be rendered powerless by a major victory against the city's enemies. In fact, the accounts which blame the Tepanecs for the death of Chimalpopoca may have been written to justify the war with them. In any case, Itzcóatl, encouraged by his nephew Tlacaelel, who shared his sense of the destiny of the Mexica to rule all the Valley of Mexico, prevailed in the council. A peace proposal was sent to Azcapotzalco, combined with a threat of war if it were not accepted. Its rejection was followed by a Tepanecan attack across the causeway from the mainland. Nezahualcóyotl had brought his Texcoco warriors to Tenochtitlán, and the Mexica of Tenochtitlán and Tlatilulco were united. As a result, the Tepanecs, completely routed, fled to Azcapotzalco, which fell to the allies after a siege of four months. It was completely destroyed, and the few of its population who did not escape were exterminated or enslaved.

In 1429-1430, the Mexica repaid Nezahualcóyotl for his support by helping him recover control of those cities east of the lake which had rebelled with the encouragement of Azcapotzalco. In 1430, Tenochtitlán asked—or demanded—that Xochimilco provide stone and logs for the expansion of the temple of Huitzilopochtli. When these materials were denied, Xochimilco was blockaded and eventually conquered. Its lands were distributed among Itzcóatl's closest supporters, and Xochimilco agreed to provide the materials and the slave labor to build a great causeway to join Tenochtitlán to the mainland from the south. A year later, Coyoacán broke off trading relations with Tenochtitlán, in effect declaring war, and was subsequently conquered. In all, according to one account (the Codex Mendoza), Itzcóatl is credited with the conquest of twenty-four towns.

In 1431, Nezahualcóyotl was crowned emperor of the three-city league, but events had already set in motion the process by which Tenochtitlán and its kings would be the dominant power in Mexico.

For a period of five or six years after the war, the slave laborers and the tribute won in the war were used to erect palaces, expand Tenochtitlán-Tlatilulco, build canals within the city, and erect greater shrines to the gods. In the center of Tenochtitlán was built the monumental shrine to the god of war, Huitzilopochtli.

The primary result of the war was the total reorganization of Mexican society. Itzcóatl created twenty-one titles for the greatest families and established a system of succession that endured until the Spanish conquest: When a king was chosen, four brothers or other close relatives were elevated to special titles, and one of them was named to be his successor. The conquered agricultural lands were distributed to a relatively small number of Mexican leaders, thus magnifying the power of the oligarchy; political power was concentrated in the hands of the king, the speaker, and the council; and the power of the military class was considerably enhanced. Above all, the cult of Huitzilopochtli, the god of war whose demands for sacrificial victims, as interpreted by the priests, were virtually insatiable, was greatly augmented. The result, in other words, was profoundly ideological—the dictatorship of the oligarchy supported by the warrior elite was justified by a constant state of war, and warfare was required by the constant need for sacrificial victims. Political, military, and religious concerns were supportive of one another.

Several accounts maintain that before the attack on Azcapotzalco the commoners were fearful of the consequences of a possible defeat. According to one account, Itzcóatl is supposed to have offered a wager to them: If the warriors failed, the king and his council would permit themselves to be killed and eaten. The commoners, in turn, agreed that if the warriors were victorious, they would accept a state of virtual slavery. This strange wager would seem, however, to be pure propaganda written after the event. In fact, most accounts agree that after the Mexica had won the Tepanec War, Itzcóatl ordered the destruction of existing accounts of the Mexican past and their rewriting to emphasize the grandeur and the justice of Tenochtitlán's rise to power. Apparently, the reforms also included a manipulation of education and of art and literature in the service of the state: Itzcóatl was the first king of Tenochtitlán to have his likeness carved in stone. Clearly, the most appalling aspect of the ideological reforms of Itzcóatl's reign was the sharp increase in the magnitude of human sacrifice.

Most accounts agree that Itzcóatl died in 1440 and was succeeded by Montezuma I, who expanded the Aztec Empire by using the methods and the ideology that his predecessor had developed.

Summary

Itzcóatl must be credited with the foundation of the Mexican monarchy, which became the dominant power in central Mexico under the rule of his successors, and he established the political and military institutions, including the political alliance with Texcoco and Tlacopán, that made possible the Aztec Empire, which endured until the arrival of the Spanish in 1519. The human cost of this achievement, however, was outrageously high.

The state which Itzcóatl was primarily responsible for creating existed for its own glorification. Even European monarchies of the time were less powerful in their control of their people—if only because they were subject to the disapproval of the Church—than was the oligarchy to which Itzcóatl gave power. Indeed, Itzcóatl, with the aid of like-minded individuals, created the kind of absolute totalitarian state which Europe did not suffer until the twentieth century. The oligarchy controlled the education of young nobles, who were taught to serve the state, and literary and artistic culture was dedicated to the glorification of the state. Furthermore, the destruction of historical chronicles and rewriting of history to make the state and its keepers the absolute political reality was something unknown in Europe until modern times.

Itzcóatl's use of the cult of Huitzilopochtli for political ends, considering that it was a cult that demanded human sacrifice, is the most extraordinary aspect of the totalitarian system he created. Admittedly, the numbers of sacrificial victims were inflated by Spanish chroniclers, but even when those numbers are reduced, the hard kernel of historical fact still horrifies. This religion of blood was put to the service of the state, and the state engaged in warfare to serve the religion. This inevitably vicious circle produced slaughter too appalling to condone, whatever the numbers. Certainly, Itzcóatl, though he had the encouragement of his colleagues, must receive the largest share of the blame. After the conquest of Azcapotzalco, he issued an edict proclaiming Huitzilopochtli the supreme god of the Mexica, and after the conquest of Coyoacán, he issued another which defined the divine mission of the Mexica as bringing all the nations of the world to the worship of that god by force of arms. The "flower wars" that provided victims for the priest-executioners of Tenochtitlán during the eighty years after Itzcóatl's death were the terrible legacy of his reign, and they contributed more than anything else to the destruction of the state which he created, for the Spanish were welcomed by the enemies those wars produced.

Considering all this, it is an error to condemn Hernán Cortés and the Spanish conquest without taking account of the fact that, in spite of the excesses of that conquest, it did not introduce to the Mexican people any violence, exploitation, or infringement of liberty that was new to them. If the priests who accompanied Cortés burned Aztec libraries, Itzcóatl had done the same before them; if they enslaved the Aztecs, the enemies of the Aztecs also had been enslaved; if they enforced conversion to Christianity, the Aztecs had sought the same ends on behalf of Huitzilopochtli, whose demands upon the common people of Mexico were infinitely bloodier.

Bibliography
Brundage, Burr Cartwright. *A Rain of Darts: The Mexica Aztecs*. Austin: University of Texas Press, 1972. The most thorough one-volume history of the Aztecs, from their obscure origins to the destruction of Tenochtitlán in 1521. Brundage has carefully weighed all the evidence of the codices, and his book provides the most likely dates for the events of Aztec history.
Conrad, Geoffrey W., and Arthur A. Demarest. *Religion and Empire: The*

Dynamics of Aztec and Inca Expansionism. Cambridge: Cambridge University Press, 1984. A comparative study, as the subtitle indicates, which thoroughly examines the political and social factors which led to Aztec expansion and evaluates the theories which modern scholars have proposed to account for it.

Duran, Diego. *The Aztecs: The History of the Indies of New Spain*. Translated by Doris Heyden and Fernando Horcasitas. New York: Orion Press, 1964. Duran was a Dominican friar who came to Mexico only twenty years after the conquest and based his account on the codices and the memory of informants. It was written to help Christian missionaries understand Aztec paganism, but it reveals considerable sympathy for the Indians.

Gillmor, Frances. *The King Danced in the Marketplace*. Tucson: University of Arizona Press, 1964. The king of the title is Montezuma I, but this book deals also with the events of Itzcóatl's reign. Based on solid research and thoroughly documented, but written in a novelistic style which makes the actual historical events sometimes difficult to follow.

Padden, R. C. *The Hummingbird and the Hawk: Conquest and Sovereignty in the Valley of Mexico, 1503-1541*. Columbus: Ohio State University Press, 1967. A thoroughly researched study of the conflict of Aztec and Spanish religious beliefs during the reign of Montezuma II, the conquest, and its aftermath, this account offers many insights into the rise of the Mexica during the reign of Itzcóatl.

Radin, Paul. "The Sources and Authenticity of the History of the Ancient Mexicans." *University of California Publications in American Archaeology and Ethnology* 17 (1920-1926): 1-150. Useful because it provides translations of various Aztec codices, including the lengthy Codex Ramírez, which deals more fully than most of the primary documents with the events of the reigns of Itzcóatl and his predecessors.

Robert L. Berner

JABIR IBN HAYYAN

Born: 721; Tus (in modern Iran)
Died: 815; Al-Kufa (in modern Iraq)
Area of Achievement: Chemistry
Contribution: The greatest alchemist of Islam, Jabir is regarded as the father of Arabian chemistry; his many works considerably influenced later Arabian and European chemists, and his alchemical ideas and recipes helped advance chemical theory and experimentation.

Early Life

It must be said at the outset that many scholars, some from as long ago as the tenth century, have believed that Jabir ibn Hayyan did not exist at all, but belief in his existence has always had its defenders. Those accepting his authenticity think that his family came from the southern Arabian Azd tribe that had settled, during the rise of Islam, in Al-Kufa, then a rapidly growing city on the Euphrates just south of the ruins of Babylon. Abu Musa Jabir ibn Hayyan, Jabir's father, was a Shi'ite apothecary in Khorasan in eastern Persia, and he supported the powerful 'Abbasid family, who hoped to overthrow the Umayyad caliph. (The Umayyad dynasty had ruled the Muslim Empire since 661.) The 'Abbasids sent Abu Musa throughout Persia to prepare the way for a revolution. In the course of this political mission he visited Tus, near the modern Mashhad in northeast Iran, and there, around 721, his son was born and named for him. Unfortunately, while the younger Jabir was still a child, his father was captured by the caliph's agents and beheaded.

Jabir was sent to southern Arabia, where he studied all branches of Eastern learning, including alchemy and medicine. Some scholars say that he was taught by Ja'far al-Sadiq, the sixth Shi'ite imam, who was a descendant of Ali, the cousin and son-in-law of Muhammad. In his later writings, Jabir often stated that he was nothing but a spokesman for Ja'far's doctrines. Besides being a Shi'ite, Jabir was also a Sufi, a mystic Muslim, and illustrators have depicted him with high forehead and curly hair and beard, and dressed in woolen Sufic robes. The Sufis taught Jabir a doctrine ascribing hidden meanings to numbers and letters, which had a great influence on his alchemical theories.

Because the Umayyads remained in power until Jabir was in his late twenties, he lived a life of concealment, roaming through various countries without settling in one place because he feared that the caliph would have him executed. Around 750, when the 'Abbasids succeeded in their revolution, he became associated with the viziers of the 'Abbasids, the powerful Barmakids. He had earned the grand-vizier's gratitude by curing one of his mortally ill harem girls. The Barmakid family became patrons of Jabir and obtained a position for him at the court of Harun al-Rashid, the famous caliph of *The Arabian Nights' Entertainments*. Jabir, for his part, deemed it an honor to compose works for this caliph.

Life's Work

In some lists the writings that bear Jabir's name number more than three thousand. According to many scholars, these works are sufficiently different in style, vocabulary, approach, and content to establish separate authorship for many of them. For example, in some of the works certain terms from late ninth century Greek translations are used, indicating that they were written long after Jabir's death. Many historians of science now regard as probable the thesis that, though some of these works may have been written by Jabir, most were composed by members of the Isma'ili, a Shi'ite sect which believed that Muhammad ibn Isma'il was the seventh imam and which was particularly interested in mysticism, numerology, alchemy, and astrology. Although some recent scholars are more willing than their earlier colleagues were to grant historical reality to Jabir and his works, all agree that many of the surviving writings contain later Isma'ili modifications and additions.

To complicate matters further, several alchemical texts that appeared in the thirteenth and fourteenth centuries with Jabir's name have no Arabic equivalents, and their style and content reveal that they were written by a Western, most likely Spanish, alchemist who lived in the later Middle Ages. This anonymous Spanish alchemist adopted Jabir's name to add authority to his work. Scholars therefore completely disregard the Latin texts by Jabir and exclusively consider the Arabic texts when discussing Jabir ibn Hayyan.

The majority of the Arabic Jabirian texts are alchemical, but others concern medicine, cosmology, astrology, mathematics, magic, music, and philosophy. The most important books include the *Kitab al-sabin* (the seventy books) and the *Kitab al-mizan* (the book of the balance). Unfortunately, the bulk of the Jabirian writings remain unstudied, even though they constitute the most significant body of alchemical works in Arabic and a principal source of Latin alchemy.

To appreciate Jabir's achievements, one must understand his relationship to Greek philosophy and early alchemy. In his theory of matter he derived many of his basic ideas from Aristotle, but not without modification. For example, Aristotle regarded the four principles, heat, cold, moisture, and dryness, as accidental qualities, whereas Jabir saw them as material natures that could be separated and combined in definite proportions to form new substances. Other Jabirian ideas can be traced to the Greek alchemists of Alexandria. These early alchemical writings, however, are often confusing and superstitious, so when Jabir used these ideas, he justified them both rationally and empirically.

In Jabir's scheme of things, science was divided into two interdependent halves, the religious and the secular. He then divided secular knowledge into alchemy and techniques. The task of the alchemist was to use various techniques to isolate pure natures, determine the proportion in which they entered into substances, and then combine them in proper amounts to give desired products. Ideally, the practice of alchemy should raise the alchemist to a higher level of knowledge where both his soul and the world will be transformed. Practically, alchemy centered on the transmutation of metals, notably the changing of base metals such as lead and iron into the valuable metals such as silver and gold.

Jabir's system of alchemy was logical and precise. For example, his classification of substances shows great clarity of thought. He divided minerals into three groups, each having certain specific qualities based on the predominance of one of the pure natures: first, spirits, or substances that completely evaporate in fire (for example, sulfur, mercury, and camphor); second, metals, or meltable and malleable substances that shine and ring when hammered (such as lead, copper, and gold); and third, pulverizable substances that, meltable or not, are not malleable and that shatter into powder when hammered (malachite, turquoise, mica, and the like).

Jabir was a firm believer in the possibility of transmutation, since this was a logical conclusion from his sulfur-mercury theory of metals. This theory suggested that all metals were composed of different proportions of idealized sulfur and idealized mercury. These idealized, or pristine, substances bore some resemblance to common sulfur and mercury, but the idealized substances were much purer than anything that could be produced alchemically. Jabir's theory probably derived from Aristotle's *Meteorologica* (335-323 B.C.), where the process of exhalations from the earth forming minerals and metals is discussed. For Aristotle, earthy smoke consisted of earth in the process of changing into fire, and watery vapor was water undergoing conversion into air. Difficult-to-melt minerals consisted mainly of the earthy smoke, while easy-to-melt metals were formed from the watery vapor. In Jabir's view, sulfur and mercury were formed under planetary influence in the interior of the earth as intermediates between the exhalations and the minerals and metals.

To explain the existence of different kinds of metals, Jabir assumed that the sulfurous and mercurial principles were not always pure and that they did not always unite in the same proportions. If they were perfectly pure and combined in the most perfect manner, then the product was the perfect metal, gold. Defects in proportion or purity resulted in the formation of other metals. Since all metals were composed of the same constituents as gold, the transmutation of less valuable metals into gold could be effected by means of an elixir.

For the alchemists, the elixir, also called the philosopher's stone, was a substance that brought about the rapid transmutation of base metals into gold. The term was initially used for a substance that cured human illnesses (the Arabic *al-iksir* was derived from a Greek word for medicinal powder). In an analogous fashion, an elixir might "perfect," or cure, imperfect metals. A peculiarity of Jabir's system was its emphasis on the use of vegetable and animal substances in the preparation of the elixir (earlier alchemists used inorganic materials). In his search for materials from which the elixir could be extracted, Jabir investigated bone marrow, lion's hair, jasmine, onions, ginger, pepper, mustard, anemones, and many other materials from the plant and animal kingdoms.

An essential part of Jabir's sulfur-mercury theory was his numerological system, used to calculate the balance of the metals necessary to achieve transmutation. Balance, or *mizan*, was the central concept used by Jabir to catalog and number the basic qualities of all substances. Therefore all alchemical work involved establishing the correct proportion of the natures—hot, cold, moist, and dry—and then expressing this proportion in numbers.

In applying this idea of balance to metals, Jabir noted that each metal had two exterior and two interior qualities. For example, gold was inwardly cold and dry, outwardly hot and moist. He determined the nature of each metal by a complex number system whose key numbers, seventeen and twenty-eight, were derived from a magic square. Its top row contained the numbers 4, 9, and 2; the middle row, 3, 5, and 7; and the bottom row, 8, 1, and 6. Adding the numbers of the top row to the bottom two numbers of the last vertical column yields twenty-eight. The numbers of the remaining, smaller square add up to seventeen. It is likely that twenty-eight, a number to which the Sufis attached great value, was astrological in origin, since it is the product of the number of planets (seven) and the number of Aristotelian elements (four). Twenty-eight is also a perfect number in that it is equal to the sum of its divisors (1, 2, 4, 7, and 14). In evaluating the nature of metals, Jabir used the numbers in the smaller square, 1, 3, 5, and 8. Thus, in his system, the contrary natures, hot and cold, or moist and dry, could fuse only in the proportions 1 to 3 or 5 to 8. The sum of these numbers is seventeen, and seventeen is the number of powers that Jabir attributed to the metals. Each quality, moreover, had four degrees and seven subdivisions, or twenty-eight parts altogether. He assigned each of these twenty-eight parts to one of the letters of the Arabic alphabet. He then composed tables interrelating the values of the Arabic letters (which depended on the Arabic name for each metal) and the amounts of the four natures.

Beyond its purely alchemical meaning, the term *mizan*, or balance, was a basic principle of Jabir's worldview. Balance also meant the harmony of the various tendencies of the Neoplatonic world soul, the organizer of the basic qualities. Balance was therefore related to Jabir's monism, which opposed the dualistic worldview of Manichaeanism (the struggle against this religion was a chief concern of Islam at the time). This religious side of Jabir's thought was based on the appearance of the word *mizan* in the Koran, where it is used in the sense of a balance that weighs one's good and bad deeds at the Last Judgment.

Astrology also played an important part in Jabir's system. The stars were not only constituents of the world but also influencers of earthly events. All natural substances had specific properties that linked them to the upper world, and this link allowed talismans to be used effectively. The talisman bore the power of the stars and, when used properly, could provide domination over events. Thus, for Jabir, the same causality determined astrology and alchemy. Both sciences imitated the Creator, since Creator and alchemist worked with the same materials and were governed by the same laws.

Despite his great fame as court astrologer and alchemist, Jabir fell out of favor in 803 because of his association with the Barmakids. When these powerful ministers had been discovered plotting against the caliph, some were executed; others were expelled. Jabir shared the banishment of the Barmakids, and he withdrew to Al-Kufa in eastern Persia. One account states that he returned to court under the new caliph, al-Ma'mun (who reigned from 813 to 833); another states that he spent the rest of his life in obscurity. The date of his death is uncertain, though it is usually given as 815. Two centuries after his death, during building operations in a quarter of Al-Kufa known as the Damascus Gate, Jabir's cellar laboratory was discovered along with a golden mortar weighing two hundred pounds.

Summary

Jabir ibn Hayyan is important for both the history of alchemy and the development of Islamic culture. Although from the vantage point of later centuries his scientific thought seems strange and superstitious, he did help to advance chemical theory and experiment. In searching for the secret of transmutation, he mastered many basic chemical techniques, such as sublimation and distillation, and became familiar with the preparation and properties of many basic chemicals. For example, he was fascinated with sal ammoniac (now called ammonium chloride), a substance unknown to the Greeks. The volatility of this salt greatly impressed the Arabs. Jabir was a skilled and ingenious experimenter, and he described for the first time how to prepare nitric acid. More clearly than any other early chemist, he stated and recognized the importance of the experimental process. In his work he also described and suggested improvements in such chemical technological processes as dyeing and glass-making.

His work also belongs to the legacy of Islam. The Shi'ites state that he is one of their great spiritual guides. Scarcely a single later Arabic alchemical text exists in which he is not quoted. When, in the twelfth and thirteenth centuries, Islamic science was transmitted to Latin Christianity, the fame of Jabir went with it. His sulfur-mercury theory persisted and was at last modified into the phlogiston theory of Johann Becher and George Stahl in the seventeenth and eighteenth centuries. In the guise of Jabir's works, Arabic alchemy exerted considerable influence on the development of modern chemistry.

Bibliography
Federmann, Reinhard. *The Royal Art of Alchemy*. Translated by R. H. Weber. Philadelphia: Chilton Book Co., 1969. This book, originally published in German in 1964, is a popular account of the history of alchemy. There is a chapter specifically devoted to Jabir's life and work.
Holmyard, E. J. *Alchemy*. Harmondsworth, England: Penguin Books, 1957. Holmyard, who has published extensively on Jabir's writings, presents a good general survey of alchemy. He accepts Jabir's existence and presents a detailed reconstruction of his life.
Leicester, Henry M. *The Historical Background of Chemistry*. New York: John Wiley and Sons, 1956. Leicester follows the evolution of chemistry through the ideas of chemists rather than their lives. His chapter on Arabic alchemy contains an insightful account of the body of writings associated with Jabir.
Nasr, Seyyed Hossein. *Islamic Science: An Illustrated Study*. Westerham, England: World of Islam Festival Publishing Co., 1976. The first illustrated account of Islamic science ever undertaken. Using traditional Islamic concepts, Nasr discusses various branches of science, including alchemy, and he places Jabir's work in its Islamic setting.
_____ . *Science and Civilization in Islam*. New York: New American Library, 1968. This book is the first one-volume work in English to deal with Islamic science from the Muslim rather than the Western point of view. Its approach is encyclopedic rather than analytic, but it does contain a discussion of Jabir's life and work in its Muslim context.
Read, John. *Prelude to Chemistry: An Outline of Alchemy*. Cambridge, Mass.: MIT Press, 1966. First published in England in 1936, this book offers a bird's-eye view of alchemy from its origins in Egypt and India to the era of the phlogiston theory. Its emphasis is on the relationship of alchemy to literature.
Schact, Joseph, and C. D. Bosworth, eds. *The Legacy of Islam*. 2d ed. Oxford: Oxford University Press, 1974. This new and completely rewritten version of a work edited in 1931 by Sir Thomas Arnold and Alfred Guillaume analyzes the contributions of Islamic civilization to the world. The chapter "The Natural Sciences and Medicine" contains brief remarks on Jabir.
Taylor, F. Sherwood. *The Alchemists*. New York: Henry Schuman, 1949. The best of the general works on alchemy. It clearly and sympathetically surveys the field from ancient to modern times.

Robert J. Paradowski

AL-JAHIZ

Born: c. 776; Basra, Iraq
Died: 868; Basra, Iraq
Areas of Achievement: Language, literature, and science
Contribution: As the first important Arabic prose writer, al-Jahiz employed his vast erudition and innovative stylistic technique to free the Arabic language from its theological and philological restraints, making it a tool for the long-term cultural cohesion of the diverse cultures of Islam.

Early Life

Abu 'Uthman 'Amr ibn Bahr ibn Mahbub al-Jahiz may have been the child of East African slaves, who were numerous in southern Iraq in the eighth and ninth centuries. His ancestry is uncertain, however. The sobriquet al-Jahiz (goggle-eyed) refers to a remarkable physical condition which observers may have attributed to African origins. People of his time described al-Jahiz as an exceptionally ugly individual.

Al-Jahiz studied in his hometown of Basra, then went off to Baghdad for advanced education. He appears to have been employed early as a clerical official or copyist for the government. His unusual stylistic flair came to the attention of high officials, and the Abbasid caliph al-Ma'mun (813-833) commissioned him to write a series of essays justifying the Abbasid seizure of power from the previous Ummayad dynasty in Damascus around 750. According to some sources, the caliph once considered employing al-Jahiz as a personal tutor for his sons, but was so unnerved by his physical appearance that he decided against him. (In fairness to the caliph, it should be noted that al-Jahiz also had a reputation for a bitter and irascible temperament.)

Al-Jahiz was an active and productive individual, involved, like many Muslim intellectuals of this time, in a variety of arenas. He followed the rationalist Mutazilite school of Islamic thought, which reveled in logical analysis and lively debate; the Mutazilite sect which he founded appears to have espoused some radical theological views. Al-Jahiz was fond of defending unpopular positions in public debate even when he did not personally agree with them. He also dabbled in the natural sciences; his zoological treatise, *Kitab al-hayawan* (book of animals), constituted one of the earliest attempts in Islam to formulate orders of living things. Of the more than 120 works attributed to al-Jahiz by thirteenth century geographer/biographer Yaqut, however, only a few are extant.

Al-Jahiz, who was fluent in Greek as well as Arabic, borrowed heavily from the Hellenistic tradition, frequently quoting or citing Aristotle and other Greek intellectual figures. Among Arabic scholars of his time, he was one of the most inclined to acknowledge his debt to Greek learning.

Life's Work

The literary career of al-Jahiz owes much to the development in Islam of the concept of *adab*, or high culture. *Adab* demanded of its practitioners not only an eclectic knowledge base but also certain mannerisms and styles of expression considered appropriate to a cultivated intellectual elite. The content of *adab* might vary according to the personality of the individual; theology and Islamic canon law (Shari'a) were considered appropriate subject matter. The keystone of *adab*, however, was literary and rhetorical expression. Eloquence was considered one of the essential virtues; indeed, in rigorously pious circles the spoken word was one of the few forms of emotional expression to which one might manifest visible reaction. Conventions of verbal elegance soon came to be applied in literary practice as well, so that good writing was elevated alongside rhetoric as a quality of the cultivated.

The evolution of *adab* raised difficulties concerning the heretofore restricted and unimaginative use of Arabic in written form. Written Arabic often adhered slavishly to Koranic expression, and in al-Jahiz's age prose style was rigid and inflexible. Writers were essentially clerks and secretaries who compiled rather than created. There was a heavy emphasis on such traditional topics as the life of Muhammad and early Islam, as well as a consuming regard for philology at the expense of experiment. Matters of everyday life and those not directly related to the Koran or canon law were addressed only in poetry.

Al-Jahiz sensed that Arabic literary expression was at a dead end—that if current trends continued, Arabic would soon be relegated to use in religious observances only. To overcome this problem, he struck out in new directions with a prose style intended, as he described it, to be both educational and entertaining and to reach a broader segment of the literate public. Al-Jahiz combined a witty and satirical style with his breadth of learning to produce a large corpus of works on all aspects of contemporary life. He made extensive use of anecdotes to make his writing accessible by varying its structure and pace. Al-Jahiz's frequent use of a rhymed, cadenced prose style called *saj'* deeply influenced *adab* culture even in media such as personal correspondence. He was also one of the first Arabic writers to employ irony as a literary device.

Among the surviving works of al-Jahiz, one that well illustrates his style is *Kitab al-bukhala'* (book of misers), in which he rebukes members of the Persian urban middle class, contrasting their behavior with the generosity of the Arabs. It is not the dubious ethnic stereotypes that make the work interesting, however, but the manner of presentation. Marked by witty, vibrant prose, the work is filled with anecdotes about well-known past and contemporary figures who serve as negative examples of the virtue of generosity. Some have suggested that the format and style of the work continues in Arabic a tradition going back to the *Charactēres ethikōi* (c. 319 B.C.; *The Moral*

Characters of Theophrastus, 1702, best known as *Characters*) of Theophrastus, in that al-Jahiz replicates the Greek philosopher's brief and vigorous descriptions of moral character types.

Never one to dodge controversy, al-Jahiz wrote on a wide variety of issues of the time. In his *Kitab al-Bayan wa-al-Tabyin* (book of eloquence and exposition), he attacked the populist Shu'ubi movement, which proclaimed the superiority of non-Arabs over Arabs in religious and cultural achievement. Not surprisingly, many Shu'ubis were Persians, who, in the view of al-Jahiz, were most responsible for the clerical and bureaucratic pedantry to which Arabic literature had been reduced. Besides an essay which extolled the virtues of the Turks, al-Jahiz wrote one on black Africans and several on corruption and venality in government.

If al-Jahiz was something of a muckraker, he was also a devout Muslim. Deeply concerned by what he saw as a growing cynicism and infidelity among the literate classes, he never lost an opportunity to weave theology into his commentaries on everyday life and his descriptions of exemplary behavior.

Summary

As a scholar and man of letters, al-Jahiz had a lasting effect on Islamic culture. His zoological treatise, which, though wide-ranging and imaginative, treats zoology almost as a branch of philology and literature, found many emulators. Among them were the cosmographer al-Qazwini and the thirteenth century Egyptian scientist al-Damiri, generally regarded as the greatest Muslim figure in early zoology.

Al-Jahiz changed for all time the nature and function of Arabic prose; without him, the development of Arabic secular writing would have been almost unthinkable. No longer would Arabic be restricted merely to government reports, theology, and the recounting of the life of Muhammad and the Arab conquests; no longer would Arabic literacy be limited to a privileged few. Al-Jahiz showed that Arabic is a subtle and supple literary language, able to express the entire spectrum of human activity and desire, a vehicle in which literary devices could be exploited to their fullest effect.

Al-Jahiz was to become something of a cultural hero in Muslim Spain, setting of one of the greatest cultural flowerings in the medieval world. Spanish Muslims who traveled to Syria and Iraq to study heard al-Jahiz lecture and eagerly sought copies of his manuscripts to take home, where they became models of literary style for several centuries to come.

Bibliography

De Somogyi, J. "Al-Jahiz and Ad-Damiri." *Annual of the Leeds University Oriental Society* 1 (1958/1959): 55-60. A brief examination of the influence of al-Jahiz on this Muslim scientist who, several centuries later, used his work as a model.

Dodge, Bayard, ed. and trans. *The Fihrist of al-Nadīm: A Tenth-Century Survey of Muslim Culture*. Vol. 1. New York: Columbia University Press, 1970. This volume contains a brief biography of al-Jahiz in traditional Muslim form, also listing some of the scholars associated with him, by a tenth century chronicler. A good example of biographical treatment at the time, it provides a sense of the intellectual environment in which al-Jahiz lived and worked.

Hirschfeld, H. "A Volume of Essays by al-Jahiz." In *A Volume of Oriental Essays Presented to Edward G. Brown*, edited by T. W. Arnold and R. A. Nicolson. Cambridge: Clarendon Press, 1922. Hirschfeld offers commentary on a previously untranslated group of essays and notes.

Hodgson, Marshall G. S. *The Venture of Islam: Conscience and History in a World Civilization*. Vol. 1. Chicago: University of Chicago Press, 1974. This volume includes a discussion of the characteristics and development of *adab* culture and the role which al-Jahiz played in articulating its literary aspects. Shows the great breadth of intellectual and literary activity embraced by *adab* and the diversity of knowledge required of its practitioners.

Marshall, D. R. "An Arab Humorist: Al-Jahiz and 'The Book of Misers.'" *Journal of the Faculty of Arts of the University of Malta* 4 (1970): 77-97. Marshall emphasizes secular as opposed to theological overtones of al-Jahiz's work and discusses the various literary devices and idioms which gave his writing wide appeal.

Pellat, Charles. Introduction to *The Life and Works of Jahiz: Translations of Selected Texts*. Translated by D. M. Hanke. London: Routledge and Kegan Paul, 1969. The essays in this volume, originally translated into French, cover topics such as politics, theology, rhetoric, science, manners, love, and society. The short introduction by Pellat is a useful discussion of the career and significance of al-Jahiz.

Zahniser, Mathias. "Source Criticism in the 'Uthmaniyya of al-Jahiz." *Muslim World* 70 (1980): 134-141. Zahniser argues that al-Jahiz belonged to a sect called 'Uthmaniyya, which opposed the claims of the Shi'is regarding the right of succession in Islam. Al-Jahiz may have written tracts for the Abbasid caliphate supporting the rightful claim of Abu Bakr, the first caliph, to leadership.

Ronald W. Davis

JAMES I THE CONQUEROR

Born: February 2, 1208; Montpellier
Died: July 27, 1276; Valencia, Spain
Areas of Achievement: Government, conquest, literature, and law
Contribution: James conquered three Islamic principalities in Spain and reorganized his many realms in Mediterranean Spain and Occitania (now southern France) into a great and prosperous state, rivaling Genoa for control of western Mediterranean naval power and trade. An autobiographer, he also founded a university and promulgated the first Romanized law code of general application in Europe.

Early Life

James I the Conqueror was born in the port city of Montpellier, whose sovereign lordship was held by his mother, Marie of Montpellier. His father was Peter II the Catholic, victor at Las Navas de Tolosa over the Islamic Almohad empire when James was a child (1212). Because of his incompetence in war, Peter lost the Battle of Muret to the French crusaders against the Albigensians—and, with it, his life and his dynasty's control over much of what is now southern France.

The crusade's leader, Simon de Montfort, kidnapped the child James, planning eventually to marry him to his own daughter. James's mother, Marie, went to Rome, persuaded Pope Innocent III to rescue her son and protect his kingdom during the child's minority, and then died (1213). Thus James was an orphan, sometimes poor and hungry, at the castle of Monzón, headquarters of the Knights Templars, who coruled his rebellious kingdom for him under papal orders.

In 1217, James began his personal rule. Although he was to call himself "king from the Rhone River to Valencia," his main realms were the inland kingdom of Aragon and the coastal county of Catalonia. Aragon was a feudal, stock-raising land; Catalonia was a far wealthier and more powerful urban region. Each had its own language, law, government, economy, and culture. James himself spoke mainly Catalan, and doubtless some Aragonese and the Occitan of his trans-Pyrenean holdings. Still a teenager, James was knighted and, to help stabilize his restless realms, married in 1221 to an older woman, Princess Leonor of Castile. The unhappy union was annulled in 1229, after the birth of a son, Alfonso.

In his prime, James was an imposing figure, taller than his contemporaries, of athletic build, with blond hair and handsome countenance. His portrait at about age fifty was to show an alert majestic personage, with a small beard and the longish hair of his generation. His character was bold, impulsive, generous, and courteously chivalric. He was also cruel on occasion, as when he had the tongue of the Bishop of Gerona cut out in 1246.

James was also notorious in Christendom as a womanizer. He dearly loved his second wife, Princess Yolande of Hungary (1235), who gave him two daughters and two sons. At her death, he married and soon repudiated his third wife, Teresa Gil de Vidaure (1255), after having two more sons. James also had at least five illegitimate children.

Life's Work

James spent much of his life conquering the Islamic regions to his south, already weakened by the breakup of the Almohad empire after his father's victory at Las Navas de Tolosa. In 1229, James gathered a large fleet and army for an amphibious assault on the emirates of the Balearic Islands. Majorca Island fell in 1229, Minorca became a tributary in 1232, and Ibiza fell in 1235. Long after young James's abortive invasion of the Islamic province, or principality, of Valencia in 1225, his raiding knights in 1232 began the long war of conquest there. James kept it going until 1245, in constant maneuvering and bypassing, with few pitched battles but with major sieges of Burriana (1233), the city of Valencia (1238), and Biar (1245). The siege of Játiva was rather a series of feints and interim arrangements from 1239 to 1252.

Meanwhile, the Franks of Francia, in the wake of the Albigensian Crusade, were absorbing ever more of Occitania; James counteracted the French moves ineffectively. In 1245, he patched up a final truce in southern Valencia with the local leader, declared his Valencian crusade finished, and plunged into Occitan affairs. He also projected in 1246 an ambitious crusade to support Latin Byzantium against Greek reconquest. As a result of all these programs abroad, the Valencian Muslims were able to revolt successfully from 1247 into 1258, to James's anger and frustration.

In 1258, James gave up all but a coastal stretch of Occitania to Louis IX of France by the Treaty of Corbeil. He continued to organize his Majorcan and Valencian conquests, each as a "kingdom" with a multiethnic population of Muslims, Christians, and Jews as parallel, semiautonomous communities. In 1261, he called the first *corts* (parliament) of Valencia, which promulgated the final version of his pioneering Roman Law code, the *Furs* (laws). When a countercrusade drove his Castilian neighbors out of the kingdom of Murcia to the south of Valencia, James reconquered that region for the Castilians. In 1269, he mounted a crusade to the Holy Land, although contrary winds and domestic worries aborted his personal role in that adventure. James had been in contact with the Mongols in 1267, exchanging diplomatic-military missions with an eye to allying with this new menace so as to reconquer Jerusalem.

During all this time, and fitted in between his crusading conquests in Spain, James led an energetic life on many other fronts. Besides his constant concern with Occitania, which involved him in the intrigues and battles of the English (from their bases in English Aquitaine) and of principalities such as

Toulouse and Marseilles, he was also involved intimately with Castile, at times lending support against the Muslims there and at times angrily on the very edge of war with its people. As the French grew stronger in Occitania, James turned to their rivals the Hohenstaufens of Sicily and Germany, marrying his son Peter to the Hohenstaufen heiress and surely already envisioning the Catalan seizure of Sicily by Peter in 1282. In between conquests and international projects, James also had to fight sporadic baronial rebellions, as well as two serious revolts by his sons.

James's greatest international triumph occurred in 1274, when he briefly became the adviser on crusade matters at the second ecumenical Council of Lyons in France. He devotes twenty chapters of his autobiography to that culminating point in his career. James died as he had lived, a conquering warrior. In the last year of his long life, the Muslims of Valencia again revolted, supported by invading armies from Granada and North Africa. James fought desperately to stem their reconquest of Valencia; when death claimed him in the process (1276), his son Peter had to bury him temporarily in Valencia and continue to subdue the Muslims. Later, James was interred in a splendid tomb at Poblet Monastery, near Tarragona.

More than a warrior and statesman, James conspicuously advanced the laws, institutions, and commerce of his realms. The *corts* of his several principalities matured under him, both in their regional and general forms. By exploiting the cheap paper available to him after his conquest of that Islamic industry at Játiva in Valencia, he built the first extensive archives of any European secular state. He multiplied a hierarchy of functionaries in a sophisticated administrative bureaucracy and tirelessly traveled his realms every year in person. James was a leader in the renaissance of Roman Law in his century; besides the Valencian *Furs* (1261), he promulgated the Aragonese *Fueros* (1247), the *Costums* of Lérida (1228), and the *Costums de la Mar* (1258) that evolved into the famed *Consulate of the Sea*. His reorganization of communal government, especially at Barcelona and in the towns of Valencia and Majorca, lent stability to his municipalities. Commerce and naval power expanded marvelously under James's direction; they may have been a major purpose of his conquests. He took over the "circle trade" between North Africa, Valencia, Majorca, and parts of southern France. His merchants became the major European presence in Tunis (effectively a client state of James) and in Alexandria, Egypt.

As part of this affluence, James encouraged Jewish immigration; despite some aggressive proselytism, as in the Disputation of Barcelona (1263), his reign is remembered as a political golden age and cultural renaissance for his Jewish communities in Spain and southern France. James presided over and contributed personally to the flowering of the Catalan language and literature. The work of historians Ramón Muntaner and Bernat Desclot, the prolific philosopher-mystic Raymond Lull, the troubadour Cerverí de

Girona—and especially the king's autobiography, *Llibre dels feyts* (*The Chronicle of James I, King of Aragon, Surnamed the Conqueror*, 1883)—exemplify this major moment in the Romance languages. Nor did James neglect higher education; he founded a university at Valencia in the wake of his conquest, and he intruded so forcefully with statutes and reorganization at the University of Montpellier that he is remembered as a kind of second founder there. In addition, his reign saw a renewed enthusiasm for building sweep over the land, from Lérida to Valencia.

Summary

James I the Conqueror is universally recognized as the founder of the greatness of the realms of Aragon and as one of the handful of main leaders of the Spanish Reconquest. He and his older contemporary Ferdinand III of Castile virtually brought that movement to its dramatic close. Since James's realms joined with Castile some two hundred years later to start the beginning of the country now called Spain, he is therefore a great figure for Spain as well. The Catalans particularly honor him as their own greatest ruler, administrator, and military figure, and as the main promoter of their rise to commercial, imperial, and cultural greatness.

His life—from helpless child-hostage and ward of the Knights Templars in a poor and unstable kingdom to eventual eminence as the most successful crusader of Christendom and head of a major world power—makes a colorful and stirring tale. Despite his solid achievements in administration, law, commerce, culture, and international affairs, James preferred to see himself in the role of chivalric knight and warrior-conqueror. His autobiography leaves out almost every other aspect of his career, concentrating, as its title says, on his deeds of war. His book's structure owes much to the Islamic ruler-(auto)biography genre, and its tone echoes the troubadour poems it often incorporates in prose form. Yet, with its naïve self-reflection and vigorous spirit, it reveals much of the private James as well—providing a rare, personal view of a remarkable medieval king.

Bibliography

Bisson, Thomas N. *The Medieval Crown of Aragon: A Short History*. Oxford: Clarendon Press, 1986. Includes a compendious summation of James's reign in chapter 3, with fine general history of the region in surrounding chapters. Especially good on the constitutional and fiscal aspects, with a long section on the king's early years and another on the conquests and foreign relations.

Burns, Robert I. *The Crusader Kingdom of Valencia: Reconstruction on a Thirteenth-Century Frontier*. 2 vols. Cambridge, Mass.: Harvard University Press, 1967. Covers the conquest and, particularly, James's use of church institutions as his main resource for consolidating his hold and restructuring the conquered kingdom's elements. With chapters on James's school system, hospitals, appointed bishops, military orders, economic foundations, and so on. Contains a bibliography.

———————. *Islam Under the Crusaders: Colonial Survival in the Thirteenth-Century Kingdom of Valencia.* Princeton, N.J.: Princeton University Press, 1973. Describes the collapse of the Almohads and Islamic Valencia, James's crusade and its extension in the form of Muslim revolts, and especially the role and transformation of Valencia's postcrusade Muslims. Covers James's surrender concessions and treaties thoroughly, his incorporation of the military elites into his feudal system, and the subject communities' law, worship, economic life, local dynasties, and organization. With a bibliography, eight maps, and seventeen contemporary illustrations.

———————. *Medieval Colonialism: Postcrusade Exploitation of Islamic Valencia.* Princeton, N.J.: Princeton University Press, 1975. Studies James's handling of Valencia's conquered Muslims, drawing social history especially from the taxes he imposed. Covers public monopolies, agrarian and commercial taxes, irrigation and similar fees, the shops and taverns, military obligations, and the means of harvesting these taxes. With a bibliography, maps, and illustrations.

———————. *Moors and Crusaders in Mediterranean Spain: Collected Studies.* London: Variorum, 1978. Sixteen selected articles on James. Chapter 1 is a psychohistorical analysis of his personality and behavior. Other chapters discuss the Muslims taken into his feudal ranks, proselytism and converts, the anti-Moor riots of 1276, James's importation of more Muslims for economic reasons, his modes of inviting surrender and making peace, and so on.

———————. *Muslims, Christians, and Jews in the Crusader Kingdom of Valencia.* Cambridge: Cambridge University Press, 1984. Discusses prominent themes in James's realms: the language barrier, redrawing the maps of the conquered kingdom, the role of his corsairs and of pirates, the king's Jews, the surrender constitutions, the proselytizing movement, the revolt of al-Azraq, and James's continuing role in southern France, especially his personal raid to kidnap the heiress of Provence in Marseilles. Contains a bibliography and maps.

———————. *Society and Documentation in Crusader Valencia.* Princeton, N.J.: Princeton University Press, 1985. Examines in detail the archival registers of James in thirty-eight specialized chapters. Describes his traveling court and household and his chancery. Six chapters cover the Paper Revolution, by which cheap paper from conquered Játiva transformed and bureaucratized James's administration. Other chapters discuss Valencia's many languages, the notarial profession, the archives, and the themes most prominent in James's records.

_____, ed. *The Worlds of Alfonso the Learned and James the Conqueror: Intellect and Force in the Middle Ages*. Princeton, N.J.: Princeton University Press, 1985. From a symposium by seven American specialists to compare and contrast these neighboring kings. Chapter 1 reviews James's accomplishments, with a five-page dateline for both Spain and Europe in synchrony with the lives of James and Alfonso. Chapter 2 analyzes kingship and constitution under James, chapter 3 Catalan literature in his day, chapter 4 his town militia, and chapter 6 his policy in southern France. With a bibliographical essay.

Hillgarth, Jocelyn N. *The Spanish Kingdoms, 1250-1516*. 2 vols. Oxford: Clarendon Press, 1976-1978. Includes an excellent assessment of James and his achievements and failures. By a specialist, this work is especially good on the chronicle sources and on the economy. The volume offers generous background for all elements of Castilian and Aragonese history from about 1250.

James I the Conqueror. *The Chronicle of James I, King of Aragon, Surnamed the Conqueror*. Translated by John Forster. 2 vols. London: Chapman and Hall, 1883. Reprint. Farnborough, England: Gregg International Publishers, 1968. The king's own *Llibre dels feyts*, or book of deeds, the main source for his personality and military achievements. Literary battles have established its authenticity and primary authorship, have clarified the inclusion of prosified poems (affecting about a sixth of the chapters), and have suggested plausible stages and circumstances of its redaction.

Swift, F. D. *The Life and Times of James I, the Conqueror*. Oxford: Clarendon Press, 1894. The only full biography of James in English. For its time, a sound and ample book, but Swift is now woefully inadequate. Most of the articles and books on James have appeared in Spain and France in the century since Swift wrote.

Robert I. Burns

JEREMIAH

Born: c. 645 B.C.; Anathoth, Judaea
Died: After 587 B.C.; Egypt
Area of Achievement: Religion
Contribution: Though Jeremiah failed to win the people of Judaea to a repentance which might have averted the catastrophe which overwhelmed them, his prophecies remained to comfort later generations of the people of Judah and to stand as a symbol of renewal for all people.

Early Life

If Jeremiah was born about 645 (some authorities place the date later), he was born into a troubled world. Israel, the northern Jewish kingdom, had been utterly crushed by Assyria (though some of the people must have remained, for Jeremiah denounced their religious laxness), and Judah itself, under Manasseh, had accepted Assyrian overlordship. Perhaps with Assyrian encouragement, pagan cults had flourished alongside the worship of the Lord (Yahweh)—cults devoted to Baal and the "queen of heaven," involving temple prostitution and even human sacrifice. With the decay of Assyrian power, however, Josiah (reigned c. 639-c. 609) was able to institute drastic reforms, which were encouraged by the finding in 622 of the book of the Law (some version of Deuteronomy). The reforms involved not only the suppression of the cults but also the centralization of the Lord's worship in Jerusalem at the expense of local shrines, even those dedicated to the Lord. Presumably, Jeremiah supported these reforms, even though they meant the decline of the shrine of Anathoth, where he had been born into a priestly family, possibly descendants of Abiathar, a high priest who had been exiled from Jerusalem for an intrigue against Solomon. Jeremiah's support of Josiah would explain the plots which the men of Anathoth directed against him. The gloomy tone of his prophecies even after the reforms could have been justified by the lingering existence of the cults, but he was also saddened by the empty ritualism that he observed and by the failure of the revival to promote social justice.

It was in this atmosphere, at any rate, that Jeremiah grew up. Some authorities date his appearance as a prophet in 627 and see the cause as the threat of an invasion by Scythian barbarians. If this was so, and no invasion took place, his powers of prediction could have been called into question. Not that a prophet such as Isaiah or Jeremiah was a mere fortune-teller: He was a preacher calling his people to abandon paganism, to worship only the Lord, and to practice social justice. Though sometimes a prophecy of disaster was unconditional, it was often a threat of a punishment which could be averted by repentance, and sometimes it was a promise of restoration, however far in the future. As for the prophet, his was a heavy burden, for he was commanded by the Lord to deliver a message which was usually unwelcome. It was perhaps for this reason that Jeremiah never married and that his prophecies express a troubled relationship to the Lord and to his fellowmen: "Why is my pain perpetual, and my wound incurable, which refuseth to be healed? Wilt thou be altogether unto me as a liar, and as waters that fail?" (This passage and subsequent quotations from Jeremiah are taken from the King James Version of the Bible, chosen partly for its literary quality and partly because some scholars believe that this translation, despite its archaisms, best reflects the style of the Hebrew text. Modern translations are sometimes preferred because they incorporate the results of recent linguistic and historical scholarship.)

Life's Work

In about 609, Josiah died in battle against the Egyptians, and Jehoiakim succeeded him as an Egyptian vassal. Jeremiah found little reason to be satisfied with the new king, who allowed the cults to return and, at a time when his subjects had to pay onerous tribute to Egypt, built a new palace with forced labor: "Woe unto him that buildeth his house by unrighteousness, and his chambers by wrong; that useth his neighbor's service without wages, and giveth him not for his work." Jeremiah's repeated denunciations of the social order (he prophesied that the king would be "buried with the burial of an ass") once brought him in danger of his life, and on another occasion he was beaten and put into the stocks overnight. Nevertheless, in 604, as the Babylonians were becoming an increasing menace to Judah, Jeremiah dictated to his disciple Baruch a kind of final warning, a scroll which Baruch read aloud in the Temple. When some of the king's advisers had it read to him, Jehoiakim took a knife and hacked off bits as it was read and burned them. Jehoiakim temporarily accepted the overlordship of Babylon, but three years later, under his son Jehoiachin, Judah rebelled. After the fall of Jerusalem in 597, King Nebuchadnezzar II carried off an immense booty and a considerable number of the most prominent inhabitants. Zedekiah (597-587) was permitted to take over the throne as a Babylonian vassal. Jeremiah, who had come to regard Nebuchadnezzar as the Lord's instrument of punishment, persistently urged Judah to submit quietly to Babylonian rule. Zedekiah may have been inclined to accept Jeremiah's advice, but he could not control his ministers, and a rival prophet, Hananiah, promised the downfall of Babylon and the return of the captives. In 589, revolt broke out, and by 588 Jerusalem was under siege.

During the siege, Jeremiah was in considerable danger as a traitor and threat to morale. In spite of the hostility of the people of Anathoth, he had exercised a kinsman's right to redeem a piece of family land put up for sale there and had symbolically buried the dead against the time of restoration, when once again people should "buy fields for money, and subscribe evidences, and seal them, and take witnesses in the land of Benjamin." When, during an interlude in the siege, he tried to go into the land of Benjamin, he was arrested and beaten as a deserter. When he urged the people to surrender, he was cast into a muddy pit and might have died if he had not been rescued by an Ethiopian eunuch, and he was thereafter kept in custody, though less rigorously, throughout the siege.

After Zedekiah, in accordance with the Law, had "proclaimed liberty" to all the Hebrew slaves in Jerusalem, and their masters pretended to let them go and then reenslaved them, Jeremiah made an especially bitter prophecy:

> Ye have not hearkened unto me, in proclaiming liberty, every one to his brother, and every man to his neighbor: behold, I proclaim a liberty for you, saith the Lord, to the sword, to the pestilence, and to the famine; and I will make you to be removed into all the kingdoms of the earth.

The end came in 587. The city fell; Zedekiah was blinded and his sons and many nobles executed; the city was utterly destroyed, and its surviving inhabitants were deported to Babylon. Nebuchadnezzar took care that Jeremiah was treated kindly, offering him a special place in Babylon. Jeremiah elected, however, to cast in his lot with Gedaliah, a native prince who had been appointed governor of the remnant "of the poor of the people, that had nothing, in the land of Judah," who had been left behind and given vineyards and fields. Some remnants of the army and the court and a number of other fugitives rallied to Gedaliah, but he was assassinated by diehards who regarded him as a turncoat. The survivors sought Jeremiah's advice, and he urged them to remain and submit themselves to Babylon, and under no circumstances to go into Egypt, where they would die "by the sword, by the famine, and by the pestilence." To Egypt they went nevertheless and carried Jeremiah with them. The last words of Jeremiah in Scripture are a report of his denunciation of some women who had sacrificed to the queen of heaven, but he had lost honor as a prophet, since the Lord had failed to save his people. According to one tradition, Jeremiah was stoned by the angry refugees.

Summary

In terms of immediate results, it would be easy to term Jeremiah's life a failure. The prophecies against foreign states, which were made without promise of renewal, did indeed come true, though it needed no prophet to foresee them; the same is true of his prophecies against the northern kingdom of Israel. The reforms of Josiah apparently gave him imperfect satisfaction, for presumably the cults revived after Josiah's death. In any case, the issue came to be overshadowed by Judah's suicidal foreign policy, and Jeremiah suffered persecution and derision for urging more prudent behavior toward Babylon. When the survivors of the consequent disaster elected to flee to Egypt, Jeremiah was powerless to deter them, and in Egypt he suffered a final humiliation when the Jewish women revived the worship of the queen of heaven, saying that as long as they had worshipped her in Judaea, they had been "well, and saw no evil." It is no wonder that "jeremiad" is a modern word for a dolorous tirade.

Yet these original jeremiads are eloquent and beautiful (much of the text is in the form of Hebrew poetry), and even more impressive (though less lengthy) are the promises of restoration:

> After those days, saith the Lord, I will put my law in their inward parts, and write it in their hearts; and will be their God, and they shall be my people. And they shall teach no more every man his neighbor, and every man his brother, saying, Know the Lord: for they shall all know me, from the least of them unto the greatest of them, saith the Lord: for I will forgive their iniquity, and I will remember their sin no more.

Perhaps inspired by these words, years later some of the exiles returned and, under Persian protection, established a state which observed the Deuteronomic code and endured until its destruction by the Romans. Still later, such passages were interpreted as announcing the coming of Jesus Christ.

Bibliography

Ackroyd, Peter R. *Exile and Restoration: A Study of Hebrew Thought in the Sixth Century B.C.* Philadelphia: Westminster Press, 1968. Ackroyd's assumptions are that Old Testament prophecy is relevant to Christian theology, that the prophetic books should be viewed as a whole, and that this whole is unique and far-reaching in its influence.

Bright, John. Introduction to *The Anchor Bible: Jeremiah.* Garden City, N.Y.: Doubleday and Co., 1965. A thorough, scholarly introduction of nearly 150 pages. Topics include the prophets of Israel, the historical background, the structure and composition of the book, the life and message of Jeremiah, and the text. The volume also contains an original translation with heavy annotation and a bibliography. Strongly recommended.

Funk and Wagnalls New Standard Bible Dictionary. Edited by Melancthon W. Jacobus, Elbert C. Lane, and Andrew C. Zenos. 3d rev. ed. Philadelphia: Blakiston Co., 1936. Gives a brief but adequate account of Jeremiah's life and times, general character of the book, personal characteristics, significance of the work, and text, with a bibliography. There are separate entries on the history of Israel, prophecy, and other related topics.

Heschel, Abraham J. *The Prophets.* New York: Harper and Row, Publishers, 1962. Attempts to attain an understanding of the prophet through analysis of his consciousness. This contrasts with an approach which either emphasizes supernatural truth or uses a psychological bias.

Perdue, Leo G., and Brian W. Kovacs, eds. *A Prophet to the Nations: Essays in Jeremiah Studies*. Winona Lake, Wis.: Eisenbrauns, 1984. An anthology representing the best modern scholarship on Jeremiah. Among the topics discussed are the date of the prophet's call, the identity of the enemy from the north, textual problems, and the composition and development of the book. On some points (for example, the dates of Jeremiah's birth and his first call, the identity of the "enemy from the north"), the conclusions differ from those given in the present essay.

Rosenberg, Joel. "Jeremiah and Ezekiel." In *The Literary Guide to the Bible*, edited by Robert Alter and Frank Kermode. Cambridge, Mass.: Harvard University Press, 1987. Aside from comment on purely literary topics, this piece is chiefly valuable for making sense out of the confused chronology of the Book of Jeremiah. Valuable notes and bibliography.

John C. Sherwood

SAINT JEROME
Eusebius Hieronymus

Born: Between 331 and 347; Stridon, Dalmatia (modern Yugoslavia)
Died: Probably 420; Bethlehem, Palestine
Areas of Achievement: Scholarship, monasticism, and religion
Contribution: Because of his scholarship, commentaries on and translation of the Bible into Latin, and role as a propagandist for celibacy and the monastic life, Jerome is numbered with Saint Ambrose, Saint Augustine, and Gregory the Great as one of the Fathers of the Church.

Early Life

Saint Jerome grew up in a world in which the influence of Christianity was rapidly expanding. He was born Eusebius Hieronymus. The names of his mother and younger sister are unknown, but his father, Eusebius, was a wealthy landowner, and Jerome had a younger brother, Paulinianus. Jerome's parents were Christians, although apparently not fervent.

Jerome began his schooling in Stridon. From Stridon he was sent to Rome for his secondary education. His parents were clearly ambitious for him: Rome was the most prestigious center of learning in the Latin-speaking part of the empire, and Aelius Donatus, the most famous master of the day, was Jerome's instructor in grammar. For at least four years, Donatus provided Jerome with a fairly typical Hellenistic education, centering on grammar and the reading and analysis of classical literature. By his adult years, Jerome had an extensive knowledge of the Latin classics. He is generally considered to be the finest of all Christian writers in Latin. In Rome he probably also acquired an elementary knowledge of Greek.

From Donatus' school, Jerome went to a school of rhetoric, also in Rome. He seems to have studied some law during this period and later could cite the Roman law with great accuracy. One of his fellow students was the Christian Tyrranius Rufinus, who was later to translate many Greek Christian writings into Latin. He and Jerome were the closest of friends, although this friendship would later break down over a theological dispute. Jerome, as a young man, had already begun to acquire many books; in his subsequent journeys he carried his library with him.

Life's Work

Jerome's baptism at Rome, sometime before 366, signaled his deepening interest in Christianity. Nothing is known of his life from approximately 357 until 367. In the next five years, Jerome traveled in Gaul, Dalmatia, and northeast Italy, particularly to Aquileia, where Rufinus lived. Although this period is also very obscure, it is clear that Jerome had become interested in current theological controversy. More important, during this period, he felt called to a more serious Christian life. For many of his contemporaries, this call was to an abandonment of the world and a life of asceticism or strict discipline. Monasticism—an institutionalized form of asceticism commonly centered on the abandonment of private property, various forms of self-denial, such as fasting and celibacy, and the attempt to live a life of perpetual prayer—had existed in the eastern part of the empire for more than a half century, but had only recently appeared in the West. Jerome did not adopt this difficult life-style suddenly. Like his younger contemporary Augustine, he first renounced further secular ambitions and committed himself to a life of contemplation and study.

Apparently, Jerome's determination to follow the ascetic life, and his success in persuading his sister to follow suit, led to an estrangement from his parents. In 372, like many pilgrims of his day, Jerome left Rome for the East and Jerusalem. As it turned out, he was not to reach Jerusalem for some years. He remained a year in Antioch, Syria, plagued with illness, but used his time there to improve his Greek and familiarize himself with the current state of theological controversy on the nature of the Trinity.

Jerome was tormented by the fact that he still had not made a clean break with the world, and probably in 374 had his famous dream, in which a Judge appeared and accused him of being a disciple of Cicero rather than Christ. That was an expression of Jerome's inability to give up reading of the classical authors in favor of purely biblical studies. Jerome records that this dream ended with him swearing an oath no longer to possess or read pagan books. He was later to say that he could not be held permanently to an oath made in a dream, but the dream does seem to mark the point at which his life's work—the study of Christian literature—came into focus. He began the first in a series of commentaries on the books of the Bible; this earliest work is not extant.

As Jerome's health returned, with it came the desire to follow through on his ascetic intentions. Many desert hermits lived near Antioch, and Jerome chose a hermit cell for himself near Chalcis. He remained in the desert two or three years, increasingly frustrated by the abuse heaped on him by the quarreling Syrian theological factions, each wishing to convert him to its position. He had his large library with him and continued his studies, learning Hebrew from a Jewish convert. Shortly after his return to Antioch, in 376 or 377, he began the second of his sustained projects, a series of translations of Greek Christian writings into Latin. His fame was growing rapidly, and he was ordained a priest by the Bishop of Antioch, although he was always to think of himself primarily as a monk.

By 379 or 380, Jerome was in Constantinople and suffering from a disease of the eyes. In 382, he was in Rome, in the service of Damasus, the Bishop of Rome, as secretary and adviser. Damasus commissioned what was to become the great labor of Jerome's life—the preparation of a standard Latin translation of the Bible. The intended scope of this project is unclear: He probably completed translations of the four Gospels and the Psalms while in Rome.

Jerome spent about three years in Rome, during which he became the spiritual guide for an extraordinary group of high-born girls and women committed to the ascetic life and led by the widows Marcella and Paula. Paula's third daughter, Julia Eustochium, was to be at Jerome's side for the rest of his life. Throughout his life, Jerome tended to create conflict with his sarcastic and combative remarks and letters. Damasus died in 384, and Jerome left Rome in 385 under pressure from both clergy and lay people whom he had offended.

Paula, Eustochium, and Jerome settled in Palestine in 386. The rest of Jerome's life was to be spent in Bethlehem and the environs of Jerusalem in a penitential life of prayer and study. Two monasteries were built at Bethlehem, one for women and one for men, and there the three friends lived until their deaths. Jerome returned to the study of Hebrew and moderated his earlier condemnation of the study of the classics. More and more, in his commentaries on and works related to the Old Testament, he relied on rabbinical interpretation and turned from the Septuagint—the Greek translation of the Old Testament commonly used in Christian circles—to the Hebrew. Jerome became convinced that a Latin translation of the Old Testament should be based directly on the Hebrew, and in about 390, he set aside the work he had done and began a new version from the original texts. Jerome's translation met with opposition and charges of Judaizing. It was not until the ninth century that his work was fully accepted; his translation of the Old Testament and Gospels, when added to translations of the remaining New Testament books by unknown scholars, became known as the Vulgate (common) Bible.

Jerome's last years were filled with tragedy. He continued to be in pain and poor health. Paula died in 404. The barbarians, who began their invasion of the empire in 375, attacked the Holy Land in 405, and Rome itself was sacked in 410. Jerome interpreted the Fall of Rome as the destruction of civilization. In 416, the monasteries at Bethlehem were burned and the monks and nuns assaulted. Jerome died in Bethlehem, probably in 420.

Summary

Saint Jerome's Christianity was a religion which at once challenged the mind of the scholar and urged those "who would be perfect" (Matthew 19:21) to detach themselves from normal worldly expectations. That a monasticism both learned and ascetic was the central cultural institution of the Middle Ages is in no small part his heritage. Although he is not, as was once thought, responsible for the entire Latin Vulgate Bible, he is responsible for the Old Testament and Gospel books of that translation. The Bible in Jerome's translation was the basis for the Wycliffe translation in the fourteenth century and the Douay version in the sixteenth century. His work was to influence Western theology and church life for centuries.

Jerome was a Latin scholar in a Greek and Hebrew-speaking world. At Bethlehem, he was one of the most important agents of crosscultural transference the world has known. Very few ancient Christians, Greek or Latin, knew Hebrew, and contacts between Jew and Christian in the ancient world regularly led to conflict. Against this backdrop, Jerome, because he saw the necessity of tracing Christianity to its most ancient Jewish roots, cultivated personal and scholarly contact with learned Jews and offered a clearer vision than had ever existed of what united, and separated, the religions.

Bibliography

Bouyer, Louis. *The Spirituality of the New Testament and the Fathers.* Translated by Mary P. Ryan. New York: Desclee Co., 1963. This first volume in the History of Christian Spirituality series is a reliable survey of ancient Christian spirituality, with a good comparison of Ambrose, Jerome, and Augustine. More sympathetic to Jerome's spiritual ideals than Kelly (see below) and much better on the theological issues involved on the relation of the literal and spiritual senses of Scripture.

The Cambridge History of the Bible. 3 vols. Cambridge: Cambridge University Press, 1963-1970. Volume 1, *From the Beginnings to Jerome*, edited by P. R. Ackroyd and C. F. Evans, and volume 2, *The West, from the Fathers to the Reformation*, edited by G. W. H. Lampe, contain useful and generally well-informed sections on Jerome. This study is often provincial, without mention of some of the best of Continental scholarship.

Courcelle, Pierre. *Late Latin Writers and Their Greek Sources.* Translated by Harry E. Wedeck. Cambridge, Mass.: Harvard University Press, 1969. One of the great achievements of twentieth century scholarship, this volume traces in detail the use and knowledge of Greek works by Latin writers. Makes clear the central importance of Jerome as a translator and agent of dissemination of Greek authors.

Hagendahl, Harald. *Latin Fathers and the Classics.* Göteborg, Sweden: Almqvist and Wiksell, 1958. This is a careful, thorough, generally reliable study of Jerome's familiarity with and use of the pagan classics. Good on his dream of the Judge and its effect on his later life.

Kelly, J. N. D. *Jerome: His Life, Writings, and Controversies.* New York: Harper and Row, Publishers, 1975. This is the best and most complete book on Jerome in English. It may nevertheless be criticized for holding Jerome to a demanding modern standard of judgment, for a lack of sympathy for his spiritual ideals, especially when they involve celibacy, and for an insufficiently sophisticated presentation of the issues involved in the relation of the literal to the spiritual senses of Scripture.

Glenn W. Olsen

JESUS CHRIST

Born: c. 6 B.C.; Bethlehem, Judaea
Died: A.D. 30; Jerusalem
Area of Achievement: Religion
Contribution: As the basis for a religious faith that has attracted many millions of adherents, Jesus' life and teachings have exerted an enormous influence on Western civilization.

Early Life

Though his name is recognized by millions and his birthday is celebrated as a holiday across the Western world, Jesus Christ's early life is shrouded in obscurity. Neither the day nor year of his birth can be fixed with certainty. Some scholars think that Bethlehem was identified as the place of his birth merely to make his life conform to old prophecies. Objective study of his life is complicated by the fact that many people believe him to be the Son of God.

The earliest Christian writer whose works are extant, the apostle Paul (died A.D. 64), makes no reference to the historical life of Jesus, aside from quoting a few of his sayings. The four canonical Gospels are not, strictly speaking, biographies of Jesus. They were written as aids to memorizing his teachings or as arguments in favor of his divinity; they do not purport to be complete accounts (John 20:30). The earliest of them, attributed to Mark (c. A.D. 70), begins with the story of Jesus' baptism by John in the river Jordan. The two attributed to Matthew (A.D. 80?) and Luke (A.D. 90?) add a story about Jesus teaching in the Temple when he was twelve and give differing accounts of his birth and genealogy. John's Gospel (A.D. 100?) is a reflective memoir, differing in chronology and in its portrayal of Jesus as a Hellenistic teacher rather than a Jewish rabbi. Other gospels, not included in the New Testament, attempted to fill the gap in Christians' knowledge about Jesus' early life by concocting fantastic stories. There are no other historical sources for the study of his life.

Matthew and Luke agree that Herod the Great was King of Judaea at Jesus' birth. Herod died in 4 B.C. Since, in Matthew 2, he is reported to have slaughtered male children under the age of two in an effort to kill the infant Jesus, scholars conclude that Jesus may have been born as early as 6 B.C. (The error in calculation was made by a sixth century monk, who compared all the then-available chronological data to determine the time of Jesus' birth.) The date of December 25 was selected by the Bishop of Rome in the late fourth century. Having a Christian festival at that time of year enabled the Church to distract its members from popular pagan festivals which occurred then. Before that time, Jesus' nativity was celebrated at various times of the year, if at all.

Jesus grew up in Galilee, where Greek influences were stronger than in the southern territory of Judaea. Though his native language was Aramaic, which is related to Hebrew, he would have had to know Greek to conduct any business. His father, Joseph, is usually described as a carpenter. The Greek word actually means something more like "builder" or "general contractor."

Life's Work

The Jews of Galilee were less conservative than those of Judaea. Rabbinic traditions and regulations were challenged in the north by a greater interest in the prophetic side of Judaism. Jesus, while not trained as a rabbi, seems to have been familiar with the standard methods of argument. He engaged in debates over interpretation of Scripture where appropriate (Mark 12:13-34) but sometimes sidestepped hairsplitting questions (Luke 10:25-37). At some points, though, he showed flashes of originality. He is never recorded as basing his teaching on the opinions of earlier rabbis—the accepted technique of the day—but taught instead on his own authority (Matt. 7:29). Parables (story-comparisons) seem to have been the foundation of his teaching technique (Mark 4:33).

Judaism was a diverse religion in the early first century A.D. Flavius Josephus describes three sects or schools flourishing at that time: the liberal and popular Pharisees, the aristocratic and conservative Sadducees, and the monastic Essenes. The Pharisees were further subdivided into the school of Shammei, which urged resistance to Roman rule, and that of Hillel, which counseled accommodation. There were also radical fringe groups such as the Zealots, who hoped to provoke a confrontation with the Romans that would lead to divine intervention and the foundation of a new kingdom of Israel.

Jesus' sudden appearance in the "fifteenth year of the reign of Tiberius" (Luke 3:1), or A.D. 29, when he was "about thirty years of age" (Luke 3:23), fit in with the general mood of discontent which prevailed in Judaea at the time. His message that "the kingdom of God is at hand" found a receptive audience. The eschatological tone was interpreted by some as an announcement of the overthrow of Roman hegemony. Even Jesus' closest disciples did not easily give up their hope for a reestablishment of the Davidic kingship (Acts 1:6).

Jesus does not, however, seem to have envisioned himself as a political revolutionary. His aim appears to have been to reform Judaism, which had become so weighted down with minute requirements that even the most scrupulous Jews had difficulty adhering to the Torah. Jesus accused the Pharisees of imposing their own restrictions on top of the commandments of Torah (Luke 11:46) and of neglecting what he called "the weightier matters of the Law: justice, mercy, and faith" (Matt. 23:23). Such utterances link Jesus with Old Testament prophets such as Amos (Amos 5:21-24), Jeremiah

(Jer. 31:31-34), and Micah (Mic. 6:7-8), who criticized the legalism of Judaism in their day and urged that obedience to the Law be a matter of inner motivation, not observance of external rituals.

Such a view was thus not a new creation of Jesus. Even his most familiar injunction, to love one's neighbor as oneself, was a quotation of Leviticus 19:18. In general, his teaching can be classed under three headings: criticism of the normative Judaism of his day (for example, Matt. 23), proposal of a new, interiorized ethic (Matt. 5-7, the Sermon on the Mount), and expectations of the imminence of the kingdom of God (Mark 13).

In addition to his teaching, the accounts of his life contain miracle stories, in which Jesus purportedly heals people with various infirmities or demonstrates his power over nature by calming storms and walking on water. The Gospels conclude with the greatest of the miracle stories, the account of Jesus' resurrection, which Paul saw as the proof of his divinity (Rom. 1:4). The other apostles also made it the center of their preaching (Acts 2:22-36).

These miracle stories are probably the major point of dispute between those who accept the divinity of Jesus and those who do not. Even those who find his ethical teachings attractive sometimes find it difficult to accept the supernatural accounts which surround them. The scientific orientation which has undergirded Western education since the mid-nineteenth century has produced an outlook on the world that makes the miracle stories seem more akin to fairy tales.

In the first century A.D., however, people were eager to believe stories of the supernatural. In Petronius Arbiter's *Satyricon* (first century A.D.), one of the characters tells a werewolf story. At the end, a listener says, "I believe every word of it," and goes on to tell a ghost story of his own. Suetonius, biographer of the first century Roman emperors, recounts as fact a story that Vespasian healed two men in Egypt in the presence of a large audience. The philosopher/mystic Apollonius of Tyana, a contemporary of Jesus, was credited with healing, resurrecting the dead, and having his birth accompanied by supernatural signs.

A major difficulty with the Gospel miracles is the inconsistency of various versions of some of the stories. For example, in Matthew 14:22-33, when Jesus walks across the waves to his disciples' boat, Peter steps out of the craft and takes a few steps before, becoming fearful, he starts to sink. Mark 6:45-51 and John 6:17-21, however, make no mention of Peter's aquatic stroll. John's is the only version which says that as soon as Jesus got into the boat, it reached the other shore.

Perhaps too much attention is devoted to the miracle stories, distracting from the more central issues of Jesus' teaching. The Gospels record his reluctance to perform miracles (Mark 8:12) because the crowds paid more attention to them than to his teachings.

Recovering Jesus' own sense of his purpose is difficult because all the documents relating to him were produced by people who believed him to be divine. Modern scholarship has concentrated on probing under the layers of interpretation which his followers added to the story in consequence of their claim that he was resurrected (see John 12:16). Jesus seems to have seen himself as a final messenger to the Jews. He claimed to have greater authority than the prophets, just as a king's son has greater authority than his servants (Mark 12:1-11).

His message was essentially a warning that the Jews had exalted ritual observance of God's Law to the point that they had lost sight of its moral implications. His criticism was directed especially against the Pharisees and scribes. They reacted predictably, by plotting to silence the troublemaker. With the collusion of one of Jesus' followers, Judas Iscariot, they seized him in a garden on the outskirts of Jerusalem.

The trial of Jesus has been a subject of much controversy as to its legality and the exact charges involved. The Romans normally left local matters in the hands of provincial officials, and the Sanhedrin had the right to try cases involving Jewish law. They do not seem to have had the power to condemn a prisoner to death. They found Jesus guilty of violating religious laws, especially those against blasphemy, but before Pontius Pilate, the Roman governor, they accused him of treason.

Pilate had been governor of Judaea for about three years at that time. According to Josephus, he had difficulty getting along with the Jews from the day of his arrival. His insensitivity to their religious traditions was a major part of the problem. His decision to crucify Jesus may have been made out of genuine concern that the man was a threat to the social order, but it was probably an effort to mollify the Jews, who had already complained to the emperor about him.

Within a few days of his death, Jesus' disciples were claiming that he had risen from the dead. Whatever one may think of that assertion, the disciples' belief in it had a remarkable effect on them. From a dispirited band of fishermen and peasants who had begun to scatter back to their homes, they were transformed into a fellowship of believers willing to undergo any difficulty or torment to proclaim their faith (Luke 24:13-35). Not even threats from the religious authorities of the day could silence them (Acts 5:27-32).

Summary

If his goal was to reform Judaism, Jesus Christ can hardly be judged successful. The Pharisees resisted his initial efforts and refused to recognize his followers as loyal Jews. Driven out of the synagogues, they founded a new faith which emphasized the spiritual values of Jesus' teachings. Jesus' assertion of the importance of love of God and fellowman—even one's enemies— and the shunning of ceremonialism and class distinctions were not original but resulted from his stress on long-neglected facets of Jewish scripture. His is the Judaism of the prophets, not of the Torah and the Talmud.

However one may regard the claims made about his divinity, Jesus' impact on Western culture has been too profound to ignore. His teaching introduced an element of humaneness that even the Greeks and Romans found remarkable. Unlike their pagan neighbors, Christians did not procure abortions or abandon unwanted children after birth. They cared for their sick, and during plagues they cared for the sick and dying pagans who had been dumped in the streets. They did not seek vengeance on those who wronged them. Several pagan writers of the first four centuries, including Aulus Cornelius Celsus, Porphyry, and the Emperor Julian (sometimes called Julian the Apostate), grudgingly admired the despised Christians and urged pagans to live up to the Christian standards of charity and philanthropy.

In summary, then, Jesus' teachings laid the groundwork for the Western world's system of morality, however imperfectly it has been observed. If Socrates gave definition to the Western intellect, Jesus implanted in it a conscience.

Bibliography

Bornkamm, Gunther. *Jesus of Nazareth*. New York: Harper and Row, Publishers, 1961. The book which reopened the question of how much can be known about the historical Jesus after a half century of pessimism engendered by Albert Schweitzer's *The Quest of the Historical Jesus* (see below).

Bowker, John. *Jesus and the Pharisees*. New York: Cambridge University Press, 1973. Comparison of the teachings of Jesus with those of the Pharisaic schools of his day. Bowker concludes that the content of much of his message was not new, but his interpretation of it was.

Brandon, S. G. F. *The Trial of Jesus of Nazareth*. London: B. T. Batsford, 1968. Discusses the problem of evidence which makes the study of Jesus' trial so problematic. The Gospels cannot be studied as if they were legal transcripts; the biases of their authors must be understood first.

Bruce, F. F. *The Hard Sayings of Jesus*. Downers Grove, Ill.: Inter-Varsity Press, 1983. Examination of some of Jesus' sayings which modern readers find particularly difficult to understand. Many of them are explicable in terms of the social or economic context of Jesus' time.

Bultmann, Rudolf. *Jesus Christ and Mythology*. New York: Charles Scribner's Sons, 1958. Bultmann is the foremost proponent of the school of thought which holds that virtually nothing can be known of the historical Jesus: The Gospels reflect only what his followers thought about him.

Goodspeed, Edgar J. *A Life of Jesus*. New York: Harper and Row, Publishers, 1950. A biography based on the first three Gospels, assuming that they present a historically accurate account.

Grant, Michael. *Jesus: An Historian's Review of the Gospels*. New York: Charles Scribner's Sons, 1977. A moderate, scholarly review of the problems related to using the Gospels as historical sources.

Jeremias, Joachim. *The Parables of Jesus*. New York: Charles Scribner's Sons, 1963. Regards the parables as the most accurately preserved part of the material relating to Jesus. Discusses principles and problems of interpretation, then analyzes the parables under subject headings.

Klausner, J. *Jesus of Nazareth: His Life, Times, and Teaching*. New York: Macmillan, 1925. Reprint. Boston: Beacon Press, 1964. A controversial classic by a Jewish scholar who surveys conditions in Palestine in Jesus' time and compares his teaching to what was current among the Pharisees.

Robinson, James McConkey. *A New Quest of the Historical Jesus and Other Essays*. Philadelphia: Fortress Press, 1983. Survey of the recent debate over the question of how much one can know about the historical Jesus on the basis of the Gospels. Robinson suggests that it is possible to learn something about his life, if one uses the sources advisedly.

Schweitzer, Albert. *The Quest of the Historical Jesus*. Translated by W. Montgomery. New York: Macmillan, 1910. Originally published in German in 1906, this study surveys nineteenth century attempts at writing a biography of Jesus and concludes that, because of the nature of the sources, it is an impossible task.

Albert A. Bell, Jr.

JOACHIM OF FIORE

Born: c. 1135; Celico, Italy
Died: 1202; Fiore, Italy
Areas of Achievement: Religion and historiography
Contribution: Joachim developed a persuasive system of historical under-
standing which evolved through three successive stages culminating in an
age of the Holy Spirit filled with bliss and understanding.

Early Life

Joachim of Fiore (archaic, Flora) was born to Maurus, a notary, and
Gemma in Celico, near Cosenza, about 1135. Although later writers would
claim that the family members were converted Jews, there is no convincing
evidence to support this statement. Joachim, who was trained to be a court
bureaucrat and notary, entered the service of King William II of Sicily at Palermo as a young man. About 1167, after an illness, he left William's service
to go on a pilgrimage to the Holy Land, where he decided to follow a religious life. While meditating on Mount Tabor, he experienced his first revelation; as a result, he believed that God had given to him a special insight into
scriptural understanding.

Joachim returned to Sicily and lived as a hermit on Mount Etna for a few
weeks, and then he traveled back to the vicinity of Cosenza, where he began
to live the life of a hermit-preacher. In 1170, he entered the novitiate at a
monastery at Corazzo and rose to the position of prior shortly after taking his
vows. Seven years later, he was elected abbot of the monastery. Either
shortly before his election or shortly thereafter, Corazzo chose to join the
Cistercian community.

As the new abbot, Joachim's first task was to seek association for the
Corazzo monastery with a Cistercian motherhouse. Thus, he began to travel
almost immediately in search of a monastery which would assume that obligation, going both to Sambucina and to Casamari. He was unsuccessful in
convincing the Cistercians in either place to accept Corazzo. Finding a
motherhouse for his monastery was doubly important to Joachim as he was
anxious to begin writing about his scheme of history and theology. The
Cistercian General Council would not authorize his scholarly activities until
Corazzo was officially within the Cistercian community. Frustrated with the
Cistercians and anxious to begin his writing, he appealed to Pope Lucius III
in 1184. Permission was granted to him to begin his studies, and the pope
also allowed him a leave of absence from his duties as abbot.

Life's Work

Joachim returned to Casamari and began to write *Liber Concordia Novi
ac Veteris Testamenti* (1519; book of concords between the Old and New Tes-

taments) and *Expositio in Apocalypsim* (1527; exposition on the Apocalypse) simultaneously. As he wrote, he realized that he still did not have a clear understanding of the relationship between the Trinity and biblical concords; thus, on Pentecost, 1183 or 1184, he received his second revelation. This revelation was so graphic that he put aside the two manuscripts on which he was working and wrote the first book of his third major treatise, *Psalterium decem chordarum* (1527; ten-stringed psaltery). Utilizing the imagery of the strings on the musical instrument, Joachim presented a full explanation of the mystery of the Trinity.

Returning to Corazzo the following year, he continued his writing; after failing to understand the meanings of the apocalyptic writings in the Bible, he received his third revelation. While he was again in deep meditation, it seemed as if curtains were lifted within his mind causing "a certain clearness of understanding before the eyes of my mind which exposed to me the fullness of this book of the Apocalypse and the entire concord of the Old and New Testaments."

In 1186, Joachim visited the new pope, Urban III, and received renewed permission and encouragement to continue his writing. In 1187, however, Urban died; Joachim traveled again to Rome in 1188 to visit Urban's successor, Clement III. Clement, too, endorsed his writings. By 1189, Joachim was feeling the pressures of growing fame and recognition as an exegete of prophecy, and he was becoming more and more disenchanted with the Cistercian Order, which he believed to be too lax in its religious life. In late winter of that year, he went deep into the Sila Mountains to seek a place of peace and quiet. In May, he settled at San Giovanni in Fiore. As a result, the leadership of the Cistercian Order considered him a renegade. He finally broke with the order when Henry VI, the Holy Roman emperor, issued a charter to Joachim on October 21, 1194, authorizing a new monastery at San Giovanni in Fiore with Joachim as its abbot. With the charter in hand, Joachim approached Pope Celestine III seeking approval of a constitution for a new religious order; the pope did so by a papal bull on August 25, 1196. Thus the Order of Fiore was born with its motherhouse located in San Giovanni in Fiore in Calabria.

Despite periodic revelations, Joachim never claimed to be a prophet. Instead, he insisted that God had given him the gift of a clearer exegetical understanding of Scripture which enabled him to display a new system of theology and historiography. Joachim's apocalyptic attitudes and theology of history were a significant departure from the Augustinian tradition in that he viewed history as dynamic rather than static. The Calabrian abbot perceived three progressive *status* (ages), or a threefold pattern of history, in which each member of the Trinity played guiding roles. The first *status*, in which God the Father directed the course of human events, began with Adam and ended with Christ's Incarnation. The second *status*, characterized by the leadership of Jesus Christ, overlapped back into the first *status* and lasted until the thirteenth century. The third *status* was more complicated. Its origins were in both the first and second *status*—a double origin and progression from the Old and New Testaments and the Father and Son; it would be guided by the Holy Spirit.

Saint Bernard of Clairvaux was the precursor to the third age. His rule had laid the groundwork for a future monastic community which eventually would encompass all Christians: monks, clerics, and laymen. Two new orders would appear and usher in the age followed by the first appearance of the Antichrist. The Antichrist would cause terrible trials and tribulations, but he would be defeated by Christians. After the Antichrist was defeated, the Holy Spirit would guide life until the second appearance of the Antichrist and Doomsday. It was with the concept of the third *status* that Joachim broke from the Augustinian tradition by placing eschatological events into human history. As a dreamer of the future, he did not look backward in time to some golden age, such as the apostolic age, in which men would emulate Christ and His disciples; rather, he concluded that the future time would be a true *renovatio*, unlike anything in the past, led by the Holy Spirit. Such ideas became fertile ground for scores of future movements of reform.

In Joachim's schema, each age was progressive toward the next; collectively, they moved toward an ideal human existence. The first age, for example, had been lived under Law, the second had been lived under grace, and the third would be lived in full freedom and understanding. Each of Joachim's three *status* was divided into seven *estates* (times) with five concordant types or species and seven *typicus intellectus*. For example, the twelve patriarchs of the Old Testament were precursors to the twelve Apostles, and one would expect a similar concordant type in the third age. Thus, history is given continuity.

Joachim has frequently been described as a "picture thinker." Toward the end of his life, he began to make elaborate and colorful drawings which graphically explained his main ideas. These drawings were compiled around 1227-1239 as *Liber figurarum* by his disciples and provide visual explanations of the intricacies of his thought.

The peace and understanding of the third age, an age which would accomplish true monastic contemplation, would be phased in exactly as the second had emerged from the first. Two new monastic orders, contemplative in the pattern of Moses and evangelical in the pattern of Elijah, would usher in the age, guiding human history from the second *status* to the third. All human history would reach fruition when "the new order of the people of God," as Joachim called it, was established. This future state of the church and society would be a physical commune based on the monastic utopian model which he drew in *Liber figurarum* and entitled *Dispositio novi ordinis pertinens ad tercium statum*. The community, which in the drawing is heavily annotated with explanatory details, would feature a contemplative society of monks, clerics, and laity living harmoniously together under the direction of a spiritual father and his councillors.

By 1200, Joachim had finished his major works, and many minor ones too, presenting them with a testamentary letter to Pope Innocent III. Joachim died just before Easter, 1202.

Summary

Joachim of Fiore was the most important apocalyptic writer and exegete of prophecy in the Middle Ages. He introduced an optimistic pattern of history which challenged future generations to view human events in terms of progress instead of deterioration.

Joachim's influence has been significant but difficult to measure, since many thinkers whose ideas reflect his tripartite scheme of history cannot be shown to have had direct access to his texts. It is certain that he influenced millenarian sects of the thirteenth century whose teachings, unlike his own, were thoroughly heretical, and references to his ideas can be tracked through subsequent centuries. The nineteenth century brought an upsurge of interest in Joachim; in particular, Joachimite thought entered the current of esoteric lore that profoundly influenced nineteenth century European literature. As a consequence, modern writers as diverse as William Butler Yeats and D. H. Lawrence were familiar with Joachim's ideas and appropriated them in fashioning their own apocalyptic visions of history.

Bibliography

Bloomfield, Morton. "Joachim of Flora: A Critical Survey of His Canon, Teachings, Sources, Biography, and Influence." *Traditio* 13 (1957): 249-311. A standard bibliography and summary of scholarship regarding Joachim up to 1957. Bloomfield updated this essay in 1980 in the volume edited by Ann Williams (see entry below).

Joachim of Fiore. *Liber de Concordia Novi ac Veteris Testamenti*. Edited by E. Randolph Daniel. Philadelphia: American Philosophical Society, 1983. This is the only modern edition of any of Joachim's major works. Introductory chapters answer perplexing questions about the abbot's extant manuscripts and technical aspects of his schema.

McGinn, Bernard. *Apocalyptic Spirituality*. New York: Paulist Press, 1979. This fine work contains a lengthy section on Joachim and his relationship to medieval apocalypticism, as well as translations of key documents.

_____. *The Calabrian Abbot: Joachim of Fiore in the History of Western Thought*. New York: Macmillan, 1985. Through both new essays and reprints of past articles by the author, this book firmly places Joachim in the history of Western thought. With Reeves's book (below), undoubtedly the best introduction to Joachim and his thought.

Reeves, Marjorie. *The Influence of Prophecy in the Later Middle Ages: A Study in Joachimism*. Oxford: Clarendon Press, 1969. This remains the classic, standard, and most complete study of Joachim, his life, his works, his teachings, and his influence up to the sixteenth century. An appendix contains lists of Joachim's authentic and spurious works.

Reeves, Marjorie, and Warwick Gould. *Joachim of Fiore and the Myth of the Eternal Evangel in the Nineteenth Century*. Oxford: Clarendon Press, 1987. An important study of the ways in which Joachim continues to influence the modern world. The book analyzes major literary figures of the eighteenth and nineteenth centuries who utilized the ideas of Joachim in their own works.

Reeves, Marjorie, and Beatrice Hirsch-Reich. *The Figurae of Joachim of Fiore*. Oxford: Clarendon Press, 1972. The most definitive study of Joachim's drawing and symbols. Chapters address major themes in Joachim's schema through his own visual portrayal of those themes.

West, Delno. *Joachim of Fiore in Christian Thought*. 2 vols. New York: Burt Franklin and Co., 1975. A sequence of journal articles in several languages which are generally unavailable in American libraries. Essays relate to Joachim and Joachimite themes studied over the twentieth century.

West, Delno, and Sandra Zimdars-Swartz. *Joachim of Fiore: A Study in Spiritual Perception and History*. Bloomington: Indiana University Press, 1983. Meant as an introduction for the general reader, this book is focused on Joachim's life and teachings as a major contribution to Western intellectual history.

Williams, Ann, ed. *Prophecy and Millenarianism: Essays in Honour of Marjorie Reeves*. Harlow, England: Longman Group, 1980. A festschrift presented to Reeves. Individual essays deal with various aspects of Joachim of Fiore and his teachings from the thirteenth century to the seventeenth century. Also, the book contains essays dealing with Byzantine and Islamic apocalypticism relating to Joachim's interpretations.

Delno West

JOAN OF ARC

Born: c. 1412; Domremy, France
Died: May 30, 1431; Rouen, France
Areas of Achievement: Government, politics, and religion
Contribution: Joan's victories initiated the withdrawal of English troops from France to end the Hundred Years' War, and she made possible the coronation of Charles VII at Reims. As a martyr to her vision and mission, she had as much influence after her death as in her lifetime.

Early Life

Usually identified with the province of Lorraine, Joan of Arc grew up a daughter of France in Domremy, a village divided between the king's territory and that of the Dukes of Bar and Lorraine. Bells from the church next to her home sounded the events of her youth. Her father, Jacques, was a peasant farmer and respected citizen. Joan learned piety from her mother, Isabelle Romée, as part of a large family. She took special pride in spinning and sewing; she never learned to read or write. By custom, she would have assumed her mother's surname, but in her public career she was called the Maid of Orléans, or Joan the Maid (with the double sense of virgin and servant).

Joan was born into the violence of both the Hundred Years' War and the French Civil War. Henry V, King of England, had gained control of most of northern France and, with the aid of the French Duke of Burgundy, claimed the crown from the insane Charles VI. The heir to the throne, Charles VII— or the Dauphin, as he was called—was young and apparently believed that his cause was hopeless. Five years after his father's death, he was still uncrowned, and Reims, the traditional coronation site, was deep in English territory. Domremy, on the frontier, was exposed to all the depredations of the war and was pillaged on at least one occasion during Joan's childhood.

Joan began to hear voices and to be visited by the patron saints of France, Saint Michael, Saint Catherine, and Saint Margaret, when she was thirteen or fourteen years old. She claimed that she heard and saw the saints, who became her companions and directed her every step. Initially, she took the voices as calling her to a holy life, and she pledged her virginity and piety. Later she came to believe that it was her mission to deliver France from the English.

Paintings and medals were made of Joan, but no genuine portrait has been identified; a contemporary sketch survives by a man who never saw her. Three carved limestone heads in helmets (now in Boston, Loudun, and Orléans) may represent near-contemporary portraits. They show a generous nose and mouth and heavy-lidded eyes. She had a ruddy complexion; black hair in a documentary seal (now lost) indicates her coloring. Sturdy enough to wear armor and live a soldier's life, she had a gentle voice. She wore a red frieze dress when she left Domremy; when she approached the Dauphin at Chinon, she wore men's clothing: black woolen doublet and laced leggings, cap, cape, and boots. She wore her hair short like a man's, or a nun's, cut above the ears in the "pudding basin" style which facilitated wearing a helmet and discouraged lustful thoughts. Later, the Dauphin provided her with armor and money for fashionable clothing. The gold-embroidered red costume in which she was finally captured may have been made from cloth sent to her by the captive Duke of Orléans.

Life's Work

In 1428, Joan attempted to gain support from Robert de Baudricourt, the royal governor of Vaucouleurs. (The pregnancy of a kinswoman living two miles from Vaucouleurs provided Joan with a pretext to leave home.) Baudricourt, after rejecting her twice—as the voices had predicted—became caught up in Joan's mission. The English had besieged Orléans, as she had told him they would, and he, similarly besieged, had to agree to surrender his castle unless the Dauphin came to his aid by a specified date. Before sending Joan to the Dauphin, he had her examined and exorcised.

Charles agreed to the interview with Joan in desperation. Orléans, besieged since October of 1428, had great strategic importance; its fall would shake the loyalty of his remaining supporters and the readiness of his cities to provide money. Joan's appearance at court on February 25, 1429, after traveling through enemy territory for eleven days, brought fresh hope. She identified the Dauphin at once in the crowded room, and she gave him some sign, "the King's Secret," which confirmed her mission but whose nature is still debated. A second exhaustive investigation of Joan occurred at Poitiers, where her piety and simplicity impressed everyone. Charles established a household for her. She had a standard made and adopted an ancient sword, discovered, through her directions, buried in the church of Sainte-Catherine-de-Fierbois.

On April 28, 1429, Joan and an expedition, believing they were on a supply mission, entered Orléans. Joan addressed the English commander, calling on him to retreat. She turned rough French soldiers into crusaders, conducting daily assemblies for prayer and insisting that they rid themselves of camp followers and go to confession. When a party bringing supplies to the city on the opposite bank found the wind blowing against them, she predicted the sudden change of wind that permitted the boats to cross. Nonplussed Englishmen allowed another shipment led by priests to pass without firing on it; they explained their lack of action as the result of bewitchment. Within the city, Joan's inspired leadership encouraged the troops to follow her famous standard and her ringing cry, "In God's name, charge boldly!" On May 7, though seriously wounded as she had predicted, she rallied the troops to victory at the Tourelles fortification, after the French captains had given up hope. The next day, the English withdrew from Orléans.

In little more than a week, with much plunder and killing of prisoners, the French drove their enemies from the remaining Loire strongholds of Jargeau, Meung, and Beaugency. Though Joan took part in these actions, her principal influence remained her extraordinary attraction and rallying of forces; she later said that she had killed no one. The troops of Arthur de Richemont, brother of the Duke of Brittany, who now joined the Dauphin, counted decisively in another victory at Patay on June 17.

Charles's coronation on July 17 at Reims, deep in enemy territory, clearly shows Joan's influence. Counselors and captains advised Charles to take advantage of his victories and move against Normandy. Joan persuaded him instead to travel to Reims, and city after city yielded to siege or simply opened its gates to the Dauphin: Auxerre, Troyes, Châlons, and Reims itself. The stunned English regent, the Duke of Bedford, offered no resistance.

After the coronation, Joan's single-minded drive to take Paris and gain the release of the Duke of Orléans conflicted with a royal policy of caution and diplomacy based on the expectation that Burgundy, too, would rally peacefully to Charles. Charles ennobled Joan and her family and provided her with attendants and money, but she was too popular to permit her return to Domremy. Her voices warned that she had little time. By September 8, when the assault on Paris finally began, the English had regained their aplomb. Joan, again wounded, unsuccessfully urged an evening attack. Charles's orders the next day forbade an attack, though the Baron of Montmorency and his men came out of the city to join the royal army, and on September 13, Charles withdrew his troops.

Joan now joined in a holding action to prevent the English forces from using the extended truce to retake their lost positions. Her men took Saint-Pierre-le-Moûtier, but lack of supplies forced her to abandon La Charité. In the spring of 1430, she led volunteers to stiffen the resistance of Compiègne against the Burgundians, contrary to the royal policy of pacification. That helps to explain Charles's failure to negotiate her release after her capture at Compiègne on May 23—an event also predicted by her voices. The Burgundians sold her to the English authorities.

Joan's trial, which ran from January 9 through May 30, 1431, tested her faith and gave her a final opportunity to uphold the French cause. Her death was a foregone conclusion; the English reserved their right to retry her if the Church exonerated her. Bishop Pierre Cauchon of Beauvais took the lead, realizing that a church trial, by proving her a witch, would turn her victories to Anglo-Burgundian advantage. Indeed, her captors may have believed her a camp trollop and sorceress until a physical examination by the Duchess of Bedford, the sister of Philip of Burgundy, proved Joan's virginity. That made it clear that she had not had carnal relations with Satan, a sure sign of sorcery.

After twice attempting to escape (for which her voices blamed her), she stood trial in Rouen. The two earlier investigations and Joan's impeccable behavior obliged Cauchon to falsify evidence and maneuver her into self-incrimination. She showed great perspicacity—her voices told her to answer boldly. Cauchon finally reduced the seventy-two points on which she had been examined to twelve edited points, on which her judges and the faculty of the University of Paris condemned her.

Seriously ill and threatened by her examiners, Joan apparently signed a recantation which temporarily spared her life. Cauchon claimed that she had renounced her voices; some historians claim forgery, admission to lesser charges, or some code by which she indicated denial. In any case, she returned to woman's clothing as ordered and to her cell. She was later found wearing men's clothing (perhaps partly to protect herself from her guards). When questioned, Joan replied that her voices had rebuked her for her change of heart. On May 29, the judges agreed unanimously to give Joan over to the English authorities. She received Communion on the morning of May 30 and was burned as a heretic.

Summary

Mystics with political messages abounded in Joan's world, but none had Joan's impact on politics. Widespread celebration in 1436 of Claude des Armoises, claiming to be Joan escaped from the flames, demonstrated her continuing popularity. Orléans preserved Joan's cult, and Domremy became a national shrine. A surge of interest beginning in the nineteenth century with Napoleon has made Joan one of the most written-about persons in history, but efforts to analyze her in secular terms reaffirm the continuing mystery of her inspiration.

Many people in the huge crowd that witnessed Joan's death believed in her martyrdom and reported miracles. English insistence on complete destruction of her body, with her ashes thrown into the Seine, underscored the point. When he took Rouen and the trial records in 1450, Charles VII ordered her case reopened, but only briefly. Too many influential living persons were implicated in Joan's condemnation, and a reversal of the verdict would also support papal claims to jurisdiction in France. A papal legate, Guillaume d'Estouteville, later encouraged Joan's aged mother to appeal to the Pope, which brought about rehabilitation proceedings and the declaration of her innocence in 1456. Even then, the revised verdict merely revoked the earlier decision on procedural grounds without endorsing Joan's mission or condemning her judges. Joan was canonized by Pope Benedict XV on May 16, 1920, and France honors her with a festival day on the second Sunday of May.

Bibliography

Fabre, Lucien. *Joan of Arc*. Translated by Gerard Hopkins. New York: McGraw-Hill Book Co., 1954. Fabre's account reflects the French and Catholic position. He calls the English "Godons," as Joan did (from their characteristic oath), and makes Cauchon a monster. He bases conclusions about the various puzzles on documents and provides a guide to the vast literature.

Guillemin, Henri. *The True History of Joan "of Arc."* Translated by William Oxferry. London: Allen and Unwin, 1972. An example of the tradition that Joan did not die in 1431. One of the many variations in this tradition makes her the sister of Charles VII. Historians have never given much credence to books of this genre.

Lightbody, Charles Wayland. *The Judgments of Joan: Joan of Arc, a Study in Cultural History*. Cambridge, Mass.: Harvard University Press, 1961. A 171-page book on a very large topic. Lightbody treats the literature on Joan through the trial for rehabilitation; by way of apology, he promises a fuller treatment, which never appeared. Worth reading, but any author who treats George Bernard Shaw's play as revelatory about Joan and her times must be held suspect.

Lucie-Smith, Edward. *Joan of Arc*. London: Allen Lane, 1976. The necessary counterbalance to Fabre's biography. An objective and scholarly accounting, but in treating Joan's voices as hallucinations the author loses touch with Joan and her times. Lucie-Smith suggests a sympathetic approach to Joan's judges.

Pernoud, Régine. *Joan of Arc by Herself and Her Witnesses*. Translated by Edward Hyams. New York: Stein and Day, 1966. A work of great integrity and judgment by the director of the Centre Jeanne d'Arc in Orléans. She has culled documents of Joan's own times for an extremely useful book.

_____ . *The Retrial of Joan of Arc: The Evidence of the Trial for Her Rehabilitation, 1450-1456*. Translated by J. M. Cohen. Foreword by Katherine Anne Porter. New York: Harcourt, Brace and Co., 1955. Though incomplete, this includes the essential 1455-1456 testimony by 144 persons who knew Joan at various stages of her life, making her one of the best-documented personalities of her century. Intended to counteract the earlier trial, it proves something of a whitewash, but it also gives a valid picture of what Joan meant to the French people.

Vale, Malcom G. A. *Charles VII*. Berkeley: University of California Press, 1974. A biography of sound scholarship which provides a better guide to the political world than do Joan's biographies. Vale, an Englishman, plays down Joan's own importance.

Warner, Marina. *Joan of Arc: The Image of Female Heroism*. New York: Alfred A. Knopf, 1981. Warner finishes what Lightbody began, ranging through the centuries. She is notably good in utilizing recent scholarship, providing, for example, a hard look at how little is really known about Joan's appearance. Warner's feminist interpretation, however, imposes modern notions on fifteenth century experience. She plays down Joan's voices and treats her fasting as possible anorexia and her adoption of men's clothing as psychologically significant.

Paul Stewart

JŌCHŌ

Born: Date unknown; probably Kyoto, Japan
Died: 1057; probably Kyoto, Japan
Area of Achievement: Art
Contribution: Jōchō established an indigenous Japanese style of wood sculpture using a joined-wood technique.

Early Life

Very little is known about the first twenty years of Jōchō's life. At the age of twenty, he became a disciple of Kōjō (also known as Kōshō), according to a book called *Chūgaishō* (compiled in the twelfth century). Kōjō was a prestigious court sculptor in Kyoto, and he and Jōchō collaborated on many projects. Their works were enshrined at the Hōjōji Muryōjuin (Amida hall) in Kyoto, which was built for the former prime minister Fujiwara Michinaga. That was the first time Jōchō met Michinaga, who was the most powerful politician in the late Heian period. To be invited to make a sculpture for Michinaga was considered a great honor.

According to an entry for the year 1020 in the *Chūgaishō*, Jōchō deeply impressed Michinaga with his sculptures. This source also maintains that, with Michinaga's help, Jōchō became one of the top artists of the late Heian period. (Jōchō's age at this time is disputed among scholars.)

Aside from the *Chūgaishō*, there is no source that describes Jōchō's early life. It is assumed that Jōchō spent his days of apprenticeship under Kōjō. Kōjō, who may have been the father of Jōchō, had the greatest influence on him. It is fair to say that Kōjō created the foundation, in both style and method, for Jōchō's achievement in art.

Kōjō was active from the end of the tenth century until his death around 1022. His style was calm and elegant, with soft modeling, refined details, and naturalistic proportions, as seen in the Fudō Myōō (Bright King) image at Dōshuin, Kyoto. His work was a great change from solid-wood sculpture images of the previous period, with their massive, powerful form but rather stiff style.

Kōjō was well connected with the upper class of society, including the court, aristocracy, and dominant monasteries. His lifetime relationship with Michinaga and his association with a monk of the Tendai Buddhist sect, Genshin, were particularly influential. According to Genshin's Pure Land teaching, the aristocracy should strive to be reborn in paradise after leaving this world.

Hōjōji was Michinaga's project to visualize paradise in this world. The nine Amida Buddhas and two bodhisattvas at the Muryōjuin were icons for the salvation of Michinaga on his deathbed. In fact, Michinaga died holding the colorful strings extending from the hands of the nine Buddhas. The late

Heian sculpture style (also called the Fujiwara style) was the art of Pure Land Buddhism. Kōjō made a great step toward this style, and after his death, Jōchō carried on the attempt to create an ideal form of the Buddha for the aristocracy.

Life's Work

Jōchō's active period was roughly from 1020 to 1057. His accomplishments cover three distinct phases: the image making for the Hōjōji, the engagement in the Kōfukuji reconstruction, and the creation of the Amida for the Byōdōin Hōōdō (Phoenix Hall). Two years after his debut at the Muryōjuin, Jōchō made thirteen images for the halls of Kondō (golden hall) and Godaidō (hall of five deities) at Hōjōji. After Kōjō's death, Michinaga assigned Jōchō to complete the Hōjōji project. Some of the statues that Jōchō made for the two halls are the Buddha figures of Dainichi, Shaka, and Yakushi, bodhisattva figures of Monju and Miroku, and various Great Kings and other deities. For this incomparable contribution, Jōchō was awarded the Buddhist rank of "Bridge of Law" (*Hokkyō*) in 1022; he was the first sculptor to be so honored. The award enhanced the social status of sculptors; during later periods, other sculptors became eligible for this honor.

In the following year, Jōchō made the images for the Yakushidō Hall in the Hōjōji. There were twenty-five statues in all. In 1026, he made twenty-seven life-size images within two months for one of Michinaga's daughters, Empress Takeko. Not only the quantity but also the size of the work was characteristic of Jōchō's sculptures. In the case of the Hōjōji, the images vary from about two to ten meters in height for standing figures and one to five meters for seated figures. During this period, the *jōroku* seated Buddha was a popular figure, measuring approximately three meters in height.

One of Jōchō's accomplishments was the establishment of a studio system. Responding to the popularity of icon making among the aristocracy, his studio increased its scale to be available for mass production of huge sculptures. About one hundred sculptors worked under Jōchō to make the Hōjōji imagery. By using a multiple-block technique of assembling wood, many images could be produced in a short time. A division of labor was established: There were *daibusshi* (major Buddhist sculptors) and *shōbusshi* (minor Buddhist sculptors). Several *shōbusshi* worked under each *daibusshi*, and Jōchō supervised all *daibusshi*. This system proved to be effective and was adopted by sculptors in later periods.

The technique popular during the early Heian period, which involved solid wood, was replaced by Jōchō's joined-wood method, which was more economical with wood, produced relatively lightweight sculptures, helped prevent cracking, and allowed for mass production. The thinner wood used in this process forced changes in the style and type of carving. Instead of deep and sharp grooves, which produced the "rolling wave" style (*honpa-shiki*) seen during previous periods, the figures now featured shallow carving, with the result that the surface had a soft, gentle quality. This change of style suited the taste of the aristocracy.

In 1048, Jōchō acquired the even higher Buddhist rank of "Eyes of Law" (*Hōgen*) for his efforts in reconstructing the images of the Kōfukuji temple. The Kōfukuji, a temple of the Fujiwara family in Nara, burned down in 1046. The next year, Fujiwara Yorimichi, son of Michinaga, began to reconstruct the temple. Jōchō's participation in this project provided a good opportunity for him to learn the Nara style of sculpture. He also made the Buddha Shaka for one of the halls of the Yakushiji temple, Tōin Hakkaku Endō, in Nara. For this image, he is said to have copied the Shaka of Daianji temple, which is one of the excellent works from the Nara period. Jōchō's study of the classic style of Nara later appeared in the perfect form of the Amida in the Phoenix Hall of the Byōdōin temple at Uji, Kyoto. Jōchō surpassed Kōjō by adopting the Nara style in his sculpture.

Among a number of Jōchō's masterpieces, the Amida image in Phoenix Hall is his only work that is known to exist in modern times. A diary of Taira Sadaie, who was Yorimichi's secretary, states that on the nineteenth day of the second month of 1053, the Amida was enshrined in the Amida hall of Byōdōin. It mentions that Jōchō received gifts for the making of the statue on the day the image was enshrined. This entry proves that the Amida at Phoenix Hall was made by Jōchō.

The Byōdōin was first the villa of Michinaga, and after his death it became Yorimichi's villa. In 1052, at the age of sixty-one, Yorimichi converted this villa into a temple. In the next year, the dedication of the Phoenix Hall was held, and the Amida image was brought from Kyoto and placed inside. The Phoenix Hall is a building with wings on each side and a tail extending to the rear, and it is completely surrounded by ponds. Two phoenix birds are set on each side of the roof of the hall. The Amida is seated on a lotus pedestal in the altar placed in the center of the hall. It is backed by a boat-shaped mandorla decorated with clouds and angels. Above the mandorla is an elaborate canopy. The fifty-two cloud-riding bodhisattvas are suspended from the walls, and the Pure Land paintings are depicted below on the door panels and walls. The ceiling, pillars, brackets, and other woodwork are decorated with bird and flower motifs. The entire hall is decorated splendidly to express a world of paradise. Phoenix Hall is an excellent representative of Fujiwara aristocratic art, which blended landscape, architecture, sculpture, painting, and craft.

Jōchō and his studio were probably engaged in the making of all the sculptural works for the hall. The Amida, however, was the supreme work. The seated Buddha is perfectly balanced and softly modeled. Every line is fluid and curvilinear; there is no distortion or imperfection. The face of the image has been described as being as round as a full moon. The facial expression is calm, tender, and full of affection. The thin robe is softly fitted to the body, and the folds of the simple drapery flow naturally. The folds are shallowly carved; Jōchō no longer used the early Heian style of carving that Kōjō used. The Buddha sits comfortably, hands folded in the posture of meditation.

The naturalness of this image reflects Jōchō's mastery of proportion. In 1134 the sculptors Inkaku and Inchō measured more than sixty sections of another Amida image made by Jōchō. The precise proportions of Jōchō's images are possible because of the innovative joined-wood method he used. Inspired by the aristocratic taste of the time, Jōchō's work reflects a sense of elegance. It is believed that Jōchō died on the first day of the eighth month of 1057.

Summary

Jōchō's Amida became a standard model for the seated Amida Buddha. During the twelfth century, the Jōchō style dominated Japanese sculpture. With the prosperity of Pure Land Buddhism, images similar to the Phoenix Hall Amida were made throughout Japan. Some of the examples include the Chūsonji and the Hakusui Amidadō, both in northern Japan. Most of these images remained faithful to Jōchō's style, reflecting little of the later sculptors' personalities. In fact, sculptors who attempted to emulate Jōchō's work tended to create stylized and lifeless figures. The limitations of Jōchō's style were those of the elite society of the period. His patrons were aristocrats and other members of the ruling class who were successful politically and economically. Thus the style he pioneered lost its vitality following the decline of the aristocracy and was eventually replaced by the Kamakura style.

Jōchō's contribution to the development of Japanese art was enormous. With Jōchō, Japanese Buddhist sculpture first achieved its own indigenous style. For centuries after the introduction of Buddhism to Japan in the early sixth century, Buddhist sculpture in Japan was imitative of Chinese and Korean art. Jōchō, following Kōjō's principle, was able to express the distinctively Japanese sense of beauty, serenity, and elegance in his images.

Bibliography

Fukuyama, Toshio. *Heian Temples: Byōdō-in and Chūson-ji.* Translated by Ronald K. Jones. New York: Weatherhill, 1976. A finely illustrated book dealing with the art of Pure Land Buddhism of the late Heian period. It contains the Hōjōji and Byōdōin Phoenix Hall of the eleventh century and the Chūsonji and others of the twelfth century.

Kuno, Takeshi, ed. *A Guide to Japanese Sculpture.* Tokyo: Maruyama and Co., 1963. Useful for a survey of the major trends of the history of Japanese sculpture. Contains helpful glossary and charts.

Moran, S. F. "The Statue of Amida Hōōdō, Byōdōin." *Oriental Art* 1, no. 2 (1960): 2-8. A complete technical study of the joined-wood method as exemplified by the Amida at the Byōdōin Phoenix Hall. It contains illustrations and diagrams for better understanding of the technique.

Nishikawa, Kyōtarō, and Emily J. Sano. *The Great Age of Japanese Buddhist Sculpture*, A.D. *600-1300*. Fort Worth, Tex.: Kimbell Art Museum, 1982. The catalog of an exhibition of Japanese Buddhist sculpture at the Kimbell Art Museum. A good source for the sculpture of Byōdōin Phoenix Hall.

Okazaki, Jōji. *Pure Land Buddhist Painting*. Translated by Elizabeth ten Grotenhuis. Tokyo: Kōdansha International and Shibundō, 1977. A useful source for understanding Pure Land Buddhism and its art, which flourished among the Fujiwara aristocracy.

Yamasaki, K., and K. Nishikawa. "Polychromed Sculptures in Japan." *Studies in Conservation* 15 (November, 1970): 278-293. A study of the techniques used to paint wooden sculptures in Japan, with examples of Buddhist statues. The Amida of Phoenix Hall and the lotus pedestal contained in the Amida are discussed.

Yoshiko Kainuma

JOHANAN BEN ZAKKAI

Born: c. A.D. 1; Judaea
Died: c. A.D. 80; Beror Heil, west of Jerusalem, Judaea
Area of Achievement: Religion
Contribution: After the destruction of Jerusalem by the Romans in A.D. 70, when the temple cult—the center of Jewish life—lay in ruins, Johanan was responsible for reorienting Jewish life around faithful observance of the Law (Torah).

Early Life

Little is known of the early life of Johanan ben Zakkai. Of the three most important sources of information for Roman-occupied Judaea during the first century, two of them, Flavius Josephus' *Peri tou Ioudaikou polemou* (A.D. 75-79; *Jewish War*) and the New Testament, contain no reference to Johanan. The rabbinical writings from the Talmud which constitute the sole source of information regarding the life of Johanan ben Zakkai were compiled between the third and fifth centuries, and at best testify to carefully handed-down memory. (For reasons of standardization, the initials B.C. and A.D. are used here to designate the chronological divisions often referred to as B.C.E., "before the common era," and C.E., "common era.")

The Talmud pictures Johanan as a leader among the Pharisees, a group of especially devout observers of the Torah (the first five books in the Hebrew Bible) who first came to prominence in the late second or first centuries B.C. and who, after the destruction of the Temple in A.D. 70 by the Romans, became the sole shapers of what is today normative Judaism. The main tradition concerning Johanan relates that he "occupied himself in commerce forty years, served as apprentice to the sages forty years, and sustained Israel forty years." He was one of four Jewish leaders believed to have lived for 120 years, the others being Moses, Hillel the Elder, and Rabbi Akiba ben Joseph. Johanan was considered to have been the last of eighty students of Hillel, who, in similar manner, "went up from Babylonia aged forty years, served as apprentice to the sages forty years, and sustained Israel forty years."

Johanan actually was born near the beginning of the first century and died during its last quarter, probably around 80. "Johanan" means "the Lord gave graciously"; Ezra and Nehemiah record 760 sons of Zakkai ("righteous man") among nearly forty-five thousand exiles returning to Jerusalem and Judah from Babylonian exile during the sixth century B.C. Johanan was descended from commoners rather than priests; his halakhic (legal) rulings sternly criticize the conduct of the upper classes toward the poor. Some of his rulings reflect a detailed knowledge of business affairs and support the claim that he engaged in business in his early or mid-life. As a young man, he entered the rabbinic academy of Hillel in Jerusalem. Whether he studied under the Master himself is problematical; Hillel died probably around A.D. 10 or at most a few years thereafter.

What is certain is that, of the two great Pharisaic schools of Torah interpretation—those of Hillel and Shammai—Johanan was schooled in the traditions of Hillel, which are generally pictured as more irenic in approach to the Law and more patient in dealing with students, as well as more widely accepted among the middle classes. Hence Johanan developed traits of flexibility in casuistry and gentleness toward students which enabled him to make a lasting contribution to the development of Judaism.

As a student, Johanan was famed for both self-discipline and intellectual acuity. He never traveled four cubits (six feet) without words of Torah, even in winter. No one preceded him into the schoolroom, nor did he ever leave anyone behind there. "If all the heavens were parchment," said Johanan, "and all the trees pens, and all the oceans ink, they would not suffice to write down the wisdom which I have learned from my masters." One of his students later made a similar statement regarding his own education at the feet of Johanan. Tradition pictures Hillel endorsing Johanan, conferring as it were his own mantle on his young student. When he completed his studies in Jerusalem, Johanan moved to a village in the northern province of Galilee—the other end of the country from Jerusalem and far removed from its scrupulous observance of the Torah. There, with his wife and his young son, he undertook his career as a teacher, a missionary for the Torah. In the Pharisaic manner, he supported himself, probably in business, while he attempted to teach the Galileans.

Life's Work

· A political event—the destruction of the Temple in A.D. 70 by the Romans—intervened in Johanan's life to thrust him, at seventy years of age, onto the center stage of Jewish history. Johanan had given his life to scholarship and teaching and was not involved in politics. His eighteen years in Galilee and the subsequent three decades which he spent as a teacher in Jerusalem together consumed his prime years. He reached the biblical "threescore and ten" offstage from history, and his decades of labor in Galilee and Jerusalem are historically noteworthy only as part of the story of a life made unexpectedly significant in the context of the destruction of the center of Judaism—the Temple—and the consequent reorientation of the Jewish religion around the Law.

There is no specific evidence that Johanan's purpose in going to Galilee was to serve as a missionary of the Torah, but it is clear that this is the significance of the years he spent there. He resided in Arav, a small village in the hill country of central Galilee, where he generally failed to make an impression on the religious life of the region. During his entire stay he had only one student, Hanina ben Dosa, and only two cases of halakhic law were brought before him for judgment. The Galileans, recent converts to the Jerusalem cult, sought a religion of miracle-working, messianic fulfillment, the piety of the Temple pilgrimage, and salvation in the next world. Johanan, by contrast, offered only the discipline of a humble life of faithful observance of the Law set forth in the Torah. A third century Talmudic source records the closing of Johanan's ministry in Galilee: "Eighteen years Rabban Yohanan ben Zakkai spent in 'Arav, and only these two cases came before him. At the end he said, 'O Galilee, Galilee! You hate the Torah! Your end will be to be besieged!'"

Disappointed, Johanan took his ailing son and wife and returned to Jerusalem. There he set up a school near the site of the Temple and spent the next three decades patiently teaching the Torah. His quiet success is demonstrated in his rise through Pharisaic ranks. Pharisaic leadership had often been shared between pairs—Shemaiah and Abtalion, Hillel and Shammai. Two halakhic rulings sent to Galilee from Jerusalem during this period bear the names of both Gamaliel I—the acknowledged leader of the Pharisees—and Johanan ben Zakkai, who probably served as his partner or deputy. Johanan, nearing his seventieth year, could look back with satisfaction upon a life of quiet scholarship, but he had accomplished nothing to earn for himself a permanent niche in history.

Just at this point in Johanan's life, an explosion occurred in the political life of Judaea. Judaean independence had been won from the Greeks in 166 B.C., but after 62 B.C., the nation had had to live in uncertain peace under Roman occupation. The Pharisees, for whom the heart of Judaism lay in personal fidelity to the Torah rather than in political sovereignty, had accepted tenuous coexistence with Rome. From 5 B.C. onward, however, there had grown among the people a Zealot movement which anticipated messianic fulfillment in the overthrow of Roman rule and the establishment of a divine monarchy in place of Caesar's. In late A.D. 65, a contingent of Zealots ambushed and defeated the twelfth Roman legion, inaugurating what is in Roman annals the famous Bellum Judaicum of 66-70. In face of the Zealot revolt and the siege of Jerusalem by the Romans, Johanan made the most critical decision of his life—one which made him for a brief moment the single most important figure in Judaism.

In 68, Johanan abandoned the war and the Zealot-controlled city of Jerusalem, fleeing for safety to the camp of Vespasian. He allowed himself to be smuggled past the Zealot watchguards and out of Jerusalem inside a coffin borne by two of his rabbinical students. Pharisaic leaders such as Gamaliel I who remained behind with the Zealots perished in the massacre which followed the fall of Jerusalem to the Romans.

The main Talmudic tradition regarding what happened next represents the following encounter when Johanan arrived at the camp of Vespasian:

They opened the coffin, and Rabban Yoḥanan stood up before him. "Are you Rabban Yoḥanan ben Zakkai?" Vespasian inquired. "Tell me what I may give you."

"I ask nothing of you," Rabban Yoḥanan replied, "save Yavneh, where I might go and teach my disciples and there establish a house of prayer, and perform all the commandments."

"Go," Vespasian said to him.

Moreover, Johanan allegedly predicted that Vespasian would become emperor, a prophecy fulfilled three days later.

A different interpretation has suggested that Johanan was held under house arrest at Yavneh by the Romans. Whether Johanan was Vespasian's guest or his detainee, however, he spent the decade following the fall of Jerusalem in the Roman-protected town of Yavneh, instructing a contingent of Pharisees who had survived the destruction. There he husbanded and nurtured the most important remnant of Pharisees, and in so doing patched together the torn fabric of Jewish national life and rescued Judaism as a Law-centered community now that it could no longer continue as a temple cult.

The period of Johanan's service at Yavneh was brief, no more than a decade. The manifest yield of his labors was sparse; few chose to sit at the feet of one who seemingly had turned his back on the nation in its hour of need. So difficult was his reception that he was even compelled to remove from Yavneh to the neighboring settlement of Beror Heil, where he died, probably around 80, surrounded by a very small number of students.

Succeeding generations, however, proved the permanent worth of Johanan's years at Yavneh. His small academy laid foundations which guaranteed the survival of Pharisaism. Furthermore, his tenure there afforded sufficient time for Gamaliel II, the true successor of Gamaliel I, to emerge from the political shadow of his family's support of the rebellion against Rome. The next decade at Yavneh—the 90's—was pivotal in the history of Judaism: Gamaliel II led five of Johanan's students, among others, in constructing the basis for what eventually emerged, in the vacuum remaining after the destruction of the Temple, as normative Talmudic Judaism.

Summary

According to rabbinic tradition, Johanan ben Zakkai acted out the nation's response to the fall of the Temple: It was he who rent his garments upon hearing the news. His physical appearance is undocumented; what is emphasized instead is the high rabbinical estimate of Johanan, whom the Jewish teachers ranked alongside Moses, Hillel, and Akiba ben Joseph as one who indeed "sustained all Israel." His title, "Rabban," indicates that he was considered the rabbi of primacy during his own period.

"My son," Johanan once replied to a student who despaired that the destruction of the Temple would mean that there could be no more atonement for sins, "be not grieved. We have another atonement as effective as this. And what is it? It is acts of lovingkindness, as it is said, *For I desire mercy, not sacrifice.*" In accord with this principle, Johanan's halakhic rulings at Yavneh readjusted the Jewish ritual calendar to suit the demands of the new situation in which the synagogue, rather than the Temple, would be the center of Jewish life.

In the age of a Judaism beset with messianic movements such as those of the Zealots themselves, of Jesus of Nazareth, and of Simon bar Kokhba, Johanan set a standard of caution which became normative in Judaism through the succeeding nineteen centuries: "If you have a sapling in your hand, and it is said to you, 'Behold, there is the Messiah'—go on with your planting, and afterward go out and receive him."

"Do not haste to tear down [the altars of Gentiles], so that you do not have to rebuild them with your own hands. Do not destroy those of brick, that they may not say to you, 'Come and build them of stone.'" So Johanan had cautioned the Zealots. His advice became the watchword of the tradition of political restraint necessary for survival during the long centuries of persecution and statelessness of the Jewish people between the fall of the second Jewish commonwealth in A.D. 70 and the establishment of the third in 1948.

Bibliography

Alon, Gedalyahu. *Jews, Judaism, and the Classical World: Studies in Jewish History in the Times of the Second Temple and Talmud.* Jerusalem: Magnes Press of Hebrew University, 1977. A series of articles on a wide variety of critical issues dealing with the history of the Jewish people from the first century B.C. through the third century A.D. Alon argues that Johanan ben Zakkai was held under house arrest at Yavneh by Vespasian.

Ben-Sasson, H. H., ed. *A History of the Jewish People.* Cambridge, Mass.: Harvard University Press, 1976. Written by six eminent scholars, this is the best one-volume interpretive history of the Jewish people. Places Johanan ben Zakkai in the context of the entire stream of Jewish history.

Neusner, Jacob. *Development of a Legend: Studies on the Traditions Concerning Yohanan ben Zakkai.* Leiden, Netherlands: E. J. Brill, 1970. A detailed criticism of the Talmudic texts which are the sole source of evidence for the life of Johanan.

_____. *From Politics to Piety: The Emergence of Pharisaic Judaism.* Englewood Cliffs, N.J.: Prentice-Hall, 1973. A brief popular account of Pharisaic Judaism during the era of Johanan ben Zakkai.

_____. *A Life of Yohanan ben Zakkai, ca. 1-80 C.E.* 2d ed. Leiden, Netherlands: E. J. Brill, 1970. The single scholarly biography of Johanan ben Zakkai written in English. Neusner contests Alon's view that Johanan was under house arrest at Yavneh and argues for the more widely accepted tradition that he was allowed to reside in Yavneh as a favor from Vespasian. Neusner published his text without notes in popular form in his *First Century Judaism in Crisis: Yohanan ben Zakkai and the Renaissance of Torah* (Nashville, Tenn.: Abingdon Press, 1975).

Zeitlin, Solomon. *The Rise and Fall of the Judaean State: A Political, Social, and Religious History of the Second Commonwealth.* Vol. 3, *66 C.E.-120 C.E.* Philadelphia: Jewish Publication Society of America, 1978. An excellent narrative account of this period of Jewish history. One chapter treats the work of Johanan ben Zakkai at Yavneh.

Marlin Timothy Tucker

JOHN OF DAMASCUS

Born: c. 675; Damascus, Syria
Died: December 4, 749; near Jerusalem
Areas of Achievement: Religion and literature
Contribution: During the Iconoclastic Controversy of the eighth century, John wrote a series of theological tracts defending the use of images in Christian worship, thus establishing the theological position of Eastern Orthodoxy.

Early Life

John of Damascus, or John Damascene, was born in the city with which he is identified at a time when Syria was under the rule of the caliphs. His family name was Mansur, meaning "victory." John's father was Sergius Mansur, a wealthy Christian who served at the court of the Umayyad caliph 'Abd al-Malik. Because of the practice of toleration by the Umayyad Dynasty, it was not unusual for Christians to serve the caliphs. When Sergius was elevated to the rank of prime minister, he was troubled at the thought that his son, John, would adopt Arab ways. He placed him under the instruction of the Sicilian monk Cosmas, who had been brought to Damascus as a slave.

It was customary for the Arabs to go on plundering excursions along the Mediterranean coasts and to return with a number of prisoners, whom they made slaves. Among a group of prisoners brought back from the coast of Sicily was the monk Cosmas. Cosmas was an ordained priest and a teacher. He knew grammar and logic, as much arithmetic as Pythagoras and as much geometry as Euclid. He had also studied music, poetry, and astronomy.

The usual practice was to sell such prisoners to farmers, who would work them in the fields until they dropped dead. There existed laws against introducing slaves into the houses of official families. John's father managed, however, to buy Cosmas for a great price from al-Malik and took him into his home; from that point onward the learned monk became John's tutor and master. Thus John acquired a formidable knowledge of theology, rhetoric, natural history, music, and astronomy. He learned from Cosmas much of the world and of spiritual theory.

John became deeply religious and, like his father, was given to good works. Upon his father's death, however, Caliph 'Abd al-Malik appointed John to the high position of chief secretary. In an Oriental court, only the position of councillor of state was higher. In time, John enjoyed the powers once possessed by his father. While serving in the Oriental court, John continued to practice the Christian virtues of charity and humility. He was obsessed by the thought of offering up all of his wealth to the poor and then following his teacher and master, Cosmas, into a monastery. It is clear that the humble Cosmas exerted more influence over John than did the mighty caliph.

Cosmas had retired to the monastery of St. Sabas in Palestine when he had completed John's education. John remained at his position in the caliph's court until approximately 730, when he, too, entered the monastery of St. Sabas. Yet already before he left the secular world, John had begun the great work of his life, the refutation of iconoclasm (the opposition to religious imagery).

Life's Work

Iconoclasm was the latest in a series of challenges—beginning with Arianism—that the Eastern church had had to face. The Iconoclastic Controversy began with Byzantine Emperor Leo III and continued through the reign of his successor, Constantine V. It was a conflict over images and the particular significance attached to them. In the Eastern (or Greek) church, the practice of venerating icons was widespread by the seventh century. The opponents of this practice maintained that Christianity, as a purely spiritual religion, must proscribe the cult of icons. This opposition was strong in the Byzantine Empire, so long the cradle of religious ferment. There were considerable remnants of Monophysitism, and the Paulicians, a sect hostile to any ecclesiastical cult, were gaining ground.

Defenders of the practice of venerating icons attributed Leo's hostility to images to Jewish and Muslim influences. Mosaic teaching requires strict repudiation of image worship, but it was contact with the Muslim world that had intensified the distrust of icons. Muslims have an abhorrence of any pictorial representation of the human countenance. They teach that "images are an abomination of the works of Satan."

In 726, the Greek islands of Thera and Therasia were shaken by a marine volcanic eruption. At the request of iconoclastic bishops of Asia Minor, Leo III responded to this natural disaster by issuing a decree declaring that the eruption was the result of God's wrath on the idolatry of the Greeks; therefore, all paintings, mosaics, and statues representing Christ and His saints had to be destroyed. Another decree ordered the destruction of the great statue of Christ over the bronze gate of the palace in Constantinople. A riot ensued when imperial officers tore down this statue. The emperor then ordered the execution of those who had tried to protect the statue; the victims were the first martyrs of the Iconoclastic Controversy.

In order to strengthen his position, Leo attempted to win over the pope and the patriarch of Constantinople. His proposals were decisively rejected by the aged Patriarch Germanus, and his correspondence with Pope Gregory II only produced negative results. After these two authorities, the emperor's principal opponent was John of Damascus.

As images, paintings, and statues were being destroyed, John wrote to the emperor. He argued that figures of the cherubim and seraphim adorned the ark of the covenant. Further, citing the Scriptures, John wrote that Solomon was ordered to adorn the walls of the Temple with living figures, flowers, and fruit. He concluded that it was fitting that Christians should adorn their churches. John's letter was reasoned and scholarly, replete with quotations from the Bible.

Leo was determined that the images be removed. He believed that Christianity needed purifying and that this could only come about with the destruction of the images. Leo was determined that Christianity survive the increasing power of Islam. Failing to get any support from Germanus, who had joined the side of the image-worshipping Christians, Leo replaced him with Anastasius.

Still in the caliph's court in 730, John issued a formidable attack, quoting the evidence of the church fathers who favored the worship of images. He quoted from Saint Basil, Dionysius the Areopagite, Gregory of Nyssa, and Saint John Chrysostom as evidence that they openly supported the use of images. The image worshippers, he wrote, were not circumscribing God but were venerating God, which was right and proper. John closed his letter by deliberately misquoting Galatians 1:8 and accusing Leo of preaching a gospel contrary to the Bible. This letter ushered in real hostility between the emperor and John.

Unable to overwhelm John by force of argument, the emperor determined to destroy him by stratagem. He forged letters addressed to himself, signing John's name to them. The letters informed the Byzantine emperor that the guards surrounding Damascus were weak and negligent and could easily be subdued. The letters urged the emperor to send an army immediately against Damascus, stating that Leo would have the cooperation of John.

These forged letters were sent by messenger to the caliph. John was summoned and asked how he could explain them. When he could offer no explanation, the caliph ordered John's right hand severed. All that night, holding his severed hand to his wrist, John prostrated himself before an icon of the Virgin Mary. According to Adrian Fortescue's text *The Greek Fathers* (1908), John said the following prayer:

> Lady and purest mother, who didst give birth to my God, because of the holy icons my right hand is cut off. Thou knowest well the cause, that Leo the emperor rages; so help me at once and heal my hand by the power of the Most High, who became man from thee, who works many wonders by thy prayers. May he now heal this hand through thy intercession, and it shall in future always write poetry in thy honour, O Theotokos, and in honour of thy Son made man in thee and for the true faith. Be my advocate, for thou canst do anything, being mother of God.

In the morning, there was only the mark of a suture to show where the knife had passed. Soon afterward, John begged the caliph to relieve him of office.

Reluctantly, for he valued his service, the caliph let him go. In the year 730, after he sold all of his worldly possessions and gave the proceeds to the poor, John set out for the monastery of St. Sabas in Palestine.

At the monastery, John did not take an active part in the Iconoclastic Controversy as it continued to rage throughout the East. The statues and paintings were destroyed, but he had nothing more to say about them. As a monk, John took the vow of complete silence; he was charged to renounce all secular learning and ordered not to write. About 735, he was ordained for the priesthood, and then the restrictions were removed.

Living in a small cell, John wrote voluminously: homilies, commentaries, ascetic tracts, liturgical canons, and hymns. One of his works, to which no definite date can be attached, was the comprehensive *Echdosis tēs orthodoxon pisteōs* (*Exposition of the Orthodox Faith*, 1899). In it, he wrote briefly about images. At first God had no form, John wrote, but God became man out of pity for man and to save man. As man, God lived upon Earth among mankind, worked miracles, suffered, was crucified, rose again, and ascended to Heaven. All these things, he wrote, actually happened and were written down for those who were not alive at the time. When man looks upon the image of God, then, he remembers God's saving passion, and he falls and worships what is represented there.

It was during his time at the monastery of St. Sabas that John formulated a fuller defense of holy images, which was his only original contribution to theology. Because of this contribution, he is recognized as the last of the Greek fathers. This defense is in the form of three treatises, collectively known as *Logoi treis apologētikoi pros toms diabollontas tas agaias eikonas* (c. 730; *On Holy Images*, 1898). The crucial argument of the treatises is the continual insistence that in the Incarnation a decisive and abiding change took place in the relationship between God and material creation. John wrote that before the Incarnation, God, being without form or body, could not be represented. Since the Incarnation, however, God has emerged in the flesh and lived among men, and representations can be made of Him. Man does not worship matter, wrote John, but worships the creator of matter.

He accused the iconoclasts, who insisted that the Old Testament's prohibition of idolatry applied to images, of quoting Scripture out of context. He proceeded to cite passages showing how God, having forbidden the making of idols, yet commanded the use of material objects and images in divine worship, instructing that His Temple be adorned with the likenesses of plants and animals—images which were not to be worshipped as idols.

On the basis of Scripture, John made a distinction between absolute worship, or adoration, and relative worship, or veneration. The Bible records many occasions when the patriarchs and prophets worshipped, venerated, and bowed before places or things to whom such honor was due, yet never with the attitude of adoration which is to be reserved for God alone. John argued that it is wrong to identify every image with its prototype. Only Jesus the Son, as the pure image of God the Father, can be said to mirror His prototype with absolute faithfulness. All other images, John wrote, whether natural, symbolic, or allegorical, are essentially different from their prototypes.

Only God, he wrote, is worthy of absolute worship, or adoration. Relative worship, or veneration, is given to the Mother of God, the saints, or sacred objects. Thus, veneration given by a Christian to an image of Christ is ontologically the same as the reverence he ought to give his fellow Christians, who are also images of Christ, but it is ontologically different from the adoration that is due God alone.

Summary

The Council of Nicaea in 787 under the Byzantine empress, Irene, restored the use of images in Christian worship. Whereas the Iconoclast Synod of Constantinople in 754 cursed John of Damascus, the church council in 787 looked upon him as a great hero. With the end of the Iconoclastic Controversy, the honor of John's name was spread throughout Christendom. An early ninth century chronicler, Theophanes the Confessor, writes that John was rightly surnamed Chrysorroas, after the chief river of his city. This name was chosen because through his life and teachings, John gleamed like gold. This name, however, did not become the common one associated with John; he has been known and honored through the centuries as John of Damascus. In the Eastern Christian church, John's feast day is December 4. Pope Leo III of the Western Christian church declared John a Doctor of the Church and appointed March 27 as his feast day. Throughout Christendom, John is known for his virtue, piety, and learning—and for defending the worship of holy images.

Bibliography

Anderson, David. *St. John of Damascus: On the Divine Images*. Crestwood, N.Y.: St. Vladimir's Seminary Press, 1980. Contains an analysis of John's three treatises on images.

Baynes, Norman H., and L. B. Moss. *Byzantium: An Introduction to East Roman Civilization*. Oxford: Clarendon Press, 1948. Contains a chapter on Byzantine education and how it relates to John of Damascus. Also includes a bibliographic index and maps.

Fortescue, Adrian. *The Greek Fathers*. London: Catholic Truth Society, 1908. Written by an expert in the field, this volume contains a chapter on John of Damascus, together with translations of some of his works. Generously documented.

Lossky, Vladimir. *The Mystical Theology of the Eastern Church*. Translated by members of the Fellowship of St. Albans and St. Sergius. London:

James Clarke and Co., 1957. Contains John of Damascus' analysis of the Holy Trinity.

Ostrogorsky, George. *History of the Byzantine State*. Translated by Joan Hussey. New Brunswick, N.J.: Rutgers University Press, 1969. Contains a section on the Iconoclastic Controversy and a bibliography. Illustrated with colored maps.

Payne, Robert. *The Holy Fire: The Story of the Fathers of the Eastern Church*. Crestwood, N.Y.: St. Vladimir's Seminary Press, 1980. Contains a chapter on John of Damascus, together with a discussion of some of his writings.

Runciman, Steven. *Byzantine Civilisation*. London: Edward Arnold and Co., 1933. Contains a chapter on Byzantine literature and makes frequent references to the works of John of Damascus. Includes bibliographic notes.

Bill Manikas

JOHN THE APOSTLE

Born: c. A.D. 10; probably Capernaum
Died: c. A.D. 100; Ephesus
Area of Achievement: Religion
Contribution: John the Apostle was one of Jesus' most trusted disciples during his lifetime; after his death, John was a leader in the early Church and by his writings made important contributions to Christian theology.

Early Life

Assuming John to have been a young man when he was called as a disciple of Jesus, he must have been born about A.D. 10, probably in Capernaum. His father was Zebedee and his mother Salome; he had a brother, James, also a disciple and presumably the elder of the two, since he is generally mentioned first and John is often identified as the "brother of James." The family occupation was fishing, and they were presumably prosperous, since they owned their own boat and employed servants; they may have been a priestly family as well. Salome figures occasionally in the Gospels; she requested that her sons be given seats of honor beside Jesus in Heaven (Matt. 20), and she was one of the women who helped to support Jesus financially (Matt. 15). James and John may have been cousins of Jesus, a fact which would explain their early call and the episode at the Cross in which Mary, Jesus' mother, was committed to the care of "the disciple whom Jesus loved," a term generally taken to refer to John the son of Zebedee. The nickname "Boanerges" (sons of thunder or perhaps anger) bestowed on James and John by Jesus suggests a certain impetuousness and aggressiveness; James's early martyrdom suggests that he had the greater share of the quality. As for John, his occupation and his besting of Peter in the race to Jesus' tomb suggest a strong, athletic man.

Life's Work

It is with the call by the Sea of Galilee that John's recorded life begins. Having called Peter and Andrew to leave their nets and become "fishers of men," Jesus immediately proceeded to James and John, who left "the boat and their father" and followed him. In general, the position of John in Jesus' ministry is clear. He appears on lists of the Twelve, and always among the first: "Simon who is called Peter and Andrew his brother; James the son of Zebedee and John his brother." When a smaller group is named, John is always among them; it is James and John who would have called down fire on a village of the Samaritans (Luke 9). Generally, however, John is linked to Peter in a subordinate role. Thus, he was present at the healing of Peter's mother-in-law (Mark 1) and of Jairus' daughter (Mark 5); he was present with Peter and James at the Transfiguration (Matt. 17) and again at

Gethsemane (Mark 14). Toward the end of the Gospel of John, there are numerous references to "the disciple whom Jesus loved," almost certainly John. He was the disciple whom Peter prompted to solicit Jesus' identification of the betrayer at the Last Supper (John 18); he was possibly the disciple who introduced Peter to the high priest's courtyard; he is the one to whose care Christ commended his mother; he is the one, along with Peter, to whom Mary Magdalene brought news of the Resurrection. Finally, "the disciple whom Jesus loved" is clearly present when the risen Jesus appeared at the Sea of Galilee, and the Gospel records a statement of Jesus which some interpreted as a prophecy that the disciple would not die before the Second Coming (John 21). John appears here, incidentally, in the same role in which Luke casts him at his first appearance: as a fishing partner with Peter.

After the Crucifixion and Resurrection, John seems to have filled much the same role as before: as a leader and spokesman for the infant Church, constantly in a subordinate role to Peter and sometimes also to his brother James, until the latter's martyrdom. John was with Peter when the lame man was healed (the first miracle performed after the death of Jesus); twice he was imprisoned, once with Peter, once with all the Apostles; he went with Peter to support the missionary effort of Philip of Samaria. Finally, he played a leading role when the Church had to decide whether Gentile converts were obliged to observe the Jewish ceremonial law, as some converted Pharisees had argued. Paul had gone to Jerusalem with Barnabas to confer on the matter and was cordially received by James (the Lord's brother) and Peter and John, "who were reputed to be pillars"; at the prompting of Peter, the Gentiles were released from the law, except with respect to unchastity and meat sacrificed to idols (Acts 15; Gal. 2). It was a crucial episode in the history of the early Church, for it meant that Christianity could no longer be regarded as a Jewish sect.

This episode took place some seventeen years after Paul's conversion and is the last biblical record of John, but church tradition suggests the shape of his later life. According to this tradition (which is not beyond dispute), John spent the latter part of his life in missionary activity at Ephesus. During the reign of Domitian (81-96), he was banished to the Isle of Patmos (an association which is still advertised in tourist literature); he is thought to have returned to Ephesus and to have lived on into the reign of Trajan (98-117). It was during this period that he is thought to have written the Gospel of John, the three Epistles of John, and (possibly) the Book of Revelation. Some scholars would make John not so much the author of these works as the authority behind them; it is evident that another hand edited the manuscript of the Gospel, with John's certification "that this testimony is true" (John 21). Perhaps John should be envisioned as the respected leader of the community, whose disciples aided him in putting together his recollections of Christ; the Gospel apparently went through several editions as material was added, perhaps in accord with specific needs of the Church. The Epistles give evidence of dissension in the churches in the Ephesus area; if the heretics mentioned indeed denied that Christ came in the flesh, in "water and blood," they may have represented an early stage of Gnosticism (which is not to say, as some authorities have, that John at one stage was Gnostic). Revelation could well reflect this same troubled atmosphere; the church at Pergamos is accused of the same offenses that were discussed at the Council of Jerusalem: fornication and meat sacrificed to idols. The latter parts of Revelation, if indeed they are John's, would reflect his exile to Patmos. The manner and even the date of John's death are unknown.

Summary

From the time of his calling (or even before), John's name was constantly associated with that of Peter—sometimes when together they were called aside by Jesus for moments that were confidential and intimate, sometimes when he and Peter (usually Peter) took the initiative. His personality came to be defined in terms of Peter: Though he and his brother James were "sons of thunder," they almost always deferred to Peter as their spokesman. The relationship continued after the Crucifixion and through the history of the early Church. Eventually, there had to be a parting: Peter went to Rome and John to Ephesus, where he became the leader of the churches in the area. Here too he developed his theology, which differed in emphasis from that of the Synoptic Gospels (Matthew, Mark, and Luke), which at least in part were based on the preaching of Peter. Specifically, John favored a higher Christology which affirmed not only that Christ was the Son of God and the Messiah but also that He was the Creator who had coexisted with God from all eternity. Apparently, some of his followers went beyond this to deny "the coming of Jesus Christ in the flesh" (2 John), like the later Gnostics. After John's death, these individuals presumably became Gnostics indeed, while John's church, which had pursued its own way apart from the "great church" of Peter and Paul, was absorbed into the greater church, taking with it the Gospel of John, which thus became canonical.

The whole issue may be summed up in the last chapters of the Gospel of John, which were apparently added in the last edition. Here John once more recalls his intimacy with Peter; there is an account of a final fishing expedition, and he records how the risen Christ charged Peter to "feed My sheep" and foretold Peter's death. Finally, as he asserted the divinity and coeternity of Christ at the opening of the Gospel, so here John asserts Christ's humanity in the striking image of his preparing a picnic breakfast for his disciples on the shore.

Bibliography

Alter, Robert, and Frank Kermode, eds. *The Literary Guide to the Bible.*

Cambridge, Mass. Harvard University Press, 1987. Contains an essay on John by Frank Kermode and another on Revelation by Bernard McGinn. Both are very fine essays, though by no means simple; they do not convey simply the authors' own impressions but also contain historical surveys of past criticism.

Brown, Raymond E. *The Community of the Beloved Disciple*. New York: Paulist Press, 1979. Though it carries an imprimatur, this volume contains all sorts of improbable hypotheses concerning John and the church at Ephesus. It does offer a useful summary of the scholarship.

——————. Introduction to "The Gospel According to St. John." In *The Anchor Bible*. Garden City, N.Y.: Doubleday and Co., 1966. Concludes that the combination of external and internal evidence associating the Fourth Gospel with John the son of Zebedee makes his authorship the strongest hypothesis. Brown's reasoning in this book has generally been accepted in the present essay.

Dodd, Charles H. *Historical Tradition in the Fourth Gospel*. Cambridge: Cambridge University Press, 1963. Seeks to reopen the historical question. Dodd argues that though the "quest for the historical Jesus" came to nothing and led many to despair of the historical approach, modern critical methods can lead to conclusions which have a high degree of probability.

Funk and Wagnalls New Standard Bible Dictionary. Edited by Melancthon W. Jacobs, Elbert C. Lane, and Andrew C. Zenos. 3d rev. ed. Philadelphia: Blakiston Co., 1936. Offers a rather conservative view of the controversy surrounding John. John's authorship of the Gospel is elaborately defended, although his authorship of Revelation is questioned. There is a good summary of what is known of John's life.

Pollard, T. E. *Johannine Christology and the Early Church*. Cambridge: Cambridge University Press, 1970. Analyzes early theological controversies which grew out of the Gospel of John. This monograph is part of a series put out by the Society for New Testament Studies. Includes an index and a bibliography.

John C. Sherwood

JOHN THE BAPTIST

Born: c. 7 B.C.; near Jerusalem, Israel
Died: c. A.D. 27; Jerusalem, Israel
Area of Achievement: Religion
Contribution: According to the biblical narrative, John was the cousin of Jesus and played a central role in introducing Jesus' ministry to the people of Palestine; as an austere, prophetic figure in the history of Judaism and Christianity, John was a stern moralist who addressed a generation of outwardly religious but inwardly corrupted people.

Early Life

The main historical record for the life of John the Baptist is the Bible, specifically the New Testament, revered by Christians worldwide as an authoritative complement to the Old Testament. Each of the Gospels records significant portions of the life and ministry of John, and three of them actually begin with his birth rather than that of Jesus, who is the central figure of the New Testament. Historical tradition suggests that John was born in a village four miles west of Jerusalem around 7 B.C. to elderly parents, Zacharias, a Jewish priest, and Elisabeth, a relative of Mary, the mother of Jesus. The Gospel of Luke provides the most extensive treatment of the early life of John and indicates that he was probably born about six months before his cousin. Like those of other famous Old and New Testament patriarchs and heroes, John's birth, Luke relates, was foretold by an angel, in this case Gabriel, who also appeared to Mary and prophesied the coming of Jesus. Gabriel, in fact, suggested the name John, and friends and relatives were shocked at the time of John's circumcision and dedication to learn that he would not be named for his father, Zacharias (Luke 1:63).

Luke's account goes on to suggest that John's education continued along the path one might expect: John, like his father, prepared for the priesthood. Sometime in his late adolescence, however, John traveled on a pilgrimage to the deserts for study, meditation, and further consecration (Luke 1:66, 80). During this extended period, John took on the appearance and habits of other prophets of Israel, especially Elijah—to whom he was compared by Jesus (Matt. 11:12-14). John is said to have eaten wild locusts and honey and to have worn coarse garments of camel hair and a leather girdle—clear associations with Elijah (Matt. 3:4; Mark 1:6; 2 Kings 1:8). After this episode of ascetic discipline and study of the Scriptures, John emerged to begin his public ministry in "all the country about the Jordan River" (Luke 3:3), a ministry which began prior to that of Jesus by at least several months.

The message John presented to the people was in many ways unique to his ministry, but it was also linked thematically to that of the prophets of old. That message can be summarized as "prepare ye the way of the Lord." John believed unequivocally that he had been called to announce some cataclysmic work of God in the first century to which he would be both witness and martyr. The message was twofold in purpose: It was a call both to radical repentance and to immersion in water for the forgiveness of sins. In his preaching, John used straightforward language, referring to some in his audience as "vipers" or "hypocrites" and imploring them to repent or change their ways and act justly toward their neighbors and manifest their love for God in obedience to the Law. The insistence on full water-immersion gave John his unique label, "the Baptist," and indicated the necessary radical break with past lackluster adherence to the Law of Moses. The repentant believer was to emerge from the water in some sense a new person, ready to behave and believe differently.

Life's Work

John's ministry attracted many followers, many more at one point than that of Jesus (Luke 7:29). In instructing his disciples, John taught them to pray and to fast (Luke 5:33, 11:1; Mark 2:18), but his work was not essentially preoccupied with personal devotion. Within and without his circle of disciples, his message was interpreted as an attack on organized religion—or the parody it had become. "The axe," he declared, "is laid at the root of the trees" (Matt. 3:10; Luke 3:9). His message focused on the necessity for a new beginning and on the emptiness of the Jews' continuing to claim some special merit as descendants of Abraham. The Coming One, or Messiah, John prophesied, would execute judgment on all but the loyal remnant of believers ready to embrace him. Late in an actually quite brief ministry, John suggested to his followers—many of whom would become Jesus' own most trusted associates—that John himself "must decrease, while [the Messiah he proclaimed] must increase." That is, as the time came closer for the Messiah to emerge, John's ministry would diminish in importance and finally come to an end.

John's ministry climaxed when Jesus himself came to be baptized by John "to fulfill all righteousness." John at first balked at baptizing "for the forgiveness of sins" the one who himself was regarded as sinless; earlier, John, upon glimpsing Jesus across a street, had told an assembled crowd, "Behold the Lamb of God who takes away the sins of the world." Jesus insisted on this act of identification with mankind and it was at this crucial event that the stunned crowd heard a voice from Heaven declare, "This is my beloved son in whom I am well pleased." This event signaled the beginning of Jesus' ministry and launched him on his itinerant preaching tours.

After this episode, John's ministry was abruptly interrupted and then ended by the antipathy he engendered in King Herod Antipas of Palestine. Herod had several motives for his displeasure with John. First, John's preaching drew large, enthusiastic crowds, a matter sure to perturb the Roman authorities at whose pleasure Herod himself served as a puppet ruler. More to the point, however, was John's radical insistence on the public morality of Israel's leaders; indeed, he had outspokenly denounced Herod for his adultery. When John refused to back down, Herod had him imprisoned, both to silence him and, in a sense, to protect him. Despite being humiliated by John, Herod was entertained by his gruff, quaint manner, much as Pontius Pilate was impressed with the sincerity and commitment of Jesus.

During his imprisonment, John sent some of his disciples to Jesus to confirm that he indeed was the coming Messiah; perhaps John wished to assure himself that his mission had been successful. Finally, during a particularly uproarious party, Herod was manipulated by his stepdaughter Salome into granting her any wish as payment for a lascivious dance she had performed (Matt. 14:6-12; Mark 6:21-28). Prompted by her mother, she requested that John be beheaded, and that his head be brought to her on a platter; Herod reluctantly acceded.

At his death, John elicited the highest praise from Jesus as the greatest of all men who lived under the Old Covenant: "The law and the prophets were until John; since that time the kingdom of God is preached" (Luke 16:16). Throughout his later ministry, Jesus continued to pay tribute to the faith and example of John. While John's baptism provided a gateway into the messianic community, the Apostles later interpreted baptism as a sacrament, a reenactment of the death, burial, and resurrection of Jesus that united the believer with the saving work of Jesus on the Cross.

Summary

The ancient Jewish historian Flavius Josephus adds historical perspective to John the Baptist's life outside the biblical account. Writing in the first century A.D., Josephus stated that John "was a good man who bade the Jews practice virtue, be just to one another, and pious toward God, and come together by means of baptism." This latter comment regarding John's teaching on baptism indicates the force and strength of John's ministry to first century Jews and to Christians. Its appearance in a secular account suggests the impact John's ministry had on Jewish culture as a whole. His call to baptism—which gave to him the name "the Baptist" or the "one who baptizes"—represented a call to radical commitment, to withdraw from a complacent, "everyday" faith to a bolder, more holy response to the God of Abraham, Isaac, and Jacob. Clearly, however, John was more dramatically an influence on the development of Christian thought and the ministry of Jesus. Jesus' appearance at John's baptisms stamped John himself as a true prophet of God in the eyes of first century Christians; later, when arguing on his own behalf, Jesus invoked the baptism of John to corroborate his own authority to command baptism and healing.

Important as it was, John's baptism is presented in the New Testament account as something that would eventually be succeeded by a peculiarly "Christian" baptism which brought believers into the kingdom of God rather than merely "preparing" them for it. The power of John's message and ministry was so strong, however, that even into the second and third decades of Christian faith, approximately A.D. 45-55, pockets of believers adhering to "John's baptism" and needing further instruction in the baptism practiced by the Apostles after the death and resurrection of Jesus could be found. For example, the New Testament Book of Acts tells how a married couple, Priscilla and Aquila, drew aside the respected teacher Apollos and instructed him in proper Christian baptism. Later, the Apostle Paul encountered a group of believers who had never heard of Christian baptism—only John's—and he instructed them further.

Contemporary scholarship has attempted to locate the origins of John's teaching in his presumed association with the Qumran community, a radical Jewish religious group whose teachings became known to biblical scholarship with the discovery of the Dead Sea Scrolls in 1945. The Qumran community stressed strict adherence to a legal code to achieve a higher degree of righteousness before God and, curiously, a water baptism, something that traditional Judaism had required of all Gentile converts. Whatever influence John's exposure to such teaching may have had, it is clear that he intended to link his own message with the prophecy of a coming redeemer, a ministry of preparation that would turn the hearts of the faithless and the faithful to a religious belief which transcended mere formalism and embraced an ongoing commitment to justice, righteousness, and peace; his mission, in his own words, was "to make ready a people prepared for the coming of the Lord."

Bibliography

Alexander, David, and Pat Alexander, eds. *Eerdmans' Handbook to the Bible.* Grand Rapids, Mich.: Wm. B. Eerdmans Publishing Co., 1973. A helpful overview of the basic message of the New Testament, the life of Christ, and the relationship of John the Baptist to Jesus, his cousin. A succinct and very practical guide to the ministries of both John the Baptist and Jesus of Nazareth and their impact on first century culture.

Foster, R. C. *Introduction and Early Ministry: Studies in the Life of Christ.* Grand Rapids, Mich.: Baker Book House, 1969. A volume that focuses primarily on the life of Christ but which includes an insightful extended discussion of the life and work of John the Baptist. Especially useful to the reader unfamiliar with the basic New Testament message and the historical context in which it arose.

Guthrie, Donald. *New Testament Introduction.* Downers Grove, Ill.: Inter-Varsity Press, 1973. A standard, scholarly overview of the entire New Testament that includes a thorough discussion of the life of John the Baptist and his ministry. Invaluable for providing the necessary context for an accurate assessment of John the Baptist's importance to later Christian faith and practice.

Hendriksen, William. *New Testament Commentary: Matthew*. Grand Rapids, Mich.: Baker Book House, 1973. An important scholarly discussion of the Gospel of Matthew, which contains the longest narratives about the birth and destiny of John. Hendriksen offers both the lay reader and the scholar an extended study and contextualization of the life of John the Baptist in relationship to the basic Christian gospel.

Malherbe, Abraham. *The World of the New Testament*. Austin, Tex.: Sweet Publishing Co., 1968. A brief but valuable overview of the entire New Testament period with special attention to the historical and theological events that served as the backdrop to the life and ministry of John the Baptist.

Thompson, J. A. *Handbook to Life in Bible Times*. Downers Grove, Ill.: Inter-Varsity Press, 1986. A standard work on the archaeology of the first century world; it continues to be one of the most comprehensive and informed overviews of the historical data gleaned from the ancient world. Overall, it provides the reader with an authentic sense of the world to which John the Baptist came, his mission, and the circumstances in which he became both a prophet to Israel and the forerunner of the Messiah of both Jews and Christians.

Bruce L. Edwards

FLAVIUS JOSEPHUS

Born: c. A.D. 37; Jerusalem, Palestine
Died: c. A.D. 100; probably Rome
Areas of Achievement: Historiography and scholarship
Contribution: Josephus' history of the Jewish revolt against Rome in 66, the
   fall of Jerusalem in 70, and the capture of Masada in 73 remains, despite
   patent exaggerations and questionable reporting, the primary source of
   information for this segment of world history.

Early Life

Flavius Josephus was born in Jerusalem into an influential priestly family.
His Jewish name, Joseph ben Matthias, indicates that he was the son of Matthias, whom he asserts to have been of noble Hasmonaean (that is, Maccabean) lineage. He claims that he was consulted at the age of fourteen by
high priests and leading citizens on the fine points of law and that, at the
age of sixteen, he conducted inquiries into the relative merits of the Pharisees, Sadducees, and Essenes. Becoming a disciple of a Pharisee named
Banus, he entered upon an ascetic existence, living with Banus in the desert
for three years and then returning, as a Pharisee, to Jerusalem at the age of
nineteen.

Seven years later, by his account, he went to Rome as an emissary to plead
for the release of some Jewish priests who were being held on what Josephus
considered to be trivial charges. The sea voyage to Rome ended in shipwreck
in the Adriatic Sea with Josephus being one of eighty survivors out of the six
hundred on board.

He reached Puteoli (modern Pozzuoli) and was befriended by a Jewish
actor named Aliturius, who enjoyed Nero's favor. Aliturius secured for Josephus an audience with Poppaea, Nero's wife, and with her assistance Josephus gained the release of the priests. He returned to Palestine a year or
two later.

His homeland at this time (66) was in a state of incipient rebellion against
Roman occupation. Josephus was opposed to insurrection and sided with the
moderate faction against the extremists. The insurgent nationalists, however,
prevailed. The Roman garrison at Masada was captured and the Roman
contingent was expelled from Jerusalem; the Roman Twelfth Legion, sent to
put down the revolt and restore order, was decisively defeated by Jewish pa-
triots. By the end of 66, the war between the Jews and the Romans was a
military reality. Josephus was pressed into service as the commander of the
region of Galilee.

Although his talents were for the priesthood and research, Josephus, like
many learned men in classical antiquity, proved to be capable in military affairs. He conceived defenses and trained fighting forces but refrained from

taking the initiative in attack. In the spring of 67 the Romans moved into Galilee. Josephus' main fighting unit was routed and he retreated to Jotapata, the most strongly fortified town in Galilee. Three Roman legions under Vespasian laid siege to Jotapata, captured it on the first of July in 67, and took Josephus prisoner.

Life's Work

The relationship of Josephus with Vespasian and the Roman imperial entourage marks the major stage in his life. Vespasian's prisoner of war became his adviser and, in time, favored client. It is this sustained association with the dominant enemy of the Jews that clouds the attitudes toward Josephus taken by his compatriots and their descendants. In his early opposition to the Jewish revolt he had been suspected of complicity with the Romans, and in view of the perquisites accorded him by the Roman leaders after Jotapata, no apologist can effectively defend him against the charge of fraternization with the enemy. He appears to have ingratiated himself with Vespasian by accurately predicting Vespasian's installation as emperor. He assumed the name of Vespasian's family, Flavius, when he Romanized his own. His account, published between 75 and 79, of the Jewish revolt against Rome carries the Greek title *Peri tou Ioudaikou polemou*, which in Latin is *Bello Judaicum*. The significance of the title (in English, *The Jewish War*) is that it denotes the Roman, not the Jewish, perspective, just as Julius Caesar's *De bello Gallico* (52-51 B.C. *The Gallic War*, or, *The War with the Gauls*) denotes the Roman, not the Gallic, perspective. Josephus had clearly staked his lot with the victorious Romans.

A telling incident prior to the fall of Jotapata makes it difficult for anyone to admire Josephus as a patriotic Jew. The besieged had agreed upon a mass suicide pact as a means of avoiding capture by the Romans. Josephus relates his attempt to dissuade them, his failure to do so, and his alternate and subsequently accepted plan to draw lots whereby number two would kill number one, number three would kill number two, and so on until, presumably, the last person left would be the only one actually to commit suicide. Josephus concludes this story with a nod to divine providence or pure chance: He and one other were the last two alive and, making a pact of their own, remained alive.

By contrast, Josephus' account of the mass suicide in the year 73 of the 960 Jews at Masada, the last citadel of resistance to the Romans, who had conclusively ended the revolt three years earlier, includes reference to no survivors save two women and five children who had hidden in subterranean aqueducts. Comparison of the respective survivors of Jotapata and Masada lends no honor to the historian of both defeats.

After the Jewish revolt of 66-70 Josephus was granted living quarters and a regular income in Rome. Thus ensconced, he produced his history of the re-

volt. His claim that he wrote the work initially in Aramaic and then translated it into Greek need not be disputed, although no Aramaic text whatso-
ever remains in either small part or citation. The Hellenistic Greek in which
this work and the other works of Josephus appear is faultlessly in character
with the *lingua franca* of the time. The idiomatic perfection of Josephus'
Greek may owe in large part to his employment of Greek-speaking assistants, but his own linguistic abilities were patently considerable.

The Jewish War was published between 75 and 79, the year in which Vespasian died and was succeeded as emperor by his son Titus. It covers not
merely the years 66 to 73 but also much of the history of the Jews, from the
desecration of the Temple at Jerusalem by Antiochus IV Epiphanes in 167
B.C. through the events culminating in the capture of Jerusalem by Titus in
A.D. 70. The work is composed of seven books, the first two of which outline
the Hasmonaean, or Maccabean, revolt, the reign of Herod the Great, and
the Roman occupation of Palestine up to the military governorship of Galilee
by Josephus.

The five books dedicated to the details of the revolt are both exciting and
graphic. Josephus mars his credibility with hyperbole and distortion of fact—
for example, he describes Mount Tabor, which has an altitude of thirteen
hundred feet, as being twenty thousand feet high, and his crowd counts are
almost invariably exaggerated, one such noting thirty thousand Jews crushed
to death in a panic rush—but, if his particulars are questionable and his narrative self-serving, his general survey of times and events has not lost its
value.

Although it may tend to disqualify him as a scientific historian, his creative
imagination undeniably enhances the grand movement of his history. In one
respect, *The Jewish War* resembles the history by the more scientific Thucydides. Both works are informed by a major theme: In Thucydides' *De
bello Peloponnesiaco libri octo* (431-404 B.C.; *History of the Peloponnesian
War*) that theme is Athenian hubris; in *The Jewish War* it is Jewish self-
destructiveness. Josephus sees the factionalism of the Jews and their imprac-
tical unwillingness to yield to the overwhelming power of Rome as suicidal
tendencies which make the Jews their own worst enemies. He underscores
this theme with many images of suicidal conflict and with depictions of individual and mass suicides.

Josephus' pride in his heritage is evident in his work and transcends both
his contempt for his Jewish rivals and enemies (especially Josephus of
Gischala) and his deference to his Roman benefactors. His second work is a
massive history of Judaism and the Jews which is entitled *Ioudaikē
archaiologia* (c. A.D. 93; in Latin, *Antiquitates Judaicae*; in English, *The
Antiquities of the Jews*). This work, in twenty books, or about three times the
length of *The Jewish War*, begins with the Creation as recounted in Genesis
and ends with the Palestinian war clouds of 66. The first eleven and one-half

books cover Jewish history up to the tyranny of Antiochus IV Epiphanes. The latter eight and one-half books cover the same material as the first book and a half of *The Jewish War* but in greater detail and with many additions. The work is addressed to Epaphroditus, an otherwise unknown figure who seems to have succeeded the emperor Titus, dead in 81, as one of Josephus' patrons.

At the conclusion of *The Antiquities of the Jews*, Josephus claims, characteristically, that his work is accurate and that no other person, Jew or non-Jew, could have enlightened the Greeks on two millennia of Jewish history and practices so well as he. In quality, however, and in importance and readability, *The Antiquities of the Jews* is discernibly inferior to its predecessor.

It must be noted, however, that *The Antiquities of the Jews* offers passages that are of notable importance to Christians. For example:

> Jesus comes along at about this time, a wise man, if indeed one must call him a man: for he was a performer of unaccountable works, a teacher of such people as took delight in truth, and one who attracted to himself many Jews and many Greeks as well. This man was the Christ. And when Pilate sentenced him to crucifixion, after he had been indicted by our leading citizens, those who had been devoted to him from the start remained firm in their devotion, for he appeared to them alive again three days afterward, as it had been prophesied about him, along with countless other wonders, by holy men. And to our own time the host of those named, after him, Christians has not dwindled.

There is a passage on the aftermath of the execution of John the Baptist and another on the stoning of Jesus' brother James. Jesus is not mentioned in the Greek version of *The Jewish War*. There is, however, an Old Slavonic (that is, Russian) version with an independent late medieval manuscript tradition that contains references to the lives of John the Baptist and Jesus, one of them being a variation of the passage quoted above.

Josephus completed the *The Antiquities of the Jews* in 93 at the age of fifty-six. His plans, announced at the end of the work, to produce an epitome of *The Jewish War*, a continuation of the same work, and a tetrad of books on the Jewish religion and laws appear not to have been realized. His brief autobiography is attached to the end of the *The Antiquities of the Jews* and contradicts some of the statements made in *The Jewish War*, in the interest, it seems, of obverting his early military opposition to the Romans and perhaps as a means of offsetting his rivals for the favor of the emperor Domitian.

The treatise which marks the end of Josephus' literary career is one that could warrant no complaint from his fellow Jews. It is called *Peri archaiotētos Ioudaiōn kata Apionos* (*Concerning the Antiquity of the Jews, Against Apion*) and is traditionally referred to simply as *Against Apion*. The work is an effective and stirring defense of the Jewish people and their religion and laws against scurrilous anti-Jewish writings of the past (by Manetho and Cheremon, for example) and by Josephus' older contemporary, Apion of Alexandria.

Having been favored by the emperors Vespasian and Titus and having enjoyed the patronage of Emperor Domitian and his wife, Josephus seems to have survived Domitian, who died in 96, by no more than a few years. Nothing is known of his reception by the emperors Nerva (ruled 96-98) and Trajan (98-117). It is significant that the last remaining works of Josephus are defenses—the autobiography a defense of his part in the Jewish revolt and *Against Apion* a defense of his Jewish heritage. It is not known whether these *apologiae*, also addressed to Epaphroditus, qualified him for a return to Judaea or, for that matter, for continued subsistence in Rome. His status with either Jews or Romans during his last years of life, as well as the actual place of his death, can only be conjectured.

Summary

The latter part of Josephus' autobiography includes a digressive apostrophe to Justus of Tiberias, who had also written an *Antiquities*, which covered Jewish history from Moses through the first century of this era and which related the insurrection and revolt of 66 to 70 in such a way as to challenge Josephus and attempt to discredit him. Justus, for example, accused Josephus of actively fomenting the revolt against the Romans. This charge, made during the reign of Domitian, would have eroded Josephus' credibility at court were it to have gone without answer, and may have done so in any case. The work of Justus stood in rivalry to that of Josephus as least until the ninth century, after which its readership, along with all traces of its actual text, disappeared. Josephus prevailed; the fact that he did attests his value, not as a benign and likable person or as an objective and fully credible historian, but as a writer of great erudition and talent, whose narrative scope and magnitude and whose personal association with many of the figures and events in his narrative make him perennially readable and provide a veritable drama in complement to scientific history.

Of especial value to general readers and to students of first century history are the detailed appraisals by Josephus of the zealotry, factions, and religious turmoil in Palestine, the political thrusts of the Roman aristocracy, and the complex relations between Rome and the Judaean principate.

Bibliography

Bentwich, Norman. *Josephus*. Philadelphia: Jewish Publication Society of America, 1914. A consideration of Josephus from the Jewish point of view. The writer is harsh on Josephus, not only as a general whom he calls traitorous but also as a scholar, claiming that Josephus was not so learned and erudite as he claims to have been and is credited as having been. According to Bentwich, Josephus misuses words such as "Gamala," an error that may have been understandable for a Roman but not for someone Jewish.

Cohen, Shaye J. D. *Josephus in Galilee and Rome: His Vita and Development as a Historian*. Leiden, Netherlands: E. J. Brill, 1979. This work, volume 8 of the Columbia Studies in the Classical Tradition, is a very scholarly study of Josephus and his sources, the literary relationship of the autobiography to *The Jewish War*, the aims and methods of the autobiography, and the historicity of Josephus' activities in Galilee and Rome.

Feldman, Louis H. *Josephus and Modern Scholarship, 1937-1980*. New York: W. de Gruyter, 1984. A massive achievement in its comparative summaries of Josephan scholarship and in bibliographical research. This work is chiefly of interest, and indeed indispensable, to the Josephan scholar; it can also be very enlightening and of considerable help to the general reader. Under specific topics (for example, "The War Against the Romans") and subtopics (for example, "The Causes and Goals of the War," "Domitian"), Feldman provides extensive bibliographic references followed by comparative commentary on works listed.

Furneaux, Rupert. *The Roman Siege of Jerusalem*. London: Hart-Davis, 1973. Furneaux's opening chapter, identifying Josephus as a "Quisling," is followed by chapters on a Zealot messiah named Judas, the Roman procurators, the emperor Titus, Pilate, and the messiah Jesus. This very readable book gives a graphic account of the systematic quelling of the Jewish revolt by the logistically superior Roman legions. Furneaux provides an appendix on the Slavonic text of Josephus.

Josephus, Flavius. *The Jewish War*. Edited by Gaalya Cornfeld, Benjamin Mazar, and Paul L. Maier. Grand Rapids, Mich.: Zondervan Publishing House, 1982. An adequate translation profusely illustrated and annotated. The photographs of sites and artifacts vary in quality from poor to very good. The maps and diagrams are excellent, and the annotations are bolstered by archaeological research and references to the Dead Sea Scrolls.

_____. *"The Jewish War" and Other Selections from Flavius Josephus*. Edited and abridged with an introduction by Moses I. Finley. Translated by H. St. John Thackeray and Ralph Marcus. New York: Twayne Publishers, 1965. Contains selections from Josephus' autobiography (including the "Polemic Against the Historian Justus"), *Against Apion*, *The Antiquities of the Jews*, and *The Jewish War*. Finley's eighteen-page introduction is well worth reading. For readers who have not the time to browse through the complete Josephus in the Thackeray-Marcus-Wikgren-Feldman nine-volume Loeb Library translation (1926-1965), this is a moderate guide.

_____. *The Jewish War*. Translated by G. A. Williamson. Harmondsworth, England: Penguin Books, 1959, rev. ed. 1970. This, in its estimable revision by E. Mary Smallwood, is the definitive English translation. Its clarity and readability are commended by Louis H. Feldman. Its introduction, notes, maps, and appendices are edifying to both the student and the general reader. A helpful companion piece to this translation is Williamson's *The World of Josephus* (1964), although Moses I. Finley cautions that it lacks scholarly depth relevant to difficult Josephan problems; this criticism should not deter the interested reader, however, who will find in both works a superb introduction to the world and work of Flavius Josephus.

Smallwood, E. Mary. *The Jews Under Roman Rule: From Pompey to Diocletian*. Leiden, Netherlands: E. J. Brill, 1976. The first twelve chapters of this study, particularly chapters 11 and 12, provide an informative reprise of the world in which Josephus was elevated to greatness and offer an appreciable survey of his place in history.

Tcherikover, Victor A. *Hellenistic Civilization and the Jews*. Translated by S. Applebaum. Philadelphia: Jewish Publication Society of America, 1959. Comprehensive exposition of the confluence of the Judaic and Hellenistic traditions; essential to an understanding of the cultural crucible in which the political identity of Josephus was formed.

Thackeray, H. St. John. *Josephus: The Man and the Historian*. New York: Jewish Institute of Religion Press, 1929. Reprint. New York: KTAV Publishing House, 1967. Six lectures given in 1928 as part of the Hilda Stich Stroock Lectures series. In its setting forth of the conspectus of Josephus (life and character; *The Jewish War*; *The Antiquities of the Jews*; Josephus and Judaism; Josephus and Hellenism; Josephus and Christianity) it is exemplary; Samuel Sandmel, however, who has provided the introduction to the reprint, finds the work lacking in an exposition of the significance and utility of Josephus' writings.

Whiston, William. *The Life and Works of Flavius Josephus*. Reprint. New York: Holt, Rinehart and Winston, 1977. This translation of the complete works of Josephus, for all its faults and verbosity, remains an important part of the Josephan tradition in the English-speaking world. Both G. A. Williamson and M. I. Finley mention its being kept alongside the family Bible in Victorian homes.

Roy Arthur Swanson

JUDAH HA-LEVI

Born: c. 1075; Tudela, Spain
Died: c. 1141; possibly Jerusalem, Palestine
Areas of Achievement: Literature and philosophy
Contribution: Judah ha-Levi, one of the greatest Hebrew poets, was also an
important medieval religious philosopher.

Early Life
The son of Samuel ha-Levi, Judah ha-Levi was born around the year 1075
in Muslim Spain. As a member of an affluent, well-educated Jewish family,
ha-Levi began the study of Hebrew and religion when he was quite young,
but his schooling was not limited to those subjects. Growing up during a
golden age of Jewish life in Spain, he was exposed to a wide range of learning—Arabic, mathematics, astronomy, philosophy. Because of the fluidity of
religious demarcations in Spain during this period, he also learned Castilian,
and the languages of all three Spanish religions (Hebrew, Arabic, and Castilian) are employed in his poetry.

When Judah ha-Levi was about fifteen, he may have gone to Lucena to
study under the noted Talmudist Isaac Alfasi. According to some sources,
after this teacher's death in 1103 ha-Levi remained at Lucena at least for a
while, serving as secretary to Alfasi's successor, Joseph ibn Megash. The
death of Alfasi and the succession and marriage of Ibn Megash occasioned
some of ha-Levi's earliest verses. Sometime in his youth, he also became
friendly with a celebrated older Jewish poet, Moses ibn Ezra of Granada.
Ha-Levi had participated in a poetry contest at Córdoba, the object being to
write an imitation of a complex poem by Ibn Ezra. Ha-Levi's entry won, and
it so impressed the senior poet that he invited ha-Levi to visit him. After
meeting the handsome, dark-haired youth, Moses ibn Ezra wrote,

> How can a boy so young in years
> Bear such a weight of wisdom sage,
> Nor 'mongst the greybeards find his peers
> While still in the very bloom of age?

The two remained lifelong friends. Ha-Levi for a time lived in Ibn Ezra's
house, and the older man's death in 1139 elicited a moving elegy from ha-
Levi.

Ha-Levi was making other important friendships as well. From Baruch
Albalia he may have derived his interest in Arabic-Aristotelian philosophy,
while Levi al-Taban of Saragossa, Judah ben Gajath of Granada, and Abraham ibn Ezra shared and encouraged his poetic interest. Abraham ibn Ezra
became an especially close friend. The two enjoyed discussing biblical exe-
gesis, and Ibn Ezra's important commentaries occasionally show evidence

of ha-Levi's influence. Tradition maintains that Ibn Ezra's son married ha-Levi's daughter.

Life's Work

Throughout his life, ha-Levi was a poet first, a physician and philosopher only secondarily. Of his literary work, some eight hundred poems survive. Though most are religious, a substantial number are secular; of these, about eighty are love poems in the manner of Arabic and Christian verses of the day. In these poems, the lady typically is cruel to her lover; the lover yearns for her and fills buckets with his tears; the lady shines even in the darkest night; her eyes slay the lover. Despite their highly stylized formula, the poems reveal technical virtuosity in the use of internal rhyme and musicality, and the imagery can be strikingly original, as when he likens a face surrounded by long red hair to the setting sun turning the sky crimson. Humor, too, surfaces in these poems:

> Awake, my dear, from your slumber arise,
> The sight of you will ease my pain;
> If you dream of one who is kissing your eyes,
> Awake, and soon the dream I'll explain.

Throughout his life, ha-Levi would admire and celebrate female beauty.

Ha-Levi was also sensitive to the beauty and grandeur of nature. Celebrating the return of spring, he wrote,

> And now the spring is here with yearning eyes
> Midst shimmering golden flower beds,
> On meadows a tapestry of bloom over all;
> And myriad-eyed young plants upspring,
> White, green, or red like lips that to the mouth
> Of the beloved one sweetly cling.

On another occasion, a storm at sea prompted him to proclaim the power of nature and to recognize man's weakness in the face of elemental rage. Commenting on these nature poems, Heinrich Graetz has observed,

One can see in his lines the flowers bud and glisten; one inhales their fragrance; one sees the branches bending beneath the weight of golden fruits, and hears the songsters of the air warble their love songs. . . . When he describes the fury of a storm-tossed sea, he imparts to his readers all the sublimity and terror which he himself felt.

Another, larger group of ha-Levi's secular poems are occasional pieces, such as those composed for the death of his teacher and the marriage of Ibn

Megash. Most of the extant poems in this category are eulogies or laments, which often combine personal grief with a sense of cosmic desolation, for in the death of a friend or fellow Jew he read the fate of the Jewish nation:

> There is no sanctuary and no rest,
>   in the West or in the East.
> Should Edom [Christianity] or Ishmael [Islam] be victor,
>   the Jew is always the vanquished.

This concern for the Jewish condition also informs ha-Levi's religious poetry. About half the surviving poems, some 350, are prayers for festivals (*piyyutim*), many of which continue to be recited. His models here were not only the biblical lamentations of Job and Jeremiah but also contemporary Hebrew and Arabic verses. Most focus on national tragedies, though he sometimes describes personal experiences and expresses a desire for salvation. The Psalms provided examples for other, more personal religious poetry in which he recorded his fears and struggles, failures and joys.

Only about thirty-five known poems deal directly with Zion, yet on these more than any others rest his fame and reputation as a poet, for into these works he poured his deepest, most powerful feelings. "My heart is in the East, and I am in the uttermost West—/ How can I find savor in food? How shall it be sweet to me?" For him, the vision of Israel was not an abstraction but a reality that he saw before him daily. Recognizing the plight of the Jews in the Diaspora, subject to the whims of mobs and petty tyrants, he asks rhetorically,

> Have we either in the east or in the west
> A place of hope wherein we may trust,
> Except the land that is full of gates,
> Toward which the gates of Heaven are open—
> Like Mount Sinai and Carmel and Bethel,
> And the houses of the prophets, the envoys,
> And the thrones of the priests of the Lord's throne,
> And the thrones of the kings, the anointed?

Of these poems, none is more moving than the "Zionide" ("Ode to Zion"), still recited in synagogues around the world each Ninth of Ab, the fast commemorating the destruction of the first and second Temples in Jerusalem and, fittingly, the 1492 banishment of the Jews from Spain, a disaster ha-Levi had feared and foreseen. In four stanzas with but a single rhyme throughout, ha-Levi expresses the Jewish longing for Jerusalem, the joy and grief for its past glories, the sense of hope unfulfilled, and the anticipation of joyful redemption when "the chosen are returned to thee/ And thy first youth in glory is renewed." The Hebrew poet Israel Efros has declared, "If the hearts of the Jews of all time could be formed into one great throbbing heart and made to turn toward the East, the song that it would sing would be" ha-Levi's "Ode to Zion."

Ha-Levi's poetry circulated widely in manuscript, and from the beginning of printing his works were incorporated into prayer books. They have been translated into German (1845), English (1851), Italian (1871), Hungarian (1910), Dutch (1929), and Spanish (1932).

Poetry could not, however, earn for ha-Levi a living, so he was forced to turn to medicine. His attitude toward the profession is conveyed in a letter to a friend.

> I occupy myself in the hours which belong neither to the day nor to the night with the vanity of the medical science, although I am unable to heal. . . . I cry to God that He quickly send deliverance to me and give me freedom to enjoy rest, that I may repair to some place of living knowledge, to the fountain of wisdom.

His disclaimer of skill notwithstanding, he apparently served as court physician to Alfonso VI of Toledo, which had fallen to the Christians in 1085. The murder of his patron, Solomon ibn Ferrizuel, in 1108 shocked ha-Levi; together with the sufferings caused by fundamentalist Muslims and the Christian Crusaders, this event reemphasized the precariousness of the Jewish position in exile.

The death of Ibn Ferrizuel seems to have driven ha-Levi from Toledo. During the following years, he traveled throughout Spain, visiting Granada, Málaga, Córdoba, and Seville. In this last city, he became friendly with the court physicians Abu Ayub Solomon ibn al-Mu'allim and Abu al-Hasan ben Meir ibn Kamniel, and here he married in 1120. Further travel took him back to Toledo (1130) and Córdoba (c. 1134). Increasingly, he felt alienated from his native land; after the deaths of his wife and his close friend Moses ibn Ezra, he resolved to follow his heart to Israel. Shortly before leaving Spain, he codified a treatise he had been developing for almost twenty years, his *Kitab al-hujja waal dalil fi nasr al-din al dhalil* (1139; *Judah Halevi's Kitab al Khazari*, 1905; best known as *Book of the Kuzari*).

The work is based on the conversion to Judaism of Bulan, King of the Khazars, a Tartar tribe in Russia, in 740. Hasdai ibn Shaprut (c. 910-970) had corresponded with Joseph, the current Khazar king, who had sent an account of the religious debates among Christians, Muslims, and Jews that had led to Bulan's decision to convert; ha-Levi was familiar with these letters and may have conversed with Khazar descendants living in Spain. The *Book of the Kuzari*, however, transcends a mere attempt at historical re-creation. Ha-Levi was concerned with the Karaite movement in Judaism that sought to reject all Talmudic tradition in favor of a literal reading of the Torah, the five books of Moses, and he was equally concerned with the inroads of Arabic-

Aristotelian philosophy. He had apparently studied Avicenna and al-Farabi, as well as their opponent, the mystical al-Ghazzali, and had sided with the latter. These concerns combined with ha-Levi's personal convictions to create a brilliant explication and defense of Judaism.

As the *Book of the Kuzari* opens, Bulan is troubled by a dream in which an angel has told him that while the king's intentions please God, his actions do not. Bulan therefore summons a philosopher to help him. The philosopher replies that purity of heart is more important than action, but Bulan's dream has already demonstrated the error of such a view. The king then calls in a Muslim and a Christian theologian; because the Jews are persecuted and universally despised, he does not invite a representative of that faith. As the Christian and the Muslim speak, though, Bulan realizes that both draw heavily from Judaism, and at the end of the first section he brings in a Jewish spokesman, the Haver (friend).

In the succeeding four sections, the king and the Haver, who serves as ha-Levi's spokesman, discuss the nature of Judaism. Bulan first wants to know how the Jews understand God. The Haver replies that actual experience is more important than theoretical speculation. He then links the Jewish people, Israel, and the Hebrew language, a fusion that ha-Levi increasingly believed to be essential: The Jew could survive only with a homeland in which he spoke his own language. In the third section, the Haver explains Bulan's dream by saying that to worship God one must fulfill His commandments. Section four finally addresses the question Bulan had asked about the nature of God. As Elohim, the Haver replies, God is remote, but as Adonai He has revealed Himself through history and prophecy. Only the Jews have enjoyed this intimate revelation from and relationship with God, so all other religions must approach God through the Jews.

Thus far, the Haver has focused on distinguishing Judaism from the other major religions. In the final section, he returns to the philosopher. Acknowledging Aristotle's authority in matters of logic and mathematics, he maintains that in spiritual matters speculation is handicapped because the philosopher knows God only indirectly. The prophet, on the other hand, has experienced God directly. Herein lies the strength of Judaism; 600,000 people saw the parting of the Red Sea and heard God's voice at Sinai. No other religion can claim such an immediate encounter with the divine, an encounter cherished through an unbroken chain of tradition. Ha-Levi thus indicates the weakness of the Karaite view: The rejection of the Talmudic heritage would leave Judaism with no stronger claim to validity than that of Christianity or Islam, since without the historical link to Sinai Judaism would lose its unique experience of revelation.

At the end of the *Book of the Kuzari*, the Haver tells Bulan of his intention to go to Israel. Why, the king replies, should the Haver undertake a dangerous journey to a perilous land? Since the destruction of the Temple, God no longer physically resides in Israel, so one can find God anywhere if one seeks with a pure heart. Speaking for ha-Levi, the Haver responds that heart and soul are perfectly pure only in the place selected by God. Though God has removed his physical presence from Israel, God's spirit remains, and therefore the Haver must go.

Still, ha-Levi's own decision to leave was not reached easily. In the *Book of the Kuzari*, Bulan anachronistically warns the Haver of the anti-Jewish sentiments of the Crusaders then controlling the Holy Land. Ha-Levi's letters express doubts about the journey, as does an introspective poem:

> Yet he feared and trembled with falling tears
> To cast Spain from him and seek shores beyond;
> To ride upon ships, to tread through wastes,
> Dens of lions, mountains of leopards.

In 1140, though, he finally set off for Israel, arriving in Alexandria on September 8. Like his Spanish compatriots, the Jews of Egypt sought to dissuade him from further travel. Why leave the comforts and safety of civilization for a desolate, war-torn land? Still, ha-Levi pressed onward toward his goal, passing through Cairo, Tyre, and Damascus.

Did he ever reach Israel? Was he able to "pass to Hebron, where the ancient graves/ Still wait for me, and wander in the dusk/ Of the forest of Carmel"? Did he "stand upon the summit of the mountains/ Where once the unforgotten brothers stood/ And the light of them was seen throughout the world"? Did he "fall to the earth and press my lips into the dust and weep thy desolation/ Till I am blind, and, blind, still comfort thee"? Were these words of his "Ode to Zion" prophecy or dream? No one knows; his final resting place, like that of Moses, remains undiscovered. Yet legend maintains that he did indeed reach the Wailing Wall, and that there, as he prostrated himself to kiss the sacred ground, an Arab horseman trampled or stabbed him to death even as ha-Levi was uttering the words of his "Ode to Zion."

Summary

Shortly after ha-Levi's death, Judah ibn Tibbon translated the *Book of the Kuzari* into Hebrew (c. 1150); ha-Levi had chosen to write in Arabic to make the work accessible to a wider audience. In later years, it was translated into many other languages and enjoyed popularity not only in Jewish but also in Christian and Muslim circles for its championship of faith above reason. The *Book of the Kuzari* impressed Johann Gottlieb von Herder, for example, who claimed that in writing his dialogues he used ha-Levi rather than Plato as his model.

Yet it was as a poet that ha-Levi saw himself, and it is as a poet that his reputation has chiefly survived. More than six centuries after his death,

Herder's countryman Heinrich Heine called ha-Levi's poetry "pure and true and blemish-free," and in 1882 Emma Lazarus published translations of a number of ha-Levi's poems in *Songs of a Semite*. Brilliant in technique, striking in imagery, adept in musicality, they reveal a talent of the first order. His contemporaries and successors repeatedly sang his praises. To Moses ibn Ezra, he was "the pearl diver and lord of most rare jewels." The thirteenth century poet Judah ben Solomon Harizi declared that ha-Levi's poetry

> shines like a crown over the congregation of Israel, adorns its neck like the most precious strand of pearls. . . . All are his followers and attempt to sing in his manner, but they do not reach even the dust of his chariot, and humbly they kiss his feet.

Later, Abraham Bedersi referred to his verses as "the Urrim and Tummim of Jewish song."

Such praise is merited; his poems are living jewels, sighing for the tragedies of the Jews and panting for salvation. He expressed the dreams of an exiled, homeless people and offered hope that despite the present darkness they might yet "behold in wonderment/ the beauteous splendor" of their land. The rhythms of ha-Levi's lines are the heartbeats of his nation. Judah ha-Levi is the enduring poet laureate of Zion.

Bibliography

Druck, David. *Yehuda Halevy: His Life and Works*. Translated by M. Z. R. Frank. New York: Bloch Publishing Co., 1941. Good introduction to ha-Levi's life and writings. Weak on specific details, but the discussions of the *Book of the Kuzari* and the poetry remain useful.

Efros, Israel. "Some Aspects of Yehudah Halevi's Mysticism." *Proceedings of the American Academy of Jewish Research* 11 (1941): 27-41. An erudite discussion of the *Book of the Kuzari*'s treatment of mysticism and rationalism. Notes ha-Levi's sources and explores the meanings of certain obscure terms in the work.

Feldman, Leon A. "Yehudah Halevi: An Answer to a Historical Challenge." *Jewish Social Studies* 3 (1941): 243-272. Based on an address given at the octocentennial observance of ha-Levi's death. Calls ha-Levi "the greatest Hebrew poet after the conclusion of the Bible." Solid historical and philosophical background on medieval Spain and the relationship of that milieu to ha-Levi's ideas. Concludes with a discussion of ha-Levi's enduring significance.

Kayser, Rudolf. *The Life and Time of Jehudah Halevi*. Translated by Frank Gaynor. New York: Philosophical Library, 1949. Kayser begins by saying that his "book does not claim to be a learned tome. It presents no new facts. Its deductions are not based on documents heretofore unknown."

The book is half finished before ha-Levi himself is discussed, for Kayser wants to place the writer within the context of the Jewish golden age in Spain and also within the context of the conflict between Western rationalism and Eastern mysticism. In the *Book of the Kuzari* and in his emigration, ha-Levi reveals his sympathy with the latter.

Minkin, Jacob S. "Judah Halevi." In *Great Jewish Personalities in Ancient and Medieval Times*, edited by Simon Noveck. Washington, D.C.: B'nai B'rith Department of Adult Jewish Education, 1959. A chronological presentation of the life and works. Draws on the poetry and the *Book of the Kuzari* to gain insights into ha-Levi's experiences and thoughts.

Zinberg, Israel. "Jehudah Halevi the Poet." In *A History of Jewish Literature*, translated and edited by Bernard Martin, vol. 1. Cleveland, Ohio: Press of Case Western Reserve University, 1972. Analyzes the evolution of ha-Levi's poetry as the writer matured. According to Zinberg, the poetry became increasingly spiritual, moving from earthly to divine love and beauty. Includes generous excerpts from ha-Levi's verses.

Joseph Rosenblum

JUSTINIAN I

Born: 483; Illyria
Died: November 14, 565; Constantinople
Areas of Achievement: Government and law
Contribution: A conscientious man of somber judgment and religious zeal, Justinian was the pivotal emperor in the transition from the later Roman Empire to the Byzantine Empire. He left a legacy of great buildings, a legal compilation that became the foundation of European law, and an enhanced autocratic tradition that helped the Byzantine Empire guard against the onslaught of Islam.

Early Life

Justinian I was born about 483 in Illyria. Nothing is known of his youth, except that his parents were from peasant families originally from Macedonia and had given their son the name Flavius Petrus Sabbatius. When Justinian was about twenty he was brought to Constantinople by his uncle, Justin I, who had risen through the ranks of the military and had become an important officer in the royal guard. Justin was married but had no children and had brought several of his nephews to the empire's capital, where they were given a good education and trained for the military. When Justinian proved the most adept and promising, he was adopted by his uncle and added the name Justinianus. In time, Justinian received a commission in the elite *candidati*, the emperor's personal bodyguard.

On July 8, 518, Emperor Anastasius I died with neither an heir nor any provision for the succession. Justin, who by this time commanded the royal guard, took advantage of the situation and arranged to have himself proclaimed emperor. He was not, however, experienced in administration or well educated (he may even have been illiterate); thus, his reign did not begin with much promise. Justinian, who had such capabilities in abundance, soon demonstrated his worth to his uncle and rose rapidly to become virtual emperor himself before succeeding his uncle on the throne when the latter died in 527. Justinian first commanded the military troops in Constantinople and kept order in the difficult early days of his uncle's reign. Justin had only one major rival for the throne, and Justinian arranged to have him assassinated by 520, with Justin's cooperation. Justinian then assumed the office of consul in 521 and of caesar in 525. Justinian was careful in these years to cultivate a popular following, which may have played a part in influencing his uncle to keep promoting him. When Justin became seriously ill in early 527, at the age of seventy-seven, he officially crowned Justinian coemperor, with the title of augustus, on Easter Sunday, April 4, 527. The old emperor died on August 1, 527, and Justinian, who had been the virtual ruler since almost 518, was now proclaimed emperor in name as well.

Shortly after Justin's accession to the emperor's throne, Justinian had met and fallen passionately in love with Theodora, one of the most remarkable women of history. She was of humble origins but a great beauty, highly intelligent and talented. There was some trouble with Justin's wife over the affair because of Theodora's questionable past as an actress, and marriage had to wait until after her death, shortly before Justin's. Although Theodora could be cruel, was often deceitful, and loved power, she had uncanny political judgment and an iron will. She was able to exercise more influence over Justinian than anyone else at court.

Life's Work

As emperor, Justinian surrounded himself with able, if somewhat flawed, advisers and assistants. Next to Theodora, John of Cappadocia, Justinian's chief financial officer, was the most important. John was infamous for his cruelty, ruthlessness, depraved personal life, and incredible greed, but Justinian ignored all that because John was also shrewd and endlessly resourceful in raising money. Justinian had inherited a full treasury, but the nearly constant warfare that faced him and the cost of his various grand projects soon depleted it. In John, Justinian found someone who could find new sources of revenue and administer the system more efficiently. John created misery and a crushing tax burden for the empire's subjects, which caused Theodora to believe that he was a threat to the public interest of the realm. For this reason, and probably because he was her rival for influence over Justinian, Theodora waged a ruthless campaign against him until she entrapped him in a bogus conspiracy against Justinian; John was banished in 541.

Another important person Justinian recruited into his service was Tribonian, a lawyer reputed to have the finest legal mind in the empire. Although Tribonian was a pagan, Justinian made him chief of the imperial judicial system. Tribonian was very nearly as avaricious as John of Cappadocia and has been accused by scholars of corrupting the whole legal system. Nevertheless, he contributed significantly to the success of Justinian's reign by directing the remarkable legal reforms that took place. Belisarius, the outstanding general of the age in tactics and administration—and who excelled as a field commander—also served Justinian well. An honest and honorable man with no ambitions beyond serving his emperor, he was trusted by everyone but the ever-suspicious Justinian.

Nearly all the major figures in Justinian's administration were of humble origins, as was the emperor himself. He was always on the lookout for talent and kept the offices of the empire filled with the best he could find. Justinian did not, however, delegate all the work to others. He was a serious and diligent monarch who paid careful attention to detail, supervised his chief officers closely, and worked such long hours that he became known popularly as "the emperor who never sleeps."

The great crisis of Justinian's reign was the Nika Riots of 532. The Blues and Greens were organizations that supported rival chariot racing teams at the Hippodrome but represented different political positions as well. When rioting broke out between the two, they forgot their differences and joined forces against Justinian when he intervened to end the violence. It looked for a time as though Justinian would be forced to flee, and several chief ministers recommended that he leave. Theodora, however, never vacillated and convinced Justinian to stand firm and await the proper moment to crush the rioters. As many as thirty thousand people may have died before Belisarius brought Constantinople under control again, and much of the city was in ruins. Two important results came from the Nika Riots. Neither the aristocratic nor the popular faction ever fully recovered, and Justinian was able to rule as an absolute monarch thereafter. Furthermore, the destruction of so much of the city provided Justinian with the opportunity for an epic building program.

Justinian was at war defending the empire's borders for most of his reign. His most celebrated military project, however, was the recovery of the territories of the Western Roman Empire which had been overrun by barbarians. In June of 533, Justinian sent Belisarius with a small force of sixteen thousand to Carthage, where he gained an easy victory over the unprepared and incompetently led Vandals. In 535, Justinian decided to attempt the next and major step by overthrowing the Ostrogothic kingdom of Italy and reestablishing imperial rule. Belisarius again had an easy victory in Sicily and in southern Italy, reaching Rome late in 536. From that point onward, however, Justinian's refusal to entrust Belisarius with adequate troops and supplies prolonged the war and brought terrible hardships to the Italian people. Believing the situation hopeless, Belisarius arranged to have himself recalled to Constantinople in 548 and went into retirement. In 550, Justinian sent Narses to Italy. Although Narses was not the military genius Belisarius was, he was given more adequate supplies, and in 552, he was able to defeat decisively the Ostrogoth forces at Taginae and had pacified Italy by 554. By this time much of Italy had been destroyed or ravaged.

There was constant trouble from the various peoples living on the northern and eastern borders which kept the empire almost constantly at war. In Spain, the Visigoths maintained constant pressure on the shrinking area in the south that remained under imperial rule. The Franks and others constantly harassed Italy. In the Balkans, the Slavs and Avars were a constant threat. The Persians to the east and Arabs to the southeast were at war with the empire on and off throughout Justinian's reign. The revenues required to sustain this military effort were actually beyond the empire's capabilities. Justinian had to use diplomacy and tribute to supplement the military effort, particularly in the Balkans and with Persia.

The role of caesaropapist emperor, one who exercises supreme authority over ecclesiastical matters, was well suited to Justinian's personality and temperament. His education had included theological training, an interest he maintained all of his life, especially after Theodora's death. Christianity was beset with schismatics, and in this age of intolerance and willingness of so many to fight and die for their particular interpretation, these divisions threatened to disrupt the empire. The chief problem was the conflict between the Monophysites, who denied that Jesus Christ had human attributes, and the orthodox Chalcedonians, who claimed that Christ was both human and divine. Justinian tried, through a variety of means, to find a compromise but never succeeded for long. In the process, however, he acquired considerable authority over the Church and its councils, including even the pope on occasion. In the end, he probably did as much as anyone to ensure the eventual split between the Roman Catholic and the Orthodox churches.

The legal system developed by the Roman Empire has been called its grandest contribution to history. By Justinian's time, the practical application of Roman law had come to be based on various collections of imperial edicts and *constitutiones*. This development made it difficult to research points of law, and much of it was obsolete or inadequate to the changed circumstances of the empire. On February 13, 528, some six months after becoming emperor in his own name, Justinian called together a commission of legal scholars led by Tribonian. Their first assignment was to prepare a new edition of the laws. The new code was to be updated, with repetitions and contradictions removed, and organized in a clear and rational manner. The first edition of the Codex Justinianus was published in late 534, but revision became necessary after later parts of the whole work were completed. The second part was a compilation of all the interpretations of the laws written by renowned Roman jurists over the centuries. These opinions, explaining the law, were important guides for the lawyers and others who applied the laws.

In 533, Tribonian and his assistants had finished the work of collating, abridging, and modernizing the old texts and the Digest was published. At the same time, Tribonian finished revising and updating Gaius' older commentaries on Roman law. This third part, known as the Institutes, was to serve as a textbook or handbook for law students. At this point the Codex Justinianus had to be revised to bring it in line with the Digest and the Institutes. Together, the Codex Justinianus, Digest, and Institutes made up the Corpus Juris Civilis, the body of civil law, which was intended to serve all the legal needs of the empire. It was in this form that Roman law was passed on to succeeding generations and Western civilization. The Codex Justinianus contained the actual laws, the Digest the definitive literature of jurisprudence, and the Institutes the official manual for law students. In time, 160 Novels, or new laws adopted by Justinian, were added. The historical impact of the Corpus Juris Civilis on the development of Western law has been enormous and stands as Justinian's greatest achievement.

Although Justinian was a conservative who perceived his duty to include preserving the empire intact in form as well as in territory, he was actually something of an innovator. In the same manner as he combined control of the political and religious life into a powerful caesaropapist concept of the emperor's office, he also streamlined and consolidated the authority of imperial administration. He dropped the now-meaningless office of consul, discarded the principle of strict separation between civil and military authority, and, in general, established precedents for future emperors to tighten imperial authority to make it more autocratic. He insisted that all subordinates be loyal and efficient servants of the state and rewarded and promoted anyone with talent. He also sought to reduce the abuses by officials of their offices but found the goal of honest government elusive, not to mention compromised by his own toleration of corrupt but efficient revenue officers. The problem with the tax system, however, was not unusual. Emperors had been trying for two centuries before Justinian to bring reform with no greater success.

Following the example of many of his predecessors, Justinian was determined to leave his mark on the empire by a building program that included practical as well as ornamental structures. Among the practical buildings, military forts on the frontiers, and sometimes in the interior of the empire as well, made up the largest category. Justinian also built many bridges, aqueducts, and roads, and various buildings for general public use, such as law courts, baths, great cisterns, storehouses, and asylums. Ornamental buildings included additions to the imperial palace and numerous monasteries and churches, many of which still stand. The great fortress-monastery of Saint Catherine of Mount Sinai is among those that have survived, and its original parts remain an invaluable repository of early Christian and Byzantine art.

Besides Constantinople, the primary focus of Justinian's church building was in and around Jerusalem and Ravenna, Italy. It is in the unusually richly decorated octagonal Church of Saint Vitalis in Ravenna that the best portraits of Justinian and Theodora were discovered. They are full-length portraits in mosaic panels. These are not particularly detailed portraits and no detailed descriptions of the two monarchs have survived. From what is known, he was of moderate height and medium build, with a pleasant, round face that seems to have been without any particularly remarkable features.

The destruction that accompanied the Nika Riots created the need for the most important category of Justinian's building projects and provided him with the opportunity to begin the process of turning the city into the most splendid of medieval Christendom. He built several giant colonnaded cisterns, two of which still survive, all manner of public buildings, and the great Augustan forum. He also substantially enlarged the Grand Palace of the Emperors and, in general, beautified the area around the city. His greatest passion seems to have been building or rebuilding churches and monasteries.

The monumental Church of the Holy Apostles, which no longer exists, was the regular site for the emperors' tombs and is reputed to have looked like the Church of San Marco in Venice.

Two other churches of particular note, both of which have survived, were also reconstructions of buildings originally erected by Constantine the Great. Haghia Eirene (Holy Peace) has suffered over the years, but Haghia Sophia (Holy Wisdom) still demonstrates the glory of Byzantine art and architecture. The Turks made it into a mosque in 1453, when they took Constantinople, covering its magnificent mosaics with whitewash. Kemal Atatürk converted it into a museum in 1935, and some of its former beauty has been painstakingly restored in the years since. It was a complex building of a then radically new design featuring a great central dome resting on a square base through the use of pendentives, semidomes on each side of the nave to add spaciousness, colonnades, and galleries. It was the greatest church of Christendom in its day and remains one of the world's great architectural masterpieces.

Theodora died of cancer on June 28, 548. The loss of her stabilizing influence and support seems to have signaled the end of the positive and creative part of Justinian's reign. Although he was to have some temporary successes in resolving the theological disputes that so plagued the empire, a permanent solution eluded him, and the problem was nearly out of control by the time he died. The crushing effects of his fiscal policies on the populace were becoming more noticeable, and the brilliance of his earlier days was giving way to exhaustion in the empire. Justinian was increasingly unable to defend the empire's borders and had to resort to diplomacy and bribes. The problem became critical in the Balkans, where the Avars and Slavs had begun pushing into the empire's territory during Justin's reign. The defensive capabilities of the empire had degenerated so far that Justinian was forced to call Belisarius out of retirement in 559 to defend the capital, while the remainder of the Balkan people were left to fend off the invaders as best they could. The Italian reconquest was brought to a successful conclusion, but at the cost of an impoverished Italy. Even the Blues and Greens circus factions reappeared to disturb Justinian's last years.

On November 14, 565, when Justinian died, at the age of eighty-two, the news was greeted with relief by his subjects. He and Theodora had had no children, and Justinian made his nephew Justin his heir. Amid popular rejoicing that the old tyrant was dead and a new era was dawning, Justinian was buried in the Church of the Holy Apostles. In truth, a great age had ended, and a terrible one was to follow.

Summary

Justinian I misunderstood the changing nature of his time. Reconquering the Western Roman Empire was a doomed effort to re-create a Christian version of the classical Roman state which left the surviving East exhausted and dangerously exposed. His lavish building program made the economic situation worse while he failed to protect adequately the empire's borders. By becoming personally involved in the theological disputes of his time, he did expand the role of emperor to a caesaropapist autocracy—but at the expense of contributing significantly to the permanent split in the Christian community between the Roman Catholic and the Orthodox churches. His misplaced religious zeal extended even to requiring adherence to Orthodox Christianity as a prerequisite to teaching in the empire and to closing the schools of higher learning in Athens in 529. Not only were those subjects with a classical education deprived of a living, but they were also driven from the empire, destroying the tradition of Plato's Academy and thus breaking an important link with antiquity. Yet he is not entirely to blame for these mistakes. Justinian was acting within the Roman tradition of what was expected of an emperor. It was only toward the end of his reign, when the consequences of these policies began to pile up, that his subjects began to complain so bitterly, not during the early years of glory and achievement.

Whatever blame may be assigned for Justinian's mistakes, it is clear that he left a remarkable legacy for the future of Western civilization, one any monarch would envy. He set a standard of dedication to duty, personal honor, and integrity rarely matched by an emperor. He sought little for himself and everything for the empire's welfare as he understood it. The Corpus Juris Civilis strengthened the empire by improving the administration of justice, establishing legal standards by which most other law in Western civilization would come to be measured, and ultimately becoming the foundation of most modern European legal systems. His building projects helped make Constantinople one of the great cities of the medieval world and an inspiration which helped sustain Byzantine civilization for centuries. These achievements, and the improvements in imperial administration, contributed to the longevity of the empire and its historic role as the bastion of Christendom in the East, guarding Europe from conquest by Islam.

Bibliography

Ariès, Philippe, and Georges Duby, eds. *A History of Private Life*. Vol. 1, *From Pagan Rome to Byzantium*, edited by Paul Veyne. Cambridge, Mass.: Harvard University Press, 1987. A rewarding historical survey of the hidden and intimate daily life of people from the rich to the poor. Especially interesting is the startling contrast of the triumph of Christianity with the undisciplined private lives of so many in Byzantium.

Barker, John W. *Justinian and the Later Roman Empire*. Madison: University of Wisconsin Press, 1966. The best and most balanced biography of Justinian and his reign. Begins with an illuminating background chapter on the Roman world before Justinian and ends with a discussion of the long-term results of his reign.

Downey, Glanville. *Constantinople in the Age of Justinian*. Norman: University of Oklahoma Press, 1960. An excellent description of Justinian's Byzantine Empire and its base in Constantinople. A useful introduction especially to the history of the city. Part of the Centers on Civilization series.

Jones, A. H. M. *The Later Roman Empire, 284-602: A Social, Economic, and Administrative Survey*. 2 vols. Baltimore: Johns Hopkins University Press, 1986. Analytical survey from Diocletian and the conversion of the Empire to Oriental despotism and the final collapse and loss of the western half of the Empire. Includes the reign of Justinian. Although the historical narrative is unbalanced, the work is a mine of information.

Procopius. *Secret History*. Translated by Richard Atwater. Ann Arbor: University of Michigan Press, 1961. Procopius wrote the most important eyewitness account of Justinian's reign. It contains vicious distortions of the historical record, however, and should be read with P. N. Ure's book (see below), which evaluates the accuracy of all Procopius' works. See also the many English translations of Procopius' other works.

Runciman, Steven. *Byzantine Civilization*. London: E. Arnold and Co., 1933. Available in numerous reprints. A brief but stylish essay by a prominent and accomplished scholar that provides an excellent introduction to the sweep of Byzantine history.

Ure, P. N. *Justinian and His Age*. Harmondsworth, England: Penguin Books, 1951. Reprint. Westport, Conn.: Greenwood Press, 1979. A balanced and detailed evaluation of accounts by Procopius and other eyewitnesses of Justinian's reign but not a chronological narrative history. Recommended only for those engaged in an in-depth study of Justinian.

Richard L. Hillard

JUVENAL

Born: c. A.D. 60; Aquinum
Died: c. A.D. 130; place unknown
Area of Achievement: Literature
Contribution: Juvenal expanded the dimensions of poetic satire in savage works that lashed out at man's vices and corruption.

Early Life

Juvenal (Decimus Junius Juvenalis) was born around A.D. 60 in the small Italian town of Aquinum. It is thought that his family was wealthy and that Juvenal entered the army to make a career in service to the emperor. Unsuccessful in his endeavors to achieve a position of responsibility, however, he turned to literature to establish or simply to express himself. He was a friend of the well-known poet Martial during this period and wrote his first satires against the flatterers and hangers-on in the imperial court. For this scathing attack, Emperor Domitian confiscated Juvenal's property and exiled him to Egypt.

Juvenal returned to Rome after the death of Domitian in 96 and wrote, recited, and published his *Saturae* (100-127; *Satires*) during the years that followed. Most of the satires written at this time do not refer to contemporary events but to the abuses of the earlier reign of Domitian. For several years, Juvenal was very poor, but eventually his financial problems were alleviated by a gift from Emperor Hadrian.

Life's Work

Juvenal's achievement can be found in the five books of satires he produced during his lifetime. There are sixteen satires in the collected works of Juvenal, and the first book contains the first five. These five satires have as their subject matter the corruption and immorality which Juvenal perceived among Roman aristocrats and leaders of his time; he considered that they were interested in wealth and sexual excess rather than the personal virtue and rectitude befitting leaders of the Roman Republic.

The first satire in book 1 is an introduction to the whole work; it is a justification for the literary mode which Juvenal created. There had been satire before Juvenal, but it did not have the tone, subject matter, or structure which Juvenal employed. Earlier satires, such as those of Horace, tended to laugh tolerantly at mankind's social foibles rather than rage about their vices. The tone set by Juvenal, then, was new: "Must I be listening always, and not pay them back? How they bore me,/ Authors like Cordus the crude, with the epic he calls the Theseid!" Juvenalian satire is an exasperated attack on those who have offended him; its realm is not the heroic but the low and the mean. He directs his hearers to the disgusting Roman scene and declares: "Then it is difficult NOT to write satire." He points to such absurdities as a eunuch marrying and Juvenal's former barber becoming richer than any patrician. Although his satire has the sweep of epic, covering "everything human" from the earliest times, its special province is contemporary life: "When was there ever a time more rich in abundance of vices?"

At the end of the poem, Juvenal brings up the problem of whether he will "dare name names," real names rather than invented ones. If he does, he is likely to end up "a torch in a tunic" in these corrupt times. He determines therefore to use only the names of the dead and reveal the type of vice if not the specific example.

The second satire is against not only homosexuality but also the hypocrisy of homosexuals who set themselves up as moral censors of society. The poem opens with a typical Juvenalian hyperbolic exclamation of frustration: "Off to Russia for me, or the Eskimos, hearing these fellows/ Talk—what a nerve!—about morals, pretend that their virtue/ Equals the Curian clan's, while they act like Bacchanal women." A list of odious examples follows this opening, the most important being that of Gracchus, a descendant of the republican Gracchi who defended the rights of the Plebeians. This Gracchus has given a large sum of money to a musician and married him in a bizarre ceremony; once more, the target of Juvenal's wrath is members of the aristocratic class, who should be offering models for the rest of society instead of pursuing debauchery. Even the great feats of Roman arms are mocked: "An Armenian prince, softer than all of our fairies" ends up in the arms of a Roman tribune, an act which Juvenal calls "the Intercourse Between Nations."

The third satire, against the city of Rome, is one of Juvenal's greatest works. The speaker in the poem is not Juvenal but his friend Umbricius. Umbricius is leaving Rome because he is "no good at lying" and therefore cannot possibly survive in Rome. One aspect of Roman life that he finds especially offensive is that the old republican Rome has become a "Greek-ized Rome," filled with subtle Greeks who can adapt to any role and thus are displacing the native aristocracy. Another target is the great value now given to wealth; poverty "makes men objects of mirth, ridiculed, humbled, embarrassed." In addition, Rome is a dangerous place; if its resident does not catch a disease, then he is likely to die in a fire or be killed by a burglar at night. The only sane course is to flee the city and relocate in a country town where civic virtue is still possible and one can live an honorable life.

The fourth satire contains two episodes. In the first, Curly the Cur spends an absurdly large sum of money for a red mullet which he devours by himself. Juvenal remarks that he could have bought the fisherman for less than he paid for the fish. This excess is paralleled by an incident involving Emperor Domitian. Domitian is given a huge turbot because his subjects fear that by purchasing it they would incur the wrath of the "baldheaded tyrant." There is no pot large enough for the fish, however, and a council of state is called to decide what to do. The councillors are all terrified of saying the wrong thing and ending up dead, so they treat the problem as a question of war. One suggests that the emperor will capture a monarch as great as the fish, while a craftier one suggests that a huge pot to cook the fish whole be created and "from henceforward, Great Caesar,/ Let potters follow your camp!" The motion is carried, and the councillors nervously depart. Juvenal adds a comment at the end of the poem to sum up the reign of Domitian: "Nobles he could kill. He was soaked in their blood, and no matter./ But when the common herd began to dread him, he perished." Once more, the Roman aristocrats are ineffectual or corrupt, and only the mob can bring down a vicious (and here ridiculous) emperor.

The fifth satire satirizes both the proud and overbearing patron and the submissive client who acquiesces to and even encourages this situation. The poem is structured as a description of a typical dinner with a patron. The patron drinks the best wines while the client is given wine that would make blotting paper shudder. The patron dines on a choice mullet, the client on an eel that looks like a blacksnake. The reason for such shameful treatment is the client's poverty; if he were rich, the daintiest morsels would be placed before him. Juvenal suggests to such clients that if they persist in seeking and accepting such treatment, "some day you'll offer your shaved-off heads to be slapped." If the client acts like a slave, the patron will surely treat him like a slave.

Book 2 of the *Satires* is composed of one long poem attacking Roman women; it is the longest and most ambitious of Juvenal's satires. His charges against women are similar to those he made against Rome's nobility: They have fallen into decadence, they care only about money, and they have forsaken old ways in favor of current fashions and modes. Women are no longer to be trusted, since so many have poisoned their husbands for wealth or convenience. Finally, even if a man were to find the perfect woman, she would not do since her perfection would be unbearable. It is an amusingly unbalanced, excessive, and effective poem.

The third book is made up of three poems. The subjects are again poverty, nobility, and ways of gaining a livelihood in first century Rome. The poor wretches in satire 7 are poets, historians, and teachers, occupations which had once been honored but are now despised. The poem piles negative example on example, but it does offer some hope for a decent life; "Caesar alone" can provide the help the public refuses to give. The eighth satire contrasts nobility of character to nobility of family; Juvenal cites examples of debased scions from famous families and declares: "Virtue alone is proof of nobility." The most telling contrast is between the noble heritage of Catiline (Lucius Sergius Catilina), who attempted to enslave the Roman people, and the relative obscurity of Cicero, who thwarted Catiline's designs and saved the Republic. The ninth satire has as a speaker, not Juvenal or one of his spokesmen but a homosexual, who is complaining about the difficulties he finds in his work as a prostitute. He is consoled at the end by a cohort who assures him that "there'll always be fairies/ While these seven hills stand." Since this is so, he can be content with a contingent of slaves, a villa of his own, and a sum of money equivalent to a thousand dollars—amenities unavailable to most poets of the time.

The highlight of book 4 of the *Satires* is "The Vanity of Human Wishes," in which Juvenal poses the question of the proper petitions of humans in their prayers to the gods. He inventories the usual requests that men make—for wealth, beauty, or power—only to find that their attainment produces dangerous results. The wealthy man, for example, has to fear the poison in the jeweled cup, while the poor man is free from such fears; the powerful man has to watch out for envy and hatred, while the weak man can be at peace. Even the desire for a long life is not appropriate, since the man to whom such a request has been granted must face burying his wife, children, and all those dear to him while he withers into a lonely old age. What then should people pray for? "A healthy mind in a healthy body, a spirit/ Unafraid of death, but reconciled to it." The rest must be left to the gods, for human beings do not know their own best interests.

The last book of satires contains only one important poem, "On an Education in Avarice." It deals not only with the dangers of the desire for great wealth but also with how the example of the parents influences the children. There is a surprising tenderness in Juvenal's tone when he speaks about the vulnerability of children. "To a child is due the greatest respect: in whatever/ Nastiness you prepare, don't despise the years of your children,/ But let your infant son dissuade you from being a sinner." Man should desire only enough to feed, clothe, and shelter himself; the rest is not only unnecessary but corrupting.

Juvenal's last book of satires was published in 127, and he died shortly after.

Summary

Juvenal's satires retain their power nearly two thousand years after they were written. Their powerful moral vision and the freshness of their language permit them to transcend the local and specific occasions which they address. Juvenal's solutions or consolations are not unusual; similar Stoic advice can be found in the writings of Horace or Sextius Propertius. No other poet of the period, however, exposed so much so fully. Some have complained that Juvenal went too far in his condemnation of mankind and that his poetic vision is unbalanced. These critics fail, however, to relate Juvenal's vision to the social and political system of the time and to take into consideration the special social role of the satirist in this period. Juvenal believed epic and lyric poetry to be entirely inappropriate forms for a corrupt age; instead, his time demanded exactly the sort of fiercely agitated satires that he produced.

Bibliography

Duff, J. Wight. *A Literary History of Rome in the Silver Age: From Tiberius to Hadrian*. London: T. F. Unwin, 1927. A broad historical survey of the literature of the period, with a specific discussion of satire as a literary form in Juvenal's time.

_____. *Roman Satire: Its Outlook on Social Life*. Berkeley: University of California Press, 1936. Reprint. Hamden, Conn.: Archon Books, 1964. Duff relates Juvenal's poems to the literary and social contexts, but he does not analyze the poems in any detail. A brief but useful introduction to the poet.

Highet, Gilbert. *Juvenal the Satirist: A Study*. Oxford: Clarendon Press, 1954. Includes a cogent discussion of each of Juvenal's satires and of their influence on later literature. The book is very thorough but accessible to the general reader.

Jenkyns, Richard. *Three Classical Poets: Sappho, Catullus, Juvenal*. Cambridge, Mass.: Harvard University Press, 1982. This very detailed study of Juvenal's style and poetic effects brings to light the satirist's techniques and methods. It is well written, but it is directed toward an academic audience.

Scott, Inez G. *The Grand Style in the Satires of Juvenal*. Northhampton, Mass.: Smith College, 1924. An early and still-valuable stylistic study of Juvenal's use of inflated language to create satiric effects. The book is appropriate for those who know something about the literary traditions of the period.

James Sullivan

KĀLIDĀSA

Born: c. 100 B.C. or c. A.D. 340; India
Died: c. 40 B.C. or c. A.D. 400; probably India
Area of Achievement: Literature
Contribution: Recognized as the author of no more than three plays and four poems, which fuse together themes of nature and love within the framework of Hinduism, Kālidāsa is generally regarded as India's greatest poet and dramatist. Sometimes characterized as the "Shakespeare of India," he is especially known in the West for his romantic play *Śakuntalā* and his metaphysical love poem *The Cloud Messenger.*

Early Life

Kālidāsa's play *Mālavikāgnimitra* (c. 70 B.C. or c. A.D. 370; English translation, 1875) has as its hero Agnimitra, a historical king of the Śuṅga Dynasty who reigned from 151 to 143 B.C. In addition, inscriptions found in the Deccan at Mandasor (dated A.D. 473) and Aihole (dated A.D. 634) quote from his poetry and laud his genius. These firm evidences are all that establish a chronological range for Kālidāsa's life. The rest is conjecture. Though the Śuṅga was an important successor to the great Maurya Dynasty and led a cultural revival, opinion holds that Hindu culture had not sufficiently developed and the times were too disturbed to accommodate a talent such as Kālidāsa's. Thus scholars suggest that the Gupta Dynasty (c. A.D. 320-c. 550), the golden age of India, marked by serenity and sophistication, was more in line with the spirit and style of Kālidāsa. It is quite possible that Kālidāsa flourished during the reign of Candra Gupta II (c. 380-c. 414), of whom a congenial relation of court poet to patron can be readily conceived. Still, students of Kālidāsa tend to attach two date ranges to his works to acknowledge the uncertainty.

Just as little is known of his dates, little is known of Kālidāsa's life—except by inference from his writings and the legends concerning him. Identified in various stories as an orphan, idiot, laborer, and shepherd, Kālidāsa may have had a difficult early life. His knowledge of religion, philosophy, the sciences, and Sanskrit probably marks him as a Brahman and a devotee of the cult of Siva. (Indeed, his name means "servant of Kali," one of the consorts of that god.) His aristocratic sensitivity, grasp of court etiquette, and familiarity with Indian geography suggest that he was not only a court poet to the Vikramaditya (Sun of Valor), his patron at Ujjain, but also a traveler and an ambassador (possibly to Kuntala, a kingdom inland from the Malabar Coast). The erotic overtones in his works make it easy to accept the legend of a princess as his lover and spouse. It is not difficult to believe that his life ended, at sixty or eighty years of age, by foul play at the hands of a courtesan in Sri Lanka, as another legend would have it.

The order of his works (rejecting the twenty or so spurious works some-times attributed to him) is unknown. Hypothetical reconstructions have been made, even to the degree of correlating the writings to his biography, but the writings are too impersonal to do this with any accuracy. Perhaps the two lyrics are early, the two epics somewhat later, while the plays are scattered at different phases of his life—*Abhijñānaśākuntala* (c. 45 B.C. or c. A.D. 395; *Śakuntalā: Or, The Lost Ring*, 1789) being the product of maturity.

Life's Work

Nearly all Kālidāsa's works were written in Sanskrit, a highly inflected lan-guage learned by an aristocratic elite—the word literally means "perfected." Sanskrit was written as poetry (*kavya*), either lyric or epic, according to pre-cise rules of grammar. The poetry, combined with other factors, created the visual immediacy of drama. Kālidāsa, using twenty-six different meters, was the king of similes, drawing from religion and nature in a style distinguished by a grace and economy that made music.

The *Ṛtusaṁhāra* (c. 75 B.C. or c. A.D. 365; English translation, 1867) is a pastoral poem mirroring a newly married man's joy of nature during the six Indian seasons (summer, the rains, autumn, early winter, winter, and spring); it is composed of 140 stanzas divided into six cantos. Though popular with the young, it is regarded as a piece of juvenilia, generally neglected by the lit-erary critics. Yet this "lover's calendar," because of its romance, may have been innovative at its first appearance.

The *Meghadūta* (c. 65 B.C. or c. A.D. 375; *The Cloud Messenger*, 1813), much adored by Johann Wolfgang von Goethe, is an elegiac monody of 111 to 127 verses, according to various recensions; it is cast in a series of seventeen-syllable quatrains in a single meter. A Yaksha, a sensual demigod, separated from his wife for a year by a curse, asks a rain cloud to transmit a love message to her. The first part of the poem contains a sweeping and detailed picture of the subcontinent via the hypostatized cloud; the second part focuses on its delivery to the wife in a celestial city of the Himalayas. The lyric plays on the pathos of love with full intensity of mood. The travels of the cloud and its detour over Ujjain lend credence to the idea of Kālidāsa as a traveler and diplomat. The poem is original and subjective; indeed, Kālidāsa pioneered a new genre. The traditional court epic (*Mahākāvya*) Kālidāsa found riddled with stereotypy and convention. Yet he was able to condense, deepen, and stylize his works into epics of aristocratic appeal, combining elevated themes with emotional verity.

The epic *Kumārasambhava* (c. 60 B.C. or c. A.D. 380; *The Birth of the War-God*, 1879) is incomplete at eight cantos, covering the courtship and mar-riage of Siva and Pārvatī only. (The birth of their son Kumāra, and his ex-ploits, are recounted in ten additional cantos which were found not to be Kālidāsa's work.) The material is drawn from the Puranas (the epic elaborating and expanding on the great epic *Mahābhārata*). Mount Himalaya's daughter Pārvatī falls in love with the meditative Yogi god Siva. Menaced by the demon Taraka, the gods determine that only a son by Siva and Pārvatī can defeat the demon; they send Kāma, the god of love, to bring about the union, but Siva burns Kāma with his third eye. Pārvatī then abandons sensuality for spiritualism, emaciating herself. Siva, in disguise, dissuades her from her course, and they come lovingly together. Thematically, self-abnegation leads to the highest form of love. Symbolically, Siva, who is Truth, combines with Pārvatī, Beauty, to produce Kumāra, Power. The risqué depiction of the lovers' honeymoon led to the charge that canto 8 is sacrilegious.

In the epic *Raghuvaṁśa* (c. 50 B.C. or c. A.D. 390; *The Dynasty of Raghu*, 1872-1895), Kālidāsa traces a line of kings descended from the sun god over nineteen cantos, dwelling on the varying aspects of the ideal king in terms of *dharma* (moral duty): Dilipa, the ascetic; Raghu, the warrior; Aja, the lover; and Rāma, the *avatāra* (incarnation) of Vishnu. Yet the line ends with Agnivarna, the consumptive voluptuary: Does this reflect the poet's tragic vision of lost ideals, or is the epic merely incomplete? Much of the poem is a brilliant summary of the classical epic *Rāmāyaṇa*. The first nine cantos of that classic deal with Rāma's forebears, cantos 10 through 15 with Rāma, and cantos 16 through 19 with his descendants. One critic wonders whether Kālidāsa preferred Raghu to Rāma, who shuns the pregnant Sītā as unclean after her abduction by Rāvaṇa the demon. When one compares these epics, *The Birth of the War-God* has singleness of legend, theme, structure, and philosophy, while *The Dynasty of Raghu* is a multifaceted pageant and chronicle.

The *Mālavikāgnimitra*, a spirited, musical harem intrigue for a spring festival, involves the love of Agnimitra, a historical figure, for a princess disguised as a maiden, Mālavikā, against the opposition of his two queens, the mature Dhārinī and the accomplished Iravati. In winning her in this parallelogram of relationships, Agnimitra has the aid of a jester, a nun, and good luck, as well as an asoka tree that responds to those that touch it by flowering or not. Perhaps the key element of the plot is Dhārinī's final acceptance of Mālavikā into the harem.

Vikramorvaśiya (c. 56 B.C. or c. A.D. 384; *Vikrama and Urvaśī*, 1851), probably intended to be sung at a royal coronation, concerns the love of a semidivine hero, Purūravas, for an immortal nymph, Urvaśī, a tale drawn from Vedic legend. Though their love is opposed by Purūravas' queen and subjected to a divine curse which separates them, the gods bring the couple together in the end. Thus, love (*kāma*), supported by wealth (*artha*), issues in progeny (*dharma*, moral duty). Act 5, when the grief-maddened king wanders in the woods apostrophizing nature, is a famous scene.

It was the eighteenth century Calcutta judge Sir William Jones, the founder of comparative philology by his "discovery" of Sanskrit, who brought Kālidāsa to the attention of the West by rendering the first English translation of *Śakuntalā* in 1789. The play remains one of the world's masterpieces. Its story of love spanning Earth and Heaven must have appealed to Europeans, as the Romantic movement was then in its infancy. Drawn from the *Mahābhārata*, the play centers on star-crossed lovers: the tender, tortured ruler Dushyanta and the natural, selfless Śakuntalā, daughter of a sage and a nymph. Their match is destroyed by a curse which erases the king's recognition of his spouse when she comes to him at his palace after a separation. Only his ring, lost and swallowed by a fish, can recover his memory of love. When the ring is found, the lovers are reunited via the aerial chariot of the god Indra, and they live happily together with their child Bharata, the first legendary emperor of India. Throughout, the play contrasts the demands of public life and the sorrow of frustrated love to the serenity of simple values and the conception of ideal love.

Summary

The drama of Kālidāsa can only be understood within its own cultural context. The theater was part of the palace complex, playing to sensitized aristocratic audiences. It combined poetry, music, dance, song, mime, and characterization in a highly stylized presentation shorn of scenery and props, with most actions occurring offstage. The absence of evil—indeed, the fusing of Heaven and Earth into a happy ending—is unique to Indian thought. The transmigration of souls, the demand of moral duty, and the consequences of fate make the cosmos ultimately moral and purposeful and eliminate the role of chance. The plays are dominated by psychological rather than plotting factors, by the power of a basic mood, or emotion (*rasa*), and the characters fill roles assigned by the cosmos rather than marked by individualism. Thus, Kālidāsa was actually a traditionalist, a believer in a finally beneficent world order (politically, he subscribed to benevolent monarchy). With such ideals as *maya* (illusion of reality), *moksa* (enlightenment), and *santa* (tranquillity) and a view of love encompassing sensual, aesthetic, and spiritual levels in different lives and worlds, Kālidāsa contributed to literature an elucidation of the cosmic pervasiveness of love.

Bibliography

Dimock, Edward C., Edwin Gerow, C. M. Naim, A. K. Ramanujan, Gordon Roadarmel, and J. A. B. van Buitenen. *The Literatures of India: An Introduction.* Chicago: Chicago University Press, 1974. This critical study complements historical and sociological approaches of earlier Orientalists. It was a cooperative venture mostly of University of Chicago faculty for the Asia Society. Covers full sweep of Indian literature. See especially sections on the epic, drama, poetics, and the lyric. Scholarly, invaluable insights.

Horrwitz, E. P. *The Indian Theatre: A Brief Survey of the Sanskrit Drama.*

Reprint. New York: Benjamin Blom, 1967. An old (originally published in 1912) but evocative description of the Indian theater. A court theater of Ujjain and imaginary performances of Kālidāsa's plays are especially well described.

Kālidāsa. *Theater of Memory: The Plays of Kālidāsa*. Translated by Edwin Gerow, David Gitomer, and Barbara Stoler Miller. New York: Columbia University Press, 1984. Contains three brilliant chapters: "Kālidāsa's World and His Plays" (by Miller), "Sanskrit Dramatic Theory and Kālidāsa's Plays" (by Gerow), and "Theater in Kālidāsa's Art" (by Gitomer). The texts of the three plays are freshly translated and accompanied by copious annotations. Most valuable.

Krishnamoorthy, K. *Kalidasa*. New York: Twayne Publishers, 1972. Literary and scholarly introduction by an Indian scholar, written in the light of both Indian and Western criticism. The author attempts a biographical analysis based on a supposed order of the works. Comprehensive but tends toward the Romantic-Victorian school of literary appreciation and consequently suffers from Kālidāsian hagiography. Includes full references to translations of all of his works.

Majumdar, R. C., ed. *History and Culture of the Indian People*. Vol. 3, *The Classical Age*. Bombay: Bharatiya Vidya Bhavan, 1954. Full treatment of the Gupta Dynasty by eighteen Indian scholars. Outlines the Gupta Empire, discusses the Sanskrit literature, and treats politics, law, religion, art, socioeconomic conditions, and education. Provides comprehensive backdrop to Kālidāsa's world (on the widely held assumption that he belongs to the Gupta age, when Hindu culture underwent its most glowing renaissance).

Ralph Smiley

KANISHKA

Born: First or second century A.D.; probably west-central Asia
Died: Probably second century A.D.; probably northern India
Areas of Achievement: Government, religion, and patronage of arts
Contribution: Kanishka, the greatest ruler of the Kushan Empire, administered an extensive realm that embraced much of modern India and Pakistan and parts of the southern Soviet Union and China. Kanishka's patronage was responsible for the introduction of Mahayana Buddhism into China and for a remarkable flowering of Buddhist iconography.

Early Life

Considering the fame of Kanishka, remarkably little is known of his life, certainly not enough to construct a proper biography. Symbolic of this gap in history is the fact that the six-foot statue of him in the archaeological museum in Mathura, Uttar Pradesh, India, is headless. The scarcity of data is further compounded by the tangled, obscure complexities of the wider history of Inner Asia and northern India during the first centuries of the common era. What is known regarding Kanishka and his achievements has been gleaned principally from folklore and archaeological artifacts dating from this period. Inscriptions, coins, sculpture, architecture, legend, and Chinese and Iranian literary sources are the raw materials from which scholars have attempted to reconstruct an understanding of Kanishka's life and times.

Even the time frame of Kanishka's reign has been the subject of much discussion; indeed, two scholarly conferences (in 1913 and 1960) were convened in London to explore the issue. One long-accepted reckoning places it roughly between A.D. 78 and 103, but more recent scholarship (agreeing with an earlier line of thought) places it between A.D. 128 and 151. Kanishka's reign has been associated, probably mistakenly, with the Saka Era dating system, which was initiated in A.D. 78 and which ultimately became the basis of the modern Indian governmental calendar.

The precise origin of the Kushans is also an open question, since they arose out of a welter of Central Asiatic races and languages in a region of complex migrations. They could have been Turkic or Iranian or, more probably, a mixture of the two. They can be traced to the Yueh-chi (or Indo-Scythians) in Chinese Turkistan on the frontier of Han China. Displaced by the Hsiung-nu (the Huns), the Yueh-chi crossed the Jaxartes River (modern Syr Darya) and occupied Sogdiana (Transoxiana) at the expense of the Saka (Iranian nomads) by 150 B.C. Then, having crossed the Oxus River (modern Amu Darya) by 130 B.C., they conquered the Indo-Greek Bactrian kingdom. The Bactrians' developed trading economy and advanced culture had a deep influence on their nomadic conquerors. One of the five tribes among these conquerors, the Kushans, rose up to assert dominance and establish political unity under Kujula Kadphises I. For unknown reasons, the Kushans eventually gravitated to the east to the Hindu Kush region and ultimately to northwest India, a world of petty states floundering in a political vacuum since the end of the Maurya Empire.

Life's Work

Precisely how, when, and how deeply the Kushans penetrated northwest India is not entirely clear, nor are the roles of Kujula, his son Wima Kadphises II, and their successor Kanishka. Until the coming of the Muslims in the twelfth century, however, no foreign power after the prehistoric Indo-Aryans gained control over as much of India—and held it for as long—as did the Kushans. There is some suggestion that Kanishka was not in the line of the Kadphises; moreover, there is the problem of a king of unknown name, "Soter Megas," who preceded him. It is thought that Kanishka may have begun a new line of succession. He may have invaded India from the north (Khotan in Sinkiang according to one authority), or he may have been one of several chiefs in India engaged in a struggle for the succession. When Kanishka came to power, he apparently used co-optation, for he shared rule with a junior, Vashishka (either his brother or his son), who ultimately succeeded him; he may have had other corulers as well.

A statue of Kanishka at Mathura shows him in Turkic warrior garb. Images of him on gold coins of the time render him as a bearded man with large, thoughtful eyes and thin, determined lips. He seems to have had a forceful personality, yet in cultural and religious matters he was more tolerant and accommodating than rigid and austere.

The Kushan Empire reached its zenith under Kanishka. An inland realm with its capital at Purushapura (modern Peshawar, Pakistan) at the foot of the Khyber Pass leading to Kabul and the Hindu Kush region, it centered on the upper Indus and the upper Ganges valleys (in modern Iran and India). It seems in India to have embraced Pataliputra (Patna) to the east, Sanchi to the south, and Bahawalpur on the Sutlej River, but its key southern city was Mathura on the Yamuna River. To the north, beyond the Pamirs, the Kushans dominated the caravan city-states of eastern Turkistan, especially Khotan, and held Bactria; to the west, in what is now Afghanistan, they held sway over Begram and Balkh. This location enabled the Kushans to connect India with China, Persia, and the Roman Empire via the Old Silk Road opened in 106 B.C. across Central Asia, combined with the old Mauryan royal highway between Taxila and Pataliputra and then through the Ganges Delta (where a Roman ship is known to have arrived about A.D. 100). Other roads led to the Arabian Sea ports of Barbaricum and Barygaza (modern Broach). The Kushans, with their command of animal power and soldiery, held the routes together and exacted great revenues through transit dues. In this way, the Kushans maintained a network of international trade that also allowed for a wide-ranging exchange of art and ideas. Within the empire, though agriculture remained important, trade profits gave rise to an urban society of guilds and merchants.

Not surprisingly, the Kushan Empire, comprising as it did many peoples, religions, and belief systems—such as Hellenism, Mithraism, Hinduism, and Buddhism—was marked by attitudes of coexistence and syncretism. The Kushans, who had spoken Bactrian (an Iranian tongue) and then Greek, in India began to adopt Sanskrit. Kadphises I had been a Buddhist, Kadphises II a Hindu; Kanishka was a Buddhist. Such cosmopolitanism was a product not only of their history and economy but also of their role as foreigners faced with the inflexibilities of *karma* (destiny) and *jati* (caste) within the Hindu system, within which the Kushans could be treated as "fallen *Kshatriya*" (warriors). Their low position within the stratified social classes of Hinduism helps to explain the Kushan tendency to embrace Buddhism (though later rulers such as Huvishka and Vasudeva were Hindu).

Such a huge and complex empire could only be governed by a feudal system allowing for significant regional autonomy. The emperor did, however, appoint satraps (provincial governors), *meridareks* (district officers), and *strategoi* (military governors). The ruler ascribed to himself a divine origin and borrowed such appellations as "King of Kings" (from Bactria), "Great King" (from India), "Son of Heaven" (from China), and "Emperor" (probably from Rome). After death, emperors were deified and temples were dedicated to them.

Religiously eclectic, to judge by his coins bearing images of a variety of gods, Kanishka came to favor the emerging Mahayana form of Buddhism over Hinduism, probably because he found the former to be more cosmopolitan and more amenable to mercantilism. It is not clear whether he underwent a genuine conversion or simply found embracing Buddhism to be politically expedient. In any case, Kanishka gave official support to Buddhist proselytization by means of education and iconography, stimulating the spread of Buddhism through Central Asia into China. Under his auspices, the Sarvastivadins, a sect of monks who favored the nascent Mahayanist Buddhism, organized the fourth Buddhist council (a gathering that cannot be called ecumenical, for the Hinayanists in the south called a separate fourth council in Sri Lanka). Rejecting Pali (the Hinayana or Theravada language) in favor of Sanskrit, the monks spent twelve years in Kashmir (or in Punjab) writing commentaries on the Buddhist canon, in the process probably launching Mahayana Buddhism. The records of this gathering, inscribed on copper plates in stone boxes, are found today only in Chinese translation.

In old age, Kanishka may have sent an army of seventy thousand over the Pamirs to oppose Chinese military thrusts into Central Asia, a venture that failed miserably. The date and circumstances of Kanishka's death are unknown.

Summary

Kanishka's policies were responsible for generating a new style in Oriental sculpture, a style that combined Greco-Roman and Iranian elements with Indian ideology to lay the basis for a Buddhist representational art with a popular appeal. The Gandhara school (in Purushapura, Taxila, and Bamian) produced more naturalistic Buddhas mostly in schist, while the Mathura school turned out more stylized images in sandstone, suggesting a Western versus an Indian inspiration in the respective schools.

Throughout the historic Punjab and modern north-central Afghanistan east of Balkh and Kandahar, more than in the Hindustan, can be found the monumental ruins of Kanishka's building projects. He erected a 638-foot stupa to Buddha at Peshawar, a monument celebrated through Asia: a five-stage, 286-foot diameter base, surmounted by a thirteen-story carved wood structure topped by an iron column adorned with gilded copper umbrellas (*chhatras*). In decay by the seventh century, the relic casket bearing an effigy and inscription of Kanishka was found *in situ* in 1908 and now may be seen in the Peshawar Museum.

The most important Kanishka inscriptions are those found on a monolith before a temple-acropolis in Greco-Iranian style at Surkh Kotal (Baghlan) in the Kunduz River Valley of northeast Afghanistan. The structure, excavated between 1952 and 1964, suggests a dynastic Zoroastrian fire-temple. In Begram (now Kāpīsā), north of Kabul, Kanishka built a monastery (*vihara*) to house Chinese royal hostages. At Bāmiān, in the high passes at the Hindu Kush west of Kabul, two colossal rock Buddhas, though carved well after his time, may have been modeled on Kanishka. Further records of Kanishka's reign are numerous coins minted during his time, many of gold, bearing images of a variety of Greek, Iranian, and Indian gods. The first Buddha coin also dates from this period.

Not only was Kanishka another Aśoka the Great in his championship of Buddhism, but he also seems to have been a patron of scholarship and the arts. It is thought that such distinguished men as the Sanskrit poet-dramatist and Buddhist popularizer Aśvaghosa (who wrote the conciliar commentaries) and the physician and medical writer Charaka may have been at his court. Imperious in nature, Kanishka could launch an army against China and carry off Aśvaghosa from Varanasi. Yet, when demanding huge booty at Varanasi, he could accept instead a begging bowl of Buddha. Kanishka stood at a crossroads of world civilization, keeping the way open for the cross-fertilization of Eastern and Western economics and culture. His patronage of Mahayana Buddhism, however, though it brought about the introduction of Buddhism to Central Asia and China, may have weakened that religion in India, for Kanishka was regarded as a foreigner, and his religion was therefore alien as well. Hinduism correspondingly came to be accorded status as India's indigenous religious system.

Bibliography
Basham, Arthur L., ed. *Papers on the Date of Kaniska*. Leiden, Nether-
    lands: E. J. Brill, 1968. Proceedings of a conference, held in London in
    1960, that attempted to resolve the question of Kanishka's dates. The date
    of Kanishka's accession to power, and its implications for understanding
    the Vikrama and Saka calendars, is the major vexing question of Indian
    history.
Davids, T. W. Rhys. *Buddhist India*. London: T. Fisher Unwin, 1903. Re-
    print. Delhi, India: Motilal Banarsidass, 1981. Chapter 26 constitutes a full
    discussion of Kanishka's historic role. Based on the ancient sources, it
    examines socioeconomic, political, and religious aspects of the Buddhist
    ascendancy from a non-Brahmin point of view. The author was a distin-
    guished Buddhologist who died in 1922.
Majumdar, R. C., ed. *The History and Culture of the Indian People*. Vol. 2,
    The Age of Imperial Unity. 5th ed. Bombay, India: Bhartiya Vidya
    Bhavan, 1980. See especially D. C. Sircar's discussion of the Kushanas, M.
    Dutt's section on the Buddhist councils, J. N. Banerjea's treatment of Bud-
    dhist iconography, and S. K. Saraswati's description of the stupa. N. R.
    Ray has a helpful discussion of Gandhara sculpture and coins, and R. C.
    Majumdar contributed a survey of Indian cultural expansion.
Narain, A. D. *The Indo-Greeks*. Oxford: Clarendon Press, 1957. The
    Kushans are actually a peripheral theme in this study, which deals at
    greater length with the Yavanas (Indo-Greeks in the Punjab). The book is
    based on a University of London doctoral dissertation. Data drawn largely
    from numismatics. Narain challenges the interpretation of W. W. Tarn (see
    below).
Rapson, E. J., ed. *The Cambridge History of India*. Vol. 1, *Ancient India*.
    New York: Macmillan, 1922. Chapter 23 includes a discussion of the Scyth-
    ian and Parthian invaders of India. The volume contains maps and plates
    showing coins of ancient Indian civilizations.
Smith, Vincent A. *Early History of India: From 600 B.C. to the Muham-
    madan Conquest, Including the Invasion of Alexander the Great*. Oxford:
    Clarendon Press, 1904, 4th ed. 1924. Offers general background informa-
    tion for the period delineated in its subtitle. Its author, however, was a
    British official in India, and his interpretations reflect an old-fashioned
    colonialist point of view.
Tarn, W. W. *The Greeks in Bactria and India*. Cambridge: Cambridge Uni-
    versity Press, 1938, 2d ed. 1951. See especially chapters 7, 8, and 9. This is
    a seminal study of the penetration of Hellenism into Inner Asia. The
    author was a scholar at the University of Edinburgh.
Warder, A. K. *Indian Buddhism*. Delhi, India: Motilal Banarsidass, 1970.
    Cites ancient sources to survey the doctrines and history of Buddhism in
    India. The first section deals with early Buddhism through the schisms of

the fourth and third centuries B.C., the second examines the eighteen schools of Indian Buddhism, and the third has to do with the Mahayana movement.

Yarshater, Ehsan, ed. *The Cambridge History of Iran*. Vol. 3, *The Seleucid, Parthian, and Sasanian Periods*. Cambridge: Cambridge University Press, 1983. See especially chapter 5, "The History of Eastern Iran," by A. D. H. Bivar, and chapter 26, "Buddhism Among the Iranian Peoples," by R. E. Emmerick, for fully updated scholarship and comprehensive examinations of the historical regions of Iran.

Ralph Smiley

KHOSROW I

Born: c. 510; probably Ctesiphon, Mesopotamia
Died: 579; probably Ctesiphon, Mesopotamia
Areas of Achievement: Government and warfare
Contribution: Through courage and shrewd practical intelligence, Khosrow I restored and revitalized the threatened Sassanian monarchy, bringing Persian civilization to a peak of wealth, prestige, and security. He also introduced administrative, civil, and military innovations that radically transformed government; thus he earned the title "Anushirvan" (of the Immortal Spirit).

Early Life

Khosrow I was born at a time when the ancient culture of Mesopotamia was disrupted by internal convulsions and threatened by several external forces—migrations of tribes displaced by the Huns and Avars, defensive maneuvers by factions of the deteriorating Roman Empire, and uprisings among the Arabs. His father, Kavadh (ruled 488-531), struggled against these forces, establishing strategies which Khosrow I would perfect. Kavadh himself had seized the throne in a rebellion of nobles fomented by the Hephthalite Huns, with whom he had lived as a prisoner or hostage. For this reason, his control was precarious. During the first part of his reign, he alienated some of his aristocratic supporters by engineering the assassination of his prime minister, Zarmiha (Sokhra), who had helped put him on the throne. His major problem, however, was with the Mazdakites, followers of the heretical Zoroastrian priest Mazdak.

Kavadh promoted the Mazdakite causes—mostly based on a revival of prescribed Manichaean principles, modified by pacifism and principles of community property—apparently because he needed the support of a cohesive group to oppose the power of the aristocracy. The strategy backfired. When rebellion broke out among the subject Armenians and Arabs, and the Byzantine emperor withheld support, the nobles conspired to depose Kavadh and replace him with his brother Zamasp. Kavadh managed, however, to escape from prison, make his way to the Hephthalite frontier, and persuade his former allies to send an army to restore him to power. Thus, in 498, Kavadh secured his power by an unusual policy of conciliation.

During the next few years, Kavadh engaged in intermittent and indecisive war with the Byzantines, which ended in a treaty in 506. Thereafter, Kavadh concerned himself with internal affairs. Mazdakite agitation persisted, and Kavadh began to moderate his earlier tolerance. He became preoccupied with the question of succession. Singling out his youngest and ablest son, Khosrow, as most likely to secure and extend his achievements, he tried for a while to persuade the Byzantine emperor, Justin I, to adopt Khosrow, thereby to gain support from that quarter. This plan fell through, and war broke out again. Khosrow began influencing policy even before his accession, taking the lead in the persecution of the Mazdakites, even bringing about the execution of Mazdak. Kavadh was able to make alliances both north and south of Persia, partly through the diplomatic efforts of Khosrow, who— young, vigorous, a splendid horseman with a commanding presence—was able to inspire immediate confidence.

Life's Work

In spite of Kavadh's preparations, Khosrow's ascent to the throne was not uncontested. His brothers Kaus and Zham launched a revolt of dissident nobles, which Khosrow suppressed with little difficulty; he then had his brothers executed. He decided that internal reforms had to take precedence over imperial ambitions, especially since the Mazdakite disruptions had damaged both economy and administration. This initial attention to the details of management set the pattern for his major achievement, a radical reform of methods of government.

Kavadh had recognized that inconsistencies in the registration of property and possessions as well as in the census itself had hampered the collection of taxes and fees. To amend this, he had begun a program of surveying and measuring the land. Khosrow completed and extended this undertaking to tabulating sources of revenue, such as date palms and olive trees, systematizing the registration of land titles, and regularizing the census. In conjunction, Khosrow replaced the old system of assessing taxes on the produce of land with a new fixed tax based on averages. At the same time, he imposed a fixed head tax on the common people. Both were to be paid in money, not kind, and payments were to be made three times a year. The effect of these reforms was remarkable: The central administration could now calculate in advance the exact revenue to be collected at any time, and that made accurate national budgeting possible.

Khosrow's army reforms were almost equally important. Previously, armies had been levied from the personal troops of the landed nobles, who served without pay, supporting their retainers by shares in plunder. Khosrow instead enrolled all nobles in the army, paying them a fixed salary and providing their equipment. This system secured the principal allegiance of the military class for the king and his army and reduced the power of the great magnates. In effect, Khosrow had created a knightly class loyal to him. During his lifetime, these nobles came to form the central class of the Persian social system: the knights who owned villages. Khosrow planted several such villages on the borders, with the explicit mission of taking up arms whenever the frontier was threatened.

Khosrow followed these reforms with further administrative changes. Dividing the empire into quarters, he appointed generals to head each part.

Thus, the empire's frontiers were secured; improved military roads and communications systems made it possible to reinforce quickly any threatened sector. Khosrow was now free to carry out military operations without having to be concerned with defending his borders. He began his military expeditions almost immediately, perhaps sensing an opportunity in Justinian I's preoccupation with the western part of his empire.

In 540, Khosrow invaded Syria, conquering Antioch. Because of his western involvement, Justinian could not employ his full military force against the Persians. Khosrow withdrew slowly, extorting ransom from Byzantine cities as he did as the price of their safety. When he actually besieged one of them to increase this forced tribute, Justinian denounced the truce and sent Belisarius, his best general, to push back the Persians.

Returning to Persia, Khosrow built a new city on the model of Antioch near Ctesiphon. He called it Veh Antiok Khosrow, or "Khosrow's Better Than Antioch," and populated it with prisoners; it became known as Rumagan, the town of the Greeks, and formed part of the opulent capital complex. When the campaign resumed, Khosrow won some initial success in the north, but eventually the war settled into a three-year stalemate. In 544, after Belisarius had returned to the west, Khosrow besieged the principal city of Edessa, intending to gain control over all Byzantine trans-Euphrates possessions. Edessa resisted the siege heroically, forcing Khosrow to retreat. Justinian was able to forge a five-year truce.

Four years later, the Byzantines broke the truce to recover the Black Sea holdings. They succeeded in retaking Petra in 551 after routing two Persian armies. This resulted in a partial truce, made permanent after the Byzantines had regained Lazica in 556. Final settlement was reached in 561 in the form of a fifty-year treaty. Khosrow agreed to this primarily to free his armies for operations in the east, where opportunities for expansion had suddenly improved. He formed an alliance with the Turks in 557 to destroy the Hephthalites and divide their territory. In this way, Khosrow dramatically extended Persian control across the Oxus River, possibly pushing all the way to India.

Khosrow also proved able to extend Persian power into southern Arabia. The Byzantines were interested in controlling this region for two reasons: to protect the various Christian interests there and to break down Persian control of the spice and silk trade routes with India. Khosrow was prevented from sending aid for a while, but in 572 he dispatched an army with a small fleet under Vahriz. After taking time to work out alliances with Arab groups, Vahriz mounted a successful campaign which made southern Arabia a Sassanian dependency in 577.

Meanwhile, Justinian was succeeded in 565 by Justin II, who was eager to recover Byzantine territory in the east. Taking advantage of an Armenian uprising in 571, he invited the rebels into the empire and sent an army to back them the following year. The Persians, however, profited from dissension among officers of the invading army, driving them back and occupying new Byzantine possessions. Justin sued for peace, but since no agreement had been reached regarding Armenia, Khosrow invaded again in 575. For the next four years, the rival empires traded successes, until the Byzantine Emperor Maurice gained the upper hand at the same moment that the Armenian rebels returned to the Sassanian fold. Negotiations for peace were taking place when Khosrow died in 579.

Summary

Khosrow I brought the Persian Empire to the pinnacle of its glory. Had that empire endured longer, it is quite possible that his name would be as well-known in Western societies as those of David and Solomon, who achieved considerably less in smaller room. His wisdom and accomplishments remain proverbial even today among the common people of the Near East, and Kisra, an Arabic corruption of his name, became the Arabs' designation for all Sassanian rulers. Peasants in Iraq still routinely point to any ruin as the work of Kisra Anushirvan, and in many cases they are right. Khosrow directed more new construction—of caravanserais, roads, bridges, official buildings, even whole towns—than had any previous Persian ruler. This network not only interconnected the parts of the empire in unprecedented ways but also promoted a remarkable economic expansion that financed Khosrow's colonial and military enterprises. He also constructed defensive walls and supporting forts on all four frontiers, designed for the protection of his four commanding generals.

The wealth supporting these activities came basically from agriculture, which expanded significantly during this period. Much of the expansion came from bringing new land under cultivation, promoted by Khosrow's painstaking survey and registration programs. He also systematically encouraged the practice of irrigation, bringing tunnel and canal systems into use throughout the empire. Irrigation had been a common practice in this region for centuries, but it was Khosrow who developed it as a state policy. Iraq owes to him the great Nahsawan canal system, which brought about a geometrical increase in that country's agricultural production.

Unlike most monarchs of his time, Khosrow permitted little religious persecution; his attacks on the Mazdakites stemmed from social and political motives. Furthermore, he advanced the cause of learning, even providing a refuge for some of the scholars and philosophers exiled by Justinian when he closed the academy at Athens. Khosrow maintained a circle of scholars at his court; a medical school established during his reign flourished into Islamic times. Numerous translations of important works date from his period.

One measure of his significance is the appellation of "the Just" attached to his name from early times. Several collections of *andarz* or "advice books"—

somewhat like how-to manuals for noblemen, especially rulers—are attributed to him, much as the Book of Psalms is to David or Proverbs to Solomon. Like these and other semilegendary figures, Khosrow's eminence was such that many tales arose concerning his special powers. That in itself, however, testifies only to his hold on the popular imagination. More concrete witnesses appear in the wealth of artifacts and architectural remnants dating from his reign, including many silver plates and engraved stones preserved in museum collections. What remains standing of the Taq Kisra in Ctesiphon, with its particularly magnificent central arch, speaks across the ages of the stature of Khosrow I.

Bibliography

Firdusi. *The Epic of the Kings*. Translated by Ruben Levy. Chicago: University of Chicago Press, 1967. An abridged translation of the *Shahnamah* (c. 1010), a monumental epic poem on the history of Persia from its eponymous beginnings through the conquest by the Muslims. Contains much information on Khosrow, both historical and legendary, presented from the perspective of Persian historiography, which is quite different from that of the Western world.

Frye, Richard N. *The Heritage of Persia*. Cleveland: World Publishing Co., 1963. Similar to the fuller account in *The Cambridge History of Iran*, though more tentative. A good discussion of Khosrow's influence on pre-Islamic Persia.

_____. "The Political History of Iran Under the Sasanians." In *The Cambridge History of Iran*, edited by Ehsan Yarskater, vol. 3. Cambridge: Cambridge University Press, 1983. The most thorough account in English of the achievements of Khosrow and their background, with complete bibliography and photographs of relevant artifacts. Other chapters on different aspects of Iranian history are also relevant to Khosrow, showing, for example, his image in Persian literature.

Ghirshman, Roman. *Iran: Parthians and Sassanians*. Translated by Stuart Gilbert and James Emmons. London: Thames and Hudson, 1962. A solid and incisive presentation, focusing on Khosrow's social, military, and civil accomplishments.

Sykes, Sir Percy. *A History of Persia*. New York: Barnes and Noble Books, 1915, 3d ed. 1969. A dated account, but it provides a substantial overview of Khosrow, his achievements, and his role in the development of Persian culture.

James L. Livingston

AL-KHWARIZMI

Born: c. 780; place unknown
Died: c. 850; possibly Baghdad
Areas of Achievement: Mathematics, astronomy, and geography
Contribution: Al-Khwarizmi is the author of several important mathematical works. The Latin translations of his writings introduced the concepts of algebra and Hindu-Arabic numerals into the mathematics of medieval Europe. He also compiled a set of astronomical tables widely used in the Islamic Near East.

Early Life

Very little is known of the life of Muhammad ibn Musa al-Khwarizmi. The name al-Khwarizmi means literally "the man from Khwarizm"; the epithet may also, however, be interpreted to indicate the origin of one's "stock." The historian al-Tabari asserts that al-Khwarizmi actually came from Qutrubull, a district not far from Baghdad, between the Tigris and Euphrates rivers. Some sources even give his place of birth as Baghdad. Historians do agree that he lived at Baghdad in the early ninth century under the caliphates of al-Ma'mun and al-Mu'tasim, whose reigns spanned the years from 813 to 842.

In *Kitab al-Fihrist* (c. 987; book of chronicles), Ibn Abi Yaqub al-Nadim's entry on al-Khwarizmi reads:

> al-Khwārizmī. His name was Muḥammad ibn Mūsā and his family origin was from Khwārazm. He was temporarily associated with the Treasury of the "House of Wisdom" of al-Ma'mūn. He was one of the leading scholars in astronomy. People both before and after the observations [conducted under al-Ma'mūn] used to rely on his first and second *zījes* [astronomical tables] which were both known by the name *Sindhind*. His books are (as follows): (1) the *Zīj*, in two [editions], the first and the second; (2) the book on sundials; (3) the book on the use of the astrolabe; (4) the book on the construction of the astrolabe; and (5) the [chronicle].

Al-Nadim's list is, however, incomplete. He mentions only the astronomical studies and omits an algebra, an arithmetic, a study of the quadrivium, and an adaptation of Ptolemy's geography. Al-Khwarizmi was apparently well-known in Baghdad for his scholarly works on astronomy and mathematics. His inheritance tables on the distribution of money were widely used.

Life's Work

Al-Khwarizmi is credited by early Arab scholars Ibn Khaldun (1332-1406) and Katib Celebi (1609-1657) with being the first mathematician to write about algebra. The word "algebra" comes from the second word of the title,

Kitab al-jabr wa al-muquabalah. It is his best-known work. Literally, the title means "the book of integration and equation." It contained rules for arithmetical solutions of linear and quadratic equations, for elementary geometry, and for inheritance problems concerning the distribution of wealth according to proportions. The algebra was based on a long tradition originating in Babylonian mathematics of the early second millennium B.C. When it was first translated into Latin in the twelfth century, the rules for the distribution of wealth, which had been so popular in the Near East, were omitted. Translated into English from a Latin version in 1915 by Louis Charles Karpinski, the book opens with a pious exhortation which reveals al-Khwarizmi's belief in an ordered universe:

> The Book of Algebra and Almucabola, concerning arithmetical and Geometrical problems.
>
> In the name of God, tender and compassionate, begins the book of Restoration and Opposition of number put forth by Mohammed Al-Khowarizmi, the son of Moses. Mohammed said, Praise God the creator who has bestowed upon man the power to discover the significance of numbers. Indeed, reflecting that all things which men need require computation, I discovered that all things involve number and I discovered that number is nothing other than that which is composed of units. Unity therefore is implied in every number. Moreover I discovered all numbers to be so arranged that they proceed from unity up to ten.

In the same introduction, al-Khwarizmi describes three kinds of numbers, "roots, squares, and numbers." He sums up the relationships among them in this way:

> Squares equal to roots,
> Squares equal to numbers, and
> Roots equal to numbers.

Karpinski explains that these three types, designated as "simple" by Omar Khayyám and other Arab mathematicians, "correspond in modern algebraic notation to the following: $ax^2 = bx$, $ax^2 = n$, and $bx = n$."

The first six chapters of al-Khwarizmi's algebra deal with the following mathematical relationships: "Concerning squares equal to roots," "Concerning squares equal to numbers," "Concerning roots equal to numbers," "Concerning squares and roots equal to numbers," "Concerning squares and numbers equal to roots," and "Concerning roots and numbers equal to a square." These chapters are followed by illustrative geometrical demonstrations and then many problems with their solutions.

Some of his problems are purely formal, whereas others appear in practical contexts. One of his formal problems states:

If from a square I subtract four of its roots and then take one-third of the remainder, finding this equal to four of the roots, the square will be 256.

His explanation is simple:

Since one-third of the remainder is equal to four roots, one knows that the remainder itself will equal 12 roots. Therefore, add this to the four, giving 16 roots. This (16) is the root of the square.

This relationship can also be stated $1/3 (x^2 - 4x) = 4x$.

An interesting chapter on mercantile transactions asserts that "mercantile transactions and all things pertaining thereto involve two ideas and four numbers." Karpinski explains:

The two ideas appear to be the notions of quantity and cost; the four numbers represent unit of measure and price per unit, quantity desired and cost of the same.

Al-Khwarizmi's last mercantile problem is:

A man is hired to work in a vineyard 30 days for 10 pence. He works six days. How much of the agreed price should he receive?

Explanation. It is evident that six days are one-fifth of the whole time; and it is also evident that the man should receive pay having the same relation to the agreed price that the time he works bears to the whole time, 30 days. What we have proposed, is explained as follows. The month, i.e., 30 days, represents the measure, and ten represents the price. Six days represents the quantity, and in asking what part of the agreed price is due to the worker you ask the cost. Therefore multiply the price 10 by the quantity 6, which is inversely proportional to it. Divide the product 60 by the measure 30, giving 2 pence. This will be the cost, and will represent the amount due to the worker.

For Muslims, al-Khwarizmi's astronomical works are perhaps even more important than his algebra. His astronomical tables were used for accurate timekeeping. In Islam, the times of the five daily prayers are determined by the apparent position of the sun in the sky and vary naturally throughout the year. In al-Khwarizmi's work on the construction and use of the astrolabe, the times of midday and afternoon prayers are determined by measuring shadow lengths. These timekeeping techniques were widely used for centuries.

Al-Khwarizmi also created tables to compute the local direction of Mecca. This is fundamental to Muslims because it is the direction in which they face when they pray, bury their dead, and perform various ritual acts. It is no wonder that in Islamic texts, al-Khwarizmi is referred to as "the astronomer."

Al-Khwarizmi's book on arithmetic has been preserved in only one version. Translated into Latin and published in Rome in 1857 by Prince Baldassare Boncompagni, al-Khwarizmi's *Algoritmi de numero indorum* appears as part 1 of a volume entitled *Tratti d'aritmetica*. The title means "al-Khwarizmi concerning the Hindu art of reckoning." This is the derivation of the word "algorithm." The arithmetic introduced Arabic numerals and the art of calculating by decimal notation. The only copy of this work is in the Cambridge University library.

His study of the quadrivium—the medieval curriculum of arithmetic, music, astronomy, and geometry—is entitled *Liber ysagogarum Alchorismi in artem astronomicam a magistro A. compositus* (1126). It was the first of al-Khwarizmi's writings to appear in Europe. The identity of the writer "A" is not certain, but he is assumed to be the scholar Adelard of Bath, who is known as the translator of al-Khwarizmi's tables. These trigonometric tables were among the first of the Arabic studies in mathematics to appear in Europe.

Al-Khwarizmi enjoyed an excellent reputation among his fellow Arab scholars. Some of his numerical examples were repeated for centuries, becoming so standardized that many subsequent mathematicians did not consider it necessary to acknowledge al-Khwarizmi as the source. Karpinski observes that "the equation $x^2 + 10x = 39$ runs like a thread of gold through the algebras for several centuries."

The geography *Kitab surat al-ard* (book of the form of the earth) differs in several respects from Ptolemy's geography. Like Ptolemy's, it is a description of a world map and contains a list of the coordinates of the principal places on it, but al-Khwarizmi's arrangement is radically different, and it is clear that the map to which it refers is not the same as the map which Ptolemy described. It is supposed that al-Khwarizmi's world map was the one constructed by al-Ma'mun. This map was an improvement over Ptolemy's, correcting distortions in the supposed length of the Mediterranean. It was far more accurate, too, in its description of the areas under Islamic rule. Because it contained errors of its own, however, the geography written by al-Khwarizmi failed to replace the Ptolemaic geography used in Europe.

Summary

Al-Khwarizmi's importance in the history of mathematics is inarguable. Two notable arithmetic books, Alexander de Villa Dei's *Carmen de Algorismo* (twelfth century) and Johannes de Sacrobosco's *Algorismus vulgaris* (thirteenth century), owe much to al-Khwarizmi's arithmetic and were widely used for several hundred years. In the ninth century, Abu Kamil drew on al-Khwarizmi's works for his own writings on algebra. In turn, Leonardo of Pisa, a thirteenth century scholar, was influenced by Abu Kamil. Numerous commentaries on Abu Kamil's work kept al-Khwarizmi's influence alive in the Middle Ages and during the Renaissance.

Karpinski states concisely what appears to be the consensus of opinion among historians:

› Mathematical science was more vitally influenced by Mohammed ibn Musa than by any other writer from the time of the Greeks to Regiomontanus (1436-1476).

Bibliography

Bell, Eric T. *The Development of Mathematics*. New York: McGraw-Hill Book Co., 1945. Begins with a historical review of the field of mathematics from the first known texts through successive stages of discoveries, ending at mid-point in the twentieth century. The chapter which is of most interest to students of Islamic science is entitled "Detour Through India, Arabia, and Spain, 400-1300."

Cajori, Florian. *A History of Mathematics*. New York: Macmillan, 1931. This rather dated work has several important characteristics which merit mention. It covers standard non-Western mathematical traditions (Hindu and Islamic). Cajori manages to give detailed information on individual mathematicians' original findings while keeping information on a sufficiently comprehensible level for the layman.

Karpinski, Louis Charles. *Robert of Chester's Latin Translation of the Algebra of Al-Khowarizmi*. London: Macmillan, 1915. Somewhat dated, but an admirable work of scholarship, with useful commentary. Contains Latin and English translations on facing pages, and pages from selected works by al-Khwarizmi in the original Islamic text.

Kennedy, E. S., ed. *Studies in the Islamic Exact Sciences*. Beirut, Lebanon: American University of Beirut Press, 1983. Provides a rather technical treatment of several scientific disciplines that flourished in early Islamic times, including the development, through trigonometry, of accurate astronomical calculations. The prospective reader should be aware that a substantial background in mathematics will be necessary to follow stage-by-stage explanations.

King, D. A. *Al-Khwarizmi and New Trends in Mathematical Astronomy in the Ninth Century*. New York: Hagop Kevorkian Center for Near Eastern Studies, New York University, 1983. Discusses some newly discovered works of al-Khwarizmi. While it presupposes a background in mathematics, this work contains interesting charts and graphs that offer a taste of al-Khwarizmi's methods.

Nasr, Seyyed Hossein. *Islamic Science: An Illustrated Survey*. London: World of Islam Festival, 1976. A carefully researched photographic record of the tools of Islamic science. Textual treatment of historical figures is more limited than in Nasr's *Science and Civilization in Islam*. Many illustrations from Islamic astronomy.

_____. *Science and Civilization in Islam*. Cambridge, Mass.: Harvard University Press, 1968. Contains no useful discussion of al-Khwarizmi, but offers a broad historical setting against which to view him.

Catherine Gilbert

KUBLAI KHAN

Born: 1215; Mongolia
Died: 1294; Ta-tu (Peking), China
Areas of Achievement: Warfare and government
Contribution: As a Mongol general and the Great Khan, Kublai helped to conquer and came to rule over an empire which encompassed 80 percent of Eurasia. He founded the Yüan Dynasty of China and brought the Mongols to the peak of their power and influence.

Early Life

Kublai was born in the year 1215, somewhere in the Mongol heartland, but the exact site cannot be agreed upon by scholars. He was the son of Tolui and the grandson of Temüjin, who had become Genghis Khan, the founder of the Mongol Empire. Kublai's three surviving brothers were Mangu, Hülagü, and Arigböge. At the time of the Genghis Khan's death, Kublai was only twelve years old, but he was already an accomplished horseman; as he matured, he gained a reputation as a warrior of great personal courage.

In 1251, Mangu succeeded his cousin Güyük (reigned 1246-1248) as Great Khan of the Mongol Empire. Güyük had succeeded his father, Ögödei (reigned 1229-1241), who previously had succeeded his father, Genghis Khan (reigned 1206-1227). Kublai served his older brother successfully as a general and led military campaigns for him in South China against the forces of the collapsing Sung Dynasty. Kublai added Szechwan, Yunnan, and Hukwang to Mangu's domains, and one of Kublai's commanders initiated the invasion of Vietnam. During his part in the conquest of the Sung, Kublai gradually came under the influence of Chinese civilization. Under Mangu, the Mongol Empire also expanded southwestward into Persia, Mesopotamia, and Syria.

When word of Mangu's death in 1259 reached Kublai in China, he quickly concluded a truce with his Sung adversaries and returned to the Mongol capital of Karakorum. On May 6, 1260, Kublai had himself proclaimed Great Khan of the Mongol Empire. Kublai's right to succeed was severely challenged by his youngest brother, Arigböge, and a four-year civil war ensued between the two, culminating in 1264 with the triumph of Kublai Khan.

Life's Work

Not surprisingly, the Great Khan Kublai took a view of China that was somewhat different from that of his predecessors. In 1264, he moved his capital from Karakorum in Mongolia to Peking in North China. He initiated new action in 1267 to complete the conquest of the Sung Dynasty in South China in 1279. Kublai had proclaimed his dynasty the Yüan (outland) Dynasty in 1271 and had ascended the dragon throne of China, thus establishing himself and his heirs as the legitimate successors to the Sung Dynasty until 1368. By 1279 he had accomplished something that the Sung had failed to do—the unification of China under one ruler. Moreover, in less than one hundred years, Kublai and his Mongol predecessors had established an empire larger than that which it had taken the Romans four hundred years to assemble a millennium earlier.

In 1276, Kublai's authority was challenged in the west by Kaidu, Khan of Transoxiana and Kashgaria (Chinese Turkistan), and the struggle that followed did not end until a decade after Kublai's death. Meanwhile, Kublai Khan's armies subjugated Burma and Indochina in the 1280's but failed in their invasions of Japan through Korea in 1274 and again in 1281 (in part because of typhoons, the *kamikaze* or "divine wind," in the Sea of Japan) and in their invasion of Java in 1293. The Mongol Empire was not a naval power, and its armies did not fare well in the tropics. Kublai also abandoned the further conquest of Europe with the destruction of the Kievan Rus as too troublesome, costly, and generally unrewarding.

China was the jewel of his empire (which eventually encompassed 80 percent of Eurasia), and Kublai tried to keep it free of war. The Sinicizing of Kublai continued after he became emperor; eventually, he even accepted conversion to Buddhism, yet was tolerant toward all religions and philosophies except Taoism. Kublai had his heirs educated as Chinese; he also established the right of succession only for his descendants. The new Mongol "square character" alphabet used during the Yüan Dynasty was designed by the Tibetan lama Pagspa for Kublai; Pagspa also governed Tibet for him. Kublai Khan introduced the use of Chinese paper money for the whole Mongol Empire and created a more unified monetary system during the years 1282 to 1287. This reform led directly not only to the stimulation and expansion of commercial activity across the Mongol Empire but also to inflation, when the new paper currency ceased to be backed effectively by or convertible to hard money.

Kublai Khan's reign also was characterized by extensive patronage of the arts and learning, and by an ambitious program of public works, including the construction of an extensive network of roads and the rebuilding and extension of the Grand Canal between Peking and Hangchow. A new law code for China was promulgated in 1291. To the Chinese, Kublai Khan was known as the Emperor Yüan Shih-tsu, the ablest and most enlightened of the Yüan rulers. He established a luxurious court, including a fabled summer retreat at Shang-tu (Samuel Taylor Coleridge's "Xanadu"). Yet he and his Mongols were never beloved by their Chinese subjects and were always viewed as alien overlords by them.

To facilitate his culturally inferior and greatly outnumbered Mongols' maintaining control over China, Kublai Khan readily employed foreigners over native Chinese as administrators and advisers, but the top offices always remained in Mongol hands. He was tolerant of Christianity, and among his subjects there were many followers of the Nestorian church. Kublai also admitted and allowed himself to be advised by Roman Catholics, the most famous of these being the Polos from the Republic of Venice.

Between 1262 and 1266, two merchant brothers, Niccolò and Maffeo Polo, journeyed across Eurasia to the seat of the Great Khan in search of trade. They arrived back in Venice with desired merchandise from the East as well as an invitation from the Great Khan for Christian missionaries to come to China and a request for an alliance with the Christian West and its Crusaders against Islamic Egypt. This tolerance of Christianity and apparent but unfulfilled promise of a joint crusade against Islam probably was responsible for the linking of Kublai Khan to the medieval Christian Prester John legends.

Under the protection of a solid gold pass (*paisa*) of safe conduct from Kublai Khan himself, the Polo brothers returned to China in 1275, this time accompanied by Niccolò's son Marco. They did not return to Europe until 1292. During these years at Kublai's court, they served him as advisers, administrators, and ambassadors. Their adventures were many, and they came to experience much of his vast but somewhat shaky empire. Marco Polo's account (dated 1324) of his travels and experiences is an invaluable European source on Kublai Khan and the Mongol Empire.

By the time of the Polos' return to Venice, Kublai's control had weakened so much that he could no longer guarantee their safety via the overland route they had originally traveled some seventeen years before. Consequently, they departed China by sea for the Middle East. Two short years later, Kublai Khan, then about eighty years old, died in Ta-tu (now Peking). He was succeeded by his grandson Temür (reigned 1295-1307). In 1368, the last Mongol emperor of China, Yüan Shun Ti, was overthrown and left Peking for Mongolia. The Mongol Yüan Dynasty was replaced by the Chinese Ming Dynasty (1368-1644), and the remaining Mongols were driven out of or absorbed by a resurgent Chinese civilization.

Summary

Kublai Khan created one of the largest empires in the history of the world; at the heart of the Mongol Empire under Kublai Khan was China. The Mongols reached the greatest extent of their power and influence under Mangu and his brother Kublai, but how unified their "state" was certainly is open to question.

Under Kublai there were no more than three million Mongols to control a domain stretching over 80 percent of Eurasia, comprising many thousands of miles and taking in numerous diverse peoples. By necessity, this empire had to be decentralized and rely heavily on Mongol-supported local administrators. This it did effectively for about two centuries. At the same time, the Mongols were forced to discriminate ruthlessly against the often culturally superior peoples they came to control. This practice was no more apparent than in the Yüan Dynasty's rule over China, enforced by a rigid caste system separating the rulers from the ruled. Despite such rigidity, even Kublai, the most effective of the Yüan emperors, had trouble maintaining control.

In the final analysis, the Mongols were spread too thin over their great empire, and their initial military-technological advantage was not sufficient to make up for their numerical and cultural inferiority to those whom they had conquered. Gradually, the Mongols were absorbed or overthrown by their conquered peoples. Hence, while Kublai Khan's military and political achievements were significant, they also were fleeting.

Bibliography

Chambers, James. *The Devil's Horsemen: The Mongol Invasion of Europe*. New York: Atheneum Publishers, 1979. This book considers the Mongol Empire from a European perspective. The concluding chapters concern themselves with the state of the empire under Kublai Khan. The decline of the empire outside Europe is not covered.

Din, Rashid al-. *The Successors of the Genghis Khan*. Translated by John Andrew Doyle. New York: Columbia University Press, 1971. This book is the classic contemporary Islamic account of the Mongol Empire from the death of the Genghis Khan through the reign of Temür Khan, grandson of Kublai Khan. The largest chapter is reserved for the life and achievements of Kublai Khan.

Hambly, Gavin, ed. *Central Asia*. New York: Delacorte Press, 1969. Contains a major chapter on the Mongol Empire at its zenith under Kublai Khan. Six chapters in total put Kublai Khan and the Mongols in historical perspective in Central Asia and to a lesser extent in Eurasia.

Howorth, Henry H. *History of the Mongols, from the Ninth to the Nineteenth Century*. Vol. 1. New York: Burt Franklin, 1876. The traditional standard multivolume study from the nineteenth century. Several important chapters touch upon the life's work of Kublai Khan.

Langlois, John D., Jr., ed. *China Under Mongol Rule*. Princeton, N.J.: Princeton University Press, 1981. Eleven essays on China under the Yüan Dynasty by a distinguished group of international scholars. Many of the selections deal with Kublai Khan and his impact on China as well as the Chinese impact on his Mongols. The Mongol Empire outside China is not considered.

Legg, Stuart. *The Heartland*. New York: Capricorn Books, 1971. Very well written. Contains a chapter dealing largely with the Mongol Empire under Kublai Khan, considered in the light of the author's interesting heartland theory of Eurasian development.

Phillips, E. D. *The Mongols*. New York: Praeger Publishers, 1969. A well-written and generously illustrated military and social history. Kublai Khan and the Yüan Dynasty are erroneously dealt with in a chapter on Mongol successor states.

Polo, Marco. *The Travels of Marco Polo (the Venetian)*. New York: Liveright, 1926. Edited by Manuel Komroff. This revised edition of William Marsden's 1818 translation recounts the classic journey of Marco Polo and his father and uncle from Venice across Eurasia to the court of Kublai Khan and the services they rendered him. A basic European primary source on the Mongol Empire of Kublai Khan.

Prawdin, Michael. *The Mongol Empire: Its Rise and Legacy*. 2d ed. New York: Free Press, 1967. Probably still the best overall history of the Mongol Empire. There is one strong chapter on Kublai Khan and another on the Polos at his court and in his service.

Rossabi, Morris. *Khubilai Khan: His Life and Times*. Berkeley: University of California Press, 1988. A readable yet comprehensive biography, of interest to both the scholar and the layperson. Includes notes, a glossary of Chinese characters, extensive bibliographies of works in Western languages and works in Oriental languages, and an index. Illustrated.

Spuler, Bertold. *History of the Mongols: Based on Eastern and Western Accounts of the Thirteenth and Fourteenth Centuries*. Translated by Helga Drummond and Stuart Drummond. Berkeley: University of California Press, 1972. Includes one major chapter on the Mongols in China under Kublai Khan. Complete with extensive primary source material on him and his people from European as well as Asiatic writings.

Vernadsky, George. *The Mongols and Russia*. New Haven, Conn.: Yale University Press, 1953. Part of a major chapter deals with the Mongol Empire under Kublai Khan. Muscovite and Novgorod Russia's commercial relations with Yüan China and elsewhere in the Far East via the Mongol caravans are discussed. The best study of its kind.

Dennis Reinhartz

FRANCESCO LANDINI

Born: 1325-1335; Fiesole, Italy
Died: September 2, 1397; Florence, Italy
Area of Achievement: Music
Contribution: Landini was the most highly regarded Italian composer and performer of his time.

Early Life

Francesco Landini (or Landino, as he is also known) was born in the small town of Fiesole, which is located approximately four miles northeast of Florence. He was the son of Jacopo del Casentino, a respected Florentine painter. Landini lost his sight as a result of smallpox while he was still a young child. Nevertheless, he received a thorough education in the liberal arts, which included the study of geometry, astronomy, rhetoric, and grammar as well as music.

Undaunted by his misfortune or, perhaps, because of it, he learned to sing and play music and write poetry with considerable skill. His primary instrument was the organ; there are a number of accounts attesting his skill at all keyboards, including the organetto, a small portative organ that could be played with one hand while being pumped with the other. His reputation as a virtuoso performer extended to other instruments as well, including the flute, recorder, lute, and rebec. He is credited with the invention of a stringed instrument, the serena serenarum, which has not survived the test of time. He also worked as an organ tuner and builder in Florence. The most important position held by him was that of organist at the Florentine church of San Lorenzo, a position he held from 1362 until his death in 1397.

In addition to his accomplishments as a skilled performing musician, Landini was a composer. His contemporaries considered him the equal of the best French composer of the age, Guillaume de Machaut. While still a young man Landini is believed to have studied composition with Jacopo da Bologna, one of the major fourteenth century Italian composers of the older generation.

Life's Work

The major Italian composers of the trecento divide into an early group located in northern Italy (perhaps best represented by the works of Giovanni da Cascia and Jacopo da Bologna, Landini's teacher) and a later group located in Florence, which catered to the tastes of the Florentine aristocracy and literati. The latter group's style is primarily represented by the works of Francesco Landini.

Landini was a secular composer who composed two- and three-part compositions. His extant work consists of 154 secular Italian compositions, including two cacce, twelve madrigals, and 140 ballate. His importance among his contemporaries can be easily deduced from the fact that an unusually large number of his compositions have been preserved, primarily in Italian manuscripts, representing approximately 20 to 30 percent of all extant Italian trecento compositions.

The most important repository of his work is the Squarcialupi Codex, named for the Florentine organist Antonio Squarcialupi, who once had it in his possession. The codex, a richly illuminated manuscript that was compiled in the early fifteenth century, contains a total of 352 secular Italian compositions. Of these, there are a remarkable 145 compositions by Landini.

Landini's style reflects the Italian penchant for beautiful melody. His music abounds with smooth, vocally oriented melodies that are in sharp contrast to the compositional practice of French composers of his time. The harmony of his music is sweeter and not as harsh or dissonant to modern ears because of his sparing use of parallel seconds and sevenths as well as an increased use of full triads. In general, the easy flow of his music impresses the listener with a sense of gracefulness and spontaneity, qualities that have been associated with Italian music for many centuries.

It would be inaccurate, however, to assume that Landini was not affected by the French compositional procedures then so prevalent. The French influence on Italian music during the fourteenth century was considerable, particularly after the return of the Papacy to Rome in 1377; examples of that influence can be seen in Landini's music as well as in that of his Italian contemporaries.

The madrigal and caccia were older Italian forms that flourished in the earlier part of the fourteenth century, while the period of the ballata's popularity began somewhat later, in the last half of the century. This changing taste can be seen in the disproportionate number of ballate composed by Landini. Almost all Landini's output, 140 of 154 compositions, is in the form of ballata— with ninety being written with two parts and fifty with three parts. The ballata, which gradually replaced the older caccia and madrigal in popularity, is believed to have been originally associated with dance. The musical form itself was the same as the French virelay, one of the very popular secular forms used during the fourteenth century. A considerable portion of Landini's three-part ballate are texted only in the upper voice; the two lower voices move in an instrumental fashion. This particular three-voice texture was so widely used in fourteenth century France that the term "French ballade style" has been widely adopted to describe it when it occurs elsewhere. Also, some of Landini's three-part compositions reveal the use of polytextuality and isorhythm, both popular practices frequently found in the fourteenth century French motet. Nevertheless, Landini's use of the French techniques should not be overemphasized. Even when it occurs, he remains true to his heritage, with the emphasis always on the vocality of the melodic line.

Landini has also been associated with a type of cadence that was quite popular with French and Italian composers of the fourteenth and fifteenth centuries. This particular cadence was an ornamented version of one commonly used in the thirteenth century in which, step-by-step, the bottom voice moved down from what in modern terminology would be described as the second scale degree to the tonic, the middle voice would move upward from the fourth scale degree to the fifth, and the upper voice would move from the seventh scale degree to the tonic. The important feature of this thirteenth century cadence was the linear movement upward of the upper two voices in parallel fourths while the lowest voice moved downward.

The fourteenth century ornamentation of this cadence occurred in the uppermost voice. The seventh scale degree would descend by step to the sixth scale degree and then skip up the interval of a third to the tonic; the overall movement is still upward. The rhythmic patterns applied to the movement of the upper voice could vary. Because of Landini's frequent use of the ornamented cadence formula, it is often referred to as "the Landini sixth."

Francesco Landini died in Florence on September 2, 1397. He was buried in the church of San Lorenzo, where he had long served as organist. His tombstone depicts him with his portative organ.

Summary

Francesco Landini, famous during his own lifetime as a composer and as an outstanding performer, was also known for his literary accomplishments. Filippo Villani, a noted Florentine chronicler, included him in his book on famous Florentine personages, telling of Landini's having been crowned with a laurel wreath in Venice by the King of Cyprus for having won a poetry contest. The composer is known to have exchanged verses with Franco Sacchetti, the Florentine poet whose texts Landini had set to music. He is also known for the extended Latin poem he wrote in support of William of Ockham's philosophical position.

Landini's fame as a composer and performer reached such proportions that, in addition to his given name, he was called and recognized by names referring to both his affliction and his instrument of choice: Francesco Cieco (Francesco the blind) and Francesco degli Organi (Francesco of the organs).

Landini held an important position as a fourteenth century Italian composer. While some of his music did reflect French influence, he maintained the vitality of the Italian tradition in the late fourteenth century. With his death, Italian music yielded to northern domination; it was not to flourish again until the sixteenth century.

Bibliography

D'Accone, Frank. "Music and Musicians at the Florentine Monastery of Santa Trinita, 1360-1363." *Quadrivium* 12 (1971): 131-151. An interesting account of old church records discovered by D'Accone that document

Landini's service as organist at the monastery of Santa Trinita in the early 1360's and his subsequent service at the church of San Lorenzo from 1365 until his death in 1397.

Ellinwood, Leonard. "The Fourteenth Century in Italy." In *The New Oxford History of Music*, edited by Egon Wellesz, vol. 3. London: Oxford University Press, 1966. A good, concise overview of the primary sources, forms, and composers of fourteenth century Italy. Contains some information about Landini.

──────── . "Francesco Landini and His Music." *Musical Quarterly* 22 (1936): 190-216. Remains one of the important sources of information about Landini in spite of its age. The article contains important biographical information and an extended discussion of his compositional output. There are seven selected compositions by Landini at the end of the article that have been transcribed into modern notation.

Fischer, Kurt von. "Francesco Landini." In *New Grove Dictionary of Music and Musicians*, edited by Stanley Sadie, vol. 10. 6th ed. New York: Macmillan, 1980. The author provides a thorough discussion of Landini and his music. The article is divided into three sections that discuss his life, extant musical compositions, and musical style. A list of his extant compositions, with short commentary, is provided, along with a lengthy bibliography.

──────── . "On the Technique, Origin, and Evolution of Italian Trecento Music." *Musical Quarterly* 47 (1961): 41-57. Provides a brief survey of compositional techniques employed by Italian composers of the fourteenth century. While several composers are discussed, the treatment of Landini is more extensive.

Hoppin, Richard H. *Medieval Music*. New York: W. W. Norton and Co., 1978. Provides an excellent survey of medieval music from chant up to music of the early fifteenth century. One chapter is devoted to the Italian *ars nova* and contains considerable information about Landini.

Pirrotta, Nino. *Music and Culture in Italy from the Middle Ages to the Baroque: A Collection of Essays*. Cambridge, Mass.: Harvard University Press, 1984. Contains a series of twenty-two essays on Italian music. The book is interdisciplinary in nature and provides a wealth of information about Italian music and Italian culture in general.

Schachter, Carl. "Landini's Treatment of Consonance and Dissonance." In *The Music Forum*, edited by William Mitchell and Felix Saltzer, vol. 2. New York: Columbia University Press, 1970. A careful and thorough analysis of how Landini used consonance and dissonance in his compositions. Schachter provides numerous musical excerpts from Landini's works to support his contentions.

Michael Hernon

LAO-TZU

Born: 604 B.C.; Ch'ü-jen, State of Ch'u, China
Died: Sixth century B.C.; place unknown
Area of Achievement: Philosophy
Contribution: Lao-tzu is widely recognized as the premier thinker of Taoism, the second of China's great philosophical schools.

Early Life

Lao-tzu (also known as *Tao-te Ching*) is the name of a slim volume from China's classical era that forms a principal text of the Taoist school of philosophy. The title literally means "Old Master," and the book has traditionally been ascribed to the "Old Master" himself—or, at least, it has been thought to reflect faithfully the philosophy of someone known as Lao-tzu. This Lao-tzu is, however, the most shadowy of all classical Chinese philosophers, and nothing at all can be said with any certainty about him.

The earliest attempt to write a biography of Lao-tzu was made in the first century B.C. by the great historian Ssu-ma Ch'ien (c. 145-c. 86 B.C.), but even at that early date the historian was only able to assemble a few scraps of information concerning Lao-tzu, many of which are mutually contradictory. Ssu-ma Ch'ien attempted to merge the stories of at least three different individuals into his biography of Lao-tzu, since he was uncertain which one was "the real Lao-tzu," and in the end the various stories proved impossible to reconcile. As Ssu-ma Ch'ien concluded, "Lao-tzu was a reclusive gentleman," and it is perhaps fitting that he remain forever elusive.

Among the few "facts" that are alleged about Lao-tzu are that his family name was Li, his given name Erh, and his "style" Tan. He was supposedly born in the southern state of Ch'u; indeed, Lao-tzu's thought does typify the lush, mystical, romantic, and sometimes erotic southern side of ancient Chinese culture that contrasts so starkly with the stern moralism of northern Confucianism.

Ssu-ma Ch'ien says that Lao-tzu served as Historian of the Archives in the court of the Chou Dynasty and that Confucius (551-479 B.C.) personally sought instruction from him in the rites. At age 160, or perhaps two hundred, disappointed with the decline of civilization in China, Lao-tzu departed. The Keeper of the Hsien-ku Pass detained him on his way out and required him to commit his wisdom to writing in the book that came to be known as the *Tao-te Ching*, before permitting him to continue his westward journey. According to a later legend, Lao-tzu subsequently went to India, where his teachings gave birth to Buddhism.

None of this information is historically reliable, however, and many modern scholars doubt that Lao-tzu is a historical figure at all. It seems more likely that there were several "Old Masters" in ancient China who taught ideas similar to those of the *Tao-te Ching* than that no such man ever existed at all. In either case, however, it ceases to be meaningful to say that Lao-tzu wrote the book that is sometimes called by his name.

The best evidence indicates that the *Tao-te Ching* was compiled sometime during the fourth or third century B.C., probably incorporating earlier fragments, and that it did not settle into its present form until the middle of the second century B.C. It may be that it is largely the product of one hand, but it can also be plausibly viewed as a jumble of anonymous Taoist sayings assembled by an editor or editors during this period.

Life's Work

The *Tao-te Ching* has been translated into English more often than any book except the Bible, and in China hundreds of commentaries have been written on it. The explanation for all this attention is that, aside from the great intrinsic appeal of the work, it is a very cryptic book that defies definitive interpretation. Each reader finds something different in the *Tao-te Ching*, and, despite deceptively simple grammar and vocabulary, it is often possible to argue at great length even about the meaning of individual sentences.

For example, the famous opening line of the *Tao-te Ching* could read, in English, "Any way that you can speak about is not The Constant Way." Alternatively, it could also read: "The way that can be treated as The Way is not an ordinary way," or, "The way that can be treated as The Way is an inconstant way." Multiply this kind of ambiguity by the more than five thousand Chinese characters in the book, and it becomes easy to understand why so many different translations of the *Tao-te Ching* are possible.

The work is divided into two sections and eighty-one brief chapters; more than half of it is written in rhyme, and it is suffused throughout with a distinct poetic atmosphere. There appears to be no particular order to the chapters, and even individual paragraphs may be unrelated to their context, thus reinforcing the impression of the *Tao-te Ching* as an anthology of Taoist maxims rather than a systematic treatise.

Interpretation of the *Tao-te Ching* must hinge, in part, upon the date one chooses to assign for its composition. Its pointed ridicule of Confucian sanctimoniousness, for example, is puzzling if the legend that Lao-tzu was older than Confucius is true, but would make sense if it was really compiled in the post-Confucian period. At least one scholar claims that the *Tao-te Ching* was not compiled until the late third century B.C.; he bases his argument on signs of opposition he sees in it to the Legalist school that was then developing.

More critical is the *Tao-te Ching*'s position within the chronology of the Taoist movement itself. Tradition gives the *Tao-te Ching* pride of place as the oldest Taoist work, but there are grounds for speculation that the other great Taoist text, the *Chuang-tzu*, might be older. Not knowing which book was written first makes it difficult to determine which book influenced which and seriously cripples scholars' ability to analyze the development of Taoism.

The principal philosophical difference between the *Tao-te Ching* and the *Chuang-tzu* is that the former advocates understanding the laws of change in the universe so as to conform to them and thereby harness them to work for one's benefit; *Chuang-tzu*, on the other hand, contends that a true understanding of the laws of change reveals all transformations to be equally valid and all differences to be ultimately relative. Hence the wise man does not try to manipulate the Tao, but simply accepts what it brings.

The Tao (pronounced "dow") is the central concept of all Taoist philosophy. The basic meaning of the word is "road" or "way," and by extension it came to refer to "the way" of doing various things. Philosophers of all Chinese schools of thought (even the Confucians) used this word and considered it to be important, but only the Taoists treated it as a universal absolute. For Confucians, the Tao is the moral Way of proper human behavior; to a Taoist, it is an amoral principle of nature.

The Tao is the constant law (or laws, since the Chinese language has no plurals) that governs the otherwise incessant change of the material universe. It is thus the one permanent, immutable thing in existence, the hub at the center of the wheel of life. Since the Tao is absolute, however, it is impossible to break it down for analysis. The mere act of giving it a name, such as Tao, is misleading, because it implies that the Tao is a thing which can be critically examined and labeled. The Tao actually transcends all humanly imposed conceptual models.

Since the Tao cannot be logically analyzed or described in words, it therefore can only be perceived holistically through intuition. This gives the *Tao-te Ching* its mystic tone and helps explain the frustrating statement in chapter 56 that "he who knows does not speak; he who speaks does not know." Ultimate truth is beyond the capacity of speech to convey. For this reason, one third century A.D. wag remarked that Confucius actually understood the Tao better than Lao-tzu, since Confucius was wise enough to keep silent about the subject.

Lao-tzu's favorite theme is the disparity between intention and result. "Reversal is the action of the Tao," he wrote (chapter 40). Striving to make oneself strong eventually exhausts and weakens a man; striving for wealth leads to poverty in the long run. The wise man instead conforms to the Tao and aligns himself with the weak, the humble, and the poor.

This philosophy was in large part a reaction to the highly competitive environment of the Warring States period in Chinese history (403-221 B.C.), when conflict was continuous and life itself uncertain. Amid such surroundings, *Tao-te Ching* taught that survival came through not competing. The solution to the problem of how to preserve life and happiness was simply to be content.

The *Tao-te Ching* contains wisdom for all men, but much of the book is directed in particular toward the ruler. It teaches a kind of laissez-faire approach to government: The state will function best if left to run itself naturally, and strenuous efforts on the part of the ruler can only cause greater confusion and disorder. The more the ruler acts, the more work he creates for himself, and the more impossible it becomes to do everything that is necessary. Far better to do nothing. The *Tao-te Ching* calls this form of government *wu-wei*, or "nonaction."

As a concrete application of this principle, the *Tao-te Ching* criticizes attempts to improve the state through moral codes or laws. The very existence of laws produces lawbreakers, and moral codes result in pretense, competition, and the very kinds of immorality they were intended to discourage. Far better, says Lao-tzu, to return to the childlike condition of original innocence that prevailed before the awakening of desires.

Summary

Lao-tzu the man is a will-o'-the-wisp—an insubstantial legend. Even a legend, however, can have important consequences. During the common era, religious Taoism (Tao-chiao) emerged under Buddhist influence out of earlier immortality cults. This Taoist religion adopted very little of the philosophical content of the *Tao-te Ching*, but its adherents came to venerate Lao-tzu himself as a god.

By the second century A.D., Lao-tzu was being worshipped as a progenitor of the universe, an incarnation of the Tao itself. The deified Lao-tzu became one of the most important members of the native Chinese religious pantheon, and the eighty-one earthly manifestations he was ultimately said to have taken included Siddhārtha Gautama (the Buddha) and Mani (Manes), the Persian founder of Manichaeanism.

The religious Taoist canon includes more than fourteen hundred separate titles, but the *Tao-te Ching*—often badly misunderstood, to be sure—ranks at the top. Even for Chinese who remained skeptical about this native religious movement, the *Tao-te Ching* continued to be regarded as an outstanding guide for living and a delightful work of literature.

The *Tao-te Ching* and *Chuang-tzu* represent the native Chinese tradition of true metaphysical speculation (as opposed to the political and social philosophy of Confucius and others) and as such have contributed immensely to the subsequent development of Chinese thought. Ch'an Buddhism (Japanese Zen), for example, owes much to Taoist influence. Taoist philosophy has always been the natural consolation of the Chinese gentleman in retirement or disgrace. The *Tao-te Ching*, one of the most profound and baffling books ever written, is a principal text in China's perennial "other" school of thought: the playful, mystical, Taoist alternative to staid and conventional Confucianism.

Bibliography

Creel, Herrlee G. *"What Is Taoism?" and Other Studies in Chinese Cultural History*. Chicago: University of Chicago Press, 1970. Contains a definitive essay on the subject, emphasizing the distinction between philosophical and religious Taoism.

Fung, Yu-lan. *A Short History of Chinese Philosophy*. Edited by Derk Bodde. New York: Macmillan, 1948. The standard survey of Chinese philosophical schools. Accessible to the general reader.

Kaltenmark, Max. *Lao Tzu and Taoism*. Translated by Roger Greaves. Stanford, Calif.: Stanford University Press, 1969. A point-by-point explanation of various Taoist terms and ideas. Its discussion of religious Taoism is especially helpful.

Lao-tzu. *Tao te Ching*. Translated by D. C. Lau. Harmondsworth, England: Penguin Books, 1963. An excellent translation, with clear and reliable introduction and supplementary materials, including an essay entitled "The Problem of Authorship."

Munro, Donald J. *The Concept of Man in Early China*. Stanford, Calif.: Stanford University Press, 1969. A rigorous analysis of early Chinese thought by a Western-trained professional philosopher.

Ronan, Colin A. *The Shorter Science and Civilisation in China: An Abridgement of Joseph Needham's Original Text*. Vol. 1. Cambridge: Cambridge University Press, 1978. An eccentric view of Taoism as proto-science, tracing the development of alchemy and the study of nature.

Waley, Arthur. *The Way and Its Power: A Study of the "Tao tê Ching" and Its Place in Chinese Thought*. London: Allen and Unwin, 1934. This work is somewhat dated, and its introduction is long and rambling. Still, it is a valuable study, and Waley's translation has been very influential.

Welch, Holmes. *The Parting of the Way: Lao Tzu and the Taoist Movement*. Boston: Beacon Press, 1957. A popular presentation of Lao-tzu's ideas, with an attempt to show their contemporary relevance. Also contains a fine—though brief—history of the Taoist movement.

Charles W. Holcombe

SAINT LÁSZLÓ I

Born: 1040?; Kraków, Poland
Died: July 29, 1095; somewhere near the Moravian border
Areas of Achievement: Government and religion
Contribution: By means of legislative reforms, diplomacy, and military bravura, László brought for Hungary both internal security and, with the annexation of Croatia, a new, more active role in the affairs of the world.

Early Life

Saint László I, also known as Ladislas, was the second of three sons born to Hungarian king-to-be Béla I, who at the time still lived in exile in Poland. Béla had fled Hungary, along with his brothers Andrew and Levente, shortly before the end of the great Stephen I's reign, when it was learned that their father, Vászoly, had been arrested for his part in an alleged pagan conspiracy and tortured to death. (His eyes were removed, and his ears were filled with molten lead.) Béla sought refuge at the court of the Polish Mieszko II and eventually married the prince's daughter, Richeza. This marriage produced three sons, Géza, László, and Lambert.

László's early life is shrouded in mystery. Essentially all that is known of it is that he spent his boyhood years at the court of his uncle, King Casimir of Poland. In that atmosphere, imbued as it was with the spirit of the Christian renaissance, László apparently was reared to be a devout Christian. Eventually, in 1046, Béla and his brothers were summoned home by the growing legions weary of the rule of Stephen's nephew and handpicked successor, Peter. When Andrew I, who had married his son Salomon to the daughter of Holy Roman Emperor Henry III, decided on his only child as his successor, Béla, who was the rightful heir to the crown, revolted. In the ensuing struggle, Béla's forces defeated those of Andrew, who died in battle. Béla thus succeeded his brother, but was himself assassinated in 1063, presumably by backers of Salomon.

Civil war was averted only through the intervention of the priests and nobles. In exchange for their oath to Salomon, Géza and László were appointed duces (*herceg*) of Nitra and Bihor counties respectively. It was during this period that László distinguished himself as a soldier. In 1068, a horde of Cumans, on their way home after raiding Hungary, were intercepted by the united front of László, Géza, and Salomon and were utterly defeated. Concerning this battle, a legend arose that László had rescued an innocent girl by chasing down and slaying the Cuman heathen who had abducted her. This Hungarian paladin, the very embodiment of courage and valor, was also blessed with a majestic appearance. With his powerful six-foot frame, László towered over his contemporaries.

In 1074, a protracted feud resulted in armed conflict and, ultimately, in the ouster of Salomon and the coronation of Géza. Finally, upon Géza's death in 1077, László was proclaimed regent of Hungary. (Salomon had absconded with the crown, thus delaying somewhat the naming of László as king.)

Life's Work

When László took power in 1077, Hungary was in serious trouble. Forty years of dynastic struggles had cast doubt on the *senioratus* principle of succession and seriously weakened the authority of the state. Lawlessness, particularly in the form of theft and robbery, was rampant. The slow spread of Christianity in Hungary began to be undermined by a resurgence of paganism. In this weakened state, moreover, the country was even harder pressed to defend its borders against the constant threats posed by Byzantium, the Holy Roman Empire, and such nomadic Turkic peoples as the Petchenegs and the Cumans. Yet, a mere eighteen years later, when László died and the crown was passed on to Kálmán, Hungary was again internally strong, indeed so much so that it had relinquished its largely defensive posture in favor of an expansionist one.

When László succeeded Géza, he was already esteemed by the nobles for his abilities as a ruler (which, as dux of Bihar, he had had occasion to demonstrate), by the churchmen for his generous financial support, and by the warriors for his prowess as a soldier. These would all be attributes of László the king as well, each of them contributing something to the restoration, indeed enhancement, of Stephen's Christian Hungarian state. László introduced new law codes, which for the most part aimed at curbing theft and robbery. He generously supported and expanded the Church, thus assuring that Hungary would remain Christian and not isolate itself from the European community. Finally, he continued to distinguish himself in the battlefield and, when diplomacy failed, defended Hungary's interests with the sword.

The new laws, including those drawn up at the Synod of Szabolcs of 1092, were extremely severe, even by the standards of the age. The theft of a hen, for example, was punishable by the lopping off of the perpetrator's hand. As László was known by his contemporaries to be as gentle and kind as he could be severe, it must be supposed that these laws were drastic measures, sorely needed to control the lawlessness which had engulfed the realm. The worst problem was clearly the one posed by theft, robbery, and a general disregard for private property. Underscoring the severity of this problem is the curious phenomenon that, in these laws, violent crimes were less severely punished than proprietary violations. The defense of private property embodied in these laws safeguarded, first and foremost, the vital economic resources of the realm.

It is ironic that it would be László, grandson of the pagan rebel Vászoly, who would take such a strong hand in preserving, indeed developing, Stephen's Christian state. Originally, there was a network of ten bishoprics, serving as the foci of Church activity, which, in theory, reached even the most outlying villages. Besides moving two of these old bishoprics to more accessible locations, László founded a new bishopric, between the Drava and Sava rivers, in Zagreb. The proliferation of churches, and with it the growing need for priests, naturally required material resources—and these László was only too happy to provide, diverting much of the income from minting, taxes, and export duties to the expansion and upgrading of the Church.

As might be expected from such a devout Christian, László had mostly good relations with the Pope. László came to power in 1077, the year Pope Gregory VII and Henry IV met at the castle called Canossa, and took the side of the Pope in the matter of investiture. While László ceded to the Pope the right to make ecclesiastical appointments, in practice he routinely did it himself. For the most part, however, the Papacy turned a blind eye to this discrepancy between theory and practice, until, in the early 1090's, László continued to act without papal consent in the newly annexed territory of Croatia.

László also cultivated a reverence for Hungary's great Christian leaders. On July 25, 1083, the body of Gerard, the bishop Stephen most relied on in his program of disseminating Christianity, was exhumed. Later, on August 20, the remains of Stephen himself were exhumed, in a ceremony attended by the king, nobles, and the masses. The subsequent canonization of Stephen and Gerard—and later that of Stephen's son Emeric—was apparently welcomed by the Pope, although he was not able to bring the matter before the synod for official approval. While there is no questioning László's basically devout nature, the elevation to sainthood of Stephen, Gerard, and Emeric was at bottom a political tool, aimed at consolidating the position of the Church.

László is also immortalized for his daring feats as a soldier, and indeed he was the hero of many a campaign. During his reign, he twice led armies to victory against invading Cuman forces, in 1085 and 1091. Yet he was not only a valiant warrior but also a crafty tactician. During the conflict between Henry IV and Rudolf, László saw the opportunity to strike and so, in early 1079, led a campaign against the German frontier resulting in the reoccupation of Moson.

When the King of Croatia, Zvonimir, died, the ensuing struggle for succession was settled when László, the late king's brother-in-law, claimed the throne for himself. By 1091, Croatia had become an indisputable dynastic acquisition, conferring upon Hungary, among other things, a passage to the Adriatic Sea. In 1095, while hurrying to the aid of the Prince of Moravia, László suddenly fell ill and died.

Summary

It might not be going too far to say that if had not been for Saint László I,

Hungary would not have developed into the Christian state for which Saint Stephen had so painstakingly laid the groundwork. László restored relative peace and tranquillity to a nation which had suffered through nearly four decades of internal strife, in large part a consequence of Stephen's failure to establish firm laws of succession. László accomplished this feat, moreover, by a variety of means: military, diplomatic, economic, and legislative.

It must be conceded, however, that when László came to power in 1077, he did so under rather favorable circumstances. Henry IV—who would have liked to turn Hungary into a vassal state and who, with this aim in mind, aided and abetted László's rival, Salomon—found himself embroiled in a struggle with the Pope over investiture. Byzantium, which had always posed a threat to Hungary, was suffering from internal conflicts of its own (in addition to the constant harassment of Turkic nomads). Russia faced similar problems. Meanwhile, the smaller Slavic nations—the Czechs, Poles, and Croatians—continued to pose no significant threat to Hungary.

Even so, the extent of László's achievement is indisputable. With the annexation of Croatia, for example, László paved the way for Hungary to become a great power. By the same token, however, he also burdened Hungary with an unassimilable alien region, one which proved an immediate source of problems and which would later contribute to the country's downfall.

Bibliography

Domjan, Joseph. *Hungarian Heroes and Legends*. Princeton, N.J.: Van Nostrand Reinhold Co., 1963. Includes a very short chapter on László, recounting some of the outstanding tales and legends associated with his name. Intended for young readers, this volume is of modest help for the serious scholar as well. With illustrations.

Kosáry G., Dominic. *History of Hungary*. Cleveland: Benjamin Bibliophile Society, 1941. Gives a fairly lengthy and readable account of László's reign in the chapter titled "The Christian Kingdom in the Middle Ages." Includes an index, bibliography, list of kings of Hungary, and genealogical tables.

Kosztolnyik, Z. J. *Five Eleventh Century Hungarian Kings: Their Policies and Their Relations with Rome*. New York: New York University Press, 1981. A heavily documented study of the Hungarian kings from Stephen to László. Features an index, bibliographical essay, and bibliography.

Sinor, Denis. *History of Hungary*. New York: Praeger Publishers, 1959. The brief account of László in this primer on Hungarian history is colorful and vivid. Has both an index and a chronology of events.

Vámbéry, Arminius. *Hungary in Ancient, Medieval, and Modern Times*. London: T. Fisher Unwin, 1887. In this venerable but rather dated work on Hungarian history, the reign of László is briefly treated in the chapter "The Kings of the House of Arpád." Includes an index and illustrations.

Yolland, Arthur B. *Hungary*. New York: Frederick A. Stokes Co., 1917. Dated though it may be, this work includes an entire chapter on László: "St. Ladislas and His Age." Features an index, bibliography, appendix, photographs, and maps.

Zarek, Otto. *The History of Hungary*. London: Selwyn and Blount, 1939. The chapter on László and his successor Kálmán is brief but informative. The text is supplemented by many study aids, including a map, an index, a bibliography, and a table of place-names in Hungarian, German, Slavonic, and Romanian (with a phonetic guide to pronunciation).

Gregory Nehler

LEIF ERIKSSON

Born: c. 970; Iceland, possibly in Haukadal
Died: c. 1035; probably near Julianehaab, Greenland
Area of Achievement: Exploration
Contribution: Though probably not the first European to sight America, Leif made the first deliberate exploration of the North American continent and provided the main stimulus for later, unsuccessful attempts at permanent settlement.

Early Life
Very little is known of Leif's early life. He was the son of Erik the Red and his wife, Thjodhild, and seems to have had two brothers, Thorvald and Thorstein, and one sister, Freydis. His father's career, however, is well-known. Erik was born in Norway but was forced to flee from there as a result of "some killings." He settled first at Drangar in Iceland but then moved to Haukadal. At that time, though land was still readily available in Iceland, the country had been known for more than a century and intensively settled for perhaps eighty years; there were many powerful and well-established families in all the areas where Erik attempted to settle.

In Haukadal, he became involved in several conflicts, killing at least two of his neighbors, Eyjolf "the Sow" and Hrafn "the Dueler." He was driven out, tried to make his home elsewhere, killed another neighbor in an argument over timber, and was then—not unreasonably—outlawed together with his family.

Erik then made the momentous decision to try to find an unsettled land. Seafarers blown off course had reported land to the west of Iceland, and in 982 Erik sailed, together with his family, to find it. He landed in Greenland near what is now Julianehaab and spent three years exploring the country. In 985 he returned to Iceland and in 986 set sail again with twenty-five ships to found a permanent settlement in Greenland. Only fourteen of the ships arrived, with perhaps four hundred people, but this landing formed the basis for the later colonization of the eastern, middle, and western settlements of Greenland, which lasted until changing climate and Eskimo hostility exterminated the colonies, probably in the early 1500's.

Nevertheless, this colonizing move had transformed Erik from a hunted outlaw in a land severely afflicted by famine to the undisputed head of a new nation, the patriarch of a land with reasonable grazing (in the more temperate climate of the late tenth century) and unparalleled hunting, trapping, and fishing opportunities. It seems reasonable to suppose that the total change of life-style also made an impression on his children, who may have wondered if they too could not become great men or great women by similar daring seamanship.

Life's Work

To reconstruct Leif's life two Icelandic sagas are indispensable: *Groehnlendinga saga* (c. 1390; *The Greenlanders' Saga*, 1893) and *Eiríks saga rauda* (c. 1263; *The Saga of Erik the Red*, 1841), the latter existing in two different versions. These sagas do not tell quite the same tale, but reasons for their deviations can often be seen. According to *The Greenlanders' Saga*, which was composed much earlier than its late fourteenth transcription date, America was originally sighted not by Leif but by one Bjarni Herjolfsson, who had been blown off course on his way to Greenland. Bjarni refused, however, to land at any of the three places he sighted (to the disgust of his crew) and finally made his way to his father's farm, located about fifty miles from the farm Erik and Leif had established at Brattahlith. Bjarni's sightings caused much discussion, and some time later, probably around the year 1000, Leif came to him and bought his ship—presumably thinking that if the ship had reached this strange destination once, it could do so again. Leif hoped to get his father, now a man of fifty or more, to lead the expedition, because of his famous good luck, but on his way to the ship Erik fell off his horse, hurt himself, and refused to go any farther. It was not his fate to discover more new lands, he said. He would leave that to his son.

The Greenlanders' Saga then relates that Leif and his men came in succession to countries they called Helluland (flatstone land) and Markland (forest land), finally arriving at a place where they stayed for the winter and by which they were much impressed. It had sweet dew, no winter frost, outdoor grazing for cattle all year, and sun visible as late as midafternoon even in midwinter—very different from the short midwinter days of Greenland or Iceland. Finally, an old attendant of Leif, the German Tyrkir, was found one day almost incoherent with delight: He had found wild grapes, from which the land was given the name of Vinland, or Wineland. Leif and his men loaded a cargo of grapes and timber—the latter in very short supply in the treeless northern islands—and went home. On their way, they sighted and rescued a wrecked ship's crew, again men who had been blown off course.

It seems likely that the story cited above is close to what really happened. In later years, however, the rather haphazard nature of the expedition was considered insufficiently inspiring, and *The Saga of Erik the Red* added a rather pointless tale of a love affair between Leif and a Hebridean lady named Thorgunna, which left him with a son, Thorgils, and a tale of how Leif went to Norway to the court of Olaf I Tryggvason, the missionary king, there to be converted to Christianity and sent back to preach the new religion in Greenland. On his return, says this saga, Leif was blown off course, sighted a land with wheat and vines on it, rescued a ship's crew, and finally arrived in Greenland to preach the faith. One can see that in this story the stubborn, unenterprising Bjarni Herjolfsson has vanished; Leif has been given entire credit for discovering Vinland, and the whole story has become vaguely tied to the advantages of Christianity. Very little is said about geography, however, and it is not at all clear how Leif had time to go to Norway, be converted, go to Vinland, explore it, and get back to Greenland, all in one short northern summer. Almost certainly the tale of Leif and the conversion of Greenland is a later addition. It is not known when Greenland was converted, but it probably occurred after the conversion of Iceland in 1000. Leif probably died a Christian, but he was probably still a pagan at the time of his landing in America.

The stories after the discovery deviate even further, but one can make out some consistent elements. Leif could and did tell people how to reach his winter settlement at Leifsbuthir in Vinland—a "booth" being the Norse term for a temporary hut. He had in fact left a house of sorts there and was prepared to lend it to people, especially family members, but not to give it away; he seems to have felt the need to keep a claim of sorts on the country. Yet later visits were not successful. Thorvald, Leif's brother, was killed by an arrow. *The Greenlanders' Saga* says it was shot by a "Skraeling"; *The Saga of Erik the Red*, with its usual attempt to improve a story, by a "uniped." Nevertheless, all sources agree that the native inhabitants of the country, called contemptuously Skraelings, or "wretches, punies," by the Norsemen, became increasingly hostile after early attempts at trade and in the end forced the Norsemen out. Another would-be colonizer, Thorfinn Karlsefni, who had married the widow of Thorstein (Leif's other brother), tried to settle near Leifsbuthir but was also compelled to leave. Finally, an expedition which included Leif's sister Freydis ended in mass murder when Freydis provoked and wiped out the crew of her companion ship, herself killing five women with an ax when no man would do it. She tried to hide the matter from her brother, but when the party returned to Greenland, Leif discovered the truth and though reluctant to punish her himself, made the killings known. The visits to Vinland had proved unlucky, and Leif and his family attempted to settle there no more—as far as is known from the sagas.

Summary

In a sense, Leif Eriksson did very little to earn his later reputation, or even his Norse nickname, Leif "the Lucky." He did not "discover" America; Bjarni Herjolfsson did. He did not try to colonize it; if anyone can be given credit for that, it should be Thorfinn Karlsefni. What Leif did was to explore the Labrador-Newfoundland-Nova Scotia coast and to publicize his exploration. In this at least he was a master, and stories rapidly became attached to his voyage: The turning back of his father, the discovery of the grapes, the use of a pair of trained Scottish "runners" given to him by King Olaf to scout large areas of land quickly and cheaply without the bother of shipping horses. Some of these stories are probably in essence true. Others were attracted to the saga by the interest taken in these western discoveries.

Furthermore, Vinland may have been visited more often than the sagas state. In the 1950's, Helge Ingstad made a careful search of the Newfoundland coast for relics of Norse settlement, trying to reconcile the geography of the area with such carefully described places in the sagas as Furdustrandir, the Wonder Beaches (perhaps the long expanse of sandy beaches south of Hamilton Inlet in southeast Labrador). In the end, Ingstad found what are claimed to be clear signs of Norse building at L'Anse-aux-Meadows in Newfoundland. Whether these are Leifsbuthir or some later establishment cannot be determined.

Finally, Vinland remained marked on maps drawn in Iceland at least up to 1590, a century after Christopher Columbus. At any time in the fourteenth or fifteenth centuries any Englishman, Italian, or Portuguese who bothered to ask an Icelander about northern geography would probably have been told that there was a large, fertile country west of Greenland. Whether anyone did ask is not known. Yet it cannot be ruled out that, for example, Columbus had sailed "beyond Thule," or Iceland, and in his 1492 expedition was encouraged by dim memories of the voyage of Leif the Lucky.

Bibliography

Gad, Finn. *The History of Greenland*. Vol. 1, *Earliest Times to 1700*. Translated by Ernst Dupont. London: Hurst and Co., 1970. A stirring account of the history of this doomed colony. Gad closely follows the Christianized version of Leif's adventures, perhaps wrongly, but the author has interesting information on the nature of Erik's and Leif's farm at Brattahlith as revealed by archaeology.

Gathorne-Hardy, G. M. *The Norse Discoverers of America*. Oxford: Clarendon Press, 1921. A conflated account of the different saga versions, making for an easier story to read but also rather obscuring the genuine discrepancies. There is a sensible discussion of textual problems and of such issues as the nature of the Skraelings.

Haugen, Einar, trans. *Voyages to Vinland*. New York: Alfred A. Knopf, 1942. This work is a translation of the various sources together with a long account of the evidence as Haugen sees it. Though largely superseded by the work by Jones, below, this book remains attractive for its clear style, and valuable because of Haugen's own status as a scholar of Norse.

Ingstad, Helge. *Westward to Vinland*. Translated by Erik J. Friis. New York: St. Martin's Press, 1969. This account gives the story of what is often regarded as the only convincing Norse archaeological site in the New World, at L'Anse-aux-Meadows in Newfoundland. Doubt is cast on this by Mowat, below, but if even the bronze pin and the spindle whorl found are incontrovertibly Norse, then it must be accepted that this is a Norse site, possibly Leif's, possibly from an unrecorded subsequent expedition.

Jones, Gwyn. *The Norse Atlantic Saga: Being the Norse Voyages of Discov-*

ery and Settlement to Iceland, Greenland, and America. London: Oxford University Press, 1964. Professor Jones traces the story of the Norse discoveries of Iceland, Greenland, and Vinland, with interesting details on seamanship and on the successive and half-planned nature of Norse exploration. The book includes translations of both *The Greenlanders' Saga* and *The Saga of Erik the Red* as well as translations of minor tales, including Eskimo ones. The most useful single work on this period and milieu.

Magnusson, Magnus, and Hermann Palsson, trans. *The Vinland Sagas.* New York: New York University Press, 1965. This work gives fresh and clear translations of *The Greenlanders' Saga* and *The Saga of Erik the Red*, using as its basis for the latter the fuller if later *Skalholtsbok* version. There is also an excellent introduction dealing with the relationship between the stories and the probable motives of the Christianizers of Leif.

Mowat, Farley. *Westviking: The Ancient Norse in Greenland and North America.* Boston: Little, Brown and Co., 1965. An exercise in wringing dry the sagas in which every paragraph is translated and commented on— often to the extent of hypothesizing the conflict, anxiety, or other motivation behind the bare facts recorded. Leif's settlement is firmly located at Tickle Cove Pond in Newfoundland. Keen though it is, this book is let down by its failure to grasp the nature of the Icelandic manuscripts on which it is based.

Tornoe, Johannes K. *Norsemen Before Columbus: Early American History.* London: George Allen and Unwin, 1965. One of many analyses of the sagas, this study is particularly good on ships, sailing directions, and other details, including Norse observations of the sun and the account of the "wild grape."

                                                                    T. A. Shippey

LEO IX
Bruno of Egisheim

Born: June 21, 1002; Egisheim, Alsace
Died: April 19, 1054; Rome
Area of Achievement: Religion
Contribution: Leo IX was one of the most important of the medieval popes. Coming to the Papacy after a long period of papal and religious decline, and during an era when the authority of the Holy Roman emperors was at its most influential, Leo instituted a number of significant reforms within the Church which had profound results not only for the Roman church in the West and the Orthodox church in the East but also for the Holy Roman Empire and other kingdoms in Europe.

Early Life

Leo IX was born Bruno of Egisheim, son of Hugo, Count of Egisheim. The family was related to Conrad II, the Holy Roman emperor. His parents were very religious, and Bruno was destined from an early age to enter the Church. The higher offices in the Church were generally reserved for members of aristocratic families, and Bruno was educated at a school for upper-class boys in Toul, an establishment noted for its atmosphere of piety and its reforming sympathies. After his schooling, he served as a deputy to Herman, the Bishop of Toul, and led the military vassals of the bishop into battle alongside the emperor (a common action by members of the clergy in that strife-torn era). Herman died in 1026, and Bruno was chosen as the new bishop of Toul, although he was only in his mid-twenties and might instead have had a successful secular career serving the emperor. Toul was a poor diocese and not an obvious choice for an ambitious cleric. Bruno was consecrated bishop in 1027.

Rampant corruption plagued the Western church in the tenth and eleventh centuries; the monastic establishments and their regular clergy, as well as various elements in the secular clergy, from the Papacy down to the village priest, had succumbed to it. There were two major abuses within the Church, and both had widespread ramifications. Simony, or the buying and selling of church offices, was rife, and there was doubt whether a clergyman tainted with simony could validly perform the sacraments upon which salvation depended. The second major abuse was that of Nicolaism, a name of unknown origin which came to stand for various types of sexual incontinence among the clergy. Requirements that all clergymen be celibate were widely disregarded and many clerics had wives, mistresses, and children.

In addition, it was a violent age, and even the Church was not immune. During the eleventh century, many clergymen, including popes, were murdered, often by their fellow clergy. There were demands for reform, both from within the Church and from secular society. Some improvement had slowly occurred, often stemming from the example set first by the monastery of Cluny, in France, founded in 910, but also by other monasteries in northern Europe. Bruno was never a monk, but he was a strong admirer of Saint Benedict of Nursia, the founder of Western monasticism in the sixth century, and many of his closest advisers were monks. Bruno was a reforming bishop in Toul, and he concentrated particularly on ending abuses in the various monastic houses. He was also active militarily in defending his diocese from threatened invasion. Bruno was a loyal vassal to his relative the Holy Roman emperor, and a staunch defender of the empire. An able diplomat, he traveled to Rome on many occasions. Even though Toul was not a prominent diocese, Bruno became widely known, not only in the empire but also in other kingdoms, in ecclesiastical as well as political and military spheres.

Life's Work

In 1048, Pope Damasus II died after serving as the Bishop of Rome, or pope, for only twenty-three days; it was widely rumored that his death was caused by poison. The selection of the new pope depended upon the wishes of the Holy Roman emperor, Henry III, for by the eleventh century the emperors had become not only secular rulers of the empire, which extended from the Germanies into Italy, but also the effective arbiters of the Church. In practice, the emperors not only chose the high officials of the Church but also invested their choices with the signs of the office, the bishop's staff and ring. The Church had periodically fought against the involvement of laymen such as the emperors in the selection of bishops, abbots, and other clergy, and various church councils had passed resolutions against the practice of lay investiture. In the feudal age, however, the needs of secular society became intertwined with those of the Church; powerful kings, emperors, and other lay persons would not allow the Church to choose its own officials unilaterally. Too much was at stake, including the possession of land, which translated into wealth and political and military power. Because of the lands they held, counts and dukes had to be loyal vassals to their lords, and in the opinion of most kings and emperors, so must bishops and abbots.

Emperor Henry III chose the new pope at Worms. His selection was his relative, Bruno of Toul. Henry was a powerful ruler of both church and state who believed himself to have been chosen by God to rule; it is doubtful that he saw himself as subordinate to the pope, even in many areas of religion. He had already chosen two previous popes. Bruno was perhaps an obvious choice, given his family connection and his already wide reputation, but even Henry could not know just how significant his selection was to become. Under Bruno, who took the name Leo in honor of Leo the Great, the Papacy became a major center of reform. The movement had not begun at Rome, but with Leo the Papacy became the driving force for reform for the next two centuries. Although the effective choice had already taken place at Worms, an election at Rome was the norm; thus, in late 1048 Leo left Toul for the Eternal City. He took with him other high-ranking clergymen, including the monk Hildebrand, who, as Pope Gregory VII, would later carry many of Leo's reforms to fruition. Early accounts of his life have Leo entering Rome barefoot, as a simple pilgrim, and being received ecstatically by the Roman populace. His papacy had begun.

Although the reform of abuses in the Church had already started, Leo gave focus and direction to the reform impetus. Because of his experience as bishop and diplomat, his intellectual capabilities, his knowledge of the problems faced by the Church in the eleventh century, and his vision of what the power of the Papacy might accomplish, Leo was ideally suited to change the Church. To do so, however, he could not remain in Rome. His own preference may have been to travel widely, and given the state of the Church and the nature of medieval society, it was impossible that the curtailment of the various abuses could be enforced without the actual physical presence of the pope where the problems were manifest. In any event, Leo was a peripatetic pope. He held many councils and synods during his reign, some in Rome but many others in Italy, France, Hungary, and the Holy Roman Empire. He preached particularly against simony and clerical incontinence, held up the canon law of the Church as the legal justification for the reforms, and, citing his authority as pope, demanded obedience. Accused and recalcitrant bishops and other church officials were summoned to Rome and in many cases were excommunicated and removed from office.

As a reformer, Leo was concerned with more than the spiritual state of the Church. As Bishop of Toul he had been involved in various diplomatic, political, and military affairs, and those interests continued when he became pope. Given the character of medieval society, the Church could not be merely an institution which dealt in spiritual and otherworldly matters; since at least the mid-eighth century, the Church had also been a temporal Italian state. At times the Papal States were under the influence and control of the Holy Roman emperor; Henry III intervened widely in Italian affairs. At other times the states of the Church had to rely upon their own resources—military, diplomatic, political, and economic—in order to survive and prosper in a violent age. It was perhaps unfortunate that the church had become a state, but it was a reality which Leo accepted.

The political and military threat to the temporal powers of the Church during Leo's reign occurred in southern Italy. Beginning before 1020, numerous bands from the duchy of Normandy in northern France had begun to loot and wage war in Sicily and southern Italy. The Normans were Christians, but much of the history of the medieval world was the story of Christians waging war on other Christians, often brutally. Leo and others complained about the ruthlessness of the Normans, but there were also political considerations. The

Church and the Holy Roman Empire had an interest in the region, as did the Byzantine Empire, which had had a toehold in southern Italy for many centuries. The Norman influx upset those established power relationships.

Henry III was at that time involved with his claims to Hungary and thus gave little support to his kinsman Leo. When, after many diplomatic exchanges, warnings, and broken promises, Leo decided to wage a holy war against the Normans, he lacked sufficient resources. He had his own vassals and the support of a number of Italian princes, but without the military might of the Holy Roman Empire, Leo's forces were no match for the Normans. Before Leo had hardly begun his campaign he was defeated in a bloody battle at Civitate, a village in central Italy, in 1053, and was forced to surrender. He was treated with honor and respect by the Normans, but if he was not broken in spirit, his physical capabilities had begun to wane. For the next several months he remained in Benevento, and he only returned to Rome in the spring of 1054.

At Benevento, Leo set into motion one of the most momentous and symbolic events of the Middle Ages. In fact if not in theory, the Christian world was not ruled by a single church. In the West, over many centuries, the bishops of Rome and the Papacy had emerged as the central focus of religious faith and practice. The Papacy had argued successfully that the popes were the apostolic successors to the first bishop of Rome, Peter, who himself had been given the keys to the heavenly kingdom by Jesus Christ. Added to this Petrine Theory, as it is known, was the Donation of Constantine, an eighth century forgery which purported to give the Papacy all of the Western lands after Constantine had abandoned them to found his city of Constantinople in the early fourth century. This document was only discovered to be a forgery in the fifteenth century, and in earlier times church officials such as Leo were sincerely convinced of its accuracy. Yet in Constantinople, in the Byzantine Empire, the Papacy's claims had never been totally accepted. Patriarchs of Constantinople, spiritual leaders of the largest city in Christendom and the wealthy and powerful Byzantine Empire, had often been reluctant to follow the lead of the Roman bishops. In the eyes of Eastern leaders, the West was more barbarous and less cultured than the East. Different historical experiences and cultural traditions, different religious practices, different languages—Greek in the East, Latin in the West—all combined to create friction and disagreements. Theologically, East and West quarreled over the issue of clerical celibacy and the so-called *Filioque* doctrine which had evolved in the West (possibly in the seventh century) and which described the Holy Spirit as coming not only from God the Father but also from Jesus Christ the Son. That was a change from the credal language agreed upon in 381, which had defined the Holy Spirit as coming only from God the Father. Through the centuries, then, Rome and Constantinople had coexisted only in an uneasy truce.

With the approval and guidance of Leo, an embassy was sent to Constantinople under the papal legate, Cardinal Humbert. Leo's temporal aim was to gain assistance from the Eastern emperor against the Normans; he also hoped, however, to attain the more far-reaching goal of uniting the Eastern and Western churches under papal leadership. Earlier popes and patriarchs had been unwilling to push their respective claims; thus, Leo's delegation, with its assertion of Western authority and supremacy and its criticism of Eastern abuses and heresies, was a new departure. It did not accomplish what Leo intended. His delegation did not receive the expected submission from the patriarch, Michael Cerularius; instead, Humbert excommunicated Michael in a dramatic confrontation. In turn, Leo's delegates were excommunicated by the Eastern church. The attempt to unite the two churches resulted instead in opening a gulf between the Roman church and the Eastern Orthodox church that has proved permanent.

Summary

Leo IX died on April 19, 1054, three months before the acts of excommunication took place in Constantinople. He had returned to Rome only a month earlier. Leo was buried in Rome; he was canonized in 1087. The reform program he had instituted as pope was continued by his successors, many of whom had been his advisers. Preeminent among them was Hildebrand, who, as Gregory VII, became pope in 1073.

The entire body of reform and the era itself would later bear Gregory's name; still, Gregory's conflict with Holy Roman Emperor Henry IV over lay investiture and his claim to papal supremacy in general were but the logical outcome of the seeds planted during the pontificate of Leo IX. Leo reigned as pope for only five years, but his reign was a watershed in the history of the Papacy, in the reform of the institutional Church, in the relations between the Church and the secular powers, and in the growth of the papal monarchy. Commentators then and since have criticized Leo for his military activities while pope and for creating the longlasting estrangement between the Roman and Orthodox churches, but his commitment to the moral and spiritual reform of the Church and the broader society cannot be in doubt.

Bibliography

Barraclough, Geoffrey. *The Origins of Modern Germany*. Oxford: Basil Blackwell, 1972. This study is the classic account of the rise of Germany from the era of Charlemagne. The author sees Leo as a key figure in resisting the claim of the Holy Roman emperors that they had been chosen by God to rule not only the state but also the church, a concept known as theocratic kingship or imperial theocracy.

Douglas, David C. *The Norman Achievement, 1050-1100*. Berkeley: University of California Press, 1969. Douglas, biographer of William the Conqueror, here describes the impact of the Normans throughout Europe, from Normandy and England to Sicily and Italy. His discussion of Leo and the Battle of Civitate particularly stresses Leo's call for a holy war or crusade against the Normans, a concept which would come to fruition in the Crusades to recapture the Holy Land from the Muslims.

Knowles, David, and Dimitri Obolensky. *The Middle Ages*. New York: McGraw-Hill Book Co., 1968. This work is the second volume in a five-volume history of the Catholic church. The authors single out Leo for considerable discussion and in the broader context of the history of the Church note that "for the first time for almost two centuries a pope of ability, energy and spirituality was in office."

Mann, Horace K. *The Lives of the Popes in the Middle Ages*. Vol. 6, *1049-1130*. 2d ed. London: Kegan Paul, Trench, Trübner and Co., 1925. Mann's account of Leo, which extends to almost two hundred pages, is one of the few extensive biographies in English of Leo's life and works. The treatment of Leo is extremely sympathetic. The volume includes, in translation, almost all the medieval sources regarding the pope and thus is indispensable.

Runciman, Steven. *The Eastern Schism*. New York: Oxford University Press, 1955. This study is a well-written narrative of the conflict between the Papacy and the Eastern Orthodox church during the eleventh and twelfth centuries. Runciman states that many persons and events bear responsibility for the Schism of 1054, but particularly singles out Cardinal Humbert for exacerbating an already difficult situation.

Southern, R. W. *Western Society and the Church in the Middle Ages*. Grand Rapids, Mich.: Wm. B. Eerdmans Publishing Co., 1970. This volume in the Pelican History of the Church is a succinct but comprehensive history of the Church during medieval times. It briefly but adequately puts Leo and such issues as the dispute with Constantinople into the historical and scholarly context.

Ullmann, Walter. *The Growth of Papal Government in the Middle Ages*. 3d ed. London: Methuen and Co., 1970. The author, who has written numerous books on the medieval Church, discusses the significance of Leo in the emergence of the Papacy as a rival to the Holy Roman Empire, and notes particularly the importance of the Donation of Constantine for Leo in his dispute with the Patriarch of Constantinople.

Williams, Schafer, ed. *The Gregorian Epoch: Reformation, Revolution, Reaction?* Boston: D. C. Heath and Co., 1964. This is a volume in the Problems in European Civilization series and includes fourteen different selections by historians from the mid-nineteenth century to the 1960's. As the title suggests, the articles concentrate on the reforms associated with Gregory VII, but many of the issues discussed relate to the years of Leo's pontificate.

Eugene S. Larson

LEONARDO OF PISA
Leonardo Fibonacci

Born: c. 1170; Pisa, Italy
Died: c. 1240; Pisa, Italy
Area of Achievement: Mathematics
Contribution: Leonardo provided Western Europe with the earliest and most heralded Latin account of the Hindu-Arabic number system and its computational methods. He helped to render Roman numerals and the abacus obsolete, contributed substantially to the acceptance of the Arabic algebraic system, and created a revolutionary mathematical technique known as the "Fibonacci sequence."

Early Life

Leonardo of Pisa, also called Leonardo Pisano or, more correctly, Leonardo Fibonacci, the surname meaning "son of Bonaccio," was born at Pisa around 1170 and probably died there circa 1240. Although very little is known about his life beyond the few facts gleaned from his mathematical writings, his father, Guglielmo, was a successful merchant who was the chief magistrate of the community of Pisan merchants in the North African port of Bugia (now Bejaïa, Algeria). As a young boy, he joined his father there and began the study of mathematics in this culturally diversified environment.

Desiring his son to be a successful merchant or commercial agent, Guglielmo sent Leonardo to study with a Muslim master who introduced him to the intricacies of Arabic mathematics, especially al-Khwarizmi's *Kitab al-jabr wa al-muqabalah* (c. A.D. 820; *Algebra*) and the practical value of the Hindu-Arabic numeral system represented by the nine Indian figures (1, 11, 111, 4, 5, 6, 7, 8, 9), the fourth through the ninth symbols representing the first letters of the Hindu names for these integers. As he grew older, he traveled around the Mediterranean area, especially Egypt, Syria, Greece, Sicily, and Provence; visited the dominant commercial centers; acquired knowledge of the arithmetical systems used by hundreds of merchants; and mastered the theoretical subtleties of Greek and Arabic mathematics, chiefly those of Plato of Tivoli, Savasorda, Euclid, Archimedes, Hero of Alexandria, and Diophantus. He even resided for a time at the court of Frederick II, the Holy Roman Emperor, where he engaged in scientific speculations with Frederick and his court philosophers, the most notable being Michael Scot, to whom Leonardo dedicated one of his works.

In his later years, Leonardo probably served Pisa administratively as an examiner of municipal accounts. This commercial expertise, however, was always secondary to his lifelong passion for mathematics.

Life's Work

The rapid improvements that marked the history of Western mathematics in the thirteenth century, particularly in the fields of arithmetic and algebra, were largely a result of the genius of Leonardo, although a second mathematician of originality, Jordanus Nemorarius, made significant contributions, especially to the theory of numbers and to mechanics. Yet Jordanus showed no trace of Arabic influence. Developing the Greco-Roman arithmetical tradition of Nicomachus and Boethius, he habitually used letters for generalizing proofs in arithmetical problems, an awkward method which Leonardo could avoid because of his employment of Arabic numbers.

Leonardo's pioneering achievements in mathematics began in 1202, when he wrote his first work, *Liber abaci* (the book of the abacus). Even though the title is a misnomer, since he eschewed Roman numerals and the methods of the abacus, the work became the earliest in the West to extol the superiority of the nine-numeral Arabic system of numbers when used in conjunction with the zero. When the *Liber abaci* first appeared, Arabic numerals were known to only a few European philosophers through the Latin translations of al-Khwarizmi's ninth century treatise. Leonardo understood fully the advantages of this system for mathematical operations. He displayed the system brilliantly in this edition and in a second, revised edition of 1228 dedicated to Michael Scot, the emperor's chief scholar, and provided more rigorous demonstrations than in any previous or contemporary work. Leonardo realized that the great merit of this system was that it contained the symbol for zero and that any number could be represented simply by arranging digits in order, the value of a digit being shown by its distance from zero or from the first digit on the left.

Predominantly theoretical in nature, the *Liber abaci* was also valuable for its commercial arithmetic, which covered such operations as profit margins, barter, money changing, conversions of weights and measures, partnerships, and interest. After his death, Italian merchants generally adopted Leonardo's Arabic system of numeration, and his book remained the standard in Europe for more than two centuries.

Besides popularizing a new system of numerals throughout the West, the *Liber abaci* was revolutionary for two reasons. First, it introduced Arabic algebra to European civilization. Leonardo's algebra was rhetorical, but it was unique because of its employment of geometrical methods in its descriptions. He dealt primarily with the extraction of square and cube roots, progressions, indeterminate analysis (an equation with two or more unknowns for which the solution must be in rational numbers, whole numbers or common fractions), false assumptions (when a problem is worked out by incorrect data, then corrected by proportion), the rules of three and five (methods of finding proportions), the solution of equations of the third degree, and other algebraic and geometrical operations.

Of even greater importance was Leonardo's famous sequence of numbers known before the nineteenth century as the "Series of Lamé" but now called correctly the "Fibonacci sequence." In answer to the problem of how many pairs of rabbits could be produced from a single pair if each pair produced a new pair each month and every new pair became productive from the second month onward (supposing that no pair died), he devised the recurrent, or recursive, series of 1, 1, 2, 3, 5, 8, 13, 21, 34, 55, 89, 144, 233, and so on. In this number sequence, in which the relation between two or more successive terms can be expressed by a formula, each term is equal to the sum of the two preceding ones. In the nineteenth century, the series proved of immense value in the study of divisibility, prime numbers, and Mersenne numbers. In the modern world, the Fibonacci sequence is used in botany for determining the patterns of natural growth.

In addition to the *Liber abaci*, Leonardo wrote three other significant works. In 1220, his *Practica geometriae* (practice of geometry) presented theorems based principally on two of Euclid's works. It applied algebra to the solution of geometrical problems, a radically innovative technique for thirteenth century Europe. In 1225, two smaller works appeared, the *Flos* (prime) and the *Liber quadratorum* (book of square numbers). More original than the *Liber abaci*, they were devoted to questions involving quadratic and cubic equations, in addition to several refinements to his earlier algebraic discourses. The *Liber quadratorum* may be considered Leonardo's masterpiece. Although the *Liber abaci* made his reputation, the *Liber quadratorum* made him the most important contributor to number theory until Pierre de Fermat, the celebrated seventeenth century French mathematician, who was instrumental in early experimentation aimed at determining the exact length of a quadrant of Earth's meridian, the scientific basis of the metric system of weights and measures.

Summary

The impact of Leonardo of Pisa on future generations was enormous. His pioneering achievements helped spread Arabic numeration and Arabic algebra throughout the West. Popular diffusion followed in the form of almanacs, calendars, and literary and poetic productions. Merchants accepted his new system—the Italians first and other Europeans by the end of the sixteenth century. Even as early as the second half of the thirteenth century, lectures in the universities incorporated the new numbering system. His use of geometry in algebraic problems and, conversely, his use of algebra in solving geometric problems, ushered in a new era in these disciplines. In time, the Fibonacci sequence revolutionized many divergent scientific fields. Last, aside from their scientific merit, his works were of tremendous cultural influence, particularly as they relate to metrology and to the major economic conditions of his time. In short, Leonardo of Pisa was the greatest Christian mathematician of the Middle Ages. The mathematical renaissance in the West dates from him.

Bibliography

Crombie, A. C. *Augustine to Galileo: The History of Science*, A.D. *400-1650*. Cambridge, Mass.: Harvard University Press, 1953. Includes much discussion of Leonardo's influence on mathematics and number theory prior to the scientific revolution.

_____. *Medieval and Early Modern Science*. 2 vols. Garden City, N.Y.: Doubleday and Co., 1959. Excellent descriptive bibliographies in both volumes, with coverage of Leonardo's precursors, his impact on popularizing Arabic numerals, and his contributions to later medieval mathematics.

Gies, Joseph, and Frances Gies. *Leonard of Pisa and the New Mathematics of the Middle Ages*. Gainesville, Ga.: New Classics Library, 1969. Contains a summary of Leonardo's life, a general survey of his works, and a brief overview of the history of numerical notation.

Hardy, G. H., and E. M. Wright. *An Introduction to the Theory of Numbers*. 4th ed. Oxford: Oxford University Press, 1960. This volume provides a detailed account of the Fibonacci numbers and sequences and is meant for the mathematician or serious student of science.

Haskins, Charles Homer. *Studies in the History of Medieval Science*. Cambridge, Mass.: Harvard University Press, 1927. Extensive coverage of the influences on Leonardo's thought, his contemporary scientific environment, and the philosophers at the court of Frederick II.

Kibre, Pearl. *Studies in Medieval Science: Alchemy, Astrology, Mathematics, and Medicine*. London: Hambledon Press, 1984. Leonardo's standing in the quadrivium (arithmetic, geometry, astronomy, and music) of later thirteenth century universities appears in the first of these republished articles.

Sarton, George. *Introduction to the History of Science: From Rabbi Ben Ezra to Roger Bacon*. Vol. 2. Baltimore: Williams and Wilkins, 1931. A separate section in chapter 33 is devoted to the life and work of Leonardo.

Sedgwick, W. T., and H. W. Tyler. *A Short History of Science*. Rev. ed. New York: Macmillan, 1939. Includes a discussion of Leonardo's books and his famous numerical series.

Ronald Edward Zupko

LI CH'ING-CHAO

Born: 1084; Chinan, Shantung Province, China
Died: c. 1155; Hangchow, Chekiang Province, China
Area of Achievement: Literature
Contribution: The greatest woman lyricist in the history of classical Chinese
   literature, Li made use of everyday language to explore the subtleties of
   human emotions, bringing the art of Chinese lyricism close to perfection.
   Her simple yet elegant style shaped the poetic expressions of the Southern
   Sung Dynasty and inspired many lyricists—even into the modern age.

Early Life

Li Ch'ing-chao was born the oldest child of a family that was very fond of
literature. Her father, Li Ke-fei, was a renowned essayist; her mother, who
came from a politically distinguished family, was also known for having literary talent. From 1086 to 1093, her father assumed a teaching position at
the Imperial Academy in the capital, K'ai-feng, and engaged himself in
composing literary works while fulfilling his scholarly obligations. This position provided him with ample opportunity to work at home. During those
seven years, Li learned from her parents much about classical Chinese literature as well as the art of literary composition. Except for a short interrup-
tion in 1094, when her father was assigned to a provincial position, Li's education at home continued well into her mid-teens.

The earliest extant works by Li, two poems of the same title, "Wu-hsi
chung-hsing sung shi" ("On Paean to Revival, Inscribed on the Cliff of Wu-
hsi"), were composed at the age of sixteen. These two poems were written in
order that they might rhyme with a poem of the same title by Chang Lei, a
famous poet in the Sung Dynasty. Taking exception to Chang Lei's traditional stance, which celebrates the restoration of the central government during the reign of Emperor Su Tzung in the T'ang Dynasty, Li was critical of
those writers who forgot and overlooked the corruption and rebellion which
preceded this restoration. The fact that Li was able to compose a poem that
rhymed with the work of such a renowned poet at a time when women were
discouraged from participating in men's social gatherings—occasions which
formed the basis of such poems—indicates the degree of recognition accorded her by her contemporaries. The efflorescence of her creativity, however, did not begin until after her marriage, which occurred in 1101.

Life's Work

Li Ch'ing-chao's marriage to Chao Ming-ch'eng inspired her to compose
many lyrics of enduring fame in the history of Chinese literature. The third
son of Chao T'ing-chih, a censor who later became the premier during the
reign of Emperor Hui Tsung, Chao Ming-ch'eng was studying at the Imperial

Academy at the time of his marriage to Li. Although arranged by their parents, as was the custom in China, the marriage proved to be a happy one for Li. She began to compose lyrics celebrating the joy of their union. As exhibited in the works at this stage—for example, "Chien-tzu mu-lan-hua" ("The Magnolia Flower") and "Yü chia ao" ("Tune: A Fisherman's Honor")—Li in her married life was a charming yet somewhat coquettish woman who was well aware of her own beauty. She not only often compared herself to a flower but also intended to rival the beauty of a flower—all to attract her husband's attention. Because of his studies at the Imperial Academy, her husband could return home only on the first and fifteenth days of each month. Consequently, her works of this time also contain melancholy expressions, lamenting her husband's absence. In such lyrics as "Hsiao-ch'ung-shan" ("Tune: Manifold Little Hills") and "Tsui hua-yin" ("Tipsy in the Flowers' Shade"), Li often refers to late spring and expresses sadness that her husband is unable to share the splendid season with her. Generally, the beautiful natural scenery described in her poetry becomes an emblem of her own beauty, which awaits appreciation.

In the second year of her marriage, a power struggle broke out at the imperial court, an event which greatly affected Li's life. Disliked by the new emperor, her father was expelled from his position as Vice Minister of Rituals and was assigned to a provincial position. In an attempt to rescue her father, Li wrote a poem of petition to her father-in-law, Chao T'ing-chih. The poem moved many people but apparently did not save her father, who served the term of five years in confinement. While Li's father fell into disfavor with the emperor, her father-in-law rose to power and soon became the vice premier. During the redistribution of political power, her father-in-law was engaged in a struggle for political domination with the premier, Ts'ai Ching, the notorious leader of the New Party. When Chao finally became the premier, Li wrote and dedicated a poem to him, calling his attention to the inherent danger of becoming an overtly powerful figure. In the midst of this political upheaval, Chao Ming-ch'eng entered public service. His official career, however, ended abruptly four years later upon the death of his father. As Li expected, after Chao T'ing-chih's death in 1107, the reinstated Ts'ai seized the opportunity to vent his anger on Chao's family.

To avoid persecution, Li Ch'ing-chao and her husband moved back to his hometown in the countryside, Ch'ing-chou, and remained there for ten years. Living in a state of seclusion, Li greatly enjoyed her life with her husband. During these years, she helped her husband with the composition of *Chin shih lu* (a record of bronze and stone vessels), a valuable reference book on Chinese antiquities. Her poetic career continued in the meantime. Since her life at this time was pleasant and peaceful, many of her works were aesthetic studies on the beauty of various flowers—cassia, chrysanthemums, lilacs, and plum blossoms. Lacking depth of human emotion or symbolic significance, these poems, such as "T'an-p'o wan hsi-sha" ("Cassia Flowers, to a New Version of the Silk Washing Brook") and "Che-ku t'ien" ("Partridge Sky"), are essentially impressionistic sketches with limited aesthetic merit.

A great change, however, occurred when Li was in her forties—a change that enabled her to perfect her art of lyricism. In 1126, several years after her husband resumed his official career, nomads from the northeast of China invaded the capital and captured Emperors Hui Tsung and Ch'in Tsung. As a result of this invasion, her husband assumed a new position in the south the following year. Having to prepare to move their belongings, Li stayed behind and did not join him until the next year. Four months or so after she left Ch'ing-chou to join her husband, their house, along with many rich collections, was burned to the ground by a rebellious troop. A year after she joined her husband in the south, her husband was again transferred and compelled to go to his prefecture, Chien-k'ang, by himself. In August of 1129, three months after he became the prefect of Chien-k'ang, Chao died. The ceaseless warring and the constant separation from and eventual death of her husband made Li particularly aware of the transience of this world. Rather than celebrating the beauty of flowers and the joy of springtime, she expressed the sorrows of separation, loneliness, and death. Because of the depth of feeling, the elegance of language, and the great musicality of her lyrics, many of her works—"Wu-ling ch'un" ("Spring at Wu-ling"), "Sheng sheng man" ("A Sad Song to a Slow Tune"), and "Ku yen er" ("On Plum Blossoms, to the Tune of a Little Wild Goose") among them—circulated widely among her contemporaries and became most popular during her time.

The latter half of 1129 witnessed not only the death of her husband but also another invasion of the nomads. To flee from the enemy, Li followed the central government, wandering from one place to another. Because of her suffering during the war as well as her need for a companion, she married again in 1132. The second marriage, lasting only about three months, ended in disaster. During the following two decades, Li led a relatively quiet life, occasionally contributing verses to the royal family when they celebrated various festivals. Like many of her contemporaries, she became a Buddhist after much suffering. As a result of her belief, her works at the last stage of her life no longer exhibited bitter grief but rather took the form of serene reminiscences of her past life. The theme of transience often manifests itself in her contemplations of the past and present. As indicated by the titles of some of her last works, "Joy of Tranquillity" and "Forever Encountering Mirth," Li accepted the end of her life with serenity.

Summary

In the long, splendid history of Chinese poetry—an area traditionally dominated by men—only Li Ch'ing-chao distinguished herself as a woman of great achievement. Shortly after their appearance, her lyrics became the representative voice of the Chinese woman confined to her house for most of her life. Many poets before Li had attempted to represent a woman's psyche in their poetry, but none was her equal in capturing the nuances of a woman's inner life. Her portrayal of a woman's joy and sorrow is equally applicable to the experience of men to the extent that it often comes to represent the joys and sorrows inherent in the human condition. Li's works not only were popular among the common people but also were greatly admired by the literati. Ever since the appearance of the first anthology of poetry, *Shih Ching* (c. 600 B.C.; *Book of Songs*), many poets who were also officials had assumed the mask of a woman to express their feelings toward their sovereigns. They regarded their relationship to their sovereigns as that of a wife to her husband. In this respect, Li's lyrical voice agreed with the sensibility of the officials, who often experienced sorrow, though of a different kind, in their relationship to their lords. Consequently, men and women, both educated and uneducated, found solace in Li's work.

In the history of Chinese poetry, Li's achievements lie not so much in the nature of her themes—love, loneliness, separation, and death—as in the manner in which she treats her subjects. Her masterly use of colloquial language, the creation of striking imagery, and the subtle structure of her lyrics place her firmly in a position of enduring literary significance. Because of the popularity of her works, her lyrical style became the model for many later poets and significantly influenced the development of Chinese lyricism, especially those lyrics composed during the time of the Southern Sung Dynasty. Apart from being a renowned poet, Li was an accomplished scholar. Completed by her years after her husband's death, *Chin shih lu* exhibits Li's talent for outstanding scholarship. This highly admired work considerably enhanced other scholars' understanding of the development of ancient Chinese culture.

Bibliography

Ch'en, Shou-yi. *Chinese Literature: A Historical Introduction*. New York: Ronald Press Co., 1961. This book is a historical study of Chinese literature from the Shang Dynasty to the beginning of the twentieth century. Its emphasis is on the historical background of various writers rather than literary criticism. The book devotes two chapters to the development of lyrical poetry in the Sung Dynasty as well as several pages to Li. The cultural milieu of her time is clearly presented.

Hsu, Kai-yu. "The Poems of Li Ch'ing-chao." *PMLA* 74 (1962): 521-528. The author uses a biographical approach in his study of Li's poems. After describing Li's life and work, he makes an assessment of her poetic achievements. Her use of colloquial expressions as a means of enriching the style of poetry in twelfth century China is emphasized.

Hu, P'ing-ch'ing. *Li Ch'ing-chao*. New York: Twayne Publishers, 1966. The only critical study in English on Li Ch'ing-chao, this book treats both her life and her works in great detail. Most of her famous poems are translated in a lucid, though sometimes prosaic, style. Despite a few blemishes in the author's interpretations of Li's works, the book provides one with a clear sense of her achievements. A selected bibliography appears at the end.

Liu, Wu-chi. *An Introduction to Chinese Literature*. Bloomington: Indiana University Press, 1966. One of the few introductions to Chinese literature that successfully blends a historical approach with literary criticism. One chapter is devoted to the study of lyrical poetry in general. The significance of Li's lyrics is discussed in the context of the historical development of lyrical poetry. An annotated bibliography is provided.

Yang, Vincent. "Vision of Reconciliation: A Textual Reading of Some Lines of Li Qing-zhao." *Journal of the Chinese Language Teachers Association* 19 (1984): 10-32. This essay is a close reading of four representative poems by Li Ch'ing-chao. Focusing on the imagery and structure of the poems, the author attempts to show Li's art of lyricism. At the end, the particular nature of her imagination is illustrated through her use of poetic techniques. The analysis is an application of Western literary criticism to Chinese poetry.

Vincent Yang

LI PO

Born: 701; Sinkiang Uighur
Died: 762; Tan Tu, Anhwei Province, China
Area of Achievement: Literature
Contribution: Li's clever, sensuous, and mystical verse has led many to consider him China's foremost lyric poet.

Early Life

According to tradition, Li Po's ancestors had been exiled to the remote area of northwestern China now known as the Xinjiang Uygur Autonomous Region early in the seventh century. When he was about five, his father, a small businessman whose income was supplemented by his wife's work as a washerwoman, successfully petitioned the authorities for permission to move his family to the city of Chang Ming in Szechwan Province, a more civilized, if still decidedly provincial, community.

In the course of their exile, Li Po's ancestors had intermarried with the Mongolian peoples of the northwest frontier, as a result of which he was taller and sturdier than the average Chinese, and his wide mouth and bulging eyes were also commented upon in several contemporary descriptions. Li Po's unusual background was reflected in his schooling, for he concentrated on the study of esoteric religious and literary works rather than the prescribed Confucian Classics, although he certainly read and was familiar with the latter. He became deeply interested in Taoism, a more mystical and romantic philosophy than the thoroughly practical Confucianism that dominated Chinese society of the time, and received a diploma from the Taoist master Kao Tien-Shih in recognition of these studies. In 720, his exceptional scholastic abilities were recognized by the governor of his province, who predicted that he would become a famous poet.

After a turbulent adolescence, during which he fell in with a group of roughnecks devoted to sword-fighting, Li Po became interested in more contemplative pursuits. Between the ages of twenty and twenty-four, he lived as a recluse with a fellow student of Taoism in a remote part of Szechwan Province, there acquiring even more of a reputation for wisdom and literary ability. Now emotionally as well as intellectually mature, he resolved to broaden his horizons by seeing what the world outside his native province had to offer.

Life's Work

Li Po began his travels by exploring those areas of China through which the Yangtze River passed. In the central province of Hubei, he met and married Hsu Hsin-shih, the granddaughter of a retired prime minister, in 727. Although they had several children and Hsu Hsin-shih seems to have been a model wife, Li's wanderlust was evidently untamed. He continued to ramble about the country, sometimes with his wife and sometimes not, visiting other poets and scholars and becoming something of a legend among his fellow intellectuals. In 735, while traveling in the northern province of Shansi, he saved the life of the soldier Kuo Tzu-i, who would later be pleased to return the favor when he rose to high political rank. A short time after this, Li Po is mentioned in accounts of a celebrated group of hard-drinking men of letters, the "Six Idlers of the Bamboo Brook," who resided in the northeastern province of Shantung.

While engaged in his travels across the length and breadth of China, Li had begun to write the deceptively simple lyrics that posterity would consider among the finest achievements in Chinese verse. The majority of his work cannot be accurately dated, but since both his life-style and his literary accomplishments remained relatively constant throughout his career, determining dates is not as important as it might be for a less precocious writer.

His early interest in Taoism was one of the most significant influences upon his poetry, one that has sometimes been insufficiently appreciated by Western commentators. Lao-tzu and Chuang-tzu, respectively the founder and the chief apostle of this philosophy, emphasized the necessity of living in harmony with the Tao, or Way, giving up the trivial concerns of conventional social life and cultivating the virtues of simplicity and directness. Withdrawal from the world was encouraged, and at their most extreme Li's verses take an almost sinful pride in their creator's capacity for achieving the heights of heavenly bliss:

> You ask what my soul does away in the sky,
> I inwardly smile but cannot reply;
> Like the peach-blossom carried away by the stream,
> I soar to a world of which you cannot dream.

As the poet grew older, however, these early expressions of mystical communion with inexpressible realities gave way to more down-to-earth recipes for pleasuring the soul. Just as twentieth century readers buy self-help books far more frequently than the classic works of religion and philosophy, so did the people of Li Po's day seek practical formulas for attaining peace of mind. Thus, when Taoist recluses discovered that the drinking of wine offered a close approximation of the mental states reached through serious meditation, alcohol soon became a respectable as well as popular means of attuning the senses to the subtle harmony of nature's underlying unities.

It was as a singer of the praises of wine that Li first impressed his fellow countrymen, and even centuries later he is a kind of unofficial patron saint of serious drinkers. Unlike those who drink to forget, however, Li and the recluses, musicians, poets, and vagabonds among whom he spent much of his life drank to heighten their appreciation of beauty and to loosen their tongues in the description of it. One of his most famous poems, a celebration of wine, asserts that "in life, when you are happy, you must drink your joy to the last drop." It is in this context of the celebration of good fortune, rather than the drowning of sorrows, that his advocacy of intoxication should be understood.

This kind of joyful imbibing often figures in the various versions of how Li Po came to meet the reigning emperor, Hsuan Tsung, and although the exact circumstances remain a matter of conjecture, it is known that by 742 he had become a favorite of this Taoist-oriented ruler. It is claimed that the emperor was once so taken with a poem praising the accomplishments of his government that he broke tradition by serving Li food with his own hands. On another occasion, the poet impressed him by dashing off a piece when obviously very drunk. The most famous poem he wrote at court, "Ching ping tiao" ("A Song of Pure Happiness"), was inspired by the emperor's beautiful concubine Yang Kwei-fei:

> Her robe is a cloud, her face a flower;
> Her balcony, glimmering with the bright spring dew,
> Is either the tip of earth's Jade Mountain
> Or a moon-edged roof of paradise.

Li seems, however, to have offended either a powerful member of the court or perhaps even the emperor himself; in 744, ordered to leave the capital, he resumed his earlier pattern of wandering about the kingdom. Shortly thereafter, he met the younger poet Tu Fu, and for a period of two or three years they traveled together, studying at remote Taoist monasteries and exchanging ideas about poetry. Tu Fu seems to have functioned as a calming influence upon his friend; he encouraged Li to write down his verses rather than simply declaim them to an admiring circle of drinking companions. Since the two were almost polar opposites in terms of poetry as well as personality, the friendship between them came to be held up as a symbol of how artistic ideals can transcend individual differences.

After parting from Tu, Li continued on his roaming life, spending most of his time in the southern and western provinces of Kiangsi and Kiangsu. In 756, he unthinkingly accepted an invitation to the court of a prince who was using the opportunity afforded by the rebellion of the Tartar general An Lushan to assert his own dynastic claims. When this prince's armies were defeated in 757, Li was imprisoned; he gained release only after his old friend Kuo Tzu-i, now the new emperor's minister of war, interceded on his behalf.

This experience was, in a way, a practical demonstration of the dangers of ignoring Taoist precepts about withdrawing from the world, and during the five years of life that remained to him, Li avoided any intrigues of this sort.

He also seems to have been reconciled with his wife and children, with whom he settled in the town of Tan Tu in the eastern province of Anhwei. There they lived a contented and—because Li was still in some political disgrace— quiet life, and when he died in 762 even old friends such as Tu Fu did not hear the news until several years later. His death, according to legend, was an appropriate one for a lover of wine: Drunk in his boat on a beautiful evening, he leaned far over the side to admire his reflection in the water, fell overboard, and drowned. In a culture where the manner of death was just as important as behavior in life, Li Po's passing ensured that he would achieve immortality as both legend and literary genius.

Summary

Li Po's poetry has been highly valued for its consummate grace and original choice of words. He wrote during a period when one of China's most revered dynasties, the T'ang, was at the apex of its power and prestige, and his verses seemed to catch the spirit of a self-confident and somewhat hedonistic age. He had, after all, been an intimate of the emperor himself, a fact which continued to fascinate succeeding generations as they preserved the many stories of the poet's brash behavior to his sovereign.

If Li Po was a sworn enemy of the mindless conformity to sterile traditions that is always a danger in highly stratified societies, he was so in a manner more like that of Henry Miller than of George Gordon, Lord Byron: It was the pursuit of pleasure, not some quixotic and suicidal act of rebellion, that marked both his life and his work. In verses that were the literary equivalent of Taoism's injunctions to accept the universe rather than strive to change it, he sang the delights of wine, women, and song in spontaneous language that appealed to nobles and ne'er-do-wells alike.

Li Po is one of the great romantic figures of Chinese literature, a poet whose adventurous and idiosyncratic life seems perfectly encapsulated in his direct and unhackneyed verses. The facility with which he wrote of mundane pleasures, gently grieved over their transience, and explored the possibilities of mystical communion with transcendent reality is just as attractive today as it was during his own time. Few readers of Chinese literature have remained immune to his charm.

Bibliography

Cooper, Arthur, comp. and trans. *Li Po and Tu Fu: Poems Selected and Translated with an Introduction and Notes.* Harmondsworth, England: Penguin Books, 1973. This is the most extensive edition of Li Po's work available in English. The translations are generally excellent, and the extensive background material on the history of Chinese poetry and literature is helpful, though marred by too many irrelevant asides. Li's connection with Tu Fu is usefully discussed.

Pulleyblank, E. G. *The Background of the Rebellion of An Lu-shan*. London: Oxford University Press, 1955. A sound historical treatment of the T'ang Dynasty's major political upheaval, with which Li Po was intimately involved. Both the specific events of the rebellion and the period's wider societal context are thoroughly covered in dry but efficient fashion.

Schafer, Edward H. *The Divine Woman: Dragon Ladies and Rain Maidens in T'ang Literature*. Berkeley: University of California Press, 1973. For those with some knowledge of T'ang poetry, Schafer's wide-ranging discussion of the era's myths and cults of goddesses will be a fertile source of suggestive connections between poetry and culture. Even those new to the field should benefit from the vivid sense of period conveyed by this extremely well-written book, which takes a broader approach to its subject than its title indicates.

_____ . *The Golden Peaches of Samarkand: A Study of T'ang Exotics*. Berkeley: University of California Press, 1963. Almost every aspect of T'ang life is dealt with in this brilliant survey, which is especially interesting in its discussion of relations with foreign states. Crammed with information, informed by great learning, and highly readable, the book is strongly recommended to anyone curious about the culture in which Li lived.

Waley, Arthur. *The Poetry and Career of Li Po*. London: Allen and Unwin, 1950. A still-useful introduction, although Waley's obsession with what he considers the immoral aspects of Li's character sometimes prejudices his judgment of the poetry. Includes many translations, which are sound if much less graceful than Cooper's.

Yip, Wai-lim, ed. and trans. *Chinese Poetry: Major Modes and Genres*. Berkeley: University of California Press, 1976. A fairly technical but nevertheless accessible study of Chinese poetic language. Includes the Chinese texts and literal translations of several of Li's poems and gives a very clear idea of the difficulties involved in rendering them into English.

Paul Stuewe

LIVY

Born: c. 59 B.C.; Patavium (modern Padua), Italy
Died: c. A.D. 17; probably Patavium, Italy
Area of Achievement: Historiography
Contribution: Livy preserved many of the early legendary traditions and mythology dealing with the earliest phase of ancient Roman history. Since many of the authors and sources he used have long been lost, his work assumes a greater importance.

Early Life

Titus Livius (Livy), according to the theologian Jerome, was born in 59, in Patavium, northern Italy. Livy makes only a few brief references to his homeland, but they indicate a patriotic pride. Unfortunately, nothing certain is known regarding his youth, but the general assumption is that he was schooled in his native town. This assumption is based on a comment made by Asinius Pollio that Livy's style was provincial. This criticism, however, is largely negated by the excellent Ciceronian style of most of Livy's historical writings.

Livy's early education must have included philosophical studies, since his writings contain many allusions and direct references to traditional Stoic values. Also, his frequent comments about religion show that he was familiar with the traditions and rituals of the Roman cults.

Livy probably did not begin writing his history of Rome until he was about thirty years old. Presumably, he had had adequate time in the previous years to read and research in preparation. By the age of thirty, he had probably moved to Rome, but regarding this there is no sure evidence. By the year 5 B.C., Livy was definitely in Rome, since at this time he was criticized by Augustus Caesar for being a "Pompeian," a person who was biased in favor of the aristocratic, senatorial views. Augustus seems not to have meant this remark too seriously, for there is ample evidence to suggest that the emperor counted Livy as a friend and took an interest in his work. Indeed, it is known that about A.D. 8 Livy helped the future emperor Claudius in his own historical studies.

Life's Work

Livy's great history was written in Latin and is generally known as *Ab urbe condita* (c. 26 B.C.-A.D. 15; *The History of Rome*) literally meaning "from the founding of the city (of Rome)." The work was exceptionally long, containing 142 books (scrolls); this length has been estimated to be equivalent to twenty-four or twenty-five crown-octavo volumes of three hundred pages each.

Probably as a result of the extreme length of the original work, abridgments and summaries were made in antiquity. Most of these have survived, but much of the original work has been lost. Only thirty-five of the 142 books have survived the ravages of time, including books 1-10 and 31-45. These surviving books deal chronologically with events between the years 753 and 243 B.C. and between 219 and 167 B.C. From the surviving summaries and fragments, it is clear that the work included information about Rome from its traditional foundation date in 753 through 9 B.C. The last twenty-two books were probably not published until after the death of Augustus Caesar in A.D. 14. The surmised reason for this is that Livy was fearful of publishing information about contemporaneous people and events.

Most scholars who have studied Livy's work in detail have noted certain distinctive features of his great history: intensely personal psychological portraits of major military and political figures, speeches of uncertain origin interwoven with the chronological narrative to reflect certain political or religious perspectives of ancient Romans, lengthy discourses on cultic religion, including references to miracles and prodigies, frequent references to the virtuous morals and ethics of the early Romans in contrast to the degeneration of morals in the more recent age, a clear sympathy with Stoic views on the providential determination of history, and a patriotic bias in favor of aristocratic, republican conservatism.

Of these features, greater scholarly attention has been devoted to two aspects: Livy's use of speeches and his emphasis on religion and morals. With regard to Livy's use of speeches, it should be noted that he was not alone among ancient historians in the use of oratorical devices. The Greek historian Thucydides, like most other ancient historians, made the most of rhetoric in his accounts. In each case, the scholar must ask whether the speeches reflect the beliefs and attitudes of the author or of the one being quoted. Unfortunately, the question cannot be resolved with certainty. Most scholars have concluded that the speeches are not verbatim (though shorthand methods of taking dictation were known), but that they represent the historian's artful summary of what he assumed must have been said on the occasion. In the particular case of Livy's history, there is evidence that Cicero was used consciously with regard to style. There are 407 major speeches in Livy's extant volumes, and if indirect speeches and minor exhortations are included, the number rises to more than two thousand. These statistics, obviously, are only from the surviving books of Livy.

One of the most lengthy of his speeches deals with Livy's other chief preoccupation, religion. Marcus Furius Camillus, who has been called the second founder of Rome, was the man who prevented the Romans from abandoning the site of Rome, which had been badly damaged by warfare with the Gauls. Though the Romans had finally defeated the Gauls, many citizens of Rome wanted to migrate to the city of Veii, which had earlier been taken from the Etruscans. Camillus convinced them, however, that such a move would be a sin, a sacrilege, according to Livy's report. Most scholars believe that references to ancient religious beliefs, whether occurring in an alleged speech or in the narrative, reflect traditional views of the time more than Livy's personal beliefs. Regardless of scholarly controversy, however, Livy's history is so full of references to religion, morals, and ethical concerns that it seems difficult to believe that he simply repeated them to fill space. Instead, he probably did believe that his age had degenerated from earlier, more austere times. Examples of dramatic concern for morality include the stories of the rape of Lucretia, the execution of the vestal virgin Minucia, the debauchery of Hannibal's army at Capua, and the introduction of the worship of the Greek god of wine, Dionysus-Bacchus.

The frequent references to religion and morals in Livy have led many scholars to conclude that he had Stoic sympathies or perhaps was actually a Stoic. Evidence for this conclusion is Livy's frequent use of such terms as *fatum* (fate), *fortuna* (chance), *felicitas* (good fortune), *virtus* (virtue, bravery), *fors* (luck), and *causa* (cause), which may indicate some sympathy with the Stoic concept of the universe.

Having enjoyed years of productive work in Rome, Livy retired to his hometown, Patavium, sometime near the end of his life; an Augustan tomb inscription discovered in the modern city of Padua honors the memory of a Titus Livius. Some scholars believe that he died as early as A.D. 12, although Saint Jerome records his death as occurring in 17.

Summary

The popularity of Livy in ancient times cannot be denied. He is also customarily covered in modern scholarly accounts of great ancient historians of Greece and Rome. The fact that he did have religious and political biases does not negate the fact that he did occasionally record his sources of information and make comments about their reliability. The ancient historian Valerius Antias is mentioned by name thirty-six times, Claudius Quadrigarius twelve times, Coelius Antipater eleven, Licinius Macer seven; Calpurnius Piso, Polybius, and Fabius Pictor are mentioned six times. In most cases, Livy tried to evaluate his sources in regard to probable accuracy and truthfulness.

Livy did, however, have undeniable weaknesses as a historian: occasional anachronisms, mistaken chronology, and topographical and geographic confusions, especially in accounts of battles. Furthermore, his patriotism makes him seem a bit prejudiced against other nations and peoples, most notably the Greeks.

Bibliography

Canter, H. V. "Rhetorical Elements in Livy's Direct Speeches." *American Journal of Philology* 28/29 (April, 1917/January, 1918): 125-141, 44-64.

1286   *Great Lives from History*

Canter shows that Livy's practice of putting speeches in the mouths of historical personages was a device used by most ancient historians. In only a few cases should the speeches be interpreted as literal quotations; generally, they are paraphrases or summaries of ideas expressed on the occasions of interest.

Duff, John W. "Augustan Prose and Livy." In *A Literary History of Rome: From the Origin to the Close of the Golden Age.* New York: Barnes and Noble Books, 1953. A brief but able analysis of Livy and other literary figures of the age of Augustus, with special emphasis on the Ciceronian literary style of Livy.

Frank, Tenney. "Republican Historiography and Livy." In *Life and Literature in the Roman Republic.* Berkeley: University of California Press, 1957. An excellent summary and analysis of Livy's predecessors in writing Roman history. Special emphasis is placed on archaeological discoveries which have confirmed some of the early legends about the founding of Rome mentioned by Livy.

Grant, Michael. "Livy." In *The Ancient Historians.* New York: Charles Scribner's Sons, 1970. He summarizes the contents of Livy's history and emphasizes his historiographical methods and aims, concluding that Livy deserves credit as a great historian. Grant complains, however, that Livy was an "armchair historian," not a participant in great historical events.

Hadas, Moses. "Livy as Scripture." *American Journal of Philology* 61 (October, 1940): 445-456. According to Hadas, Livy's references to miracles, prophecies, and religion are somewhat comparable to such references by biblical authors; Hadas concludes that Livy was probably sincerely religious, or at least sympathetic to Stoicism.

Laistner, M. L. W. "Livy, the Man and the Writer" and "Livy, the Historian." In *The Greater Roman Historians.* Berkeley: University of California Press, 1947. A detailed treatment of Livy as an adherent of a Stoic view of history in which religious signs were considered valid. Laistner describes Livy as a good example of a patriotic historian praising Roman virtues.

Walsh, P. G. "Livy." In *Latin Historians*, edited by T. A. Dorey. New York: Basic Books, 1966. Describes Livy's themes, such as the decline of Roman morality, his political views (senatorial and conservative), and his philosophical views (Stoic). Walsh also points out Livy's weaknesses: He is too rhetorical and too concerned with individual psychological factors in history.

John M. Lawrence

PIETRO LORENZETTI and AMBROGIO LORENZETTI

Pietro Lorenzetti

Born: c. 1280; probably Siena
Died: 1348; probably Siena

Ambrogio Lorenzetti

Born: c. 1290; probably Siena
Died: 1348; probably Siena
Area of Achievement: Art
Contribution: The Lorenzetti brothers recognized the problems of depicting three-dimensional space on a two-dimensional surface. Although they did not fully solve the problems of perspective, their experiments with space provided a necessary stage for the development of Italian Renaissance painting.

Early Lives

Since Pietro and Ambrogio Lorenzetti lived and worked in a period during which the lives of artists were not considered important, biographical information is based on a few public records, existing paintings (some of which are damaged and many of which are neither signed nor dated), and guesswork. For example, in 1306 the Sienese government paid 110 lire for a painting intended for the Palazzo Pubblico to a "Petruccio di Lorenzo." Because Petruccio is a diminutive form of Pietro, most historians have concluded that the recipient was in fact Pietro Lorenzetti and that he was a relatively young man in 1306. In order to receive payment directly, however, the artist had, by Sienese law, to be at least twenty-five years old. Therefore, 1280 is generally given as the approximate date of Pietro's birth.

Unfortunately, no similar documentation has been found in relation to Ambrogio's birth date. Consensus that the two men were brothers is based on an inscription from a public hospital which has long since been torn down. On the façade of the Sienese hospital was a series of frescoes depicting the various stages in the life of Mary, Jesus' mother. These frescoes, dated 1335, listed Pietro and Ambrogio as the two artists and also identified the artists as brothers. Because Pietro's name appeared first, it is assumed that Pietro was older.

Pietro's earliest work that can be dated with certainty is a panel for the altarpiece in the Church of the Pieve in Arezzo, a town in central Italy. On April 17, 1320, Pietro signed a contract for the composition, which is not one painting but nineteen. The central portion is a Madonna and Child with pictures of various saints in the side panels and an Annunciation immediately above the Madonna and Child.

This work illustrates one of Pietro's chief concerns, the emotional state of his figures. In the central portion, the Christ Child gazes happily at his mother, and the saints, each of whom is encased in a separate archway, turn toward one another, almost as though they were in conversation. In the Annunciation panel, Mary's eyes are locked into Gabriel's as the young Virgin, awestruck by the news of her impending pregnancy, clutches at her throat. Some historians have theorized that the model for the bearded Saint Luke may have been the artist himself, a portrait signature common among later artists. Another trademark of Pietro that is evident in the Arezzo panel is the interest in spatial relationships. Although the figures seem flat by High Renaissance standards, Pietro employs the techniques of modeling and overlapping.

The only dated evidence of Ambrogio's early work is also a Madonna and Child. Painted in 1319 for Vico l'Abate, a small church just outside Florence, Ambrogio's panel depicts a stiff Virgin staring straight ahead. Although she is seated, Mary seems to have no lap. On the other hand, the baby seems much more realistic. His tender gaze almost manages to focus on the mother's face, while the toes on his left foot curl backward in a touchingly realistic gesture which stands as an Ambrogioian signature. After painting the *Vico l'Abate Madonna*, Ambrogio may have remained in Florence for several years, as the next document related to him, dated 1321, indicates that creditors in Florence seized a suit of clothes belonging to the artist for payment of a debt that he owed.

Life's Work

The work that marks the transition into Pietro's mature style is an altarpiece of 1329. This work for the Carmelite Church in Siena contains a Crucifixion, another Madonna and Child surrounded by saints, and a narrative sequence depicting scenes from the history of the Carmelite Order. The figures in the main part of the altarpiece are not very interesting, because the crucified Christ could almost as easily be lying on a flat table as hanging from a cross, the crowned Virgin is stiff and joyless, and the Christ Child is weightless. On the other hand, the narrative scenes on the predella panels at the base of the altarpiece illustrate Pietro's experimentation with perspective through the use of diagonal lines and proportion.

For the Church of Saint Francis in Assisi, Pietro worked on a funeral chapel for the Cardinals Napoleone and Giovanni Orsini. The huge altarpiece is arranged on two levels. The central level contains figures of various saints with scenes from their lives. Above is a Passion cycle composed of eleven scenes from the last days of Christ, including the Crucifixion and the Ascension. Below the main level was originally a predella containing thirteen scenes—the major portion of which is now in the Uffizi in Florence, while two small panels are in Berlin. Much of the work is thought to have been done by students of Pietro, but the master's hand is evident in the later scenes from the Passion cycle, especially the powerful *Descent from the Cross*. In this scene, the angular body of Christ is being lifted off the Cross by his friends. Mary tenderly cradles the head of her son as their left eyes almost touch. Particularly interesting is the state of Christ's body, which, through line and modeling, is depicted in the early stages of rigor mortis.

Because Mary was considered the patron saint of Siena, the Sienese took a special interest in the Virgin. The Cathedral of Siena commissioned a whole cycle of altarpieces depicting the life of Mary. Pietro's contribution, the *Birth of the Virgin*, signed and dated in 1342, is the artist's latest work for which documentation exists. This painting, which has been moved to the Opera del Duomo in Siena, depicts Saint Anne, Mary's mother, lying on her bed with its checkered bedspread while the baby Virgin is being bathed. The *Birth of the Virgin* is important for two reasons. One innovation is the secular setting for a religious subject. In addition to the aforementioned checkered bedspread, the water pitcher and basin, trunk, and blankets are all objects that could be found in a middle-class Sienese household. Another innovation is the use of space. The diagonals in both the bedspread and the rug seem to disappear in a single vanishing point, a technique which was to be used by artists for the next one hundred years to give the appearance of three-dimensional space. Also, the frame of the triptych and the architecture in Anne's house are the same style and shape, so that the two appear to be part of the same system. The result is that the viewer seems to be looking not at a picture but through a window into the saint's bedroom.

Ambrogio, a more introspective artist than Pietro, is generally considered the more talented of the two brothers. Around 1330, Ambrogio completed work on an altarpiece at Massa Marittima, a town to the south and west of Siena. This work, a *Maestà*, or "Madonna in Majesty," emphasizes Mary's position as Queen of Heaven. A *Maestà* differs from a simple "Madonna Enthroned" because of the larger, more complicated design with the Madonna and Child being accompanied by a host of angels, prophets, and saints. Two other Sienese artists who are roughly contemporary with Ambrogio, Duccio di Buoninsegna and Simone Martini, also painted *Maestàs*. In contrast to Duccio's and Martini's figures, those of Ambrogio seem to be more energetic and less somber, and the supporting characters are more emotionally involved with the Madonna and Child. Also, in a marked improvement over the stiffness of the *Vico l'Abate Madonna*, the Virgin gazes tenderly into the Child's eyes while the Child, curling the toes on his right foot, clutches at Mary's collar.

Although most of Ambrogio's paintings and frescoes concerned religious subjects, the work for which the artist is most famous is political in nature. Apparently in competition with his brother, Ambrogio won the commission for a fresco series entitled *Good and Bad Government* for the Sala della Pace in the Palazzo Pubblico of Siena. This signed work, dated 1338-1339, is monumental. Covering three walls of the chamber, it depicts good and bad government allegorically and the effects of each type of government in both town and country realistically. Ambrogio chose the better-lighted wall for the allegory of Good Government. Of all the figures, the semireclining Peace is the most often reproduced, because the body's casual stance and enfolding drapery show a strong classical influence upon which Renaissance artists were to build.

It is, however, the section called "The Effect of Good Government in the Country" that is the most innovative. The first large-scale landscape since classical times, it is a panorama of the countryside surrounding Siena. Citizens are climbing up the hillside toward the cathedral, fields are being plowed, grain is being harvested, and peasants are bringing their meats and produce into the city. This portrayal of man in command of nature rather than the other way around marks an important stage in the concept of man's relation to the universe. Floating above the scene is an allegorical figure named Securitas, whose semiclad figure marks another innovation in artistic thinking. The notion that the human body should be an object of joy and celebration rather than a source of shame, while only hinted at here, would be explored in detail by artists of the Renaissance.

In 1342, at the same time that his brother was painting the *Birth of the Virgin* in the cathedral in Siena, Ambrogio was painting the *Presentation in the Temple*. In this altarpiece, all the adults are depicted as separated and distinct individuals of varying ages, and the Christ Child is a real baby instead of a small adult. The thin, straight hair frames oversized eyes, while the baby sucks his finger. Even more interesting is the setting of this work, supposedly a medieval cathedral, whose immense space is suggested by the use of diagonal perspective, a system in which farther objects are higher on the picture plane than nearer objects and are aligned along an oblique axis.

Summary

Of necessity, Pietro and Ambrogio Lorenzetti both concentrated on religious subjects. Tracing their many versions of the Madonna and Child is instructive, as both evolved from painting stiff, frontal Virgins to depicting tender, naturalistic mothers. Ambrogio from the first was more successful in capturing the essence of a baby and toward the end of his career was creating almost realistic infants.

Ironically, both brothers' highest achievements occurred when they moved away from religious subjects, perhaps because they felt more free to experiment. Pietro's *Birth of the Virgin* succeeds primarily because of the addition of everyday details whose arrangement contributes to the appearance of space on the picture plane. Ambrogio's sensuous Peace and Securitas in the

Good and Bad Government frescoes would have been unthinkable in a religious context.

Of the eight different ways of achieving perspective, the brothers experimented with at least five. Even so, Pietro's most successful use of perspective, the *Birth of the Virgin*, seems stiff, crowded, and crudely executed by Renaissance standards. Although Ambrogio's *Presentation in the Temple* presents the architectural space very convincingly, the figures are too large for the space they inhabit. As a result, to those who are accustomed to viewing work by High Renaissance artists, it is easy to dismiss the achievements of the Lorenzettis. Yet it is the concepts and experiments of Pietro and Ambrogio and other pre-Renaissance artists that laid the groundwork for their successors.

Bibliography
Becherucci, Luisa. "Lorenzetti." In *Encyclopedia of World Art*. New York: McGraw-Hill Book Co., 1964. Gives an exhaustive, chronological history of the dated works by both Ambrogio and Pietro Lorenzetti as well as every known detail relating to their personal lives in a clear, readable manner. Includes an extensive bibliography.
Berenson, Bernhard. *The Italian Painters of the Renaissance*. London: Phaidon Press, 1952. Expresses a negative view of the brothers' work, arguing that Pietro's flamboyant depiction of pain and suffering took precedence over other artistic values, such as composition, and that Ambrogio's paintings tended to be too crowded with details.
Hartt, Frederick. *History of Italian Renaissance Art: Painting, Sculpture, Architecture*. New York: Harry N. Abrams, 1969. Traces the development first of Pietro and then of Ambrogio and places the artists in the context of the works of other Sienese artists who were at work during the early Trecento.
Janson, H. W. *History of Art: A Survey of the Major Visual Arts from the Dawn of History to the Present Day*. Englewood Cliffs, N.J.: Prentice-Hall, 1969. Places the Lorenzettis in the context of artistic development through the centuries. Contains an excellent bibliography.
Rowley, George. *Ambrogio Lorenzetti*. 2 vols. Princeton, N.J.: Princeton University Press, 1958. Contains a detailed analysis of the stylistic features of Ambrogio's work and traces the artist's development through his dated as well as his undated works. A highly controversial commentary, partially because Rowley seeks to assign many works thought to be by Ambrogio's hand to that of other artists. Includes an excellent bibliography and helpful chronology.
Seymour, Frederick. *Siena and Her Artists*. Philadelphia: George W. Jacobs, 1907. An individualistic account. Seymour places the work of the Lorenzetti brothers in the context of other Sienese artists.

Vasari, Giorgio. *The Lives of the Painters, Sculptors, and Architects*. Translated by A. B. Hinds. 4 vols. New York: E. P. Dutton, 1927. Vasari (1511-1574), an Italian painter and architect, wrote one of the earliest biographies of Italian artists. Contains a complimentary account of the work of Ambrogio but does not mention Pietro. Although known to include many inaccuracies, this work provides many useful details about paintings that have either disappeared or disintegrated.

Sandra Hanby Harris

LOUIS II THE GERMAN

Born: c. 804; possibly Aquitaine
Died: August 28, 876; Frankfurt
Area of Achievement: Government
Contribution: As the ruler who founded the kingdom that later became known as Germany, Louis, while supporting the idea of the unity of the Carolingian Empire, protected his kingdom from the covetousness of his relatives, patronized the Church, and defended his lands from numerous attacks by such peoples as the Vikings, Hungarians, Bohemians, Moravians, and Slavs.

Early Life

The third son of Louis the Pious and Ermengard, Louis was born about 804. His father, the third son of Charlemagne, would become sole ruler of the Carolingian Empire in 814. His mother was the daughter of a government official, Count Ingram. Probably Louis spent most of his early years at the courts of his father and grandfather. When Charlemagne died, Louis the Pious had to make numerous arrangements for the governance of the empire. The new emperor granted the rule of Bavaria and Aquitaine to his two eldest legitimate sons, Lothar and Pepin, respectively. Because of his youth, Louis continued to live in his father's household.

Three years later, Louis the Pious issued the Ordinatio Imperii of 817, in which he proclaimed the disposition of the empire for the remainder of his reign as well as after his death. Louis received Bavaria, which Lothar had ruled since 814. On the death of the emperor, Louis' share of the empire was to be increased to include Carinthia and the Bohemian, Slavic, and Avar marches. Lothar would act as coemperor and succeed their father as sole emperor, who would then maintain a loose supervision over the kingdoms ruled by his Carolingian relatives. In the future, the various Carolingian kingdoms were to be passed on without further subdivision. Thus, Louis the Pious was able to preserve the unity of the empire while conforming to the Frankish practice of dividing a man's patrimony equally among his sons.

From 817 to early 832, Louis acted as a loyal son and his father's lieutenant. At eighteen, he commanded a flank of the expedition that Louis the Pious mounted against Brittany in 824. Beginning in 825, Louis actively governed Bavaria while annually returning to France to attend his father's court. Some of his attention was spent on wars against the Slavs in 825 and the Bulgars in 828 that accomplished little. In 827, Louis married Emma, a daughter of Count Welf, who was also the father of Judith of Bavaria. Nine years earlier, the emperor had married Judith, by whom he had a son, Charles "the Bald," in 823. During the summer of 829, Louis the Pious took two actions that produced dissension in both the royal family and the government. He granted some lands to Charles, his youngest son, and replaced a number of his governmental officials. The result was a revolt led by the displaced ministers, who seized control of the government and gained the support of Lothar and Pepin. Despite being under house arrest, Louis the Pious arranged an understanding with Pepin and Louis and in October, 830, reclaimed control of the empire's government. From 829 until 843, the rule of the empire would be contested by Louis the Pious' sons and elements of the empire's governmental bureaucracy. Upon recovering the government, the emperor sent Lothar to Italy and rewarded Pepin, Louis, and Charles with more lands. To Louis' lands were added Thuringia, Saxony, Frisia, Flanders, Brabant, Hainault, most of Austrasia, and part of Neustria. On the emperor's death, the three brothers would be allowed to act independently one another, to aid one another in defense of the empire's borders and the Roman church, and to ignore Lothar, who would rule in Italy. Furthermore, the emperor expected his three younger sons to remain loyal or he would punish them by removing lands from their rule. Distrust had become so great on all sides, however, that the remaining decade of the emperor's life was to see continual plotting and intermittent rebellions by his three older sons.

Life's Work

From 832 onward, Louis the German followed a policy of protecting his German lands while occasionally acting as a mediator in family disputes. During the 830's, Louis often found himself in opposition to his father's plans and particularly to those concerning Charles. After Pepin began a revolt late in 831, Louis made plans to invade Alemania, an area recently given to Charles and which contained a number of Welf estates, in early 832. When the emperor entered Bavaria in May, Louis sought and obtained a pardon. The spring of 833 saw an attempt by Lothar, Pepin, and Louis to seize the empire's government from their father. Supported by Pope Gregory IV and various imperial ministers, the three brothers confronted their father at Rothfield. With his followers slipping away, the emperor surrendered. Lothar was declared sole emperor, and Louis the German returned to Bavaria in the late summer. When Lothar tried to harass his father into becoming a monk, Louis, somewhat distressed by this, and Pepin marched on Paris, where Lothar and their father were. Lothar fled, leaving Louis the Pious to reclaim the emperorship in early March, 834. Then, in October, 837, the emperor gave to Charles the territories between the Seine and Meuse rivers in northeast France, lands that had been held at different times by Lothar and Louis the German. In late 838, after a meeting with Lothar and two with the emperor, Louis the German declared war against his father; this war continued until his father's death in June, 840. In the spring of 839, Louis the Pious again divided the empire; this time it was evenly split between Lothar and Charles, while Louis the German was allowed only the rule of Bavaria. With the emperor's death, Lothar continued the war against his brother Louis, who faced a Saxon revolt at the same time. Unable to arrange an accord with Lothar, Charles reluctantly joined Louis. On June 25, 841, at Fontenoy, they defeated Lothar, who was again defeated in September. In order to protect themselves and defeat Lothar, at Strasbourg on February 14, 842, Louis and Charles exchanged the famous Strasbourg oaths that bound them together in a defensive alliance against Lothar. By operating together, Louis and Charles forced Lothar to open negotiations. At a meeting near Mâcon on June 15, the three brothers agreed to divide the empire into three equal parts. A year of further discussions among their representatives produced the Treaty of Verdun in August, 843. By this treaty, Louis retained the Germanic territories east of the Rhine plus three counties to the west of it and the whole of Alemania; Charles kept the French kingdom; and Lothar held Italy, plus a corridor of counties between his brothers' kingdoms, as well as continuing his use of the title of emperor. The political unity of the Carolingian Empire had come to an end.

With the passage of time, the Treaty of Verdun became the cornerstone of the kingdom of Germany. Louis' immediate concerns were the protection of his borders from the Vikings and various peoples to the east, the maintenance of the Church, and future relations with his brothers. For the most part, the wars against the Bohemians, Moravians, and Slavs were successful. The Vikings, however, remained a threat to both Germany and the rest of the Carolingian lands, despite Louis' efforts to keep them at bay. Within Germany, Louis supported the Church by means of numerous grants, received the support of his clergy, and endorsed its efforts to convert the neighboring pagan peoples. Nevertheless, it was the clergy of Aquitaine in the 850's and those of northeastern France between 858 and 860 who thwarted the attempts of segments of the Aquitanian and French populations to replace Charles the Bald with Louis.

During the dozen years between the settlement at Verdun and the death of Lothar in 855, relations among the three brothers were precarious. At Meerssen in March, 847, the brothers agreed to cooperate against external threats and in sorting out internal problems that were common to the kingdoms. Yet the distrust among them, especially between Charles and Lothar, clouded the arrangement. After attempts in 849 and 850 to patch up differences, the brothers in May, 851, again at Meerssen, came to a consensus. As relations between Lothar and Charles improved, Louis began to drift away from them. Early in 855, Louis sent his eldest son, Louis the Younger, to assist the Aquitanians in a revolt against Charles. The rebellion's failure and a mediation undertaken by Lothar restored peace. Lothar then died, leaving a complex division of his lands that would dominate the rest of his brother Louis' life.

Lothar had divided his kingdom equally among his three sons, Emperor

Louis II in Italy, Charles, King of Provence, and Lothar II, King of Lotharingia, all of whom would have no legitimate son. Because of the weaknesses of their small kingdoms, Lothar's sons found themselves somewhat at the mercy of their two uncles. A party to a barren marriage and directly caught between the large kingdoms of Louis the German and Charles the Bald, Lothar II tried to divorce his wife and marry his mistress. Actions by his uncles and the Papacy blocked these efforts, thereby virtually ensuring that Lothar's kingdom would fall at his death to his two uncles. Louis the German was ill when Lothar II died in August, 869, and so could not forestall Charles the Bald's seizure of Lotharingia. A year later to the day, August 8, 870, faced with the possibility of an attack by Louis the German, Charles agreed to honor an arrangement the two had made in 869 to partition Lotharingia. By this Treaty of Meerssen, the kingdom was split from north to south along a line that would be disputed again and again in future centuries. Because Emperor Louis II had only a female heir, the possibility of obtaining the emperorship came to interest his two uncles. Engelberga, Louis II's wife, favored Louis the German's ambitions in this regard, while Popes Hadrian III and John VIII sided with Charles the Bald. Although Engelberga claimed after her husband's death that his wish was for Carloman, Louis the German's eldest son, to have the emperorship, Charles the Bald, combining diplomacy and fighting skill, outmaneuvered his brother's armies and raced to Rome in late 875. As Pope John crowned Charles emperor on Christmas Day, Louis the German with his son Louis the Younger was leading a fruitless invasion into France. The French magnates remained loyal to Charles, so Louis the German had to abandon his attack and return to Germany. After Charles and Pope John solidified the new emperor's hold on Italy, on August 28, 876, they dispatched an embassy to meet with Louis the German. On that day, however, Louis had died at Frankfurt. Immediately Charles tried to negate the 870 Treaty of Meerssen by seizing Lorraine, only to be decisively defeated by Louis the Younger.

Summary

On balance, Louis the German achieved success as a medieval king. As a warrior, he had protected his lands from external threats from the east as well as from his brothers, Lothar and Charles the Bald. Louis overcame the several internal rebellions led by his sons in the early 860's, along with the occasional one by a magnate, with his position strengthened further. His reputation as a good ruler is evidenced by the willingness of various French magnates to seek him out as a king for both Aquitaine and France. His generosity to the German church resulted in its clergy's continual support of their king, even at times against the wishes of the Papacy, which often involved itself in ecclesiastical affairs north of the Alps.

Of Louis the German's private life, little is known. Indications are that he spent his youth in the household of Louis the Pious and possibly that of Charlemagne. How this experience developed his character is not clear, but through much of his life, Louis the German defended the concept of a unified empire, an idea supported in both households. Although Louis had no illegitimate children, as both Charlemagne and Louis the Pious had had, he did follow a common Carolingian policy regarding marriages of daughters. All three of his surviving daughters, Hildegard, Ermengard, and Bertha, were placed in nunneries and died unmarried. He allowed his sons at first to maintain relationships with mistresses; later they married the daughters of counts. His own death followed so quickly on that of Emma in January, 876, that one cannot be sure if he might have remarried.

Louis the German's greatest accomplishment was the founding of a kingdom, Germany, that would survive as a separate entity. He provided it with three future kings, the youngest of whom, Charles the Fat, would become an emperor as well. By the time Louis' line died out in 911, the concept of a German kingdom separate from the rest of the old Carolingian Empire was strong enough that the German magnates chose to remain distinct from troubled France and selected a German duke as their king.

Bibliography
Cabaniss, Allen, trans. *Son of Charlemagne: A Contemporary Life of Louis the Pious*. Syracuse, N.Y.: Syracuse University Press, 1961. Cabaniss has translated the ninth century *Vita Hludovici*, written by an anonymous author, probably of Louis the Pious' household. This history provides considerable information about the emperor's relations with all of his sons, including Louis the German. With it and Nithard's account (below), the reader may develop a good picture of Louis the German's early life.
Deanesly, Margaret. *A History of Early Medieval Europe from 476 to 911*. London: Methuen and Co., 1956, 2d ed. 1960. Deanesly's study provides an excellent introduction to the Carolingian period and the basic outline of Louis the German's activities.
Gibson, Margaret, and Janet Nelson, eds. *Charles the Bald: Court and Kingdom*. Oxford: British Archaeological Reports, 1981. This is a collection of twenty-one papers presented at a colloquium held in London in 1979, covering a wide range of subjects beyond Charles the Bald.
Halphen, Louis. *Charlemagne and the Carolingian Empire*. Translated by Giselle de Nie. Amsterdam: North-Holland Publishing Co., 1977. Originally published in French in 1947, Halphen's book is the basic work available in English on the ninth century. It details Louis the German's relationships with his father and brothers and as such is the starting point for anyone interested in the first German king.
Nelson, Janet L. *Politics and Ritual in Early Medieval Europe*. London: Hambledon Press, 1986. This collection of seventeen articles published

since 1967 illustrates the complexity of the scholarship required to understand the world of Louis the German, who repeatedly is mentioned in its
pages. Nelson is especially good on the institution of kingship and the narrative sources of the ninth century.

Nithard. "Histories." In *Carolingian Chronicles*. Translated by Bernhard
Walter Scholz with Barbara Rogers. Ann Arbor: University of Michigan
Press, 1970. Here is the basic source for the struggle between Louis the
German and his brothers from 840 to 843. Reading it provides the reader
with the flavor of the troubles that dogged the brothers through most of
their lives.

Kenneth G. Madison

LOUIS IX

Born: April 25, 1214; Poissy, France
Died: August 25, 1270; near Tunis (modern Tunisia)
Areas of Achievement: Government and religion
Contribution: Louis IX reformed and centralized the French government and
   judiciary and increased the prestige of the royal house of France through
   his saintly life.

Early Life

Louis IX was born at Poissy, near Paris, the son of the Crown Prince of
France, Louis the Lion. His grandfather, Philip Augustus (Philip II), a contemporary of Richard I the Lion-Hearted, was still vigorous and ruled until
Louis was nine years old. In 1214, the year of Louis' birth, Philip won at
Bouvines over John of England and annexed the French territories of the
English royal family. Louis' mother, Blanche of Castile, a niece of John, had
a claim to the English throne which led to an unsuccessful invasion of England by her husband in 1216. Blanche and Louis had twelve children, of
whom nine survived infancy.

At the death of Philip Augustus in 1223, Louis the Lion succeeded to the
throne as Louis VIII and pursued vigorous policies of expansion of crown
territories and repression of heretics. He died suddenly on November 8,
1226, upon returning from a successful crusade against Albigensian heretics
in southern France. Queen Blanche, regent through the terms of his will,
arranged for the immediate coronation of her twelve-year-old son as King
Louis IX.

The early years of the regency were marked by attacks from all sides. The
great nobles of the realm often owed feudal allegiance to the crowns of both
England and France and were likely to play one against the other. They were
also tempted to replace the boy king with one of their own number. Hugh,
Count of La Marche, stepfather to Henry III of England, and Peter of Dreux
or Peter Mauclerc, Count of Brittany, actually invited Henry III to invade
France but were unable to provide sufficient troops and supplies and eventually surrendered to the royal forces. Blanche succeeded in holding even the
most vulnerable territories for her son.

Louis IX led his first military campaign at the age of fourteen and was
soon recognized as an able and inspiring commander. By the time he married
Marguerite of Provence in 1234, the worst of the domestic uprisings were
over, and the realm of France settled into a period of peace. Along with her
concerns of government, Blanche had devoted herself to the religious education of her children. Louis developed into a particularly devout man and
maintained a close attachment to his mother. (Relations between Blanche
and her daughter-in-law were notoriously poor.) The young Louis is de-

scribed as tall and slender, blond, and with the face of an angel. He was firm in his character and endowed with humor and intelligence.

Life's Work

No formal date is given for the end of Blanche's regency. She continued as royal counselor and regent in Louis' absence until her death in 1252. Gradually, Louis assumed more responsibility for government. His understanding of Christian monarchy demanded a high standard of personal virtue and continual effort to make salvation a possibility for all of his subjects. To that end he pursued peace and justice in his kingdom. Under Louis IX the royal government began to regularize and expand its role in administration and the judiciary. Originally, the king had ruled only within those territories that were his by feudal succession. Louis ruled a greatly expanded area through the gains made by Philip Augustus and Louis VIII; as he extended the limits of his judicial power to these areas, he also assumed the same power in territories held by the great lords who owed him feudal allegiance. This process was a gradual one. Military considerations forwarded centralization, as did Louis' growing popularity.

Louis IX was an exceptionally devoted Christian, practicing charity in unostentatious sincerity. He contributed liberally to cloistered religious orders and participated in the heavy manual labor of building the Cistercian monastery Royaumont. His unassailable piety allowed him to maintain the temporal rights of the French nation against the worldly power of the Catholic church. He supported French bishops in their resistance to the papal practice of appointing Italians to open positions in the French church. He opposed the bishops when they demanded that he use royal authority to enforce decrees of excommunication. He insisted on the maintenance or expansion of his own jurisdiction in contested areas.

Louis inherited a system of *baillis* and *sénéchaux*, royal administrators sent to govern the regions of France, to administer justice, to assist in military levies, and otherwise to represent the Crown. Louis regularized and reformed this governmental system, making administrative posts merit appointments and guarding against corruption by sending out a body of traveling *enquêteurs*, auditors and inquisitors who went to each region and investigated complaints.

Louis was deeply involved in the judicial system and is pictured by chroniclers such as Jean de Joinville as giving personal justice while seated under a huge oak tree near his castle at Vincennes. Since the laws were not codified, a judgment in any matter depended upon regional tradition. Louis formed his decisions with a knowledge of feudal tradition, Roman and canon law, and his own vigorous common sense. He applied these decisions throughout his expanded realm. Many feudal nobles were incensed when he outlawed the practice of trial by combat. He did not hesitate to call the highest nobles to account and in many cases reversed decisions made in the courts of his royal brothers or the nobles.

Louis IX faced an unstable world. England and France had been at war for decades. The Holy Roman Empire was in disarray; Frederick II of Sicily had been handpicked to rule by Pope Innocent III, but conflicts had arisen, and even though Frederick recovered Jerusalem in 1229, Pope Gregory IX excommunicated him and preached a crusade against him. Hordes of Mongols were beating at the gates of Europe. A succession of crusades were preached by the popes of these times—crusades to rescue the Holy Land (Jerusalem fell again in 1244) and crusades against heretics within Europe.

In his international policy, Louis IX worked consistently for the twin goals of peace within Christendom and redemption of the Holy Land. He went on two crusades himself, the Seventh (1248-1257) and the Eighth (1270). His endeavors to remain on good terms with Frederick II as well as with the Papacy reflect his desire for Christian peace and his need of aid from both sources for the prosecution of his crusades. He was able to arrange a stable truce with Henry III of England before leaving France in 1248. On his return, he worked for the establishment of a formal peace with England and succeeded with the Treaty of Paris of 1259.

At the beginning of Louis' reign, the abbey of Royaumont was built as a memorial to his father. He took great interest in the process. He also presided over the translation of the remains of his royal ancestors to the royal necropolis of Saint-Denis. In 1239, Louis acquired several relics of Christ's Passion, including the Crown of Thorns, and he began the construction of the Sainte Chapelle next to the royal residence on the Île de la Cité in Paris to house them. In all these things, Louis responded to his own sense of religious fervor and his role as anointed leader of his people. Following his recovery from a serious illness in 1244, he determined to go on a crusade. His departure with the flower of French nobility in 1248 was seen as a special grace.

Louis' Crusade began with elaborate preparations, provisions stockpiled during a period of years, the building of a French Mediterranean port at Aigues-Mortes, and a general settling in order of all temporal concerns. Queen Marguerite accompanied her husband and bore three children while on crusade. The city of Damietta in Egypt was the first target; it fell almost without a fight and she remained there, holding the city. In 1250, Louis and his men were captured as they retreated in disarray from the city of Mansourah. Near death from dysentery, Louis refused to leave his troops and insisted on staying with them until every survivor was ransomed. Damietta was part of the payment. Louis remained in the East, fortifying the Christian kingdoms of Outremer. Only the death of Queen Blanche in November, 1252, succeeded in calling him home. The news reached Louis in Sidon during the summer of 1253; he arrived in Paris in early September,

1254. The Crusade, in spite of early good luck, was a fiasco fatal to many, including Louis' favorite brother, Robert of Artois, and nearly cost the king his life.

Louis' long absence damaged France less than it might have, thanks to Blanche's able regency, but disorders had arisen, and Louis set to work to clean house. He was a humbled man, conscious of the failure of his Crusade and seeking a renewal of his own spiritual life through redoubled asceticism and penitence. From his first moments back in France he began to plan a return trip to the East, and his efforts to amend any disorder may be seen as tending toward this goal. While in Syria, he had been distressed to see that the libraries for Islamic scholars were superior to those available to Christians in France. On his return, he assembled a royal library, copied as many manuscripts as possible, and gathered what would be the beginning of the French National Library. He encouraged the University of Paris and favored the establishment of the Sorbonne by his counselor Robert de Sorbon. He gathered the greatest biblical scholars of his day and delighted in their debates. Thomas Aquinas dined at his table. The years between the Crusades were also devoted to the pleasant duties of education and marriage of his children, the last of whom was born in 1260.

The Treaty of Paris with Henry III of England dates from this time of peace and order. This treaty, unpopular on both sides of the Channel, ended Plantagenet claims to French lands, at the price of large money grants from Louis IX to Henry III. Louis made Henry the gift of several parcels of land from his own properties and accepted Henry's feudal homage, making him a Peer of France. Louis was also called upon by the English barons to arbitrate their disputes with Henry III. In January, 1264, he gave an award, the Mise of Amiens, which upheld Henry on almost every point. The barons ignored it, and by August, 1264, Henry had relinquished almost all the concessions made to him in the Treaty of Paris for money to use in civil war against his barons.

The death of Frederick II in 1250 left the Holy Roman Empire in complete disarray. Charles of Anjou, Louis IX's brother, became King of Sicily by papal invitation and ruled from 1266 to 1285. His influence may have guided Louis' plans for his Second Crusade. In spite of the king's frail health, Louis and his sons sailed from Aigues-Mortes in early July, 1270. Louis' First Crusade had attacked Egypt. This Crusade was directed against Tunis, directly across the Mediterranean from Charles's Sicily. The heat and unsanitary conditions led to an almost immediate outbreak of severe dysentery among the French. Louis' son, John Tristan, born at Damietta in 1250, died on August 3, 1270. Louis himself died on August 25. His remains were returned to France by his heir, Philip III, and entombed at Saint-Denis in May, 1271. Almost immediately after his funeral, his tomb was credited with miracles. His canonization was celebrated in 1297.

Summary

Louis IX's great genius and great folly was to incarnate the thirteenth century ideal of kingship. Even his faults, such as his anti-Semitism, were consistent with his desire to further the salvation of his people. He was extremely generous to converts, but the unconverted Jew or heretic was a danger to wavering Christians. His Crusades were disasters on a worldly level, costing many lives and resources, yet they served to give a focus to Louis' reforms and reorganization in France. As a simple nobleman would set the affairs of his estate in order before going on crusade, so the king did for his kingdom.

Louis saw the performance of government at all levels as a reflection of his personal performance as monarch. This view gave a special resonance to his administrative reforms. In 1254, the Great Ordinance was promulgated, formulating and regularizing the higher standards of justice and tighter royal control in the courts which Louis sought throughout his reign. Crown officials were publicly sworn to accept a severely practical code of ethics and stringent auditing. His Treaty of Paris of 1259 was not a simple political gesture but an idealistic personal one. His intent in making generous personal concessions to Henry III was to assure friendship between their children and to gain Henry's personal loyalty to him as feudal lord. In his most idealistic actions, Louis was also most immediately personal. It was his embodiment of the medieval Christian ideal that made Louis the focus of French national spirit and mystic prestige for the crown of France for centuries to come.

Bibliography

Dahmus, Joseph. *Seven Medieval Kings*. Garden City, N.Y.: Doubleday and Co., 1967. This readable book presents Louis IX as one of seven outstanding monarchs spanning the period of the Middle Ages (the others: Justinian, Harun al-Rashid, Charlemagne, Henry II of England, Frederick II of Sicily, and Louis XI of France). Louis' character and achievements are placed in the perspective of a historical continuum.

Fawtier, Robert. *The Capetian Kings of France: Monarchy and Nation, 987-1328*. New York: St. Martin's Press, 1960. Translated by Lionel Butler and R. J. Adam. This is the standard secondary work on France under the Capetian Dynasty, to which Louis IX belonged, and includes a substantial section dedicated to him and France under his rule. Bibliography.

Hallam, Elizabeth M. *Capetian France, 987-1328*. New York: Longmans, 1980. This excellent and scholarly book is firmly grounded on the most basic and practical aspects of the Capetian era. Chapter 5, "Louis IX: The Consolidation of Royal Power, 1226-1270," directly discusses Saint Louis. The book as a whole places Louis within the context of his ancestors and descendants. Hallam provides the reader with maps, genealogical tables, and a bibliography.

Joinville, Jean, Sire de. *The Life of Saint Louis*. London: Sheed and Ward,

1955. This basic primary work, a memoir by a friend and crusading companion of Louis IX, was written in the author's old age for Louis' grandson. It is referred to by all writers on the period and is the source for many personal anecdotes which succeed in revealing the more human side of Saint Louis. The most easily accessible English translation of this work is to be found in M. R. B. Shaw's *Chronicles of the Crusades* (London: Penguin Books, 1963).

Jordan, William Chester. *Louis IX and the Challenge of the Crusade: A Study in Rulership*. Princeton, N.J.: Princeton University Press, 1979. This study concentrates on the development of Louis IX's character and his philosophy of rulership through his preparation for and involvement in his Crusades. Jordan unites psychological analysis with detailed economic and political data, accompanying the text with maps, illustrations, appendixes, and an exhaustive bibliography.

Labarge, Margaret Wade. *Saint Louis: Louis IX, Most Christian King of France*. Boston: Little, Brown and Co., 1968. This complete, readable, and well-documented biography of Louis IX presents maps, illustrations, a table of dates, a chart of family relationships, an annotated list of sources, and a general bibliography.

Pernoud, Régine. *Blanche of Castile*. London: Collins, 1975. Translated by Henry Noel. This extremely readable biography of the mother of Louis IX illuminates his family background, childhood, and early reign. Pernoud supplies family charts, illustrations, and a bibliography.

Anne W. Sienkewicz

LUCRETIUS

Born: c. 98 B.C.; probably Rome
Died: October 15, 55 B.C.; Rome
Areas of Achievement: Literature, natural history, and philosophy
Contribution: Though he in no sense offered an original philosophical outlook, Lucretius' *On The Nature of Things* synthesized primary tenets of
Greek Epicureanism and atomism and offered a rational, nontheological
explanation for the constituents of the universe; just as remarkable is the
fact that he did this in Latin hexameter verse and developed a philosophical vocabulary required for the task.

Early Life

It is much easier to show why most of what has been written about the life
of Titus Lucretius Carus is incorrect, doubtful, or malicious than it is to
arrive at a reliable account. Relatively little can be deduced from his poem,
and there are no substantive contemporary references to him. Consequently,
too much credence has been given to the jumbled biographical note written
by Saint Jerome, which itself was derived from an unreliable account by the
Roman historian Gaius Suetonius Tranquillus. Jerome miscalculates Lucretius' dates of birth and death; also, it is unlikely that Lucretius was driven
insane by a love potion and wrote *De rerum natura* (c. 60; *On the Nature of
Things*) during periods of lucidity. The latter story seems to have arisen from
Lucretius' treatment of love in section 4 of the poem.

Several details of Lucretius' early life can, however, be inferred with relative certainty. His name is a strange combination which implies both servile
(Carus) and noble origins (from the kinship grouping *Gens Lucretia*), but he
was likely closer to the middle class of his contemporary Cicero. Though Cicero himself did not emend Lucretius' poetry, as Jerome reports, it is likely
that his brother Quintus Cicero oversaw its publication. Like Cicero, Lucretius appears to have evinced an early interest in philosophy, influenced by the
Alexandrian movement, though his own poetry has an old Roman spirit reflecting his readings of Quintus Ennius. Cicero considered that Lucretius had
the "genius" of Ennius and the "art" of the Alexandrians.

Lucretius lived through the turmoil caused by the civil war between aristocrat Lucius Cornelius Sulla and populist Gaius Marius as well as the
conspiracy of Lucius Sergius Catilina. He also witnessed the consequent
decline of Roman republican government. Perhaps this political uncertainty
directed him to the comfortable philosophy of Epicurus, which held that the
goal of human existence should be a life of calm pleasure tempered by morality and culture. The atomism of Democritus and Leucippus, which held that
the material universe could be understood as random combinations of minute particles (*atomoi*), provided a rational and scientific means of explain-

ing the cosmos and avoiding what Lucretius came to see as the sterile superstitions of religion.

In all, the impressions one has of Lucretius at this early stage in his life are
of a young man of good background and a good education, who is eager not
for the political arena or personal advancement but to explain the world in a
reasonable way to Romans with similar education who would read his verse.
In addition, he aimed to make living in that rationally explained world as
pleasant an experience as possible.

Life's Work

One can only guess how Lucretius lived during the years he was writing *On
the Nature of Things* from its dedication to Gaius Memmius. Memmius held
the office of praetor in 58 and fancied himself a poet, primarily of erotic
verse in the style of Catullus. Memmius' shady political dealings eventually
caught up with him, and he was driven into exile; nevertheless, it is reasonable to assume that Lucretius received some financial support from him.
Memmius figures less importantly in the body of the poem, however, and his
name is used in places only for metrical convenience.

Details of the poem show the kind of atmosphere Lucretius wished to escape, essentially that of his own city in the final years of the Republic. The
world is filled with gloom, war, and decay. The poet wishes to stand on a hill,
far removed from wickedness and ambition, and watch the waste and
destruction. Passages such as these reveal a man who yearned for tranquil
anonymity. Other writers, such as Cicero, would find themselves propelled
into a political maelstrom which would ultimately destroy them; Lucretius
was determined to avoid this fate.

The times in which Lucretius lived cried out for reasonableness. Educated
Romans saw the obvious conflict between their elaborate mythology and
their religion, which glorified deities who did everything from seducing
women to causing mildew. Even so, Rome continued to fill the various
priestly colleges, to take auspices as a means of determining favorable out-
comes, and to celebrate public games in honor of these very deities. A century later, Rome would deify its emperors, partly to shift its religious observances to personalities who were incontestably real, and partly to curb the
spread of imported cults such as Mithraism and what came to be known as
Christianity.

Lucretius had solved this problem, for himself at least, and outlines his
position on religion in *On the Nature of Things*. The creative force of nature is
real; it is personified in the goddess Venus. The deities are simply personi-
fications of various aspects of nature, and human beings can free themselves
of superstition by seeing the world as constantly recombining *atomoi*. Death
itself is nothing more than atomic dissolution, a preparation for new arrangements of atoms and new creation. If human beings can accept death in these

terms, they can cast aside the fear that binds them to religious superstition. This acceptance will prepare them to see that life's purpose is to maximize pleasure and minimize pain.

Neither of these theories is new; they are derived from the atomism of Democritus and Leucippus and the teachings of Epicurus. What is new is Lucretius' synthesis and his offering it as rational scientism to educated Roman readers. One reason almost nothing is known about Lucretius' personal life is undoubtedly his determination to practice these ideas. Removing himself from the fray to seek philosophical calm necessarily results in a lack of contemporary biographical references, but it is precisely on this score that Lucretian Epicureanism is most misunderstood. It is just the opposite of egocentric gratification, because Lucretius couples it with the mechanics of atomism. Seen in this way, the individual is merely a part in the world machine; immortality exists, but only in the myriad indestructible *atomoi* which constitute each part.

One can only guess how Lucretius first encountered Epicureanism. There were Greek professors in Rome during the first century B.C. who taught the theories of Epicurus. Cicero mentions non-Greek Epicureans who wrote treatises Lucretius might easily have read. The ease with which Lucretius deals with the technical vocabulary of atomism suggests that he was accomplished in Greek. (This would be expected of any educated Roman.) He no doubt read Epicurus, Democritus, and Leucippus in the original language.

Reading Greek gave Lucretius access to other sources such as Empedocles, the philosopher-poet who wrote *Perì Phýseōs (On Nature)*. What the modern world calls "natural selection" comes to Lucretius through Empedocles, as does the principle of attraction and repulsion, which Lucretius sees as "love" and "hate." Lucretius' hexameter meter is used by Empedocles but also by Homer. Indeed, Lucretius borrows from Homer, Euripides, Thucydides, Hippocrates, and various early Roman poets.

Though his philosophy is Greek, Lucretius maintains a very Roman insistence on the primacy of law. In *On the Nature of Things*, for example, he notes that human beings moved from primitive status to society only after they had agreed upon a social contract. Language improved upon gesture, and social order prevailed. It is worth noting that similar ideas later appear in the creation account of Ovid in *Metamorphoses*. Though Lucretius failed to convert the Roman masses, he obviously made inroads among his successors in poetry. Vergil read him, too, and while Vergil's work is more elegant, there can be little doubt that he was impressed by Lucretius' descriptions of nature; one can easily see their influence in Vergil's pastoral poems.

The random nature of the *clinamen* ("swerve") that atoms make when they recombine must have troubled Lucretius, since he is generally insistent on the orderly cycle of nature. This bothered others, too, but is the only way to explain natural differences atomically. The *membranae* ("films"), which are thrown from objects and thereby produce visual impressions, are another artificial means of describing a natural phenomenon, but *On the Nature of Things* is, on the whole, free of such difficulties.

The poem's six books show evidence of unfinished composition, but one cannot deduce Lucretius' premature death from this fact. The Victorian poet Alfred, Lord Tennyson, perpetuated Suetonius' marvelous fiction of Lucretius' insanity and death by a love potion, but the author of *On the Nature of Things* was a very sane man whose entire reason for living was to bring rationality to an irrational world.

Summary

Lucretius privileged the creative force of nature, but he in no sense resembled the English Romantic poets in their wonderment at its powers. He was the rare combination of natural scientist, philosopher, and poet, and he strove for clarity and reasonableness in what he wrote. He clearly was not the gaunt, love-crazed, mad genius of Suetonius and Jerome, but an evangelizer who appealed to an educated audience, much like twentieth century writers of popular science.

Lucretius thus became a symbol which served the purposes of those who wrote about him. Because the facts of his life remained a mystery, even to the generation which immediately followed his own, he could be portrayed by Suetonius as foreshadowing the Empire's vice, by Jerome as representing pagan degeneracy, and ultimately by Tennyson as typifying egocentric gratification. Even so, as is true of many great lives, work overshadows personality, and this is clearly what Lucretius intended, for *On the Nature of Things* opened a world of what would otherwise have remained esoteric Greek philosophy to a popular audience. What is more important, Lucretius presented these ideas as a means of dealing with his own troubled world.

Were one to cancel out Lucretius' masterly synthesis of Epicureanism and atomism, his contribution to both Roman poetry and the Latin language would remain. Nearly one hundred technical words adapted from the Greek appear within six books of hexameter verse, the epic meter of Homer and of Lucretius' fellow Roman Ennius. That Lucretius' work inspired the succeeding generation of Roman poets, which included both Vergil and Ovid, attests its immediate influence. The modern reader, armed with contemporary science and psychology, can object only to the mechanics of the natural phenomena Lucretius discusses; his plea to cast aside superstition and fear strikes a welcome note.

Bibliography

Bailey, C. "Late Republican Poetry." In *Fifty Years (and Twelve) of Classical Scholarship*, edited by Maurice Platnauer. New York: Barnes and Noble Books, 1968. This fine article, in an anthology which surveys all major aspects of classical studies to the mid-1960's, discusses Lucretius with special emphasis on editions and translations of his poem, possible sources, textual criticism, and Lucretian thought, philosophy, and natural science.

——————————. *Lucretius*. 3 vols. Oxford: Oxford University Press, 1947. This standard edition of *On the Nature of Things* presents not only the full Latin text and apparatus but also a readable and accurate translation on facing pages. A "Prolegomenon" in the first volume analyzes what little is known about Lucretius' life against the background of his poem as well as various aspects of scholarship relating to Lucretius.

Duff, J. Wight, and A. M. Duff. *A Literary History of Rome from the Origins to the Close of the Golden Age*. New York: Barnes and Noble Books, 1960. This companion volume to the Duffs' study of Silver Age Latin literature devotes a sizable chapter to Lucretius. It records the basic meager details of Lucretius' life, analyzes his poem, and makes several interesting cross-references to English Romantic and Victorian poets.

Latham, R. E., trans. *Lucretius: On the Nature of the Universe*. Baltimore: Penguin Books, 1951. This accurate translation has the great virtue of an introduction which discusses what is known about Lucretius' life and, more, outlines his poem section by section with line references. It is, by far, the best introduction to Lucretius for one unable to read Latin.

Leonard, William Ellery, and Stanley Barney Smith, eds. *T. Lucreti Cari De rerum natura*. Madison: University of Wisconsin Press, 1942. Though this is a Latin text with full apparatus, its special feature for non-Latinists is an introductory essay by Leonard, "Lucretius: The Man, the Poet, and the Times." Virtually a book-within-a-book, this essay discusses the period in which Lucretius lived, what is known and conjectured about his life, and what impelled Lucretius to write his poem.

Robert J. Forman

RAYMOND LULL

Born: c. 1235; Palma de Mallorca
Died: early 1316; at Tunis, on Majorca, or on the voyage to Majorca
Areas of Achievement: Literature, philosophy, and religion
Contribution: As the Doctor Illuminatus (enlightened teacher), Lull devised a unique and influential Neoplatonic and non-Scholastic philosophy. As a mystic and lay missionary, he founded a school of Arabic, composed Arabic books, and dialogued with Islamic savants in North Africa. As an author and poet, he helped create the Catalan language. Friend of rulers, prelates, and the powerful, he wandered the courts of Europe relentlessly as a propagandist for his many enterprises.

Early Life

Raymond Lull (Ramon Llull in his native Catalan) was born about 1235 to a Crusader who had helped conquer Islamic Majorca island some three years before. Like most youngsters of his affluent class, he apparently received a gentleman's education in the vernacular but called himself "illiterate" in the learned Latin. As was fashionable, he became a troubadour composer and gave himself to a life of womanizing and trivialities. A disputed report makes the boy Lull a page at the court of James the Conqueror, the ruler of the various realms confederated around Catalonia and Aragon; he held the post of majordomo, or head of household, at the subordinate court of the Conqueror's son, James II of Majorca. Lull's marriage to Blanca Picany in 1257 gave him a son Domènec and a daughter Magdalena, though he continued to live a dissolute life.

In later years, he confided many details of his life to monks of Vauvert in Paris, from which a fascinating *vita coetanea* (contemporary life) was composed in 1311. In it Lull tells of five apparitions of the crucified Christ in 1263 which frightened and then converted him to a life of religious fervor at age thirty.

Lull's Majorca was a cosmopolitan center of western Mediterranean trade and culture, with a third of its population still Muslim, with a large Jewish community, and with merchant colonies and an immigrant society from many countries. It was natural for Lull to focus on converting Muslims and to learn Arabic. Leaving a fund to support his abandoned family, he set about acquiring a formal education in Latin, while adopting the coarse cloth and mendicant life-style of a wandering holy man. During nine years of intensive study on Majorca, he learned Latin and Arabic passably well, and studied the Koran, the Talmud, and the Bible as well as the works of Plato, Aristotle, and the standard European authors. A book written by a disciple six years after his death shows Lull as a thin, serene figure, his bald head capped and his beard unusually long.

Life's Work

Lull was both a meditative thinker and a man of restless action. The two personas were fused: action in the service of his contemplative vision. His active life can be followed in his constant travels during thirty years, until his death at the end of a journey. During these travels, he wrote an average of nine or ten books a year. Some of these works were treatises or booklets, but seven ran to 150,000 words, three to 250,000, one to 400,000, and one to nearly a million. During his studies Lull had made a compendium in Arabic of al-Ghazzali's logic; more significant, he also wrote in Arabic *Libre de contemplació* (1273; *Book of Contemplation*, 1985). *Book of Contemplation* is an encyclopedic summa of mysticism; some scholars think it his greatest work. At the end of his studies, during two sessions of intense contemplation on Mount Randa on Majorca, he received a cosmic illumination and then a vision of a Christlike shepherd, which set the direction of his future thought and books. As a guest at La Real Abbey, he now composed the first version of his celebrated work on the ultimate constitution of reality and its symbolic expression in systems, which he called *Ars compendiosa inveniendi veritatem* (1274; a brief Art of finding truth). Later he devised a machine with crank and revolving wheel to demonstrate his Art graphically as propositions revolved in circles, squares, and triangles.

Acclaim for his books led James II of Majorca-Roussillon to invite Lull to his court at Montpellier in 1274-1275. Lull persuaded the king to endow a center or priory on Majorca called Miramar, where relays of thirteen Franciscan friars would learn Arabic for missionary work, a foundation Pope John XXI confirmed in 1276. Lull seems to have spent the next decade writing on Majorca, though older scholars have him traveling widely in Europe and Africa. The fourteen books finished on the island include *Libre de l'ordre de cavalleria* (1279; *The Book of the Order of Chivalry*, 1484), *Doctrina pueril* (1282; teaching of children), *Libre del gentil e dels tres savis* (1274-1276; *The Book of the Gentile and Three Wise Men*, 1985), and works on law, medicine, logic, theology, and angels. At Montpellier in 1283, he wrote his novel *Blanquerna* (English translation, 1925), named after its hero, and two more books on his Art. At Rome in 1287 seeking papal multiplication of language schools, Lull discovered that the Pope had died; he therefore journeyed to Paris to lecture on his Art at the university, to visit Philip the Fair, and to write his novel *Libre de meravalles* (1288-1289; *Felix: Or, Book of Wonders*, 1985) and five other works. Back at Montpellier, perhaps after a side trip to Rome, he lectured and wrote on his Art. A brief residence in Genoa allowed him to translate the latest work on his Art into Arabic, before pleading again at the papal court for schools and for a crusade; *Libre de passatge* (book of passage), his petition to Pope Nicholas IV, and his treatise on converting infidels date from this Roman stay of 1292.

Though his chronology is sometimes difficult to establish, Lull seems to have announced at Genoa his intention to preach to the Muslims in Tunis, but out of cowardice, he refused to sail. The resultant popular scorn induced a grave psychosomatic illness. Stirred by two visions, he tried unsuccessfully to enter the Dominican Order and then became a Franciscan external affiliate or layman-tertiary. He did voyage to Tunis in 1293, where his preaching on the Trinitarian Art to Muslim savants caused the Hafsid sultan Abū Hafs to imprison and then to expel him. At the Franco-Angevin court of Naples, Lull lectured on the Art, preaching also to the Muslim colony of nearby Lucera and conferring with the new pope, Celestine V, at Naples, in 1294-1295. Lull fitted in a trip to Barcelona and to Majorca, where he dedicated a philosophical work to his son; later, he returned in 1295 to Rome, where he presented two books to the latest pope, Boniface VIII. Stopping at Genoa to compose several books, Lull visited James II at Montpellier and traveled on for a prolonged stay lecturing at the University of Paris from 1297 to 1299. At Paris he consulted with Philip IV and composed thirteen of his most important works—on topics ranging from theology, mathematics, and astronomy to love, proverbs, and encouragement for the Venetian prisoners of war (including Marco Polo) at Genoa.

Staying at the court of James II of Aragon at Barcelona in 1299, Lull wrote two books and preached by royal permission to subject Muslims and Jews. In 1300-1301, he preached to Majorca's Muslims and wrote seven books. At the news that the Mongol khan Ghazan was conquering Syria, Lull embarked for Cyprus, intending to oppose him; once arrived, Lull found that the rumor was false. He visited Henry II of Cyprus, hoping that the king would send him to preach to the local Muslims and to the ruler of Islamic Egypt. Lull wrote two books on Cyprus, including his *Rhetorica nova* (1301; new rhetoric). Illness and an attempt by two assistants to poison him frustrated his efforts on the island. He visited Cilician Armenia, writing a book there on belief in God (1302). Perhaps after a trip to Jerusalem, he wrote *Mil proverbis* (1302; thousand proverbs) at sea on his way back to Italy. From 1303 to 1305, he worked alternately in Genoa and Montpellier, producing at Montpellier fifteen of the nineteen books written by him during this period.

At the court of James II of Aragon at Barcelona in 1305, Lull composed *Liber de Trinitate et Incarnatione* and *Liber praedicationis contra judeos*. In 1306, he worked at the University of Paris as well as at the court of Pope Clement V at Lyons. Back on Majorca, he took ship for Islamic Bougie, where he preached in the center of town and barely escaped being stoned. Jailed for six months and scheduled for execution, he wrote in Arabic a Christian-Muslim dialogue. Later, expelled, shipwrecked, and nearly drowned off Pisa, he took advantage of his recuperation in that city to finish his greatest work, *Ars generalis ultima* (1308; last general Art). At Pisa he composed a total of eight books, including one on memory, and tried to persuade the city council to found a crusading military order. He visited Genoa and Pope Clement V at Avignon, before settling down at Montpellier to write eighteen books during 1308-1309. While lecturing at the University of Paris in 1310-1311, he produced thirty-five books, many against the work of the philosopher Averroës.

When the ecumenical council met at Vienne in France in 1311-1312, Lull appeared before it to argue successfully for a statute mandating chairs of Oriental languages at the major universities. He also urged consolidation of the military orders for more effective crusading. The suppression of the Knights Templars in 1312 was the result. Back at Montpellier briefly in May, 1312, to write a book on angels, he continued on to Majorca, writing there seventeen books and making his will. He spent the year from spring, 1313, to spring, 1314, at the Messina court of his supporter Frederick III of Sicily, where thirty-seven books were published. He was in Tunis again in 1314-1315 and produced twenty-six more works, mostly small in size. Lull died prior to March, 1316, at Tunis, or Palma de Mallorca, or aboard ship on the way from Tunis.

Summary

Raymond Lull was the first European to write on philosophy in the ver-nacular. Since his goal was to unify the three faiths of Abraham (Judaism, Christianity, and Islam), revelation and mysticism were prime components of his philosophy as well as the reason for his writing and debating in Arabic. He joined elements of Islamic and Jewish learning to Christian thought, especially to the tradition of Augustinian Neoplatonism. Fundamentally syncretistic rather than innovative, his conceptual and stylistic patterns are puzzlingly complex. Lull is also the first great name in Catalan prose, and his *Blanquerna* is the first European novel on a contemporary theme. Audacious and immensely vigorous, he traveled tirelessly around the western Mediterranean as a propagandist and reformer. His writings are astonishing for their variety and number. The ten large volumes of the modern Mainz edition hold only fifty of his 280 works. Lull is famous as a mystic and a poet; he even has reputations as an occultist and a martyr. Attempting to organize all knowledge, his Art mechanizes logic and thought processes into what Anthony Bonner calls "an extraordinary network of systems" in symbolic computation, foreshadowing computer science.

For centuries after his death, theologians and philosophers were divided over his writings. In 1376 the inquisitor Nicholas Eymerich condemned one hundred Lullian "errors," and Pope Gregory XI condemned twenty of Lull's books; Pope Martin V reversed this condemnation in 1416. Jean de Gerson battled Lull's great influence at Paris and around 1400 had his Art banned from the Sorbonne. Nevertheless, Lullism continued to excite academics and mystics. He enjoyed a transcendental influence in the Renaissance, especially on Heinrich Cornelius Agrippa, Cardinal Bessarion, Giordano Bruno,

Nicholas of Cusa, Lefèvre d'Étaples, and Giovanni Pico della Mirandola. A chair was founded in Lull's name at the Renaissance university of Alcalá in 1508, and Philip II of Spain projected a Lullian academy in 1582. Lull's *The Book of the Order of Chivalry* was one of the first books published by William Caxton when printing came to England. Sir Francis Bacon, René Descartes, François Rabelais, and Jonathan Swift mocked Lull, but Gottfried Leibniz was deeply influenced by him. Though never canonized, the layman Lull was allowed a limited cultus within the Franciscan Order, with his feast day on July 3 confirmed in 1858 by Pope Pius IX.

Bibliography

Bonner, Anthony, trans. *Selected Works of Ramon Llull, 1232-1316*. 2 vols. Princeton, N.J.: Princeton University Press, 1985. Bonner's first one hundred pages of introduction provide an excellent short biography, including Lull's own semiautobiography. The footnotes are often important. Introductions, before each of the seven works (including two on his Art), add considerable information. Includes a revised catalog of Lull's works, by date and place, as well as a bibliography and an index.

Hillgarth, Jocelyn N. *Ramon Lull and Lullism in Fourteenth-Century France*. Oxford: Clarendon Press, 1971. Though concerned with Paris as the most important center of Lullism after Lull's death, Hillgarth also offers the best short biography of Lull in English. He also has a detailed chronology, bibliography, index, and clear plates of all twelve illustrations of Lull's life.

_____. *The Spanish Kingdoms, 1250-1216*. 2 vols. Oxford: Clarendon Press, 1976-1978. Besides giving full background on Lull's times, this eminent scholar has a long chapter comparing Lull with contemporary Spanish literary figures King Alfonso X, Don Juan Manuel, and Juan Ruiz, Archpriest of Hita.

Johnston, Mark D. *The Spiritual Logic of Ramon Llull*. Oxford: Clarendon Press, 1987. A scholarly philosophical survey of Lull's logic in its fundamentals and development. Johnston argues that Lull adapted his scholastic predecessors so that his Art was applied in a unique way to logic and became a program both of thought and of argumentation. Johnston concludes that Lull was not a philosophical genius, as most scholars think, but one of the greatest moral teachers. He includes a brief biography.

Peers, Edgar Allison. *Ramon Lull: A Biography*. New York: Macmillan, 1929. Outdated, especially on the disputed chronology of works and voyages, Peers's work is still the only full-length biography. Peers was an early Lull scholar who translated several of his works. This lengthy presentation in traditional biographical format should not be confused with Peers's later brief version, *Fool of Love: The Life of Ramon Lull* (1946).

Robert I. Burns

LYSIPPUS

Born: c. 390 B.C.; Sicyon, Greece
Died: c. 300 B.C.; place unknown
Area of Achievement: Art
Contribution: A sculptor whose career spanned virtually the entire fourth century B.C., Lysippus was not only a major transitional figure between classical and Hellenistic styles but the most renowned portraitist of the century as well.

Early Life

Though relatively little contemporary evidence survives about the man or his life, a considerable amount is known about the era in which Lysippus produced his art and about the key events and a number of the significant individuals that helped shape his career. Lysippus was born in Sicyon, in southern Greece. His early work is said to have reflected certain values and preoccupations of the fifth century B.C., when Greek civilization, led by Athens, defined for the West the essence of the classical in art. With the work of his later career, Lysippus' artistic concerns show dramatic change, as he established himself as perhaps the most renowned portraitist of antiquity, defining forever in sculpture the essence of Alexander the Great. There is perhaps no other ancient artist whose style evolved more dramatically or whose work more clearly reflects the significant changes of an era.

Subsequent to the great wars with Persia (490-478 B.C.), the Greek city-states, though independent political units, fell generally under the influence of either Sparta or Athens. These two city-states had achieved their ascendancy chiefly by force of arms; Sparta had been the dominant military power in Greece since at least the sixth century, and Athens had converted an alliance of coastal and island states in the early fifth century into a naval empire. Although it eventually fell to Sparta in 404, Athens for the last half of the fifth century was the cultural and intellectual center of all Greece. Here was defined the classical in the arts, notably in architecture (chiefly by the Parthenon) and in sculpture.

The fourth century witnessed in its early decades a series of attempts by different city-states to repeat the fifth century achievements of Athens and Sparta. Some, such as Thebes and Athens and Sparta themselves, met with limited success, but none had the resources, economic or military, to sustain it. Internally divided and weakened by constant warfare, the city-states by the mid-fourth century began to be pressured by the ambitions of outsiders, including Mausolus, dynast of Caria in Asia Minor, Jason of Pherae in Thessaly, and finally, Philip of Macedonia. Abruptly and decisively, the uncertainties of the mid-fourth century Greek world were brought to an end in 338, when Philip and his eighteen-year-old son, Alexander, overwhelmed a

Greek allied army at Chaeronea in central Greece. With defeat, the states of Greece were obliged to follow the lead of Macedonia, and during the next sixteen years stood, cowed and helpless, as Alexander succeeded his father and marched east, conquering by the time of his death in 323 most of the then-known world. By the time of his death, Alexander had been formally acknowledged a god by the Greeks, though his kingdom quickly suffered irreparable division at the hands of his successors. All of this Lysippus witnessed, from the attempts early in the century to replicate the achievements of the classical era to the partitioning of Alexander's empire in the last decades of the century. What Lysippus witnessed is reflected in his art.

Life's Work

While Lysippus is said to have been especially prolific during the course of his long career—it is claimed that he produced as many as fifteen hundred pieces—none of his works is known in fact to have survived, a consequence in part of his having worked primarily in bronze. What has survived is written testimony about a number of his more important pieces—mainly in the work of the first century A.D. Roman encyclopedist, Pliny the Elder—and some stone copies, which in subject matter and manner of execution seem consistent with what is known of Lysippus' work.

Lysippus' style early in his career is said to have been influenced by the work of Polyclitus, also a southern Greek and unquestionably one of the most important sculptors of the fifth century B.C. Polyclitus in his sculpture is said to have sought to express a sense of the Good and the Beautiful; that is, he attempted to represent in sculpture abstract values. It was Polyclitus' belief that there existed an underlying order in the universe and that this order could be understood in terms of mathematical ratios, much as the order of music can be understood. Polyclitus wrote a treatise (now lost) detailing his views and executed a piece that was to embody them, entitled the *Doryphorus* or *Spear Bearer* (dated c. 450-440 B.C.). This statue of an athlete standing, poised with spear held over the left shoulder, of which only stone copies survive, was so sculpted that each element stood in what Polyclitus judged to be a perfect ratio to every other element. Thus it possessed a perfect order and expressed Polyclitus' ideal of the Good and the Beautiful. Such preoccupation with form, with principles of organization, and with effecting a tension between the abstract and the concrete, the universal and the individual, became central characteristics of fifth century Greek classical style.

As he matured, Lysippus moved away from conformity to the classical norms of Polyclitus. Though no copies of his earlier works survive, those that do from the middle part of his career mark a turning from the abstract and universal toward a more explicit expression of the individual, the concrete, and the momentary. Not only is the statue of the athlete scraping himself with a strigil (called the *Apoxyomenos* and dated c. 330) executed in proportions more elongated (and thus visually more realistic) than those of the *Doryphorus*, but the statue is also fully three-dimensional: The arms are outstretched and actually intrude into the viewer's space and thus make more immediate the relationship between figure and viewer. Indeed, the action of the figure, cleansing after exercise, is intimate and private. Here, then, in the uncertainty of the mid-fourth century, the confidence that had been expressed by classical form gives way to the exploration of the momentary and transient.

Exploration of the individual in sculpture is effected most naturally through portraiture; in his later career, Lysippus became the master of this medium. An example that has survived, though again only in stone copies, is the statue of the seated Socrates. There is nothing in this statue to suggest the idealization of the human form. The philosopher, balding, eyes bulging, with satyrlike features and an exposed upper torso exhibiting the physical softening brought on by old age, sits gazing ahead in reflection or in mid-dialogue. The effect of realism is genuine and remarkable, especially since Socrates had been tried and executed in Athens in 399 and thus would never have been seen by Lysippus. As illustrated by this statue, Lysippus' portraiture sought to capture the essence of the subject. Like Polyclitus, Lysippus explored beneath the surface of things, but whereas Polyclitus sought with his art to define the ideal, Lysippus sought to define the real.

Such became the reputation of Lysippus that he was retained by the Macedonian court and later in his career served as the official sculptor of Alexander the Great. So prized was Lysippus' ability to capture Alexander's character that the young Macedonian king is alleged to have allowed no one else to render a likeness of him. Again, stone copies constitute the only visual evidence, but these are suggestive. Consistently in these copies, Alexander's head is turned to the side, tilted slightly upward, eyes deep-set and gazing, and hair folded back in waves. The essence captured is of a man in search, looking longingly beyond the present—an attitude attributed to Alexander by the historian Arrian. Lysippus would have seen Alexander and thus there is reason to believe the likeness truer to the person than is the portrait of Socrates. Confirmation comes from a story told by the ancient biographer Plutarch, who notes that Alexander's former rival and successor, Cassander, while walking in the sanctuary at Delphi, encountered a statue of Alexander, presumably by Lysippus, and was seized by a shuddering and trembling from which he barely recovered.

The realism of Lysippus' work was heightened, so it seems, by the attention he devoted to detail. He was recognized throughout his career as an especially skilled craftsman. In fact, Pliny notes that Lysippus was said to have been a student of no one but originally to have been a coppersmith. Other of his works known from copies are the *Agias* of Pharsalus, the copy of which is nearly contemporary with the original, a series of works on Heracles, who, like Alexander, attained the status of a divinity as a consequence of his heroic exploits, as well as depictions of a satyr, the god Eros, and Kairos (Fortune) made a divinity. Of his other works, only written testimony survives.

Summary

With the death of Alexander the Great in 323, a new era dawned in the eastern Mediterranean. Alexander's kingdom, lacking a designated heir, quickly was divided among his generals and companions into a series of rival monarchies and remained so until absorbed by Rome in the second century B.C. With the defeat at Chaeronea, the city-states of Greece had ceased to exercise internationally significant political or military influence. Greek culture, on the other hand, during this the so-called Hellenistic era was suffused throughout the entire Mediterranean. Much that was characteristic of Hellenistic visual art had been anticipated by Lysippus in the fourth century. In brief, Hellenistic sculpture explored the unique and the individual; it investigated internal emotional states and sought to extend the appreciation of form beyond the canons of the classical. Beyond the particular achievements of his own career, Lysippus may also be regarded as one of the significant transitional figures in the history of art.

Bibliography

Beazley, J. D., and Bernard Ashmole. *Greek Sculpture and Painting to the End of the Hellenistic Period*. Cambridge: Cambridge University Press, 1932, reprint 1966. This is a standard, scholarly handbook on Greek sculpture and painting from the early archaic period to the Hellenistic era. The text is concise; the illustrations are numerous and of excellent quality. There is a separate chapter on the sculpture of the fourth century.

Boardman, John. *Greek Art*. Oxford: Oxford University Press, 1964, rev. ed. 1973. Part of The World of Art series, the volume surveys systematically and with numerous illustrations the arts of Greece, major and minor, from the post-Mycenaean through the Hellenistic eras. Lysippus is examined in two chapters, one on classical sculpture and architecture, the other on Hellenistic art.

Carpenter, Rhys. *Greek Sculpture: A Critical Review*. Chicago: University of Chicago Press, 1960. Although a survey of sculpture from the archaic to Hellenistic eras, the work also focuses on the evolution of style in sculpture. Consequently, it makes no claim to completeness. The plates are excellent, though there are none of Lysippus' work.

Hammond, N. G. L. *A History of Greece to 322 B.C.* Oxford: Clarendon Press, 1959, 3d ed. 1986. This is an excellent standard survey, detailed and clearly written, of ancient Greek history: political, military, and cultural.

Lysippus is noted in a chapter on the intellectual background of the fourth century.

Jex-Blake, K., and E. Sellers. *The Elder Pliny's Chapters on the History of Art*. New York: Macmillan, 1896. Reprint. Chicago: Argonaut, 1968. This work includes the appropriate chapters from the text of Pliny the Elder's *Historia naturalis* (A.D. 77; *The Historie of the World*, 1601, better known as *Natural History*) with a translation by Jex-Blake and a commentary and historical introduction by Sellers. In addition, there is a preface and select bibliography on Pliny by R. V. Schoder. Pliny is the principal ancient source on Lysippus.

Johnson, Franklin P. *Lysippus*. Durham, N.C.: Duke University Press, 1927. A revised doctoral dissertation, this remains the most complete work on Lysippus available, though it is somewhat dated. The appendix is especially valuable, since it preserves all the ancient notices on Lysippus with English translations. There are numerous and excellent plates.

Pollitt, J. J. *Art and Experience in Classical Greece*. Cambridge: Cambridge University Press, 1972. This is an excellent analysis of Greek classical art, chiefly sculpture and architecture, and the intellectual and cultural context in which it was produced. Lysippus is examined in some detail. The plates are numerous and of a high quality.

Richter, G. M. A. *The Sculpture and Sculptors of the Greeks*. New Haven, Conn.: Yale University Press, 1929, 4th ed. 1970. This remains the standard volume on Greek sculpture from the early archaic through the late Hellenistic eras. As the title suggests, there are two main sections, one on sculpture, the other on known sculptors, including Lysippus. There are approximately three hundred pages of plates.

Edmund M. Burke

MA YÜAN

Born: c. 1165; Ho Chung, Shansi, China
Died: c. 1225; Hangchow, Chekiang, China
Area of Achievement: Art
Contribution: Together with his somewhat younger contemporary, Hsia
  Kuei, Ma Yüan formed the Ma-Hsia school of Chinese painting. In some
  ways, the school served as the prototype for Chinese landscape painting
  and heavily influenced both Chinese and Japanese painters.

Early Life
Ma Yüan belonged to what was probably the most prolific and distinguished family of painter-scholars in Chinese history. Altogether, seven members of his family served the Northern and Southern Sung imperial families. This service lasted from the time of Yüan's great-grandfather Ma Fen in the late eleventh century, to that of his son Ma Lin in the mid-thirteenth century. Besides Yüan, the Ma artists included his great-grandfather, Fen; his grandfather, Hsing-tsu; Shih-jung, his father; Kung-hsien, an uncle; K'uei, his brother; and his son Lin. Each of them received accolades from the imperial court, but unquestionably Ma Yüan became the most famous, and his legacy was the most profound.

Despite the acclaim which surrounded the Ma painters, little is known about their personal lives, and exact dates for their professional careers are generally missing. In part, the absence of such information reflects the turbulence of the times in which they lived. Ma Fen painted at a time when the Chinese rulers of the Northern Sung Dynasty were conspiring with a Tungusic people, the Juchen, to end the Khitan control over northern China. While this alliance did manage to displace the Khitans in 1126, the subsequent rupture between the Sung and the Juchen resulted in a further loss of territory and a rather ignominious Chinese retreat to the south. The imperial court abandoned the capital, Kai-feng, and moved to Hangchow at the mouth of the Che estuary in the Yangtze area. Despite the fact that Hangchow became the most beautiful of Chinese capitals, the sting of losing northern China to "barbarians" marked the Southern Sung in Chinese eyes as less than respectable. One Chinese critic, for example, has said that Ma's "incomplete" paintings were a reflection of a "divided and less than complete empire."

During Ma Yüan's lifetime, the Southern Sung was in even further military retreat, a time when Genghis Khan was forming the Mongol nation and setting it on the path toward world conquest. The Mongols would become the first foreigners in Chinese history to conquer all China, and the Southern Sung would bear the stigma of being the first dynasty to have lost all China to a "barbarian" conqueror.

Despite the Southern Sung's so-called military weakness, a point which many Western scholars claim has been exaggerated by Chinese historians, the dynasty was a glorious and sophisticated one. During the late twelfth and early thirteenth centuries, Hangchow was surely the most cosmopolitan city in the world, and the imperial Chinese court surrounded itself with scholars, historians, poets, and painters. Neo-Confucianism flourished, and poetry and prose of great excellence abounded. The wealthy lived luxurious and generally tranquil lives.

It was in such a milieu that Ma Yüan worked. No doubt he was highly literate and something of a scholar, as were most of the court dignitaries of that period. If the reign of the Southern Sung was not known as a great military period of Chinese history, it was certainly one of the most enlightened in terms of scholarship and governmental support of artists. Thus, Ma Yüan received numerous awards, such as the Golden Girdle, and was artist-in-attendance at the imperial court.

The earliest suggested painting by Ma Yüan purportedly dates from the reign of Kao Tsung (1127-1162), although such an early date is unlikely. At the latest, Ma was said to have still been artist-in-attendance during the reign of Li Tsung (1225-1264). Certainly he was very active during the reign of Ning Tsung (1195-1224), receiving as he did the patronage of the empress Yang and her family. This patronage is verified by several seals bearing the empress Yang's name, together with inscriptions on Ma Yüan's paintings. These inscriptions not only offer some of the very few concrete dates connected to Ma Yüan but also corroborate the generally held view that Ma's career was principally that of a court painter.

Life's Work

Ma Yüan's paintings offer a glimpse of court life in Hangchow. Many of the works attributed to him depict favorite aristocratic pastimes, such as nighttime entertainment in a villa or scenes from the panoramic West Lake. Yet, Ma Yüan was much more than a reflection of the grandeur of the Sung court. Consciously or not, he began a style unique to him and his younger contemporary, Hsia Kuei, which would make his career a watershed in the history of Chinese art.

In addition to his nicknames Ch'in-shan and Ho-chung (the latter indicating that he was from Ho Chung, Shansi), Ma was also known as "One-Cornered Ma." The latter name reveals the innovative aspects of Ma's career. "One corner" refers to a tendency in many of Ma's works to emphasize one corner of a scene. This was described by some Chinese critics as "leaning to one corner," or—as mentioned earlier—being incomplete.

Ma's one-corner emphasis may have been a reflection of Taoist beliefs concerning the illusory nature of appearances; certainly, mood and imagination are more important in his art than is detailed reproduction. Critics and detractors of Ma Yüan's style and paintings often refer to his lyric and poetic qualities. Empty spaces are, in his works, opportunities for the viewer's imagination to soar.

Ma's one-cornered style calls to mind the approach of the great Taoist historian of the Early Han, Ssu-ma Ch'ien (fl. 100 B.C.), who often narrated a biography of a particular subject from the narrow perspective of the subject himself, and left other perspectives to the biographies of the subject's contemporaries. In a sense, this too was a one-cornered approach. One final explanation for Ma's style is that, as part of China was occupied by a "barbarian" state, the Juchen Chin Dynasty, the Southern Sung constituted only a corner of the true Chinese empire and was—as mentioned above— incomplete.

Regardless of whether Ma's peculiar quirk was a political statement or a philosophical expression, the result resembles the work of a photographer who consciously blurs all but the focal point of a shot. In Ma Yüan, this technique was executed with great subtlety, and it endowed his paintings with an almost eerie sense of transience.

Not all aspects of Ma Yüan's style were original. Like Hsia Kuei, Ma often used what has been described as the ax-stroke method of depicting rocky mountains. This technique, which is generally attributed to the great Northern Sung painter Li T'ang (fl. 1100), has been described as "hacking out the angular facets of rocks with the side of the brush." Sharp contours can be seen elsewhere in Ma Yüan's works, and critics have referred to his "exact severity" and use of a "squeezed brush" to define leaves. Furthermore, the seemingly restless movement of water in many of his works is often said to be typical of the "fighting-water" technique. While precedents for all but the one-cornered style can be found, the combinations which Ma used emerge as singularly his.

His works, often in the form of fans, album leaves, and (less frequently) scrolls, painted in ink with traces of color, can be found in numerous museums around the world. In the United States, paintings by Ma Yüan and very close Ming copies of his work are located in the Cincinnati Art Museum, the Cleveland Museum of Art, the Fogg Museum, and the Freer Gallery. Many more of his works hang in Japanese galleries. The reason for this is his great popularity during the Ashikaga period (1338-1573) in Japan. Unfortunately it is also a consequence of Japanese collectors' helping themselves during their country's wartime occupation of China. In China, the majority of Ma's works available for viewing are in either the Beijing or the Taipei palace museums. A major problem for those wishing to examine his art lies in the fact that forgeries and imitations are common, and not a few of the paintings bearing his name were done by his students or by later admirers. With a few exceptions, however, art experts have been able to distinguish the genuine works from imitations with considerable confidence.

Summary

The impact of Ma Yüan on subsequent Chinese painting was slow in developing. In some measure, this was a result of Chinese art critics' characterizing Ma and Hsia Kuei as belonging to the northern school of painting, at a time when the southern school was considered to be the proper school for China's literati. Such distinctions were social as much as they were aesthetic; the professional court painters were criticized in contrast to the literati, who pursued painting strictly as a gentlemanly hobby. Furthermore, the Ma-Hsia school was sometimes derided as being an academic school whose style was easily learned. During the Ming Dynasty (1368-1644), however, interest in Ma Yüan and appreciation of his worth began to develop.

Even before the Ming resurrection of the Ma-Hsia school, the Japanese had begun to admire these two painters and their school. Because the paintings were not yet highly collectible and therefore could be acquired without great difficulty, the Japanese brought back numerous fine examples of both painters, particularly during the shogunates of Yoshimitsu (1358-1408) and Yoshimasa (1435-1490) of the Ashikaga period. The Ma-Hsia school has remained popular in Japan to this day. Moreover, in recent years Western critics have come to consider Ma Yüan and Hsia Kuei the best of the Chinese landscape painters. An interesting development is that Chinese critics may be taking their cue from Japan and the West in elevating Ma to the highest echelon of China's artistic pantheon.

Bibliography

Bush, Susan. *The Chinese Literati on Painting: Su Shih, 1037-1101, to Tung Chi Chi-ch'ang, 1555-1636.* Cambridge, Mass.: Harvard University Press, 1971. Quotes several Chinese scholars' views of Ma Yüan and Hsia Kuei.

Cahill, James. *Chinese Painting.* New York: Rizzoli International, 1977. Contains a chapter devoted to Ma Yüan, Hsia Kuei, and Ma Lin, with examples of their work.

——————. *An Index of Early Chinese Painters and Paintings: T'ang, Sung, and Yuan.* Berkeley: University of California Press, 1980. Contains a lengthy list of paintings attributed to Ma Yüan which are located in museums and private collections.

Edwards, Richard. "Ma Yuan." In *Sung Biographies*, edited by Herbert Franke. Wiesbaden, West Germany: Franz Steiner, 1976. The most detailed discussion of Ma Yüan in English, with an excellent discussion of Ma's impact on Chinese art.

Gernet, Jacques. *Daily Life in China on the Eve of the Mongol Invasion, 1250-1276.* New York: Macmillan, 1962. Simplistic but useful description of Southern Sung and Hangchow shortly after Ma Yüan's life.

Loehr, Max. *The Great Painters of China.* New York: Harper and Row, Publishers, 1980. Contains a very brief sketch of Ma Yüan's family and life, together with several photographs of paintings attributed to Ma Yüan.

Munsterberg, Hugo. *The Landscape Painting of China and Japan*. Rutland, Vt.: Charles E. Tuttle Co., 1955. In Munsterberg's chapter on the Southern Sung period, there is a brief discussion of Ma Yüan and Hsia Kuei, their paintings, and their impact on later Chinese art.

Sirén, Oswald. *Chinese Painting: Leading Masters and Principles*. Vol. 2. London: Ronald Press, 1956. Contains a glowing critique of Ma Yüan's paintings.

_____. *A History of Early Chinese Painting*. Vol. 2. London: E. Weyhe, 1932. Contains a brief discussion of the Ma-Hsia school with examples of their work.

Sullivan, Michael. *The Arts of China*. London: Thames and Hudson, 1973. Contains a brief passage about Ma Yüan and Hsia Kuei with an example of the work of each.

Swann, Peter C. *Art of China, Korea, and Japan*. New York: Praeger Publishers, 1963. Contains a very brief discussion of the Ma-Hsia school, with examples of their paintings.

Waley, Arthur. *An Introduction to the Study of Chinese Painting*. New York: Grove Press, 1958. Authoritative discussion of the Ma-Hsia school.

Hilel B. Salomon

GUILLAUME DE MACHAUT

Born: c. 1300; Machault, near Reims, France
Died: Possibly April, 1377; Reims, France
Areas of Achievement: Music and literature
Contribution: Generally acclaimed as the most important figure of the French *ars nova*, Machaut—poet, musician, courtier, and diplomat—was among the first to compose polyphonic settings of the fixed forms of medieval poetry (ballade, rondeau, virelay), to write songs for four voices, and to compose an integrated setting of the entire Ordinary of the Mass.

Early Life

Guillaume de Machaut was born around the beginning of the fourteenth century, most probably in the village of Machault in the Champagne region of France, not far from the cathedral city of Reims. Some music historians surmise that he may have been born in Reims itself, but as practically nothing is known of his early life, such speculations remain mere guesses; one scholar, however, has traced the existence of a Wuillaume Machaux—who may have been the poet's father—at Reims around 1310. The little information available indicates that Machaut was educated by clerics in an ecclesiastical venue, probably in Paris and Reims, and that he eventually earned a master of arts degree, although he never took Holy Orders.

Sometime around 1323, Machaut joined the entourage of John of Luxembourg, the blind King of Bohemia, a well-admired ruler and exemplar of chivalry and courtesy and a lover of war and the battlefield. For the next several years, Machaut's life involved constant travel—primarily because John involved himself in various military campaigns, although much of the travel was simply for entertainment—to places such as France, Lithuania, Poland, Prussia, and Silesia. One of Machaut's earliest known works, *Bone pastor Guillerme* (1324), a Latin motet celebrating the installation of Guillaume de Trie as the new Archbishop of Reims, was written during his early years in King John's service. Another work, *Le Jugement dou Roy de Behaingne*, although undated, was almost certainly written during the years Machaut spent with John. As clerk, personal secretary, and general assistant to King John, Machaut frequently benefited from the king's influence on Popes John XXII and Benedict XII: In 1330, he was named canon at Verdun; in 1332, he became canon at Arras; and in 1337, he was awarded a more desirable canonicate in Reims. Machaut appears to have settled in Reims in the late 1330's, leaving that city only to accompany King John on occasional journeys. After the king's heroic suicide in the battle at Crécy in 1346, Machaut continued his association with the royal family through King John's daughter, Bonne of Luxembourg, who later became the wife of John II of France. He also maintained close ties with other nobles, among them Charles of Navarre, Jean de France, the future Charles V of France, and Amadeus VI of Savoy.

Life's Work

Although Machaut remained linked with the royal courts of Europe, he spent the rest of his life as a canon at Reims Cathedral, having relinquished his other canonicates. Evidence points to the probability that the Reims canons—who were either tonsured clerics, as Machaut probably was, or priests who had taken Holy Orders—functioned as choristers for cathedral services. As churchmen, they were bound by innumerable rules of behavior and dress: They were required to dine together at the refectory on certain days of the week as well as certain holy days; they had to reside within the city walls of Reims; and they had to sing a minimum of thirty-two masses during the year. Although this restrictive and semicloistered life in a cathedral city was markedly different from the exciting years of foreign travel with King John, it provided Machaut with both the time and the artistic environment in which to write poetry and compose music.

Machaut's *Remède de Fortune*—a long poem generally considered an early work, although it is difficult to assign specific dates to much of Machaut's output—is a didactic narrative in which a lover passionately delineates the physical and moral beauty of the lady he adores and asserts that his love for her has instilled in him all the virtues. A collection of examples of both the lyric forms he favored (ballade, *lai*, rondeau, and virelay) and older forms (*complainte* and *chanson royale*) which he used only in this work, the *Remède de Fortune* is something of an anthology of fourteenth century lyric forms. Many of the individual forms look back to *trouvère* compositions of the thirteenth century with their occasional reliance on the old rhythmic modes and stanzaic forms and in their three-voice structure, which suggests French polyphony of the age preceding that of Machaut; the ballades, however, have four voices—a decided innovation—although the fourth voice may have been intended as an alternate to one of the other three.

La Fonteinne amoureuse (written between 1360 and 1362) has attracted critical attention for its treatment of the story of Paris of Troy and his judgment of the three goddesses. In this poem, the narrator overhears a young nobleman lamenting his unrequited love. The two men discuss at length the fountain of love from which the nobleman has drunk, and then they fall asleep. They both dream that Venus appears and recounts Paris' story and then produces the lady whom the nobleman loves. The lovers exchange rings, the dream fades, and the two men awaken. On the nobleman's finger is the lady's ring, and he vows to spend his life serving Venus and building a temple in her honor. Although this poem has traditionally been seen as a flattering portrait of Jean de France on the eve of his marriage, recent scholarship refutes that theory by indicating that the poem is, in reality, a critical look at the results of a nobleman's devoting himself to love instead of to the responsibilities of his position as a member of the nobility.

Around 1364, Machaut completed his *La Messe de Nostre Dame*, a complex work and the first complete surviving polyphonic setting of the Ordinary of the Mass. In the following century, such settings would become common, but in Machaut's day his achievement was monumental. The mass is in four voices and without instrumentation, although in its performance an organ may have doubled the tenor part in some sections. Machaut broke from the custom of his predecessors in using more ornamentation and contrary motion between voices, ensuring that the text was emphasized and therefore heard. Pope John XXII, who had been responsible for Machaut's comfortable position at Reims, had in his Bull of 1324-1325 required that the text of the Mass be clearly heard and not submerged in the music.

Machaut's most interesting and most famous work is probably *Le Voir-Dit* (1365), a nine-thousand-line romance that features different meters, forty-six letters in prose, and several lyric poems, some of them set to music. The work is particularly interesting to medieval scholars because it supplies much biographical information about Machaut, not only concrete facts but also commentary on his psychological state during specific incidents. In the piece, Machaut, then in his sixties, describes in some detail his love affair with a seventeen-year-old noble lady whose identity has long occupied scholarly interest. Initially thought to be Agnes d'Evreux, sister of Charles the Bad of Navarre, Toute-belle (Machaut's name for his lover) is now generally held to be Peronne d'Unchair, Dame of Armentieres, a wealthy heiress from Machaut's home province of Champagne. *Le Voir-Dit* contains one of the famous correspondences of literary history in its series of letters between the narrator and the young lady, who insists that he publicize their affair in songs and poems, some of them supposedly of her own composing. It is clear from the letters that the lady enjoys the notoriety of her affair with a celebrated poet, as she alternately teases her elderly lover and chides him for being afraid to visit her. Machaut's narrator is a decided departure from the typical courtly lover in that he describes himself as aged, gouty, blind in one eye, and undignified. Such a lover would become common in later narrative poetry, much of it influenced by Machaut's works.

As a composer, Machaut produced a body of work that is larger than that of any other fourteenth century musician and noteworthy for its range of form and style. Early in his career he had concentrated on traditional forms such as the motet, but he became more and more interested in secular song and polyphony, combining the two traditions in his ballades and rondeaux, many of which were incorporated into his long narrative poems, such as *Remède de Fortune* and *Le Voir-Dit*.

In his later years, Machaut seems to have devoted his time to supervising the production of his works in elaborately illuminated and very expensive

manuscripts for some of his royal patrons, among them Amadeus of Savoy
and Jean de France. Machaut died sometime in 1377 in Reims, where he had
produced so much of his best work.

Summary

As Master of Reims, Guillaume de Machaut enjoyed fame and prestige
during his lifetime and remained a major figure for some time after his
death. His real contribution, however, lies in his influence on other, later poets, not only in France but also in England. Not a true innovator (the fixed
forms he favored had evolved in the work of others), he took the literary
heritage in which he had been educated and adapted and reworked it, thus
creating a synthesis of past and present. In one way or another, Machaut was
indirectly responsible for several of the major developments in the verse narrative of the Middle Ages; his corpus of work includes early examples of the
judgment poem, the poem of complaint against Fortune, the consolation
poem, the Marguerite poem, the poem containing classical *exempla*, and the
poem with an elderly man as narrator. He helped to introduce into lyric verse
some elements—the woman's point of view, the psychology of dreams, the
combination of allegory and autobiography—which would become common-
places in the poetry of later eras. Yet many of his works represent nearly perfect manifestations of older genres that fell into disfavor soon after his death;
among these are the *lai*, virelay, motet, and *dit amoreus*.

In the prologue to *Le Dit dou Vergier* (generally considered, on the basis
of its style and allusions, to be his first long narrative poem, although no date
is available), Machaut describes his theory of poetry: Because poetry is language ornamented with rhyme and meter, it is allied to both music and rhetoric; its function should be lyrical, allegorical, didactic, and personal. Machaut clearly believed that poetry and music belonged together. Eustache
Deschamps, the self-proclaimed disciple of Machaut (and probably his
nephew), re-elaborated Machaut's ideas in his *L'Art de dictier* (1392), in
which he illustrated the interrelationship of music and poetry and the idea of
poetry as song.

Praised by many medieval poets in various countries, Machaut was a major
influence on Jean Froissart, Christine de Pisan, and certainly Geoffrey Chaucer, whose *The Book of the Duchess* (c. 1370) clearly derives in part from at
least seven of Machaut's narrative poems, as well as from a few motets and at
least one *lai*.

Bibliography

Brownlee, Kevin. *Poetic Identity in Guillaume de Machaut*. Madison: Uni-
    versity of Wisconsin Press, 1984. An in-depth analysis of Machaut's pro-
    logue and his seven long narrative love poems, with special attention to
    Machaut's development of a distinct poetic identity. Brownlee shows that

Machaut created his identity as a poet by conjoining the clerkly narrator of Old French romance, the first-person voice of the court lyric, and the persona of the professional artist. The notes to each chapter are informative and valuable, as is the select bibliography listing both primary and secondary sources.

Caldwell, John. *Medieval Music*. Bloomington: Indiana University Press, 1978. A straightforward historical overview of Western music from about 950 to 1400. A chapter on fourteenth century French music provides a good introduction to Machaut's musical milieu and devotes several pages to a detailed discussion of Machaut's work, especially his handling of polyphony.

Calin, William. *A Poet at the Fountain: Essays on the Narrative Verse of Guillaume de Machaut*. Lexington: University Press of Kentucky, 1974. A series of essays examining the narrative verse of Guillaume de Machaut.

Cosman, Madeleine Pellner, and Bruce Chandler. *Machaut's World: Science and Art in the Fourteenth Century*. New York: New York Academy of Sciences, 1978. A collection of essays covering such topics as scientific thought, paper manufacturing, and Gothic architecture, all in the context of the fourteenth century that Machaut knew. The most valuable group of essays specifically discusses Machaut as a poet in the modern sense of the word, rather than as simply a poet-composer.

Ehrhart, Margaret J. *The Judgment of the Trojan Prince Paris in Medieval Literature*. Philadelphia: University of Pennsylvania Press, 1987. A study of several medieval versions of the story of the Trojan prince Paris, his judgment of the rival goddesses, and the consequences of that judgment. Included in the study is a detailed analysis of Machaut's *La Fonteinne amoureuse*, in which a lovesick young nobleman reenacts Paris' judgment and thus receives from Venus the object of his desires.

Patterson, W. F. *Three Centuries of French Poetic Theory: A Critical History of the Chief Arts of Poetry in France (1328-1630)*. New York: Russell and Russell, 1966. This three-volume work studies fourteenth, fifteenth, and sixteenth century treatises on the art of poetry in relation to the poetic production of those three centuries. Includes discussions of Machaut's work as a whole as well as several of his individual lyrics.

Wilkins, Nigel. Introduction to *La Louange des Dames*, by Guillaume de Machaut. New York: Barnes and Noble Books, 1973. Precedes a collection of Machaut's lyric poetry and musical settings. This introductory material, which is in English, contains valuable information on Machaut, including a good short biography, a bibliography of selected secondary sources, a chronology of Machaut's works and manuscript sources, and brief essays on Machaut's lyrics and his poetic form.

Wimsatt, James I. *The Marguerite Poetry of Guillaume de Machaut*. Chapel Hill: University of North Carolina Press, 1969. A monograph on Machaut's contribution to the body of fourteenth century love poetry addressed to the mysterious Lady Marguerite. Among other things, the study reveals that Machaut may well be the originator of most of the Marguerite imagery, that Marguerite almost certainly was a historical person connected with Pierre of Cyprus, and that Machaut's poem was a major influence on Geoffrey Chaucer's *The Legend of Good Women* (1380-1386).

Edelma Huntley

GAIUS MAECENAS

Born: April 13, c. 70 B.C.; probably Arretium
Died: September 30, 8 B.C.; Rome
Areas of Achievement: Literature and government
Contribution: Maecenas was one of the most powerful men in Rome of the
first century B.C., often functioning as diplomatic arbiter and city administrator. His most significant role was as patron to a circle of writers who
became known as the poets of the Golden Age of Latin literature.

Early Life

Gaius Maecenas Cilnius was born in Arretium (modern Arezzo, Italy) to a
wealthy equestrian family that traced its origins to Etruscan kings. Nothing is
known of the first thirty years of his life, but he must have received an aristocratic education, for he knew Greek as well as Latin. He first emerges in
ancient writers as the intimate friend and financial and political supporter of
Gaius Octavius (called Octavian before 27 B.C., Augustus thereafter), the
heir of Gaius Julius Caesar, the junior member of the Second Triumvirate,
and the future first Emperor of Rome.

Maecenas greatly preferred the life of a private citizen, but he shocked
Rome. He hosted extravagant parties, drank excessively, and wore his tunic
unbelted (in opposition to proper Roman fashion). Two eunuchs frequently
accompanied him through the streets. Although he became notorious as self-
indulgent and effeminate, Maecenas appears to have been popular with the
Roman people.

Octavian also liked, and trusted, Maecenas. In the years directly following
44 B.C., the young heir found himself faced with the monumental task of
avenging his adopted father's murder and making all Italy safe from disen-
franchised Romans. Initially, he struck an alliance with Marcus Antonius
(Mark Antony), then with Sextus Pompeius, whose bands were raiding the
southern coast of Italy. Repeated setbacks with these two, however, convinced Octavian to enlist the aid of friends. Marcus Vipsanius Agrippa
became his general, and Maecenas his diplomat and politician.

At Octavian's request, Maecenas arranged an engagement between Octavian and Scribonia, Sextus' sister-in-law, in the hope of allying Octavian
with Sextus. When relations grew strained between Octavian and Antony,
Maecenas helped arbitrate reconciliations at Brundisium, in 40, and at
Tarentum, in 37 B.C. For unknown reasons, he was present at the Battle
of Philippi (42 B.C.), where Octavian and Agrippa defeated the forces of
Gaius Cassius Longinus and Marcus Junius Brutus, the major surviving assassins of Julius Caesar. Octavian again inexplicably summoned him to Actium
(31 B.C.), where the troops of Antony and Cleopatra were defeated. He may
also have been present at the campaigns against Sextus.

When Maecenas' services were not required in the field, he was governing Rome and the rest of Italy. Octavian had entrusted Maecenas in his absence with temporary administration of the city, hoping to bolster popular support for himself and quash any resurgent popularity for his opponents. Maecenas now held all the powers of City Prefect, but without the title. His power even extended to issuing official proclamations. He quelled a civil riot in 37 B.C., and in 30 B.C. he quietly crushed the assassination plot against Octavian which was led by the son of the recently deposed Triumvir, Marcus Aemilius Lepidus. Maecenas made the city streets safe after dark and may have helped rid Rome of magicians and astrologers. All these duties without benefit of public office endowed Maecenas with powers greater than those of any elected official.

Life's Work

Octavian's return to Rome in 29 B.C. ended Maecenas' role as public servant, but not his influence in Rome. While he had been acting as diplomat and administrator, Maecenas had also begun befriending at Rome a number of writers whose talents he could use to the advantage of Octavian's new political order. To this growing group of friends he had assumed the role of literary patron, a role to which he now devoted all his energy. Literary patronage frequently included gifts of money or possessions. In addition, it usually included a larger audience for a poet's writings, circulation of his poems, and their publication. Maecenas entertained certain of his friends at his mansion to provide these benefits. Scholars disagree as to what extent Maecenas actually used his patronage to foster a state propaganda literature, but the works of his poets make it clear that they realized some expectation on the part of Augustus. In several of his *Odes* written in 23 B.C. (for example, 1.20) the poet Quintus Horatius Flaccus (Horace) answers with a polite refusal (*recusatio*) a request from his patron to write on a suggested topic. Sextus Propertius (*Elegies* 2.1, c. 25-28 B.C.), does the same when Maecenas suggests a change in theme from love to state matters. Since the literary refusal was standard in Alexandrian verse, it is uncertain how strongly Maecenas actually made his requests for propaganda poems. He may have done no more than give general guidance.

Maecenas' circle included many people who have become little more than names to posterity: Gaius Melissus, Lucius Varius Rufus, Domitius Marsus, and Plotius Tucca. His three most famous poets, however, whose works have survived to modern times have immortalized Maecenas. Publius Vergilius Maro (Vergil) may have become Maecenas' protégé as early as 40. His three major works, the *Eclogues* (43-37 B.C.), the *Georgics* (c. 37-29 B.C., written in honor of Maecenas), and the *Aeneid* (c. 29-19 B.C.), all glorify ideals which Octavian was trying to reinstate in society. In 38, Vergil and his friend Varius Rufus introduced Horace to Maecenas, who invited the young man to become one of his special "friends" eight months later when he returned from a diplomatic mission to the east on Octavian's behalf. Horace's lyric poetry, while not as universally patriotic as Vergil's, does reflect his respect for Octavian and the new regime. Propertius, who was already an established elegiac poet, became one of Maecenas' circle about 25 B.C. and dedicated the first poem of his second book to Maecenas, though his poetry is least indicative of Augustan ideals.

It is a paradox that the man who sought out and encouraged the most talented group of literary artists of his day was himself an author of the worst type. Enough fragments of his works survive to reveal that his compositions were oddly expressed and affected. Augustus disliked his style and parodied it unmercifully.

From his semiretirement in 29 until about 20, Maecenas reigned as the predominant literary patron in Rome. This era saw the publication of Horace's *Odes* (books 1-3), Vergil's *Georgics*, and the second book of Propertius' *Elegies*. Thereafter, Augustus personally assumed the role of patron, and Maecenas returned completely to private life.

Ancients and moderns have speculated on this shift in literary power. Ancient historians supposed that Augustus never forgave Maecenas for telling his wife, Terentia, of the discovery of her brother's conspiracy against the emperor. Others say that Augustus' passion for his friend's wife led to the rift. Maecenas, for his part, may have wished, for personal or health reasons, to resume the life of a private citizen. Many modern scholars believe that Augustus was the real patron, Maecenas only his interim manager. Augustus, now secure in his position as princeps (first citizen) and at leisure to pursue more than war, no longer needed Maecenas as an intermediary between himself and the writers. Since Maecenas always preferred the life of a private citizen, his retirement may have been mutually desirable.

Even in retirement, however, Maecenas retained influence with the emperor in public and private matters. Several times, Maecenas' sound judgment restored Augustus to an even temper. Moreover, it was supposedly on Maecenas' advice that Augustus married his daughter, Julia, to his general, Agrippa, in 21 B.C.

The life of private citizen seems to have suited Maecenas' tastes well. Despite his years as Augustus' factotum, Maecenas chose to limit his involvement in politics, refusing all elective offices and remaining an equestrian all of his life. He erected a huge mansion on the Esquiline Hill, which he transformed from a plebeian cemetery into a magnificent residential area. The estate included a large house, a magnificent tower, lush gardens, and even a swimming pool. There he lived with his wife, Terentia, a beautiful but faithless woman from whom he may eventually have been divorced.

Despite his eccentricities, Maecenas retained his popularity with the Roman people and his intimacy with individual friends. After recovering from a serious illness, for example, Maecenas was greeted with resounding applause from the audience as he entered a theater. Whenever Augustus was ill, he slept at Maecenas' house. Vergil had a house on the Esquiline Hill very near Maecenas'. Horace, who became his personal as well as professional friend, was buried near the tomb of Maecenas on that same hill.

Maecenas' excesses, though tolerated by Augustus and the Roman people, seem to have caught up with him. He suffered from a chronic fever for the last three years of his life. When Maecenas died, he was mourned by his friends and especially by Augustus, to whom he had devoted so much of his life, talents, and energy.

Summary

Maecenas, through his lifelong friendship with Augustus and his almost fifteen years' government service, helped Augustus establish a firm foundation for a smooth transition from the Roman Republic to the Roman Empire. It is his discovery, support, and nurturing of some of the greatest poets of Latin literature, however, that accounts for Maecenas' most lasting effect on the ancient world. He provided a buffer between the emperor and the poets, a role which had advantages for both factions. On the imperial side, Augustus was protected by the figure of Maecenas from the embarrassment of being eulogized by any poet unworthy of his theme. On the other hand, poets who might have felt compelled to yield to a suggestion from Augustus as if it were a command still exercised their prerogative of saying "no" to Maecenas. In this way, the illusion of the Roman Republic which allowed freedom of choice was maintained. Maecenas' patronage supported Augustus' assertion that the Republic had been restored.

Maecenas believed in the idea of merit rather than wealth or social class. In the poets he selected he must have recognized their ability to form their own judgment and must have trusted that judgment to guide them in their writings. While he may have provided encouragement and general guidance to the poets, Maecenas shrewdly avoided demanding particular types of poems from his authors. This policy of nonintervention distinguished him from preceding centuries of literary patrons and set the standard for later generations of patrons in Europe. By fostering such poets as Vergil, Horace, and Propertius, Maecenas became identified with the Golden Age he helped Augustus establish. By giving the poets the freedom to express themselves as they saw fit, Maecenas became the model for all future literary patrons. Immortalized by the Golden Age poets, Maecenas' name has become synonymous with the term literary patron.

Bibliography

Dalzell, A. "Maecenas and the Poets." *Phoenix* 10 (1956): 151-162. Provides an interesting argument, based on the evidence of ancient texts, that

Maecenas was not really Augustus' special patron of state propagandist literature. Most notes are from secondary sources (commentators), and more than half are in English.

DuQuesnay, I. M. Le M. "Horace and Maecenas: The Propaganda Value of *Sermones* I." In *Poetry and Politics in the Age of Augustus*, edited by Tony Woodman and David West. Cambridge: Cambridge University Press, 1984. A look at the *Satires* in the atmosphere of 38-36 B.C. and a convincing argument for the propagandist nature of the poems dedicated to Maecenas. Copious notes and a fine bibliography are useful to readers wishing to pursue the subject of Augustan propaganda through Maecenas.

Fraenkel, Eduard. *Horace.* Oxford: Clarendon Press, 1957. Focuses especially on Maecenas' personal relationship to Horace, with occasional references to the public Maecenas and fewer to the person. No bibliography, and the footnotes are in general good only for readers of Latin.

Gold, Barbara K. *Literary Patronage in Greece and Rome.* Chapel Hill: University of North Carolina Press, 1987. Bibliography, index, and copious notes are useful for both the general and the experienced reader. Maecenas' role as patron is explored especially in part 3, chapter 5, "Maecenas and Horace," which carefully explores their dynamic relationship as seen through Horace's writings.

Griffin, J. "Augustus and the Poets: *Caesar Qui Cogere Posset.*" In *Caesar Augustus: Seven Aspects*, edited by Fergus Millar and Erich Segal. Oxford: Clarendon Press, 1984. Cites practical reasons for Maecenas, not Augustus, being the patron of the literary set. Endnotes provide little explanation but instead refer the reader to ancient works, most of which can be found in English translation. Citations of foreign texts are of limited use to the general reader.

Reckford, Kenneth J. "Horace and Maecenas." *Transactions and Proceedings of the American Philological Association* 90 (1959): 195-208. Abundant bibliographical notes on the ancient sources that recount Maecenas' life and activities. A number of citations in Latin are of limited use to the general reader, but the first part provides good background for Maecenas.

Shackleton Bailey, D. R. *Profile of Horace.* Cambridge, Mass.: Harvard University Press, 1982. Maecenas is mentioned everywhere in this excellent literary criticism of Horace's *Epodes* and *Satires*. Gives more of a sense of who Maecenas was as a patron than actual data on his life. Latin passages are translated. Limited bibliography.

Syme, Ronald. *The Roman Revolution.* Oxford: Clarendon Press, 1939. Maecenas is mentioned often as the close friend of Augustus, running personal and political errands for the leader and acting as a diplomat of invaluable skill. No straightforward biography. Minimal notes.

Joan E. Carr

MOSES MAIMONIDES

Born: March 30, 1135; Córdoba, Spain
Died: December 13, 1204; Cairo, Egypt
Areas of Achievement: Religion, philosophy, and medicine
Contribution: Through his classification of Jewish law, life, and observance, as defined in the Torah, Mishnah, and Talmud, and his further interpretation of the philosophical bases of Judaism in the light of Aristotelian thought, Maimonides influenced Jewish and Christian scholarship and trends, an influence which continues to the present. His work combining psychology and medicine may be interpreted as one of the early foundations of psychotherapy.

Early Life

Moses Maimonides was a child of destiny, recognized as such by the family and society into which he was born. His birth as son of the renowned Maimon ben Joseph was regarded as so important that the day, hour, and minute were recorded, as well as the fact that it occurred on the eve of Passover, which fell on the Sabbath. The young Maimonides (sometimes referred to as the "Second Moses") was extraordinarily sensitive to his religious and intellectual heritage and to an awareness of his destiny—to be a leader of his people. As a result of this precocity, the child spent no time playing or attending to his physical health, lest such activities interfere with his life's mission.

Although Maimonides' boyhood and physical characteristics are not recorded, biographical accounts place much emphasis upon his intellectual development. His major teacher was his father, who was a Talmudic scholar, a member of the Rabbinical Council, *dayan* (judge) of Córdoba (a position held for generations in the family), and an acknowledged scholar and writer in the areas of Bible exposition, Talmudic commentary, astronomy, and mathematics. The young boy's knowledge expanded from other sources as well: Jewish scholars, his relatively untroubled interactions with the life and scholars of the Spanish and Arab communities of Córdoba, and countless hours reading the manuscripts in his father's library. In turn, Maimonides, entrusted with the education of his younger brother, David, began to develop his classification skills as he transmitted his own knowledge to the younger boy.

When Maimonides was thirteen, the religiously fanatical Almohad faction captured Córdoba. Jews and Christians were initially forced to choose between apostasy and death but later were allowed the third option of emigration. Historical sources are unclear as to how long Maimonides' family remained in Córdoba, in what other cities they lived, or whether they formally converted or professed belief in the other monotheistic religion while continuing to practice Judaism. In their writings, both Maimonides and his father addressed the difficulties of living as a Jew and the minimum expectations afforded the still-practicing Jew in a hostile environment. Clearly, between 1148 and 1160, when the family settled in Fez in Morocco, Maimonides, in addition to his other activities, was collecting data for the three great works of his career.

In Fez, Maimonides studied medicine, read extensively, and wrote while his father and brother established a thriving jewelry business. While ostensibly involved with the Arabic community, the family remained faithfully Jewish. This period of accommodation with Muslim leaders and thought was broken by the prominence given to Maimonides' *Iggereth Hashemad* (c. 1162; *Letter Concerning Apostasy*), which reassured the many Jews who were similarly accommodating to their environment. Because this leadership position thrust upon Maimonides threatened the family's security, they emigrated to Palestine in 1165. After remaining five months in Acre, the family settled in Egypt, living first in Alexandria and then in Cairo.

During the family's stay in Alexandria, Maimonides' father died, and his brother David drowned. David's death was particularly grievous, as Maimonides wrote: "For a full year I lay on my couch, stricken with fever and despair." At age thirty, Maimonides began to support himself and David's wife and children financially by putting to use the medical career for which he had prepared during his years in Fez. Embarking upon his dual career of Jewish scholarship and medicine, Maimonides made notable contributions which remain relevant and significant to the present day. His personal life remains obscure, but his letters indicate that his first wife died young. He remarried in 1184 and fathered both a girl and a boy, Abraham, who later followed in his father's path of scholarship and leadership. In fact, ten generations of the Maimonides family followed as leaders of the Cairo community.

Life's Work

Maimonides' twofold scholarly approach throughout his life was to examine existent knowledge in a field through classification followed by integration. In clear and succinct form, he would then publish the results, which had a major impact as each succeeding generation continued to find new, contemporaneous, and ever-relevant meanings in his writings.

The achievements of Maimonides, one of history's "men for all seasons," are broad and deep. He has been equally influential in four areas: religion, philosophy, psychology, and medicine. In the fields of religion and religious thought, Maimonides made his significant impact primarily through two major works: *Siraj* (1168; *The Illumination*) and *Mishneh Torah* (1180; *The Code of Maimonides*, 1927-1965). The first was written in Arabic, the second in Hebrew. *Siraj* is a commentary on the Mishnah, the early compilation of Jewish law. Maimonides' intent in this work was to clarify for Jews the complex discussion of law of which the Mishnah is composed and to provide an understandable framework of guidelines for living a life satisfactory to God. Probably the most important section of the *Siraj* is the statement of Maimonides' articles of faith, the basic principles of Judaism, which include the existence of a Creator, the unity of Deity, the incorporeality of God, the external nature of God, the worship and adoration of God alone, the existence of prophecy, the greatness of Moses as a prophet, the gift of the Law to Moses by God on Sinai, the immutability of the Law, the knowledge by God of the acts of man, reward for the righteous and punishment for the wicked, the coming of the Messiah, and the resurrection of the dead.

The *Mishneh Torah* continues the explanation of Jewish law with a codification by subject of the content of the massive Talmud in fourteen books, each representing one area of Jewish law. The work begins with a statement of purpose, followed by book 1 on God and man. It ends with a poetic longing for the Messianic Age, when "the earth will be filled with the knowledge of God as the waters cover the sea."

Maimonides' contributions to religion and religious thought overlap his contributions in philosophy. His major philosophical contribution, however, is *Dalalat al-ha'rin* (1190; *Guide of the Perplexed*, 1881), in which he addresses and reconciles the rationalist Aristotelian philosophy with Jewish beliefs and faith. His treatments of philosophical constructs include discussions of God, Creation, prophecy, the nature of evil, Divine Providence, and the nature of man and moral virtue.

More than his other writings, *Guide of the Perplexed* has become part of mainstream philosophy of all society rather than remaining unique to Judaism. One reason for its generalized significance may be that it represents the beginnings of psychotherapy. In the section on the nature of man and moral virtue, Maimonides defines a life satisfactory to God as one which approaches happiness through development of intellect and control of appetites by morality, referring especially to control of the sexual drive. This work also represents a bridge between Maimonides' contribution in the second area, philosophy, and his major contributions to both the third and fourth areas: psychology and medicine.

In the study of medicine, Maimonides' significant contribution was in his clear, textbook descriptions of major areas of the discipline which he describes metaphorically as one of the "strange women [in addition to his betrothed, the Torah] whom I first took into my house as her handmaids [and who have] become rivals and absorb a portion of my time." Maimonides' medical writings date between 1180 and 1200 and include most notably *A Physician's Prayer*; his "aphorisms" (*The Medical Aphorisms of Moses Maimonides*, 1970, 1972); an encyclopedia; a glossary of drug names; treatises on asthma and poisons and their cures; and *Physiology and Psychology of Married Life*.

Summary

Maimonides' contributions span and integrate history. His contributions begin with his scholarship in religion and religious thought which explores concepts and events from Creation to the giving of the Torah, to the canonization of prophetic thought in the Mishnah and the Talmud. His scholarship then moves to philosophical contributions that integrate the Jewish world of antiquity with the Greek world of Aristotle and with the Arabic worlds of Spain and Egypt of the twelfth century. In his contributions to psychology and medicine, Maimonides foreshadows today's practices in healing and Freudian thought.

History shaped Maimonides' insights as he codified and synthesized Jewish literature. In turn, Maimonides guided the insights of his contemporaries and those of succeeding generations as he responded to the realities of medieval Spain and the traditions of Aristotle, developing a new blend of faith and rationalistic thought. He influenced the thought of succeeding scholars by providing new religious, philosophical, psychological, and medical foundations upon which to build the concept of a good life.

Bibliography

Bratton, Fred. *Maimonides: Medieval Modernist*. Boston: Beacon Press, 1967. Bratton's purpose is to acquaint the Christian world with the life and works of Maimonides from the viewpoint of a Christian. His easy-to-follow text, which places Maimonides in perspective in the environment of medieval Spain, evaluates the scholar's writings in relation to their impact on the Jewish-Christian worlds and European thought.

Cohen, Abraham. *The Teachings of Maimonides*. Reprint. New York: KTAV Publishing House, 1968. Cohen's treatise summarizes the teachings and views of Maimonides in a systematic classification. The prolegomenon by Marvin Fox that precedes this edition is a valuable introduction to the understanding of the various strong reactions throughout history to the teachings of Maimonides.

Goodman, Lenn Evan. *Rambam: Readings in the Philosophy of Moses Maimonides*. New York: Viking Press, 1976. This careful translation and commentary on Maimonides' *Guide of the Perplexed* and *Eight Chapters* (part of the commentary on the Mishnah) is also valuable for its long and helpful general introduction to the life and works of Maimonides and for the annotated bibliography of his writings, which follows the text.

Katchen, Aaron L. *Christian Hebraists and Dutch Rabbis*. Cambridge, Mass.: Harvard University Press, 1984. A recent treatment of Maimonides' influence, Katchen's work concentrates on seventeenth century Holland, in which the *Mishneh Torah* began to be translated and distributed widely. Included are an extensive bibliography and indexes to biblical passages from specific works, to specific titles from the Mishnah, to the Babylonian Talmud, to the Midrashic literature, and to other general literature.

Katz, Steven T., ed. *Maimonides: Selected Essays*. New York: Arno Press, 1980. One work of the series Jewish Philosophy, Mysticism, and the History of Ideas, the volume contains reprints of fourteen essays in four languages (English, French, German, and Italian) with original publication dates ranging from 1864 to 1937. Together, the essays represent the best of pre-World War II scholarship on Maimonides' writings.

Munz, J. *Maimonides: The Story of His Life and Genius*. Boston: Winchell-Thomas, 1935. This first volume of the Jewish Bookshelf series is a simply written, although flowery, introduction to the life and works of Maimonides.

Roth, Leon. *Spinoza, Descartes, and Maimonides*. New York: Russell and Russell, 1963. More than 60 percent of this book is devoted to an excellent exposition of the thinking of Maimonides, especially in his *Guide of the Perplexed*, in relation to the writings of Baruch Spinoza. Although the book supposedly focuses on Spinoza, Roth notes strongly that Maimonides influenced not only Spinoza but also "the course of European speculation," from Albertus Magnus and Thomas Aquinas to G. W. F. Hegel.

Yellin, David, and Israel Abrahams. *Maimonides, His Life and Works*. 3d ed. New York: Hermon Press, 1972. This third, revised edition of the classic originally published in 1903 remains the most complete treatment of the life of Maimonides, also embodying within its chronology a treatment of his most famous works. Noteworthy are the selected bibliography of books by and about Maimonides in English, the extensive notes, and the genealogical table of Maimonides' descendants through four generations.

June H. Schlessinger
Bernard Schlessinger

MANSA MŪSĀ

Born: c. 1280; probably Niani, Mali
Died: 1337; Niani, Mali
Area of Achievement: Government
Contribution: Mūsā was the ruler of the empire of Mali, the dominant political and cultural force in West Africa in the fourteenth century and a major influence in the development of an Islamic intellectual and religious environment in the region.

Early Life

Mansa Mūsā (also known as Kankan Musa) was a member of the powerful Keita clan, whose members ruled the West African empire of Mali from around 1250 until some two centuries later. According to the Muslim historian Ibn Khaldun, Mūsā was the ninth ruler of Mali and a grandnephew of its founder, Sunjata. ("Mansa" is an honorific title analogous to "highness" or "excellency" in Europe.)

Almost nothing is known about Mūsā's childhood, since the various chronicles that mention him are little more than dynastic narratives. It is reasonable to suppose that he was educated as a Muslim, a matter of importance in assessing his later achievements. Mali was the first large Islamic polity in West Africa, and the Keita dynasty was generally Islamized by Mūsā's time. There is considerable disagreement over whether Sunjata, the founder of the line, was a Muslim; he is usually depicted as a pagan sorcerer-king. For a time, the use of Arabic names for the Keita rulers was observed only indifferently, but by Mūsā's reign, the practice was firmly established.

Life's Work

Historians generally identify Mūsā's reign with the height of Malian prestige and cultural achievement. This tendency is, in part, a result of the fact that much more is known about Mūsā than about others of his clan. Ibn Khaldun covers Mali, particularly the career of Mūsā, extensively, despite the empire's position on the edge of the Islamic world, and the historian is effusive in his praise. Shortly after Mūsā's death, the accomplished traveler Ibn Battutah made his way to Mali and passed on a detailed and positive account of its culture. Mūsā also made himself more accessible to posterity by undertaking the *hajj*, the pilgrimage to Mecca, together with an enormous entourage. In 1324-1325, his party passed through Cairo, where he was interviewed by Egyptian government secretaries, and in 1338, some of these interviews were recorded by Ibn Fadl Allah al-'Umari, whose work still survives.

Evidence suggests that Mūsā was a devout Muslim, in contrast to the rather nominal piety of some of his predecessors. Although he was the third

ruler of the Keita dynasty to undertake the *hajj*, the first two did not take
Arabic names, and one of them died en route under mysterious circumstances. Mūsā appears to represent the growing Islamic influence in Mali,
but local traditions about him also imply that pagan religious and political
elements resented this development and on occasion may have resisted it.

Mūsā was the builder of a strong and growing empire, rather than the
caretaker of a kingdom in its golden age as some popular accounts suggest.
Even during his pilgrimage, Malian armies were active, and the capture of
the enormous Songhai principality of Gao, east of the great bend of the Niger River, may have forced the king to end his travels early and hasten back
to Mali. By the end of Mūsā's reign, Mali extended from the Atlantic coast,
near modern Senegal, close to the borders of contemporary Nigeria in the
east, and far into the Sahara Desert in the north. Only the forest fringe of
the West African coast from Liberia to Benin remained outside direct Malian
authority. Some historians describe Mali as being substantially larger than all
Europe. Though probably accurate as far as area is concerned, these estimates imply a far larger population than actually existed. A fairer comparison of the size and population of Mali would be to the Inca Empire in South
America.

Mali's livelihood derived principally from the export of gold across the Sahara to entrepôts on the Mediterranean, where it was purchased by European merchants. The trade itself began as early as Roman times, but during Mali's period of development and greatest strength, it expanded by at
least an order of magnitude. In the thirteenth and fourteenth centuries,
many European governments, pressed by expanding economies and currency
demands, returned to minting gold coins after a hiatus of many centuries.
The frantic demand for gold drove prices up and encouraged the systematiza-
tion of gold production in Mali. Under Mūsā and other Malian kings, the
gold trade became a state monopoly, and the revenue doubtless was critical
to the ability of the empire to expand and consolidate in Mūsā's time. In this
sense, Mūsā and the Keita clan were as much a part of the medieval economic surge in the Mediterranean world as any European family of bankers
or princes.

It was in religion and culture, however, that Mūsā may have had his greatest impact. He actively encouraged the spread of Islam and the development
of Islamic institutions. His efforts included a campaign for the construction
of mosques throughout his domain. Among the intellectuals who accompanied Mūsā back to Mali after his pilgrimage was Abu Ishaq al-Sahili, possibly the most outstanding architect of medieval Islam. His varied talents
included not only architecture and city planning but also poetry and music,
and they indicate the richness of Islamic culture with which Mūsā seeded his
kingdom. Abu Ishaq perfected techniques of mosque construction using
West African materials, including the difficult task of building minarets out

of mud brick. Some of his mosques still stand in the cities of modern Mali.

Mūsā also encouraged the development of systematic study and education. At the Sankore mosque in the fabled city of Timbuktu, near the northernmost part of the Niger's course, theologians, geographers, mathematicians, historians, and scientists gathered into a community which continued to publish until well into the eighteenth century. Just as Christian thinkers collected around cathedrals and thus began the European university tradition, Muslim intellectuals congregated around mosques, and Sankore was one of the best. Its fame spread as far as Egypt and Morocco. Professors summoned to teach in Timbuktu from some of the intellectual hotbeds of Islam often became the students of the Timbuktu scholars rather than their instructors. Mansa Mūsā probably died in 1337.

Summary

Under Mansa Mūsā, Mali achieved a level of wealth and international prestige never before experienced in West Africa. It carried on diplomatic relations with Egypt, North African kingdoms, and other African states, and occasionally came to the notice of Europeans. Malian administrative and economic elaboration was crucial to driving the forces of medieval European expansion, trade, and capital accumulation. Thanks to Mūsā's determination, Islam was able to sink its roots deeply into West African culture.

There was, however, a tragic element in Mansa Mūsā's story. His was a tempestuous family; no firm rules of succession could be established. Mūsā himself may have come to the throne in circumstances of intrigue: He told the Egyptians a story of his predecessor having disappeared on an ocean voyage. Owing in part to this dynastic instability, much of the cultural efflorescence under Mūsā did not survive.

Nor did a substantial amount of his contrived Islamic influence. Underneath the struggles for power in Mali and the Keita clan lay a network of pagan priests and other royal families who regarded Islam as an adversary. Later, the Songhai broke away from Mali and eventually overwhelmed it. They were more disposed to paganism, and in the Songhai period, many elements of Islamic culture and influence in West Africa vanished or were seriously diminished. Most historians, more familiar with recent African history than with the medieval period, consequently have undervalued the influence of Islam in West African history.

The greatest irony of Mūsā's career is something he himself could not have known. When his pilgrimage entourage arrived in Cairo in 1324, it brought so much gold that it dumbfounded local observers. In obedience to Muslim piety, the pilgrims distributed incredible amounts of wealth throughout Egypt, so much that some medieval historians believe that the gold standard in the eastern Mediterranean nearly collapsed. Inevitably, news of this phenomenon traveled along the commercial intelligence network in the Mediterranean, until it reached the famous guild of Jewish cartographers in the Balearic Islands. By 1375, Mūsā's likeness was appearing on European maps of West Africa, where previously there had been only fabulous beasts to conceal Europe's ignorance of the region. On those maps, Mūsā was shown seated on a throne of gold. It was the beginning of the end. Almost at the same time as the pagan Songhai began to run amok, Portuguese mariners began probing their way down the African coast, electrified by tales of unbelievable wealth: Mali was doomed.

Bibliography

Bell, Nawal Morcos. "The Age of Mansa Mūsā in Mali: Problems in Succession and Chronology." *International Journal of African Historical Studies* 5 (1972): 221-234. A summary of problems in Keita dynastic structure and chronology. Concludes that scholars have relied too heavily on Ibn Khaldun's assurances of legitimate succession and that it was really an ad hoc affair without clearly established rules.

Bovill, E. W. *The Golden Trade of the Moors*. London: Oxford University Press, 1968. A description of Mūsā's era, emphasizing his contributions to the cultural and intellectual life of the empire.

Davidson, Basil, ed. *The African Past: Chronicle from Antiquity to Modern Times*. Boston: Little, Brown and Co., 1964. A translation of selected descriptions of Mūsā in Cairo during the pilgrimage to Mecca, and a portion of Ibn Battutah's account of Mali. Also see *The Lost Cities of Africa* (Boston: Little, Brown and Co., 1959), by the same author.

Ibn Battuta. *Travels in Asia and Africa, 1325-1354*. Edited and translated by H. A. R. Gibb. London: George Routledge and Sons, 1929. The famous traveler's description of Mali during and shortly after the reign of Mansa Mūsā.

Levtzion, Nehemia. "The Thirteenth- and Fourteenth-Century Kings of Mali." *Journal of African History* 4 (1963): 341-354. Summarizes the history of the Keita dynasty, more or less according to Ibn Khaldun. Describes how Mūsā usually received more favorable treatment from chroniclers because he was a Muslim and shows how nearly every achievement in the history of Mali has been associated with his reign. Also see *Ancient Ghana and Mali* (London: Methuen and Co., 1973), by the same author.

Trimingham, J. Spencer. *A History of Islam in West Africa*. London: Oxford University Press, 1962. An extensive treatment of the empire of Mali, constructed both from the work of major Arab geographers and chroniclers and from Arabic-language sources written by contemporaneous West African scholars.

Ronald W. Davis

MARCUS AURELIUS

Born: April 26, 121; Rome
Died: March 17, 180; Sirmium or Vindobona (modern Vienna)
Areas of Achievement: Government and literature
Contribution: Although renowned as the last of Rome's "good emperors," Marcus Aurelius is best remembered for the *Meditations*. These simply written private notes reflect the emperor's daily efforts to achieve the Platonic ideal of the philosopher-king and are the last great literary statement of Stoicism.

Early Life

Marcus Aurelius Antoninus was born Marcus Annius Verus in Rome. His father was Annius Verus, a magistrate, and his mother was Domitia Calvilla, also known as Lucilla. The emperor Antoninus Pius was by virtue of his marriage to Annia Galeria Faustina, the sister of Annius Verus, the boy's uncle. The emperor, who had himself been adopted and named successor by Hadrian, eventually adopted Marcus Annius Verus. The young man then took the name Marcus Aelius Aurelius Verus. The name Aelius came from Hadrian's family, and Aurelius was the name of Antoninus Pius. The young man took the title Caesar in 139 and, upon becoming emperor, replaced his original name of Verus with Antoninus. Hence, he is known to history as Marcus Aurelius Antoninus.

Marcus Aurelius was well brought up and well educated. Later, he would write of what a virtuous man and prudent ruler his uncle and adoptive father had been. To the fine example set by the emperor was added the dedicated teaching of excellent masters. Letters exist which attest the boy's industry and the great expectations engendered by his performance as a student. He studied eloquence and rhetoric, and he tried his hand at poetry. He was also trained in the law as a preparation for high office. Above all, Marcus Aurelius' interest was in philosophy. When only eleven years of age, he adopted the plain, coarse dress of the philosophers and undertook a spartan regimen of hard study and self-denial. In fact, he drove himself so relentlessly that for a time his health was affected. He was influenced by Stoicism, a sect founded by the Greek philosopher Zeno of Citium in the fourth century B.C.

Life's Work

Antoninus Pius became emperor upon the death of Hadrian in July, 138. He adopted not only Marcus Aurelius but also Lucius Ceionius Commodus, who came to be called Lucius Aurelius Verus. The adoptive brothers could scarcely have been more different. Verus was destined to rule alongside Marcus Aurelius for a time despite his manifest unworthiness. He was an indolent, pleasure-loving man, whereas Marcus Aurelius was proving himself worthy of more and more responsibility. The year 146 was a highly significant one, for it was at about that time that Antoninus Pius began to share with him the government of the empire. Further, the emperor gave him Faustina, his daughter and the young man's cousin, in marriage. A daughter was born to Marcus Aurelius and Faustina in 147.

At the death of Antoninus Pius in March, 161, the senate asked Marcus Aurelius to assume sole governance of the empire. Yet he chose to rule jointly with Verus, the other adopted son. For the first time in its history, Rome had two emperors. Apparently, and fortunately for the empire, Verus was not blind to his inadequacies. He deferred to Marcus Aurelius, who was in turn tolerant of him. Marcus Aurelius cemented their relationship by giving his daughter Lucilla to Verus as wife. That their joint rule lasted for eight years was really a credit to them both.

The first major problem to be faced by the joint rulers was the war with Parthia. Verus was sent to command the Roman forces but proved ineffectual. Fortunately, his generals were able, thus achieving victories in Armenia and along the Tigris and Euphrates rivers. The war was concluded in 165, but as soon as Marcus Aurelius and Verus received their triumph—a huge public ceremony honoring the victors in war—Rome was struck by a virulent pestilence. As the plague spread throughout Italy and beyond, the loss of life was great.

At this time, barbarians from beyond the Alps were threatening to invade northern Italy. Although Marcus Aurelius was able to contain them, they would periodically renew their efforts. For the rest of the emperor's life, much of his time and effort was spent in holding these warlike people at bay. Verus died suddenly in 169, and Marcus Aurelius became the sole emperor of Rome. His reign continued as it had begun, beset by difficulties on every hand. He was almost constantly in the field, campaigning against one enemy or another. He was on the Danube River for three years, prosecuting the German wars, and by 174 he had gained a series of impressive victories.

In 175, Avidius Cassius, who commanded the Roman legions in Asia, led a revolt against the emperor. Up to that time, Cassius had been a fine general, but when he declared himself Augustus, the emperor marched east to meet the threat. Before the emperor arrived, however, Cassius was assassinated by some of his officers. Marcus Aurelius' treatment of the family and followers of Cassius was magnanimous. His letter to the senate asking mercy for them has survived. During this time, Marcus Aurelius suffered a severe personal tragedy. The empress, Faustina, who had accompanied her husband on the Asian march, abruptly died. Some historians have written that she was scandalously unfaithful and promiscuous, but their reports are contradicted by her husband's pronouncements. He was grief-stricken at her death, and his references to her are loving and laudatory.

It was during this decade of constant warfare, rebellion, and personal grief that Marcus Aurelius began to write the lofty, dignified contemplative notes that were originally known as *Tōn eis heauton* (c. 171-180) and would come to be called his *Meditations* (1634). They were meant for no eyes but the emperor's, and their survival down through the centuries is a mystery (although scholars have no doubts as to their authenticity). They reflect his sense of duty, his high-mindedness, his apparent inner peace. Two themes dominate the *Meditations*: that man, to the utmost of his ability to do so, should harmonize himself with nature and that it is not the circumstances of one's life that produce happiness, but one's perception of those circumstances. According to the emperor, happiness always comes from within, never from without. The *Meditations* are also marked by their author's common sense. He observes that when one is seduced by fame and flattered by others, one should remember their want of judgment on other occasions and remain humble. A great emperor might be expected to be self-assured, perhaps even self-centered and self-satisfied; Marcus Aurelius strikes the reader as more self-composed and self-contented.

Although the emperor's campaigns were generally successful (one victory, in which a fortuitous storm threw the enemy into a panic, was even viewed as a miracle), his reign was not unblemished. He was often forced to make concessions which allowed large numbers of barbarians to remain in Roman territory and which eventually resulted in a proliferation of barbarians within his own armies (some of his legions were already identifiably Christian in makeup). He also seems to have been blind to the vices of Commodus, his son and successor. It is the persecution of the Christians, however, which brings his record into question.

The constant state of war, aggravated by widespread pestilence, caused the populace to demand a scapegoat. The Christians were a natural target, since their repudiation of the ancient gods was thought to have brought divine retribution upon Rome. An ardent persecution was begun, especially in the provinces. At first, the persecutions seem to have progressed ad hoc. Eventually, however, a provincial governor appealed to the emperor for guidance. His directions were, by contemporary standards, severe. If the Christians would deny their faith, they should be released. Otherwise, they must be punished. Those unrepentant Christians who were Roman citizens were beheaded. The others were put to death in a variety of imaginative ways. Apologists for Marcus Aurelius have maintained that he had little to do with these persecutions, and they do seem out of character for the author of the *Meditations*. Still, in order to argue that Marcus Aurelius was in no way culpable, one must read history quite selectively.

In 180, the emperor was conducting yet another successful, though somewhat inconclusive, campaign, this time along the upper Danube. He fell ill with the plague or some other contagious malady and died on March 17 of that year.

Summary

The commemorative bust of Marcus Aurelius features a noble head indeed. Framed by a full head of curly hair and neat chin whiskers, the countenance is strong, honest, and handsome. Any idealization of the likeness is appropriate, for the emperor's demeanor as well as his words set one of the greatest examples in history. When his ashes were returned to Rome, he was honored with deification and, for long afterward, he was numbered by many Romans among their household gods. Commodus erected in his father's memory the Antonine column in Rome's Piazza Colonna. The emperor's statue was placed at the top of the column and remained there until Pope Sixtus V caused it to be replaced by a bronze statue of Saint Paul. The substitution is symbolic, as it was meant to be.

Throughout the Christian era, attempts have been made to associate the *Meditations* with Christian thought. Such efforts are understandable, for the emperor's self-admonitions to virtuous conduct for its own sake, steadfastness, magnanimity, and forbearance are congenial to the mind of the Christian apologist. The weight of evidence, however, indicates otherwise. Marcus Aurelius seems to have known little about the Christians, and what he knew he did not like. Even granting that he was not deeply involved in their persecution, he clearly regarded them as fanatical troublemakers. He should be viewed, then, not as an incipient Christian but as the voice of paganism's last great moral pronouncements.

The emperor was an able but not a great military figure. He was an intelligent but not a brilliant thinker. As a writer, he was a competent but not a formidable stylist. In short, Marcus Aurelius was great because he brought a human quality to his leadership and made optimal use of his limited talents.

Bibliography

Arnold, E. Vernon. *Roman Stoicism*. London: Routledge and Kegan Paul, 1911, 2d ed. 1958. A series of lectures by a classical scholar, arranged in seventeen chapters. The thought of Marcus Aurelius receives ample treatment, as he is discussed in four chapters.

Aurelius Antoninus, Marcus. *The "Meditations" of the Emperor Marcus Aurelius Antoninus*. Translated by R. Graves. London: Robinson, 1792. The editor's translation, reproduced in the Library of English Literature, is accompanied by a biography and notes. Graves was a clergyman and an Oxford don. His assessment of Marcus Aurelius, written toward the end of the Enlightenment, is of historical interest.

_____. "The *Meditations* of Marcus Aurelius." Translated and edited by George Long. In *Plato, Epictetus, Marcus Aurelius*, edited by Charles W. Eliot. New York: P. F. Collier and Son, 1909, 2d ed. 1937. An entry in the Harvard Classics series. Long's translation of Marcus Aurelius' work is accompanied by his brief and readable life of the author. His companion essay, "The Philosophy of Antoninus," includes a very useful explanation of Stoicism and traces its progress and decline in the Roman world. Long, writing in the freewheeling academic style of the late nineteenth century, is occasionally pugnacious in making his point, but he is always lucid and direct.

Guevara, Antonio de. *Archontorologion: Or, The Diall of Princes, Containing the Golden and Famovs Booke of Marcvs Avrelivs, Sometime Emperour of Rome*. Translated by Thomas North. London: Alsop, 1619. North's translation, reproduced in the Library of English Literature, of a sixteenth century book by a Spanish bishop. The work is a sort of romance, founded on the life and character of Marcus Aurelius. A view of the emperor from the Renaissance perspective, the book was written to put before the emperor Charles V the model of antiquity's wisest and most virtuous prince. The final edition of North's translation has corrected "many grosse imperfections."

Wenley, R. M. *Stoicism and Its Influence*. New York: Cooper Square, 1963. An entry in the series called Our Debt to Greece and Rome. A defense of the importance of Stoicism against historians of philosophy who have tended to dismiss it lightly. Discussions of Marcus Aurelius are liberally sprinkled throughout the text.

Patrick Adcock

MARGARET OF DENMARK, NORWAY, AND SWEDEN

Born: 1353; Søborg, Denmark
Died: October 28, 1412; Flensburg, Denmark
Area of Achievement: Government
Contribution: Margaret was the first ruler to unite Scandinavia (under the Kalmar Union) and the first ruling queen of Denmark, Norway, and Sweden.

Early Life

Born in 1353, Margaret was the younger daughter of King Valdemar IV Atterdag of Denmark and Queen Hedevig (the sister of the Duke of Slesvig). Betrothed at the age of six to Haakon VI of Norway, born in 1340, she became his wife in 1363, when she was ten and he twenty-three.

She did not go to the court at Akershus until she was sixteen, however, but spent her early married years in Norway in the household of Märta, the married daughter of the Swedish Saint Bridget, a mystic visionary and the founder of a monastic order. At Märta's house, Margaret must have heard daily of political happenings in all the Scandinavian kingdoms, for Bridget was an international celebrity, better known than any other Scandinavian citizen. Her children similarly were well traveled, educated, and cosmopolitan. Margaret in her later life worked tirelessly for Bridget's canonization, accomplished in 1391.

Margaret's son Olaf was born in 1370, when she was seventeen, a year after she joined Haakon at the Norwegian court. When Olaf was five, Valdemar Atterdag died. Now only twenty-two, Margaret persuaded the council of state to elect Olaf king with herself as regent, even though her sister's son Albrecht of Mecklenburg was the logical heir as son of the elder daughter. The Danish council did not like the Germans, however, and had many quarrels with the Prussian nobility. War with Mecklenburg and Holstein followed, but Albrecht was defeated. On the death of her husband, Haakon, in 1380, Margaret managed to secure Olaf's election as King of Norway (he was only ten years old), again with herself as regent. By this time, she was only twenty-seven years old.

Some background should be remembered for fourteenth century Scandinavia. Denmark, Norway, and Sweden had been isolated from the rest of Europe for a thousand years, developing a culture of their own, free from the influences of both Rome and the Teutonic cultures of Germany. They had produced one of the world's great literatures (that of the Nordic sagas), given women a position they had nowhere else, practiced rotation of crops, invented their own system of writing (runes), and discovered new lands in the West. Feudalism came to these cultures very late, and the system that developed in Scandinavia had no serfdom, no lifetime service to an overlord. Instead, all three countries were unified kingdoms from early in their history; military service was owed to the monarch not by the person but by the district. Laws had more than a local application, because the whole of each kingdom was united and easily connected by water transportation.

The fourteenth century, however, was disastrous for Scandinavia. The cities of the Hanseatic League, as well as the various northern German states such as Holstein and Mecklenburg, conquered much of the wealthiest Scandinavian territory—Skåne (in Sweden), the islands of Bornholm and Gotland, the Baltic states, and Slesvig (part of the Jutland peninsula).

Worse, the Black Death was particularly difficult for sparsely populated Norway and Sweden. Brought to Bergen by ship in 1349, the plague killed one-third to one-half of the population before the end of the century. By 1400, there were only sixty of the more than three hundred noble families remaining in Norway. Farms lay in ruin, crops were neither planted nor harvested, the clergy death rate left parishes without religious leadership, famine and poverty were everywhere. A letter exists from young Queen Margaret written to Haakon in 1370, in which she begs for basic provisions for herself and the servants:

> You must know, my lord, that I and my servants suffer and are in dire need for lack of food and drink, so that neither they nor I get the necessities. And so I beg you that you will find some way out so that things may improve and that those who are with me shall not leave me on account of hunger.

Members of the royalty were often in straitened circumstances for years. Haakon's mother, Queen Blanche, for example, left at her death only some linens for bed and table, a few spices, and "a few table knives and four silver spoons."

Margaret's father, Valdemar Atterdag, was called "another day" because of his characteristic expression and the "new day" which he brought in for Denmark. After twelve years without a king, under the chaos of the rule of the German dukes, he reunified the country, bought back lost land (such as Gotland), and made favorable treaties with Hanseatic cities such as Lübeck. Margaret continued his policies and strengthened the monarchy.

Life's Work

Margaret's great achievement was the uniting of all Scandinavia under one sovereign. Olaf died suddenly at age seventeen in 1387. With no clear heir, only Margaret remained—and no woman had ever been queen. Nevertheless, in preference to Albrecht of Mecklenburg, she was chosen "all-powerful lady and mistress," regent of Denmark and Norway, with the right to name her successor.

In Norway, a disaffected faction reported that Olaf was not dead. The impostor claimed the crown and gained followers by revealing information that only Olaf and Margaret could know. Margaret hurried to Norway and proved that the impostor was the son of Olaf's nurse by showing that he did not have a large wart on his back, Olaf's birthmark. The false Olaf was tortured and burned at the stake.

Soon Margaret named her grandnephew Erik of Pomerania as her successor; both the Norwegian and the Danish clergy and nobility agreed with this move. In Sweden, the nobles opposing King Albrecht, led by Birger, Bridget's son and Märta's brother, called on Margaret for assistance. She accepted on the condition that she be made Queen of Sweden. Albrecht had insulted Margaret, calling her "a king without breeches" and the "abbot's concubine," as well as claiming both Denmark and Norway for himself. He also sent her a hone to sharpen her needles, swearing not to put on his nightcap until she surrendered.

The battle lines were drawn for civil war in Sweden. In September, 1388, the Battle of Falköping was fought, with about twelve thousand men on each side. Both sides incurred great losses, but in the end, Margaret's forces were victorious; both Albrecht and his son Erik were captured. When the prisoners were brought before her, she had a nineteen-yard-long paper nightcap put on Albrecht, proportioned to his verbal offenses. He was imprisoned in Skåne for seven years. Margaret was now the undisputed Queen of Sweden as well as of Norway and Denmark.

Sweden, too, accepted Erik of Pomerania, and in 1397 Kalmar, Sweden, was the site for a gala coronation ceremony. Erik was crowned king of all the Scandinavian countries by the archbishops of Uppsala and Lund. At the same time, Margaret called together a large group of nobles and clergy from all three countries, and together they drafted an arrangement for a closer union of the three governments. The resulting document had three articles. The first provided that the three kingdoms should have the same king, to be chosen successively by each of the kingdoms. The second article decreed that the monarch divide his time equally among the three kingdoms. The third article directed that each kingdom should continue its own laws, customs, and councils, but that foreign alliances concluded with one country would be binding on all three, that all must aid the others in time of war, and that banishment or treason in one country would be treated the same way in all.

Nevertheless, the document, called the Kalmar Union, is inconsistent. The six parchment copies called for do not exist; they seem never in fact to have been drawn. The single copy extant is on paper, not parchment, and has only ten seals, instead of the requisite seventeen. These wax seals are stamped on the paper, rather than attached to the document. Perhaps this copy is a draft, and the others were never agreed upon or made. There are no Norwegian seals at all, and only three Danish ones. Scholars continue to debate the issue, wondering who exactly was opposed to the union and for what reasons. Despite these problems, the union existed de facto for the lifetimes of Margaret and Erik, and the union of Denmark and Norway continued until 1814.

Margaret continued to consolidate and strengthen her power. She kept close, personal contact with all levels of government in the three kingdoms and was an indefatigable traveler, spending more time away from Denmark than at home. She appointed administrators and bishops, having them serve away from their home countries in order to strengthen their personal loyalty to her. The Danehof, or Danish Assembly, was never called, since she made decisions personally. She continued to win back the Danish lands lost to German states, through battle, treaty, or outright purchase. She negotiated marriage contracts to strengthen alliances, first Erik's marriage to Philippa, daughter of Henry IV of England, and later a marriage treaty with Bavaria. Nevertheless, she remained steadfastly neutral in the bloody wars between England and France and in other European conflicts.

Margaret transformed the coinage, minting coins of pure silver rather than of copper, thus strengthening the Crown's economic position. Even though she had inherited heavy debts from her father, after 1385 her economic situation was markedly improved when she regained the Swedish castles in Skåne. Earlier, she had had to borrow from the Bishop of Roskilde; now, she was able to make large donations of money and property to the Church. According to some scholars, these gifts were cleverly arranged, however, so that the property reverted to the Crown after a certain income had accrued. In any event, she was well loved for her generosity to religious establishments such as the motherhouse of the Bridgettine Order at Vadstena, Sweden.

Margaret's last years were especially concerned with the perennial problem of regaining lost Danish territory in Slesvig. In 1412, not yet sixty years old, she died suddenly, probably of the plague, on board her ship in Flensburg harbor in Slesvig after she had been welcomed into the city and negotiations had begun.

Summary

Called the "Semiramis of the North" after the Queen of Babylon, Margaret was one of the strongest monarchs of the three kingdoms. She had a gift for avoiding strife and persuading factions to come to terms under her strong leadership. She managed to influence public opinion in controversial matters, such as heavy taxes and the appointment of Germans to administrative posts. Tactful but assertive, she could be charming even while ruthless. She was restrained and lovable, knowing how to keep both the Church and the nobility happy. She used her considerable resources to strengthen the kingdoms by means of alliances and contributions and kept clear of expensive foreign wars.

Margaret's achievement at a time when all Scandinavia was being threatened by German cultural and economic domination was to unite the kingdoms and not only hold back the Germans but also regain lands lost to the south. At the time of her death, the Scandinavian Union was by far the most powerful force in the Baltic; it was also the second largest accumulation of European territory under a single sovereign. It is not too much to say that she almost single-handedly kept Scandinavia independent at a time when the kingdoms could easily have been made subservient to various German states.

Bibliography
Andersson, Ingvar. *A History of Sweden*. Translated by Carolyn Hannay. Stockholm: Natur och Kultur, 1955. Chapter 8, "The Union of Kalmar," deals with the subject from the Swedish perspective, giving much detail about the controversy surrounding the document.
Derry, T. K. *A History of Scandinavia*. Minneapolis: University of Minnesota Press, 1979. The best history in English, this work is particularly good on social and cultural history. Chapter 3 deals with Margaret and the Kalmar Union as well as giving a contextual discussion on life in the Middle Ages. Includes maps, family trees, and a helpful time line of parallel events in all the Scandinavian countries. Excellent bibliography.
Jochens, Jenny M. "Denmark." In *Dictionary of the Middle Ages*, vol. 4. New York: Charles Scribner's Sons, 1984. This long and helpful article gives a historical overview of Denmark in the medieval period, focusing on political history and connections between all the Scandinavian countries. A bibliographical essay surveys scholarly work in English and Scandinavian languages.
Larsen, Karen. *A History of Norway*. Princeton, N.J.: Princeton University Press, 1948. The best English source on Norway, this study is particularly good on the social-historical context. Chapters 9 and 10 cover the years of Margaret's reign, evaluating her somewhat negatively from the Norwegian perspective. Good bibliography.
Scott, Franklin D. "A Saint and a Queen: Two Indomitable Figures of the Fourteenth Century." In *Scandinavian Studies: Essays Presented to Dr. Henry Goddard Leach*, edited by Carl F. Bayerschmidt and Erik J. Friis. Seattle: University of Washington Press, 1965. One of the few scholarly articles on Margaret available in English. Treats Margaret and Saint Bridget of Sweden, focusing on the international and Scandinavian values that each espoused as well as the many connections between the two women.
Sinding, Paul C. *History of Scandinavia, from the Early Times of the Norsemen and Vikings to the Present Day*. New York: Pudney and Russell, 1858. This study has more detailed information on Margaret, in chapters 2 and 3, than do most contemporary texts. Each chapter begins with an outline, making it easy to find topics.

Margaret McFadden

MARIE DE FRANCE

Born: c. 1150; Île de France
Died: c. 1215; probably England
Area of Achievement: Literature
Contribution: The earliest known French woman poet, Marie de France is still admired for her narrative and poetic skill and for her psychological insight.

Early Life

Marie de France's identity is still a matter of conjecture. Her name is known because in an epilogue to *Fables* (after 1170; English translation, 1898) she said, "My name is Marie, and I come from France." It has been pointed out that during the twelfth century "France" was actually the Île de France, the area within the rivers around Paris, as opposed, for example, to Normandy. The phrase "from France" and other evidence indicate that she was not living in France when she composed her works; it is fairly clear that she was in England, and that the king to whom she dedicated *Lais* (c. 1167; *Lays of Marie de France and Other French Legends*, 1911, better known as *The Lays*) was Henry II of England.

Marie de France was almost certainly a member of the nobility. She was well read and knew English and Latin as well as her native French. She was influenced by Ovid, and she claimed to have taken her fables from those of Alfred the Great; regardless of whether she actually did, she was familiar with earlier English literature. Beyond this, conjecture begins. Scholars have suggested that she might have been the abbess of Reading, a noble lady in Herefordshire, or a countess. Some evidence exists that she could be the abbess of Shaftesbury, King Henry's illegitimate half sister, the daughter of Geoffrey Plantagenet. There has been much speculation as to the identity of the "Count William" to whom *Fables* is dedicated, but because the name was so popular at Henry's court that clue has not been helpful. At any rate, because her work does not include any borrowings from the influential Chrétien de Troyes, it is assumed that her first poems, the *lais* (lays), were composed in the latter part of the 1160's.

Because so little is known about her life, her personality must be deduced from her work. She is a member of the privileged classes, compassionate toward her inferiors but impatient with their attempts to rise above their proper station. Highly intelligent and well read, she is gifted also with the common sense evident in *Fables* and with the insight into human nature which can be seen in *The Lays*.

Life's Work

Marie de France's first work was a group of twelve *lais*, or narrative poems retold from stories, many of Celtic origin, which she had probably heard sung by Breton bards. Generally they are either set in Brittany or attributed to a Breton source. Marie de France formulated her own structure for these poems: a prologue, the story, and an epilogue, all in octosyllabic couplets. *The Lays* vary in length from one hundred to one thousand lines. Their theme is the power of love, which sometimes shapes lives for good, sometimes for bad. The stories include temptation, infidelity, treachery, seduction, betrayal, frustration, imprisonment, suffering, and death, as well as fidelity, forgiveness, and reunion. In addition to the thematic unity, the stories are unified by the voice of the poet, a realist who reveals the subtle differences among her characters, despite the similarity of the intensity of their passions.

The Lays have been divided between those which are realistic and those which draw upon folklore or in some way include supernatural elements. Sometimes the realistic stories end sadly, sometimes happily. "La Fraisne," for example, ends with a young girl's reunion with the mother who had abandoned her; "Milun," with the marriage of the lovers and their reunion with their son. "Chaitivel" and "Les Dous Amanz," on the other hand, end in bitterness and death.

Interestingly, adulterous loves are treated sympathetically in some stories and unsympathetically in others. "Chievrefueil" is a touching story of a brief, idyllic tryst between the Queen of Cornwall and her banished Tristan. In "Laostic," too, the sympathy is with the lovers, not with the old husband. The scheming lovers in "Équitan" on the other hand are scalded to death. In "Eliduc," the faithful mate, in this case the wife, is the sympathetic character. Nobly desiring her husband's happiness, she retires to a convent so that he can be with the princess he loves. Later, both Eliduc and his new wife follow the first wife's lead and give up human love for divine.

Although the supernatural tales will support some interesting symbolic or allegorical analyses, on the surface they deal with the same problems and passions as the realistic lays. The hero of "Bisclavret" is a werewolf with a wife just as treacherous as the wife in "Équitan," and as the faithful mate, he is rewarded. True love, however, is not necessarily marital love. In Marie de France's other three lays, the supernatural forces are on the side of true love. In "Guigemar," a magic boat brings a lover to a lady whose husband has locked her up; in "Yonec," a lover comes to an imprisoned wife as a falcon and even fathers a child, who grows up to kill the cruel husband. In "Lanvel," it is a supernatural lady who rescues her knight and carries him off to Avalon, where Guinevere cannot endanger his life with false accusations. Whether realistic or supernatural, the poems of the *The Lays* were particularly significant; instead of the artificial patterns of courtly love, they dramatized the play of overpowering passions which could persist through suffering, absence, and death. If there was danger in such emotions, there was also sometimes grandeur.

Marie de France's next work, *Fables*, was quite different in tone. Whether

her source was really Alfred the Great, as she claimed, or some other writer in the tradition of Aesop, Marie de France made the materials her own, much as she had done with the Breton lays. Her collection consists of 102 fables, ranging in length from eight lines to more than one hundred. Like *The Lays*, the tales are told in octosyllabic rhymed couplets. There is a standard format: After a general statement, the story is told, and the poem concludes with a moral.

While the romantic *lais* had been limited to love among the upper classes, *Fables* dealt with every social class. Nevertheless, Marie de France emphasizes the importance of hierarchy, as in fable 15, when an ass mimics the dog by jumping on his master. The moral is that one should stay in one's own station. In fable 38, a flea thanks a camel for a ride to his destination and even offers to return a favor. Like the flea, the poet says, when the poor get close to the rich, they overestimate their own importance.

On the other hand, Marie de France gives practical advice to all levels of society, as in fable 47, in which she warns that one should be careful in legal matters, or in fable 74, in which she shows the way that the arrogant bring about their own downfall. Her compassion for victims of injustice is evident in fable 4, in which a dog sues a sheep and by his clever lies deprives the innocent sheep first of his wool and then of his life. Most of the fables, however, are not so pessimistic. Their very structure suggests that man can learn to live more wisely as well as more safely. If human beings use their reason, they will understand that society is a whole, functioning properly only when every element in it is treated justly. In fable 27, the poet tells the story of the man who refused to give his stomach food, only to discover that neither his hands nor his feet could perform their proper functioning without the help of the organ he had despised.

Marie de France's final work was *L'Espurgatoire Seint Patriz* (English translation, 1894), which has been dated from 1180 to 1215. Written in the same couplet form as her other works, *L'Espurgatoire Seint Patriz* is based on a Latin work written by an English monk, Henry of Salisbury, whose popularity is demonstrated by the fact that Marie de France's version is only one of seven which appeared during the period. In taking an Irish knight through Purgatory, this kind of story anticipates Dante's *La divina commedia* (c. 1320; *The Divine Comedy*, 1802). As her final work, it illustrates the intellectual depth and versatility which place her among the finest poets of the twelfth century.

Summary

Despite the paucity of biographical details about Marie de France, her fame as a writer has never diminished since her lifetime when, as one of her contemporaries attests, *The Lays* brought her popular success. That *Fables* was also popular is evidenced by the fact that it is preserved in no less than twenty-three manuscripts.

It would be difficult to overestimate Marie de France's influence on later writers. From the thirteenth to the fifteenth centuries, *Fables* was translated or adapted frequently. In fact, as Mary Lou Martin points out, for several centuries it was *Fables* for which she was best known. She is also credited with inventing or refining the *lai* form, however, and although her poems in that genre were the models for all the later lays, critics believe that her poems were never surpassed by those of her successors. With the development of Romanticism in the late eighteenth century, writers such as Johann Wolfgang von Goethe rediscovered *The Lays*; they are now generally considered her most important production. Certainly they are emphasized by twentieth century critics, who find a depth of symbolic meaning beneath their deceptively simple surface.

Marie de France should be remembered as the first woman writing in French whose name is now known. Her importance, however, is not merely historical. Because of her knowledge of human nature, her skill in storytelling, and her poetic genius, she deserves recognition not only as an early woman writer but also as one of the finest poets of the medieval period.

Bibliography
Crosland, Margaret. *Women of Iron and Velvet: French Women Writers After George Sand*. New York: Taplinger Publishing Co., 1976. Despite the seeming limits of the title, in the second chapter the author discusses Marie de France from a feminist perspective, thus providing a different view of her importance.
Damon, S. Foster. "Marie de France: Psychologist of Courtly Love." *PMLA* 44 (Spring, 1929): 968-996. An outstanding study of the subject, Damon's article is structured as a systematic analysis of the similarities and differences among the characters in the various *lais*. An illustrative chart supports author's hypotheses.
Donovan, Mortimer J. *The Breton Lay: A Guide to Varieties*. Notre Dame, Ind.: University of Notre Dame Press, 1969. Donovan includes an initial chapter on Marie de France, which is followed by other chapters detailing the later development of the lay form. Contains useful plot summaries of *The Lays*. A carefully researched and clearly written book, with an excellent bibliography.
Ferrante, Joan M. *Woman as Image in Medieval Literature: From the Twelfth Century to Dante*. New York: Columbia University Press, 1975. The works of Marie de France are used to illustrate various points made throughout this well-written critical work. Of particular interest is the section on the lays in which an imprisoned woman invents or calls forth an ideal lover, which Ferrante sees as indicating the power of the female imagination.
Ferrante, Joan M., et al., eds. *In Pursuit of Perfection: Courtly Love in*

Medieval Literature. Port Washington, N.Y.: Kennikat Press, 1975. Although the specific discussion of Marie de France in this book is brief, pointing out elements of the courtly love tradition but insisting that "Eliduc" represents her rejection of that tradition, the various essays provide a good background for the study of medieval literature which deals with love.

Holmes, Urban Tigner, Jr. *A History of Old French Literature: From the Origins to 1300*. New York: Russell and Russell, 1936, rev. ed. 1962. One of the authoritative books on medieval literature. Because of the frequent references to scholarly arguments, it is sometimes difficult to follow; nevertheless, in his careful assessment of the merits of various opinions, Holmes helps the reader to make sound judgments. Has interesting speculations about a possible identification of Marie de France.

Martin, Mary Lou. *The Fables of Marie de France: An English Translation*. Birmingham, Ala.: Summa Publications, 1984. The translator's fine introduction to this book provides an interesting thematic analysis of the fables as well as a discussion of their literary reputation. The translations themselves are provided opposite the Old French texts.

Rosemary M. Canfield-Reisman

GAIUS MARIUS

Born: 157 B.C.; Cereatae
Died: January 13, 86 B.C.; Rome
Areas of Achievement: Warfare and politics
Contribution: Marius was a successful Roman general whose military innovations created the professional army of the late Roman Republic and early empire. Representing the Popular Party, he was elected consul seven times.

Early Life

Gaius Marius was born on a farm near the village of Cereatae in the district of Arpinum, about sixty miles southeast of Rome. He was the son of a middle-class farmer. Marius received little formal education and grew to manhood with a certain roughness in speech and manner which characterized him throughout his life. He first saw military service in 134 in Spain under Scipio Aemilianus in the campaign against the Numantines. Marius readily adapted to military life and was decorated for valor. For the next ten years, he served as a junior officer in Spain and the Balearic Islands.

Returning to Rome, Marius began his political career. With the help of the powerful Metelli clan, he won the election for tribune of the people in 119. During his tribuneship, he showed his independence by carrying a bill for election reform despite opposition from the Metelli and the Senatorial Party. In the next year, Marius stood for the office of aedile but was defeated. In 115, he was elected praetor but only with difficulty. In the following year, he was appointed propraetor for Further Spain. About the year 111, Marius contracted a highly favorable marriage alliance with the ancient Julian clan. His marriage to Julia, a future aunt of Julius Caesar, gave him an important link to the aristocracy.

Life's Work

The Jugurthine War soon brought Marius to a position of prominence in Roman affairs. In 109, he was appointed staff officer to Quintus Caecilius Metellus, who as consul was given command of the army in the war against Jugurtha, the revolting King of Numidia. Bringing his army to Africa, Metellus waged war against the wily Jugurtha for two years without success. Amid growing criticism of the slowness of the campaign, Marius determined that he would seek the consulship for the year 107. If successful, he hoped to replace Metellus as commander and reap the glory of ending the war. Returning to Rome, he boldly attacked Metellus and the senate and promised to capture or kill Jugurtha if elected. He was supported by members of the business class, who desired stability in North Africa, and the plebeians, who used the war as an opportunity to criticize senatorial leadership. Marius won the consulship by a wide margin. Although the senate voted to extend the command of Metellus for an additional year, the tribal assembly passed a measure directing that the command be transferred to Marius.

In raising an army, Marius chose not to rely upon conscription, which involved a small property qualification. Instead, he called for voluntary recruits from the proletariat, promising land at the end of military service. The innovation was made by Marius out of necessity, since conscription was viewed as a burden by the small farmers, whose numbers were diminishing and who were reluctant to leave their farms. Those who joined the army were often the poorest citizens. For them, the army offered hope for the future.

After arriving in North Africa, Marius began seizing and occupying the fortified strongholds of Jugurtha. By the end of 107, most of eastern Numidia was under Roman control. Jugurtha retreated westward, joining forces with his father-in-law, Bocchus, King of Mauretania. During the year 106, Marius marched across the western half of Numidia. He reached the river Muluccha, five hundred miles west of his base of operations, and seized the war treasure of Jugurtha in a remote mountain fortress. As the Roman army returned eastward, Bocchus and Jugurtha attacked but were repelled. Convinced now that he was on the losing side, Bocchus secretly offered to make peace. Marius sent his quaestor, Lucius Cornelius Sulla, to the Mauretanian camp. Sulla persuaded Bocchus to betray Jugurtha, who was kidnapped and turned over to the Romans. With the capture of Jugurtha, the war ended. Marius took credit for the victory, overlooking the critical role played by Sulla, who was to become his bitter rival. Marius returned to Rome in triumph with Jugurtha in chains; a few days later, Jugurtha was executed.

Marius had returned from Africa at a critical time, for two Germanic tribes, the Cimbri and the Teutons, had invaded the Roman province in southern France. In 105, the Cimbri had annihilated a Roman army at Arausio (Orange) in the lower Rhone Valley. Marius was elected consul for 104 even before he returned from Africa. With Italy threatened by invasion, the Romans disregarded the law requiring a ten-year interval between consulships. The need for Marius' military ability was so great that he was elected consul repeatedly between 104 and 101. Fortunately for Rome, the Cimbri migrated to Spain and the Teutons to northern France, giving Marius time to prepare for their return. In raising an army, Marius again used voluntary recruits from the propertyless class. He increased the strength of the legion to six thousand men; each legion was divided into ten cohorts of six hundred men. Marius completed the process of making the cohort the standard tactical unit of the legion, replacing the smaller maniple. The cohort was subdivided into six centuries, led by veteran centurions who had risen through the ranks. Weapons were standardized to include the short sword and the hurling pilum. Each soldier was required to carry his own pack. Marius introduced the silver eagle as the standard for each legion; each developed its own traditions and *esprit de corps*.

In 102, the Cimbri and Teutons reappeared. The Teutons advanced toward Italy along the southern coast of France. Marius met them at Aquae Sextiae (now Aix). The battle took place in a narrow valley, with the Teutons advancing uphill against the Romans. At the height of the battle, the Teutons were attacked from the rear by a Roman force that had been concealed behind a hill. The Teutons panicked, and the battle became a rout. As many as 100,000 Teutons may have perished. The Cimbri invaded Italy through the Brenner Pass. The other consul, Quintus Lutatius Catulus, brought an army northward to intercept them but was driven back south of the Po. In the spring of 101, Marius joined Catulus with additional troops. The decisive battle was fought on the Raudine Plain near Vercellae, located between Milan and Turin. The Cimbri, facing a burning sun, advanced against the Roman center. As soon as they were overextended, Marius attacked on the flanks. The Cimbri were dealt a severe defeat from which they could not recover. With the threat of the German invasion ended, Marius and Catulus returned to Rome to celebrate a joint triumph.

After these victories, Marius began a new phase of his career as a politician, but he failed miserably. He formed a coalition with two political opportunists, Lucius Appuleius Saturninus and Gaius Glaucia. In the elections for the year 100, Marius won the consulship for the sixth time; Glaucia was elected praetor and Saturninus tribune. Soon afterward, Saturninus introduced bills to establish land grants for Marius' veterans in Transalpine Gaul and colonies in the east. Marius was to be given the right to bestow citizenship upon a select number of the settlers. When the senate objected, Saturninus took the unprecedented step of requiring all senators to take an oath supporting the bills after passage or suffer exile. The urban proletariat also protested, for they judged the measures overly generous to the Italian allies who made up a large part of the veterans. The bills were finally passed after Saturninus used Marius' veterans to drive off the opposition in the assembly.

In the elections for 99, Saturninus again won the tribuneship. Glaucia stood for consul but was defeated by Gaius Memmius. Seeking to intimidate their opponents, Saturninus and Glaucia ordered their henchmen to murder Memmius. The reaction to the slaying restored momentum to the senate, which passed a decree directing Marius to arrest Saturninus and Glaucia. After some hesitation, Marius ordered his veterans to seize his former friends, who were encamped on the Capitoline. He placed them in the senate building for protection, but the angry mob tore off the roof and pelted the prisoners to death with tiles. Marius completed his term as consul, but his influence and prestige disappeared. Under the pretext of fulfilling a vow to the goddess Cybele, he departed for the east.

After returning to Rome, Marius remained in relative obscurity until the outbreak of the Social War. When the revolting allies gained early victories in the war, Marius was recalled to military service in the year 90. Although serving in a subordinate status, he was responsible for inflicting two defeats on the Marsi. Despite his success, he was given no assignment for the following year. The glory of concluding the war went to Sulla. In the year 88, when Mithridates, King of Pontus, led a revolt in the east, Marius sought to gain the command for the approaching war. The senate, however, ignored him and bestowed the command on Sulla, who was consul for 88. Marius gained the support of the tribune Publius Sulpicius Rufus, who initiated a tribal assembly measure transferring the command to him. Sulla, who was with his army in Campania, marched on Rome and ordered the executions of Marius and the leaders of the assembly. Sulpicius was captured and put to the sword; Marius fled to the coast, hiding in the marshes near Minturnae. At length he found refuge on the island of Cercina off the coast of Africa.

When Sulla departed for the east in 87, Marius returned to Italy and raised a new army. He joined forces with the democratic leader Lucius Cornelius Cinna, whom the Senate had recently driven from Rome. With their combined armies, they advanced against Rome and forced its surrender. Marius now vented his anger after years of frustrations and disappointments by ordering wholesale executions of his enemies in the senate and among members of the nobility. Dispensing with the election process, Marius and Cinna appointed themselves consuls for the year 86. Marius, now seventy-one years of age, entered his seventh consulship, but by this time he was gravely ill. He died of fever a few days after taking office in January, 86.

Summary

One of the foremost generals of his age, Marius showed his resourcefulness and capability as a military commander in his successful campaigns in North Africa, Gaul, and Italy. His innovative recruitment of troops was of major significance for the future of Rome. By relying on volunteers from the proletariat class, Marius created an army of professional soldiers who were ready to serve for extended periods of time. The new system was vastly superior to the short-term conscript militia of the past, but it also posed dangers. The soldiers of the professional army identified their interests with their general and expected to be rewarded with land following their service. They gave allegiance to their general rather than to the state. This system gave extraordinary power to any general who might desire to use the army for his own political ends. It led directly to the civil wars of the late republic, when military strength became the key to political power. Marius also introduced important reforms to improve the fighting ability of the army. His innovations in organization, weapons, and tactics produced a highly efficient fighting machine at a time when Rome was sorely pressed by its enemies. The new Marian army became the Roman army of the late republic and early empire.

Although Marius was a successful general, he failed as a politician. His successive consulships are attributable not to political adroitness but to his skill as a general at a time when Rome was severely threatened. The year 100 marked a turning point in Marius' career. Elected consul for the sixth time and immensely popular after his recent victories, Marius devised no program for social reform beyond that of acquiring land for his veterans. Inept as a public speaker and vacillating in his political decisions, Marius allowed himself to be led by the demagogues Saturninus and Glaucia, whose radicalism and violence precipitated his fall. Driven by ambition, Marius spent the remaining years of his life trying to recover his former power and prestige. At his death, Rome had entered a new era of civil war and bloodshed that would last more than half a century.

Bibliography

Badian, Ernest. "From the Gracchi to Sulla." *Historia* 11 (1962): 214-228. An examination of the political career of Marius set against the background of the Roman Revolution and the accompanying contest between the Senatorial and Popular parties. Special attention is devoted to the political factions which supported and opposed Marius. Extensive notes review the progress of Marian studies. Bibliography.

Carney, Thomas F. *A Biography of Gaius Marius*. Chicago: Argonaut, 1970. This book is a new printing of the author's article published in the *Proceedings of the African Classical Associations*, Supplement 1, in 1962. The work is a concise, highly technical treatment of Marius' career. The notes present several new directions in research. Numerous references. Appendix with tables listing all existing and nonextant contemporary sources.

Kildahl, P. A. *Gaius Marius*. New York: Twayne Publishers, 1968. Highly readable, sympathetic account of the life of Marius. This book is intended for students and the general reader but will also be useful for scholars. Preface contains an analysis of contemporary sources. Chronology, map, useful notes, and select bibliography.

Last, Hugh. "The Wars of the Age of Marius." In *The Cambridge Ancient History*. Vol. 9, *The Roman Republic*. Cambridge: Cambridge University Press, 1932. Causes and historical background for both the Jugurthine War and the Cimbrian War are discussed. Detailed accounts of military campaigns, strategy, and battle tactics. Maps with physical features, mileage scales, and Roman place-names for areas of military operations. Description of military reforms under Marius. Lengthy discussion of sources. Notes and bibliography.

Parker, H. M. D. *The Roman Legions*. Oxford: Clarendon Press, 1928. 2d ed. New York: Barnes and Noble Books, 1958. A study of the composition of the Roman army through the periods of the Republic and the Empire. The chapter on the Marian army reforms offers technical explanations and details regarding Marius' innovations and contains valuable references to contemporary sources. The introduction provides a description of the pre-Marian army.

Scullard, H. H. *From the Gracchi to Nero*. New York: Barnes and Noble Books, 1959. The best account for the general background of the last century of the Roman Republic. Highly readable with sound scholarly judgment. Detailed chapter on the career of Marius. Extensive notes include a discussion of sources for Marius, problems and conflicting interpretations arising from the sources, and numerous references for additional study.

Norman Sobiesk

MARTIAL

Born: March 1, c. A.D. 40; Bilbilis, Spain
Died: c. A.D. 104; Spain
Area of Achievement: Literature
Contribution: Martial perfected the epigram, the witty, sometimes salacious poem, typically of two to four lines, which points out the moral and social ills of the poet's day or lampoons prominent people.

Early Life

Everything known about Martial comes from his own poems and from one letter of Pliny the Younger, written at the time of the poet's death. Martial alludes to his Spanish origins in an early poem, but by the age of fifty-seven he had already spent thirty-four years in Rome. His parents, of whom nothing more than their names is known, provided him with the standard rhetorical education designed to equip him to be a lawyer. In one of his poems, Martial depicts them as already in the underworld. Martial seems to have been in Rome by 64, perhaps under the patronage of the powerful Seneca family, also natives of Spain.

At some point he received the status of knight and an honorary military tribunate, but he does not mention which emperor bestowed on him those privileges. By contrast, it is clear that Titus gave Martial the privileges of a father of three children and that Domitian renewed the grant. His silence about the emperor who had provided the two earlier honors leads scholars to suspect that it was Nero, who fell into disgrace upon his death in 68. It was important to Martial to have his honors known but impolitic to boast about who had given them to him.

Martial probably practiced law during Vespasian's reign (69-79), though it does not seem to have suited him. His comments about the profession are unkind, yet fairly late in his life he gibed someone who had failed to pay him for pleading his case in court.

Exactly when or why Martial turned to poetry cannot be determined. His first published effort was *Spectacula* (80; *On the Spectacles*), a collection of short poems in honor of the dedication of the Flavian Amphitheater (the Colosseum) in 80. Between 86 and 98 he published his epigrams at the rate of roughly a volume a year. Publication order is not necessarily the order of writing. Epigrams 2.59 and 5.26, for example, refer to the same incident but were published several years apart. The twelfth and final volume appeared in 101, after he had returned to Spain. There are also two volumes of incidental poems which were meant to accompany gifts given at banquets. Probably written between 80 and 85, these are sometimes numbered books 13 and 14 of his collected works, but this classification does not seem to have been Martial's intention.

One of the great puzzles about Martial's early life is how he supported himself. Many of his poems complain about his poverty and the necessity of flattering the rich in the hope of a handout or a dinner invitation. He mentions his wretched third-floor apartment, and his ragged toga is a frequent subject of lament.

In other poems, however, Martial refers to his "Nomentan farm," a suburban villa not far from Rome, and to his private home in the city. He invites guests to dine with him and boasts about his kitchen and his cook, luxuries beyond the means of the urban poor who inhabited Rome's apartment houses. He asks permission from the emperor to tap into the city water supply and pipe the water directly into his house, a privilege reserved for the ruler's wealthy friends. The image which he tries to project of a poor poet scrounging handouts from stingy patrons may be nothing more than a literary pose.

Life's Work

This problem of the poetic persona complicates enormously the study of Martial's life and work. His poems are the only source of information about his life, but there is doubt that what he says about himself is to be taken seriously. For example, in one poem he complains about his wife having a lover, while in another he objects that she is too moralistic to engage in the deviant sexual behavior which he enjoys. Can these poems be talking about the same woman? As a result, some modern scholars contend that Martial was never married and that any reference to a wife is merely a literary convention. Another possibility is that he was married several times, something that was not at all uncommon in Rome in the late first century A.D.

If one cannot be certain whether, or how many times, Martial was married, it is difficult to ascertain anything else about his life. In one poem, he refers to a daughter, but only once in passing. In another, he mourns deeply the death of the slave child Erotion, tending her grave for years and requiring the next owner of the property to observe the same rituals. Could this have been his daughter by a slave woman on his farm?

It is virtually impossible to know Martial himself from his poems, as the contradictions in his work are numerous. In some of the poems he pictures himself engaging in homosexual relations; in others he ridicules men who do the same. He praises the joys of simple country life, but he lived in Rome for thirty-five years. He claims that, although many of his poems are bawdy, his life is decent.

Every writer must please his readers, and Martial seems to have been slanting his material to the tastes of his audience; in one poem he claims that he "could write what is serious" but emphasizes entertainment value, for that is what makes people "read and hum my poems all over Rome." Most of his poetry was produced in the reign of Domitian, a cruel, self-indulgent emperor (according to the biographer Suetonius) who enjoyed brutal sex with prostitutes and initiated mixed nude bathing in Rome's public baths. After his death, the emperors Nerva and Trajan brought about a kind of Victorian reaction to the loose morality of Domitian's day. Martial found that his poetry no longer appealed to the general public, so he retired to Spain.

While he does not reveal himself to the reader, Martial does draw an intimate portrait of Roman society in the late first century. One commentator says that he "touched life closely at all levels." One of his poems describes a Roman's daily schedule and several others focus on certain daily activities.

Martial's day would begin with a visit at daybreak to his patron, a wealthy man who would give him a small daily handout in exchange for Martial's accompanying him to public meetings and generally boosting his ego. Every Roman aristocrat had as many such clients as he could reasonably support. His status was measured by the size of the throng which surrounded him as he walked through the streets. Since Rome lacked a governmental welfare system, this informal arrangement redistributed some of the wealth which was concentrated in the hands of the aristocracy, a minute percentage of the population. In addition to the daily *sportula*, clients expected to receive gifts on their birthdays and at the festival of the Saturnalia in December. Martial's poems show that the clients would complain vociferously if the gift was not as large as they had expected.

One of the client's duties was to accompany his patron to court, an obligation which the litigious Romans faced frequently. Lawyers seem to have had difficulty collecting their fees, which was perhaps one reason that Martial abandoned the calling. The speeches in court were long and often irrelevant, but the client was expected to applaud his patron's case in the hope of influencing the jury.

By midday, everyone was ready for a rest, followed by exercise and a bath. Martial frequented the baths and pointed out the flaws—the stretch marks, the sagging breasts, the brand of the former slave—which other patrons tried to hide. From the numerous poems that discuss the baths, one can conclude that they served as Rome's social center. People went there to see and to be seen, to catch up on the latest gossip, and to wangle invitations to dinner. This last function was the most important to a client such as Martial. Failure to obtain an invitation meant that he had to provide his own meal, which marked him as a social outcast.

Dinner began in the late afternoon, since the Romans did not eat much, if anything, for breakfast or lunch. The city's social life revolved around these huge meals, at which the food was often intended to impress the guests as much as to nourish them. The seating arrangement indicated the guests' social standing, with the more prominent individuals reclined on couches closest to that of the host. Many aristocrats served two meals at once: elegant food for those eating immediately around them and cheaper fare for those in the farther reaches of the dining room. That this practice was common is evidenced by Pliny the Younger, who in a letter to a friend assured him that he did not engage in such habits.

Though these dinners did not often turn into orgies, the Romans had no compunctions about promiscuous sexual activity. Martial seems to have engaged in his share of such activity and was aware of what everyone else in his social circle was doing. His language is so explicit that no one dared to translate all of his poems into idiomatic English until 1968.

Summary

Scattered through Martial's epigrams are the people of Rome, from the aristocracy to the prostitutes. He exposes their posturing and the vices they thought would remain secret. His picture of Roman society may be the most accurate available, for he does not adopt the bitterly satiric tone of Juvenal or the staid disdain of Pliny. Martial's poetry gained for him renown in his own lifetime, something which he openly pursued. What made him successful, he believed, was the shock value of his epigrams. Martial once wrote that it is the nature of the epigram, as he refined it, to jolt the reader while it amuses, just as vinegar and salt improve the flavor of food.

Martial's clearest statement of his purpose is found in epigram 6.60: "Rome praises, adores, and sings my verses./ Every pocket, every hand holds me./ Look, that fellow blushes, turns pale, is stunned, yawns, hates me./ That's what I want. Now my poems please me." Pliny's judgment on Martial's epigrams was that they were "remarkable for their combination of sincerity with pungency and wit. . . . His verses may not be immortal, but he wrote them with that intention." Later generations have agreed with Pliny's critique. Though the church fathers frowned upon him in the Middle Ages, Martial's technique was much admired and palely imitated from the Renaissance until the eighteenth century. His Erotion poems directly influenced Ben Jonson's "Epigrammes XXII on My First Daughter," and Robert Herrick's "Upon a Child That Died."

Bibliography

Adamik, T. "Martial and the *Vita Beatior.*" *Annales Universitatis Budapestinensis* 3 (1975): 55-64. Martial's personal philosophy of life seems to be closest to Epicureanism. He satirizes Cynics and Stoics especially.

Allen, Walter, Jr., et al. "Martial: Knight, Publisher, and Poet." *Classical Journal* 65, (May, 1970): 345-357. Discusses the problem of Martial's persona and concludes that he was not actually a poor, struggling poet but a reasonably successful writer and publisher.

Ascher, Leona. "Was Martial Really Unmarried?" *Classical World* 70 (April/May, 1977): 441-444. Surveys scholarly opinion on the question of Martial's marital status and finds the evidence inconclusive.

Bell, Albert A., Jr. "Martial's Daughter?" *Classical World* 78 (September/ October, 1984): 21-24. Suggests that the girl Erotion, who is the subject of several of Martial's poems, was his daughter by a slave woman.

Bellinger, A. R. "Martial, the Suburbanite." *Classical Journal* 23 (February, 1928): 425-435. Depicts Martial as a "professional beggar," dependent on handouts from aristocrats to maintain himself.

Carrington, A. G. *Aspects of Martial's Epigrams.* Eton, England: Shake-speare Head Press, 1960. A nonscholarly introduction to selected poems, especially those discussing Martial's life, Roman history, and the process of creating a book in antiquity.

Semple, W. H. "The Poet Martial." *Bulletin of the John Rylands Library* 42 (1959/1960): 432-452. Discusses what can be known of Martial's life and analyzes some of the major themes or categories of his epigrams.

Spaeth, John W., Jr. "Martial and the Roman Crowd." *Classical Journal* 27 (January, 1932): 244-254. Making allowances for Martial's tendency to satirize and lampoon his contemporaries, one can gain valuable insights into the social history of the late first century.

_____. "Martial Looks at His World." *Classical Journal* 24 (February, 1929): 361-373. Martial shows more interest in the lower classes than do most Roman writers, although he is not sympathetic by any means. The antilabor prejudice characteristic of his day is evident in his poems.

Sullivan, J. P. "Martial's Sexual Attitudes." *Philologus* 123 (1979): 288-302. Though graphic by modern standards, Martial was merely expressing contemporary sexual values in his poetry. His explicit language is a convention of the epigram, as seen in Catullus and earlier poets.

                                                              Albert A. Bell, Jr.

SIMONE MARTINI

Born: c. 1284; Siena
Died: 1344; Avignon, France
Area of Achievement: Art
Contribution: Through his innovative painting techniques and sophisticated
use of color, Martini expanded on the French Gothic style.

Early Life

Simone Martini was born in a section of Siena known as San Egidio. Little
is known about his parents, but it is believed that he had a brother, Donato,
who was also his student. It is probable that Martini spent the first years of
his life in Siena and received his early training in the studio of Duccio di
Buoninsegna, the master painter of the city. Yet no record of Martini's early
training has been found, and historians know little of his life before 1315. In
that year, Martini produced a masterpiece, the Siena *Maestà*, a work so
advanced in technique and so important politically—it was placed in the
council chamber of the Palazzo Pubblico (city hall) in Siena—that it has fostered an ongoing search for Martini's apprenticeship works. Art historians
suspect that several other works, including *Christ Blessing* and *Saint John the
Evangelist*, also date from that period.

Other attempts have been made to locate Martini's presumed lost earlier
works by tracing his connection with Duccio. Four years earlier, in 1311,
Duccio had painted a *Maestà* of his own in the cathedral and naturally expected to receive the commission for the city hall. Still others, because of the
unusual French Gothic style of Martini's paintings, have sought in vain to
find evidence that he spent his early life in France. It is generally agreed that
the Italian historian Giorgio Vasari is in error in assigning Martini's training
to the school of Giotto in Siena; Vasari's claim that Martini was the pupil of
his father-in-law Memmo di Filippuccio is also believed to be false.

When Martini was thirty-three, he was invited to the Angevin Court of
Naples, where he was granted a yearly payment of fifty ounces of gold and
where, on July 23, 1317, he was knighted, the first painter in history to be so
honored.

Life's Work

Martini lived at a time when the Byzantine style flourished in Italy under
the guidance of the master painters Giotto (of Florence) and Duccio (of
Siena). Because Siena and Florence were flourishing cities with rapid economic growth, they became cultural centers as well, attracting writers and
artists eager to engage the budding ideals of the Italian Renaissance. Florence, the larger and more progressive city, became a tourist and industrial
center. It was known particularly for its modeling and enormous art pro-

ductivity. Siena, locked deep in the Tuscan hills without natural resources, was not suited for industry but survived on banking and trade. For years, the Sienese were the Pope's bankers, a fact that may have helped Martini establish contacts outside his isolated city. In the world of art, Siena became known for its decorative detail and its daring, innovative style.

The so-called Sienese school, of which Martini was a leading figure, thrived for more than 150 years. Few of the early Sienese paintings survive, but one of the earliest is a dossal dated 1215, heavily wrought with a gold-covered surface, called *Blessing Christ and Six Scenes*. Then came the work of such well-known artists as Nicola Pisano, Guido da Siena, Giotto, Duccio, Martini, the Lorenzetti brothers, and Barna of Siena. Following this great flourishing of painters, the Siena school became suddenly, mysteriously quiet.

The influence of the two leading painters of the time, Giotto and Duccio, can be seen clearly in Martini's art. From Giotto, he derived a sort of Gothic freedom; from Duccio, he learned structural technique. Martini's work represents a rather radical shift from the Greco-Roman-Byzantine style from which all painters were struggling to free themselves (a shift neither of the two other painters could achieve) toward a newly emerging, humanistic style. His art, therefore, is a struggle of its own, an attempt to break loose from the restrictions of the physical canvas into a visual essence of being. He was at the same time trying to wean himself from the power of his early teacher Duccio, straining to achieve an independent, vibrant style.

Martini's earliest known painting, the great *Maestà* fresco in the Siena city hall incorporates both the Gothic and the humanistic. The Gothic style is characterized by greater emphasis on curved lines, the use of nature as subject matter, and a heightening of motion and emotion in art. Martini was able to achieve this style by carving out wider spaces between his objects and by rendering a closer focus on reality. For example, in Duccio's *Maestà* the main panel is packed with angels and saints to the point of overcrowding, but Martini's *Maestà* loosens up the spacing. Using a blue background, which also gives an impression of open space, Martini pared down the massive throne and set a Gothic queen squarely in the seat under a Gothic canopy, instead of the vague, abstract character used by Duccio. Yet it is in the mastery of the musical lines, its rhythms, its flowing grace, its light undulations and modulations, where Martini's paintings achieve a distinctive Gothic movement and feeling.

Art historians are somewhat puzzled as to how Martini developed his style. Some critics claim that he obtained his taste for the Gothic and the Oriental from Giotto. Others argue that he analyzed imported cloth, jewelry, furniture, and art in Siena trade centers. Both views are certainly plausible. Since Martini was in such demand from commissions and traveled widely, he gained a broad, empirical, cultural base for his art.

In addition to his Gothic style, Martini is noted for highlighting his paintings in a manner that makes his subjects appear three-dimensional. The effect is the creation of a sensuous outer beauty with an inner mysticism. Such an effect comes partly from his own expansive range of human feeling, partly from the awakening of the period to humanistic sympathies, and partly from his later contact with the Humanist poet Petrarch. The rediscovery of sensibilities and of beauty in life engendered in Martini a search for more responsive artistic subjects. The *dolce stil nuovo* was a vital issue of the period, in both the visual and verbal arts, and Martini was at the forefront of the search for a visual language to express it.

As a result of his spreading fame, Martini was summoned to the French Angevin Court of Naples to be knighted by King Robert of Anjou. The most noted work attributed to his four-year stay in Naples is the altarpiece showing King Robert being crowned by his brother Louis, who gave up the right to the crown in order to be canonized in 1317. In the *Saint Louis of Toulouse* painting, he again employs early Gothic forms instead of the heavier Byzantine forms, in this case a truncated gable which recurs in other paintings. This work also introduces, perhaps for the first time in Italy, a five-part *predella* exhibiting scenes from the life of Saint Louis.

In 1319, Martini moved to Pisa, where he composed the large polyptych for the Dominican church dedicated to Saint Catherine and from there to the small town of Orvieto, where he painted another polyptych for the Dominican Order. The inner trefoiled units of these two polyptychs show an interesting evolution of Martini's style from the Romanesque oval shape in the Pisa work (1319) to the more Gothic ogival shape in the Orvieto work (early 1320's). Here, too, the Christ child, unlike the earlier Byzantine models, stands with curled hair on his mother's knee, more in the style of Gothic sculpture. Finally, his preference for the clearer and brighter enamel-like colors acts to free up more space than do Duccio's subdued hues.

In 1321, Martini returned to his home in Siena and repaired his damaged *Maestà* while composing several other works now lost, including the famous *Madonna* (1321) for the chapel in the Palazzo Pubblico. It was during this period, also, that Martini began collaborating with the painter Lippo Memmi. By 1324, the partnership was already close, for in that year Martini married Giovanna, the sister of Lippo Memmi and the daughter of painter Memmo di Filipuccio. According to Petrarch, Martini was not a handsome man, but his wife loved him dearly and remained his companion for the rest of his life.

During the sixteen-year period from 1324 to 1340, Martini is known to have been in and around the three cities of Assisi, Florence, and Siena (all fairly close together). Evidence points to several lost portraits he must have painted of castles and towns under the control of the Sienese. In an eight-year span (from 1328 to 1336) he painted some of his greatest works, including the two best of his career: the large *Guidoriccio da Fogliano* fresco (1328) and the *Annunication* painting (1333) in the Cathederal of Siena, but most of the remaining works are missing. Internal evidence in these later paintings appears to show that his brother-in-law's conservative style acted as a brake on Martini's style, since the more creative and energetic Gothic spirit seemed to erupt when Martini worked alone.

Martini is known to have bought a house in Siena in 1340. In that same year he departed for the French city of Avignon, where he spent the last four years of his life. It is likely that this city appealed to Martini because it was a commercial as well as a religious center of power. While there, Martini formed a close friendship with Petrarch, composing a miniature portrait (now lost) of the famous Laura of Petrarch's poems, in exchange for which Petrarch immortalized Martini's name in two sonnets. In addition to the Laura portrait, Martini composed for Petrarch an illuminated title page for one of his manuscripts.

What is most significant about this phase is that Martini was for art what the new literary voices in Italy at the time (Petrarch, Giovanni Boccaccio, Dante) were to literature. Since Martini had more than a passing interest in the freeing of art from the highly Romanesque mannerism, he and Petrarch would have had much in common. Martini's paintings of the period are more volumetric and palpable, calling for a greater attention to human sensibility.

Summary

It is unclear whether the Black Plague ended the Sienese school or the school died of artistic inbreeding resulting in inertia. What is clear it that Simone Martini's exploitation of the Gothic style at a time when art thirsted for new ideas, his slight traces of Oriental flavor, his freeing of color tones, his vivid figures, and his sensitivity to humanistic values all served to doom the highly stylized Byzantine art and to usher in a more expressive style. Through perspective, color, and design, Martini created new ways to use space, and his approach to realism broke the shackles of the Romanesque style. That he was at the forefront of this striving toward a loftier representation of humankind in all the arts shows both his importance as an artist and his acute awareness of the direction painting needed to go at that time in history.

Martini's designs and his iconography show a sophisticated artistry far beyond the expectations of fourteenth century theory. His brilliant style was to have a major impact on the history of Italian painting for the next hundred years. His influence can be seen in the full, clear faces depicted in the work of his brother-in-law Lippo Memmi, and other, little-known artists such as Lippo Vanni and Bartolo di Fredi carried on Martini's tradition in a mediocre fashion. While the Sienese influence was felt in Hungary, France, and Bohemia, the dazzling styles of Duccio, Martini, and the Lorenzetti brothers eventually died out, except in the works of Barna of Siena, who alone advanced the art beyond that of his predecessors.

Bibliography

Cole, Bruce. *Sienese Painting: From Its Origins to the Fifteenth Century*. New York: Harper and Row, Publishers, 1980. Contains excellent, succinct material on Martini but little about his life. A well-written work, it covers the Sienese school from its beginnings, in 1215, to 1450, providing a much-needed update of the Sandberg-Vavalà book cited below. With black-and-white illustrations.

Paccagini, Giovanni. *Simone Martini*. London: Heinemann, 1955. Still the best complete work in English on Martini's life and works. One of the few books in which the paintings are in color. The prints are large, and there are generous historical and critical notes. Although he overstates the influence of Giotto on Martini, Paccagini is a seasoned writer and an astute scholar. This book is essential to any study of Martini.

Sandberg-Vavalà, Evelyn. *Sienese Studies: The Development of the School of Painting of Siena*. Florence: Leo S. Olschki, 1952. One of the earliest surveys of the Sienese school of painters, this volume begins with the oldest known paintings of Siena and provides a chapter on each of the Sienese artists. There are some errors on places and dates of the paintings, but this work is a scholarly analysis of the events and styles of the movement.

Vasari, Giorgio. *Lives of the Most Eminent Painters, Sculptors, and Architects*. 6 vols. London: H. G. Bohn, 1850-1907. Outside legal documents and art prints, this work is the earliest source of material on Martini's life. Although it is suspect in some details and totally unreliable in others, it is the most comprehensive study of Martini prior to the twentieth century and the only work that provides specific details not gathered from analysis of paintings or from legal documents.

Weiglet, Curt H. *Sienese Painting of the Trecento*. New York: Harcourt, Brace and Co., 1930. Reprint. New York: Hacker Art Books, 1974. One of the better books on the Sienese school of painters. It contains five chapters, one of which is on Martini. He provides much material on Gothic influence. Two-thirds of the book is composed of black-and-white art reproductions conveniently keyed to paragraphs in the text. Unfortunately, the work is outdated.

White, John. *Art and Architecture in Italy, 1250-1400*. New York: Penguin Books, 1966. This study of the early Renaissance is divided into three sections of fifty years each. It covers painting, architecture, and sculpture set against a social and historical backdrop. The three hundred paintings and thirty-three drawings are reproduced in black and white, but the selection is excellent.

Ernest R. Pinson

AL-MAS'UDI

Born: c. 890; probably Baghdad, Iraq
Died: 956; al-Fustat (Old Cairo), Egypt
Areas of Achievement: Historiography, geography, and exploration
Contribution: A pioneer Arab historian, geographer, and chronicler, al-Mas'udi traveled extensively, gathering enormous quantities of information on poorly known lands. His work helped set the tone for future Arabic scholarship; he has been called the Herodotus of the Arabs.

Early Life

Abu al-Hasan 'Ali ibn Husain al-Mas'udi came from an Arab family in Baghdad which claimed descent from one of the early Companions of the Prophet Muhammad, though some sources erroneously describe him as of North African origin. His educational background is unknown, but his career reflects a catholic and almost insatiable thirst for knowledge.

By the standards of the tenth century, al-Mas'udi was a peerless traveler and explorer, whose feats surpass those of Marco Polo more than three centuries later. He began his travels as a young man, visiting Iran, including the cities of Kerman and Istakhr, around 915. Subsequently, he fell in with a group of merchants bound for India and Ceylon. Later, al-Mas'udi seems to have found his way as far as southern China. On his return from China, he made a reconnaissance of the East African coast as far as Madagascar, then visited Oman and other parts of southern Arabia. There followed a visit to Iran, particularly the region of the Elburz Mountains, south of the Caspian Sea.

On yet another journey, al-Mas'udi visited the Levant. He examined various ruins in Antioch and reported on relics in the possession of a Christian church in Tiberias in 943. Two years later, he returned to Syria, settling there for most of the remainder of his life. From Syria, he paid several extended visits to Egypt. Although it is uncertain whether he traveled there, al-Mas'udi's writing also demonstrates detailed knowledge of the lands of North Africa.

Al-Mas'udi's written work is characterized by his adherence to the rationalist Mutazilite school of Islamic thought. The Mutazilites, who applied logical analysis to fundamental questions of human existence and religious law, combined an intellectual disposition with a preference for vocal activism.

Life's Work

Regrettably, much of al-Mas'udi's literary work has been lost, so that in modern times it is known only by the references of others and from his own summaries in extant material. Only a single volume remains extant, for example, out of perhaps thirty that constituted al-Mas'udi's monumental attempt to write a history of the world. The surviving volume covers the myth of creation and geographical background as well as the legendary history of early Egypt.

The major work of al-Mas'udi which has survived is *Muruj al-Dhahab wa-Ma'adin al-Jawhar* (947; partial translation as *Meadows of Gold and Mines of Gems*, 1841). Apparently, there was a considerably larger, revised 956 edition of this work, but it is not extant. Al-Mas'udi laid out his philosophy of history and the natural world in *Kitab al-Tanbih w'al-Ishraf* (book of indications and revisions), a summary of his life's work.

In his books, al-Mas'udi presents a remarkable variety of information. His material on peoples and conditions on the periphery of the Islamic world is of vital importance, as modern knowledge of this aspect of Islamic history is extremely scanty. For modern scholars, however, al-Mas'udi's style and critical commentary leave something to be desired. His presentation jumps from subject to subject, without following a consistent system. Al-Mas'udi made little attempt to distinguish among his sources or to obtain original versions of information, as, for example, the eleventh century geographer/historian al-Biruni was careful to do. He treated a sailor's anecdote or a folktale in the same way as he did a map or a manuscript.

On the other hand, al-Mas'udi's uncritical approach doubtless led to the preservation of material, much of it useful, which would not have found its way into the work of a more conventional scholar. Al-Mas'udi expressed none of the condescension one sometimes finds in other writings of the time for non-Muslim authorities; he displays as much enthusiasm for learning what lay outside Islam as he does for Islamic teaching. The broad scope of his investigations was without precedent.

The juxtaposition of sources of varying authority in al-Mas'udi's work is enough to raise skeptical questions in the minds of modern readers. In discussing the geography of the Indian Ocean, for example, he first presents the "official" version, heavily dependent on erroneous ideas borrowed from Ptolemy and other Hellenistic writers, who regarded the sea as largely landlocked and accessible only through a few narrow entrances. Al-Mas'udi then lays out contrary—and more accurate—information about the Indian Ocean drawn from sailors' tales and from his own experience, indicative of the vastness of the ocean and the cultural diversity of the countries surrounding it. He also presents the orthodox notion of his time that the Caspian Sea and the Aral Sea were connected, followed by an account of his own explorations which revealed that they are separate bodies of water.

Al-Mas'udi departed from established form in presenting his information in a loosely topical manner, organized around ethnic groups, dynasties, and the reigns of important rulers instead of the year-by-year chronicle method typical of the time. In this respect, he anticipated the famed fourteenth century Islamic historian Ibn Khaldun, whose work, in turn, represents a major step toward modern historical scholarship.

A noteworthy feature of al-Mas'udi's observations of nature is his attention to geologic forces which shape the environment. Although his comments sprang mostly from intuition, they were often prescient of modern scientific theory. He wrote, for example, of physical forces changing what once was seabed into dry land and of the nature of volcanic activity.

Summary

Al-Mas'udi deserves to be included among the major Arabic historians, despite the loss of most of his work. His career marks the introduction of a new intellectual curiosity in Islam, one that sought knowledge for its own sake and paid scant attention to the boundaries between Islam and the rest of the world. His fascination with geographical elements in history and human affairs would be taken up by many later Arabic scholars.

Western historians have suggested that al-Mas'udi's intellectual disposition reflects the development of Hellenistic influence in Islamic scholarship, foreshadowing the pervasive Greek character in nontheological Islamic writing in the eleventh and twelfth centuries, particularly in Mediterranean lands. He has been compared both to Herodotus of the fifth century B.C. and to the first century A.D. Roman geographer/historian Pliny the Elder. Lack of knowledge about al-Mas'udi's training and education makes such judgments problematic, but there can be no doubt that his work is in many respects prototypical of what was to come in Islam.

Bibliography

Ahmad, S. Maqbul, and A. Rahman, eds. *Al-Mas'udi Millenary Commemoration Volume*. Aligarh, India: Indian Society for the History of Science and the Institute of Islamic Studies, Aligarh Muslim University, 1960. These essays examine the career of al-Mas'udi after one thousand years. Every major aspect of his thought and writing is covered, including his sources, his geographical and scientific ideas, his use of poetry and other devices, and his knowledge of peoples as far away as Western Europe. Several essays also discuss how al-Mas'udi's writings have been used as resources for modern scholars in various fields.

Ahmed, S. Maqbul. "Al-Mas'udi's Contribution to Medieval Arab Geography." *Islamic Culture* 27/28 (1953/1954): 61-77, 275-286. This detailed account of al-Mas'udi's life and work suggests that he was somewhat defensive about scholarship. Points out that Ptolemy was also indiscriminate about sources; al-Mas'udi may have tried to justify his eclectic sources in terms of ancient predecessors. He rejected most astronomical sources because of their reliance on astrology. Ahmed describes al-Mas'udi as a "roads and countries" scholar, heavily descriptive, less enamored with traditional cosmography.

——————. "Travels of Abu'l Hasan 'Ali B. al-Husain al-Mas'udi." *Islamic Culture* 28 (1954): 509-524. Ahmed summarizes al-Mas'udi's travels, based on his own accounts; he speculates that all travel inferences cannot be taken for granted and that some information may have been gleaned at second hand, even though the geographer's writings do not say so explicitly.

Modi, Sir Jivanji Jamshedji. "Macoudi on Volcanoes." *Journal of the Bombay Branch of the Royal Asiatic Society* 22 (1908): 135-142. Here it is shown that al-Mas'udi's descriptions and notions of volcanic activity are broadly similar to ancient ideas of Hell and to myths derived from the fantastic shapes perceived in vapor clouds. Yet al-Mas'udi also displays intuition about the concentration of volcanoes in certain geographical areas and reports volcanic activity from as far away as Java and Sumatra.

Tarif, Khalidi. "Mas'udi's Lost Works: A Reconstruction of Their Content." *Journal of the American Oriental Society* 94 (1974): 35-41. Tarif discusses the growing realization among scholars of al-Mas'udi's importance. A total of thirty-four titles have been attributed to him; his historical works apparently were produced after a long period of reflection on law, philosophy, science, and theology. Thus he relied on scientific explanations for historical schema, anticipating the methods of Ibn Khaldun.

Ronald W. Davis

MENANDER

Born: c. 342 B.C.; Athens, Greece
Died: c. 292 B.C.; Piraeus, Greece
Areas of Achievement: Theater and drama
Contribution: Noted for his careful plotting, his accurate depiction of middle-class society, and his sympathetic treatment of character, Menander is considered the finest writer of Greek New Comedy.

Early Life

Although there is some disagreement about the exact date of his birth, Menander was probably born in 342 in Athens, Greece. His father was Diopeithes of Cephisia.

Menander's family was evidently involved in both the social and the cultural life of Athens. His uncle Alexis was an important playwright in the tradition of Middle Comedy; he had some two hundred plays to his credit. Menander attended the lectures of Theophrastus, who had succeeded Aristotle as head of the Peripatetic school and who was also a notable writer, now known chiefly for his *Charactēres ethikōi* (c. 319 B.C.; *Characters*), sketches of human types, which undoubtedly influenced Menander and the other dramatists of New Comedy.

Like all Athenian men, between the ages of eighteen and twenty Menander served a year in the military. It was at that time that he became a close friend of Epicurus, whose philosophy was influential in Menander's works. Another of Menander's early friends was important in his later life: Demetrius Phalereus, a fellow student. When Menander was in his mid-twenties, Demetrius was appointed by the Macedonians as ruler of Athens. During the following decade, Demetrius constructed magnificent buildings in the city and drew the most brilliant and talented men of Athens to his court. Among them was Menander, who was already recognized as a playwright, having written his first work when he was nineteen or twenty.

The bust which has been identified as that of Menander suggests what an addition he would have been to the court of Demetrius. The classic features, well-defined profile, penetrating eyes, and strong jaw testify to strength of mind and character; the sensitive mouth and wavy hair soften the general impression. All in all, he was a strikingly handsome man.

When Demetrius fell, Menander is said to have been in some danger, and he was offered the protection of Ptolemy Soter if he would follow his friend Demetrius to Alexandria, Egypt. The playwright declined, however, as he also is said to have declined an invitation to Macedonia, and he spent the remainder of his life in Athens.

Life's Work

In somewhat more than thirty years, Menander wrote some one hundred comedies. Most of his work, however, has been lost. Until 1905, he was represented primarily by hundreds of lines quoted by other writers and by the four plays of Plautus and four others of Terence which were based on certain of his lost plays. Then, a fifth century A.D. papyrus book was discovered in Egypt; it contains one-third to one-half of three of Menander's plays, *Perikeiromenē* (314-310 B.C.; *The Girl Who Was Shorn*), *Epitrepontes* (after 304 B.C.; *The Arbitration*), and *Samia* (321-316 B.C.; *The Girl from Samos*). In 1958, another papyrus book was found in a private collection in Geneva; it holds not only a complete play, *Dyskolos* (317 B.C.; *The Bad-Tempered Man*), but also half of *Aspis* (c. 314 B.C.; *The Shield*) and the almost complete text of *The Girl from Samos*.

Because so much of Menander's work is lost, and because the dating of those plays and fragments which have survived is very uncertain, it is difficult to analyze the playwright's development. It is known that his first work was written about 322 B.C. The only complete play which has survived, *The Bad-Tempered Man*, is an early one, performed in 317, which incidentally was the year that another of Menander's plays, now lost, won for him his first prize.

In *The Bad-Tempered Man* one can see the careful plot construction and the realistic but sympathetic treatment of characters for which Menander was noted. The title character of the play is Cnemon, a misanthrope, whose wife has left him because of his nasty temper and who lives alone with his daughter and a servant, while his virtuous stepson lives nearby. In the prologue to the play, the god Pan announces that he intends to punish Cnemon because he has offended against the principles Pan prizes, in particular good fellowship and love. It is not surprising, then, that this comedy, like Menander's other plays, must move toward suitable marriages, which symbolize reconciliation and which sometimes are accompanied by the reform of an older man who is angry, obstinate, or miserly. In this case, it must be admitted that the most interesting character, Cnemon, is not really reformed, but instead is forced into participating in the final marriage feast. Other typical Menander characters in *The Bad-Tempered Man* include the parasite who profits from his attachment to a rich young friend, a fussy chef who does not realize how stupid he really is, and various comic servants.

The Girl from Samos is based on an even more complicated plot, involving the births of two illegitimate babies, one to a poor girl, the other to a woman from Samos. When the Samian woman's baby dies, it is decided that she will pretend that the other is hers. The result is a series of misunderstandings as to who is making love to whom, who are the parents of the baby, and who is related to whom. This plot enables Menander to analyze relationships between children and their fathers, who can move from love to anger to compassion as their perceptions of the truth alter. At the end of the play, the baby's parentage is revealed, the lovers marry, and parents and children are reconciled.

In *The Girl Who Was Shorn*, too, there is a problem of identity, in this case that of twins who were separated in infancy, while in *The Shield* the confusion arises from the supposed deaths of two men, who naturally must be resurrected in the final section of the play.

Because they see a greater depth in *The Arbitration*, critics believe it to be a later play. The basis of the play is a serious situation: Pamphila was raped by a drunken reveler, and the baby to whom she later gave birth was abandoned. When she married, she concealed the truth from her young husband, and when he learned from a servant about her past, he rejected her and threw himself into a dissolute life. At this point, the play begins. As single-minded as a tragic heroine, Pamphila remains faithful to her husband throughout the play, and though there are comic scenes, such as that in which a charcoal burner argues like a lawyer, and deliberate deception, masterminded by clever slaves, finally the husband is won by his wife's nobility. The baby reappears and is revealed to be the child of Pamphila and her husband, who did not remember raping her. At that point, presented with a grandchild, even Pamphila's father is happy.

Although *The Arbitration* has many of the elements of the other plays, such as the complex plot, the love intrigue, and the stock comic characters, the profound theme elevates it above the other surviving plays of Menander and suggests the basis of his high reputation. In *The Arbitration* can be seen not only the comic confusion which was the essence of New Comedy but also the compassionate treatment of human problems for which Menander was particularly admired.

In his early fifties, Menander drowned while swimming in the harbor of Piraeus, the seaport near Athens. According to Plutarch, Menander died at the height of his dramatic powers. It is unfortunate that his literary career lasted only slightly more than thirty years and that almost all of his plays have been lost. All that remains is a name, a reputation, and an influence.

Summary

In his plot elements and stock characters Menander was probably similar to many of the other playwrights of New Comedy; his superior reputation rests upon the fact that he rejected mere Dionysian horseplay for the presentation of a real moral drama. In this may be seen the influence of his friend Epicurus. In his penetration of character, he undoubtedly followed the tragedian Euripides.

Unfortunately, audiences of Menander's own time seem to have been less than enthusiastic about his kind of play, preferring the bawdy productions of his rivals. Of his one hundred plays, only eight won the coveted prize for comedy. After his death, however, his reputation rose rapidly. Among the Romans he was highly valued. Ovid admired him; Plutarch ranked him above Aristophanes, and others placed him just below Homer. During the period of the empire, his philosophical maxims were frequently quoted and even collected.

Menander's greatest influence, however, came through the Roman playwrights Plautus and Terence, who adapted and imitated his works, devising their own complex plots, dramatizing Roman everyday life as Menander had the life of his own people, and working toward resolutions in which folly is exposed and lovers united. Through Plautus and Terence, he survived to help establish the pattern of Renaissance drama. Menander's influence can be seen in the exaggeratedly humorous characters of Ben Jonson and the romantic lovers of William Shakespeare. Finally, his satire set in ordinary society provided the basis of the comedy of manners genre. Even though most of his work has been lost for centuries, Menander's comic vision persists in the plays of his successors.

Bibliography

Allinson, Francis G. Introduction to *Menander: The Principal Fragments.* Translated by Francis G. Allinson. Cambridge, Mass.: Harvard University Press, 1921, reprint 1964. This brief but extremely scholarly introductory essay includes a clear description of Menander's historical placement, concise comments about the playwright's use of prologue, plot, and character, and even a statement about his Greek style. Contains some material not generally available.

Bieber, Margarete. *The History of the Greek and Roman Theater.* Princeton, N.J.: Princeton University Press, 1939, rev. ed. 1961. A lavishly illustrated volume whose text is somewhat confusing because it seems to proceed from one statue or vase to another rather than in the ordinary chronological order. Used with a more conventional history, however, extremely interesting, both for its text and for photographs of sculptures—for example, those depicting Menander at different ages.

Dover, K. J. *Ancient Greek Literature.* Oxford: Oxford University Press, 1980. A concise and accurate treatment of the subject. For a full understanding of Menander's place in Greek literature, it would be helpful to read the entire book, although Menander is specifically treated in the chapter headed "Comedy."

Goldberg, Sander M. *The Making of Menander's Comedy.* Berkeley: University of California Press, 1980. An outstanding scholarly discussion of Menander's work. Explains clearly his relation to Old and Middle Comedy, delineates the problems of scholarship, and then proceeds to a lucid analysis of each of the surviving works.

Pickard-Cambridge, Arthur W. *The Dramatic Festivals of Athens.* Oxford: Clarendon Press, 1953, rev. ed. 1968. The authoritative account of the production of Greek drama, ranging from the descriptions of the various festivals themselves to detailed explanations of acting style, costuming, and music, even including an analysis of the composition and character of the audience. Well illustrated.

Reinhold, Meyer. *Classical Drama: Greek and Roman*. Woodbury, N.Y.: Barron's Educational Series, 1959. In outline form, an excellent guide to its subject. Chapters 5 through 11, dealing with Euripides, Old, Middle, and New Comedy, and Menander's Roman successors, are particularly recommended. Contains plot summaries, with hypothetical suggestions as to missing elements, of four of Menander's plays. With glossary and bibliography.

Sandbach, F. H. *The Comic Theatre of Greece and Rome*. New York: W. W. Norton and Co., 1977. An excellent study of comedy from Aristophanes to Terence, with a particularly illuminating discussion of Menander's themes, in the light of the newly discovered texts. Well written. Glossary and selected bibliography included.

Rosemary M. Canfield-Reisman

MENANDER

Born: c. 210 B.C.; probably Kalasi, Afghanistan
Died: c. 135 B.C.; probably in northwest India
Areas of Achievement: Government and religion
Contribution: Menander extended the Greco-Bactrian domains in India more than any other ruler. He became a legendary figure as a great patron of Buddhism in the Pali book the *Milindapañha.*

Early Life

Menander (not to be confused with the more famous Greek dramatist of the same name) was born somewhere in the fertile area to the south of the Paropamisadae or present Hindu Kush Mountains of Afghanistan. The only reference to this location is in the semilegendary *Milindapañha* (first or second century A.D.), which says that he was born in a village called Kalasi near Alasanda, some two hundred *yojanas* (about eighteen miles) from the town of Sāgala (probably Sialkot in the Punjab). The Alasanda refers to the Alexandria in Afghanistan and not to the one in Egypt. No evidence exists on the question of whether Menander was an aristocrat or a commoner or of royal lineage. All surmises about the life of Menander are based on his coins, for information in Greek sources is very sparse indeed. All that remains of a more extensive history of the east by Apollodorus of Artemita are two sentences in Strabo's *Geography* (c. first century A.D.) that the Bactrian Greeks, especially Menander, overthrew more peoples in India than did Alexander. Strabo is dubious that Menander "really crossed the Hypanis River [Beas] toward the east and went as far as the Isamos [Imaus, or Jumna River?]." Plutarch in his *Ethica* (first century A.D.; also known as *Moralia*) calls Menander a king of Bactria who ruled with equity and who died in camp, and after his death, memorials were raised over his ashes. If Menander became a convert to Buddhism, this could mean that Buddhist stupas, covering reliquaries, were built over his remains, which were divided among different sites. The final classical source which mentions Menander, Pompeius Trogus, simply calls him a king of India together with Apollodotus.

The Pali *Milindapañha*, a series of questions put to a Buddhist sage by King Milinda, along with their answers, contains no historical data save those about Menander's birth, which may be legend, as well as moral precepts beloved to Buddhists. Another text of the period, the *Vāyū Purāna*, only mentions him as a Greek king in India. The last reference to Menander occurs in an inscription on a relic casket dedicated in the reign of Mahārāja Minedra (Menander), which is not informative. Modern students are left with the coins, the styles and legends of which have provided the basis of hypothetical reconstructions of the life of Menander. That he was married to a certain Queen Agathocleia, daughter of Demetrius, is suggested by W. W.

Tarn on the basis of the coin style of Agathocleia, especially the figure of Pallas Athena, the favored deity of Menander's coins on the reverse, and the similarity in portraits between goddess and queen. The usual epithet on Menander's coins was the Greek word *soter* (savior), but what he saved, if anything, is unknown.

From the great number of extant coins of Menander and the widespread location of find spots, one may surmise that he had a fairly long rule over a kingdom extending from the Hindu Kush Mountains into the present-day United Provinces of north India. His rule over Mathura and especially Pā-taliputra on the borders of Bengal is uncertain and disputed, although the former is more likely than the latter. In any case, he obviously was that Greek king of India who made the greatest impression on the Indians, especially the Buddhists.

Life's Work

One of the two achievements which have earned for Menander a place in history books was the great extension of Greco-Bactrian rule in India, to the extent that his rule was probably the high point of Greek rule on the subcontinent. The second and equally significant factor in the life of Menander was his role in Buddhist legend. The *Milindapañha* was not popular only among Indians; a Chinese translation exists as well as the Pali version. Although it is unproven whether Menander became a convert, and there is no tradition that he propagated Buddhism as Aśoka the Great and Kanishka are supposed to have done, he holds an eminent position as an enlightened Buddhist ruler in their tradition. Whether he was considered by his Indian subjects a Chakra-vartin, a supreme Buddhist ruler who conquered lands by persuasion and justice rather than by the sword, is unknown. If Plutarch's statement that memorials were raised over his ashes can be interpreted as meaning Buddhist stupas containing some part or ashes of him, then it is plausible that Menander was a Buddhist. The fact that legends did grow up about him at least indicates his importance in Buddhist circles.

The suggestion of Tarn that the Pali book was modeled after a Greek original which might have had the title "Questions of Menander" is intriguing. It would imply that the Greek presence in India was neither simply a short-lived foreign military occupation nor a diluted, mixed Iranian-Indian culture with a thin Hellenistic veneer, but that it did have a strong purely Greek content. Furthermore, that content was responsible for the introduction into India of Greek genres of literature and philosophical and other ideas, as well as the canons of Greek art which were to flower later under the sobriquet of Gandharan art.

Summary

It may be argued not only that Menander was responsible for extending

Greek arms on the Indian subcontinent to the fullest extent but also that he was much more than a conqueror. Since he has become a legend in Buddhist tradition and is praised by Plutarch as a just king, it may be further surmised that under his rule, Greek philosophy and culture met and influenced Indian civilization, which in the middle of the second century was dominated by Buddhism. Whether a hypothetical Greek "Questions of Menander" influenced not only the Buddhists in India but also Hellenistic literature in Alexandria, Egypt, and elsewhere, as Tarn suggests, is even more speculative. The flowering of Gandharan art in the second century A.D., when Hellenistic origins are overwhelmingly indicated, probably owed as much to the legacy of Menander and his many successors as it did to the influence of Roman provincial art forms. Thus, Hellenism in India and Central Asia may owe much more than is now known to Menander and his legacy.

Bibliography

Bivar, A. D. H. "The Sequence of Menander's Drachmae." *Journal of the Royal Asiatic Society*, 1970: 128-129. A basic work on the coins of Menander's reign, with historical interpretations of their presence in certain locations.

Frye, Richard N. *The Ancient History of Iran*. Munich: Verlag C. H. Beck, 1984. A summary of the milieu and events in which the life and activities of Menander may be placed.

Majumdar, N. G. "The Bajaur Casket of the Reign of Menander." *Epigraphica Indica* 24 (1937): 1-8. An analysis of the only extant inscription of Menander's reign; includes translation and commentary.

Narain, A. K. *The Indo-Greeks*. Oxford: Clarendon Press, 1957. A response to Tarn's book (below) concentrating on translations of Chinese and Indian sources. Written from the Indian perspective.

Tarn, W. W. *The Greeks in Bactria and India*. 2d ed. Cambridge: Cambridge University Press, 1951. The basic study on Menander. Includes translations and analyses of classical sources. Highly speculative, but fascinating reading.

Richard N. Frye

MENCIUS
Meng-tzu

Born: c. 372 B.C.; Tsou, China
Died: c. 289 B.C.; China
Area of Achievement: Philosophy
Contribution: Through a lifetime of reflection, Mencius clarified and expanded the wisdom embodied in Confucius' *Analects*, rendering Confucian ideas more accessible. His *Meng-tzu* eclipsed other interpretations of Confucius and gained acceptance as the orthodox version of Confucian thought.

Early Life

Mencius was born probably about 372 B.C. in the small principality of Tsou in northeastern China, not far from the birthplace of Confucius, whose work Mencius spent his life interpreting. Knowledge of Mencius' early life is scarce. What evidence exists must be extracted from his own writing, most notably the *Meng-tzu* (first transcribed in the early third century B.C.), although many biographical observations are found in the great historian Ssu-ma Ch'ien's *Shin chi* (c. 90 B.C.), a large work which has been translated in part many times and is best known by its original title.

Mencius was probably a member of the noble Meng family, whose home, like that of Confucius, was in the city-state of Lu, in what is now southwestern Shantung Province. Certainly Mencius' education was one that was common to the aristocracy, for he was thoroughly familiar with both the classical *Shih ching* (c. 500 B.C.; *Book of Odes*, 1950) and the *Shu ching* (c. 626 B.C.; *Book of Documents*, 1950), which together provided the fundamentals of his classical training. Moreover, he had a masterly grasp of Confucius' work and quoted it frequently, leading to the assumption that he studied in a Confucian school, purportedly under the tutelage of Confucius' grandson, who was himself a man of ministerial rank in the central state of Wei.

Known as Meng-tzu to his students, Mencius assumed the role of teacher early in his life and never abandoned it. Rejecting material well-being and position as ends in themselves, he, like many Confucians, nevertheless aspired to hold office inside one of the courts of the Chinese states. He did indeed become a councillor and later the Minister of State in Wei. In such positions, he tutored students, not all of them noble, in classical works: the dynastic hymns and ballads anthologized in the *Book of Odes* and state papers from archives (from 1000 to 700 B.C.) which formed the *Book of Documents*. These were works from which, by the end of the second century B.C., Confucian precepts developed. During these early years of observation and teaching, Mencius gained disciples, furthered his interpretations of Confucius, and enjoyed considerable renown in many parts of China.

Life's Work

Meng-tzu was Mencius' principal work. It appeared late in his life. Had it incorporated less wisdom than his many years of diverse experiences and reflections allowed, or a less lengthy refinement of Confucius' thoughts, it would not be likely to rank as one of the greatest philosophical and literary works of the ancient world.

Mencius garnered experience through his wanderings and temporary lodgments in various Chinese courts and kingdoms. He was fortunate to live in an age when, despite continuous political turmoil, dynastic rivalries, and incessant warfare, high levels of civility prevailed in aristocratic circles. Teacher-scholars, as a consequence, were readily hosted—that is, effectively subsidized—by princely families eager to advance their children's education and to instruct and invigorate themselves through conversation with learned men.

Some of Mencius' temporary affiliations can be dated. Between 323 and 319, Mencius was installed at the court of King Hui of Liang, in what is now China's Szechwan Province. He moved eastward about 318 to join the ruler of the state of Ch'i, King Hsuan. Prior to his sojourn to Liang (although the dates are conjectural), Mencius visited and conversed with princes, rulers, ministers, and students in several states: Lu, Wei, Ch'i, and Song.

Mencius' journeyings were not feckless. They related directly to his philosophical and historical perceptions. Like Confucius, Mencius believed that he lived in a time of troubles in which—amid rival feudatories and warring states, divided and misruled—China was in decline. Also like Confucius, Mencius looked back fondly on what he thought had been the halcyon days of Chinese government and civilization under the mythical kings (2700 B.C.-770 B.C.), when a unified China had been governed harmoniously.

Drawing on Chinese legends incorporated into literary sources familiar to him from the *Hsia* and the Shang and Chou dynasties, Mencius concluded that the ideal governments of these earlier days had been the work of hero kings—Yao, Shun, and Yu—whose successors had organized themselves into dynasties. These were the Sage kings, who, like kings Wen and Wu of the Chou family, had been responsible for China's former greatness. Their dissolute successors, however, such as the "bad" kings of the *Hsia* and the Shang Dynasty, were equally responsible for the subsequent debasement of the Sage kings' remarkable achievements and erosion of their legacy.

For Mencius, a vital part of this legacy was the concept of the Mandate of Heaven. It was an idea that he ascribed to the early Chou kings, who justified their authority by it. These kings asserted that they had received the mandate directly from the deity, who designated Chou rulers Sons of Heaven, viceroys of Heaven. Effectively, that charged them with the responsibilities of being the deity's fief holders. The Chou kings, in turn, proceeded to impose lesser feudal obligations on their own fief holders and subjects. In

Mencius' view, this arrangement was more than merely an arbitrary justification for Chou authority; it was also a recognition of authority higher than man's. Because the Mandate of Heaven was not allocated in perpetuity, it was essentially a lease that was operative during good behavior. When rulers lost virtue and thereby violated the mandate, the punishment of Heaven descended upon them. Their subjects, their vassals, were constrained to replace them. It was on this basis, as Mencius knew, that the Chou kings had successfully reigned for four centuries.

Equally important in this hierarchical scheme developed around the Chou conception of the Mandate of Heaven, of Sage kings functioning in response to it, were the roles of Sage ministers. It was these ministers whom Mencius credited with the rise and harmonious rule of the Sage kings. In times when the Mandate of Heaven had obviously been forgotten or ignored, Mencius wished not only that this ideal past would be restored but also that his presence at various courts would allow him to identify, assist, and guide potential Sage kings, fulfilling the role of Sage minister himself or through his disciples.

King Hsuan of Ch'i was one of the rulers at whose court he served and for whom he envisioned greatness as the Ideal King. Hsuan, however, appeared lacking in will. King Hui of Liang also showed some promise, but Mencius despaired of Lui when he revealed his desire to rule the world by force. Briefly, Mencius saw potential in the king of T'eng, who ruled a small principality that, nevertheless, afforded a sufficient stage for a True King. That potential also went unrealized. To critics who charged that Mencius was simply unperceptive, his reply was that such rulers possessed ample ability but had not availed themselves of his services. After these encounters, despairing, he returned home to kindle his belief in the Ideal King in the hearts of his disciples.

The basis for Mencius' initial optimism lay in his interpretation of China's history, for it reassured him that great kings had appeared in cycles of about five hundred years. Half a millennium lay between the reign of T'ang, founder of the Shang Dynasty (c. 1384-1122 B.C.), and Wu, first ruler of the great Chou Dynasty (1122-221 B.C.). Consequently Heaven's dispatch of another Sage king, according to Mencius, was overdue. In this interim and in expectation of the Sage king's appearance, men such as himself—"Heavenly instruments"—had divine commissions to maintain the ideal.

There is no evidence that Mencius, any more than Confucius, was successful in the realization of such dreams. Although Mencius served briefly as a councillor, and although his knowledge was profound as well as wide-ranging, he revealed more disdain for than interest in (or understanding of) practical politics in his own highly politicized environment. Furthermore, areas of intellection such as religion, ethics, and philosophy were densely packed with rivals. A number of these, such as Micius the utilitarian or Yang

Chu the hedonist, enjoyed greater recognition and higher status than he did. Nor was Mencius ranked among the leading intellectuals or scholars of his day who were inducted into the membership of the famous Chi-Hsia Academy.

Later generations would honor him, but in his own time Mencius was a relatively obscure, evangelizing teacher whose views were merely tolerated, a pedagogue who never penetrated beyond the fringes of power, a man without a substantial following. These conditions help explain his occasional haughtiness, manipulative argumentation, and assertive promulgation of Confucianism. Nevertheless, not until two centuries after his death did Confucian principles gain significant influence.

Thus, Mencius' work can be examined for its intrinsic merit, outside the context of his own lifetime. He was, foremost, a devoted follower of Confucius. As such, he never wavered in the belief that it was not enough to be virtuous; men also had to model themselves after the Sage kings. Antiquity represented the epitome of good conduct, good government, and general harmony. Consequently, the ways of old—or his interpretations of them—had to be accepted or rejected completely.

This position inevitably raised the issue of how the Sages of yesteryear had become, both as men and as governors, such ideal models. Had such gifts been divinely bestowed? Mencius believed that they were like all men. This response led him therefore into an elaboration of the central tenets of his philosophy, into an embellishment of Confucius, and ultimately into formulating his major contribution to thought.

Whereas Confucius left only one equivocal observation on human nature, Mencius—probably because the contention of his time demanded it—placed the essence of human nature at the center of his work. Discussions of humanity (*jen*) and of justice (*yi*) accordingly became his preoccupations, and, subsequently, because of Mencius, became the focus of Chinese philosophy.

In defining humanity, he declared unequivocally that all men were born sharing the same human nature and that human nature is good. Mencius sought to demonstrate this belief through his maxims and parables: All men were endowed with sympathy for those whose lives were at risk or who had suffered great misfortune; all men felt best when they were instinctively being their best. Thus, all men who cultivated *jen* were capable of indefinite perfectibility; they were capable of becoming Sages. Furthermore, men would find *jen* irresistible, for it nullified the menaces of brute physical force (*pa*). Writing with fewer logical inhibitions than had been displayed by Confucius, Mencius asserted that all things were complete within every man: Everyone, in microcosm, embodied the essences of everything: the macrocosm.

Consequently, men who knew their own nature also knew Heaven. In asserting this, wittingly or not, Mencius again went beyond Confucius, for

knowing oneself first in order to know everything suggested meditative introspection, whereas Confucius had disparaged meditation and insisted on the
superiority of observation and the use of the critical faculty. Mencius stressed
the real incentives for the cultivation of one's humanity. Those who did so enjoyed wisdom, honor, and felicity. When such men became kings, the state
was harmoniously governed and prospered. In turn, such kings won over the
allegiance of the world—which to Mencius, as to all Chinese, meant China.
Jen therefore also afforded men prestige and moral authority that constituted
power (*te*) far greater than any physical force.

Mencius was all too aware of the extent to which his everyday world indicated just the opposite, that is, the appalling conditions men had created for
themselves. He was also aware of misapplications of force, either as a result
of these problems or as a result of attempts to resolve them. Yet to Mencius,
the failure to cultivate one's humanity lay at the root of these difficulties. He
was not naïve about some of the causes of inhumanity. Poverty and the misery of men's environments, he conceded, often left little chance for cultivating one's humanity, but that lent urgency to the search for a Sage king who
could mitigate or eradicate these conditions. He was also aware that men's
appetites, as well as the conditions in which they lived, left little to differentiate them from other animals. Yet, the difference that did exist was a vital
one: namely, their ability to think with their hearts.

Justice (*yi*) was a concomitant to Mencius' concept of humanity and was
also central to his teaching. By justice, Mencius meant not only doing the
right thing but also seeing that others received their rights. Clearly the "right
things" consisted in part of rituals and formal codes of manners and of traditional civilities. They also embraced rights which were not necessarily embodied in law: the right of peasants to gather firewood in the forests, the
right to subsistence in old age, and the right to expect civilities and to live
according to traditional codes to behavior. If feeling distress for the suffering
of others was, according to Mencius, the first sign of humanity, then feelings
of shame and disgrace were the first signs of justice.

Mencius spent his lifetime forming his maxims and parables to illustrate
what humanity and justice meant to him—or what he believed they should
mean to all men. Appropriately for a teacher, he provoked more questions
than he answered; he never arrived at his goal, nor did his disciples. He died
about 289, probably near his place of birth on the Shantung Peninsula.

Summary

A devoted Confucian, Mencius expanded and clarified Confucius' *Lun-yü*
(late sixth or early fifth century B.C.; *Analects*) and the principles of his master as they were being taught and debated a century after Confucius' death.
Mencius, however, went beyond Confucius by placing human nature and his
belief in its essential goodness at the center of philosophical discussion. Of-

ficially ranked a Sage, he stands among the world's most respected literary and philosophical geniuses.

Bibliography

Creel, H. G. *Chinese Thought from Confucius to Mao Tse-tung*. Chicago: University of Chicago Press, 1953. A very informed, bright, readable work, with a brief bibliography and selected readings. Includes a useful index.

Dobson, W. A. C. H., trans. *Mencius*. Toronto: University of Toronto Press, 1963. Splendidly translated and arranged for general readers. Mencius' thoughts are reordered for coherence. A fine introduction is followed throughout by excellent annotations. Includes thorough notes, which more than compensate for lack of a glossary or index.

Lau, D. C., trans. *Mencius*. Hong Kong: Chinese University Press, 1984. Contains an interesting but dense introduction addressing the problems of dating events in Mencius' life. Five very informative appendices. With useful notes, glossary, and index.

Legge, James, trans. *The Chinese Classics*. 7 vols. Rev. ed. Oxford: Clarendon Press, 1893-1895. The standard scholarly translation of Mencius, this set includes the works of Mencius in volume 2. With fine notes and an index.

Mote, Frederick W. *Intellectual Foundations of China*. New York: Alfred A. Knopf, 1971. Brief but superb for placing Mencius in context. These are brilliant, reflective, and well-crafted scholarly essays by a leading sinologist. Contains a select bibliography and an index.

Richards, I. A. *Mencius on the Mind: Experiments in Multiple Definition*. London: Kegan Paul, 1932. Richards concentrates on Chinese modes of meaning as revealed in Mencius. The exploration is designed to see if beneath linguistic barriers there is material for comparative understanding. Thus, though ranking Mencius among the world's great thinkers, Richards deals critically with Mencius' methods of argument.

Waley, Arthur. *Three Ways of Thought in Ancient China*. Winchester, Mass.: Allen and Unwin, 1939. Fine basic intellectual history which for years has been standard among scholars. Readable, informative, and reflective. Contains a brief bibliography and a useful glossary and index.

Clifton K. Yearley
Kerrie L. MacPherson

MI FEI

Born: 1052; Hsiang-yang, Hupeh, China
Died: 1107; Huai-yang, Kiangsu, China
Area of Achievement: Art
Contribution: An accomplished calligrapher and the paragon of Chinese artist-connoisseurs, Mi Fei played a pivotal role in the transmission of the classical tradition of Chinese calligraphy.

Early Life

Mi Fei (also known as Mi Fu, Yüan-chang, Hsiang-yang, and Hai-yüeh Wai-shih) was born at the beginning of the year 1052 in Hsiang-yang County in Hupeh Province, China. Although he did not come from a distinguished family tradition, he was reared on the palace grounds, as his mother served as a palace lady of the empress and wife of Emperor Ying Tsung (reigned 1064-1067).

Together with Su Shih (1036-1101), Huang T'ing-chien (1045-1105), and Ts'ai Hsiang (1012-1067), Mi Fei is known as one of the four great masters of calligraphy of the Sung Dynasty (960-1279). He was a gifted artist with deep perceptions and passionate sensitivity. He possessed an irrepressible urge to rise above stuffy conventions and had a tendency to protest against accepted practices. Outspoken and unbridled, Mi Fei liked to wear loosely fitted robes with sweeping sleeves, in the style popular during the T'ang Dynasty (618-907), and had an idiosyncratic fixation on cleanliness, refusing to share towels and utensils with even his closest associates. Furthermore, he had a passion, if not an obsession, for grotesquely shaped rocks, before which—according to tradition—he would even prostrate himself and worship. It is therefore not at all surprising that Mi Fei acquired the nickname Mi-tien, or Mi the Eccentric.

Life's Work

Mi Fei was a collector, art critic, connoisseur, painter, and calligrapher. He was appointed a collator in the Imperial Library at the age of twenty and subsequently served for two decades in minor official posts in the southern provinces. His home on the palace grounds and successive travels in the south afforded him ample opportunity to cultivate social contacts and to study many calligraphic works in private collections. He completed his first book on classical calligraphic works, *Pao-chang tai-fang lu* (records of searches for precious scrolls), in 1086. He was widely acclaimed as a leading calligrapher in 1088, at the age of thirty-six, when he wrote his famous *Shu-su t'ieh* (calligraphy on coarse Szechwan silk).

In 1092, Mi Fei was appointed subprefect in Yung-ch'iu, Honan; he was then close to the capital, Kai-feng, where famed collectors and dealers were easily accessible. According to his necrology, in 1103 he was given the title Doctor of the Imperial Sacrifices (*t'ai-ch'ang po-shih*) for his calligraphic skills. Mi Fei reached the pinnacle of his official career in 1105, when he was invited to become Doctor of Calligraphy and Painting (*shu-hua po-shih*) and, shortly thereafter, assistant division chief of the Board of Rites (*li-pu yuan-wai-lang*). He was given an audience with Emperor Hui Tsung (reigned 1100-1125), to whom he presented his own handwritten copy of the "Thousand-Character Essay" following the foremost example of pre-T'ang standard script (*k'ai-shu*).

Mi Fei maintained close contacts with some of the outstanding intellectuals of his time. At the age of thirty-two, he was fortunate enough to make the acquaintance of Su Shih. Su Shih was a towering figure in an influential circle of scholar-officials, and he considered Mi Fei his protégé. He encouraged Mi Fei to begin a serious study of calligraphic works of the masters of the Eastern Chin Dynasty (A.D. 317-419), particularly those of Wang Hsi-chih (c. 307-379) and Wang Hsien-chih (344-386). Mi Fei equipped himself with a boat which he called Shu-hua fang, or Boat of Calligraphy and Painting, and sailed it up and down the waterways in southeastern China, eagerly participating in the privileged social game of collecting and trading art objects.

A unique combination of connoisseur and artist is immediately discernible in Mi Fei. For him, connoisseurship and artistic skills complemented each other—one was the *sine qua non* of the other. This view is particularly understandable in the cultural climate of which Mi Fei was a part, for nearly all the original brushwork art of the classical period was lost and copying the works of the early masters was an integral part of practicing calligraphy. Copies of the originals, or copies of the copies, served as the primary source of information for the study of early masterpieces. One could only depend on the expert judgment of the connoisseurs, who might have viewed more originals and better copies.

Mi Fei had diligently practiced the art of calligraphy since his early childhood. He copied most laboriously works of masters of the Eastern Chin Dynasty—works he regarded as stylistic prototypes, embodying the highest standards of fine calligraphy. Few artists, in fact, have ever engaged in such a prolonged and fruitful study of the works of their predecessors. Mi Fei became known for his extraordinary ability to copy faithfully works of early masters down to the minutest details. He frequently borrowed masterworks from his associates and copied them meticulously. His skill reached such perfection that even some of the most discerning connoisseurs were confounded and could not differentiate his copies from the originals. Through his ardent and creative absorption of the skills and artistic spirit embodied in the works of earlier masters, Mi Fei achieved an unprecedented level of brush mastery. His calligraphic works demonstrate a refreshing style and a distinctive cultivated air.

Mi Fei's critical writings are widely regarded as the foremost source of information for the history of calligraphic work before the Sung Dynasty. He transmitted an image of the Chin masters' art through his personal interpretations. Although Mi Fei's writings lacked systematic integrity, he presented himself forcefully and methodically. He scrutinized an enormous volume of painting and calligraphic pieces and offered candid (though often cantankerous) and trenchant comments in the form of discussions. Although Mi Fei wrote on the history of calligraphy and painting, connoisseurship of ink stones and paper, techniques of scroll mounting, and the use of seals, those observations on calligraphy have had the most lasting influence.

According to Mi Fei, extensive and continuous stylistic explorations within the classical tradition are paramount: They are directly beneficial to the development of the theoretical proficiency required of an artist. This proficiency helps facilitate the formation of the artist's personal style. In addition, Mi Fei regarded the development of calligraphy as a social phenomenon, not to be dictated by the particular style of an individual. He wrote most frequently in running script (*hsing-shu*), most popular during the Sung. This style combines the legibility of standard script with the creative freedom of cursive. Mi Fei also left behind specimens written in the traditional seal (*chuan-shu*) and clerical (*li-shu*) styles. In fact, a wide spectrum of styles and a variety of shapes and strokes are found in his oeuvre. His brushstrokes seem to have been made in rhythmic bursts; they display restless energy and effortlessness. Fluidity and spontaneity characterize his work. Mi Fei's calligraphy, as the twentieth century scholar Ch'en Chih-mai shrewdly observed, "can be compared to a Gothic cathedral, fretted, restless, dynamic, mysterious, and even playful." Artistic creation, according to Mi Fei, must demonstrate quintessential artistic qualities such as *ch'ao-i* (transcendence), *p'ing-tan* (plain tranquillity), and *t'ien-jen* (natural perfection). This view decisively and profoundly influenced many artists in China after him.

While his calligraphic works are better known than his paintings, Mi Fei's landscapes did give rise to a new school of painting, known as the Mi school. His creative inner impulse led him to break with accepted conventions. It is said that in his landscape paintings he abandoned drawn lines altogether in favor of blobs of splashed ink, thus giving more vitality to his creations. The term "Mi mountains" (*Mi-chia-shan*) refers to the landscapes of Mi Fei and his son Mi Yu-jen, who was an accomplished artist in his own right.

Summary

Calligraphy was the art form most widely practiced in traditional China. Everyone who aspired to enter into officialdom was expected to be a proficient calligrapher. Exquisite and refined calligraphy was regarded by the Chinese as their supreme artistic and, simultaneously, moral achievement. That brushwork mirrored the personality and the moral character of the artist was a concept accepted since the early Han Dynasty (207 B.C.-A.D. 220). For the Chinese, calligraphy is an effective means through which one cultivates his inner strength and morality. Thus, in China, Mi Fei—calligrapher, art historian, and connoisseur *par excellence*—is immortalized for his artistic eminence.

Bibliography

Ch'en Chih-mai. *Chinese Calligraphers and Their Art*. Melbourne: Melbourne University Press, 1966. This book offers a panoramic view of both the history and the various styles of Chinese calligraphy. The chapter "Sung: The Age of Hsing Shu" and the three chapters on calligraphy as an art provide the layman with a quick overview.

Chiang Yee. *Chinese Calligraphy: An Introduction to Its Aesthetic and Technique*. 3d ed. Cambridge, Mass.: Harvard University Press, 1972. A good introductory work for general readers. The discussion of the basic concepts of calligraphy and the skills required of a calligrapher is informative and helpful.

Fu, Shen C. Y., et al. *Traces of the Brush: Studies in Chinese Calligraphy*. New Haven, Conn.: Yale University Art Gallery, 1977. This work is the catalog which accompanied an exhibition held at the Yale University Art Gallery and the University Art Museum, University of California, Berkeley, in 1977. The author, an eminent scholar of Chinese art, addresses himself in this study not only to questions of connoisseurship but also to a preliminary outline for a comprehensive history of Chinese scripts.

Ledderose, Lothar. *Mi Fu and the Classical Tradition of Chinese Calligraphy*. Princeton, N.J.: Princeton University Press, 1979. The most scholarly, comprehensive, and detailed study of Mi Fei. It discusses the pivotal role Mi Fei played in the transmission of the classical tradition of the Chin masters' art. The author traces the evolutionary patterns in the history of Chinese calligraphy through a study of the methods Mi Fei used to investigate the past. Mi Fei's historical and aesthetic concepts are carefully examined. Numerous illustrations help enliven the author's skillful discussions.

Sullivan, Michael. *The Arts of China*. 3d ed. Berkeley: University of California Press, 1984. A good textbook on the Chinese artistic tradition. Useful to both the general reader and the serious student. The author concerns himself not only with art but also with Chinese philosophy and religion.

San-pao Li

MILTIADES THE YOUNGER

Born: c. 554 B.C.; probably Attica, Greece
Died: 489 B.C.; probably Athens, Greece
Areas of Achievement: Politics and warfare
Contribution: Through innovative tactics and inspired battlefield leadership, Miltiades led Athens to victory over the Persians at the Battle of Marathon. He thus helped to secure Greek civilization from engulfment by Near Eastern influences and greatly enhanced Athenian prestige in the Greek world.

Early Life
Very little is known about the first thirty years of Miltiades' life. His family and clan relationships, however, would prove to be highly influential in the shaping of his career, as was commonly the case in ancient Athens. He was born into the very old and wealthy Philaidae clan, whose members had long played an active part in Athenian politics. This family's estates were located in rural Attica (the countryside which bordered Athens). As a member of a prominent, aristocratic family, Miltiades probably enjoyed the benefits of a fine education and certainly profited from extensive political connections.

Miltiades' father, Cimon, however, was notorious for his failure to advance in the Athenian political arena, a source of considerable shame for aristocrats in Greek society. He was widely known for intellectual torpidity, a trait which earned for him the nickname *koalemos*, meaning "the nincompoop." Nevertheless, Cimon's failure to earn a prominent place in public life was probably more a result of his opposition to the Peisistratidae clan, an aristocratic family and political faction which exercised an authoritarian rule over Athens from 560 to 510 B.C., with considerable popular support.

In order to secure his own place in politics, Miltiades was forced to disavow his father's opinions and seek allies elsewhere. He did not have to search outside his own clan, because his uncle, Miltiades the Elder, and his older brother, Stesagoras, had acquiesced to Peisistratidaen rule and had been dispatched to the Chersonese (modern Gallipoli Peninsula) to conquer, colonize, and rule the region for Athens. In roughly 524 or 523, Miltiades served as archon, a judicial-administrative post which he secured through his acceptance of the Peisistratidaen tyranny.

Sometime before 514, Miltiades married an Athenian woman, about whom nothing definite is known. Some historians believe that she was a relative of the Peisistratidae. This union produced at least one child. Around 516, the Peisistratidae sent Miltiades to the Chersonese to assume the duties formerly performed by Miltiades the Elder and Stesagoras, both having recently died childless. Miltiades would utilize this opportunity to achieve renown in the Aegean world.

Life's Work

The Peisistratidae had entrusted Miltiades with an important assignment. By the latter half of the sixth century, Athens was importing unknown quantities of wheat from Black Sea regions through the Hellespontus strait to feed its burgeoning population. The Philaidae's mission was to preserve free access to the waterway by protecting the coastal regions from the depredations of pirates, Thracian tribes, and those Greek cities on the Asian side of the Hellespontus. Ancient sources tell little about the quality of Miltiades' service in the Chersonese, except that he continued the authoritarian rule over Athenian colonists and natives begun by his relations.

Miltiades' fame had its origins in the events surrounding the Scythian expedition, undertaken by Darius the Great, King of Persia. The Persians had extended their rule over the Greek cities of eastern Asia Minor (known as Ionia) in 545 and governed this region through Greek tyrants supported by their armies. From Ionia, around 513, Darius launched the first Persian invasion of Europe, utilizing the Greek fleets for logistical support. Initially, he was successful, subduing Thrace and reducing Miltiades to vassalage. His difficulties began when his army plunged into the lands of the Scythians, just north of the Danube River in modern Romania. The Persian army was doggedly harassed by the enemy and forced to retreat toward the Danubian boat-bridge maintained by the Ionians and their ships. At this crossing point, Miltiades urged the other Greeks to destroy the bridge and abandon Darius to his fate. Although his compatriots refused, Miltiades withdrew his forces to the Chersonese. His anti-Persian stand would serve him well politically in the future.

In the meantime, however, Darius' escape across the Danube left Miltiades in a precarious position. As the Persians retreated through the Chersonese into Asia, they were pursued by the Scythians. Miltiades and his family were expelled from their small kingdom. His whereabouts during the next eighteen years are not made known by the ancient sources, but it is likely that he spent time at the court of Olorus, King of Thrace.

There, sometime between 513 and 510, he married Olorus' daughter, Hegesipyle. The fate of his first wife is unknown. This marriage produced four children: Cimon, destined to achieve greater fame than his father in the mid-fifth century as rival to Pericles and a founder of the Athenian Empire; Elpinice, a woman admired for her beauty and notorious for her free sexual behavior; and two other daughters whose names are unknown.

While Miltiades bided his time in exile, events in Ionia offered new political and military opportunities. In 499, the Ionian cities rose up in revolt against their Persian-imposed tyrants and thus began a six-year-long war in the eastern Aegean for Greek independence. Miltiades entered the fray in 495, when the inhabitants of the Chersonese invited him to return to rule over them. Installed once again in his kingdom, he utilized the Persians' preoccupation with the Ionian Revolt to seize the islands of Lemnos and Imbros, turning them over to the Athenians.

The Persian riposte was not long in coming. After suppressing Ionian resistance, their attentions focused on the Chersonese. When a Phoenician fleet in the service of the Persians closed in on Miltiades, he fled for the island of Imbros. In 493, he arrived in Athens, armed with vast political, and especially military, experience and widely admired for his consistently anti-Persian stance.

Politics in the Athens to which Miltiades returned had changed significantly since the days of his youth. Hippias, the last of the Peisistratidaen tyrants, had been expelled in 510. Around 508, Cleisthenes had introduced democratic reforms to the Athenian constitution, a political maneuver which greatly increased the strength of his clan, the Alcmaeonidae. Aristocrats seeking political power were thus forced to court the favor of the populace more strongly than ever before. It was a political culture alien to Miltiades' previous experience, but the looming Persian threat to Greek security— Athens had assisted the Ionian Revolt—made his military knowledge of the Persian Empire an important asset.

Traditionally, historians have viewed Athenian politics during the 490's as a contest between political parties supporting well-defined ideologies. Some were appeasers of the Persians, while others were decidedly in favor of resistance to them. Some favored the new democratic constitution, and others longed for a return to an era of aristocratic predominance. Recently, most historians have rejected such theories, because they do not jibe with ancient sources, which describe political rivalries largely in personal and familial terms. Modern interpretations stress the general agreement of Athenian politicians on essential issues: strong opposition to the Persian threat and a generalized acceptance—if not preference—for the democratic constitution. An exception to this rule was the Peisistratidae, still led by Hippias, who wanted to restore their tyranny with the backing of the Persians.

Miltiades' arrival on the political scene threatened to upset a delicate power balance. His appeal as a "Persian-fighter" instantly secured for him a power base, which promised to be troublesome to those clan factions which had grown used to the absence of the Philaidae. Although nearly all aristocratic politicians agreed with Miltiades' views, the essential issue in Athens in this era was not to what purposes power should be used but who should enjoy the benefits and prestige of power itself.

Shortly after Miltiades' arrival in Athens, he was brought to trial for exercising a tyranny over the Chersonese, possibly at the instigation of the Alcmaeonidae. During these proceedings, Miltiades probably strained to disassociate himself from his former affiliations to the Peisistratidae, giving rise to later legends of his youthful hostility to that clan. In any case, he was acquitted, thus foiling clever attempts to depict him as a reactionary aristocrat and to boost his enemies' popularity with the people.

In 490, with a Persian invasion imminent, Miltiades was elected to the ten-man board of generals from his tribe. Although this position was largely a command post—the Athenian army was organized tactically along tribal divisions—the board also functioned as an advisory council to the supreme commander, the polemarchos. Miltiades' expert advice was to play a crucial role in the impending campaign.

In July of 490, a Persian fleet, commanded by Datis and Artaphernes, sailed west from Ionia. King Darius' objectives were to punish Athens and another city-state, Eretria, for assisting the Ionian Revolt and to establish a base from which all mainland Greece could later be conquered. Ancient sources give grossly exaggerated numbers for this invasion force. Modern historians have variously estimated its military strength at fifteen thousand to thirty thousand infantry, including five hundred to one thousand cavalry. After subduing the Cyclades Islands and ravaging Eretria on Euboea Island, the Persians landed on the plain of Marathon, about twenty-file miles northeast of Athens. Most Athenian strategists favored a tough defense of the city's walls as the key to victory. Miltiades, however, who had personally observed skilled Persian siegecraft during the Ionian Revolt, argued for a pitched battle in the open field. He sponsored a decree to this effect in the Assembly. On its authority, the commander Callimachus led the ten-thousand-man hoplite force out to Marathon to meet the enemy.

For several August days, the Persians and Athenians observed each other across the plain. Both sides had compelling reasons for delay. The Persians were waiting for Hippias, who had accompanied them, to rally the Peisistratidaen faction to the invasion. The Athenians were anticipating the arrival of troops from Sparta, the most militarily powerful of the city-states in Greece.

Miltiades had different ideas about how this campaign should be fought. He persuaded Callimachus at a divided meeting of the board of generals to attack the Persians in the plain immediately. Ancient sources do not give explicit reasons for this precipitate decision to engage in battle, although modern historians have generally agreed that the Athenian commanders feared the collusion of the Peisistratidae—and possibly the Alcmaeonidae—in the invasion. An immediate victory would save Athens from the treachery of these opponents.

In the ensuing battle on August 12, Miltiades' innovative tactics capitalized on Persian weaknesses: a lack of heavy armor and reliable shock weapons and an overdependence on the missile power of their archers and cavalry. As the Greek hoplites advanced toward the Persian lines, their pace accelerated. Once within missile range, they rushed headlong into contact with the enemy. The vaunted Persian archery skills were thus rendered useless. The Persians were surprised by this tactic, as Greek armies normally walked into combat to preserve the solidity of their battle lines.

To avoid being outflanked, Miltiades had deliberately extended his weaker army to match the frontage of the Persians. This formation involved weakening the center of the phalanx. As the battle developed, this emaciated center gave way before the enemy onslaught. His stronger wings, however, were triumphant. Exercising firm control over his men, Miltiades diverted these flank hoplites from pursuit in order to turn them in against the Persian center. This section of the enemy army was almost annihilated. More than six thousand Persians fell in the battle. As the Persians sailed away in retreat, Miltiades and his men could congratulate themselves on a victory which had saved Greece from tyranny.

In the aftermath of this battle, known as the Battle of Marathon, Miltiades' popularity soared. His career, nevertheless, was already very close to an ignominious end. From the Assembly, he secured funds for a secret military mission which, he promised, would enrich Athens. His subsequent assault on the island of Paros ended in failure, while Miltiades himself received a critical leg wound. Back in Athens, he was brought to trial for deceiving the people, an accusation brought forth by Xanthippus, who had married into the Alcmaeonidae clan. Miltiades was convicted and assessed an enormous fine. Jealous political rivals had triumphed. He died shortly thereafter from gangrene.

Summary

Miltiades' career provides a fine case study in the extremely competitive nature of Greek politics, a competition wherein clan and family loyalties, while very important, played a secondary role to the overpowering imperative to succeed. Aristocrats who won the political game were regarded as virtuous, while those who failed—such as Miltiades' father—were disgraced or shamed. Athenian political culture holds interesting clues to the reasons for the individual brilliance of the Greeks and their inability to achieve stable political organizations.

Bibliography

Burn, A. R. *Persia and the Greeks: The Defence of the West, c. 546-478 B.C.* Rev. ed. Stanford, Calif.: Stanford University Press, 1974. The best overall account of the titanic struggle between the Greeks and Persians, superseding the outdated, but ubiquitous, *The Great Persian War* (1901) by G. B. Grundy. Interspersed with short sections on Miltiades' activities in this era, with references to the ancient sources on him. Also includes the most precise chronology of the Battle of Marathon.

Bury, J. B., S. A. Cook, and F. E. Adcock, eds. *The Cambridge Ancient History*. Vol. 4, *The Persian Empire and the West*. New York: Macmillan, 1926. Chapter 6 contains the most accessible of the traditional interpretations of Athenian politics in the 490's. Readers are warned that J. H.

Munro's reconstruction of the campaign and Battle of Marathon in this volume is no longer regarded seriously by historians.

Herodotus. *The Histories*. Translated by Aubrey de Sélincourt. Harmondsworth, England: Penguin Books, 1954. By far the most important ancient source on Miltiades and the Battle of Marathon—the place to start for those doing research. Aspiring scholars should use this volume only in conjunction with modern accounts, because historians have discounted some of what Herodotus wrote.

Hignett, Charles. *Xerxes' Invasion of Greece*. Oxford: Clarendon Press, 1963. Despite its title, this book contains the best scholarly account of the Battle of Marathon. Provides references to nearly all the ancient sources and criticism of many of the modern attempts at reconstruction of the great event. Explains the modern tendency to regard Herodotus' writings as the most reliable of ancient sources on the Persian Wars.

Lloyd, Alan. *Marathon*. New York: Random House, 1973. A popular history which suffers from serious errors of interpretation and an unabashed idolization of the Greeks. Part 4, however, contains a dramatic and well-written narrative of the battle, drawn from reliable scholarly sources.

Sealey, Raphael. *A History of the Greek City-States, 700-338 B.C.* Berkeley: University of California Press, 1976. Written by a prominent proponent of the prosopographical approach to Greek politics, that is, the concept that personal and familial relations overrode ideological issues in shaping events. Includes discussion of major aspects of Miltiades' life, with ancient sources referenced.

Michael S. Fitzgerald

MITHRADATES THE GREAT

Born: Probably 134 B.C.; probably Sinope, Kingdom of Pontus
Died: 63 B.C.; Panticapaeum, Crimea
Area of Achievement: Government
Contribution: Mithradates fought three wars with Rome in the first half of
the first century B.C., resulting in the destruction and transformation into a
Roman province of his own Kingdom of Pontus.

Early Life

Mithradates Dionysus Eupator (good father) was probably born at Sinope,
the capital of the Kingdom of Pontus (in modern northern Turkey), in
134 B.C. He was the son of the Pontic king Mithradates V Euergetes (benefactor) and his wife, Laodice. When his father was assassinated in 120, Mithradates succeeded to the throne, possibly in conjunction with his brother
Mithradates Chrestus (the good), under the regency of their mother. Further
details of his life at this time are shrouded in mystery. According to the Latin
historian Pompeius Trogus, whose work in summary form is the only literary
source to describe Mithradates' activity in these years, Mithradates went to
live in the wild for the next seven years to avoid falling victim to various palace conspiracies. It is clear that this story is not strictly accurate, for a series
of inscriptions in honor of Mithradates and other members of the Pontic
court, dated to 116, found on the island of Delos in the Aegean Sea and an
inscription discovered in southern Russia show that he was a presence in the
palace during these years. The Kingdom of Pontus was characterized by the
difficult fusion of Greek and Iranian cultural traditions, as, indeed, was the
court itself. It is therefore possible to interpret Trogus' story as a folkloric
development stemming from the basic education of an Iranian noble in
horsemanship and the hunt.

Whatever the case may be, it is clear from the course of his later life that
Mithradates received a good education in Greek as well as in the traditional
Iranian arts of war and the hunt. He was a man who truly represented the
amalgam of these two powerful cultural traditions, and throughout his career
there are many signs of these two sides in his upbringing. His coins suggest
that he tried to model his appearance on that of Alexander the Great, for
when he made war on Rome he presented himself to the cities of the Greek
East as a champion against the Romans—the "common enemy"—and surrounded himself with officials of Greek descent. At the same time, he gave
these officials titles such as "satrap," which evoked the memory of the
ancient Persian kingdom swept away by Alexander, and he offered massive
sacrifices to the high god of the Persian pantheon, Ahura Mazda. In general
terms he was a man of tremendous physical and intellectual gifts, preternat-
ural brutality, and, evidently, severe paranoia. He could speak twenty-two

(or, according to another tradition, twenty-five) languages and was a patron of the arts and a lover of music. He is said to have been able to control a chariot drawn by sixteen horses and in his late sixties could still ride a hundred miles in a day. He included prophylactics against poison in his meals, murdered three of his ten sons, and, in the course of his wars, perpetrated massacres which were to become legendary in antiquity.

Life's Work

In 115 or 114 B.C., Mithradates established himself as the sole ruler of Pontus, murdering his mother and then his brother in the process. At about the same time, he began a series of campaigns to extend his control in the areas of the Crimea, in southern Russia, and along the coast of what is now Bulgaria and Romania. He appears to have undertaken these operations for several reasons. One was to increase his prestige in the Greek world as a whole, since a result of these campaigns was that he emerged as the protector of these Greek cities against neighboring barbarian tribes. Another reason was to increase the overall power of Pontus, whose natural economic base was not sufficient to support a great nation. The territories which now came under his control were extremely wealthy; they had for centuries been an important source of grain and dried fish for the Aegean world and were to become an important source of revenue for Mithradates. In the next few years, he sent his armies to establish control over the eastern shore of the Black Sea as well. The success of these operations was vital for what seems to have been Mithradates' great ambition: the establishment of Pontus as a major power in Anatolia and the Aegean world, an ambition which he could achieve only if he could match the hitherto irresistible power of Rome.

In addition to strengthening his kingdom through acquisitions along the Black Sea coast, Mithradates worked to enhance the economic base of his ancestral territories, which extended along the northern coast of modern Turkey and just across the Caucasus Mountains into the Anatolian plateau. Many parts of this realm were at the time of his accession quite backward. The settled areas south of the mountains had retained their basic political structure from the time of the Persian Empire, or, indeed, of the Hittites, while the mountainous regions had always been the preserve of wild tribes whose primary occupations were the pasturing of flocks and brigandage. Mithradates sought to encourage urbanization, founding cities in the mountain valleys and bringing the tribesmen out of the hills. He was not altogether successful in this, but the effort is a good illustration of his comprehensive planning to build up the power of Pontus.

In the final decade of the second century, Mithradates began to turn his attention to the kingdoms which lay to his south and west: Bithynia, which bordered Pontus at its western extremity in Asia Minor; Paphlagonia, to the southwest; and Cappadocia on the central Anatolian plateau to the south.

All these areas were essentially under the influence of Rome, which had established a presence in what is the central portion of modern western Turkey when in 132 it had accepted this area as a bequest from the last king of Pergamon (who had ruled these areas). This land had become the Roman province of Asia. As a result of the potential might of Rome, Mithradates at first had to move against these areas through diplomacy and the promotion of domestic discord. On several occasions between 109 and 89, he sought to establish his relatives or supporters as the rulers in both Paphlagonia and Cappadocia. On each occasion, Roman embassies had ordered him to withdraw, and Mithradates, who did not believe that he could risk armed conflict, had done so.

The situation changed in 90 as a result of two events. First, a major civil war broke out in Italy between Rome and her Italian subjects, which initially went badly for Rome. Second, the incompetent Roman governor of Asia, Manius Aquillius, in conjunction with Cassius, the head of a Roman embassy which had recently ordered Mithradates out of Bithynia (from which he had expelled King Nicomedes), encouraged Nicomedes to attack the territory of Pontus. In 89, Mithradates struck with overwhelming force, thinking that he could no longer tolerate the intervention of Rome in his affairs and that Rome was now so weak that it would not be able to take effective action against him. His armies overwhelmed all resistance in Asia Minor, captured Aquillius (whom Mithradates executed by pouring molten gold down his throat) and Cassius, and began a wholesale massacre of Romans and their supporters throughout the region. In 88, at the height of his power, his forces were established in Greece while he remained to administer his newly won territories.

In the same year, after the war against the Italians had turned decisively in Rome's favor, the Roman general Lucius Cornelius Sulla, after temporarily securing his personal domination by a military occupation of the city, set out to engage Mithradates. From 87 to 86 Sulla besieged Athens, the main base of the Pontic armies in Greece; in 86, he captured Athens, defeated in two battles the two main Pontic field armies, commanded by Mithradates' lieutenants, and prepared an invasion of Asia. At the same time, a Roman army under the command of one of Sulla's rivals (Sulla's enemies had occupied Rome after heavy fighting in 87) moved directly against Mithradates. Although this army defeated him in several battles, it proved to be his salvation. When Sulla arrived in Asia Minor in 85, he was more interested in doing away with his rival and reestablishing his power in Italy than he was in destroying Pontus. Sulla struck a deal with Mithradates to restore the state of affairs before the outbreak of hostilities in return for a large indemnity, which Sulla could use to support the war that he then undertook in Italy. This deal, the Treaty of Dardanus, was signed in 85.

The treaty with Sulla saved Mithradates' kingdom and enabled him to rebuild his forces. He was able to do this rapidly enough to repulse an invasion by Murena, the officer whom Sulla had left in charge of Asia, in 82. This event is traditionally referred to as the Second Mithradatic War, even though it seems to have been no more than an unsuccessful plundering expedition. In the next several years, aided by Romans who had fled Sulla's bloody return to Italy and had continued the struggle abroad, Mithradates assembled a new army. At the same time, it is said, he offered encouragement to the pirates based in southern Asia Minor in their raids on Roman shipping.

Mithradates' third and final war with Rome began in 73 B.C. It was precipitated by the death of the King of Bithynia, who bequeathed his kingdom to the Romans. At first, Mithradates was completely successful. He defeated a Roman army, overran Bithynia, and again sent his troops into the Province of Asia. Yet his success was short-lived. At the end of the year, the Roman general Lucius Lucullus encountered Mithradates' main force as it was besieging the city of Cyzicus. At the beginning of 72, Lucullus destroyed this army and invaded Pontus itself. In 71, he drove Mithradates out of his kingdom.

Mithradates fled to Armenia, where he convinced his son-in-law, King Tigranes, to support him. Lucullus continued his invasion in 69 and defeated the combined forces of the two kings, leaving Mithradates roaming the hills with a small band of followers. Mithradates' career would have ended had it not been for a crisis of command on the Roman side. In 68, Lucullus' army mutinied and he was forced to withdraw to Asia. Mithradates was then able to defeat the Roman army which had been left behind to occupy Pontus. This defeat led to the removal of Lucullus from command, though no effective officer relieved him until 66 when Pompey the Great arrived. Mithradates used this interval in an unsuccessful effort to consolidate the defenses of his old kingdom. At the end of 66, Pompey drove him from his kingdom and he was forced to withdraw, at the head of a small army, around the coast of the Black Sea to the Crimea. It was a difficult march and its success is testimony to the enduring energy of the king.

In 63, while planning a new campaign against the Romans, which is said to have involved the grandiose scheme of marching on Italy through the Balkans, Mithradates faced a serious palace revolt. His son, Pharnaces, launched a successful coup and took command of the army. Mithradates withdrew to his palace and, after killing his harem, tried to commit suicide. His efforts to poison himself failed, as a result of the drugs he had taken against poison throughout his life, and he had to call upon one of his officers to stab him to death.

Summary

Mithradates was a man of tremendous energy and ambition. It must also be conceded, however, that this energy and ambition were fatally misdirected. No matter what steps he took, he would never have been able to match the power of Rome, and despite initial successes, he was never able to hold his own when Rome turned its superior military might against him. In fact, he was able to survive his first failure only because Sulla thought that he had more pressing business elsewhere.

Although Mithradates' determination, his refusal to admit defeat, and the broad vision he brought to the organization of his kingdom were impressive, his accomplishments were essentially negative. He initiated a series of wars which led to the expansion of Roman control in Anatolia and proved to be of great importance for Rome's subsequent organization of this area, precisely the end which he sought to avoid. Furthermore, the process involved massive devastation by both Mithradates and his enemies. There can be no doubt that the course of Roman expansion would have been very different if it had not been for Mithradates, but it can scarcely be argued that the course which Mithradates initiated was beneficial to those involved, as it resulted in the undoing of all that he had accomplished in the early part of his reign.

Bibliography

Appian of Alexandria. "The Mithridatic Wars." In *Appian's Roman History*, translated by Horace White, vol. 2. New York: Macmillan, 1912. Appian's account of the Mithradatic Wars, written in Greek during the first half of the second century A.D., is the basic source for Mithradates' reign. This translation by White for the Loeb Classical Library is the best in English.

Jones, Arnold H. M. *The Cities of the Eastern Roman Provinces*. Oxford: Clarendon Press, 1971. This work contains a useful chapter on the history of Pontus.

McGing, Brian. *The Foreign Policy of Mithradates of Pontus*. Leiden, Netherlands: E. J. Brill, 1984. The most detailed study of Mithradates' reign, this good, thorough treatment replaces previous studies.

Magie, David. *Roman Rule in Asia Minor to the End of the Third Century After Christ*. Princeton, N.J.: Princeton University Press, 1950. Several chapters on Mithradates, including detailed analysis of the sources in extensive notes.

Plutarch. *Fall of the Roman Republic*. Translated by Rex Warner. Harmondsworth, England: Penguin Books, 1954. This volume contains Plutarch's biographies of Sulla and Pompey, both of which provide much information about the campaigns of Mithradates. The life of Sulla is of particular interest, as it is based closely on Sulla's own autobiography.

Sherk, Robert, ed. and trans. *Rome and the Greek East to the Death of Augustus*. Cambridge: Cambridge University Press, 1984. This volume contains translations of a number of documents (inscriptions, papyruses, and classical texts for which other translations are not readily available) that are relevant to the career of Mithradates. Several of these texts provide information which enables modern scholars to correct accounts preserved in other sources, chiefly those of Appian and Plutarch.

Sherwin-White, Adrian N. *Roman Foreign Policy in the East, 168 B.C. to A.D. 1*. Norman: University of Oklahoma Press, 1984. The central portion of the book deals with the history of Mithradates' reign, including valuable studies of the military aspects.

David Potter

MOSES

Born: c. 1300 B.C.; near Memphis, Egypt
Died: c. 1200 B.C.; place unknown
Area of Achievement: Religion
Contribution: As the leader of tribal Israel who brought his people to the brink of nationhood in the thirteenth century B.C., Moses may be seen as the father of many governmental, social, and religious ideals that continue to influence the contemporary world. The codification of religious and ethical laws in the Pentateuch, the first five books of the Old Testament, is traditionally attributed to him.

Early Life

According to the biblical narrative, Moses was born to Jochebed, a Hebrew woman, during a period in which the children of Israel were under slavery to Egypt. The people of Israel had come to Egypt at the invitation of Joseph, one of Jacob's sons, who had become a prominent Egyptian leader in friendship with the pharaoh. Then, as the biblical text relates, "there arose a Pharaoh who knew not Joseph." As the Israelites grew in number and threatened the stability of Egyptian society, a more ruthless pharaoh began a policy of genocide toward newborn Hebrew males (Ex. 1:22). Immediately after Moses' birth, to spare him this fate his mother hid him in an arklike cradle and floated it down the Nile River, where it was discovered by an Egyptian princess who was bathing (Ex. 2:5-10). This princess found that Moses, whose name means "one drawn out of water," satisfied her longing for a son. Moses thus grew to manhood in the Egyptian palace, learning its language and culture, sheltered from his Hebrew heritage. Here Moses was exposed to the most sophisticated philosophies and science of the then known world, and he most likely learned how to write not only in the cuneiforms and hieroglyphics of Egyptian textuality but also in the proto-Semitic alphabetic script known to have been used near Mount Sinai even before the historical period in which Moses may be placed.

One day in his young adulthood, when visiting among the Hebrews, Moses was roused to justice on behalf of a Hebrew laborer who had been struck by an Egyptian (Ex. 2:11). In Moses' defense of his fellow Hebrew, he killed the Egyptian; he was then forced into exile in Midian. There Moses began a new life with a wife, Zipporah, and family and tended the flock of his father-in-law, Jethro. It was evident that Moses' destiny lay in a higher calling, however, when the angel of the Lord appeared to him in a burning bush and God Himself spoke to him. Moses heard God's call to lead the Israelites out of Egyptian bondage (Ex. 3:1-17). In this divine commission, Moses was promised, on behalf of his people, a "land of milk and honey." It was during this encounter that God revealed His name to Moses as "Yahweh," or "I am that

I am," the self-existing One who had chosen Israel to be His special people. Despite his initial hesitance, Moses accepted the call and was promised that his testimony would be corroborated with miracles.

Life's Work

The first part of Moses' life had been exhilarating, as he grew from infancy to adulthood in a pharaoh's house. The remainder of his life, however, was spent in turmoil, verbal and physical warfare, and continuing challenges to his authority by his own people. Upon returning to Egypt, Moses called upon his brother Aaron to accompany him and be his spokesman. In several bold and audacious audiences with the pharaoh, Moses demanded that the Egyptian leader free his people and allow them to worship Yahweh, who had called them to tabernacle at Mount Sinai. The pharaoh, amused by Moses' claim to authority and power, rejected his repeated pleas. There ensued a series of ten plagues that brought Egyptian society to its knees, including the final plague—the death of the firstborn. That plague killed many Egyptian children while sparing the Hebrews, who had spread blood over their doorposts to avert the angel of death, who "passed over" them. This event came to be celebrated on the Hebrew holy day of Passover, which commemorates the preservation of the Hebrews and their deliverance from bondage in Egypt (Ex. 12-14).

When the pharaoh finally relented, Moses led his people in a mighty throng into the Red Sea, whose waters were miraculously parted for them and then closed upon their Egyptian pursuers (Ex. 14-15). From their mountain encampment, Moses went to Mount Sinai for a momentous encounter with Yahweh, who revealed Himself so spectacularly that Moses returned from the mountain with his countenance shining. The thunder and lightning that accompanied these events caused great fear among the people, and they asked Moses to be their intercessor lest they be consumed by Yahweh's omnipotence. Moses brought back to them the Covenant, a body of laws and relationships that was to bind Yahweh and the people of Israel together in a partnership (Ex. 19-20). Their task was to live in obedience to Yahweh's precepts—attributes of His holy character (justice, righteousness, peace, joy, and love)—for which He would continue to bless and protect them from their enemies. They were called upon to acknowledge Him as the only God and the surrounding civilizations as pagan and idolatrous.

Almost as soon as the people agreed to the covenant, they plunged into turmoil and rebellion. While Moses went to the mountain to receive further instruction from Yahweh, the people, impatient with Moses' absence, built a golden calf to worship, a reflection of their immaturity and naïveté and an action strictly forbidden by the covenant they had just ratified. Enraged at this apostasy, Moses returned from the mountain with vengeance, breaking the tablets on which the Ten Commandments had been written, destroying the idol, grinding it into powder, and forcing them to drink it. This lack of faith prefigured the continued disbelief and sin of the people, as the generation of Israelites who first left Egypt were destined to falter in their journey, never reaching the land promised them when Moses was called to God's service in Midian. During this time, however, Moses continued to meet with Yahweh and continued to build a record of Israel's experiences with this God who had brought them out of Egypt. Among the things that were presented to the people were the plans for building a tabernacle for worship, an elaborate ecclesiastical structure; detailed specifications for its construction and use in the corporate life and worship of the Jewish people were supplied.

The other pivotal event in the history of this first generation who left Egypt is recounted in the Book of Numbers. Moses sent spies into the land of Canaan to determine when and how the Israelites might occupy the land promised to them by Yahweh. Of the twelve spies sent out only two, Joshua and Caleb, brought a positive report. As a result, only Joshua and Caleb and their families were eventually permitted to enter Canaan. The other members of the first generation were refused entry by God as a result of their disbelief.

The Book of Deuteronomy records Moses' farewell speeches to the generation of Israel who would enter the Promised Land—a reiteration of the first covenant and an exhortation to obey the God who had called them out of bondage. In recounting the blessings and cursings that were to accrue to the Israelites, depending upon their behavior, Moses advised, "I have set before thee this day, both death and life. Choose life" (Deut. 30:19).

Moses' egotism, briefly revealed in the biblical narrative, eventually prevented Aaron and Moses themselves from entering Canaan. During one trying episode, Moses became frustrated with the Israelites' continual bickering about the availability of food and water. At one point, Moses exclaimed, "Hear now, you rebels; shall we bring forth water for you out of this rock?" (Num. 20:10), thus presumptuously attributing to himself the power to provide for Israel's needs. This sin weighed heavily on Moses toward the end of his life. Psalm 90 in the Old Testament Book of Psalms is attributed to Moses; it contains this bittersweet comment on the brevity of life: "Thou dost sweep men away; they are like a dream, like grass which is renewed in the morning: in the morning it flourishes and is renewed; in the evening it fades and withers. For we are consumed by thy anger; by thy wrath we are overwhelmed."

Near the end of his days, Moses passed the mantle of leadership over to his aging comrade, Joshua, who would lead Israel into the land that had been promised. A heroic and dutiful life was then brought to rest with a series of blessings that Moses pronounced upon the people of Israel. The concluding words of Deuteronomy offer this understated editorial judgment: "There has not arisen a prophet since in Israel like Moses, whom the Lord knew face to face" (Deut. 34:10).

Summary

The Law of Moses, his written legacy to subsequent generations, is matched only by Greek and Roman poetics and rhetoric in its impact on Western culture. Whatever editorial interventions there may have been over the centuries, it is clear that the five books of Moses—Genesis, Exodus, Leviticus, Numbers, and Deuteronomy—were intended to be histories of the Jewish people, beginning with the creation of the heavens and the earth. As a slave people fresh from redemption, this fledgling nation had few common experiences and little religious identity to bind them. Consequently, the Mosaic account of God's decision to choose the people of Israel as the blessed descendants of Abraham and to allow them to influence many civilizations can be seen as a primary attempt to solidify their nationhood during a precarious time. Moses' narrative gives the people of Israel a historical and moral vantage point from which to interpret their past and present experiences and, most important, to give praise to Yahweh, who called them out of Egypt to worship Him.

The religious foundation begun in the codification of legal and moral teaching became the scaffolding for Christianity, as Jesus Christ and his followers directly traced their heritage not only to Abraham but also to Moses. During his ministry, Jesus claimed to have come to fulfill the Law of Moses and to inaugurate a new covenant of grace that would subsume and complete the covenants made with Abraham, Isaac, and Jacob. Islam, whose sacred text is the Koran, also owes much of its message to the framework established in the works attributed to Moses. Muhammad, the Prophet of Islam, claimed Abraham and Moses as his forerunners, proclaiming that he and his message stood in the same historical and intellectual genealogy as theirs.

It is not difficult to understand the nearly universal recognition of Moses as a pivotal leader in history. He was holy and devout, a man of action and contemplation, a diplomat and military strategist, and a shrewd political adviser. In witnessing the ongoing direct and indirect influences of Mosaic thought in contemporary Judaism, Christianity, and Islam as well as the continuing political significance of the lands that he helped secure and develop for his people, one must conclude that, indeed, Moses was a man of remarkable gifts.

Bibliography

Alexander, David, and Pat Alexander, eds. *Eerdmans' Handbook to the Bible*. Grand Rapids, Mich.: Wm. B. Eerdmans, 1973. A comprehensive handbook to biblical history and geography, with helpful interpretations that trace the history of Israel under Moses' leadership and rise to power in the ancient Middle East. Particularly useful are maps and word studies that illuminate Israel's relationships with Egypt and other Middle Eastern nations of 1400-1200 B.C.

Allis, Oswald T. *The Five Books of Moses*. Grand Rapids, Mich.: Baker Book House, 1949. An older but still-valuable historical and theological defense of the Mosaic authorship of the Pentateuch, by one of the most outstanding Old Testament scholars of the twentieth century. While the archaeological data Allis supplies are clearly somewhat dated, the cogency of his arguments remains unsurpassed.

_____. *God Spake by Moses*. Philadelphia: Presbyterian and Reformed Publishing Co., 1958. An outstanding and thorough biographical and theological analysis of the Pentateuch, the life of Moses, and his unique role as a prophet of God. The volume illuminates the life of Moses and the birth and growth of Israel as a nation.

Bright, John. *A History of Israel*. Philadelphia: Westminster Press, 1975. Probably the most thorough and compelling nontheological treatment of the history of Israel available. Sections on the kingdoms and civilizations contemporary with Moses illuminate the story of his life and sustain the interest of both the common reader and the scholar.

Friedman, Richard Elliot. *Who Wrote the Bible?* New York: Summit Books, 1987. Friedman is representative of the majority of modern biblical scholars in rejecting Mosaic authorship of the Pentateuch. In this book, intended for the general reader, Friedman draws on a synthesis of current scholarship to present his own, controversial answer to the question of authorship. Includes notes and a bibliography; lightly illustrated.

Harrison, R. K. *An Introduction to the Old Testament*. Grand Rapids, Mich.: Wm. B. Eerdmans, 1972. A complete overview of the origin, message, and impact of each book in the Old Testament. The volume addresses directly and comprehensively the issues of the chronology, authenticity, and influence of the life of Moses on the people of Israel in ancient times and in the present. A massive, comprehensive scholarly work with extensive documentation.

Kitchen, K. A. *The Bible in Its World*. Downers Grove, Ill.: Inter-Varsity Press, 1977. An insider's look at the world of archaeology and how it functions in validating ancient records and narratives. Particularly helpful in its extensive examination of antiquity's cultural artifacts and social conditions against the backdrop of the age of Moses and his people's sojourns in Egypt and wanderings in the wilderness.

Schultz, Samuel J. *The Old Testament Speaks*. New York: Harper and Row, Publishers, 1970. Written for the lay reader, this cogent and lucidly written volume presents an objective historical analysis of the lives of the patriarchs. Includes a major section on Moses and the Pentateuch and their role in the evolution of ancient and modern Israel.

Thompson, J. A. *Handbook to Life in Bible Times*. Downers Grove, Ill.: Inter-Varsity Press, 1986. A colorful, lavishly illustrated reference tool with key sections on the domestic life, travel, family customs, and cultural preoccupations of the biblical world. The work illuminates the birth of Israel and its development under Moses' theological and political leadership.

Wenham, John. "Moses and the Pentateuch." In *New Bible Commentary: Revised*, edited by Donald Guthrie, Alec Moyer, Alan Stibbs, and Donald Wiseman. Grand Rapids, Mich.: Wm. B. Eerdmans, 1970. A concise and singularly wise assessment of the career of Moses, his personality and leadership qualities, and his continuing impact on both Jewish and Christian thought.

Bruce L. Edwards

MOSES DE LEÓN

Born: 1250; probably León, Spain
Died: 1305; Arévalo, Spain
Areas of Achievement: Religion and philosophy
Contribution: Through his lifework, the *Zohar*, Moses de León exercised the
greatest influence on Judaic religious thought after the Talmud and the
Bible.

Early Life

Rabbi Moses ben Shem Tov de León was an itinerant scholar who spent
the greater part of his life wandering from town to town in his native province of Castile. Although few concrete personal details are known of these
years, his writings reflect the social and religious unrest of his times. In the
thirteenth century, Spain was still divided, Muslim and Christian, with Christian Spain slowly but steadily gaining the upper hand. Large numbers of Jews
were now Christian subjects either as a consequence of the Reconquest or
because they were forced to flee Muslim Spain during the increasingly violent
persecutions of the Almoravids and the Almohads, who had entered Spain in
the eleventh and twelfth centuries and tolerated no religious dissension even
among their own people. During the era of the *taifas*, the previous Arab rulers, before the arrival of the fanatical newcomers, the Jewish communities
had been prominent and respected, and Jewish intellectuals had blossomed
in the civilized cosmopolitan atmosphere of al-Andalus. In fact, the peninsula, both Christian and Muslim, was to produce some of the greatest philosophers of Jewish history.

The most famous and most controversial of the religious thinkers was
Moses Maimonides (died 1204) of Córdoba, who interpreted basic Judaic
religious beliefs and traditions in the light of Aristotelian rationalism. His
Dala-lat al-Ha'rin (1190; *Guide of the Perplexed*, 1881) became one of the
cornerstones of medieval Jewish philosophy and, through its Latin translations, influenced the writings of men of many divergent beliefs, not least
among them Saint Thomas Aquinas. As conditions in the Jewish communities began to worsen, however, for many there was cold comfort in pristine
rational arguments. Earlier, in the name of faith and revealed truth, many
Jewish traditionalists, scandalized, had attacked Maimonides' teachings as a
form of heresy. Now their protests were united with the yearnings of a belea-
guered people who needed something in which to believe.

Both groups found a source of strength in the uniquely Jewish mystical
expression of the Cabala. The tradition of the Cabala, which literally means
"received," traces its roots back to Abraham, but the term came to mean the
mystical beliefs and practices which entered Europe through Italy from Palestine and Babylonia in the twelfth and thirteenth centuries. There were

originally two great schools of Cabalistic thought in Germany and the Provençal region of France, but the movement reached its zenith in Spain in the Jewish communities of Barcelona, Burgos, Gerona, and Toledo. Here the new theosophy merged with an intellectual Judaic tradition well into its golden age and refined its characteristic admixture of Gnostic and Neoplatonic elements.

The basic tenet of the Cabala is that the visible world is merely a reflection of a greater unseen world; the two worlds are interdependent, their influences flowing back and forth. An action in one will cause an equal repercussion in the other. Glimpses of this hidden reality could be read, for example, in every word, name, number, and syllable of the Torah, if one knew the code. This reading was the task and obligation of the Cabalistic masters who could interpret these mysteries of spiritual revelation. Moses de León was one of the teachers of the Cabala who spread its doctrines during his travels through Castile and through his writings. In *Shoshan Edoth* (*The Rose of the Testimony*) and *Sepher Hermon* (*The Book of Hermon*), he attempted a mystical Cabalistic treatment of the Ten Commandments. He seems to have used Guadalajara as his home base until around 1292, when he finally settled in Ávila. The rabbi then dedicated the rest of his life to the reworking and circulation of the manuscripts of the work that was to become the bible of Cabalistic thought, the *Sefer ha-Zohar* (the book of splendor; usually called simply *Zohar*).

Life's Work

The *Zohar* was the overriding preoccupation and great accomplishment of de León. It is not one work, but rather a miscellanea, written partly in Aramaic and partly in Hebrew, of biblical interpretation, mystic theology, prophecy, and moral and ethical teaching generally expounded by well-known rabbinical philosophers. The most famous and most quoted passages constitute a commentary on the Pentateuch, the first five books of the Bible. A summary of the prevalent Cabalistic concepts of its time, the *Zohar*, with a vocabulary and set of correspondences all its own, sets out to reveal not only the mystical significance underlying all Judaic theology and edicts but also the hidden relevance of all material creation. Man is acclaimed as the unifier, the conjunction of the visual and spiritual worlds. By the end of the Middle Ages, the *Zohar*, with its appeal to faith and the heart, passionate at times in its lyrical beauty, had captured thousands in its mystical web. Paradoxically, however, the man whose crowning achievement it was, disclaimed the honor.

De León never accepted authorship of the *Zohar*. Instead, he circulated the manuscripts, ostensibly as a type of editor, and attributed their actual writing to Rabbi Simon bar Yohai, a famous Hebrew sage who lived in Palestine in the second century. Pursued by victorious Romans, bar Yohai hid in a cave for thirteen years, legend asserting that he spent the time mastering the secrets of the universe. When questioned as to how he obtained the document, de León revealed that Moses Nachmonides (1194-1270), a fellow Cabalist of great prestige, had discovered the work in Palestine and, shortly before his death, had sent it to the Spanish rabbi. Although there was much discussion over de León's claims, his account of events was never seriously doubted during his lifetime, with one exception. Isaac de Acre, a close friend of Nachmonides, but who surprisingly had never heard of such a manuscript, demanded that de León swear to its authenticity. De León did so and promised to show him the original, but died on the way to Ávila. Isaac, however, did not give up. He continued the journey and enlisted the aid of prominent Jewish leaders in Ávila. One of these, Joseph of Ávila, promised de León's widow, who was in great financial distress, a great sum of money and even a marriage between his son and her daughter if she told the truth concerning the authorship of the *Zohar*. The widow finally admitted that her husband had written the entire work himself without any outside references, recently discovered or not.

That is the position taken by most modern scholars. There are, indeed, glaring anachronisms in the work. For example, bar Yohai, who himself appears as one of the characters, mentions other rabbis who died centuries after. Also, the Aramaic dialect in which the *Zohar* was partially written was seldom used by the Jewish writers of the second century (the time period to which de León attributed the work), who preferred Hebrew. Although there are a few proponents for an unknown ninth or tenth century Palestinian Cabalist as author, it is generally agreed that de León, a poverty-stricken, virtually unknown wanderer, wrote the *Zohar* and attributed it to the legendary bar Yohai in order to endow his work with importance and prestige.

Self-protection may also have been a principal motive. During the thirteenth century, the Jews in Spain not only faced Muslim and Christian persecution but also were divided in bitter social strife within their own communities. There was widespread hatred and resentment of the dominant Jewish courtier class. It was believed that while they had enjoyed influence and power in the Castilian court, they not only had forgotten their own people but also had manipulated them for their own and their Christian masters' political ends. One of the aims of the Cabalist movement from the very beginning had been the elevation of religious and moral conduct and standards together with the overthrow of the wealthy aristocracy. The *Zohar*, therefore, is not simply a mystical treatise, but contains a bitter attack against the rich and the religious leaders who looked the other way and failed to chastise their influential patrons. The rabbinical scholars in the *Zohar* were meant to exemplify the conduct and theology of the true religious man and provided de León with camouflage for his acid criticism. His arguments were reinforced by the vivid memory of the execution of several important

Jewish courtiers in 1280-1281. They were not mourned by many in the Jewish communities.

The *Zohar*, therefore, was widely accepted as a guide to proper Jewish behavior. In addition, with its glorious visions of the coming of the Messiah and the resurrection and vindication of his true followers, it gave spiritual comfort amid suffering; as the intensity of the persecutions increased, so did the importance of the *Zohar*, its influence reaching its zenith after the final, terrible expulsion of the Jews from Spain in 1492. The exiles spread the ideals of their beloved *Zohar* throughout the world. The chief center of Cabalist thought became, fittingly, Safed in Palestine, close to the burial place of Simon bar Yohai. By the sixteenth century, the *Zohar* and its Cabalistic teachings held sway in Judaic religious philosophy as important scholars such as Isaac Luria (1534-1572) interpreted and refined its tenets and practices. Its influence started to wane only with the coming of the Enlightenment and the emergence of a new generation of rationalists. Nevertheless, the Cabala did greatly inspire the powerful Hasidic movement of the eighteenth century, which still has thousands of modern-day adherents. The Hasidic appeal to strength of faith and purity of heart is pure *Zohar*.

The understanding of the Cabala, however, has suffered a progressive deterioration throughout the centuries as the underlying significance of its philosophy and terminology has been forgotten or misused. The name itself has become synonymous with superstition and magic as an aura of pseudo-religious, medieval occultism has encircled it. Sequences of its numbers and letters are evoked in magical incantations, and its symbols are worn to ward off evil spirits. Therefore, it is not surprising that the Cabala and its textbook, the *Zohar*, have been furiously attacked by contemporary Jewish scholars. Zohartic concepts, with their pagan and Gnostic elements, have come to represent, in the opinion of many, all that should be alien to progressive Jewish thought. It has not helped that Christian scholars, entranced by its mystical insights and unaware of its source, have used de León's vindication of Judaism to strengthen such Christian articles of faith as the explanation of the Trinity and the identification of Jesus Christ with the biblical Messiah. De León wished to write a guide for the strong in faith. He realized that his concepts and terminology were complex, but even he could not have understood their ramifications.

Summary

De León wrote, or "edited," a controversial work whose influence has been profound and varied throughout the centuries. At times, his teachings have been used in ways that would have horrified him. Itself an attack on declining religious values and practice, the *Zohar* has become for some a handbook of occult lore and ritual. This view, however, in no way negates its religious and historical importance. The *Zohar* is not only a reflection of prevalent Judaic mystical thought; it provides valuable insights into the background and philosophy behind the mystical fervor that swept through all faiths in the twelfth and thirteenth centuries. In many ways, it is startlingly similar to Christian apocalyptic literature, and the wandering Judaic sages portrayed in its pages could, with a slight change of name, be taken for Franciscan mendicant friars. More important, in its portraits and indictment of the conduct of the wealthy, the powerful, and the apostate, it illustrated the social and moral climate in which a movement such as the Cabala could be born and gain momentum.

The *Zohar* also stands as a symbol. The exiled Spanish Jews cherished it as a living link in the spiritual chain of their heritage, which had been so cruelly broken in 1492. Other Jews, in empathy, seeing this self-identification of the Sephardim with the *Zohar*, came also to regard the book as a tribute to the tenacity of faith. The great work of an exiled people seemed expressly made for a religion that saw itself in continual exile.

An ardent Cabalist, de León believed himself to be capable of interpreting the hidden signification underlying all material objects. In his philosophy, the *Zohar* not only attempted to decipher these meanings but also was in itself a further cipher in the chain of correspondences between the higher and lower worlds. He could not have foreseen how later readers would find so many different codes and meanings.

Bibliography

Baer, Yitshak. *A History of the Jews in Christian Spain.* Translated by Louis Schoffman. Vol. 1, *From the Age of Reconquest to the Fourteenth Century.* Philadelphia: Jewish Publication Society in America, 1961. Baer traces century by century the deteriorating social conditions in the medieval Jewish communities which influenced the rise of the Cabala.

Cahn, Zvi. *The Philosophy of Judaism.* New York: Macmillan, 1962. Contains a chapter on Moses de León and discusses the problem of authorship of the *Zohar.*

Caplan, Samuel, and Harold U. Ribalow, eds. *The Great Jewish Books and Their Influence on History.* New York: Horizon Press, 1952. Contains an interesting discussion of the reasons behind the growth of Zohartic thought emphasizing not only historical factors but also the beauty and power of the text itself, using selections from the original as illustrations.

Epstein, Isidore. *Judaism: A Historical Presentation.* Harmondsworth, England: Penguin Books, 1959. Concise information and clear explanations of prevailing Judaic philosophical trends during the Middle Ages, many of which have Spanish origins.

Moses de León. *The Zohar.* Translated by Harry Sperling and Maurice Simon. 5 vols. London: Soncino Press, 1931-1934. The most complete and faithful English translation of the original.

O'Callaghan, Joseph F. *A History of Medieval Spain*. Ithaca, N.Y.: Cornell University Press, 1975. Detailed description of Spain as the philosophic battleground between the proponents of Maimonides' rationalism and the mystical, "irrational" tenets of the *Zohar*.

Charlene E. Suscavage

MUHAMMAD

Born: c. 570; Mecca, Arabia
Died: June 8, 632; Medina, Arabia
Areas of Achievement: Religion and government
Contribution: Through Muhammad, the Koran was recited and propagated as the revealed word of Allah; through his teachings and leadership, Islam was established as a religious system and a way of life which has possessed extraordinary influence and persuasive powers in many parts of the world.

Early Life

Muhammad ibn 'Abdallah was the only child of his parents' marriage. His father, 'Abdallah ibn 'Abd al-Muttalib, from the tribe of Quraysh, was a merchant who transported goods on camel caravans along routes into Syria and Palestine. The boy's mother, Aminah bint Wahb, was from another clan of the same tribe. It is known that Muhammad was born, probably during the year 570, in the city of Mecca, which at that time was important as a commercial outpost as well as a religious center. At about that time, or shortly thereafter, his father died; the family's means were so modest, according to one account, that apart from personal possessions they were left with little more than five camels and a few sheep. Muhammad's mother died when he was about six years old; he was then reared in turn by a grandfather and an uncle.

Relatively little is known with certainty about his early years. It would seem that for quite some time he lived in relative poverty. It is probable, however, that his intelligence and tact gained some recognition for him among local traders. When he was about twenty-five, he married Khadijah bint Khuwaylid, a wealthy widow with several children. According to tradition, though she was about fifteen years older than he, four daughters were born to them, as well as sons who died in early childhood. Throughout their life together, he was devoted to her.

Muhammad was subject to periods of introspection and abstraction, and at times he would meditate alone among the hills and caves north of Mecca. His own recollections and the verses recorded as the holy writ of Islam furnished an account of the divine inspiration which he maintained had appointed his destiny for him. Probably during the year 610, he received some definite indications of the mission he was to assume.

One day, Muhammad heard a voice from on high declare that he was the messenger of Allah. Subsequent revelations seemed to confirm this calling. Further manifestations appeared, sometimes in the form of visions, and as forms could be discerned more clearly, Muhammad came to believe that the powerful being appearing to him was the archangel Gabriel (Jibril). An encounter which took place on what was later called "the night of destiny" began with the mighty spirit calling upon him to recite; inquiring about what he should recite, Muhammad struggled three times with the great being before uttering the lines which would be placed at the very beginning of the Koran.

By this time, because of the intensity of his mystical experiences, Muhammad determined to consult others. He confided in his wife, and she referred him to one of her cousins, an elderly religious scholar; he suggested that Muhammad had received guidance of the sort which had been instrumental in the development of Judaism and Christianity. Other revelations, at times accompanied by images of an angel, seemed to confirm further Muhammad's growing conviction that he had been chosen to convey Allah's tidings to the world. Increasingly, he was given to recitations that would eventually be incorporated in the Koran (though not always in chronological sequence). As the means of transmission seemingly became more regular and certain, Muhammad also felt moved to convey his message to those around him.

At that time, several different gods and goddesses were worshipped in Arabia; one of them resembled the Allah of Muhammad's prophecies. In Mecca, a celebrated black stone shrine, known from its shape as the Ka'bah, or Cube, served as the centerpiece for religious practices. In the beginning, there were relatively few converts to Muhammad's message that there was only one God, who would not countenance idolatry. Khadijah and others in the prophet's household were the first to accept the new faith; also prominent among the early Muslims was Abu Bakr, a moderately successful local merchant whose dauntless loyalty and resolute good sense were to prove invaluable in many ways.

Others who accepted Islam included some younger members of influential clans, men from outlying families or tribes, and former slaves. Most local people, however, preferred to remain with their ancestral beliefs; some of them claimed that Muhammad was mad or possessed by spirits. Wealthy citizens were no doubt put off by his statements condemning distinctions of riches and poverty.

In about 615, some Muslims emigrated for a time to Abyssinia, in the hope that there they might find a more congenial reception. It was probably during this period that Muhammad delivered some of the ringing denunciations of unbelief that were subsequently recorded in the Koran; graphic descriptions of Hell probably were meant to illustrate the fate of those who rejected him. Still, though there was little overt persecution beyond throwing stones and casting thorns in the prophet's path, the Meccans by and large rejected the new religion; indeed, for some time a boycott was organized against the small Muslim community. Muhammad's fortunes as a religious leader seemed to have reached their nadir; in 619 he was further saddened by the death of his wife and of his uncle Abu Talib, who had encouraged his efforts without actually embracing Islam.

Life's Work

Somewhat more favorable prospects presented themselves in other Arabian cities. Although little progress was made in Taif, southeast of Mecca, Muhammad had reason to believe that Medina (Yathrib) would prove more receptive to his preaching. In 622, the celebrated emigration or departure (*hijrah*) took place: Muhammad and many of his disciples removed themselves to Medina. The year 622 later was adopted as the beginning of the Muslim calendar. In Medina, Muhammad confronted many problems essentially of a political order; a compact he reached with residents of the city recognized the interests of the Muslims as a separate group and established that his authority as the messenger of Allah would be binding for the settlement of their disputes.

Military expeditions also became important to the new Muslim polity, and raids were mounted to harass Meccan caravans. The first outbreak of major violence, which occurred near Nakhlah, between Mecca and Taif, took place during a month which Arabian tradition had held holy. The Muslims insisted that combating unbelief served a greater good than the observance of time-honored truce periods. In 624, in a major battle fought at Badr, southwest of Medina, a party of Muslims defeated a larger force of their opponents; relatively few men were killed on either side, but the Meccans lost their commander. Engagements of this sort undoubtedly had the effect of strengthening solidarity and morale among the various groups that had embraced Islam. The doctrine of *jihad*, or war for the faith, arose during this period. Some setbacks were encountered; north of Medina, at Uhud, in March, 625, the prophet for the first time took part personally in combat; he was struck by a stone and wounded, and he may have killed one of his opponents. The Muslims were compelled to retreat, however, when their adversaries launched a successful flank attack. Hamzah ibn 'Abd al-Muttalib, the prophet's uncle, was acclaimed a martyr for the faith after he was killed by an enemy's javelin. Their pagan opponents attempted to follow up their victory with a full-scale expedition against Medina. Although they raised an army of about ten thousand men, they were unable to penetrate the entrenchments Muhammad's forces had dug about the city. In the spring of 627, after some desultory skirmishes, the Meccans abandoned their siege, leaving the Muslims victorious in the Campaign of the Ditch (al-Khandaq).

Some portions of the Koran were revealed during Muhammad's sojourn in Medina; many of these verses are notable for their striking imagery and resonant tone. It would appear that the prophet was acutely sensitive to comments from others about the literary quality of his teachings. In keeping with Muhammad's position within the Muslim community, many passages established legislative norms that were taken as binding upon believers. Sumptuary regulations and the prohibition of wine were among the obligations imposed on the faithful. For those who were able, the giving of alms was also enjoined. Many matters affecting marriage and divorce were also subject to religious law; it is possible that the permission for men to take four wives derived from concern for women who had been left widowed after the Battle of Uhud.

The eschatology formulated by Muhammad bore some resemblance to those of previous faiths but was distinctive and original on many points. The Last Judgment, which is to come suddenly and in the midst of cosmic upheaval, is vividly depicted in some of the earlier revelations. The Resurrection, when the living are to be spirited away while the dead will be summoned from their graves, is to be followed by a reckoning when the book of each person's life is opened. Some later lines supply detailed descriptions of the afterlife; others speak of the presence of angels. The Prophet warned against the intrigues of Satan (Shaytan, or Iblis), who was portrayed as an angel who fell from grace and ever after has been devising temptations to lure people from the straight path; he has lesser servants at his beck and call, who also lay traps for unwary mortals.

Clearly, many of Muhammad's teachings reflect Jewish and Christian doctrines; indeed, some later verses make reference to Moses, King David, and Jesus Christ, all of whom were venerated as predecessors of the Prophet. It seems likely, however, that Muhammad's knowledge of other scriptures was incomplete; some of his ideas may have been suggested by oral accounts which had circulated in various forms. In other ways, Islamic beliefs diverged from those of Judaism and Christianity. Muhammad rebuffed requests that he provide signs or other evidence of miraculous powers; he maintained that Allah, who alone could act in such ways, would do so only when it accorded with the divine purpose. Muhammad's criticisms of Christian beliefs later came to figure prominently in Muslim polemics; he asserted, for example, that the doctrine of the Trinity was not compatible with faith in one God. According to the Koran, Muhammad was the last and the seal of the prophets; his teachings were universal in character and were meant to be received by all mankind. (In Medina, Muhammad was dismayed and perplexed when local Jewish groups rejected the message of Islam; some of them were expelled from the area and, when it was feared that others might assist Meccan forces, in 627 the tribe of Banu Qurayzah was summarily eliminated.)

Surviving descriptions of Muhammad's manner and bearing suggest that he was a man of impressive dignity. He had a broad and powerful torso, thick black hair, a long beard, and a hooked nose. His eyes were very dark and piercing. Although he had a pleasant smile, he tended to laugh infrequently. It is said that he retained a youthful appearance even in his later years. His personal life became a matter for subsequent speculation, and his character and motivations were questioned, but it seems likely that some of the criticisms concerning his relations with women were misplaced. By the end of his life, Muhammad had accumulated nine wives. Among them were 'A'ishah bint Abi Bakr, who reputedly was his favorite, and Zaynab bint Jahsh, a maternal cousin; a concubine, Mariyah the Copt, was the mother of the only child born to the Prophet's household during these later years, but their son, Ibrahim, died during his second year. Some later critics charged that the Prophet was driven by sensual impulses, but there is little evidence to support this accusation. It would appear that some of Muhammad's marriages were undertaken in order to forge alliances with key clan leaders. Jealousy did sometimes erupt among Muhammad's wives, despite his practice of staying one day with each of them in turn.

After the Muslims had successfully withstood the siege of Medina, Muhammad seized upon certain diplomatic stratagems which displayed political foresight and adroit statesmanship. Outlying tribes, impressed by the stalwart example of the Islamic community in Medina, began to accept the new faith. In March, 628, Muhammad embarked upon what ostensibly was a pilgrimage to Mecca. On the way, at al-Hudaybiyah, he and his men halted to negotiate a truce whose terms seemed quite unfavorable to the Muslims. This apparent setback, however, produced a period of peace that allowed the forces of Islam to gather their strength. During the next year, when, in keeping with this agreement, about two thousand Muslims entered the city as pilgrims, it would appear that the Meccans were daunted by their numbers; certain key Meccans even converted. In November, 629, a quarrel that arose over one of the tribes that had aligned itself with the Muslims provided an occasion for Muhammad to abrogate the peace of al-Hudaybiyah; an army of ten thousand men was assembled, and in January, 630, they marched into Mecca, which yielded after very little fighting. The Prophet solemnly proclaimed an end to the practice of idolatry; a general amnesty was also announced. Excepting four men who were sentenced to death, even those regarded as criminals or long-standing enemies were pardoned.

Shortly thereafter, the most dangerous Bedouin tribe which still opposed the Prophet in the Hejaz was vanquished at Hunayn, to the east of Mecca. The Arab Islamic state had already become a force to be reckoned with; Muhammad had sent embassies to the Byzantine emperor, the King of Persia, and other heads of state. Although for the time being efforts to expand beyond Arabia met with little success, the Muslims held sway in the Prophet's homeland. Muhammad spent most of the time that remained to him in Medina; in March, 632, he made his last pilgrimage to Mecca, where he uttered what has been regarded as his final revelation. Upon his return, he was affected briefly by an illness; without designating a successor he died, apparently rather peacefully, in Medina on June 8, 632.

Summary

Despite its small and inauspicious beginnings, the faith Muhammad taught eventually came to be accepted in many parts of the world. In the unsettled conditions which prevailed during the early seventh century, Arabia was ready to receive the teachings of Islam; the Muslim faith, with its austere monotheism and its specific moral guidelines, answered clear spiritual needs. Islam provided a way of life which applied to many spheres of human activity, for Muhammad's prophecy extended to legislation and guidance of the community as well as to strictly spiritual matters.

Some commentators, particularly from Western countries, have given particular attention to Muhammad's military endeavors and his many marriages, but the traits which recommended him most to the faithful were his sincerity, his simple eloquence, and his skill and insight in attending to his community. Also striking was the essential humility which, in keeping with his faith in one God, restrained him from claiming that he was more than the messenger by whom Allah's word was made known. While by some standards his life fell short of the perfection to which religious leaders are called, Muhammad's intense devotion and masterful leadership set a compelling example by which his essential aims were realized. In so doing, he secured wide acceptance of the Allah of his revelations.

Bibliography
Andrae, Tor. *Mohammed: The Man and His Faith*. Translated by Theophil Menzel. New York: Charles Scribner's Sons, 1936. This brief but informative study begins and ends with discussion of the life and character of the Prophet; his religious revelations and teachings are summarized in the middle chapters, along with an examination of the sources of his theological inspiration. The author concludes with a sympathetic evaluation of Muhammad's personality in relation to comparable figures from other religions.
Cook, Michael. *Muhammad*. Oxford: Oxford University Press, 1983. In this brief survey, various problems of Islamic doctrine which arose during the prophet's lifetime are considered from a critical perspective.
Gabrieli, Francesco. *Muhammad and the Conquests of Islam*. Translated by Virginia Luling and Rosamund Linell. New York: McGraw-Hill Book Co., 1968. The considered judgments of an Italian specialist are presented in this work, which deals with Muhammad and his mission in the first four chapters and then discusses the expansion of Islamic empires which took place under the caliphs who followed him. The author's remarks about the Prophet may seem perceptive to some and rather acerbic to others.
Glubb, John Bagot. *The Life and Times of Muhammad*. London: Hodder and Stoughton, 1970. This sympathetic work by a British writer, who for some time was the commander of the Arab Legion in Jordan, is of interest partly for its depiction of Arabian life and customs and for its reconstruction of desert battles.
Haykal, Muhammad Husayn. *The Life of Muhammad*. Translated by Isma'il

Ragi A. al-Faruqi. Indianapolis, Ind.: North American Trust Publications, 1976. A modern Islamic treatment of the Prophet is afforded by this biography by an Egyptian scholar. Although apologetics and polemics surface at times, the author does provide a full and detailed account of Muhammad's work.

Ibn Hisham, 'Abd al-Malik. *The Life of Muhammad: A Translation of Ishaq's "Sirat rasul Allah."* Translated with an introduction and notes by Alfred Guillaume. London: Oxford University Press, 1955. This version of a biographical chronicle from a traditionist of the second century after Muhammad shows how the Prophet's life was perceived by early Muslims. A work that is highly regarded by scholars.

Khan, Muhammad Zafrulla. *Muhammad: Seal of the Prophets*. London: Routledge and Kegan Paul, 1980. A full and sympathetic study by a Pakistani scholar who has served as a jurist and a diplomat. The interpretation advanced here, that Muhammad was an exemplar of religious piety, may have its roots in the author's affiliation with the Ahmadiyah movement, which has heterodox missionary inclinations.

Lings, Martin. *Muhammad: His Life Based on the Earliest Sources*. New York: Inner Traditions, 1983. A useful and detailed work. In attempting to convey the sense and style of original materials, however, Lings has incorporated archaic language that can be perplexing.

Rodinson, Maxime. *Mohammed*. Translated by Anne Carter. New York: Pantheon Books, 1971. This effort by a French scholar to provide a modern interpretation of the life of the prophet, though well-informed on many points, has some awkward moments when the author attempts to apply Marxist or psychoanalytical explanations.

Schimmel, Annemarie. *And Muhammad Is His Messenger: The Veneration of the Prophet in Islamic Piety*. Chapel Hill: University of North Carolina Press, 1985. Since early times, the life and teachings of Muhammad have occupied a special place in the literature and thought of Muslim culture; this work depicts the variety and profusion of such motifs as they have been found throughout the Middle East and Asia. Also of interest is a chapter dealing specifically with biographical studies that have appeared in Islamic lands.

Watt, W. Montgomery. *Muhammad at Mecca*. Oxford: Clarendon Press, 1953. In this and the following work, significant research has produced a carefully traced narrative of the Prophet's life, considering matters of historical fact in the light of current scholarship. Here Muhammad's early years, the first revelations he received, and the origins of the Koran are discussed in a study which depicts his activities through the year 622.

_____. *Muhammad at Medina*. Oxford: Clarendon Press, 1956. The rise of Islam had immediate political and theological implications, and the author takes up these concerns, as well as biographical matters, in this work dealing with the Prophet's life during his last ten years. This volume and its predecessor were abridged and combined in the author's *Muhammad: Prophet and Statesman* (1961), from the same publisher.

J. R. Broadus

MURASAKI SHIKIBU

Born: c. 978; Kyoto, Japan
Died: c. 1030; Kyoto, Japan
Area of Achievement: Literature
Contribution: The foremost writer of the Heian period, Murasaki authored
   The Tale of Genji, one of the greatest works in Japanese literature and the
   world's earliest novel, defining in it the aesthetic sensibility of the aris-
   tocratic courtier class whose lives and culture her writings reflected.

Early Life

Murasaki Shikibu began her life in the late tenth century when the Fujiwara family dominated politics at the capital of Kyoto. Controlling the
posts of chancellor and regent, the Fujiwara permitted the emperors to reign
but not rule. Moreover, the Fujiwara influenced the succession to the throne
by marrying their daughters into the imperial line. Fujiwara no Michinaga,
the most powerful family member in the mid-Heian period, married four of
his daughters to emperors and was the grandfather of three emperors.

Fujiwara no Tametoki (born c. 945) was a member of a cadet branch of
this clan. A low-ranking member of the court bureaucracy, he was adept in
the Chinese Confucian classics and poetry—talents he inherited from his father and grandfather, who were literary figures in their own right. Eventually,
Tametoki—through the assistance of his powerful kinsman, Michinaga—
rose to a post in the Bureau of Ceremonials (*Shikibu-shō*). He married a
daughter of Fujiwara no Tamenobu and about 975 they had a daughter. This
daughter's real name is unknown, but history has come to know her as
Murasaki Shikibu. Since surnames were uncommon, women frequently were
known by names derived from a brother's or father's official post. "Shikibu,"
her father's title, became part of her name and "Murasaki" ("violet" or "pur-
ple") perhaps was derived from the color of the wisteria flower, whose Chinese character made up the first syllable of the name "Fujiwara" (wisteria
plain). Some sources call her "Tō" no Shikibu, Tō being another way of
reading the first part of Fujiwara.

Heian women were expected to be educated at home in calligraphy, playing the koto, embroidery, painting, and other feminine arts. Males, on the
other hand, were to learn the Chinese classics and the histories in preparation for official careers. Murasaki, however, received a broad education in
both the feminine arts and the traditional Chinese classics. In fact, she was
better at composition in Chinese than her brother Nobunori. She often
delighted her father by quoting from the Chinese histories, composing poems
in imitation of Chinese masters, and displaying a command of literature that
normally would have been expected only of boys. She also was well versed in
Japanese literary genres and Buddhist writings.

In addition, Murasaki was proficient at kana writing. The Japanese, lacking a written script for their language, had borrowed the Chinese system about the time that Buddhism was introduced from the continent (via Korea) in the sixth century. Unfortunately, the Chinese characters, linked as they were to the monosyllabic Chinese syntax, were awkward for expressing the very different polysyllabic Japanese language. As a result, the Japanese eventually used the cursive, written form of certain Chinese graphs for sound value alone. This new syllabary, called hiragana, was used with katakana (a script, also derived from Chinese characters, reserved for writing foreign words) and kanji (Chinese characters). Thus, kana blended three different systems into one written language.

Writing thus became less intimidating; in addition, Japanese ideas could be liberated from Chinese models wedded to the foreign script. Men, however, looked down on using the easy kana syllabaries, preferring to use characters alone in imitating Chinese genres. Women, who were not expected to know Chinese, were given free rein to write in kana, and they experimented with new literary forms to express uniquely Japanese sentiments. In fact, the Heian period marked the emergence of an original Japanese literature liberated from Chinese stereotypes; much of it was produced by talented women such as Murasaki.

When her father was assigned to the post of governor of Echizen, she accompanied him in 996 and evidently spent several years in the provinces. In 998, Murasaki returned to Kyoto to marry Fujiwara no Nobutaka, a man nearly her father's age. While her husband had had children by three other women and had a reputation for high-handedness when he was the provincial governor of Yamashiro, their marriage was nevertheless a happy one. In 999 Murasaki gave birth to a daughter, Kenshi, who would become a poet as well. Soon after, Murasaki's husband died in an epidemic.

Life's Work

Perhaps seeking consolation for her husband's death, Murasaki turned to writing. About 1002, she started work on a tale (*monogatari*) about the romantic escapades of a fictitious character: a handsome, talented son born to an emperor by a low-ranking consort. The hero's name was Genji (the shining one) and the work was called *Genji monogatari* (c. 1004; *The Tale of Genji*, 1925-1933).

Highly cultured and living among the aristocratic class, Murasaki drew on her own experiences, which were augmented by her profound knowledge of human nature, to capture in this story the ambience of Heian life. It is said that her penchant for gossip and her curiosity may have given her access to privileged information about real court personalities, which then became the stuff of her tale; some even suggest that she had an affair with Michinaga. Yet such theories do not do justice to her truly creative ability.

Around 1005 Murasaki was brought to court by Michinaga to serve as a tutor and companion to his daughter Shōshi, the nineteen-year-old consort to the Emperor Ichiyō. Chapters of *The Tale of Genji* were read at court and the young emperor once complimented Murasaki on her literary erudition.

Murasaki also kept a diary (*nikki*) and some poetic memoirs (*kashū*), works, surprisingly, which reveal little about herself. In one telling remark, though, Murasaki recorded that fellow ladies-in-waiting resented her aloofness. She denied that she was conceited and considered herself a misunderstood, gentle person victimized by court gossip. Her novel was being written not as a self-serving display of her learning but, as she has Genji say at one point, because she "was moved by things, both good and bad," and wanted "to commit [them] to writing and make it known to other people—even to those of later generations."

While in imperial service, she enriched her impressions of aristocratic life at court and eventually produced more than fifty chapters incorporating, in a fictitious way, what she was observing at first hand. Her Genji epitomized the idealized Heian aristocrat. Adept at all the genteel arts, he romanced a bevy of women by being a cultured lover in a world sensitized to beauty. Included among Genji's many paramours was one to whom he returned frequently—the Lady Murasaki, a sensitive, gentle character perhaps personifying qualities for which the author hoped that she herself would be remembered.

On the surface a book about romantic and sexual love, *The Tale of Genji* is in reality a complex, almost psychological, exploration of human emotions and relationships. Plot development is minimal and time references are muted. Karmic retribution and a sense of impermanence seem to bracket the amorous trysts of Genji, making the work a reflective analysis of the human predicament. As the story darkens in its final chapters (one theory holds that they were completed by someone other than Murasaki), the author herself seems to retreat from the glitter of the court, fatalistically preparing for her own end.

It is not known how Murasaki ended her days. Reportedly she retired to a Buddhist nunnery to reflect on the impermanence of the material world, just as many of the characters of *The Tale of Genji* did. She may have died in her mid-thirties, although some historians say that she lived on to 1025 or 1030. Tradition has it that a certain grave in Kyoto is the site of her burial.

Summary

The Heian period was a singular time in Japanese literary history, one in which women writers dominated all genres. Murasaki Shikibu's contribution was to define the ideal of the cultivated aristocrat—Genji—living and loving in the effete, rarefied world of courtiers. The Heian sensibility of *mono no aware* (the pity of things), a feeling that Murasaki vividly depicted in her prose and poetry, permeated this milieu, evoking melancholy enjoyment of ephemeral pleasures; her writings would preserve for generations of readers the pleasure of eavesdropping on an age unsurpassed in cultural richness. Her characters and their emotional responses to one another provided the inspiration for picture scrolls (*e-maki*), Nō dramas, puppet plays, Kabuki theater, and other art forms celebrating the aesthetic sensitivity that Murasaki codified in Japanese literature.

Bibliography

Bowring, Richard. *Murasaki Shikibu: Her Diary and Poetic Memoirs*. Princeton, N.J.: Princeton University Press, 1982. Chapter 1 is an up-to-date, concise summary of what Western and Japanese scholars know about Murasaki's life. Reproduces scenes from *The Tale of Genji* picture scroll. Includes a bibliography mostly of Japanese works.

Keene, Donald. *Landscapes and Portraits: Appreciations of Japanese Culture*. Palo Alto, Calif.: Kodansha International, 1971. Reprints Keene's 1967 essay, "Feminine Sensibility in the Heian Era," which explores the emergence of women writers and the kana writing system. Murasaki and *The Tale of Genji* are analyzed as part of this phenomenon. Includes illustrations and a bibliography.

Morris, Ivan. *The World of the Shining Prince: Court Life in Ancient Japan*. Baltimore: Penguin Books, 1964. Morris' study is the best interpretative work on the historical and cultural milieu of *The Tale of Genji*. Chapter 9 is an excellent biographical account of Murasaki. Includes a complete glossary listing historical figures in Murasaki's life. Bibliography is dated.

Murasaki Shikibu. *The Tale of Genji*. Translated by Edward G. Seidensticker. New York: Alfred A. Knopf, 1976. The award-winning, most complete translation.

Puette, William J. *Guide to "The Tale of Genji" by Murasaki Shikibu*. Rutland, Vt.: Charles E. Tuttle Co., 1983. Includes a useful précis plot of *The Tale of Genji*, supplemented by background chapters on topics relevant to understanding the novel. Chapter 4 gives a brief biography of Murasaki. Good bibliography.

Seidensticker, Edward G. "Eminent Women Writers of the Court: Murasaki Shikibu and Sei Shonagon." In *Great Historical Figures of Japan*, edited by Hyoe Murakami and Thomas J. Harper. Tokyo: Japan Cultural Institute, 1978. This authoritative essay by a respected translator of *The Tale of Genji* compares and contrasts the lives and literary works of Murasaki and her court rival.

William M. Zanella

JOHANNES DE MURIS

Born: c. 1300; Lisieux diocese, Normandy
Died: c. 1351; probably in or near Paris
Area of Achievement: Music
Contribution: De Muris was a leading proponent of the notational reform of music in the early fourteenth century.

Early Life

Johannes de Muris has been most widely known by the Latinized version of his name, leaving open to speculation his country of origin and the original spelling of his name. Modern scholarship has established that he was not Swiss or English, as has been speculated, but French and that the French version of his name is Jehan des Murs.

The French mathematician, astronomer, and musical theorist was born in Normandy in the diocese of Lisieux. While nothing is known about his childhood or background, much is known about the activities and accomplishments of his adult life. This is a result in part of the recent discovery of a manuscript, located in El Escorial library near Madrid, Spain, that contains a number of biographical annotations. Most of these are believed to be in de Muris' own hand.

De Muris is known to have been a student in Paris, where he pursued an education in astronomy and mathematics. His earliest extant writings are from this period and may be dated as early as 1317. A Vienna manuscript, the earliest dated manuscript attributed to him (although the date may be erroneous), finds de Muris working on a calendar in an attempt to determine the date of Easter. While there are far more than one hundred extant manuscripts attributed to him, the authenticity of many remains in question.

De Muris wrote on astronomical, mathematical, and musical topics, but it is his writings on music that are the most significant and for which he is best known. Of the five musical treatises attributed to him, *Ars novae musicae* (1321) and *Musica speculativa secundum Boetium* (1323) are generally regarded as the most important. The mathematical treatise entitled *Opus quadripartitum numerorum* (1343), which was written two decades later than either of the two musical treatises cited above, remains one of his best-known nonmusical writings.

De Muris completed his studies sometime in the early 1320's. He is generally believed to have taught at the University of Paris shortly thereafter. It was during those early days as a student and teacher in Paris that he became friends with Philippe de Vitry, the other major French theorist of the early fourteenth century; both men advocated fundamental changes in music.

Life's Work

The first of de Muris' treatises on music may be his most important. This work, entitled *Ars novae musicae*, may have been written as early as 1319, when de Muris was still a student in Paris. Clearly, musicians, and certainly theorists, were aware that they were breaking new ground; this awareness is reflected in titles such as *Ars novae musicae*, which means the art of new music and de Vitry's *Ars nova* (1320; English translation, 1961), which means the new art. *Ars novae musicae*, itself controversial, was born in an era of controversy, instability, and change.

While the thirteenth century had been a period of relative stability, with the Church enjoying a position of authority not only in religious matters but in affairs of state as well, that began to change in the fourteenth century. The early years of the century witnessed the challenge of papal authority, ultimately resulting in the relocation of the Papacy to Avignon from 1309 to 1377, a period known as "the Babylonian Captivity." The ensuing years until 1417 were little better; occasionally, there were as many as three different men claiming the papacy at the same time. Confusion in leadership, emerging and newly redefined limitations of authority for church and state, as well as corrupt and immoral clergy led to a general disillusionment with the Church.

Religious instability was accompanied by economic decline, wars, the Black Death, which decimated more than one-third of the population of Europe, and civil turmoil. While all these events did not occur at once, a new environment was created which precipitated a dramatic change in the arts; this change was reflected in music. French composers of the fourteenth century created more secular music than sacred music, and much of it reflected a heightened interest in intellectual games which frequently manifested itself in rhythmic intricacies. The trend toward greater rhythmic complexity, which had begun in the late thirteenth century, placed demands upon the older Franconian notational system that it could not accommodate.

Ars novae musicae, along with de Vitry's *Ars nova*, is one of the important early fourteenth century treatises advocating notational reform. De Muris' work, which may predate de Vitry's, addressed one of the hotly debated musical issues of the day, advocating acceptance of duple division of the note value on an equal basis with the traditional triple division of note values. De Muris' logically argued yet restrained presentation, which could be described as a masterpiece in diplomacy, raised considerable concern among those who supported the "old art."

Most notable among those who vigorously opposed the new art was Jacques de Liège, who produced a treatise in 1330 entitled *Speculum musicae*; in it, he defended the "old art." In addition, the writings of de Muris and de Vitry prompted a papal bull issued by Pope John XXII in 1324 in which the innovations of the new school were condemned. Nevertheless, the conservatives could not stem the change, and their objections were largely ignored.

Even the emphasis of de Muris' treatise reflects the changing times, as is clear when de Muris' work is compared with a treatise by a conservative theorist from the same era. For example, de Liège's *Speculum musicae*, which, ironically, was mistakenly attributed to de Muris at one time, follows a standard format. It may be broken into two basic divisions, material that falls into the realm of the speculative and philosophical and material that is concerned with practical matters and their application. Most of de Liège's treatise is focused on the speculative material, which is typical of a medieval work. De Muris' treatise, however, while broken into the same two divisions, treats the speculative material in an obligatory fashion and moves quickly to the second division, *Musica practica*, to deal with substantive issues that affect working musicians. The new focus of de Muris' treatise is indicative of the change that was beginning to occur in writing about music in the fourteenth century.

The other musical treatise for which de Muris is best known is *Musica speculativa secundum Boetium*, which was written around 1323, while he was in Paris. In it, de Muris explains selected passages taken from the writings of Boethius, who was the most famous and influential writer on music in the early Middle Ages. De Muris again combines mathematics and music in an explanation of musical proportions. The treatise also contains a section on the division of the monochord, a device consisting of a single string stretched over a long, wooden resonator with a movable bridge that allowed the vibrating string length to be varied. The monochord was very popular in antiquity and the Middle Ages for the demonstration of acoustic principles as they related to music.

Other music treatises attributed to de Muris are *Questiones super partes musicae* (c. 1322), *Libellus cantus mensurabilis* (c. 1340), and *Ars contrapuncti secundem Johannes de Muris* (c. 1340).

Scholars have dated de Muris' death as no earlier than 1351 because of a letter thought to have been written by him congratulating de Vitry on his appointment as Bishop of Meaux in that year. While his death is generally accepted as around 1351, the authenticity and date of the letter itself remain in question. De Muris is believed to have died in or near Paris.

Summary

While Johannes de Muris is best known for two of his five treatises on music, it should be remembered that these were the works of a young man whose primary interest was in mathematics and astronomy. De Muris produced a number of works on astronomy and mathematics during his lifetime, but they have not attracted the same attention in their respective disciplines as have his treatises on music. Nevertheless, he must have enjoyed a certain reputation in the scientific community; he was invited to Avignon by Pope Clement VI in 1344 for a conference on calendar reform. Later, in collaboration with a Firminus de Bellaville, who had also been invited to the conference, de Muris presented the pope with a recommendation for reforming the calendar, although it was not implemented.

De Muris is not believed to have been a composer, since no compositions are mentioned in his writings and none has been attributed to him. Nevertheless, he was held in high esteem as a theorist by his contemporaries and also in subsequent generations. After his death, his reputation eclipsed even that of de Vitry. De Muris' writings on music became an important part of the university curriculum in the fourteenth and fifteenth centuries, rivaling the authority of Boethius' works. As de Muris' fame grew, so did the legend of his accomplishments. The creation of certain note values was even attributed to him in the sixteenth century.

Bibliography
Besseler, Heinrich. "Johannes de Muris." In *Die Musik in Geschichte und Gegenwart*. Kassel, West Germany: Barenreiter Verlag, 1949. While this encyclopedic work is in German, it remains a major source of information about de Muris. Particularly valuable is the comprehensive bibliography. This source may be found in most university music libraries as well as in large public libraries.

Carpenter, Nan Cooke. *Music in the Medieval and Renaissance Universities*. Norman: University of Oklahoma Press, 1958. Carpenter deals with the study of music at medieval and Renaissance universities. The work contains some biographical information on de Muris. Includes some discussion of his writings on music and information about his posthumous impact upon university curriculum.

Gallo, F. Alberto. *Music of the Middle Ages II*. Cambridge: Cambridge University Press, 1985. This volume contains an excellent treatment of the music of fourteenth century France. Included is a brief breakdown of de Muris' *Ars novae musicae*. Also includes a good discussion of the "old art" versus the "new art."

Gushee, Lawrence. "Johannes de Muris." In *New Grove Dictionary of Music and Musicians*, edited by Stanley Sadie, vol. 9. 6th ed. London: Macmillan, 1980. The best and most comprehensive source in English on the life and works of Johannes de Muris, this lengthy article is divided into four major sections that discuss his life, his nonmusical writings, his musical writings, and the influence of his writings. An excellent bibliography is included.

_____. "New Sources for the Bibliography of Johannes de Murs." *Journal of the American Musicological Society* 22, no. 1 (1969): 3-26. Gushee's article deals with a recently discovered Spanish manuscript that contains valuable biographical information about de Muris. The article, a good update to the Besseler article (see above), sheds new light on this important fourteenth century figure. One of the most important sources of information on de Muris.

Hoppin, Richard. *Medieval Music*. New York: W. W. Norton and Co., 1978. While only brief references are made to de Muris, the book provides an excellent survey of medieval music from chant to music of the early fifteenth century. One chapter, devoted to the *Ars Nova*, discusses the musical innovations of the fourteenth century.

Karpinski, Louis. "The *Quadripartitum numerorum* of John of Meurs." *Bibliotheca mathematica* 13 (1912-1913): 99-114. A detailed and highly technical discussion of de Muris' famous mathematical treatise.

Lang, Paul Henry. *Music in Western Civilization*. New York: W. W. Norton and Co., 1941. An authoritative work on the history of music and its role in the culture of Western civilization. The book assumes that the reader already has a basic knowledge of music history.

Reaney, Gilbert. "Ars Nova in France." *Ars Nova and the Renaissance 1300-1540*. Vol. 3 in *The New Oxford History of Music*, edited by Egon Wellesz. London: Oxford University Press, 1966. An excellent overview of the musical forms and composers of fourteenth century France. Contains some information about de Muris and a good discussion of the notational innovations of the fourteenth century. Also includes some information about major and minor French composers of the period.

Thorndike, Lynn. "John de Murs and the Conjunction of 1345." In *A History of Magic and Experimental Science*, vol. 3. New York: Macmillan, 1923-1941. An excellent source concerning the scientific activities, accomplishments, and writings of de Muris. Some biographical material is included at the beginning of the article.

Michael Hernon

NABU-RIMANNI

Born: early first century B.C.; probably Babylonia
Died: late first century B.C.; probably Babylonia
Area of Achievement: Astronomy
Contribution: Nabu-rimanni was a Babylonian scribe who copied and preserved astronomical tables for the computation of lunar, solar, and planetary phenomena. By providing accurate numerical parameters for the
prediction of astronomical phenomena, Babylonian astronomy furthered
the development and success of Greek spherical astronomy, developed to
its fullest in the Ptolemaic system.

Early Life

Because the nature of Babylonian sources is such that authors and authorship remain obscure, it is not possible to reconstruct for Nabu-rimanni a
biography in the strict sense. The historical period with which he is associated, however, may be sketched. While the years of Nabu-rimanni's floruit
were in the mid-first century B.C., one may also define this period more
broadly, that is, from roughly 300 B.C. to the beginning of the common era,
as the Hellenistic period. As a result of the spread of Greek political influence across the Near Eastern territories once belonging to the empires of
Persia, Babylonia, and Assyria, this era produced notable cultural and intellectual change from the cities of mainland Greece to Egypt in the south and
Mesopotamia in the east. In particular, science flowered in Hellenistic intellectual centers such as Alexandria, and Greek astronomy, which had already
begun in the fifth century, reached its height during the Hellenistic period, in
part as a result of the transmission of astronomical knowledge from Mesopotamia.

Life's Work

The Hellenistic authors Strabo (64 or 63 B.C.-c. A.D. 25) and Pliny the
Elder (A.D. 23-79), who traveled and produced encyclopedic compendia of
the knowledge and customs of the day, mention Babylonian astronomical "schools" and a few of the Babylonian astronomers by name. Thus, one
finds in book 16 of Strabo's *Geōgraphia* (*Geography*) the name Naburianos
(=Nabu-rimmani), and also Kidenas, Sudines, and Seleucus, all associated
with Babylonian cities such as Babylon, Uruk, and possibly Borsippa. Nabu-
rimanni's particular or distinguishing role in the history of Babylonian astronomy, however, cannot be determined either from the Greek account or from
Babylonian cuneiform sources. Cuneiform texts yield information about the
scribes only in the colophons at the end of the inscriptions. These colophons,
when complete, note the names of the owner of the document and the scribe
who copied it, as well as the date the tablet was written and who was king at

the time. Nabu-rimanni's name is preserved on the colophon of an astronomical tablet from Babylon. The only fact, therefore, that can be established about him from Babylonian sources is that he was a scribe who copied, or possibly computed, a table of dates and positions in the sky of new and full moons for the year 49-48 B.C. This particular colophon is the source for the claim that Nabu-rimanni was the inventor of the method of astronomical computation represented in his tablet. Far from showing this scribe as an innovator of Babylonian astronomy, however, Nabu-rimanni's tablet is one of the youngest of Babylonian lunar ephemerides; the oldest such tablets stem from the third century. Nabu-rimanni can therefore be credited only with preserving the tradition of Babylonian astronomy, not inventing it.

Since Nabu-rimanni is associated with a particular method of astronomical computation, but his individual contribution cannot be determined from the sources, the focus of any examination of his life's work must be Babylonian astronomy itself. Babylonian mathematical astronomy of the last three centuries B.C. is known from only two identifiable archives, one found in Babylon and the other in Uruk. The bulk of the texts are lunar or planetary ephemerides, which are supplemented by a smaller group of procedure texts outlining the steps necessary to generate ephemeris tables. The ephemeris tables contain parallel columns of numbers in specific sequences which represent occurrences of characteristic lunar and planetary phenomena. Each column represents a different periodic phenomenon—for example, new moons, eclipses, first visibilities, stationary points. The consecutive entries in each column correspond to dates, usually months. In the case of the ephemeris for the moon, the objective is to predict the evening of the first visibility of the lunar crescent. The appearance of the new moon defines the beginning of the month in a strictly lunar calendar. Indeed, the control of the calendar seems to have provided a major motivation for the development of mathematical methods for predicting astronomical phenomena.

For calculations, the Babylonians utilized a number system of base 60; that is, numbers are represented with special digits from 1 to 59, while 60, or any power of 60, is represented by 1. These "sexagesimal" numbers were written using a place-value notation system similar to decimal notation, so that for each place a digit is moved to the left, the value is multiplied by 60. The positional system was extended for fractions, which were expressed by moving digits to the right of the "ones" place, thereby dividing each time by 60. The Babylonian sexagesimal system is still preserved in the counting of time by hours, minutes (1 hour equals 60 minutes), and seconds (1 minute equals 60 seconds).

Babylonian lunar and planetary theory comprised two separate but coexistent systems, designated A and B, which are defined according to two different arithmetical methods of describing the distance covered each month by the sun. In this way, the velocity of the sun could be measured in terms of the progress of the sun in longitude, or degrees along its apparent path through the stars, the ecliptic. In system A, the progress of the sun along the ecliptic is described as being 30° per (mean synodic) month for one part of the zodiac (from Virgo 13° to Pisces 27°) and 28° 7' 30" for the other part (from Pisces 27° to Virgo 13°). A mathematical model is thereby created whereby the sun moves with two separate constant velocities on two arcs of the ecliptic. If the sun's velocity, reckoned in terms of progress in longitude (degrees along the ecliptic), is plotted against time, the resulting graph represents a "step function." System A also implies a certain length of the solar year, namely 1 year equals 12;22,8 months, expressed sexagesimally. (Sexagesimal numbers are represented in modern notation with a semicolon separating integers from fractions.) This method and its complementary system B were both used during the period from c. 250 B.C. to c. 50 B.C.

System B assumes the motion of the sun to increase and decrease its speed steadily from month to month. The variation in velocity is bounded by a minimum and a maximum value, and within this range of velocities, the monthly change is always by a constant amount. To plot the progress of the sun by this model produces a graph representing a "linear zig-zag function." The name Kidenas, mentioned by Strabo, Pliny, and Vettius Valens (A.D. second century), may be associated with System B, as a scribe by the name of Ki-di-nu (=Kidinnu) is known from colophons of system B-type ephemerides for the years 104-101 B.C. The Greeks credited him with derivation of the relation 251 synodic months = 269 anomalistic months. This numerical relation is in fact seen in system B computations.

Systems A and B constitute theoretical mathematical models of the motion of the sun that account for the varying lengths of the seasons of the year. By analogy with solar motion, the methods of systems A and B were applied to many celestial phenomena of a cyclic character. A Babylonian lunar table deals with the determination of conjunctions and oppositions of sun and moon, first and last visibilities, and eclipses, all of which are cyclic phenomena. Planetary tables for the planets Jupiter, Venus, Saturn, Mercury, and Mars predict the dates and positions in the zodiac of the cyclic appearances of planets, such as first visibilities, oppositions, stationary points, and last visibilities. The fact that each phenomenon had its own period enabled the Babylonians to compute them independently. No general theory of planetary and lunar motion was needed, since the strictly arithmetical methods of the two systems were sufficient to predict the individual appearances of the heavenly bodies. The goal of Babylonian astronomy was, therefore, to predict when the moon or planets would be visible. In contrast, the Greeks' goal was to develop a single model which would serve to describe and account for the motion of celestial bodies in a general sense, and from which the individual appearances of celestial bodies would follow as a consequence. The achievement of this goal was found in geometrical methods and kinematic models (explaining motion), developed by Apollonius of Perga (third century B.C.) and perfected by Ptolemy in *Mathēmatikē suntaxis* (c. A.D. 150; *Almagest*). Such geometrical concepts are not found in Babylonian astronomy.

The question of the identity of the Babylonian astronomers is not answered by the cuneiform astronomical texts. One scribe is hardly distinguished from another when the extent of one's information is the appearance of the scribe's name in a text colophon. Nevertheless, the question as to the significance of the scribes Nabu-rimanni and Kidinnu, whose names are remembered by later Greek and Roman authors, remains. The belief that they were the inventors of the systems A and B gains no support from the cuneiform texts. Indeed, the establishment of dates for the invention of systems A and B has proved difficult; thus, statements concerning the origins of Babylonian mathematical astronomy, in regard to both chronology and the role of individual scribes, must for the time being remain inconclusive.

Summary

Babylonian lunar and planetary theory became the foundation for the development and further refinement of astronomy by the Greek astronomers Apollonius, Hipparchus, and Ptolemy. In very general terms, one can enumerate the various Babylonian contributions to Greek astronomy and thereby to the development of science in general as follows. About 300 to 200 B.C., the Greek astronomers adopted the Babylonian sexagesimal number system for their computations and for measuring time and angles (360 degrees in a circle with degrees divisible by minutes and seconds). The use of arithmetical methods characteristic of Babylonian astronomical tables continued, particularly in the procedures used by Hellenistic astrologers. While Greek astronomical theory depended upon geometrical and kinematic models, neither of which was used in Babylonian astronomy, the parameters used in constructing those models were Babylonian. Indeed, the success of Greek astronomical theory rests upon the accuracy of the parameters established by Babylonian astronomers (such as the length of the solar year given above). The concepts related to the parameters must also have been transmitted. Such concepts were, for example, the following components of lunar motion: longitude, latitude (angular distance of the moon from the ecliptic), anomaly (irregularity in motion), and the motion from east to west of the line of nodes (the two diametrically opposed points where the moon's orbital plane intersects the plane of the ecliptic) in a nineteen-year cycle. Also of use for Greek planetary theory were the period relations essential to the determination of successive occurrences of a periodic phenomenon in Babylonian astronomy. Through the wide acceptance of the Ptolemaic tradition, as evidenced by Indian and Islamic astronomy, the direct influence of Babylonian astronomy on the Greek world had even greater impact as the ultimate impetus for the quantitative approach to celestial phenomena.

Bibliography

Aaboe, Asger. "Observation and Theory in Babylonian Astronomy." *Centaurus* 24 (1980): 14-35. Suggests a reconstruction of the process by which the Babylonian systems of computing astronomical phenomena were developed.

──────── . "Scientific Astronomy in Antiquity." In *The Place of Astronomy in the Ancient World*, edited by F. R. Hodson. London: Oxford University Press, 1974. Summary and explanation of the mathematical content of the Babylonian astronomical ephemerides and discussion of what constitutes a "scientific" astronomy.

Neugebauer, Otto. *Astronomical Cuneiform Texts*. London: Lund Humphreys, 1955. A transliteration and translation of the cuneiform astronomical texts, accompanied by an analysis.

──────── . *The Exact Sciences in Antiquity*. Providence, R.I.: Brown University Press, 1957. Reprint. New York: Dover Press, 1968. Concise history of mathematics and astronomy in Babylonia, Egypt, and Greece.

──────── . *A History of Ancient Mathematical Astronomy*. Heidelberg, Germany: Springer Verlag, 1975. Definitive and extremely technical treatment of Babylonian, Egyptian, and Greek astronomy (pre-Ptolemaic and Ptolemaic systems).

Van der Waerden, B. L. *Science Awakening*. Vol. 2, *The Birth of Astronomy*. Leiden, Netherlands: Noordhoff International Publishing, 1974. More accessible and less technical but also less reliable than Neugebauer. Gives an overall account of the phenomena of interest in Babylonian mathematical as well as pre-mathematical astronomy.

Francesca Rochberg-Halton

NEBUCHADNEZZAR II

Born: c. 630 B.C.; place unknown
Died: 562 B.C.; Babylon
Areas of Achievement: Conquest and government
Contribution: One of the most ambitious and successful military leaders of
   ancient times, Nebuchadnezzar possessed excellent governing ability which
   made Chaldean Neo-Babylon the most powerful and feared nation in
   Western Asia.

Early Life

Nebuchadnezzar II, the eldest son of Nabopolassar, King of the Chaldean
Neo-Babylonians, who reigned from 625 to 605, entered the world's military
arena in the early 600's. As crown prince, he led Chaldean forces against the
remnants of the Assyrian army and a sizable Egyptian contingent in the decisive Battle of Carchemish, fought in what is modern Syria. For the remainder of his life, Nebuchadnezzar expanded upon his father's conquests, until
Babylon was the richest, most prominent, and most renowned nation in the
ancient world.

Nevertheless, his exploits, considerable though they were, would not have
been so well-known to later generations if he had not been the monarch who
burned and looted Jerusalem, forcing its most able inhabitants into temporary exile in Babylon. By so doing, Nebuchadnezzar unwittingly fulfilled
the prophecies of Jeremiah, the most noted Jewish prophet of the time.
Thus, the Bible has preserved the Babylonian ruler's most notable accomplishments.

After he succeeded his father as king in 605, Nebuchadnezzar gave the city
of Babylon its most famous feature, the Hanging Gardens, as well as fiery
furnaces used both for commercial enterprises and for the torture and
destruction of Babylon's foes; its grand celebrations of Marduk, Babylon's
patron god, and the goddess Ishtar; and its huge brick outer walls, which
dominated the desert for many miles. By these gifts, Nebuchadnezzar transformed Babylon from a dusty, shabby provincial city into an elegant world
capital. With no remaining Assyrian enemy to engage or any significant
Egyptian threat to counter, Nebuchadnezzar turned his attention not only to
the rebuilding of Babylon but also to its territorial expansion. He and his architects created enormous stepped ziggurats for the glory of Marduk and
Ishtar, while he planned further forays against neighboring states.

Using the Code of Hammurabi as his basis, Nebuchadnezzar created a stable, generally lawful Babylonian society. Criminals faced severe penalties
ranging from torture to death. The most notorious punishments, however,
were reserved for enemy rulers and their retainers; upon capture, these
people were often flayed alive, partially dismembered, and cast alive into the

furnaces, or were blinded and had gold clasps affixed to their tongues; with a leash attached to the clasp, the afflicted could be led around Babylon. By rigidly adhering to the Code of Hammurabi, Nebuchadnezzar reinforced his reputation for ferocity.

Life's Work

The battles which occurred after the flight of the Egyptian army brought many victories to the Chaldeans; each victory brought destruction and death to the vanquished tribe or nation. In 601, Nebuchadnezzar's forces were defeated by Necho II, the King of Egypt, an event which elevated the hopes of the kingdom of Judaea. Although Jehoiakim, appointed king of Judah by the pharaoh, had once submitted to Nebuchadnezzar, he had shortly thereafter covertly joined forces with the Egyptians in order to war against Babylon. Jeremiah, one of the principal Old Testament prophets, warned his people that God intended to punish them for their worship of foreign gods and for their allegiance to Egypt.

Nebuchadnezzar fulfilled Jeremiah's prophecy by marching on Judah and its largest city in 597. King Jehoiakim had died before the city was captured, but Nebuchadnezzar took his son Jehoiachin into Babylonian exile. Later, in 586, after an eighteen-month siege, Jerusalem was burned and its leading citizens sent into exile. As much as possible, Nebuchadnezzar attempted to erase all signs of Jewish civilization from the former kingdom. Zedekiah, the ruler of Judah-in-exile, paid for his dealings with Egypt by being blinded after witnessing the murder of his sons by Babylonian captors.

The enslavement of the Jews was nothing like the total servitude they had faced centuries before when Egyptian pharaohs forced them to make bricks for the Pyramids and treated them like beasts of burden. Nebuchadnezzar, while never allowing them to return home, did allow them many freedoms, including the rights to work at trades and to mingle freely with the populace of Babylon. Yet the Jews were a miserable people who dreamed of one day going back to their ancestral towns and villages. In their midst was the prophet Ezekiel, Jeremiah's counterpart. Ezekiel prophesied that the Jews would be delivered from Babylonian captivity by a great king from the East, a vision that came true when Cyrus the Great of Persia invaded Babylon in the year 539.

After the destruction of Jerusalem and the capture and blinding of Zedekiah in 586, Nebuchadnezzar sent his armies against the Egyptians once again, finally capturing the important Phoenician city of Tyre in 571, thus adding considerably to the wealth, power, and authority of Babylon. With Egyptian influence flagging, Babylon became the unquestioned power of Asia Minor. Commerce with surrounding nations accompanied the empire's ascent as Babylon became the mercantile center of western Asia. A storehouse of gold, silver, and precious gems taken as tribute from vassal nations,

Babylon could buy and trade virtually any commodity.

Nebuchadnezzar made certain that waterways and highways were constructed, making the city readily accessible to the heavy trade flowing into it. His earlier building program was intensified in the middle years of his reign so that Babylon would be an impregnable fortress as well as a center of commerce. The temples and ziggurats were made enormous and the city walls rose higher than they had previously, decorated with enameled figures of beasts. The Hanging Gardens were made even more elaborate so that the king and his harem could enjoy the delights of a large oasis in the middle of a desert city.

Little is known about the last years of Nebuchadnezzar. The final major event to occur before he faded from history was a battle with the Median leader Cyaxares, who had sacked Uratu and headed toward the kingdom of Lydia, which was close enough to Babylonian territory to make Nebuchadnezzar uneasy. Bitter fighting ended in May, 585, when darkness caused by a solar eclipse enveloped the Medes and the Neo-Babylonians; the event was interpreted as a sign from the gods to stop fighting. A truce was signed; nevertheless, the Medians remained a source of anxiety for Nebuchadnezzar, who ordered that a high wall be built around the city.

There is much speculation about his final days. Some scholars believe that he gradually grew weary of the burdens of kingship and retired from active life, others that he may have suffered from senility or even madness. Perhaps the best-known source for the latter theory is the biblical account of Daniel, in which the King of Babylon is depicted as an insane old man, an eater of grass. In any event, his immediate successor, his son Evil-Merodach, the man he had hoped would continue his life's work in Babylon, died in 559 (or, as some accounts have it, 560) after being overthrown. The short-lived Chaldean dynasty founded by Nebuchadnezzar's father finally ended with the death of Nabonidus in 539, when Cyrus' army swept into Babylon and established Achaemenid rule.

Summary

Nebuchadnezzar II's genius for conquering rival nations and tribes and then paralyzing them by taking their best-educated, most talented people into exile, as well as his great civic and military planning abilities, makes him one of history's most influential leaders. He took chances in his military campaigns, but such risks were shrewdly calculated. By using the punishment of exile, he placed hostile governments directly under his own surveillance and, by so doing, nipped any potential revolution before it could grow into a threat. His cruelty toward certain unrepentant foes was unrivaled in the ancient world and established him as an enemy not to be resisted. Those who did resist brought upon themselves death and destruction. A lover of pomp, he made the city of Babylon into a magnificent fortress, its gardens, palaces, courtyards, and walls the marvels of their time. Almost single-handedly, the king magnified the power and prestige of his nation. Yet the end of Babylon was soon in coming, foretold by Ezekiel and those who shared his prophetic vision; its magnificence was destroyed by enemies within and without, leaving it a warren of broken walls in the midst of a desert.

It is ironic that the Jews whom Nebuchadnezzar took into bitter exile were to portray him most memorably for later generations. To readers of the Old Testament, he is the cruel but brilliant monarch who fulfilled Jeremiah's predictions by destroying Jerusalem and creating the lengthy Diaspora as well as the man who threw Daniel into the den of lions and Shadrach, Meshach, and Abednego into a furnace. Like Daniel and his companions, the Jews survived Nebuchadnezzar's tortures, but Babylon itself, largely the creation of its king, left few traces after Cyrus made it into a wasteland. Like many empires, it had its golden age, followed by rapid decay. This golden age could not have occurred had it not been for the consummate genius of Nebuchadnezzar.

Bibliography
New Catholic Edition of the Holy Bible. New York: Catholic Book Publishing Co., 1957. The books of Jeremiah, Ezekiel, and Daniel deserve special attention, although references to Nebuchadnezzar are found elsewhere in the Bible. One of the most revealing sources of information about how Nebuchadnezzar was viewed by one of his enslaved peoples.
Oates, Joan. *Babylon.* London: Thames and Hudson, 1979. Considers many aspects of life in Babylon under various kings including Nebuchadnezzar. Discusses Babylonian law, religion, social customs, festivals, and military conquests and defeats and gives a fine overview of each king's contribution to Babylon's rise and fall. An in-depth look at a sophisticated, complex society.
Oppenheim, A. Leo. *Ancient Mesopotamia: Portrait of a Dead Civilization.* Chicago: University of Chicago Press, 1964. Written by one of the foremost scholars dealing with the region, this work considers the development of the nation of the Tigris and Euphrates basin. Gives much insight into relationships between strong and weak nations.
_____. *Letters from Mesopotamia: Official, Business, and Private Letters on Clay Tablets from Two Millennia.* Chicago: University of Chicago Press, 1968. These letters shed light on the inner dynamics of the nations of the Near East in ancient times.
Saggs, H. W. F. *The Greatness That Was Babylon: A Survey of the Ancient Civilization of the Tigris-Euphrates Valley.* New York: Frederick A. Praeger, 1969. Written for both general and scholarly readers, this study covers the Babylonian monarchies. Invaluable for its lively depiction of the lives of both noble and worker. Well-illustrated; extensive bibliography.

Tabouis, G. R. *Nebuchadnezzar*. New York: McGraw-Hill, 1931. Tabouis, a member of the Académie Française, gives readers an imaginative glimpse of life in Nebuchadnezzar's court. Historical fiction at its best.

John D. Raymer

ALEXANDER NECKAM

Born: 1157; St. Albans, Hertfordshire, England
Died: Probably March 31, 1217; Kempsey, Worcestershire, England
Areas of Achievement: Science, education, and religion
Contribution: Neckam typifies the broadening humanistic interests of the twelfth century through his writing and teaching in many areas, including grammar, science, and theology.

Early Life

Alexander Neckam was born in 1157 at St. Albans in England. Little is known about his family except that his mother, Hodierna, was probably nurse to Richard the Lionhearted, the future King of England, who was also born in 1157. He began his education at the monastery school of St. Albans. His pleasant memories of the school as well as its high reputation suggest that his early education fostered the abilities that were to produce his later literary achievements.

He continued his education in Paris, which, in the second half of the twelfth century, was the preeminent European intellectual center in the liberal arts and theology. Neckam was associated with the school of Petit Pont which the logician Adam made famous for its subtle disputation in the mid-twelfth century. Neckam's studies also included theology, medicine, and canon and civil law. He probably taught as a master and also began writing during his years in Paris. Although they contain no definitive date of composition, several of his works fit well into probable interests connected with his studies in Paris. The *Commentary on Martianus Capellus* (c. 1177-1190) deals primarily with mythology based on the standard treatise on the liberal arts by this late antique author. The *Novus Avianus* (c. 1177-1190; new aviary) and *Novus Esopus* (c. 1177-1190; new Aesop) contain bird and animal fables which probably represent exercises in his ability to write on set themes. *De nominibus utensilium* (c. 1177-1190; on the names of utensils) is characteristic of elementary school instruction: It is a list of words taken from all facets of everyday life, from household furnishings to ships and sailing, put together in sentences whose purpose was to teach boys the Latin equivalents of these words. Its basic idea comes from a treatise on more difficult words by Adam of Petit Pont.

Life's Work

When Neckam returned to England around 1182, he spent about twenty years as a teacher. First, he was a master at Dunstable, a school under the control of St. Albans monastery. After about a year, he obtained a teaching position at the St. Albans school during the abbacy of Warin (1183-1195). Variations on a story based on his name—*nequam*, meaning worthless, naughty, or bad in Latin—are connected with his assumption of the position at St. Albans. According to the thirteenth century account of Matthew Paris, Abbot Warin summoned him with a wordplay on his name: "Si bonus es venias; si nequam nequaquam" (if you are a good man, come; if worthless, by no means). In other versions, the abbot gives this response to Neckam's petition to become a monk at St. Albans.

During the 1190's, Neckam taught at Oxford University. Although he is considered the first scholastic theologian at Oxford, only a few traces of his teaching or lectures can be detected in his later writings. About fifty sermons, mainly from his Oxford period, survive. They are addressed to a variety of audiences, including scholars, laymen, and monks. Their form is simple, and they make only sparing use of the compositional techniques, rhetorical devices, and exempla that became characteristic of the developed sermon of the thirteenth century.

Neckam considered the monastic vocation the highest calling in life, and he fulfilled this ideal by entering the Augustinian abbey of Cirencester in Gloucestershire between 1197 and 1202. He became abbot in 1213. As an Augustinian canon, his learning and experience were called into service for both ecclesiastical and royal business. In 1212-1213, at the time of the interdict, he took part in royal affairs. In 1213, for example, King John ordered him to inquire into royal rights in the priory of Kenilworth. On several occasions, he was an ecclesiastical judge and a papal judge delegate. In 1215, he left England to attend the Fourth Lateran Council, and he returned in 1216. He died in March of 1217 at Kempsey, a manor of the Bishop of Worcester, and was buried in Worcester Cathedral.

Most of Neckam's literary production on which his reputation primarily rests comes from his later life when he was a canon at the abbey of Cirencester. In some of his writings, he continued his interests in grammar. The *Sacerdos ad altare* (c. 1200-1210), whose title of convenience comes from the first words of the treatise, is similar to the earlier *De nominibus utensilium* in its presentation of words put together into sentences with lengthy glosses on points of grammar following each section. The types of words, however, are different since they represent a higher social and intellectual level with an emphasis on priests and their vestments, the church and monastery with furnishings, the royal court, and the student and his reading list. This course of study is of particular interest because it gives some insight into the curriculum of the schools at Paris in the late twelfth century.

The *Corrogationes Promethei* (c. 1200-1204) is the primary source of Neckam's grammatical teaching. The meaning of the title, "collections of Prometheus," is uncertain. It may refer to one medieval view of Prometheus, the brother of Atlas, as instructing men in the arts; thus, the work would be a collection for a basic education in the arts which began with grammar. The first part concerns the art of grammar, including figures of speech, construction of sentences, accents, and orthography, with much material based on Arelius Donatus and Priscian, the main Roman authors of grammatical texts that were used in the Middle Ages. The second part glosses difficult words or passages from the Bible.

Science was another area of intellectual inquiry to which Neckam made an important contribution. Although many of his works contain scattered pieces of scientific information, two of his writings are devoted primarily to scientific questions. The *De naturis rerum* (on the natures of things), written before 1205, is the earliest and most extensive. It serves as an introduction comprising the first two books to his *Commentary on Ecclesiastes* (before 1205). As such, Neckam considered it a moral treatise, and a moral or spiritual interpretation follows descriptions of natural phenomena. The subjects he discusses, however, represent the state of knowledge of natural sciences in England in the late twelfth century. He begins with creation and the firmament, discussing astronomy, including eclipses and the marks on the moon. The remainder of *De naturis rerum* is structured according to the elements. He begins with air and some of its properties as seen in the theory of the vacuum. He also catalogs birds which inhabit the air. Similarly, he discusses some properties of water followed by aquatic creatures. For the earth, he begins with minerals, then vegetables, and finally ends with animals, culminating with humanity.

The *Laus sapiente divine* (c. 1213; praise of divine wisdom) was composed just before he became abbot of Cirencester; in the last year of his life, the *Suppletio defectum* (1216), which is a supplement of lacking material, was added to it. The *Laus sapiente divine* is, in some ways, a versified form of the *De naturis rerum*. Its organization into ten distinctions differs, however, and the omission of many stories and more extensive treatment of some subjects, such as an enumeration of the stars and the theory of the elements, makes it an equally interesting source for Neckam's scientific views. The *Suppletio defectum*, also in verse, is divided into two sections. The first dealing with birds, animals, and plants covers material familiar from his other writings. The second section on problems about mankind as well as astronomy introduces some new information.

Because he was a cleric and canon educated at Paris, a substantial portion of Neckam's writings concerns theological matters. Most are commentaries on books or passages in the Bible in the older monastic form consisting of lengthy discussions explaining the four senses of Scripture: literal or historical, allegorical, tropological, and anagogical. These works include the *Solatium fidelis anime* (after 1197; consolation of the faithful soul), a moralized interpretation of the days of creation; the *Commentary on Ecclesiastes* which the two books of *De naturis rerum* introduce; the *Commentary on the Song of Songs* (before 1213), which emphasizes the relationship between Christ and the Virgin; the *Commentary on Proverbs* (before 1213); and the

Tractatus super mulierem fortem (after 1213; treatise on strong women), which comments on Proverbs 31: 10-31 in honor of Mary Magdalene, the Virgin, and the Church. The newer scholastic commentary of the schools appears in his *Gloss on the Psalter* (after 1197), which follows the scholastic reading of text and gloss on the Bible and the second part of the *Corrogationes Promethei*, which utilizes the scholastic *distinctio* on the meaning of biblical words. He expounds his theological views in the four books of the *Speculum speculationum* (before 1213; mirror of speculations), which is notable for his discussion of grace and free will in the fourth book. Also surviving in parts or excerpted collections (*florilegia*) are several hymns and minor works such as the *Laus beatissime virginis* (after 1197; praise of the most blessed Virgin).

Summary

Alexander Neckam is significant because in both his career and his writings he represents a transition from the developing schools and humanistic learning of the twelfth century to the expanded sources, new methods of teaching, and scientific interests of the later Middle Ages. In education, he was among the first authors of basic and practical descriptive vocabularies for primary instruction in Latin, although his grammatical glosses remained close to traditional expositions of Donatus and Priscian. While he was instrumental in introducing scholastic disputation in his Oxford teaching, his sermons and theological writings generally followed more traditional forms. For related theological and scientific problems, he demonstrated an early awareness of a broader corpus of the writings of Aristotle, whom he highly praised as great and most acute. Nevertheless, although various citations in his scientific writings point to some familiarity with Aristotle's works on natural science, Neckam relied most heavily on the more widely known Aristotelian treatises on logic. Also, while he evidenced interest in scientific observation and gave perhaps the earliest references to the compass and to glass mirrors, he repeated much information, often fabulous, from older authors such as Isidore of Seville. Through his prolific writings in many fields, his teaching at several educational levels, and his active participation in monastic life as well as royal and ecclesiastical service, Alexander Neckam was important in transmitting and transforming the widening intellectual interests of the twelfth century into their scholastic form of the late medieval period.

Bibliography

Esposito, M. "On Some Unpublished Poems Attributed to Alexander Neckam." *English Historical Review* 30 (1915): 450-471. This article attributes several poems in a manuscript at the Bibliothèque Nationale in Paris to Neckam. The appendix provides a list of Neckam's work in printed editions and manuscripts.

Gaselee, Stephen. "Natural Science in England at the End of the Twelfth Century." *Proceedings of the Royal Institution of Great Britain* 29, no. 3 (1937): 397-417. This piece contains a brief biography of Neckam. It is the fullest description of the contents of Neckam's *De naturis rerum*.

Haskins, Charles Homer. *Studies in the History of Mediaeval Science*. Cambridge, Mass.: Harvard University Press, 1924. Chapter 28 ascribes the *Sacerdos ad altare* to Alexander Neckam. It provides a transcription of the section on a student reading list.

Hunt, R. W. Edited and revised by Margaret Gibson. *The Schools and the Cloister: The Life and Writings of Alexander Nequam, 1157-1217*. Oxford: Clarendon Press, 1984. This book is a biography of Neckam with a discussion of all of his writings. It contains a complete list of the writings, in chronological order, giving all known manuscript sources and printed editions. It also has thorough bibliographical references to other works about Neckam.

Russell, Josiah C. "Alexander Neckam in England." *English Historical Review* 47 (1932): 260-268. Discusses the documentation for Neckam's life and career in England. An appendix contains emendations to M. Esposito's list of Neckam's works.

Thorndike, Lynn. *A History of Magic and Experimental Science*. Vol. 2. New York: Macmillan, 1923. One chapter discusses Neckam's life and learning, concentrating on his scientific writings and their contribution to scientific knowledge.

Karen Gould

NEZAHUALCÓYOTL

Born: 1402; probably Texcoco
Died: 1472; Texcoco
Area of Achievement: Government
Contribution: Nezahualcóyotl, who was primarily responsible for the creation
of the Aztec Empire, was a proponent of a religious vision which, if it had
prevailed, might have made possible that empire's survival.

Early Life

Nezahualcóyotl (Hungry Coyote) was the son of Ixtlilxóchitl, King of
Texcoco, and therefore a descendant of Xólotl, who led a Chichimec tribe
into the northern part of the Valley of Mexico in the mid-thirteenth century
and established the Kingdom of Alcolhuacán. Quinatzin, who established his
Alcolhuacán capital at Texcoco in 1318, was the great-grandson of Xólotl and
the great-grandfather of Nezahualcóyotl, who also had connection with the
Mexica Aztecs of Tenochtitlán through his mother, Matlalcihuatzin, who was
the daughter of a Tenochtitlán king.

To understand why the childhood of Nezahualcóyotl was a time of great
peril for the royal house of Alcolhuacán, the reader must take account of the
wars fought in the valley in the period before the rise of the Mexica Aztecs of
Tenochtitlán. The arena of these wars was a relatively small area in the vicinity of modern Mexico City, and the powers engaged were all cities on or
near the shores of Lake Texcoco or on its islands. Because the various
codices upon which one depends for knowledge of these events were written
from memory after the Spanish Conquest, they do not agree in detail, but
their description of the wars that tore the Valley of Mexico apart in the years
before Nezahualcóyotl came to the throne of Texcoco are in agreement on
the basic events.

The dominant power on the western shore of the lake was the Tepanecans
of Azcapotzalco, whose great King Tezozómoc, though he was himself a
grandson of Xólotl, was determined to extend his control over the valley by
conquering Texcoco, which dominated the country between the lake and the
mountains to the east. In 1412, Tezozómoc launched a three-pronged attack,
sending armies against Alcolhuacán around the north and south ends of the
lake and sending his Mexican allies from Tenochtitlán directly across the lake
in their war canoes. Ixtlilxóchitl repulsed the southern attack and drove off
the war canoes; then, in a war that lasted three years, he defeated the armies
of Tezozómoc in every battle in the country north of the lake and laid siege
to Azcapotzalco itself.

At this point, Tezozómoc sued for peace, and Ixtlilxóchitl, who had virtually won the war, magnanimously chose not to demand unconditional surrender. This stance ensured his own downfall, because Tezozómoc chose not to

abide by the terms of the peace treaty, which called for both sides to disarm. In 1418, he launched a treacherous attack, and Ixtlilxóchitl was defeated and forced to flee to the mountains with Nezahualcóyotl. There, hiding in the branches of a tree, the boy saw his father make his last stand before he was cut down by the pursuing Tepanecans. From that moment, apparently, Nezahualcóyotl was determined to have his vengeance on Azcapotzalco.

Though the chronicles may rely only on popular legend, they all suggest that after fleeing across the mountains to Tlaxcala, where he found refuge with relatives, Nezahualcóyotl spent the next few years traveling incognito in Alcolhuacán, preparing his people for the day when he would lead them in a war of liberation against Azcapotzalco. In any case, during this period he was in great peril as a result of a reward posted by Tezozómoc, and he eventually was captured at Chalco, a city on the southeast shore of the lake subject to Tezozómoc. According to the chronicles, Tezozómoc ordered him caged and starved to death, but his guards, remembering the greatness of his father, secretly fed him. Later, when he was to be put to death, one of his guards permitted him to escape and was himself killed in his place.

Eventually—in 1425 according to one account—two of his aunts, related to the royal houses of both Texcoco and Azcapotzalco, persuaded Tezozómoc to permit the young prince to return, and he was allowed to live in Texcoco and with his mother's relatives in Tenochtitlán. In his last days, however, Tezozómoc regretted giving the prince even this limited freedom and sent an assassin to kill him. Again, Nezahualcóyotl survived as a result of the prestige he enjoyed as the son of Ixtlilxóchitl; the assassin warned him of the plot.

In 1426, Tezozómoc died. Nezahualcóyotl, as an Aztec prince related by blood or marriage to all the royal houses of the valley, attended the funeral, apparently keeping his own counsel as he observed the final rites performed for the tyrant against whom he had sworn vengeance. Even then the sons of Tezozómoc were arguing about the succession, and Nezahualcóyotl, whose political instincts were strong, must even then have been planning the conspiracy by which he would destroy them and their city. The accession of Maxtla to the throne of Azcapotzalco in 1426 set in motion the events which led eventually to the destruction of Azcapotzalco, the rise of Tenochtitlán to prominence, and the return of Nezahualcóyotl to his rightful place on the throne of Texcoco.

Life's Work

In 1420, Tezozómoc had rewarded his allies in Tenochtitlán with suzerainty over Texcoco. Now with Tezozómoc's death, Chimalpopoca, the King of Tenochtitlán, granted the rule of Texcoco to Nezahualcóyotl, who immediately conspired with Chimalpopoca against Azcapotzalco's new king, Maxtla. The plot was a failure, and Nezahualcóyotl was again forced to flee. In 1427, however, Chimalpopoca was killed—either by agents of Maxtla or by the most aggressive elements în Tenochtitlán itself—and Ixtcóatl (or Itzcóatl, as the name is also transliterated) succeeded him on the throne of Tenochtitlán. The way was now prepared for the alliance which would bring Maxtla down.

Though Maxtla's henchmen ruled in Texcoco, Nezahualcóyotl was able to call upon the goodwill he had earned among the people in the other cities east of the lake during his exile. The alliance of these cities now became part of a grander alliance of all those city-states that had grievances against Azcapotzalco. They were a mixed lot. Besides Nezahualcóyotl's cities, the alliance included his allies in Huexotzinco and Tlaxcala beyond the mountains east of the lake, Cuauhtitlán on the northwest shore of the lake, and Tlacopán on the west shore. Above all, it included Tenochtitlán. These Mexica Aztecs had fought against Nezahualcóyotl's father, they had opposed Nezahualcóyotl himself, and they had reduced him for a time to the status of a tribute-paying prince. He knew that the alliance against Azcapotzalco would not succeed without their warriors, however, and the alliance which resulted was primarily the result of his recognition of the political realities of the valley. Tenochtitlán, more or less imprisoned on its island in the lake, needed land, and Nezahualcóyotl used this land-hunger as a means of wreaking vengeance on Azcapotzalco.

As a result, he took a force of his best warriors to Tenochtitlán to aid in its defense. Maxtla's Tepanecans attacked across the causeways which linked Tenochtitlán to the western shore, and the Mexica and Nezahualcóyotl's Acolhua repulsed it. Meanwhile, armies from Huexotzinco and Tlaxcala were advancing on Azcapotzalco from the north. In 1428, the allies laid siege to Azcapotzalco and eventually destroyed it. The primary result of the victory was the ascendancy of Tenochtitlán in the political and military life of the valley and the rise to dominance of the most warlike and aggressive elements in that city.

Nezahualcóyotl remained in Tenochtitlán for several years, even building a palace there, while planning his campaign to regain the throne of Texcoco from the henchmen of Maxtla. The Mexica, keeping their part of the bargain, assisted him from 1429 to 1430 in the recovery of Texcoco. Now firmly allied with Tenochtitlán, he assisted them in their campaigns against the other cities on the shores of the lake, including Coyoacán and Xochimilco. In 1433, the fall of Cuitláhuac ended the Tepaneca War.

In 1431, Nezahualcóyotl was crowned emperor of the three-city league of Texcoco, Tenochtitlán, and Tlacopán, which he, more than anyone, had created. He realized that the kind of empire his ancestor Xólotl had achieved, a single state ruled by a single overlord, was no longer possible. Peace in the Valley of Mexico, therefore, depended on the maintenance of a loose confederation of the Acolhua of Texcoco, the Mexica of Tenochtitlán, and the Tepaneca of Tlacopán. Whatever the faults of this "empire," it endured until the Spanish Conquest.

In 1433, Nezahualcóyotl returned to Texcoco and embarked on a program which inaugurated that city's golden age and made it the most beautiful city in the Valley of Mexico and its intellectual and cultural center. He was a patron of science, industry, art, and literature; he was himself a poet of considerable renown; and he encouraged the creation of historical archives which at the time of the Spanish Conquest were the most extensive in Mexico.

In 1440, when King Itzcóatl of Tenochtitlán died, Nezahualcóyotl rededicated himself to the friendship of the three cities and gave his support in the election of a new king to Moctezuma (or Montezuma) I. Apparently he believed that Moctezuma would be a less ambitious threat than any other candidate to the integrity of Alcolhuacán and was willing to make concessions to ensure this election, which in time proved to be disastrous. The Mexica under Moctezuma's leadership became the dominant power in the valley, though Nezahualcóyotl continued as emperor.

In 1450, when torrential rains raised the level of the lake and flooded Tenochtitlán, Nezahualcóyotl, who was perhaps the most distinguished engineer and builder in Mexico before the Conquest, proposed the great dike which stretched nine miles north to south down the lake and isolated Tenochtitlán from the east side of the lake, which received the heaviest runoff from the mountains. In the next few years, however, the Valley of Mexico was afflicted with a long drought. Nezahualcóyotl distributed food from his own supplies and resisted the charge of some of his subjects that the gods had withheld the rain because Nezahualcóyotl had neglected to maintain the rites of human sacrifice. Characteristically, he preferred to build an extensive irrigation system to bring water from the mountains.

Nezahualcóyotl's antipathy to human sacrifice, which is in itself enough to make him the most remarkable political figure of his time and place, apparently derived from his sympathy with the cult of Tloque Nahuaque. This god, who was assumed to be unfathomable, all-present, and formless, was the one god in the pantheon that did not demand human sacrifice, and in the encouragement of his cult, Nezahualcóyotl seems clearly to have been attempting to lead his people toward a religion based on a benevolent monotheism.

One of Nezahualcóyotl's concessions to Moctezuma was his agreement to assist his ally in future wars of aggression. From 1455 to 1458, therefore, he contributed to the success of Tenochtitlán's war against the Mixtecs, and in 1464 he sent an army that helped Tenochtitlán destroy Chalco.

In 1467, Nezahualcóyotl completed in Texcoco the temple to the war god Huitzilopochtli, which was required as a further concession to the Mexica of Tenochtitlán. In the same year he completed a temple to the peaceful, benevolent Tloque Nahuaque. The coincidence of these two events must be considered an indication of the tragedy inherent both in the life of Nezahualcóyotl and in the history of Mexico. In the next half-century, that tragedy would play itself out to its inevitable conclusion as the adherents of Huitzilopochtli, with their doctrine of war, aggression, and human sacrifice, would triumph over the cult of peace and benevolence of which Nezahualcóyotl had been the champion.

Summary

Nezahualcóyotl was a supreme example of the Aztec knight, but he was also a poet, a lawgiver, a skillful politician and diplomat often called upon to mediate disputes, a builder and engineer, and a great patron of culture and learning. When he dedicated the temple to Huitzilopochtli in 1467— which in the Aztec calendar was called One Reed—he predicted that when One Reed returned in fifty-two years, the Aztec Empire would be destroyed. This prediction, along with the popular assumption that the benevolent god Quetzalcóatl would return in One Reed, was part of a complex of fears that haunted the last years of Aztec supremacy in Mexico with visions of the end of their civilization.

The demands of the Aztec war god for ever-increasing gifts of blood caused wars waged to capture sacrificial victims and ultimately dissension within the empire, which an astute conqueror would find easy to exploit. For this reason, Nezahualcóyotl's political decision to make concessions to Tenochtitlán—and thus to the cult of Huitzilopochtli—for the sake of peace within the empire must be considered an unfortunate development in the religious history of Mexico. If he had been able to unite the empire under the protection of a god of brotherhood and benevolence, the Spanish Conquest would undoubtedly have been more difficult. As it happened, however, when One Reed came around again (in 1519), it brought the Spanish and, as Nezahualcóyotl had predicted, the destruction of the civilization of which he was the outstanding representative.

Bibliography

Brundage, Burr C. *A Rain of Darts: The Mexica Aztecs*. Austin: University of Texas Press, 1973. Based on enormous scholarship, this book is the single most important work in English on Aztec history, with a thorough and well-balanced account of the Kingdom of Alcolhuacán and the life and achievements of Nezahualcóyotl.

Gillmor, Frances. *Flute of the Smoking Mirror*. Tucson: University of Arizona Press, 1949. A biography of Nezahualcóyotl, based on extensive scholarship but written in a novelistic style which requires the reader to check the narrative against the thoroughly documented end notes.

Padden, R. C. *The Hummingbird and the Hawk: Conquest and Sovereignty in the Valley of Mexico, 1503-1541*. Columbus: Ohio State University Press, 1967. Padden treats primarily Aztec affairs during the reign of the last Aztec emperor and the early colonial period, but his book includes a useful account of the religious conflicts in Mexico during Nezahualcóyotl's lifetime.

Peterson, Frederick A. *Ancient Mexico*. New York: Capricorn Books, 1962. A splendid survey of Mexican history and culture before the Spanish Conquest, with a useful discussion of Nezahualcóyotl's achievements and their historical background.

Radin, Paul. "The Sources and Authenticity of the History of the Ancient Mexicans." *University of California Publications in American Anthropology and Ethnology* 17 (1920-1926): 1-150. Includes the text of the Codex Xólotl, the most important original chronicle to discuss Nezahualcóyotl and the history of Texcoco.

Robert L. Berner

NICHIREN

Born: 1222; Kominato, Japan
Died: 1282; Sochu-ji Temple, Ikegami, Japan
Area of Achievement: Religion
Contribution: Through extraordinary dedication, Nichiren founded the Lotus sect of Buddhism, which, in turn, gave rise to a fervent Japanese nationalism.

Early Life

Japanese sources trace the lineage of Nichiren, most famous of Japan's Buddhist leaders, to the illustrious Fujiwara family of early Japan. Feudal power struggles, exile, and dispossession reduced Nichiren's family to humble circumstances. Born to one Shigetada, a fisherman, Nichiren was first named Zennichi-maru; Nichiren (lotus of the sun) is a Buddhist name which he adopted later as a monk—*nichi*, the sun, symbolizes Japan, and *ren*, the lotus, is the prime Buddhist symbol.

For ten years, Nichiren conscientiously studied Buddhism as a monk of the prominent Tendai sect centered at Mount Hiei-zan, near Kyoto. He came to believe that he alone could help the Japanese people and save the nation.

Life's Work

In 1253, Nichiren began a turbulent ministry marked by confrontation with various governmental authorities. He propagated a new doctrine believed to have been preached by the historic Buddha, Siddhārtha Gautama, in his later career, a doctrine centered mainly on the Mahayana Buddhist sutra *Saddharma-pundarika*. He referred to himself as a reincarnation of the bodhisattva Vishish-ṭachāritra, ancient disciple of the Buddha.

Early in his career, Nichiren became convinced that he would establish the true sect of Buddhism, a sect that would dominate the world from a holy see in Japan. This sect was known as the Lotus sect of Buddhism, and Nichiren's role in history is inseparable from the rise and continuing influence of this doctrine.

Nichiren's life and work, although rooted in traditional Japanese society, heralded an entirely new spirit of nationalism and religious intolerance. While most great religious leaders came from southern Japan, Nichiren came from the eastern provinces. His religion was permeated with a patriotic fervor and bore a strong, independent spirit—an offensive, temperamental disposition characteristic of the eastern samurai warriors of medieval Japan.

Just as the rise of Protestantism in early modern Europe is understandable only against the background of the dominant Catholic church, so Nichiren's form of Buddhism must be understood in relation to the other sects which dominated Japanese history. Some of these sects had fallen into corrupt practices and were scorned by the populace, and much of Nichiren's career was marked by vitriolic criticism of them. For example, Nichiren criticized the Tendai sect, of which he himself was a member; this sect was popular among the elite of Japan and stressed ornate ritualism and "high church" ceremonies. Nichiren also railed against the most popular sect, Amadism, or the Pure Land sect, which emphasized simple salvation by faith and complete trust in Amida Buddha. Pure Land Buddhism was popular with the poor and downtrodden, to whom it gave comfort for the battle of life and consolation in the hour of death. While the older forms of Buddhism were weakening, the Pure Land sect had matured during the great strife and chaos of a country in perpetual civil war and would compete with Nichirenism as the dominant belief.

All Japan's traditional Buddhist sects, except that of Nichiren, had counterparts in China. The Zen sect, for example, appealed to the samurai class, with its simple and direct approach to salvation and emphasis on intellectual effort, self-reliance, and meditation. Buddhist sects were generally pacifist by nature and not exclusive. Yet Nichiren's new sect was seen as an unorthodox doctrine, hostile to other forms of Buddhism and given to militant, intolerant attitudes and behavior. This was the first sect of Japanese origin, a new doctrine whose time had come among a people prepared for its distinctive claims.

Nichiren and his adherents held that truth and salvation were to be found only in the Lotus Sutra, and an important part of their ritual was the repeated utterance of the mystic words *Namu-myōhō-renge-kyō*, meaning "homage to the wonderful law of the Lotus Sutra." This new doctrine, like most new types of protestant Buddhism that emerged in medieval Japan, was characterized by a highly dogmatic form of teaching. It offered a message similar to messages of some Western religions, placing much emphasis on the "last days" and stressing a preparation for the advent of a savior. During this dark period of Japanese history, Nichiren and others emphasized the idea of *mappo*, or the "end of the holy Buddhist law." Some historians speculate that this idea emerged from the pessimism of a degenerate era of feudal Japan characterized by misery, epidemics, and internecine warfare. Others challenge this notion and call attention to the eastern provinces of Japan, where the warrior clans were characterized by a vigorous creative spirit and a mood of confidence. Whatever the case, Nichiren emerged with a new apocalyptic creed in which some, such as the historian George Sansom, see a corollary with the apocalyptic vision of John the Apostle, who foretold an era of dreadful misery that would end in the coming of a messiah, a savior of the world. This idea of a savior is not a central theme in traditional Buddhism, but there is mention in early Buddhist texts of a savior, Maitreya Buddha, who was to come in the dark ages. The apocalyptic characteristics of his doctrine distinguish Nichiren's brand of Buddhism from various popular religions that emerged during his era.

Nichiren declared that he was a reincarnated bodhisattva who had come forth specifically to preach a singular truth that the "latter day of the Buddhist law" was to give way to a new era of salvation. This promise of a new era was the cardinal feature of the Lotus sect. His birth and mission, Nichiren maintained, were clearly described in the twelfth and thirteenth chapters of the *Hokke* scripture.

The general spiritual aspects of Nichiren's teachings are fairly close to traditional Buddhism. The sect's uniqueness was its emphasis on the role of the Lotus Sutra as the means of spiritually unifying the world and establishing peace. Nichiren preached and wrote often about peace, although he himself was very quarrelsome in his manner. He once admitted that he was the most uncompromising man in Japan, and he used strong language to condemn other Buddhist leaders; his sermons and invective against them were marked by such epithets as "devil," "liar," and "fiend."

Nichiren used the same strong language against the military government (*bakufu*) at Kamakura. His antagonism made him many enemies, and he was exiled for a time and subsequently released in 1263, only to return with renewed criticism of rival religions and government officials.

Nichiren's mission must also be seen in the context of a special crisis which faced Japan—a Mongol invasion. Nichiren distressed the high officers of the government by sharply criticizing their handling of the crisis and castigating them for lack of foresight and courage. The adherents of other Buddhist sects which he had attacked then plotted against him, and he was condemned for treason. Sentenced to death, Nichiren gained a stay of execution on the very site where he was to be beheaded. The details of this incident are not clear, but Nichiren disciples interpret his evasion of death as a miracle.

In exile for three years on the bleak island of Sado (1271-1274), he studied and meditated, perfected his doctrinal interpretation, and reached the conclusion that he was the savior about whom much had been said.

There were samurai warriors who admired Nichiren's courage and facilitated his return to the capital in 1274, on the eve of the Mongol invasion. Government officials attempted to resolve their confrontation with this influential monk, but he was uncompromising. Until his death in Sochu-ji Temple at Ikegami in 1282, he demanded that the government condemn all other sects as apostate, suppress their heresies, and unite Japan under the *Hokke* religion. Nichiren did have a more charitable side to his personality, apparent as he went among his poor followers. During his lifetime, however, the main body of his believers were the samurai warriors, attracted by his militant, crusading spirit.

Apart from his charismatic character, Nichiren was an eccentric scholar with a keen mind and a vigorous style, the author of religious treatises of great literary excellence. It is in this connection that Nichiren made an additional contribution, in the realm of Japanese national consciousness, that emerged only after his death. His influence here was probably even more significant than his founding of the religion that bears his name. Japan was the first nation in Asia, indeed the first non-Western nation, to experience the phenomenon of nationalism, and Nichiren contributed to this important development. This is best seen in his treatise *Risshō ankoku ron* (1260; *On the Establishment of the Orthodox Teaching and the Peace of the Nation*, 1980), which stressed the national crisis and maintained that only by espousing Nichiren Buddhism could the nation be saved.

His vision was actually broader than the country of Japan, for he claimed that his doctrine had universal validity, that his truths would emerge from Japan to be propagated throughout the world. He had visions of a universal Buddhist church, with a holy see located in Japan. This nationalistic aspect of religion was unique to Japan.

Nichiren left an indelible mark on the religious history of Japan. Indeed, while some religions have had a limited appeal and impact on the life of a nation, Nichiren's religion has had a lasting appeal to the Japanese, many of whom have seen themselves as special and belonging to a nation that somehow has a mission in the world. No religion has done as much as Nichiren Buddhism to identify Buddhism with the national life of a country. Also, no other sect of Buddhism has been so characterized by an apocalyptic mysticism as that of Nichiren.

Following Nichiren's death in 1282, the perpetuation of his particular brand of Buddhism was left in the hands of six disciples, and there was considerable sectarian conflict among rival factions that continued for centuries. The main headquarters of the dominant sect continued at Mount Minobu, with a rival branch of the religion located nearby. Fairly reliable reports indicate that, after World War II, the Nichiren sect numbered some ten million adherents, with more than five thousand temples, while the rival sect numbered 300,000 adherents with two hundred temples.

Summary

Nichiren's life was a series of crises, and his religion was a crisis-born, militant sect. It is generally seen as the culmination of a process of Japanization of the Buddhism introduced from China and Korea, and it bore the seeds of nationalism.

Nichiren's brand of Buddhism is not to be dismissed as past history, for in the 1930's, there appeared a Buddhist renaissance inspired by Nichirenism. The movement was quickly eclipsed when it came into conflict with Japan's military leaders on the eve of World War II. Following the war, however, the religion reemerged and produced a remarkable revival, the most rapidly growing religion in Japan (if not in the world) in the 1950's. The religion was again characterized by Nichiren's deep-rooted doctrine and militant conviction. *Soka gakkai*, as this revivalistic, intolerant religion was called, claimed to be the wave of the future for the Japanese people and the world. It gained millions of adherents, mainly among workers and less educated people, and by 1955 had even influenced the political arena: Vigorous campaigns were waged to elect its representatives to the national assembly of Japan. This marriage between religion and politics harks back to Nichiren himself, who asserted that religion and national life were inseparable.

Bibliography

Anesaki, Masaharu. *Nichiren: The Buddhist Prophet.* Cambridge, Mass.: Harvard University Press, 1916. This classic study on Nichiren was written by a recognized authority on Japanese history. Illustrated with maps.

Eliot, Charles N. E. *Japanese Buddhism.* New York: Barnes and Noble Books, 1959. A standard treatment of the Buddhist world from which Nichiren emerged.

Nichiren. *Nichiren: Selected Writings.* Translated by Laurel R. Rood. Honolulu: University of Hawaii Press, 1980. A selection of important primary writings by the prophet himself. Includes a lengthy bibliography and a helpful index.

Papinot, Edmond. *Historical and Geographical Dictionary of Japan.* Rutland, Vt.: Charles E. Tuttle Co., 1972. A useful resource for the study of Japan, this volume gives a concise treatment of Nichiren. Illustrated.

Sansom, George B. *Japan: A Short Cultural History.* London: Cresset Press, 1931. A standard work by a British scholar and diplomat that gives the historical context of Nichiren's career.

Paul Hyer

NICHOLAS OF AUTRECOURT

Born: c. 1300; Autrecourt, near Verdun
Died: After 1350; probably Metz, Lorraine
Areas of Achievement: Philosophy and religion
Contribution: A philosopher whose thinking reflected the intellectual themes of his time, Nicholas contributed to the end of High Scholastic thought by proposing a form of radical nominalism which was critical of the Aristotelian notions of substance and causation. Far ahead of its time, Nicholas' thought anticipated some of the discoveries of David Hume, later rationalists, and later empiricists.

Early Life

Nicholas was born about 1300 in Autrecourt, in the French diocese of Verdun. This region was also the birthplace of two other iconoclastic contemporaries, James of Metz and John of Mirecourt. Of Nicholas' early youth, little is known, though he apparently proved himself a bright boy, matriculating at the University of Paris and living as a Fellow of the Sorbonne between 1320 and 1327.

During the time Nicholas was a student, the University of Paris was, intellectually, an especially exhilarating place. Change was in the air. By the fourteenth century, the seams of the much-patched fabric of Scholastic synthesis had begun to unravel rapidly because the internal oppositions between Christian theology and Aristotelian metaphysics and Aristotelian logic were becoming more and more obvious.

The criticism of Scholasticism which resulted from the need to resolve these oppositions was not, however, an entirely new creation. It was an outgrowth of the logical methods of Scholasticism itself. Thus when John of Ockham personally carried his nominalistic philosophy to France to answer the charge of heretical and erroneous opinions before the papal commission at Avignon in 1324, he was greeted by the professors of the University of Paris as a fellow laborer. It is impossible to discount the influence of both the rise of nominalism and the Parisian intellectual atmosphere on Nicholas' intellectual development, even though Nicholas' philosophy cannot, in any proper sense, be considered a form of Ockhamism.

Shortly after completing his studies in 1327, Nicholas received his licentiate in theology and the degrees of master of arts and bachelor of theology and laws. Appropriately equipped, he embarked upon an academic career at his alma mater. His tenure at the University of Paris, which lasted from 1327 to 1340, represents the period of his greatest accomplishment.

Life's Work

It was during his tenure as an academic that Nicholas wrote the controversial works which helped shape the intellectual scene of the fourteenth century. Unfortunately, the fragmentary nature of the surviving corpus makes it impossible to describe the full scope of his thought. Of Nicholas' commentaries on the writings of Aristotle and Peter Lombard, all that survives comes from the replies of Jean Buridan in his commentaries on Aristotle's *Physica* (c. 335-323 B.C.; *Physics*) and *Metaphysica* (c. 335-323 B.C.; *Metaphysics*) and those of Thomas of Strassburg in his commentary on Peter Lombard's *Sententiarum libri IV* (1148-1151; four books of sentences). The only surviving Nicholatian texts are two complete letters and fragments of five others written to Bernard of Arezzo, an almost complete letter to Egidius, an answer to a theological question, and a philosophical treatise entitled *Exigit ordo executionis*. All were written before 1340, the *Exigit ordo executionis* apparently being the last. Only the two complete letters have been translated into English in their entirety. It is on the basis of this motley collection of works that any reconstruction of the main themes of Nicholas' philosophy proceeds.

Nicholas' philosophical starting point is the logical principle of noncontradiction: A thing cannot be and not be something at the same time. All arguments formed to arrive at truth which do not follow from the principle of noncontradiction are merely probable. Only deductive arguments which presuppose this principle are absolutely certain.

Nicholas distinguishes two kinds of certainty which characterize different forms of experience: the certainty of faith and the certainty of evidence. The certainty of faith is guaranteed by God's grace, is subjective, and is thus beyond the criticism of philosophers. One who has it finds it supernaturally indubitable, and nothing more can be said; it is its own proof. The second variety of certainty is the proper province of philosophers. It is called the certainty of evidence and is characterized by admitting no degrees. Either the evidence produces certainty or it does not. Nicholas does maintain that the certainty of evidence comes in two varieties: the certainty of evidence about simple things and the certainty of evidence about complex things. By the former, Nicholas means the certainty of inner perception or experience; by the latter, he means the certainty of propositions. The principle of noncontradiction can be used to test both varieties.

In some of his writings, Nicholas provides demonstrations as to how the criterion of noncontradiction can be applied to simple and complex judgments. In the case of perception (simple certainty), he argues the impossibility of separating judgments of existence associated with perception from the perceptions themselves. In other words, to perceive a color and to be aware that one is perceiving a color are inseparable acts. To maintain that one perceives a color and that one is not, at the same time, conscious of perceiving a color is a contradiction. From this Nicholas draws the inference that everyone perceives his or her own existence. To maintain that the perception of existence is possible without a consciousness of that existence is a contradiction; to maintain this is to assert that there can be a perception without something doing the perceiving.

In the case of complex things (or propositions), Nicholas provides a number of analogous arguments which show that the certainty of propositions, too, depends upon the principle of noncontradiction. If it were possible to be certain about a proposition which was not dependent upon the principle of noncontradiction, then this act would be tantamount to saying that one could be certain about a proposition which could be either true or false, or—more subtly—that one could be certain about a proposition which appears true and yet is possibly false. Yet certainty does not allow the possibility of falsehood. The only recourse, then, is to rest the judgment of propositions on a principle which guarantees that certainty is achieved only when conclusions are reached that cannot fail to be true or about which there is no possibility of falsehood. The principle of noncontradiction alone meets this requirement.

Nicholas characterizes certain propositional knowledge as that variety which modern logical positivists term "tautologous." When Nicholas asserts that "A is P and therefore it is not the case that A is not P," he construes that relationship not in the manner of medieval Aristotelians, who thought of it either as the relation between a substance and another higher genera or as the relation between a substance and its accident. Rather, he construes that relationship in the manner of some modern logicians who see the relationship between A and P as being simply that between an object and one of the predicates that make it what it is. According to Nicholas, there is no substance underlying the perceptions of the object.

Since the Aristotelian substance is beyond the five senses, it can never be an object of a perception. Nor can it be an object entertained in a proposition, because propositions depend upon the five senses to flesh out their content. The Scholastic discussions of substance, accidents, and efficient causation were mere babble to Nicholas. In their place, he substitutes a kind of phenomenalistic Democritean atomism. The only realities are atoms of quality which in momentary confluence present themselves as things; the only real things are the perceptible combinations of these qualities.

It is possible to have certainty about the judgment of perception associated with these things, but this certainty lasts only as long as the things are present. Certainty is momentary and cannot be extended to judgments about the past or future behavior of things. The existence of a thing at one time cannot be inferred from the existence of another thing at another time, because neither can be put into a relation of identity or of part to whole. One's only recourse is to count up the number of conjunctions and decide the probability of their occurring together in sequence. Moreover, if that is the best one can do for perceptible things, then it is impossible to talk about the causal relations which hold between nonperceptible things such as sub-stances, because probable demonstrations require, at the very least, percep-tible things. Since an Aristotelian substance is not perceptible, and since only correlations, not perceptible relations, can be found between perceptible things, it is impossible to establish a probable correlation between a sub-stance and a perceptible thing or a substance and another substance.

With arguments such as these, Nicholas was able to challenge some of the most cherished thinking of the accepted Aristotelian metaphysics. Of all of his criticisms, the most devastating were his critiques of the Scholastic proofs of God's existence. Because these proofs relied heavily upon the Aristotelian notions of substance, cause, and accident, Nicholas was able to demonstrate that even a probable proof making use of these notions was impossible. The irony of Nicholas' critique is that he used the most fundamental principle of Aristotelian logic: the principle of noncontradiction.

The controversy surrounding the audacity, brilliance, and rigor of Nich-olas' philosophy spread across France like a brush fire. By 1338, his promi-nence as an academic had become so great that he was made a canon of the cathedral at Metz and given a Prebend's stall. This honor did not come with a condition of residency but was a comfortable stipend which allowed Nicholas to pursue advanced study. This he did in comfort, until 1339, when a decree was issued by the faculty of arts accusing students and some of the faculty of insubordination as evidenced by their study of nominalistic philosophy and the meeting of secret nominalistic conclaves. This decree was followed, in December of 1340, by further, more severe decrees against Ockhamism as well as a request from Pope Benedict XII that Nicholas and other Parisian professors critical of Scholastic Aristotelianism appear before the papal curia at Avignon. The first papal inquiry was postponed because Benedict died shortly after issuing his summons, but on May 19, 1342, Pope Clement VI re-opened the inquiry by appointing a commission of inquisition under the directorship of William, Cardinal Curty.

Before this commission, Nicholas defended himself with great skill and subtlety. He made it clear that his thought was proposed with the intention of fruitful discussion alone, that his philosophy was designed to reveal the weaknesses of the Scholastic synthesis so that these might be remedied; it was not designed to pull the Scholastic edifice down. He also pointed out that at no time had he denied any of the dogmatic declarations of the Church and urged that when one of his probable arguments stood in contradiction to dogma the argument should be understood as false. Cardinal Curty, for the most part, remained unmoved. He termed Nicholas' counterarguments "foxy excuses" and produced a list of sixty condemned propositions.

Uncertain of his fate, Nicholas fled from Avignon and went briefly into hiding, probably in the court of Ludwig of Bavaria. In 1346, he was sum-moned to Paris to recant the condemned propositions, to burn his writings, and to be stripped of his academic credentials. On November 25, 1347, after recanting his philosophy and being discharged from the faculty of the University of Paris, Nicholas watched as his collected works were publicly burned.

Although disgraced in the eyes of the Church, Nicholas lived the rest of his life in its bosom. In 1350, he was made a deacon at the cathedral of Metz, and in the document recording this event is found the final mystery in this controversialist's life: He is described as possessing the licentiate in sacred theology, a license which ought to have been taken from him when he was discredited. It is possible that the authorization to teach sacred theology was officially restored by the Church sometime after his public recantation, or perhaps this mention was merely an act of charity upon the part of the clerics at Metz, who had always appreciated Nicholas' brilliance. About the remainder of his life, little is known. Nicholas died sometime after 1350.

Summary

It is difficult to measure the direct influence Nicholas of Autrecourt had upon Western theological and philosophical development since no Nicholatian school survived the conflagration of 1347. Nicholas is most important not for the direct force he exercised in shaping Western thought but for his part in the rise of nominalistic philosophy which characterized the fourteenth century and which was the herald of empirical natural philosophy, the death of the Aristotelian metaphysic, and the birth of the Reformation.

Even so, Nicholas' philosophy did directly shape the fashion in which more traditional theologians and philosophers, such as Jean Buridan and Thomas of Strassburg, read and interpreted Aristotle and their more immediate predecessors. Moreover, in many respects, Nicholas' thought was modern, and in fact, quite prescient. In accepting the law of noncontradiction as the cornerstone of certainty, he anticipated the thought of the rationalists and their *more geometrico*. In his insistence upon the primacy of perception and the certainty associated with judgments of perception, he anticipated later empiricists. In arguing that causation could be established as probable at best, he anticipated some of the arguments of David Hume.

Finally, perhaps the most significant thing about the career of Nicholas of Autrecourt was his intellectual honesty. Using logic like a sharp scalpel, he ruthlessly cut away many of the contradictions living in the body Scholastic. The audacity of his intellectual project provides an example for anyone who finds the formulaic repetition of tired old answers unsatisfying.

Bibliography

Copleston, Frederick C. *A History of Philosophy*. Vol. 3, *Late Medieval and Renaissance Philosophy*. New York: Image Books, 1963. Copleston's history stands as the most thorough history of philosophy written in English in this century. Volume 3 provides an extensive, but very compact, exposi-

tion of Nicholas' life, arguments, and influence within the context of fourteenth century nominalism. The end of this volume contains notes referring to the Latin sources and a multilanguage bibliography.

——————. *Medieval Philosophy*. New York: Harper and Brothers, 1963.
This is Copleston's pointed summary of the history of medieval philosophy.
More general and accessible than the volumes in *A History of Philosophy*,
it provides a brief overview of the period, discussing only Nicholas' general
significance to philosophy. It contains a brief bibliography of French and
English works.

Hyman, Arthur, and James J. Walsh, eds. *Philosophy in the Middle Ages*.
New York: Harper and Row, Publishers, 1967. Hyman and Walsh provide
English translations of the first and second letters of Nicholas to Bernard
of Arezzo. They also provide a brief but detailed biography of Nicholas
and some comments on his importance. A short bibliography of journal
articles and books follows the translation, with a longer multilanguage bibliography at this work's end.

Weinberg, Julius R. *Nicholas of Autrecourt: A Study in Fourteenth Century
Thought*. Princeton, N.J.: Princeton University Press, 1948. This is the
seminal work on Nicholas' thought and has yet to be superseded. It contains chapters on the theories of evidence, probability, change, and causation as well as a bibliography of the standard works. The work's level of difficulty presupposes some philosophical sophistication.

——————. *A Short History of Medieval Philosophy*. Princeton, N.J.:
Princeton University Press, 1969. This work contains a chapter on the criticism characteristic of nominalism. Weinberg is the authority on Nicholas in
the English-speaking world, and his discussion can be trusted in all particulars. Lucid summaries of Nicholas' logical arguments are provided in
abbreviated form. This book contains a multilanguage bibliography.

Thomas Ryba

NICHOLAS THE GREAT

Born: c. 819-822; Rome
Died: November 13, 867; Rome
Area of Achievement: Religion
Contribution: Nicholas strengthened the power of the Papacy by actively promoting the primacy of the Holy See in all Church matters and in secular cases of moral consequence.

Early Life

Nicholas the Great was born to a noble family in Rome shortly before or after the year 820. His father was Theodorius, a man of great learning, who served as a regionary notary and worked for Pope Leo IV. No facts are extant about Nicholas' mother. As a youngster, Nicholas was serious, intelligent, and eager to learn, traits he inherited from his father and which Theodorius encouraged in the boy. Nicholas was always a good student; he became well read in both secular and theological writings. The clergy at Rome anticipated a bright future for the young scholar.

In 845 Pope Sergius II called Nicholas to serve him as a subdeacon and a member of the Curia at the Lateran palace. Nicholas was made a deacon by Sergius' successor, Pope Leo IV, and during the reign of Benedict III, Nicholas became a highly valued adviser to the Holy See. Benedict was extraordinarily fond of Nicholas as a personal companion and respected his counsel. Benedict died on April 17, 858; Nicholas is said to have wept openly and profusely at the funeral.

Nicholas' success as a scholar and adviser for almost fifteen years in Rome also brought him to the attention of Emperor Louis II, who befriended him. When a successor was being considered after Benedict's death, Louis remained in Rome and pressed for Nicholas' acceptance by the balloting clergy. On April 22, 858, Nicholas was elected to the Papacy. His formal installation took place on April 24, 858. Nicholas is thought to have been the first pope to be fitted with a gem-encrusted secular crown at his consecration the following October, although no records exist to confirm this fact positively.

Nicholas' rise to the Papacy resulted from several factors, all involving his personal attributes. He was a handsome man with fine facial features and a graceful bearing, winning laymen and clergy alike to his favor. He was very learned but at the same time modest, and he also had a reputation as an eloquent speaker. When Nicholas held to a principle, he did so faithfully and with more courage and commitment than did most men. He was also sincere, just, and honest in his dealings with all, whether of noble or humble rank.

Nicholas would have to call on all of these traits to aid him through a short but difficult papacy. He reigned for nine years, at a time when anarchy threatened Western Europe. The descendants of Charlemagne had divided his empire into three sections. These rulers often quarreled among themselves; they had unruly offspring as well. This civil discontent also made for some anarchic acts by the clergy. Some corrupt bishops held small kingdoms of their own, where they ruled over both civil and spiritual issues. Others came under the influence of powerful civil leaders. Some ambitious and undisciplined clergy took goods and property from their parishioners and guided these people ineffectively, if at all. When Nicholas became pope, the issues created by such disobedience and strife fell to him to resolve.

Life's Work

Nicholas' papacy is marked by three major crises that occurred almost simultaneously with one another. The first crisis involved his disciplining of corrupt and ambitious clergymen. Nicholas came into conflict with the powerful, independent Archbishop Hincmar of Reims. Hincmar had dismissed a member of the clergy for being an unworthy administrator; that bishop, Rothad of Soissons, appealed to Pope Nicholas, complaining that Hincmar had judged him unfairly. Nicholas, as defined in canon law, was the spiritual authority to whom all bishops when in conflict with their archbishops were to appeal. Hincmar had deposed Rothad at a synod in 862, after which time that bishop was imprisoned. Nicholas overturned the decision of this synod, since at the time that it met Rothad had already begun an appeal to Rome. Hincmar was forced to abide by the Pope's pronouncement and reinstate Rothad at Soissons during Christmas week of 864.

In a similar case of a tyrannical church leader, Nicholas came into conflict with Bishop John of Ravenna. John had begun to confiscate lands in his area, even some belonging to the Holy See. In addition, Nicholas learned that John made exorbitant demands on his congregation for his housing, food, and entertainment. John also had dismissed any clergymen who disagreed with his method of administration. Nicholas sent warnings to the bishop to end his misconduct, but they were ignored. Nicholas intervened and went to Ravenna personally to restore property to its rightful owners. In November of 861, John came to Rome to beg the Pope's pardon; Nicholas reinstated him as bishop, with the stipulation that John personally report annually to Rome on his activities.

The second area in which Nicholas had to intervene for the sake of justice was in royal marriages in Europe. The most famous case of Nicholas' defending an oppressed, defenseless spouse came in the two marriages of King Lothair II, a Frankish ruler. Lothair had taken a wife, Waldrada, in 855 in what was then a Germanic traditional ceremony but not a Church-sanctioned marriage. Waldrada, a noblewoman from Lorraine, had three children by Lothair. In 857, he married Theutberga, the daughter of Count Bosco of Burgundy, in the Church; this marriage was a politically feasible union, but it produced no children. In 860, Lothair decided to return to Waldrada. The Frankish archbishops whom Lothair requested to dissolve his marriage to Theutberga readily complied with their civil ruler. Nicholas, after Theutberga made an appeal to him, intervened and declared Lothair's marriage to her to be the only valid union. Emperor Louis II marched on Rome with his imperial army to protest what he believed was an unfair decision about Lothair's choice of wife. Nicholas retreated inside the buildings of St. Peter's to fast and pray, while Louis' troops angrily smashed up religious processions in the Roman streets. Finally, after two days, both men agreed to discuss the case. Possibly, this meeting was mediated by Louis' wife. The result of the discussion was that Theutberga would remain Lothair's legitimate wife and that he was to cease living with or meeting with Waldrada. Nicholas was so eager to see full justice done in this case that in October, 863, he called to Rome the two archbishops who had supported Lothair in his renunciation of Theutberga. These two Frankish archbishops, Günther of Cologne and Theutgard of Trier, were deposed by Nicholas and replaced. Nicholas also excommunicated Waldrada and her principal supporters.

These conflicts concerning corrupt and ambitious church officials and immoral imperial marriages are relatively minor in comparison with the one great crisis that Nicholas faced in his papacy. For several reasons, including cultural differences between Rome and Constantinople and the personal ambitions of a learned Constantinopolitan layman, Nicholas' papacy was marred by a serious schism between the Western and the Eastern churches.

At Constantinople, Emperor Michael III had an adviser named Bardas who lived an immoral personal life; Bardas had left his wife to live with his son's young widow. When ordered by the patriarch, Ignatius, to return to his wife, Bardas refused. After that incident, Ignatius did not allow the adulterer to receive Communion at Mass on the Feast of the Epiphany in 857. When the emperor saw how his favored adviser was being treated, he dismissed Ignatius in late 858. Michael replaced Ignatius with Photius, a learned Greek layman and his imperial secretary; in less than a week, Photius was consecrated through all the various stages of the clergy, from lector to priest. Then, on December 25, 858, he assumed the office of patriarch. Protests arose from angered supporters of Ignatius, who was in exile at Terebinthos. Michael announced that Ignatius had resigned his office, but historical evidence does not exist to prove that claim. One particularly vocal supporter of Ignatius, the monk Theognostos, traveled to Rome, where he lodged an appeal with Pope Nicholas to intervene on Ignatius' behalf.

As an investigation into this incident at Constantinople began, Nicholas declared that no one was yet to recognize Photius, since his case had to be reviewed. When Photius wrote a courteous letter to Nicholas requesting that he be sanctioned as the patriarch, the Pope answered by sending two legates to Constantinople to study the situation. The two trusted legates that

Nicholas sent on this delicate mission, Radoald of Porto and Zachary of Agnani, immediately had trouble in the Byzantine city. They were pressured by Photius and the emperor to vote at a council held on the patriarchal dispute. Nicholas had sent these two clergymen only to investigate and to report back to him; they were not authorized to represent him in any voting assembly. This Council of Constantinople, convened in late 861, voted to accept Photius as the legitimate patriarch.

When the two legates returned to Rome in 862, Nicholas immediately deposed them, their votes, and the decision of the Council of Constantinople. Nicholas then convened his own Council of Rome in early 863, at which Photius was threatened with excommunication if he did not restore Ignatius to the patriarchy. When Photius learned of this decision and ignored it, the split between the Eastern and the Western churches grew wider.

In August of 867, Photius conducted a council of his own, at which time he declared Nicholas to be deposed and excommunicated. On September 24, 867, Michael was assassinated; his successor, Emperor Basil, reinstated Ignatius to the See of Constantinople on November 26, 867, and Photius was deposed. Pope Nicholas did not live to hear of these events; he died on November 13, 867. Each November 13 the Roman Catholic church celebrates the Feast of Saint Nicholas in honor of the canonized pope.

Summary

Nicholas the Great was a persistent and courageous fighter for the rights of all oppressed people. His actions in defending parishioners from corrupt clergymen and betrayed spouses from cruel husbands clearly show how uncompromising he was in the pursuit of justice. Nicholas also gained a reputation throughout Europe as a friend to the poor. He established an innovative program by which all the poor of Rome were fed on a regular schedule. Anyone blind or disabled had a daily meal sent to him. The able-bodied reported to the Lateran palace once a week to receive a food ration. Nicholas even devised a special token to be carried by each person to remind him on which day of the week to report for food.

This Pope was also a very organized and eloquent letter writer. On his ascension, he had appointed Anastasius the Librarian his personal secretary. Nicholas' choice of such a highly literate man proved valuable, especially when the Pope's health failed. Nicholas, in his last years of life, was frequently incapacitated by a painful illness and also from general exhaustion from his zealous attention to his numerous duties. In such instances, Anastasius helped the weakened Pope to draft his typically long letters.

Nicholas sent missionaries to Scandinavia to convert people there to Christianity. He was also chiefly responsible for the conversion of Bulgaria in the time of King Boris I. Boris had been baptized by the clergy at Constantinople, with Michael as his godfather. When Boris became disappointed with what he believed was the Eastern Church's lack of enthusiasm and of useful aid in their missionary efforts in Bulgaria, he turned to Nicholas for advice. Nicholas immediately sent to Boris two bishops and a very lengthy, meticulously detailed letter. This letter, known as *Responsa Nicolai ad Consulta Bulgarorum* (866), answers the 106 questions that Boris had concerning Christianity and his role as a Christian ruler. Nicholas responded to these questions with precise answers and in terminology Boris could understand. Theologians to this day praise Nicholas' response to Boris as one of the greatest documents in papal history.

Nicholas was also responsible for a great secular achievement during his time in office. He was able to unite Western Europe by providing a strong central authority for all church matters. Europe in the mid-800's lacked cohesion, consisting of several small, bickering kingdoms. Nicholas continually kept Rome at the forefront of European life, both in religious and in civil matters. When King Boris requested that a code of civil laws be sent to him, it was Latin laws Nicholas sent.

Pope Nicholas' greatest lasting achievement was his maintaining and strengthening the supreme authority of the Roman See. When arrogant and independent clergymen attempted to rule their parishioners with no input from Rome, Nicholas swiftly ended their autonomy. He reserved for himself and future popes the right to intercede in any church affairs gone wrong. Nicholas was one of the most powerful, beneficent, and active popes of the Middle Ages.

Bibliography
Cheetham, Nicholas. *Keepers of the Keys: A History of the Popes from St. Peter to John Paul II*. New York: Charles Scribner's Sons, 1983. Cheetham summarizes Nicholas' personality and his effectiveness as pope. The author also clearly explains the major crises Nicholas faced in office; here he makes some use of contemporary accounts of Nicholas' conduct. A helpful chronological chart serves as an appendix to this book.

Dvornik, Francis. *The Photian Schism: History and Legend*. New York: Cambridge University Press, 1948. Dvornik is the leading authority on the events leading to and widening the schism between Nicholas and Photius. This book serves two purposes: to dispel the myths about how the schism occurred and to replace these myths with accurate historical evidence about it. An extremely well-documented and scholarly study.

Gontard, Friedrich. *The Chair of Peter: A History of the Papacy*. New York: Holt, Rinehart and Winston, 1964. A well-illustrated text with an appendix on the popes in office. Nicholas' papacy is discussed in the context of European politics in the mid-800's. Gontard presents a balanced view of Nicholas' tactics and accomplishments in office.

Mann, Horace K. *The Lives of the Popes in the Early Middle Ages*. St. Louis:

B. Herder Books, 1925. Mann offers a very thorough analysis of Nicholas' papacy. Mann, more than any other author listed here, provides the reader with a full background to the problems that beset Nicholas and the political climate of his era. A well-documented study.

Ullmann, Walter. *A Short History of the Papacy in the Middle Ages*. London: Methuen and Co., 1972. This book contains a substantial section of bibliographical notes giving Ullmann's sources for each chapter. He points out the long-term significance of Nicholas' solutions to the various crises he faced. Much space is devoted to a discussion of the conflict between Nicholas and Photius and the strategies that each man employed in dealing with the other.

Patricia E. Sweeney